STEPS ON THE PATH TO ENLIGHTENMENT

STEPS ON THE PATH TO ENLIGHTENMENT
A Commentary on Tsongkhapa's Lamrim Chenmo

Volume 1: The Foundation Practices
Volume 2: Karma
Volume 3: The Way of the Bodhisattva
Volume 4: Śamatha
Volume 5: Insight

STEPS ON THE PATH TO ENLIGHTENMENT

A Commentary on Tsongkhapa's
Lamrim Chenmo

Volume 5: Insight

GESHE LHUNDUB SOPA
with Dechen Rochard

Wisdom

Wisdom Publications
199 Elm Street
Somerville, MA 02144 USA
wisdompubs.org

Library of Congress Cataloging-in-Publication Data for Volume 1
Lhundub Sopa, Geshe, 1925– 2014
Steps on the path to enlightenment : a commentary on Tsongkhapa's
Lamrim chenmo / Geshe Lhundub Sopa ; David Patt, senior editor ;
Beth Newman, editor.
p. cm. Includes bibliographical references and index.
ISBN 0-86171-303-6 (alk. paper)
1. Tsoṅ-kha-pa Blo-bzaṅ-grags-pa, 1357–1419. Lam rim chen mo.
2. Lam-rim. I. Patt, David. II. Newman, Beth. III. Tsoṅ-kha-pa
Blo-bzaṅ-grags-pa, 1357–1419. Lamrim chenmo. IV. Title.
BQ7950.T754L359 2003
294.3′444—dc22
2003017363

ISBNs for Volume 5: Insight
ISBN 978-1-61429-323-1   ebook ISBN 978-1-61429-334-7
21 20 19 18 17
5 4 3 2 1

Cover and interior design by Gopa & Ted2, Inc. Set in Diacritical Garamond
Pro 10.5/13. Cover image © C&N Photography, www.candnphoto.com.
Frontispiece photo courtesy of Kalleen Mortensen.

Contents

Foreword

THE *Great Treatise on the Stages of the Path to Enlightenment (Lamrim Chenmo)*, composed by Tsongkhapa and explained here by Geshe Lhundub Sopa, is a commentary on the *Lamp for the Path to Enlightenment*, by Atiśa. The primary goal of these teachings is to discipline and transform the mind. These texts have their source in the sutras and the other teachings of the Buddha himself, but their special virtue is that they convey the thought of the Buddha in a format that is easy to apply in actual practice.

The authors of these wonderful texts composed them in order to help all living beings. Since they developed the altruistic attitude to benefit mother sentient beings, we too should follow their example, irrespective of our own weak situation.

The Buddha and the great teachers who followed him gave clear instructions on how to proceed from a state of suffering to a state of peace and happiness. Following such teachings of the great masters of the past, Atiśa summarized them in his famous text, the *Lamp for the Path to Enlightenment*. It is a wonderful text, and Atiśa's disciples, such as Dromtonpa and Potowa, put what it teaches into practice. It was then transmitted through the Kadam lineages, finally coming down to Tsongkhapa.

He was an unparalleled scholar, who composed the *Great Treatise on the Stages of the Path to Enlightenment*, the marvelous text explained here in the manner of the great masters of Nālandā monastic university. We are indeed fortunate after so much time to have access to such a great work and to be able to read and think about what it contains. With this publication of Geshe Sopa's commentary, Tsongkhapa's words are brought to life and illuminated for a modern audience, continuing the lineages of scripture and realization that the Buddha set in motion more than 2,500 years ago.

The two principal aspects of practice described here are a proper understanding of emptiness and the awakening mind of *bodhicitta*. A correct understanding of the view of emptiness is very important, for whether you are taking refuge, or cultivating the awakening mind of *bodhicitta*, all other practices are enhanced by such an understanding. At the same time, it is extremely important that our insight into the ultimate nature of reality is supported by compassion and the awakening mind of *bodhicitta*.

In my own case, regardless of my limited capacity, I try my best to develop these two minds: the wisdom understanding emptiness, and *bodhicitta*—the wish to achieve enlightenment for the sake of all sentient beings. Merely trying to approach and cultivate these two minds brings greater peace and happiness. The development of these two minds is really the heart of Buddhist practice. It is the essential meaning of this *Stages of the Path to Enlightenment.* If we were to examine all the sutras and words of the Buddha, along with the subsequent treatises that are commentaries on them, we would find that they can be summed up in these two practices. Therefore, we should study these teachings motivated by an aspiration to achieve enlightenment for the sake of all sentient beings.

Today, Buddhism is spreading throughout the Western world, encountering new cultures and new languages. During such a period of transition it is very important that the Dharma be transmitted by scholars and practitioners who possess a deep and vast understanding of the teachings, because that is the only way to protect the authenticity and purity of the teachings.

Atiśa exemplified this role by bringing the pure teachings from the great monastic centers of North India and establishing them in Tibet in an authentic and complete form that was, at the same time, suitably adapted to the Tibetan personality. He reestablished monasticism in Tibet and emphasized ethical conduct as the heart of Buddhist training. He dispelled the many misconceptions and erroneous customs that had entered the practice of the Dharma in Tibet. In this way he reestablished the pure Buddhadharma in many places where it had been lost, and enhanced it where it survived.

Requested by Jangchub Ö to give a teaching that would be beneficial to the Tibetan people in general, Atiśa composed the *Lamp for the Path to Enlightenment,* which condensed the essential points of both sutras and tantras into a step-by-step method that would be easy to follow. This text inaugurated the grand tradition of the study and practice of the stages of the path method in Tibet. Atiśa also worked with his Tibetan students on the translation of many texts from Sanskrit into Tibetan and so made a rich contribution to the flourishing of Buddhism in the Land of Snows.

Geshe Sopa, the author of this commentary on the *Lamrim Chenmo,* was one of the several good students of Geshe Lhundrub Tabke and was therefore chosen to debate with me during my final examination. Geshe Lhundrub Tabke, who became the abbot of Sera Je, was in turn one of the several good students of Geshe Tsangpa Lhundrub Tsondru, who was a renowned scholar at the time of the Thirteenth Dalai Lama and later ascended the throne of

Ganden Tripa. Geshe Sopa is therefore the third generation of high-quality scholarship commencing from Geshe Tsangpa Lhundrub Tsondru, and he continues the excellent tradition today.

He is an exemplary heir of Atiśa's tradition conveying the pure Dharma to a new world in an authentic and useful way. He has been a pioneer among those bringing Buddhism to the West. He left for America in 1962. In due course, Geshe Sopa was invited to the University of Wisconsin, where he became one of the first Tibetan language instructors at an American university. He later rose to become a tenured faculty member, and his career as a professor of Buddhist studies eventually spanned more than thirty years.

All Tibetans should feel honored and proud that Geshe Sopa, a man from far-away Tibet, could rise to the highest levels of Western academic attainment largely on the basis of his Tibetan monastic education combined with his own brilliance and personal qualities. Publication of this excellent series of books is a fitting tribute to an illustrious career.

Tenzin Gyatso, the Fourteenth Dalai Lama

Editor's Preface

WORKING WITH GESHE Sopa Rinpoche on this volume has been a life-changing experience for me, and I hope that reading it will be a life-changing experience for others. Although parts of this text appear very technical, it is composed entirely of teachings to be taken to heart. As Geshe Sopa humorously declared, it is like chewing hard bones to get to the juicy marrow. The effort required to engage in this material is both painstaking and joyous, and the learning curve is steep. However, gentle perseverance over a long period of time is rewarded by gradual understanding that opens the mind to the holy truth, which can eventually transform our minds completely. I cannot find words to express my gratitude to the holy guru for his most illuminating, vibrant, and patient guidance. In working on this text with Geshe Sopa over the years, I held fast to his every word, to every nuance in his voice. This was absolutely necessary, whether listening to his live presentations or to his recorded teachings. Going over difficult points again and again, Geshe Sopa's patience was boundless, his mind ever unperturbed and joyous. It has been an enormous privilege to witness his fresh yet authentic presentation of Tsongkhapa's words and to contribute to the process of putting his penetrating explication into printed form for the benefit of all beings.

After completing the first draft of this volume, having worked on it for six years, I was obliged to take some time away from the project for academic reasons. I handed the text over to Wisdom Publications for the line edit. Beth Newman was asked to take on this task, which she very kindly accepted. She is the person most familiar with the style required, having already translated and edited volume 3 and having assisted with the editing of volume 1. Beth worked extremely hard on this volume for the next couple of years and succeeded in making it more readable. She has a special talent for bringing space into a text and letting it breathe. I am most grateful for her input. The new edit of volume 5 enabled me to work further with Geshe Sopa to revise and refine the philosophical content. This was a period of most intensive endeavor. Sadly, it was cut short when Geshe-la contracted pneumonia. Most happily, he recovered. But he never regained his former physical strength, so we could not resume reading the draft together after this point, the middle of chapter 18. Nevertheless, I had the opportunity to spend more than a year going over the text again while Geshe-la was still present, able to answer questions and give it his blessing. I have done my best to present Geshe Sopa's commentary on the insight section of *Lamrim Chenmo* as accurately as possible in all its full and magnificent detail. However, with a text of this complexity and length, it is almost inevitable that some errors remain. Any such errors are undoubtedly my own.

This project would never have come into being in the first place were it not for David Patt, who initially conceived of it in discussion with the former Wisdom director Nick Ribush. David worked dedicatedly on the first two volumes, and I am most grateful to him for recommending me to work on volume 5, and to Geshe Sopa Rinpoche and Lama Zopa Rinpoche for accepting his recommendation. Lama Zopa Rinpoche is the rock on which this project has been built. As a devoted disciple of Geshe Sopa, he has both generously funded the project and lovingly managed its progress over the years. He has also been an inspiring presence at Geshe Sopa's annual teachings on Tsongkhapa's major texts, held at Deer Park Buddhist Center from the late nineties onward, which has been a great blessing to all.

I have found it a delight to interact with staff members of Wisdom Publications, notably Tim McNeill and David Kittelstrom, who have been consistent sources of support and guidance. During the final phase of this project, I greatly benefited from the beautifully light and accurate editorial assistance of Harmony DenRonden and Mary Petrusewicz. I would like to express my deep appreciation for all their hard work.

There are many people whom I would like to thank for their kind assistance: the 104th Ganden Tripa, H.E. Lobsang Tenzin Rinpoche, heart disciple of Geshe Sopa Rinpoche, who illuminated some difficult philosophical points; Geshe Tenzin Dorje and Geshe Tenzin Sherab, resident teachers at Deer Park Buddhist Center, who addressed some poignant questions; David Farrell and Vicki Schuknecht, who provided ready access to recordings of Geshe Sopa's teachings; Ven. George Churinoff, who located sources difficult to find and proved to be a valuable conversation partner; Ven. Sherab and Ven. Chowang, who took phone calls from me to Geshe-la and relayed messages between us when speaking became impossible; Ani Drolma and other residents of Phuntsok Choeling, who accommodated me as Geshe-la's guest and were most amiable companions; Ani Jampa (Alicia Vogel), Christina Yousafzi, Patrice Kennedy, Frank Barone and Cathy Kennedy, who accommodated me in their own homes and became my very dear friends; and all my Dharma brothers and sisters attending Geshe Sopa's teachings over the years, who warmed my heart with their affectionate friendship. I am most grateful to you all.

Finally, I would like to express my deep appreciation for the wonderful work of Jim Blumenthal, who died of cancer in 2014 at the peak of his career. A renowned scholar and sincere practitioner, he will be sorely missed by many people throughout the world. He completed volume 4 of this series just in time before passing away in the wake of Geshe Sopa himself, and will surely be born close to Geshe-la in his next life. Although Geshe-la's physical passing is a great sorrow to all who knew him, his holy mind pervades everywhere. We can rejoice in his continuing influence in our hearts through the teachings he so kindly bestowed in this world. I would like to dedicate the merit of the present volume to the swift reincarnation of Geshe Sopa Rinpoche and to the continuing presence of all our teachers, especially His Holiness the Dalai Lama. May all our gurus' holy wishes be fulfilled and may all beings attain the state of enlightenment as soon as possible. As the *King of Concentrations Sutra* instructs:

> If you analyze the selflessness of phenomena,
> And if, having analyzed, you meditate upon it,
> This will cause the result: the attainment of nirvana.
> There is no peace from any other cause.

Sarva Maṅgalaṃ
Dechen Rochard
Bristol, England

Technical Note

REFERENCES

All works mentioned are referenced by their titles in English. Although there are many ways to render a particular title, in most cases we have employed the versions used in the Cutler et al. translation of the *Lam Rim Chenmo—The Great Treatise on the Stages of the Path to Enlightenment*—to make it simple for the reader to use the two works together.

At the first mention of a particular work we provide the title in its language of composition. Again, although scholars may find some irregularities, for the ease of the general reader in most cases we have followed the Sanskrit titles as they appear in *The Great Treatise on the Stages of the Path to Enlightenment*. The bibliography allows the reader to find an English title and see the same title in Sanskrit (if applicable) or Tibetan.

Quotations not drawn from *The Great Treatise on the Stages of the Path to Enlightenment* are cited by the English title, chapter, and stanza or page number. Quotations drawn from *The Great Treatise on the Stages of the Path to Enlightenment* are not cited in notes. Since in general we utilize the subject headings from Cutler's translation for the ease of the reader, such quotations can be easily found in those volumes.

PRONUNCIATION

Terms from Sanskrit and Tibetan that have become part of the English language appear without diacritic marks or Tibetan spelling.

Tibetan technical terms and names are spelled phonetically for ease of use of non-Tibetan speakers. Sanskrit technical terms that are not commonly used in English appear in this work with diacritic marks. These terms appear in the glossary in English alphabetical order.

The following rough guide to Sanskrit pronunciation is from *The Wonder That Was India*, by A. L. Basham.

The vowels *ā, ī, ū, e, ai, o,* and *au* are long and have approximately the same pronunciation as in Italian, or as the vowels in the English words *cam, machine, rule, prey, time, go,* and *cow*, respectively. The vowels *a, i,* and *u* are short and equivalent to the vowels in the English words *cut, bit*, and *bull*. Ṛ is classed as a short vowel and pronounced *ri* as in *rich*.

The aspirated consonants *th* and *ph* are pronounced as they are in the words *pothole* and *shepherd*; they are never pronounced as the English *thin* or *photo*. *C* is pronounced *ch* as in *church*. Ś and ṣ are both generally pronounced *sh* as in *shape*. The distinction between the other subdotted retroflex consonants (ṭ, ṭh, ḍ, ḍh, ṇ) and the dentals (without subdots) is not important to the general reader.

STYLISTIC NOTE

Steps on the Path to Enlightenment is based on an oral commentary on Tsongkhapa's *Lamrim Chenmo* that Geshe Sopa gave to his students over the course of more than a decade. In turning Geshe-la's presentation into a series of books, the editors have chosen mainly to use an informal second-person voice. In contrast, the Tibetan language generally leaves person understood and is often rendered with an abstract third person: "one can do this" or "one should do that." We chose the second-person style in order to preserve something of the oral nature of the original and to create a more intimate bond between the author and the reader. The intent of Tsongkhapa and of Geshe Sopa was to give those who wish to embark on the path to enlightenment advice on how to proceed. This advice is offered here in the direct address of a teacher to his students.

STRUCTURE OF THE BOOK

The outline of headings in this book is drawn from Tsongkhapa's own outline of the *Lamrim Chenmo*. The full outline for this volume is reproduced in the appendix.

Introduction

The lamrim

A FORTUNATE HUMAN LIFE, with freedom and opportunity such as we have now, is so incredibly special. On the basis of this very life we can completely free ourselves from suffering and its causes and attain genuine happiness and lasting peace. We cannot find such peace and happiness through acquiring material goods, because this does not remove our mental afflictions, those of attachment, hatred, jealousy, pride, ignorance, and so on. We can find genuine happiness only by actualizing the stages of the path to enlightenment.

Lamrim literally means "stages of the path." A spiritual path or any of its stages is a special kind of realization. So the lamrim is really a series of realizations culminating in enlightenment. We cannot jump from a lesser realization to a higher realization—there are many steps involved. Je Tsongkhapa gathered together various teachings of Buddha and placed them in a specific order to show us how to develop these realizations gradually.

The words of Buddha are contained in one hundred large volumes of the Kangyur, each of which emphasizes a different subject. Some texts explain impermanence and emptiness, whereas others focus on suffering and compassion, and so on. When we approach such a vast collection of books, it is difficult to know where to find specific teachings or in what order to read them. Tsongkhapa's presentation of the lamrim places them in a precise order relevant for the practitioner. This systematic organization of Buddha's teachings was first introduced to Tibet by the great Indian master Atiśa. Following his innovation, other scholars and practitioners used this format to further explain the extensive collection of Buddha's word. Tsongkhapa wrote three different lamrim texts. Among these the *Lamrim Chenmo* or *Great Treatise on the Stages of the Path to Enlightenment* is the most extensive version. It is a detailed presentation of the Buddhist path to enlightenment incorporating many quotations from the Kangyur as well as passages from the scriptures by great Indian and Tibetan scholars; it also includes stories and examples of earlier Tibetan scholars and yogis. This volume that you are reading now is a detailed commentary on the insight chapter of Je Tsongkhapa's *Lamrim Chenmo*.

The *Lamrim Chenmo* is like a window through which we can see a vast landscape. All the different features of the view from it, such as trees, rivers, and sky, do not fit into the space of a small window—yet we can see them there. Likewise, though relatively short, the *Lamrim Chenmo* introduces us to the ultimate goal and shows us how to get there. It tells us what inner obstructions we need to remove and how to remove them, and what realizations we need to develop and how to develop them. The entire path to enlightenment is presented in the *Lamrim Chenmo*, and in particular a full explanation of how to develop the perfection of wisdom is explained in this volume.

THE CORRECT MOTIVATION

As spiritual practitioners our goal in life is not just to experience temporary sensual pleasures such as good food and comfortable accommodation. Sleeping when we are tired and eating when we are hungry provides short-term satisfaction and relief from manifest suffering. But real spiritual practitioners are dissatisfied with such transitory pleasures; they want to attain the everlasting peace and happiness of enlightenment. Enlightenment is not an external place; it is not some paradise we can fly to by physical means. Enlightenment is an inner state of being. To attain it we must accomplish our own mental purification—no one can do it for us. We engage in spiritual practice to purify our mindstreams, gradually removing mental afflictions and other inner obstructions. These levels of mental development constitute the path to enlightenment. Just as in the Western system of education—where first you have elementary school, then you go to high school, and then on to professional training—the lamrim method consists of three sets of progressively more advanced practices to purify and train the mind. We begin with the practices for beings of lesser spiritual capacity, motivated by a wish to prevent rebirth in the lower realms and attain the temporary goal of a good rebirth. Then, wishing to be free from all samsaric rebirths, including the upper realms, we move on to the practices for those of medium spiritual capacity. After that we engage in the practices for beings of great spiritual capacity in order to attain complete enlightenment. These practices are for courageous bodhisattvas, whose main wish is to benefit others and alleviate their suffering; for this purpose alone they are willing to undergo any hardship in their effort to attain enlightenment. Spiritual practitioners of all three capacities generate the desire to achieve their respective goals through learning about the paths. But desiring to attain the goal is not enough. Each person has to engage in the particular methods and actualize the particular paths that result in their desired goal. In other words, we must study and practice the Dharma precisely as explained in the teachings.

The practice of Dharma begins with morality, which refers to any kind of virtuous activity that leads to liberation or enlightenment. We engage in Dharma practice when we read a Dharma book, when we listen to a Dharma teaching, and when we meditate on its meaning. Our Dharma practice is our main refuge. Going for refuge to the Dharma does not mean that we put external Dharma objects in a high place and go for refuge to them! That is not real Dharma refuge. We take real refuge in the Dharma within our own mindstreams. For example, if we take monastic vows and keep them purely, this inner practice will protect us from misery and suffering. It will lead us to liberation.

The Sanskrit word *dharma*, or *chos* in Tibetan, has many meanings. The root of the Sanskrit word *dharma* is *dhṛ*, which means "hold." Anything that exists, whether virtuous or nonvirtuous, holds its own identity and is *dharma* or *chos*. So one meaning of the word *chos* or *dharma* is that which "holds its own identity" (*rang gi ngo bor 'dzin pa*), which is equivalent to "exists." In this sense, *dharma* refers to all phenomena or existent things. But when we go for refuge to the Dharma, the word *dharma* has a different meaning. It specifically refers to religious truth or virtuous conduct. In this context, "hold" indicates "holding away from lower rebirth." Virtuous things have a special power to hold, not just in terms of holding their own identity but in terms of holding us away from falling into misery. Any virtuous activity, such as generosity, morality, and patience, as well as any realization of truth within our own mindstreams, is our Dharma refuge. We should think, "Now I want to rely on this Dharma; this Dharma has the ability to protect me." Instead of regarding certain things on the altar or something in space as Dharma, we should regard the Dharma within us as the real Dharma. Our own Dharma is more important. People usually do not think like this. They forget their own Dharma and think of the Dharma as something external.

Practitioners of lesser spiritual scope fear the misery of rebirth in the lower realms and want to be free from that in their future lives. So they strive to be born in higher realms and to have a good life as a human or a god. Although a higher rebirth is only temporary, it is beneficial. It is extremely fortunate to be born where there is an opportunity to hear the Dharma teachings and learn about the truth. If we act on this properly, we can progress higher and higher on the spiritual path. We have the potential to attain permanent cessation of our own suffering or even complete enlightenment for the benefit of others. Both of these are possible because we have four excellent qualities: a human body with clear sense organs; the necessary conditions of food, clothing, shelter, and medicine, obtained without too much difficulty; helpful religious friends and spiritual teachers who present the excellent teachings of Buddha;

and the power to accomplish our Dharma activities. The last quality refers to being able to complete whatever we undertake. Some people cannot carry their activities through to the conclusion. They begin to do something but soon give up and start something else; then before they finish that, they turn to something else yet again. It is an excellent quality to have a natural inclination to complete whatever we start—especially to carry our spiritual practice through to the end.

In order to improve our mind and to progress from path to path, these four qualities are essential. Without these four excellent qualities we cannot develop either the method side of the path—compassion, patience, and so on—or the wisdom side of the path—an understanding of the ultimate truth of emptiness, or *śūnyatā*. Humans who lack these four qualities, and beings such as animals who have taken lower rebirths, cannot complete the accumulations of method and wisdom. It does not matter how beautiful one's body may be, being born as an animal is an obstacle to spiritual development. This is true even if one is born as a pampered pet belonging to a rich owner. Pets in the West are so well cared for; they have excellent food, a beautiful home, and are much loved and cherished. But even though they have such luxuries, they do not have the mental capacity necessary for attaining enlightenment. However much you might talk to an animal and even give it teachings on the *Lamrim Chenmo*, it will just shake itself and walk away. Maybe, if it is in a good mood, it will wag its tail. That is all it can do.

Taking birth as a human or god is not a perfect goal. Even if you are born healthy, wealthy, and famous, maybe as royalty with magnificent possessions and power, it is not totally faultless. It is not a state of final liberation or enlightenment. It is merely the result of previous virtuous action or karma; as soon as that result is finished you will descend to the lower realms if you have not created additional virtuous karma. Recognizing this, you evolve into a person of middling spiritual capacity and want to become completely free from samsara, not just from the lower realms.

What is samsara? Dharmakīrti explains in his *Commentary on Valid Cognition* (*Pramāṇa-vārttika*), where he introduces the four noble truths:

> Suffering is the samsaric aggregates. (5.147a)

Samsara is not primarily external, like the sky and trees, though these things are part of the situation. Samsara is the collection of one's own contaminated aggregates, which have arisen through the power of karma and mental afflictions. Samsara is one's own continuous rounds of birth, sickness, aging, and death—all in the nature of suffering. This process has no beginning, and we keep creating it over and over again. Therefore samsara is called *cyclic existence*. Nāgārjuna says in his *Precious Garland* (*Ratnāvalī*):

> As long as there is grasping at the aggregates,
> Then there is grasping at myself.
> If there is grasping at myself there is action,
> And from these there is rebirth. (1.35)

"Grasping at the aggregates" is mentioned first because as soon as the aggregates appear, they appear to exist inherently—and because of that appearance, we usually hold them to exist inherently. Based on holding the collection of one's own body and mind as inherently existent, each of us holds them to be inherently "me" or "mine." This egotistic view immediately results in aversion to unpleasant experiences and desire for pleasant experiences. Motivated to gain good things for oneself and avoid painful things, we create both nonvirtuous and virtuous karma, which eventually gives rise to another birth. It would be wonderful if nothing happened to us after we died, no matter how much and what kind of karma we created in this life! But that is not what happens. We will be reborn in accordance with the karma we have created. In the next stanza Nāgārjuna explains how this occurs:

> The three paths, without beginning, middle, or end,
> Circle around like a wheel of flaming torches;
> Continuously revolving, they cause each other:
> This is cyclic existence. (1.36)

In this context the "three paths" are the samsaric paths: the thoroughly afflictive path of mental afflictions, the thoroughly afflictive path of contaminated karma, and the thoroughly afflictive path of suffering or contaminated rebirth. Here the term *afflictive* does not refer just to the mental afflictions. It includes all the misery of samsara that comes along with rebirth. These three paths do not have a beginning, middle, or end—just like the riddle "Which comes first, the chicken or the egg?" it is impossible to locate an original cause. From one point of view it is the mental afflictions that create karma, and then karma creates suffering and birth. From another point of view it is birth that gives rise to the mental afflictions, which then create karma, suffering, and yet another birth. So everything circles around like a wheel: We are born, age, and finally die. Then we are born again, create karma, and experience suffering, aging, and death. It is like the appearance of a ring of fire created by spinning a wheel of firebrands around on a dark night. This looks like a complete circle of light but is just a single torch moving quickly through points in space. In each place there is only a momentary point of light; the fast movement makes it look like a continuous circle. Samsara is like that—its different components mutually generate one another so they seem like a continuous circle. In this way we have been cycling around without beginning or end.

All the miseries of samsara arise from mental afflictions created by ignorance. These mental afflictions pollute and influence our actions. If we cut the root of our afflictions, our actions will become pure. As a result, we will cease to have contaminated aggregates. So to become free from suffering, we need to cut the root of the mental afflictions: ignorance. Ignorance is the innate misunderstanding that things truly exist as they appear to our ordinary perception. Until we develop a correct understanding that things have an illusion-like nature and do not exist as they appear, we act under the power of ignorance. How can we cut the root of ignorance? The only weapon is the supreme wisdom understanding emptiness, the ultimate truth. Such wisdom is called *special insight*. We need to develop this special insight because without it we cannot achieve freedom from samsara or attain full enlightenment.

Buddhahood, or full enlightenment, is the highest spiritual goal. A courageous bodhisattva yearns to become a buddha because only a buddha can lead all sentient beings to perfect peace and happiness. This supreme altruistic intention is known as *bodhicitta*—the mind or heart of enlightenment. Buddha taught various special practices to his bodhisattva disciples. All these practices are included, directly or indirectly, within the six perfections: generosity, ethical conduct, patience, joyous effort, meditative concentration, and wisdom. Each of the first five perfections has its own special qualities, and when combined they are like a powerful vehicle that can transport us to another place; but without the sixth they lack direction. Wisdom is like the eyes of a careful driver who steers the vehicle so as to arrive at the desired destination: enlightenment. In a similar analogy, blind people need someone with sight to take them to a particular place. They need a guide who can see the path and any obstacles on it in order to arrive at their destination. In the *Verse Summary of the Perfection of Wisdom* (*Ratna-guṇa-saṃcaya-gāthā*) Buddha says:

> The multitude of blind people, without a leader,
> Cannot see the route, so how can they enter the city?
> The first five sightless perfections, without wisdom,
> Have no leader, so they cannot reach enlightenment. (7.1)

Blindly engaging in any spiritual practice without wisdom will not lead to the final fruit of enlightenment, yet if we want to arrive at supreme buddhahood, we need more than wisdom alone. Just as a bird needs two wings to fly in the sky, we also need two wings—method and wisdom—to reach the highest goal of enlightenment. The first five perfections are called *method*. The sixth is *wisdom*. Wisdom alone is not enough, and method alone is not enough. Only when we have completed the collections of both wisdom and method and joined them together, like a pair of wings, can we fly to buddha-hood. Candrakīrti puts it like this in his *Introduction to the "Middle Way"* (*Madhyamakāvatāra*):

> With great white wings of the conventional and ultimate reality,
> The king of swans soars ahead of common beings.
> Borne aloft by the powerful wind of virtue,
> He reaches the far shore of the ocean of royal qualities. (6.226)

In the first four volumes of this series, I commented in detail on Tsongkha-pa's explanation of the method side of practice—from the fundamental practices on the path for those of lesser spiritual scope through to the development of bodhicitta and the practice of the first five perfections for those who have great spiritual capacity. Attainment of any spiritual goal, whether individual liberation from samsara or complete enlightenment for all beings, depends on wisdom. We can say that all the teachings on the method side are directly or indirectly for the purpose of presenting the perfection of wisdom. Śāntideva says in his *Engaging in the Bodhisattva's Deeds* (*Bodhisattva-caryāvatāra*):

> All these branches were taught
> By Buddha for the sake of wisdom. (9.1a–b)

WISDOM

We need to develop superior wisdom, or insight, to uproot the fundamental cause of suffering within our own mindstream. All types of suffering arise from their general and particular causes—contaminated actions of body, speech, and mind. The suffering of cyclic existence includes pleasant, unpleasant, and neutral experiences, which result from contaminated virtuous, non-virtuous, and neutral actions, respectively. Contaminated actions include all actions that are propelled by ignorance. Ignorance is not a simple case of not knowing the truth; it is the *opposite of knowing* the truth, a fundamental misunderstanding of reality. Upon perceiving things to exist objectively, as if bearing their identity from their own side, ignorance grasps them as existing in that way. If something appears ugly, the mind of ignorance holds it to be ugly objectively; if something appears beautiful, it holds it to be beautiful objectively. To a mind influenced by ignorance things appear to exist from their own side, independently of being perceived; then a manifest mind of ignorance naturally arises that holds the appearance to be true. But that appearance is not reality; nothing really exists as it appears to our ordinary awareness.

There are many aspects or factors of our mind, each of which may also be called a *mind*. Ignorance is one of the six root mental afflictions, and it misapprehends the way things exist. Ignorance is a very deep and powerful mental factor that influences other aspects of our mind. It causes us to grasp things incorrectly, and we act on that wrong conception. Any ordinary actions propelled by ignorance lead to cyclic existence, including virtuous contaminated actions. Ignorance also gives rise to all our other mental afflictions, such as attachment, hatred, jealousy, and pride. We can see in our daily lives how much these mental states control our minds. Through the power of these afflictions we engage in nonvirtuous actions, whether verbally or physically. Nonvirtuous actions can only ever lead to misery in the end. The fundamental cause of all these problems is ignorance.

Ignorance is the root of all suffering, including rebirth itself. So we need to ask ourselves, Can I get rid of ignorance? Tsongkhapa addresses this question in a stanza praising Buddha and his profound teaching:

> Ignorance is the root of all
> The manifold misery in the world,
> So he teaches dependent arising—
> The seeing of which reverses it.[1]

To remove ignorance we need to apply its antidote: a special kind of wisdom that sees the truth of dependent arising. In order to see everything as dependently arising, we must understand the emptiness of inherent existence, śūnyatā. Emptiness and dependent arising have the same profound meaning. They are like two sides of the same coin. *Emptiness* does not mean nothingness or nonexistence; it means that all things lack something—they are empty of inherent existence. To say that a thing is empty of inherent existence means that it does not exist independently of a perceiving mind. There are different ways of being dependent, ranging from gross to subtle: dependent on causes, dependent on parts, and dependent on imputation by mind. When Tsongkhapa says that a realization of dependent arising will reverse ignorance, he is referring to the subtlest understanding of dependent arising: nothing exists inherently from its own side, independently of a mind that perceives or conceives it. If we do not comprehend emptiness, we cannot see the truth of dependent arising or relativity. A direct realization of emptiness, corresponding to the subtlest level of dependent arising, clears away ignorance.

Chewing hard bones

The insight chapter in the *Lamrim Chenmo* provides a full explanation of how to develop the perfection of wisdom—the special insight that understands the true nature of reality. However, this is a very complicated subject and it covers a vast area. Tsongkhapa even discusses wrong views so that we students can learn their pitfalls and see how to negate them. He shows us how misinterpretations can be eliminated and replaced by the right view. Some of the quotations from the sutras and the great Indian commentaries are very difficult to interpret, and their implications are hard to understand. It is like chewing hard bones to reach the juicy marrow. But no matter how tough they may be, it is important to work with these teachings. So let us look a little more closely at ignorance and its opposing force, wisdom.

Fundamental ignorance is often referred to as the *egotistic view*. The great Indian scholar and spiritual master Śāntideva says:

> All the injuries, harm, fear,
> And suffering that exist in the world
> Arise from the egotistic view;
> What use is that great devil to me?[2]

The combination of the egotistic view with a profoundly selfish attitude gives rise to every unkind thought and harmful attitude toward others. We mistakenly think that pleasure, wealth, success, and fame are desirable and appropriate goals in life. Day and night, from birth until death, we try to gain these "goods" for ourselves. Automatically we follow our desires for attractive objects of the five senses and continuously hanker for pleasure. We want to have the best and to be the best and are always trying to obtain desirable things and avoid unpleasant things. If someone else gets the things we want, we become jealous and angry. We may even want to destroy those things or hurt those people. This harmful attitude is rooted in the egotistic view. When such a nonvirtuous attitude arises, we can see clearly how the egotistic view is functioning and how it dominates our awareness.

What is the egotistic view? Is it something external with horns or tusks? Is it something that you carry around in a bag? No. It is our own ignorant mind that grasps strongly at "I" or "me" as though it were an independent entity. Candrakīrti says:

First, thinking "I," grasping at a self arises;
Thinking "This is mine," attachment to things arises.
Thus sentient beings are powerless, like a bucket on a water wheel;
I bow to the bodhisattvas' compassion for them.[3]

As soon as we think "I" we think "mine." We are attached to my body, my house, my friend, my town, my country, and my world. Out of attachment we perceive "I" and "mine" on this side and "others" on that side. At a primitive level we do not want others to have good things—we do not even want them to exist! We think that only "I" and "mine" are worthy of existence. Even if we do not explicitly think this way, this attitude is always present under the surface. From the moment we get up in the morning, the thought of "I" and "mine" arises. We worry about what we will do today, what we will gain, what we want to get rid of, and so on. These thoughts are based on the egotistic view.

Śāntideva calls it "the devil." When something goes wrong, we consider ourselves innocent and blameless. We immediately blame others. We may even think we are the victim of some evil external force. But the real devil is present in our heart, in our mind: it is the egotistic view that grasps at a truly existent "I" based on the five aggregates. We think of this "I" as unique, enduring, and perfect. We feel we are the best, most deserving, and most precious person in the whole world. We honestly believe there is nobody as wonderful as "me," there is nobody better than "me." Based on that attitude we indulge in all kinds of selfish behavior, harming others in thought, word, and deed. In this way we hurt ourselves most of all—for our actions give rise to many problems in our present life and result in our future rebirth in the lower realms. This selfish, egotistic attitude is the source of all suffering. Therefore it is the real devil. If we manage to see that our real enemy is this inner foe, then we will stop feeling any desire for it. When we no longer want this inner enemy, then we will determine how to destroy it. So to do this, first we must clearly recognize that our greatest enemy is our own egotistic view.

The egotistic view gives rise to all kinds of selfish attitudes, which are the opposite of universal love and compassion. If we remove the egotistic view from our mindstream, then those selfish attitudes can no longer arise because they have no basis. Until then, however, the cause of those selfish attitudes exists within us. Can those selfish attitudes ever give rise to bodhicitta, the desire to attain enlightenment for the benefit of other sentient beings? No, they cannot, because selfish attitudes and bodhicitta are completely opposite attitudes. When selfish attitudes are active in our mind, then there is no bodhicitta active at that time, and thus there is no Mahayana practice. If there is no Mahayana activity, how can we attain buddhahood? No matter how many times we say

"I want to become a buddha," this will not happen if we create causes that lead in the opposite direction. So in order to get rid of the cause of selfish attitudes, we must get rid of the egotistic view.

The term *egotistic view* is a convenient way of referring to what is literally called the "view of the perishable collection." It is important to have a clear understanding of what is meant by this phrase. In general the phrase "perishable collection" refers to the five aggregates.[4] The term "perishable" indicates that the aggregates are transitory, changing moment by moment. The term "collection" indicates that they are not a partless unit. In a special sense the phrase "perishable collection" may also refer to the person that is merely imputed on the five aggregates—for the person or self is both transitory and nonunitary.[5] According to some non-Buddhist philosophical systems, the self or soul is a permanent, single unit without parts; it is not an aggregation of several transitory elements that are then identified as a whole and given a name. Buddha showed that there is no such permanent, partless self. The self that exists is impermanent and composed of parts and merely imputed on a perishable collection, the aggregates. Now, contrary to what its name suggests, the phrasing "view of the perishable collection" refers to a distorted mind that holds the self to be not a perishable collection at all! Although the phrasing suggests that this view holds its *object* to be a perishable collection, in fact it grasps its object wrongly as inherently existent. This wrong view grasps the self, which is imputed on the aggregates, to be inherently existent. It holds the self to exist in a way that is opposite to what is really the case. This view of the perishable collection is the fundamental ignorance that is the root of samsara.

The main thing to consider is the way in which the self exists and the way in which it does not exist. Everybody has a self; it exists in dependence on its causes, on its parts, and on its basis of imputation. There is a correct way of apprehending the self and a wrong way of apprehending the self. The basic object in both cases is the conventionally existent self. There is no problem with this self. The problem is with how it is held by the mind perceiving it or conceiving it. The object held by the correct way of viewing the self does conventionally exist—it is the self held to be dependently existent. But the object held by the wrong way of viewing the self does not exist at all—it is the self held to be inherently existent. That object held by the egotistic view is the self that is to be negated. Actually there are two kinds of self to be negated: the self of persons and the self of phenomena. Although the basis is different (a person or a phenomenon), the object negated—inherent existence—is the same in both cases. The egotistic view concerns only the self of persons. Moreover, it only apprehends the self of persons based on the subject's own aggregates. You cannot have an egotistic view based on someone else's body and mind. You do not think of someone else's aggregates as "I" or "me" in any way; you only think of your own aggregates as such.

The egotistic view that grasps at a self of persons creates all the misery in the world. Every sentient being is under its power and totally lacks freedom. We cannot choose when we die, when we are born, or where we are born. We do not know what today will be like or what will happen next in life. Everything that we experience is under the influence of our past karma. Candrakīrti uses the example of a bucket on a water wheel to illustrate this. In ancient India water was obtained from wells by means of wheels with attached buckets. When the wheel went down, the buckets descended; when the wheel circled up, the buckets ascended. The buckets had no freedom of their own. In a similar way we sentient beings have no independence; we are trapped in cyclic rebirth due to the power of our karma. We have had many lives, one after another continuously, sometimes going up into human and celestial realms and sometimes going down into animal, hungry ghost, and hell realms. Good karma takes us up and bad karma carries us down.

Until this point in time we may have tried to control our experiences on a temporary basis by creating good karma and avoiding bad karma. But because we have not tried to get rid of the root of contaminated karma, our rebirths continue owing to the force of cause and effect, and we remain traveling in samsara. The last line of Candrakīrti's stanza praises great bodhisattvas who understand the truth. Having uprooted their own causes of suffering, they have great compassion for sentient beings that continue to suffer. They fervently want them to be free of those causes and work selflessly toward that goal.

This is the key point. You are receiving these teachings in order to understand the supreme wisdom that removes all misery and its causes. I shall do my best to explain Tsongkhapa's great insight chapter. However, I do not see myself as someone who really knows the meaning of all the quotations he has collected. Please do not think that I am omniscient and you are stupid. In this commentary I share what I have understood, through the teachings I have received and through my own studies. I have the lineage of transmission of the complete *Lamrim Chenmo*. However, I have not heard a detailed explanation of this section on special insight. It is rare to receive an extensive teaching on wisdom. Even in Tibet and India, a great number of scholars and teachers with the capacity to benefit and train others teach only the first half of *Lamrim Chenmo* in detail. Once they get to the insight chapter, where the subject is śūnyatā, they go through it very quickly. Perhaps even some of these great lamas do not understand it. So although I received some teaching on it and developed a deeper understanding of it through debate and studying various commentaries, I too enjoy this opportunity to further chew these hard bones.

Some of these bones are very hard indeed, and you may not be able to swallow them right now. But at least you will know they are there. Even if you do not understand the ideas perfectly, you are trying. This is a rare and excellent opportunity.

HOW TO PROCEED

So how should we use our human rebirth with excellent qualities? We should use it to achieve a definite spiritual goal in this life. Instead of falling under the influence of the mental afflictions, we should practice the spiritual path to develop the wisdom that understands the ultimate truth. Maitreya says in the *Ornament for the Mahayana Sutras* (*Mahāyāna-sūtrālaṃkāra-kārikā*):

> Never go under the power of delusions
> And do not pervert your actions. (17.2c–d)

The direct realization of emptiness will gradually free us from ignorance, attachment, and hatred. In addition, we must take care that the activities we undertake are not motivated by selfish egotistic attitudes. To properly understand what to do with our body, speech, and mind, we need a special kind of wisdom that understands conventional reality. Both kinds of wisdom—the wisdom that understands ultimate reality and the wisdom that understands conventional reality—are powerful and necessary attributes. Without them, any abilities we have might fall under the sway of delusions and turn into something evil. Thus wisdom is the essence of the *Lamrim Chenmo* teaching.

Do not read this volume on wisdom with the aim of becoming a scholar. Do not arrogantly think, "Now I will know śūnyatā." Base your motivation on a deep appreciation of all the previous stages of the path explained in the *Lamrim Chenmo*, particularly the wish to free all beings from the causes of suffering. The altruistic intention of bodhicitta is the motivation for coming to understand the essence of both sutra and tantra. By studying and practicing the lamrim method in this way, you can develop the wisdom that is free of wrong views and beyond the power of delusions. The wisdom that sees ultimate truth is the weapon that directly severs the root of all mental afflictions. Developing this wisdom gradually reduces and eventually removes even the subtlest obstruction to perfect knowledge. If we do not develop the wisdom that realizes śūnyatā, we will not get rid of the source of the mental afflictions—even if we realize all the other stages of the path, from relying on the spiritual teacher up to developing bodhicitta. Remember this as you make your way through the book. Contemplate your life's wonderful potential and generate in your heart a beneficial motivation. Then with great patience and joyous enthusiasm, gently chew on these teachings and slowly try to digest them. That is how to use your mind in the best possible way.

‡ 1 ‡

Why Insight Is Needed

(ii) How to practice insight

――――◈――――

THE TITLE OF THE final section of the *Lamrim Chenmo* says:

> *How to practice insight, the essence of wisdom, after practicing the bodhisattvas' deeds on the stages of the path of the great being.*

Here we find an explanation of the latter stages of the Mahayana path. A "great being" is someone who has developed universal love and compassion and who always takes more care of others' problems than his or her own. The heartfelt wish of a great being is to free all sentient beings from cyclic existence. Therefore a great being takes on the responsibility to lead all sentient beings away from suffering and place them in a state of freedom and lasting peace. Such a being will sacrifice him- or herself in order to benefit others. When this heartfelt sense of responsibility arises spontaneously it is called *bodhicitta*. Bodhicitta is literally the mind of enlightenment; it is the wish to attain buddhahood as soon as possible solely for the purpose of benefiting others. When bodhicitta arises spontaneously within one's mindstream, one enters the Mahayana path; at this point one becomes a bodhisattva.

Bodhicitta alone is not enough to attain enlightenment. So what else must we do? We must practice the various stages of the path from the basic level, through the intermediate level, and finally through all the practices of a being of great spiritual capacity. After a practitioner has developed bodhicitta, he or she engages in the bodhisattva's deeds or activities. This means taking the bodhisattva vows and practicing the six perfections. The vows embrace all physical, verbal, and mental actions, whereby whatever we do is only for the benefit of others and never just for ourselves. The great waves of the bodhisattva's deeds can be summarized as the six perfections: generosity, ethical conduct, patience, joyous effort, meditative concentration, and wisdom. The first five perfections are the method side of a bodhisattva's practice, which have already been explained in earlier volumes of this series.[6] The sixth perfection is wisdom. The subject of this volume, except for a short section at the end of the text on how to practice tantra, is how to develop wisdom or insight.

(ii) How to practice insight

Before beginning a discussion about how to develop insight, it is helpful to recall briefly the nature of the fifth perfection, meditative concentration. This is the ability of the mind to settle calmly on the object of one's choice for as long as one wishes. With meditative concentration the mind can comfortably focus without distraction. Usually when we try to think about something the mind stays with the object for a short while—but before we know it, the mind goes off somewhere else without control. When we develop a special type of single-pointed meditative concentration known as *samatha*, the mind no longer has this negative quality. It can remain focused on a chosen object for any length of time effortlessly and without distraction.

However, special conditions and great effort are needed to train the mind to focus this way. So when striving to develop *samatha*, yogis usually go to live in quiet solitary places like mountain caves or forests. They know that if they stay close to distracting activities and interfering people, their minds will be filled with disturbing thoughts. If they are in the presence of alluring objects of the senses, they will fall under the power of attraction to them. In contrast, when sitting in a deep cave without hearing or seeing much of the outside world, concentration can arise more easily. Silence and solitude are required to free the mind to focus joyfully on an object of meditation.

Meditative concentration has many wonderful qualities, but three special ones should be noted in particular. The first is that when we have mastered *samatha*, all discursive thought ceases. Although some meditation techniques employ analysis, the purpose of *samatha* meditation is for the mind to stay on its object for as long as may be desired without any distraction or agitation. Once we find the object, we do not examine it. In this meditation the mind is like a butter lamp; once lit, it burns continuously for as long as the fuel lasts. The second special quality of *samatha* is a mental clarity that is free of laxity and dullness. Generally we are able to focus on an object for only a short while. At a certain point we lose our clarity regarding the object and our mind becomes more and more dull, until finally we fall asleep. This is laxity or sinking. Both gross and subtle sinking are obstacles to meditative concentration.

Tsongkhapa explained mental clarity in detail earlier in the *Lamrim Chenmo*,[7] specifying how the object appears and how the mind holds the object with an awareness that is neither too tight nor too loose. The third special quality of śamatha is a mental and physical pleasure, a naturally arising delight. Usually when we sit for a long time the body starts to ache and does not want to cooperate with the mind. But with continuous mental training, a special energy-wind becomes active in the body. The body's lack of cooperation with the mind slowly diminishes, and it becomes closer to the mind, which has already developed some mental pliancy. As the mind and its subtle physical vehicle, the energy-wind, begin to function in tandem, a physical pliancy is produced. Associated with this is a subtle sensual bliss beneficial for meditation because it eliminates any feeling of tiredness. As a result, yogis can remain for a long time in śamatha meditation. Some can stay in meditative absorption for days or even weeks without any hardship or without even noticing that they have a body.

In brief, there are two types of pliancy: mental pliancy, which arises first, and then physical pliancy. Each of these produces a subtle feeling of pleasure or bliss. Here we should note that each pliancy and the bliss that it causes arise at different times. The bliss associated with physical pliancy arises first, which then influences the mind to experience an even more subtle bliss. These pleasurable feelings are a little gross upon first arising, but gradually they calm down. Eventually the physical and mental enjoyment subsides and rests at a perfect level without disturbing the yogi's meditation. These subtle pleasures cannot be described in words.

Although meditative concentration possesses the special qualities of non-discursiveness, clarity, and bliss, it is only a temporary peace. It is not the final goal. Many practitioners achieve śamatha, but by itself this is a worldly goal. There are two kinds of goals: mundane and supramundane. Mundane goals are included within samsara, whereas supramundane goals are the liberation from samsara and the attainment of complete enlightenment. Here in conjunction with śamatha we must develop the supreme wisdom, or *vipaśyanā*, that investigates reality and sees it clearly. Analytical investigation and single-pointed concentration may seem contradictory, but when they are fully developed they are not. Some monastic textbooks explain how they function together using the example of a tiny fish in a huge bowl of clear water. The water is completely still, with no wind rippling the surface, and the tiny fish swims gently without disturbing the water at all. In a similar way the main part of the mind remains stable and focused, while a subtle analytical wisdom investigates and comes to understand the nature of reality. This illustration is given in the context of combining śamatha with vipaśyanā that analyzes the ultimate, for the purpose of gaining freedom from samsara or attaining enlightenment. This is what we really need to practice. But to accomplish a lesser goal śamatha may be combined in a similar way with vipaśyanā that analyzes the mundane.

The supreme mundane goal is the highest level of the formless realm. According to Buddhist cosmology there are three realms within cyclic existence: the desire realm, the form realm, and the formless realm.[8] These three realms can refer to places; however, in the context of śamatha meditation they primarily indicate different levels of mental development. Above the desire realm are the four mental stages of the form realm. Above this is the formless realm, also divided into four levels: limitless space, limitless consciousness, nothingness, and the peak of samsaric existence. If we count the desire realm as one and add the four levels of the form realm and the four levels of the formless realm, there are nine divisions altogether. We distinguish these mental levels by the type of attachment manifesting in the mind of a being dwelling there. For example, the desire realm is identified by attachment to the objects of the senses, whereas the formless realm is identified by attachment to the bliss of concentration.

Both mundane and supramundane paths require the development of meditative concentration. This is not easy to achieve. To develop śamatha we must be free of strong attachment to sensual pleasure, though we will still have subtle, innate attachment. If we are addicted to enjoying the objects of the senses, such as visual beauty or sexual touch, the mind will have no place to abide calmly. So the way to achieve śamatha is to reduce worldly attachment and attraction to sensual pleasures. This is not a uniquely Buddhist practice; even non-Buddhist yogis engage in this practice to achieve śamatha. As soon as a person develops śamatha, his or her mind is superior to the rough and low mind of ordinary beings living in the desire realm. The next step for practitioners on a mundane path is to develop insight so as to remove the manifest mental afflictions associated with the various levels of samsara—though the innate afflictions will still remain. First they try to remove the mental afflictions of the desire realm, which are the roughest and most powerful. Then they try to remove the intermediate mental afflictions of the form realm. The subtler mental afflictions of the formless realm are the most difficult to remove, so they are left until last.

The mundane insight meditation to remove the mental afflictions of the desire realm involves comparing the desire realm with the first level of the form realm. We reflect on the nature of the desire realm, the ugliness and dirtiness of the body, the shortness of life, and the pain endured by all the various beings, from the lowest hell being to the highest desire-realm god. In every part of the desire realm there is the physical suffering of birth, aging, sickness, and death. Life in the desire realm is more gross and more painful than life in the first concentration, or *dhyāna*, which is the lowest level of the form realm. Life in the form realm is characterized by peacefulness, a long life span, and being unburdened by a physical body made of flesh and bones. Form-realm beings have subtle mental bodies that are free of physical suffering; just as a ray of light cannot be cut with a knife, their bodies of light cannot be hurt.

Those who engage in śamatha combined with analytical meditation that compares the characteristics of the desire realm and the first level of the form realm are on the path of the first dhyāna. This is the way to remove attachment to the desire realm and attain the first level of the form realm. The antidote that removes the obstructions is the union of śamatha and insight. While the practitioner engages in this particular meditation practice, the desire-realm afflictions do not manifest in the mind. They are completely subdued. When these mental afflictions are removed we obtain the fruit of our efforts, a deep mental absorption. In the next life we rise above the desire realm and are reborn in the first dhyāna. A practitioner of any spiritual tradition can rise through the levels of the form and formless realms in this way. Comparing the roughness of the first dhyāna with the peace of the second dhyāna, we remove the mental afflictions of the first dhyāna and attain the second level. Then we compare the roughness of the second dhyāna with the peace of the third dhyāna and so on through the levels of the formless realm until we reach the peak of samsara.

In the context of the mundane path, "remove" means to temporarily remove. The meditation practice combining śamatha and mundane insight removes the mental afflictions respective to each stage of mental development only for the present. In other words, the manifest mental afflictions are suppressed, but their seeds are still in the practitioner's mindstream.[9] Since the mental afflictions are only suppressed, the cessation of the misery of each level is merely temporary. We can temporarily stop the mental afflictions; we can also stop gross consciousness altogether for a period of time in a way that is much more subtle than deep sleep.[10] But even if the mental afflictions and their results have ceased for a number of years, the situation is not permanent. They will arise again. Every being born into any level of the form and formless realms is still under the power of karma and mental afflictions. Someone may be born in a good place, but when that karmic ripening or experience is finished they can fall down into a lower rebirth.

Furthermore, this type of meditation can only temporarily remove the mental afflictions up through the third level of the formless realm, nothingness. It cannot remove the mental afflictions of the highest formless realm, the peak of samsaric existence. So the achievement of even the highest level of the formless realm is not a true cessation. Temporary cessations are not real cessations;

they are just called cessations. A true cessation is a permanent cessation of a portion of the obstructions to liberation, which are the mental afflictions and their seeds.[11] To remove the mental afflictions permanently one must practice a supramundane path combining meditative concentration with the insight cognizing emptiness. In other words, in conjunction with a śamatha that is peaceful, stable, and blissful, we must develop a vipaśyanā or wisdom that properly understands reality. Wisdom is a mind that arises from investigating the way things actually exist; it sees emptiness, śūnyatā, clearly. We should not be satisfied with any lower level of attainment. Śāntideva says:

> Vipaśyanā conjoined with śamatha
> Destroys the mental afflictions;
> Having understood this, first search for śamatha
> Achieved through the joy of being unattached to the world.[12]

Tsongkhapa's point is that to remain for an incredibly long time in a subtle state of bliss is not the main reason for developing śamatha. We begin by developing meditative concentration. However, not only must we not be satisfied with mere meditative concentration, or śamatha conjoined with mundane insight, but we should also join śamatha to supreme insight in order to destroy the mental afflictions permanently. Permanent cessation of mental afflictions begins by way of a much higher level of insight meditation than those on the mundane paths. Only with supramundane insight can we get rid of the seeds of the mental afflictions and thereby achieve any permanent cessation. In short, the purpose of developing meditative concentration is to unite it with supreme insight so that we can eliminate all the mental afflictions with their seeds.

If we do not have a realization of śūnyatā, then no matter how skillfully or how long we engage in śamatha meditation, we will not eliminate the two kinds of self-grasping: grasping at a self of persons and grasping at a self of phenomena. The primary problem is the grasping at a self of persons, or more specifically, the egotistic view that holds oneself to be truly existent. Although we do not consciously use these descriptions, whenever we think or say something about ourselves, we usually feel that there is a "me" that is absolutely real. If somebody says, "You are stupid, and I am better than you," our sense of self rears up and angrily objects. We have an innate attitude that "I" have a special kind of existence, an identity that is almost different from the aggregates making up the body and mind, which feels solid and absolute. Likewise, when we consider "my body" we usually grasp at the self of phenomena; we have an underlying assumption that our body possesses an inherent characteristic of bodyhood that is substantial and unique. What is the body? When we look at it carefully all we can find is hair, skin, flesh, bones, muscles, blood, an upper part, a lower part, inside and outside, and so on. There is no actual "body" existing from its own side.

Usually we do not analyze things this way. We naturally hold things to be inherently and absolutely existent. Simply seeing that they exist, we feel that they exist from their own side. This is called *self-grasping*. Every ordinary being has self-grasping. Even animals have it, though they do not have the language to express it. They recognize danger, experience fear, and know how to protect themselves. Even little animals that live underground will stick their heads out of their burrows and glance in every direction before they come out. I do not think they are trying to exercise their necks! They are checking to see if it is safe to leave their holes. They recognize when an enemy comes close, then they run and hide or attack in order to defend themselves. They are attached to themselves, to their friends, and to their offspring. They have a robust sense of self and a strong self-centered attitude.

We need to differentiate between the self that exists, which is dependently imputed on the aggregates, and the self that is held to exist from its own side, which does not exist at all. Only by means of the analytical wisdom realizing selflessness can we understand that there is no such thing as the latter kind of self, the object of self-grasping. There is no way to get rid of self-grasping until we achieve this insight. Just as light clears away darkness, the wisdom understanding emptiness that arises from engaging in ultimate analysis clears away ignorance. Ignorance is the distorted view holding things to be truly and objectively existent, just as they appear to the ordinary mind. Ignorance pervades all the other mental afflictions, such as desire, attachment, hatred, and jealousy. We naturally hold things to exist in the way that we see them. The innate mind of ignorance grasps whatever appears *as* it appears and holds it like that without any examination. Āryadeva says in his *Four Hundred Stanzas* (*Catuḥ-śataka*):

> Just as the tactile sense power pervades the whole body,
> Ignorance abides in all [the mental afflictions].
> Therefore by destroying ignorance
> All mental afflictions are destroyed. (6.10)

The body has many parts and various sense faculties, such as the eyes and visual sense power, the ears and auditory sense power, and so on.[13] But the tactile sense power pervades all of them. It is present from the top of the head to the tips of the toes. In a similar way ignorance pervades and influences all the mental afflictions. They all arise in dependence on ignorance. Therefore we can eliminate all the eighty-four thousand mental afflictions by destroying their root, ignorance. Thus the most important antidote is the antidote to ignorance; it is the wisdom directly realizing emptiness that we must develop and utilize in meditation. It will completely uproot ignorance and its seed.

The great Indian scholar Kamalaśīla wrote in detail about the objects and techniques of meditation. He too says it is not sufficient to rely simply on meditative stabilization, or *samādhi*, because it is not able to remove mental afflictions from the root. In the first *Stages of Meditation (Bhāvanākrama)*, he says:

> When you have stabilized your mind on the object, you must analyze it with wisdom. The dawning of this wisdom clears away the root of all mental afflictions. If you do not do this, then, just like the non-Buddhists, you will not abandon the afflictions through mere samādhi alone. The *King of Concentrations Sutra (Samādhi-rāja-sūtra)* says:
>
>> Although worldly ones cultivate samādhi,
>> That does not destroy the false notion of self;
>> Afflictions return and disturb them,
>> Like Udraka, who cultivated samādhi up to this level.

Non-Buddhist yogis can achieve very high levels of samādhi, including the absorption of cessation, which stops the mind and mental factors and leads to rebirth in the highest level of the formless realm. But even this meditation does not get rid of the mental afflictions completely. It can only temporarily eliminate them up to the level of nothingness, the third level of the formless realm.

Kamalaśīla is not merely asserting this; he quotes from the *King of Concentrations Sutra* to prove his point. The first line of the stanza refers to "worldly ones." These are ordinary living beings imputed in dependence on what is perishable and a mere aggregation—the mental and physical aggregates. Neither the body nor the mind is a single absolute thing. Each is an aggregation of many interdependent components. The body is a combination of flesh, blood, bones, and so on. The mind is a combination of feelings, perceptions, and so on. These aggregates are contaminated, impermanent, and subject to birth, aging, sickness, and death, without any freedom or power of their own. Even though mundane beings may cultivate meditative concentration and come to possess its special qualities—nondiscursiveness, clarity, and joy—they have only temporarily subdued certain obstructions. No matter how much they engage in this kind of meditation practice, it cannot get rid of the seeds of mental afflictions. The afflictions arise again because these yogis have not first abandoned grasping at the self. Until they have accustomed themselves to a direct realization of emptiness and uprooted ignorance, the necessary causes and conditions will gather together and ripen into a manifestation of the egotistic view, giving rise to the other mental afflictions. This leads to the creation of karma and to further rebirth in samsara.

The last line of the sutra mentions Udraka as an example. He was a non-Buddhist yogi who spent so many years in meditation that he accomplished all four concentrations of the form realm and the first three absorptions of the formless realm up to and including the level of nothingness. The mental afflictions on these seven levels no longer arose within his mental continuum, and those afflictions on the highest level of the formless realm, the peak of samsaric existence, are so very subtle that the meditator almost appears to be an arhat. At this point Udraka no longer experienced any noticeable attachment, hatred, or other affliction, so he thought that he had achieved liberation from samsara. During the time it had taken him to achieve this level, Udraka's hair had grown very long. One day he awoke from his meditation and found that his hair had been eaten away by mice. This disturbed him. Seeing that his mind was agitated, he realized that mental afflictions were still present in his mental continuum. This made him angry. The karma of anger later caused him to fall into a lower rebirth. This story shows that Udraka's concentration was limited to the mundane level, indicated by the final phrase "up to this level" in the preceding verse, without touching the supramundane.

If such an accomplished yogi cannot gain freedom from samsara through his meditation, then what kind of meditation do we need to do in order to gain liberation? The answer is given in the next stanza of this sutra:[14]

> If you analyze the selflessness of phenomena,
> And if, having analyzed, you meditate upon it,
> This will cause the result: the attainment of nirvana.
> There is no peace from any other cause.

Only through precisely analyzing the nature of phenomena can we generate the wisdom that sees selflessness, which is the cause of the final result, nirvana. Emptiness cannot be realized without refined logical examination. We must investigate how the subject and its object exist. Realizing emptiness does not mean making the mind empty by letting go of all thoughts. Some people think that every thought is pervaded by the mental affliction of ignorance and thus having no thoughts at all is the realization of śūnyatā. Tsongkhapa and Kamalaśīla strongly attack this interpretation. They say that if emptiness simply means making one's mind empty so that nothing appears to it, nothing is known, and nothing is grasped, then it is like not having a mind at all.

Cultivating a practice that makes the mind dull, as if it were deeply asleep, is not productive. Some animals hibernate during the winter; they sleep without any thoughts arising, and nothing bothers them for several months. But even though they spend all this time without thinking, they do not realize the truth. Their long sleep does not get rid of their mental afflictions. When they wake up in the spring they are still in samsara. The way to realize emptiness is to develop an understanding of emptiness through analysis and then meditate on what has been understood. In this way the object gradually becomes clearer and clearer until one finally has a direct realization. In brief, first we must examine in what way things are empty. Once we find the correct view of emptiness, we meditate utilizing that wisdom continuously. That meditation is the cause for attaining the final result, nirvana.

Suppose someone asks, "Is there another way to obtain liberation without needing to realize emptiness?" In the last line of the preceding stanza, Buddha clearly says, "No, the permanent peace of nirvana has no other cause. It is impossible to pacify suffering and the cause of suffering without the special wisdom that directly realizes emptiness. Meditation on any path that does not have this wisdom cannot free you from suffering and its cause." Indeed, if there were another way we would not bother trying to understand śūnyatā.

Tsongkhapa draws this *King of Concentrations Sutra* quotation from the first of Kamalaśīla's three *Stages of Meditation* texts. He quotes from all three texts at various points in his *Lamrim Chenmo* to support his views on emptiness. So it is helpful to know how and why Kamalaśīla wrote them. Buddhism first came to Tibet during the reign of King Songtsen Gampo in the seventh century. Later, in the eighth century, King Trisong Detsen fostered the spread of Buddhism in Tibet. He invited the great Indian master Śāntarakṣita to give monastic ordinations and teachings on the sutras. At that time the original religion of Tibet, called Bon, was still very popular. Bon involves the worship of local spirits and nature gods, such as tree gods and water gods. Each family also had their own gods that had to be worshiped so that they would not cause harm. Many of the king's ministers were followers of Bon and were critical of the new religion from India. They tried to influence the king to protect Bon and prevent Buddhism from taking root in Tibet. In response, Śāntarakṣita urged the king to invite to Tibet the great Indian tantric adept and magician, Guru Padmasambhava. Padmasambhava spread the Dharma by dealing with the superstitions of the people and subduing the local demons. With his powers he overawed the local spirits; those gods promised to abandon their harmful ways and protect people engaged in virtuous activities. They are now called Dharma protectors because they assist practitioners of Buddhism. Padmasambhava also gave tantric teachings and initiations to the members of the royal family, the nobility, and certain restricted gatherings of people.

In the eighth century there was a strong relationship between China and Tibet. The Buddhism being brought to Tibet from China was quite different from the teachings transmitted by Śāntarakṣita. Indian Buddhism focuses on abandoning the ten nonvirtuous actions, engaging in virtuous activities, taking vows, and all the other basic practices. In contrast, a form of Chinese Buddhism exemplified by the teachings of the great Chinese master Hashang Mahayana seemed very simple. He gave Dharma teachings that everyone, even ordinary laypeople, could practice easily. He taught, "Do not think anything and do not do anything." He told people not to engage in discursive thought. Why? The reason he gave is that all thoughts—judgments about things being good or bad, and so on—are obstructions to enlightenment in the same way that white clouds and black clouds both obstruct the sunlight, golden chains and iron chains both tie you down, and white dogs and black dogs both bite. He claimed that good thoughts and bad thoughts function in this way, so they should be stopped altogether. The mind should be completely blank. Hashang and his followers propounded that the mind is like a clear, colorless crystal. If we put a colored cloth underneath this clear crystal each of the colors will be reflected in it, though the crystal itself remains free of color. Similarly, the mind is influenced by sensory awareness and thoughts, but once we put these discursive thoughts aside the pure mind is revealed; this pure mind is the essence of buddhahood. Hashang's followers contend that everyone is already a buddha; the nature of the mind is already completely pure. This teaching on the nature of the mind is special, but it needs to be understood properly. It is not to be taken literally.

However, in those ancient times some Tibetans were attracted to a literal interpretation of the approach taught by Hashang. They thought it was simple and marvelous; it did not require any scholarship or effort. There was no need to worry, no need to do anything, no need to engage in complicated meditation—just sit there and relax! Hashang had masses of followers from eastern Tibet all the way up to Lhasa. The king found himself in a difficult situation and wondered what to do about the rivalry between these two very different kinds of Buddhism. Hashang's approach appeared to be opposite to the Indian Buddhist approach, which insisted on thinking carefully, abandoning nonvirtuous behavior, and replacing it with virtuous behavior. The king did not want to have two conflicting views in his land. Śāntarakṣita, prior to leaving Tibet, had advised the king that if a situation like this were to arise he should invite Kamalaśīla, Śāntarakṣita's own disciple, to come from India to clear up the confusion about Buddhist philosophy and practice.

So King Trisong Detsen invited Kamalaśīla and a few of his Indian follow-ers to come to Lhasa, where Hashang and his disciples had already gathered. The king and the Chinese master, with their respective entourages, went to welcome Kamalaśīla at the Tsangpo River, south of Lhasa. The party from Lhasa was on the north bank of the river, and the party from India approached on the south bank. Before they met, each of the great Buddhist masters wanted to check the skill and intelligence of the other. Kamalaśīla raised his walking stick and turned it in a certain way to ask, "What is the cause of samsara?" In response the Chinese master held the two sleeves of his coat to indicate, "Grasping at the duality of subject and object is the cause of samsara." In other words, he was expressing his view that there should be no thought or any kind of mental grasping.

The king asked the two teachers to debate. He proclaimed that whoever lost the debate must offer a flower garland or silk scarf to the winner and then return home. The winner would remain in Tibet to teach the Dharma, and Tibetans would thereafter follow the winner's view. Scholars have not deter-mined whether the debate took place in Samye, Lhasa, or western Tibet. How-ever, it does not really matter where it took place. As you may know, Indian scholars are great logicians; if there is a debate they will definitely win. So Kamalaśīla won. Hashang lost and had to go back to China. From that time onward, just as the king had proclaimed, Tibetans would follow the Indian Madhyamaka view and practice. The king recognized that his subjects needed clear and practical instructions on how to do that, so he asked Kamalaśīla to write a text explaining the teachings.

Based on this request Kamalaśīla wrote the three *Stages of Meditation* texts. In these texts he negates wrong views and proves the correct view by means of logical reasoning supported by a great many scriptural quotations. In the second *Stages of Meditation* he says we must be certain that the wisdom real-izing selflessness is necessary to sever the root of cyclic existence. Many great non-Buddhist yogis had developed the highest level of mundane meditative concentration and thereby attained five types of supernormal knowledge: the divine eye, divine hearing, the ability to see past lives, miraculous pow-ers, and the ability to read the mind of those whose attainments are lower than or equal to one's own. However, there is a sixth supernormal knowledge not attainable merely through developing mundane meditative concentra-tion: a direct realization that one's mental afflictions have been permanently removed. This knowledge cannot be attained by non-Buddhists because they still have a strongly entrenched egotistic view. According to Buddhism these non-Buddhist yogis have many virtuous qualities, so most likely they would be reborn in the god realms. However, all their achievements occur within cyclic existence, not beyond it. Without the correct view of selflessness they have no means to obtain the sixth supernormal knowledge and be freed from samsara. It is impossible to attain liberation from cyclic existence without developing the wisdom realizing selflessness through analytical reasoning. The *Scriptural Collection of the Bodhisattvas (Bodhisattva-piṭaka)* says:

> Being satisfied by mere meditative concentration, without realizing reality as explained in the scriptures, gives rise to pride—thinking that you have attained the path cultivating the profound meaning. Thus you will not be liberated from cyclic existence. Having considered this, I say: "It is through hearing others that you will be liberated from aging and death."

Here Buddha clearly specifies that merely emptying the mind is not enough. The phrase "mere meditative concentration" refers to mastering the nine stages of developing śamatha, through which we can keep the mind steady and free of distracting thoughts. But if, as a result of this practice, we view all thoughts as obstructions to enlightenment and see the mind's true nature as free of thought and without any reflection of objects, then we will be greatly misled. Buddha voices his concern that if we give rise to this experience we may feel pride, thinking, "I have found the true nature of the mind, the profound reality." Such a thought prevents us from gaining liberation from cyclic existence, because this experience is not the realization of emptiness that destroys ignorance. In this quotation, "the path cultivating the profound meaning" refers to a realization of emptiness; the error is to think that *emptiness* refers to the mind being empty of all perceptions and conceptions rather than to the emptiness of inherent existence. When we make this mistake, we view all thoughts as obstructions to enlightenment.

Some people think that they do not need to study or hear the teachings from another person. They think that wisdom arises from within, simply through keeping the mind contained and stopping all thoughts and perceptions. But this is a misconception. Therefore Buddha says that we need to hear the teachings from others in order to become free of aging and death. We do not naturally have knowledge of ultimate reality, so we must learn about it from reliable, holy teachers. In this way we can develop the wisdom that arises from hearing about selflessness. After this we must study and analyze the meaning of the teachings we have heard. This is how to develop the wisdom that arises from thinking. Then we must meditate on what we have understood by means of this wisdom arisen from thinking and analyzing. In this way we develop the wisdom that arises from meditation. Through the development of these three kinds of wisdom we will be liberated from the misery of aging and death. *Aging and death* is the last of the twelve links of dependent arising. Each link arises in dependence on the previous one. So to become free of aging and death and the entire cycle, we move back through the twelve links to reach the root of the whole process—ignorance of the way things actually exist. Ignorance can only be uprooted by its opposite: the special wisdom that sees the true nature of reality, which arises from hearing, thinking, and meditating.

If the wisdom perceiving reality arose simply by stopping all thought and activity, why would Buddha have given so many teachings on wisdom? Why would so many scriptures state that we should hear, study, and concentrate on these teachings to gain a realization of the ultimate truth? Some Buddhist scriptures unambiguously explain reality, whereas others explicitly address other topics such as the truth of suffering and its cause or Mahayana practices such as boundless love, compassion, and bodhicitta. However, even the texts that explicitly explain the method side implicitly point toward developing the correct view of emptiness. Just as all the great rivers and little streams in the world—whether flowing from the east, west, north, or south—eventually reach the ocean, all the Buddhist scriptures—no matter what their subject and whether they are directed to practitioners of the lower, intermediate, or great spiritual scope—lead directly or indirectly to a realization of emptiness. The key point is that only through clearly understanding emptiness will we remove the root of cyclic existence, ignorance. Until we have a direct realization of reality, we cannot destroy the darkness of ignorance. Understanding śūnyatā is the light that makes the darkness disappear completely. Pure wisdom will not arise by merely developing the single-pointed mind that is śamatha. For this reason we should search without hesitation for the special wisdom that understands reality, the meaning of selflessness. Kamalaśīla's second *Stages of Meditation* says:

> When you have achieved śamatha, you should cultivate vipaśyanā. You should think, "All Buddha's teachings were excellently taught. Whether directly or indirectly elucidating reality, they incline toward it. If I understand reality, it will remove all the tangled nets of wrong views, just as the light of dawn eliminates the darkness. Śamatha alone will not produce pure wisdom nor clear away the mental obstructions. However, if I use understanding to meditate correctly on reality, I will generate pure wisdom and realize reality. Only through this wisdom will I completely abandon the obstructions. Since that is so, I must abide in śamatha and use understanding to thoroughly search for reality. Thus I should not be satisfied with mere śamatha." You may ask,

"What is reality?" Ultimately all things are empty of a self of persons and a self of phenomena.

Being entangled in nets of wrong views, especially the egotistic view, gives rise to many wrong perceptions, such as considering what is impure to be pure, what is in the nature of suffering to be blissful, what is impermanent to be permanent, and what is selfless to have a self. These nets of wrong views are cut away by the special insight that realizes emptiness. A yogi must understand that all phenomena—whether external or internal, subject or object—do not exist ultimately. They are free of ultimate existence as a person or as a phenomenon. They exist relatively or dependently. Ultimate reality, the emptiness of existing ultimately, is known by the sixth perfection: the perfection of wisdom. The other five perfections, including meditative concentration, cannot directly realize emptiness. Those perfections are blind; wisdom alone sees the truth. So we must not confuse mere meditative concentration with perfect wisdom. We must develop special insight itself. Eventually we must actualize the union of śamatha and supreme vipaśyanā. In *Basic Path to Awakening*, Tsongkhapa says:

> I do not see the ability to cut the root of cyclic existence
> Merely with single-pointed concentration;
> Yet no matter how much you analyze using wisdom without śamatha,
> You will not get rid of the mental afflictions.
>
> The wisdom reflecting deeply on the meaning of reality,
> Having mounted the horse of unwavering śamatha,
> Destroys all the objects of grasping at the extremes
> With the sharp sword of reasoning of the Middle Way free from extremes.
>
> Through the vast wisdom of correct analysis,
> The vipaśyanā realizing reality flourishes.[15]

Right now we have erroneous perceptions as well as wrong views and an incorrect understanding of reality. We fall to one extreme or the other continuously. The logical methods of the Middle Way establish a view of emptiness that is free from the extremes of nihilism and eternalism. Nāgārjuna uses reasoning to establish the correct view in all twenty-seven chapters of *Fundamental Treatise on the Middle Way* (*Mūla-madhyamaka-kārikā*). To prove the correct view of emptiness, he presents many different arguments from many points of view, such as time, agent, and action. By properly examining the object of inquiry in this way, our wisdom gradually increases, and we understand that things are not absolutely, independently, or inherently existent. However, this logical understanding of emptiness is not sufficient by itself. We must unite it with meditative concentration. Wisdom alone without śamatha is dry and cannot remove the mental afflictions. So having understood the very depths of reality, we must put this wisdom into practice by conjoining it with the meditation technique of śamatha. In this way we will finally generate a powerful vipaśyanā that can cut the root of cyclic existence. This kind of wisdom is special insight. In Tsongkhapa's analogy śamatha is like the horse and vipaśyanā is like the warrior riding it, wielding the weapons of Nāgārjuna's sharp arguments. Mounted on a horse, a warrior can move very fast, turn in any direction, and manipulate powerful weapons to gain victory over the enemy in battle. Similarly, using the weapons of logical analysis, wisdom rides the obedient and powerful horse of śamatha to destroy the objects of wrong perceiving and wrong conceiving, thereby cutting the root of cyclic existence.

Buddha turned the wheel of Dharma three times. This does not mean that he taught only three times; it means that he presented three fundamental approaches to understanding reality. In the first turning of the wheel Buddha taught that everything exists in a real sense; he explained the four noble truths, the six realms of rebirth, cause and effect, and so on. In the second turning Buddha presented a doctrine that seems to reject what he taught in the first turning of the wheel. He taught the perfection of wisdom so as to show the empty nature of all phenomena. The teachings in this turning include, for example, the *Heart Sutra*, which says that form, feeling, discernment, the four noble truths, and even buddhahood do not exist. In the third turning of the wheel Buddha deals with this apparent contradiction. It is said that at Vaiśāli the bodhisattva Avalokiteśvara pretended not to understand these ostensibly contradictory teachings. He made a special request to Buddha: "First you taught the four noble truths, cause and effect, and so on, to be real things. Then you taught us that none of them exist. For us this seems to be a great contradiction. However, you are an omniscient being; for you there is surely no contradiction. So please explain to us what you mean, especially with regard to the second set of teachings." In response to this supplication Buddha taught the *Sutra Unraveling the Intended Meaning* (*Saṃdhi-nirmocana-sūtra*). In this sutra Avalokiteśvara asks Buddha:

> Bhagavan, through which of the perfections do bodhisattvas behold the absence of essential nature of phenomena?

In reply Buddha says:

> Avalokiteśvara, they behold this through the perfection of wisdom.

Similarly, in the *Sutra of Cultivating Faith in the Mahayana* (*Ārya-mahāyāna-prasāda-prabhāvanā-sūtra*), Buddha says, "If you lack the perfection of wisdom, I do not say that you gain release from samsara, no matter what Mahayana practices you do with faith in the great vehicle of bodhisattvas." In short, wisdom is the most important of the six perfections. No matter how much faith a bodhisattva has in the Mahayana, no matter how sincerely or how much a bodhisattva practices the first five perfections, he or she will not gain release from cyclic existence without wisdom.

BUSINESS REPLY MAIL
FIRST-CLASS MAIL   PERMIT NO. 1100   SOMERVILLE, MA

POSTAGE WILL BE PAID BY ADDRESSEE

WISDOM PUBLICATIONS
199 ELM ST
SOMERVILLE MA 02144-9908

Wisdom

WISDOM PUBLICATIONS

Please fill out and return this card if you would like to receive our catalogue and special offers. The postage is already paid!

NAME

ADDRESS

CITY / STATE / ZIP / COUNTRY

EMAIL

Sign up for our newsletter and special offers at wisdompubs.org

Wisdom Publications is a non-profit charitable organization.

Relying on Definitive Sources

(a') Fulfilling the prerequisites for insight
    (1') Identifying the scriptures of provisional and definitive meaning
    (2') The history of commentary on Nāgārjuna's intended meaning

———✦———

THE WAY TO DEVELOP insight is explained in four main topics:

    (a')   Fulfilling the prerequisites for insight (chapters 2–21)
    (b')   Classifications of insight (chapter 22)
    (c')   How to cultivate insight in meditation (chapters 22–23)
    (d')   The measure of achieving insight through meditation (chapter 24)

Tsongkhapa now describes the causes and conditions that give rise to insight. This is the main topic. Next we learn about the divisions of insight and then how to employ insight meditation. The fourth section describes how to determine when we have achieved insight. These topics occupy the majority of this book; only a short summary and conclusion follow.

(a') FULFILLING THE PREREQUISITES FOR INSIGHT

If you want to understand emptiness, you must learn about it from somebody who understands it well. In other words, the first step is to rely on a spiritual master who has great knowledge of the essence of the scriptures. It is very important to study the teachings that have been passed down from master to disciple, including the sutras as well as the commentaries of great masters. There are many ways to gain a correct initial understanding of the teachings: you can attend the teachings of a lama, listen to recordings, watch videos, read books, discuss various topics with your friends, and so on. After this you need to use logic to analyze what you have heard. This will clarify your understanding until you are very sure about what is correct and what is incorrect. The correct view of emptiness arises from the wisdom that comes from hearing and thinking about the subject. If you have neither listened to the teachings nor thought about them, then you have nothing to meditate on and so cannot generate genuine insight. There is a Tibetan saying that goes, "A person who claims to be a great meditator without having heard many teachings is like someone without hands trying to climb a steep, rugged mountain." Mountain climbers need their hands to ascend a cliff; similarly, the understanding arising from hearing and thinking is indispensable for developing genuine insight into the nature of reality.

The nature of reality is emptiness. Emptiness is the ultimate truth; it refers to reality as it is. When you directly realize something as it is, the object exists as it appears. There is nothing to be changed. Only emptiness is stable in this sense; it appears exactly as it is. All other phenomena appear in various ways that are different from how they exist; but they are, in reality, empty of that way of appearing. Emptiness alone is free of this variation. The ultimate nature of reality, emptiness, is such a very deep subject. After attaining enlightenment Buddha initially thought that no one would understand it. He says:

> Profound, peaceful, free of elaborations, radiant, unproduced:
> I found a truth like nectar.
> No one I teach this to will understand it.
> So I will not speak about it; I will hide in the forest.[16]

If Buddha had immediately declared, "There is no form, no sound, no smell," and so on, everyone would have thought that he was crazy![17] They would have wondered why a man from a royal family, after many years of meditation, came back to say that nothing exists. So for a time Buddha taught what was best for beginners, such as cause and effect expressed in the four noble truths. Eventually he gave explicit teachings on emptiness—because, as we have seen, only a direct realization of emptiness can free one from contaminated cyclic rebirth.

Understanding emptiness comes about in dependence on studying the scriptures and teachings given by others. When we search for the truth we have to depend on what is known as the four reliances:

> Do not rely on the person, rely on the teaching;
> Do not rely on mere words, rely on their meaning;
> Do not rely on the provisional meaning, rely on the definitive meaning;
> Do not rely on conceptual understanding, rely on direct realization.

Buddha was very clear that we should not be swayed by a charismatic person. He never said or implied, "I am great, and so you should accept whatever I say." We should rely on what someone teaches, the Dharma. However, we should look deeper than the words; we should rely on what the words mean. The meaning of a text can be either *provisional*, in that the words require further interpretation to establish the intended meaning, or *definitive*, where the words require no interpretation to establish the ultimate meaning. We should rely on the definitive meaning. In relying on the definitive meaning, we should not depend merely on our conceptual understanding. Although we need this kind of understanding, it is not sufficient. In the end we have to rely on understanding that arises from our meditation: a direct realization of emptiness that is free of thought.

In order to develop a direct realization of emptiness, we must start by studying the meaning of the definitive scriptures. To do that we need to recognize which scriptures are definitive and which are provisional. Initially we do not know which teachings to follow; we do not know whom to trust. We are like a blind person, liable to walk into danger because we are without a guide. We should not trust just anyone; we should trust only someone who knows the truth directly and can explain it clearly, logically, and in detail. If we find that kind of person, then we should follow them absolutely.

Tsongkhapa says we should rely on Nāgārjuna and Asaṅga, the two great openers of the chariot way. This may seem like a strange epithet to you; when I first studied this topic, I did not understand it either. When I was a child there were no wheeled vehicles in Tibet. Reading this appellation, I often wondered, "What is a chariot?" But it makes sense when you think that in ancient India kings and queens traveled in elaborate chariots or coaches that required wide roads. As time went by, these roads ceased to be used. The jungle would grow over them, and the thoroughfare would disappear until someone rediscovered and reopened it. A similar thing happened to the Mahayana teachings. Buddha taught the Mahayana, but over time people became more interested in their own liberation and so focused on the Hinayana teachings. Gradually the teachings on universal compassion, bodhicitta, and the extensive presentation of emptiness became less common. The Mahayana tradition was virtually lost to the world because the scriptures explaining the subtle way to understand emptiness, as well as those who practiced it, had disappeared.

Buddha prophesied that the Mahayana would dwindle until it almost vanished, but then two individuals would reestablish it. Asaṅga would place special emphasis on reopening the method side of Mahayana practice, and Nāgārjuna would reopen the teachings on emptiness. There are many sutras and tantras in which Buddha prophesied that Nāgārjuna would clearly explain the profound reality that is free of the extremes of nihilism and eternalism. For example, in the *Descent into Laṅka Sutra* (*Ārya-laṅkāvatāra-sūtra*) he says:

> In the south, in the area of Vidarbha,
> There will be a monk known widely as Śrīman
> Who will also be called Nāga.
> Destroying the extreme positions of existence and nonexistence,
> He will thoroughly teach in the world
> My vehicle—the unsurpassed Great Vehicle.
> Then he will achieve the Very Joyous stage,
> And upon passing away go to the Blissful Pure Land.[18]

This prophecy says that after Nāgārjuna explains the unsurpassable Mahayana vehicle, he will achieve the first bodhisattva stage, the first moment of the path of seeing. Some other texts say that he reached as high as the seventh bodhisattva stage. This account does not contradict the previous one if we understand it to mean that Nāgārjuna accomplished at least the first stage, without mentioning whether he might also have progressed further.

There are many other prophesies about Nāgārjuna. He is said to be famous in the three worlds: below the earth, on the earth, and in the heavens above the earth.[19] According to legend, Nāgārjuna was particularly famous underground in the nāga kingdom. Not only did he teach the nāgas, but he also retrieved the *Perfection of Wisdom Sutras* from the nāga kingdom, where they had been kept safe since the passing away of Buddha. Nāgārjuna reintroduced the teachings on emptiness here on the earth. He explained from many points of view what Buddha taught, using various logical reasons and examples. Without his detailed explanation to guide us, we would find it very difficult to understand such statements as "There is no form, no sound," and so on. Candrakīrti emphasizes the importance of understanding Nāgārjuna:

> Those outside the path of the honorable Nāgārjuna
> Have no means to find peace;
> They deviate from the ultimate and conventional truths;
> Diverging from these, there is no achievement of liberation.[20]

Tsongkhapa agrees with this assessment of Nāgārjuna, and he follows Nāgārjuna's views closely throughout the *Lamrim Chenmo*. He gives reasons why we too should rely on Nāgārjuna's system to develop the correct view: because Buddha prophesied that Nāgārjuna would be the reopener of the

Mahayana and because Nāgārjuna wrote excellent commentaries on the *Perfection of Wisdom Sutras* to guide us toward an understanding of emptiness.

The prerequisites for developing insight are explained in three subtopics:

(1') Identifying the scriptures of provisional and definitive meaning
(2') The history of commentary on Nāgārjuna's thought
(3') How to determine the view of emptiness (chapters 3–21)

(1') IDENTIFYING THE SCRIPTURES OF PROVISIONAL AND DEFINITIVE MEANING

Those who wish to understand reality must rely on Buddha's scriptures. His teachings are many and varied because they were given to disciples with differing attitudes and capacities. He had particular purposes for saying different things at different times—just as parents tell their children different things, some true and some not, in order to help them in a specific way. So you may wonder, "With all these different scriptures, how are we to discern the correct explanation of reality?" Tsongkhapa says we will know the nature of reality through relying on scriptures of definitive meaning.

So we must be able to distinguish which scriptures are definitive and which are provisional. There are different ways to divide the scriptures into these categories: some differentiate them from the point of view of the words of the text and others from the point of view of the text's subject matter. The Madhyamaka school of thought differentiates scriptures from the point of view of their subject matter. The scriptures and commentaries that principally explain the ultimate truth are classified as definitive. Although the textbooks of different monasteries define the characteristics of the scriptures differently, they all agree that the main subject of a definitive scripture is the ultimate truth. Scriptures that principally explain conventional truth are classified as provisional scriptures. The *Teachings of Akṣayamati Sutra* (*Akṣayamati-nirdeśa-sūtra*) says:

> What are the definitive scriptures and what are the provisional scriptures? Sutras that teach conventional things are provisional. Sutras that teach ultimate reality are definitive. Sutras that teach various [referring] words and terms are provisional. Sutras that teach profound reality, which is difficult to see and difficult to realize, are definitive.

Are all scriptures that teach conventional things provisional? Not necessarily; we qualify this by saying: those scriptures that *principally* show conventional things are provisional, and those scriptures that *principally* show ultimate truth are definitive. So the question is, "How does a text teach conventional things so as to be labeled provisional?" Likewise, "How does a text teach the ultimate truth so as to be labeled definitive?" The answer is given in the sutra just quoted:

> Sutras called provisional are those that teach about an owner, even though there is no owner, using various terms such as self, sentient being, living being, nourished being, creature, person, vital being, able being, agent, and experiencer. Sutras called definitive are those that teach the three doors to liberation—emptiness, signlessness, and wishlessness—as well as no composition, no birth, no production, no sentient beings, no living beings, no persons, and no owners.

Provisional scriptures use various terms, labels, and synonyms to teach the diverse characteristics of conventional things. For example, there are many ways to refer to the person or the self. Each of these words, such as "experiencer" or "sentient being," highlights a slightly different function of a living being.[21] Even though there is no substantial or inherently existent self, the language used makes it look as if there is such a self. Let us consider an easier example. In the ancient Indian tradition various terms are used to refer to the moon. One name is given from the point of view of the white color of its light. Another name indicates that the temperature becomes cooler when the moon rises and the sun sets. Another describes the moon's appearance as having a rabbit-shaped form on its surface. All these epithets—White Circle, One with Cooling Rays, Rabbit Bearer—refer to the same object, the moon. They simply show the conventional nature of the moon—its color, temperature, and appearance—from different points of view.

Whereas provisional scriptures elaborate the various aspects of the self, a living being, a person, and so on, definitive scriptures cut away those elaborations by teaching no self, no production, and so on. Elaborations—such as good and bad, beautiful and ugly, cause and effect—do exist conventionally. However, definitive scriptures cut through these elaborations by showing that they do not exist in an ultimate sense, an understanding of which gradually eliminates the wrong view holding them as such.

Definitive scriptures teach about the emptiness of inherent existence and that the realization of emptiness is the door to liberation. This can be divided into three aspects: emptiness, signlessness, and wishlessness. Emptiness indicates that everything has the nature of being empty of inherent existence. Signlessness shows that although conventional things, such as trees, water, and fire, have their own sign—which can be interpreted as their own name, mark, or cause—ultimately there are no signs. Things look as if they truly exist, in that they have their own unique qualities or causes. However, they do not have any real or inherent existence. They exist conventionally. The third door of liberation, wishlessness, relates to the future arising of a result. In a conventional sense things are compounded through the accumulation of causes and conditions, but in an ultimate sense there is no such thing. There is nothing arising inherently (with regard to the future) and nothing produced inherently (with regard to the past). Likewise there are no inherently existent sentient beings, living beings, or persons, and neither is there any inherently existent ownership. Thus the three doors show the emptiness of inherent existence of nature, cause, and effect, respectively. Nāgārjuna also presents his arguments in these terms, showing the emptiness of inherent existence from the point of view of action, agent, and object of action.[22]

The *King of Concentrations Sutra* says we can categorize the scriptures based on whether they primarily teach conventional or ultimate reality:

> Know to be instances of definitive sutras
> Those that teach emptiness as explained by Buddha;
> Know to be provisional all teachings
> That explicate sentient beings, persons, living beings.

The subjects explained in the definitive scriptures, such as the emptiness of the self, emptiness of production, and emptiness of cause, are themselves ultimate; they are ultimate truth. Likewise the subjects explained in the provisional scriptures, such as birth, person, self, cause, effect, and sign, are themselves conventional; they are conventional truth. Kamalaśīla says in the *Illumination of the Middle Way* (*Madhyamakāloka*):

> Therefore you should understand that only those scriptures presenting the ultimate truth are of definitive meaning; the converse ones are of provisional meaning. The *Ornament for the Light of Wisdom That Introduces the Object of All Buddhas* (*Sarva-buddha-viṣayāvatāra-jñānālokālaṃkāra*) says, "Anything of definitive meaning is the ultimate." Also the *Teachings of Akṣayamati Sutra* shows that the absence of production and so on are called "definitive meaning." Thus it is certain that only the absence of production and so on are called "ultimate."

Emptiness is the ultimate truth and therefore definitive meaning. Subjects other than emptiness are conventional truths and therefore provisional meaning. Emptiness is definitive because it cannot be interpreted to mean something else. In contrast, provisional indicates something temporarily arranged or adopted for the time being in the place of something permanent or final. It is accepted in default. It is interpretable in that it serves to set forth the meaning of something else. Consider, for example, form and the emptiness of form. Form is provisional. The emptiness of form, or form's lack of inherent existence, is definitive. When we look at form we see various characteristics—shape, outline, color, and so on. But when we look for how form really exists, its final nature, we find nothing absolute in itself. The object we are examining does not exist from its own side. In the end we find only that negation; yet that negation is not nothing.

Similarly, the person has various characteristics—the body, mind, and so on. When we look for the true nature of the person—the self, the soul, or whatever we choose to call it—we find that there is no inherent self or soul. That lack of inherent existence itself is the final nature. From there we cannot go any further. That is the final meaning. We can see and further analyze the characteristics of form, such as its color and shape. We can see and further investigate the characteristics of oneself, such as one's sense powers and consciousness. But when we arrive at the final truth, the emptiness of inherent existence, that is the end. There is nowhere further to go. That is the meaning of reality. If we look at reality itself, we find it is also empty of inherent existence. We cannot interpret the final meaning in any other way than the emptiness of inherent existence. This is why it is called the definitive meaning.

So according to this system, the definitive and the provisional meaning as well as the definitive and the provisional scriptures are differentiated on the basis of the two truths. All types of emptiness are the definitive meaning and are explained in the definitive scriptures. The remaining phenomena are the provisional meaning and are presented in the provisional scriptures. Kamala-śīla's *Illumination of the Middle Way* says:

> To what does *definitive meaning* refer? It refers to whatever has validity and expresses the ultimate truth, because it cannot be interpreted as something else by anyone else.[23]

This statement presents two aspects of definitive meaning. First, whatever is explained as definitive must be established by valid knowledge—either valid reasoning or valid perception.[24] It cannot be proved in any other way. In addition, the definitive must have as its subject matter the ultimate, the final nature of reality, which is the furthest limit of investigation. Thus a definitive scripture must fulfill two requirements: it must be valid, in that it cannot be disproved as it is expressed, and its subject matter must be the final nature of reality, which cannot be interpreted in any other way—not even by a buddha. This quotation also implicitly shows us how to understand *provisional meaning* and *provisional scriptures*. The provisional is the converse of the definitive: it is not suitable to be held as it is expressed, and it must be interpreted to mean something else. In other words, its meaning is not the final meaning; it is a text whose subject matter is not the ultimate.

To clarify this distinction let us look at a statement such as the first of the four seals, "All products are impermanent." This statement is valid. It can be proved logically, and there is no valid way to prove the contrary, that is, that any products are permanent. However, even though the statement "All products are impermanent" is established by valid knowledge and can be taken literally, it is still not a definitive teaching. It is provisional because it does not concern the ultimate nature of reality. Even if we understand that form is impermanent, and that is indeed true, the impermanence of form is not the ultimate truth. We can subject form to ultimate analysis if we want to search for its final nature. However, when we search for the impermanence of form existing from its own side, we will not find it; all we find is emptiness. The final nature of each thing is its emptiness. So the meaning of any scriptures presenting conventional things must in the end be interpreted further.

There is some difference among the Buddhist philosophical schools regarding the categorization of provisional and definitive scriptures. Some schools say that scriptures that are acceptable literally as expressed are definitive scriptures, and those that are not literally acceptable are provisional. Based on this understanding an opponent may pose the following question. Any definitive sutra must be literally acceptable; so if it says "There is no production" or "There is no person" and so on, we would have to conclude that there is no production and no person at all. Otherwise that sutra would not be literally acceptable and instead would be a provisional scripture. Tsongkhapa says that this position appears to be incorrect. Indeed there are many definitive teachings, such as the *Heart Sutra*, that say there is no production, no cessation, and so on; however, at certain critical points in the sutra Buddha applies a special qualification to this list of negations. When a qualifying term, such as "ultimate" or "inherent," is used in one place, it does not need to be repeated continuously. It should be understood to apply to the whole list of negations as a common attribute.

For example, the *Heart Sutra* says, "Perfectly see that even the five aggregates are empty of inherent existence." According to the Prāsaṅgika-Madhyamaka system, this means that the aggregates exist conventionally but not ultimately. Having stated the word "inherent" on the first occasion, in the rest of the sutra the word is dropped. It is not necessary to repeat it all the time; occasional occurrences are enough. So where it says that there is no form, no feeling, no discernment, no conditioning factors, no consciousness, and that there is no suffering, no cause of suffering, no cessation, and no path, it means that these things do not exist ultimately or inherently. Because this qualification is not specifically stated in each case, the individual phrases cannot be taken literally; we have to understand what is intended. There are many similar instances where the negations are explicitly qualified by terms such as "ultimate" and "inherent." In places where they are intended but not explicitly stated, you should add them yourself. Thus, since the ultimate reality of phenomena is the subject matter, and the qualification "inherently" is applied implicitly to all the particular cases mentioned, how could such a sutra not be definitive? Otherwise, if the statement "There is no production" were to be held literally so as to be a definitive teaching, then we would end up negating production in general. If we negate the generality, this necessarily implies that we negate the particular instances, in which case there could not be even one thing that is produced. The unintended consequence is that even the words we use to talk about these things could not exist. Therefore, Tsongkhapa concludes, although a scripture may contain a few individual words or phrases that cannot be accepted literally on their own, this does not disqualify such a text from being a definitive scripture. That is how it is understood in the Prāsaṅgika system.

The Svātantrika-Madhyamaka and Prāsaṅgika-Madhyamaka schools differ a little regarding this point. According to the Prāsaṅgika-Madhyamaka system of Buddhapālita and Candrakīrti, the following six terms are synonymous and indicate ways of existing that are to be rejected: *ultimately existent, truly existent, inherently existent, existing by way of its own characteristics, existing from its own side*, and *existing by its own nature*. The absence of these modes of existence is the Prāsaṅgika understanding of emptiness. The Svātantrika-Madhyamaka system of Bhāvaviveka, Śāntarakṣita, and Kamalaśīla defines emptiness very differently. They say that *truly existent* and *ultimately existent* mean the same thing and are to be rejected. The absence of these two modes of existence is the Svātantrika understanding of emptiness. However, in their system the following four terms are synonymous and indicate ways of existing that are accepted: *inherently existent, existing by way of its own characteristics, existing from its own side*, and *existing by its own nature*. In short, the Svātantrikas accept things to exist inherently, by their own characteristics, or by their own nature, whereas the Prāsaṅgikas do not accept anything to exist in that way at all.

The Prāsaṅgika and the Svātantrika systems are both Madhyamaka systems; they equally reject anything to be truly existent or ultimately existent. Both understand the emptiness of true existence and the emptiness of ultimate existence to be the actual profound emptiness, śūnyatā. The Prāsaṅgika system is more encompassing; they say that inherent existence is synonymous with true existence and ultimate existence, and thus the emptiness of inherent existence is also the profound emptiness, śūnyatā. This is not the case for the Svātantrika; they accept that things do inherently exist.

Therefore, according to the Svātantrika system, the *Heart Sutra* is provisional because even though it explains ultimate truth, it is not valid as it is expressed. The phrase "Perfectly see that even the five aggregates are empty of inherent existence" is not literally acceptable according to them. As discussed earlier, the term "inherent" here should be understood to apply throughout the text to all statements such as "There is no form, no feeling, no discernment, no causal factors, and no consciousness." None of these statements with the implied qualification can be taken as definitive by the Svātantrikas, because doing so would contradict their view that form and so on are inherently existent. According to the Svātantrika system it is insufficient to interpret "There is no form" to mean "There is no inherently existent form." The real meaning of such a statement must be: "There is no ultimately inherently existent form" or "There is no truly inherently existent form." They must add the terms "ultimately" or "truly" to the negation of existence or to the negation of inherent existence in order to correctly indicate the ultimate truth. Since such terms do not appear in the *Heart Sutra* at all, this text is taken to be a provisional scripture. Although this text discusses the ultimate as its subject matter, for the Svātantrikas it does not present a view of the ultimate that can be taken as valid in the way that it is literally expressed.

The Prāsaṅgika-Madhyamaka system does not require a definitive scripture to be valid as it is literally expressed. The single requirement that a scripture primarily discusses the ultimate is enough to make it definitive. Thus, according to Tsongkhapa, whether the meaning of a text can be accepted literally is not a sufficient criterion to determine if it is definitive. The main issue is the primary subject matter of the text. A definitive scripture must principally show the ultimate truth, śūnyatā, the final nature of reality. If it principally shows conventional things, it is a provisional scripture. The Svātantrika system agrees that texts that describe conventional things are provisional; however, they include other texts in this category also.

This is an important difference between these two philosophical systems because according to the Prāsaṅgika-Madhyamaka system both types of scripture sometimes use language in a way that cannot be held literally. A common example from a provisional scripture is the statement "One's father and mother are to be killed." These particular words were said to particular disciples, in a specific situation, and were meant to be understood in a particular way. The words "father" and "mother" do not refer to one's biological father and mother;

here "father" refers to karma, and "mother" refers to mental afflictions, both of which are to be destroyed. This kind of provisional or interpretable language is the obvious kind; everyone accepts that such language needs to be interpreted.

(2') The history of commentary on Nāgārjuna's thought

Nāgārjuna's six treatises correctly explain the view expressed in scriptures such as the *Perfection of Wisdom Sutras* that all phenomena are without any kind of inherent production, inherent cessation, and so forth.[25] There are various interpretations of Nāgārjuna's great treatises, and later scholars endeavor to explain what Nāgārjuna really means. Nāgārjuna's direct disciple, Āryadeva, is considered by later Madhyamaka scholars to be as valid and reliable as Nāgārjuna himself. Even great commentators of the Svātantrika and Prāsaṅgika schools, such as Buddhapālita, Bhāvaviveka, Candrakīrti, and Śāntarakṣita, trust Āryadeva in the same way that they trust Nāgārjuna. Thus Nāgārjuna and Āryadeva are referred to as the father and son; they are the source of all the other Madhyamaka commentaries and make no division into what later came to be called the Svātantrika-Madhyamaka and Prāsaṅgika-Madhyamaka views. Prior to the time of Tsongkhapa, Tibetan scholars referred to Nāgārjuna and Āryadeva as "great Mādhyamikas" or "Mādhyamikas of the great texts" and to the later Mādhyamikas as "one-sided Mādhyamikas."

Scholars have divided the Madhyamaka into subschools of thought in a number of ways. One earlier Tibetan scholar posits two types of Mādhyamikas in accordance with their way of presenting conventional truth: those Mādhyamikas who accept conventionalities in a way that is closer to the Sautrāntika system versus those Mādhyamikas who accept conventionalities in a way that is closer to the Yogācāra system. Sautrāntika-Mādhyamikas assert that conventionally there are independent external objects that are not of the nature of the mind, which act as causes that give rise to specific types of consciousness, and that consciousness is a different entity from external things. Yogācāra-Mādhyamikas assert that conventionally there is no duality of subject and object, there are no independent external objects, and everything is of the nature of the mind. When we make a twofold division of the Madhyamaka based on how conventional reality is understood, Śāntarakṣita and Kamalaśīla belong to the system called Yogācāra-Madhyamaka.

This earlier scholar also posited two types of Mādhyamikas in accordance with their way of asserting the ultimate: the Proponents of Rationally Established Illusion, who assert the combination of appearance and emptiness to be ultimate truth, versus the Proponents of Thorough Nonabiding, who assert ultimate truth to be the mere negation of elaborations with respect to appearances. This scholar says that Śāntarakṣita and Kamalaśīla are included in the former division. The terms characterizing these two divisions used by the earlier Tibetan scholars, namely, *illusion-like* and *thorough nonabiding*, were even used by some Indian scholars. Although some Indian and Tibetan scholars divide the Madhyamaka this way, Tsongkhapa does not bother too much with it. He says there are a lot of people with different ideas, views, and terminologies—so who in the world could possibly explain all of these different approaches? It is more important to understand the views of the great Mādhyamikas who follow Nāgārjuna. Tsongkhapa agrees with the great translator from Ngog, Loden Sherab,[26] who said that only fools are impressed by the twofold division of Mādhyamikas based on how they present ultimate truth.

A brief explanation of this division of the Madhyamaka will illustrate why Tsongkhapa does not go into detail here. The Proponents of Rationally Established Illusion are given this name because of the way they say that emptiness is understood. When people first try to understand śūnyatā, they attempt to logically prove that things are not truly existent. They may reason, for example, that because a thing, such as a sprout, dependently arises, it is not truly existent. One begins by thinking about what a sprout is and how it exists. A sprout arises as a result of planting a seed, which then germinates, and from which a shoot appears. A sprout arises in dependence on many things: the seed from which it grew, the soil, water, warmth, and so on. When all the necessary conditions come together, the sprout appears. Therefore it dependently arises. If a sprout were truly or absolutely existent, then its appearance would not depend on those other factors. It would exist through its own nature. But that is not how it is; it is dependently related. This inferential understanding occurs by first imagining a sprout and then thinking about how that sprout exists. Based on this one develops an inferential understanding that a sprout does not exist inherently, and one forms a mental picture of that. Then these two images, of subject and attribute, are combined together. The subject is the *sprout*; the attribute is *not truly existent*. To ordinary perception the sprout seems to be truly existent, but with this inferential understanding one knows that this appearance is not real. In other words, through inferential knowledge one understands that the appearance of a truly existent sprout is illusion-like. Hence the name of those following this approach: the Proponents of Rationally Established Illusion.

The Proponents of Rationally Established Illusion hold that the object of knowledge that is the combined appearance of the illusion-like nature and emptiness is ultimate truth. Having an illusion-like nature means that although something appears to exist in a particular way, one knows that it does not truly exist in that way. Because the appearance of emptiness is mixed with a conventional appearance, it is like an illusion: the image of śūnyatā, the attribute, is combined with the image of the subject, in this case a sprout. This inferential knowledge of śūnyatā is not as pure as a direct realization. A direct realization of emptiness arises in the mind as the perception of a mere absence—the emptiness of true existence.

Tsongkhapa says that the combined subject and attribute of such an inferential understanding—emptiness of true existence in combination with an appearance of the sprout as illusion-like—is not ultimate truth. It is not śūnyatā because the combination of a sprout and nontrue existence is an implicative negation.[27] It implies a nontruly existent sprout. Śūnyatā is a mere negation; it does not imply the existence of anything else.[28] The way to arrive at a genuine understanding of emptiness is to start by examining the subject or basis—in this case, a sprout. The appearance of the sprout is a conventional truth. Through examining whether it exists truly, we will succeed eventually in negating *truly existent* on the basis of the sprout. Then we meditate on that. In time just the pure negation, *not truly existent*, appears to the mind unmixed with the subject. When we actually perceive the emptiness of true existence, the subject or basis no longer appears to the mind. There is no combination of the appearance of emptiness and the appearance of the conventional object that is its basis.

Inferential understanding of śūnyatā, such as is generated by the Proponents of Rationally Established Illusion, relies on logical analysis; it arises in dependence on thought, not on direct perception. In general an object does not appear directly to a thought apprehending it; it appears mixed with a conceptual image of that object. However, the mind comprehends the object through this conceptual image. For example, when we look at a statue of Buddha we see it directly with our visual consciousness. When we close our eyes and try to recollect it, we see an image of that statue in the mind and can describe it to someone else. But it is not the same as seeing it directly with our eye consciousness. The mind is focused on a mental image of the statue, not on the statue. However, without the image appearing to our conceptual awareness, we would not understand the object. Every thought has this kind of quality. In the beginning we cannot realize emptiness without a conceptual image of emptiness. It is through the appearance of emptiness mixed with a conceptual image of it that we come to understand that there is no true existence. The appearing object of this inferential understanding based on reasoning, however, is not ultimate truth. It is an image of ultimate truth.

Śāntarakṣita's *Ornament for the Middle Way* (*Madhyamakālaṃkāra*) and Kamalaśīla's *Illumination of the Middle Way* both say that the object of an inferential understanding of emptiness "approximates ultimate truth," and therefore it is sometimes called *ultimate*—but it is not genuine ultimate truth. Other Mādhyamikas also say that the object arrived at when logical reasoning cuts away the elaborations of true existence is too rough to qualify as ultimate truth. Ultimate truth is the mere emptiness of inherent existence. It does not refer to something else that appears to the mind when the elaborations of true existence are conceptually eliminated. A direct realization does not directly rely on thought. So Tsongkhapa concludes that the twofold division of Mādhyamikas into the Proponents of Rationally Established Illusion and Proponents of Thorough Nonabiding is not appropriate.

Regarding the history of commentary on Nāgārjuna's thought, Yeshe De[29] mentions that Nāgārjuna and Āryadeva did not clearly specify whether external objects exist. Mādhyamikas do not accept anything to be ultimately existent; so the question here is whether, on a conventional level, an object exists as a separate entity from the mind apprehending it. Bhāvaviveka rejects the Yogācāra assertion that there are no external objects and that everything is of the nature of mind. According to the Yogācāras, the mind is truly existent; so if everything is of the nature of mind, then everything would be truly existent. The two lower philosophical schools, the Vaibhāṣika and the Sautrāntika, assert that physical things exist externally and are separate substances from the minds apprehending them. External things are made up of tiny partless atoms, which collect together to form bigger substances—such as the different elements of earth, water, fire, and air. Gross objects are formed from these elements coming together in certain ways. When objects are large enough they can be perceived by the senses and recognized as specific things, such as mountains, elephants, people, and houses. So according to these two schools, external objects are formed first and then the minds that perceive them arise. Bhāvaviveka accepts this differentiation between object and subject and rejects the Mind Only interpretation, so his system is called Sautrāntika-Madhyamaka.

Yeshe De further reports that Śāntarakṣita, a later commentator on Nāgārjuna, relies on the Yogācāra texts, such as those by Asaṅga, to show that conventionally there are no external objects. In contrast to the two lower schools, the Yogācāra says that the mind is primary and functions as the substance out of which externally appearing things are formed. Śāntarakṣita applies this to the Madhyamaka teachings. He shows that conventionally there are no external objects—there is just the mind. However, ultimately the mind does not exist by way of its own nature—there is no mind ultimately. Śāntarakṣita adopts a Mind Only position, so his system is called Yogācāra-Madhyamaka. In this way two Madhyamaka systems arose, the earlier being

Bhāvaviveka's Sautrāntika-Madhyamaka and the later being Śāntarakṣita's Yogācāra-Madhyamaka.

Tsongkhapa says that from the point of view of the order in which they historically appeared, this way of labeling these systems is correct. However, it is not correct from the point of view of a representation of their assertions. A division into Yogācāra-Madhyamaka and Sautrāntika-Madhyamaka should not be made based on whether they accept or reject external objects conventionally. It is incorrect to say that any Mādhyamika who accepts external objects to be conventionally existent should be called a Sautrāntika-Mādhyamika. For example, Candrakīrti accepts external objects to be conventionally existent but not in the way that a holder of Sautrāntika philosophical tenets believes them to exist. Likewise, it is totally incorrect to label Candrakīrti as being similar to the Vaibhāṣika system simply because of his acceptance of external objects. Thus Tsongkhapa does not accept this early division of the Madhyamaka system into Sautrāntika-Madhyamaka and Yogācāra-Madhyamaka.

The terminology for another twofold division of the Madhyamaka system evolved in Tibet: the division into Svātantrika-Madhyamaka and Prāsaṅgika-Madhyamaka. This division of the Madhyamaka accords with Candrakīrti's commentary on Nāgārjuna's *Fundamental Treatise on the Middle Way*, called *Clear Words* (*Prasanna-padā*), so Tsongkhapa concludes that later Tibetan scholars did not invent it. In fact he shows that this division developed in India as the great Madhyamaka scholars attempted to explain Nāgārjuna's ideas. The terms *Prāsaṅgika-Madhyamaka* and *Svātantrika-Madhyamaka* refer to the different systems of Buddhapālita and Bhāvaviveka, respectively. Buddhapālita wrote a commentary on Nāgārjuna's *Fundamental Treatise on the Middle Way* in which he presents the arguments they contain in the form of logical consequences (*prasaṅga*): *P* entails *Q*; if you cannot accept *Q*, because it contradicts your own assumptions, then you must reject *P*.[30] So Buddhapālita began what was later called the Prāsaṅgika school—those who follow the system of consequences. This form of argument differs from the more traditional positive proof statement. A proof statement is usually expressed as a three-part inference: *X* is *Y* because of being *Z*. In other words: every *Z* is *Y*, *X* is *Z*, and therefore *X* is *Y*.

According to Buddhist philosophy the word *inference* (*anumāna*) refers to the understanding that arises within a person's mental continuum on the basis of some other correct understanding. Logical arguments are employed to engender that new understanding, so these are often called inferences too. Both logical consequences and trimodal proof statements are inferences in this sense. In order to differentiate between them, this volume uses the term *syllogism* to indicate a trimodal proof statement (rather than adopt a restricted notion of "inference" that excludes logical consequences—a popular approach among academics).

A syllogism is called *autonomous* (*svatantra*) if it presupposes that the referents of the elements of the syllogism exist by their own nature. Bhāva-viveka, having studied Buddhapālita's commentary, considers many aspects of Buddhapālita's work to be very good and relies on them in his own text. However, he rejects Buddhapālita's reliance on logical consequences, which do not assume the inherent existence of anything. Bhāvaviveka says that logical consequences are not enough for a realization of emptiness. A final realization, he says, must depend on inferential knowledge consisting of inherently exist-ing, autonomous, positive proofs. This is one of the major points that differ-entiates the Madhyamaka systems, based on which they may be divided into Svātantrika-Madhyamaka and Prāsaṅgika-Madhyamaka; this concerns how to develop the correct view of emptiness within one's mindstream.

Now which of those great scholars should we follow when trying to under-stand Nāgārjuna and Āryadeva? The great Atiśa considers Candrakīrti's sys-tem to be the best. Many early Tibetan masters follow Atiśa. Probably most of Tsongkhapa's teachers follow Atiśa's and Candrakīrti's interpretation of the Madhyamaka view. Candrakīrti says that among the eight great famous com-mentaries of Nāgārjuna's *Fundamental Treatise on the Middle Way*, Buddha-pālita gives the most complete explanation of Nāgārjuna's thought.[31] Therefore he takes Buddhapālita as his basis. Candrakīrti feels that Bhāvaviveka also made many good points; these Candrakīrti incorporates into his system. How-ever, he rejects Bhāvaviveka's refutation of Buddhapālita. Tsongkhapa sees the commentaries of the two great masters, Buddhapālita and Candrakīrti, as the best explanations of the texts by Nāgārjuna and Āryadeva. So he says that he will explain the thought of Nāgārjuna following them.

❖ 3 ❖
The Stages of Entering into Reality

(3') How to determine the view of emptiness
    (a") The stages of entering into reality

———◦∎◦———

(3') HOW TO DETERMINE THE VIEW OF EMPTINESS

Establishing a correct philosophical understanding of śūnyatā has two parts:

    (a")   The stages of entering into reality
    (b")   Actually determining reality (chapters 4–21)

(a") THE STAGES OF ENTERING INTO REALITY

We cannot attain any kind of enlightenment unless we actualize the perfection of wisdom, the true path. This applies to all three ultimate spiritual goals: the nirvana of the śrāvaka, the nirvana of the pratyekabuddha, and the perfect nirvana or full enlightenment of a buddha. According to the Prāsaṅgika system, Hinayana and Mahayana goals are impossible to accomplish without a direct realization of śūnyatā, the true path. All three final attainments are based on completely abandoning the root of samsara: the ignorance that holds things to exist in a way that is completely opposite to reality. Ordinary beings cannot distinguish between actual existence and inherent existence. Things naturally appear to exist from their own side, and we believe them to exist just as we perceive them rather than merely through the power of thought and labels. We generally think that if things were not truly existent, then they would be merely imaginary, like objects in a dream. So we have a tendency to hold things to exist as totally objective. This grasping at inherent identity is the root of samsara. All the mental afflictions—attachment, hatred, and so

forth—as well as any actions and results based on them, spring from this ignorance. So we need to get rid of this ignorance, the root of all suffering. We need
to destroy the view that holds things to exist inherently. To accomplish this, we
need to gain a direct realization of śūnyatā.

As a practitioner seeking to understand Nāgārjuna's view of śūnyatā we
should not begin by asking, "What is śūnyatā?" or "How are things empty?"
We must begin by considering how to enter a spiritual path. We need to know,
"What is the goal to be attained?" and "How do we attain that goal?" First we
must determine the goal. The goal is nirvana. So what is nirvana? According
to the Madhyamaka system, nirvana is a special type of ultimate truth. More
generally we can say that nirvana has two aspects: the ultimate nature of all
things and the purified state to be attained. The first is not actual nirvana,
though it is ultimate truth and totally pure; the second is actual nirvana, of
which there are three types.[32] In the first case, the mind is naturally empty of
inherent existence from the very beginning, just like everything else. This is
called *natural nirvana*, though it is not actual nirvana. Our minds are already
naturally empty and naturally pure in this sense, so it is not something to be
attained. Yet we have inner obstructions, impurities, and mental afflictions
that cause our suffering. These are temporary and can be removed; they are not
part of the true nature of the mind. We can remove them with certain methods
and eventually attain actual nirvana.

Right now as unenlightened beings our mindstreams are not purified.
External and internal phenomena appear to us to be inherently existent, even
though they do not exist in that way; based on this appearance, we grasp
them to be inherently existent. This grasping at inherent existence is a mental
affliction, a mind of ignorance, which leaves two kinds of potentialities in the
mental continuum. One is called a *seed*, which gives rise to further grasping at
inherent existence. The other is called an *imprint*, which gives rise to the mistaken appearance of things as inherently existent as soon as we perceive them.
Seeds are abandoned together with the mental afflictions themselves by means
of the first seven grounds of the Mahayana path of meditation. Imprints,
which are the subtlest obstructions, are purified by the three highest stages of
the Mahayana path of meditation. A *ground* or *stage* of the path of meditation
is a special type of wisdom that directly perceives śūnyatā and removes the
root of certain obstructions. The absence of those obstructions at each stage
of purification is known as the different levels of cessation. Each of these cessations is permanent, being the mere absence of those specific obstructions
that will never arise again. When all the gross and subtle obstructions have
been removed from the mental continuum, that stream of awareness becomes

the infinitely compassionate and holy mind of a buddha: the Dharma body (*dharmakāya*).

The Dharma body has both an ultimate nature and a conventional nature, neither of which ultimately exists. Its conventional nature is the completely purified immaculate mind itself, known as the *wisdom Dharma body* (*jñāna-dharmakāya*). Its ultimate nature is the emptiness of the immaculate mind, its śūnyatā, known as the *nature body* (*svābhāvikakāya*). There are two aspects of the nature body: the aspect that is naturally pure and the aspect that is puri-fied of all temporary stains. The latter is the final true cessation.[33] This is a very special type of śūnyatā because not only is its basis naturally pure, but its basis is also completely purified of all temporary obstructions and faults. This emptiness is called nonabiding nirvana.[34]

Tsongkhapa identifies this aspect of the Dharma body, nonabiding nirvana, as the primary goal of the spiritual path. Now we need to consider, "How do we enter into this reality? How do we attain the Dharma body?" First we must critically reflect on the faults of samsara. When we become completely dis-gusted by the suffering nature of samsara, we will feel a strong desire to be rid of it. Seeing that we cannot eliminate it without eradicating its cause, we seek to discover the root of samsara. In short, the motivation to practice Dharma is the desire to discover and eliminate the fundamental cause of samsara. If the root cause were outside us and beyond our control, such as God, Truth, or Universal Nature, then we would not be able to change it. Such a cause would always be out there, independent, untouchable, and absolute. No matter how much we want to get out of samsara, we would have no way of doing so because we could not affect its cause, much less remove it. It would be a hopeless situa-tion. But from the Buddhist perspective the situation is not hopeless. When we become thoroughly disgusted with samsara and are desperate to get out, there is something that we can do. Since our suffering has a cause, which is internal, we can remove it and attain the longed-for freedom. What is this cause? After searching for it deeply, we discover that it is fundamental ignorance, the ego-tistic view—literally, the view of the perishable collection.

Why is this ignorant view called the *view of the perishable collection*? The phrase "perishable collection" is often used to refer to the aggregates because they are momentary and usually considered as a group. Buddha explained the conventional nature of the aggregates to be impermanent and a collection of causes and conditions. However, the meaning of the phrase in this context is more profound. Buddha taught that all caused things are impermanent and nonunitary. Each and every produced thing, whether the self, the body, an atom of matter, or a moment of thought, is just composed of fleeting parts.

The *view of the perishable collection* actually holds the opposite of what its name suggests. It does not hold its object to be a perishable collection. Somewhere within our own aggregates, which are in fact transitory, we think there is an absolute controller that owns them. We identify this as "I" or "me," existing from its own side. The mind that identifies it in this way is the egotistic view, the view of the perishable collection. This mind is the opposite of the correct view, which understands the self to be dependently imputed on the aggregates. But our innate self-grasping mind does not think of the self as merely imputed on its parts. Instead, to our natural way of thinking, our "I" seems to be a unit, something single, with its own identity. When we say "my eyes," "my body," and so on, we feel that there is one thing, "me," to which these things belong in an objectively established sense.

We have become accustomed to the false perception and wrong conception of "I" and "mine" throughout all our countless previous lives. This way of see-ing and thinking of ourselves as objectively identifiable is deeply rooted. We do not need any effort to *see* things in the wrong way—it happens all the time—or to *think of* things in the wrong way—it occurs quite naturally. Without questioning our notion of ourselves we just assume it is correct. This grasping "me" and "mine" as inherently existent is the egotistic view that gives rise to all our daily frustrations. Our feeling of being an independent self is at the center of our lives, and everything revolves around that. We have a natural urge to be supremely successful, most highly cherished and honored, and in every way better than anybody else. If we see that someone else has accom-plished more than us, we get jealous and fearful that his or her success may hinder our own. Each of us naturally feels, "Everyone should notice me and appreciate me, and if they do not, they are fools!" This attitude arises from the deeply entrenched notion that we are truly or inherently existent. Based on this distorted grasping, we act out of desire, worry, frustration, and fear. This is how the egotistic view functions. It is a fundamental misunderstanding of how the self actually exists. It influences all our other thoughts and perceptions, thereby contaminating our actions and leading us to rebirth in samsara. Fur-thermore the egotistic view produces all our other mental afflictions, thus giv-ing rise to miserable experiences and leading us to rebirth in the lower realms. Buddha taught that the mental afflictions and contaminated karma together give rise to samsara, represented as a chain of events known as the twelve links of dependent arising. This contaminated cycle of existence begins with igno-rance, which in the next moment gives rise to conditioning action and so on throughout the links, to birth, then aging and death. It ends in death every time, and then from ignorance another cycle begins.

When we have examined this process thoroughly and fully understood it, we will see that the root of samsara is the egotistic view. At that point we will have identified the real enemy that causes us to suffer, and we will spontaneously wish to be free from it from the depths our hearts. We do not have to go out to destroy the enemy. The real enemy is within, lurking in the depths of our experience. When we understand this, we will not complain so much about others, blaming them for our problems. When we recognize that the real enemy is the ignorance within our own mind, then the wish to be liberated from that spontaneously arises. You may have already managed to develop a slight wish to leave samsara, based on some teachings that you have heard or read, but that is something artificial and constructed. It is not spontaneous. Genuine renunciation of samsara arises spontaneously as a result of deep reflection, meditation, and understanding. It is a complete change of heart—an all-encompassing desire to get rid of the inner enemy, the view of the perishable collection, which is the root of samsara.

How can we get rid of it? Eliminating this wrong view that grasps at the self depends on generating the wisdom that understands selflessness. We must recognize that what this egotistic view holds as its object—an independent, inherently existing self—is in fact not there. We have to see that no such self exists at all. In order to see this, we must study various logical proofs that demonstrate that there is no such independent, absolute self. The egotistic view is a wrong understanding; it holds its object incorrectly. It is like confusing a coiled piece of rope in the corner to be a big poisonous snake. As long as we believe that there is a large snake in our room, we experience fear. To get rid of that fear we have to see the object clearly; we must see that it is a piece of rope. It is completely empty of being a snake. Until we recognize that, we will not be able to get rid of the view that it is a snake, and we will have problems until we get rid of that view.

To develop the right view, we must prove to ourselves that the object of this wrong view does not exist. An inherently existent self is already nonexistent, but we naturally conceive it to exist. We have to realize for ourselves that it does not exist, by negating it through logical inference and scriptural quotations. We need to develop a firm understanding, because without true conviction we will not be able to attain liberation. If you are sincerely seeking liberation, the wisdom understanding śūnyatā is crucial. Without it, no matter how much you pray "May I attain liberation," there is no way to eliminate the egotistic view. It will not happen. So first we have to find the correct view—an understanding that there is no inherently existent "me" or "mine." But just understanding the right view is not enough; we have to meditate over and over again on what we have understood. Meditation influences the mind much more deeply than mere conceptual understanding. So we must familiarize ourselves with the right view by meditating for a long time.

The word commonly translated as "meditation" literally means to become accustomed to something. In order to become accustomed to the correct view, we need to use a special method that combines profound wisdom with single-pointed concentration. Our situation until now has been that all our mental states have been under the influence of the egotistic view. Right now we are trying to turn this whole process around, which requires meditation over a long period of time. If we do this meditation properly we can purify all the mental afflictions and their seeds as well as their imprints. However, this final result will arise only if we are motivated by bodhicitta, the wish to attain buddhahood solely for the benefit of others. With this special motivation we can use these powerful meditation practices to influence our minds; this gradually enables us to complete the two collections of profound wisdom and vast merit and eventually obtain the Dharma body. Candrakīrti's *Clear Words* says:

> Just as a celestial city is not reality, mental afflictions, karma, bodies, agents, results, and all such things are not reality, but they appear to the spiritually immature as reality. If one asks in this context, "What is reality? How does one enter into it?" it must be explained as follows. Through not seeing internal and external things [as reality], the grasping at internal and external things as the self or as belonging to the self is completely extinguished: that is reality in this context.[35] As for entering into reality, look in the *Introduction to the "Middle Way,"* which says:
>
> > All afflictions and faults without exception
> > Arise from the view of the perishable collection;
> > Seeing this with wisdom and realizing the self to be its object,
> > The yogi negates the self.

Internal and external things conventionally exist, but they do not exist exactly as they appear to ordinary beings. They appear to exist inherently but are in fact empty of inherent existence. Hence we say that they have an illusion-like nature. There are many analogies for this illusion-like nature in the sutras, such as a celestial city, a face reflected in a mirror, a moon reflected in water, an echo in a cave. None of these are even conventionally real as they appear. Ārya beings understand everything to be like reflections because they have directly realized conventional and ultimate truth. When they see conventional things, they know that those things do not exist as they appear. Based on this under-standing the mental afflictions naturally do not arise so strongly. So they have less attachment, hatred, and so on. Ordinary beings, on the other hand, have not directly realized śūnyatā; they are like children who naturally think things are real, just as they appear. Śāntideva says:

> When their sand castles collapse,
> Children howl in despair.[36]

Ordinary beings are not so different from little children who cry when their sand castles fall down because they think they are really their own houses. Thinking that everything is real, just as it appears, is a spiritually immature view. Candrakīrti asks and then answers the questions, "What is reality? How does one enter into a realization of it?" The general situation is that internal and external things do not exist as they are held by the egotistic view. Conventional things appear to ordinary beings to be inherently real, but that is not their final nature.

It will help here to clarify the use of the word *exist*. To exist means to be known, proved, or established by valid knowledge. If something is known, it exists; if it is not known, it does not exist. So, *not known* and *not existent* indicate the same thing.[37] In this context, to say that the yogi does not per-ceive or know inherently existent things means that inherently existent things do not exist. The afflictive mind grasping at internal and external things as an inherently existent self or as belonging to such a self is the egotistic view, the view of the perishable collection. A mind grasping at these is a distorted awareness. The wisdom that understands the absence of inherent existence of the self and of belonging to the self gradually and completely brings to an end such grasping. This realization also purifies the grasping at internal and exter-nal phenomena as an inherently existent self or as belonging to such a self, along with the seeds of this grasping. We should remember here that through their meditation on emptiness, bodhisattvas on the paths of accumulation and preparation gradually reduce the intellectually acquired grasping at inherent existence. This contrived grasping is totally removed by a direct realization of emptiness occurring at the second moment of the path of seeing. It takes much longer to eliminate the innate grasping at inherent existence, which is accomplished gradually on the path of meditation up to the eighth ground. Upon attaining the eighth ground, the gross obstructions blocking liberation are finally removed. Then on the eighth, ninth, and tenth grounds, bodhisatt-vas meditate on emptiness as an antidote to the subtle obstructions blocking omniscience. These are finally removed upon attaining buddhahood.

Candrakīrti urges the practitioner to look for the way to understand reality as he expresses it in *Introduction to the "Middle Way."* In the first line of the stanza that he quotes in *Clear Words* above, the word "faults" refers to all samsaric suffering, which are the karmic results of the mental afflictions. The afflictions themselves are always instances of mind. Mental afflictions and suffering arise from the egotistic view, which is a distorted mind that observes the self imputed on the aggregates and holds it to be inherently existent. It directly observes the self. Indirectly it observes any of one's own five aggregates and holds them to be lasting, independent, and inherently existent, thus grasping them to exist in a way that is contrary to their actual nature when in fact they are fleeting, dependently arising, and noninherently existent. After much analysis, the yogi sees, by means of his or her supreme wisdom, that all the problems of samsara arise from the view of the perishable collection. This understanding is a special kind of wisdom that directly realizes emptiness and indirectly realizes this particular cause-and-effect relationship. Having seen this, the yogi recognizes that the object of this view is the wrongly grasped self. So he or she tries to negate the wrongly grasped self by means of logical proofs and scriptural citations.

There are two possible ways to explain the two occurrences of the word "self" in the last two lines of Candrakīrti's stanza. According to one explanation, both occurrences of the term refer to the wrongly grasped self—the self as it is held by the egotistic view. That is my preferred explanation. According to another explanation, the first use of the term "self" refers to a general undifferentiated notion of self, whereas the second refers to the self as it is held by the egotistic view. It is the latter self that is negated.[38]

Tsongkhapa immediately quotes another passage from Candrakīrti's *Clear Words*:

> A yogi who wants to abandon all mental afflictions and faults completely and enter into reality carefully investigates, "What does this samsara have as its root?" When he investigates in this way, he sees that samsara is rooted in the view of the perishable collection, and he sees that the self is the object of the view of the perishable collection. Based on this he sees that by not perceiving the self to exist, the view of the perishable collection is removed; by removing it, all mental afflictions and faults are reversed. So at the beginning he carefully investigates just the self, asking, "What is this so-called self that is the object of self-grasping?"

The term "object" in this passage simply indicates that the self rather than the aggregates is the object of the view of the perishable collection. It does not indicate a more specific object—differentiated as either the basic object or held object of the egotistic view. When a yogi investigates the source of samsara, he sees that it is the result of the view of the perishable collection. What is the view of the perishable collection? It is a view that wrongly grasps its main object, the self, as inherently existent. Again there are two possible explanations of the two occurrences of the term "self" in this passage. According to my preferred explanation, the yogi recognizes that the inherently existent self is the object held by the wrong view of the perishable collection. Upon analyzing the self, which is wrongly held by this view, he or she understands that this wrongly held self does not exist and thus gradually abandons the egotistic view. The yogi realizes that the object (the self) as it is held by that view (as inherently existent) does not exist at all; in other words, an inherently existent self does not exist. By meditating on this for a long time he or she eventually destroys the view of the perishable collection. Seeing that all mental afflictions and suffering are gradually eliminated by abandoning this wrong view, the yogi tries to discover the nature of the so-called self that is the held object of the egotistic view.

According to another explanation, the yogi recognizes that the self in general is the object in general of the wrong view of the perishable collection. Upon analyzing this general self more deeply, he or she distinguishes between the mere self, which is an appropriate basis, and the inherently existent self, which is the wrongly held object of the egotistic view. The basic object, the conventionally existent self, exists; but the held object, the inherently existent self, does not exist. The egotistic view holds the basic object, the conventionally existent self, wrongly—as inherently existent. The phrase "the self that is the object of self-grasping" refers to the held object, the inherently existent self that does not exist at all. So the yogi begins by analyzing just the general self; then he sees that the conventional self, which is the basic object of the egotistic view, is held wrongly by that view as inherently existent, and he finds that such an inherently existent self does not exist at all. In this way the yogi abandons the wrongly held object of the egotistic view. That view is gradually destroyed when the yogi realizes that the object as it is held by that view does not exist at all.

Both of these explanations present a situation that is similar to the case of believing that a certain coiled rope in a dark place is a poisonous snake; when you see that it is a rope and not a snake after all, then your fear of the poisonous snake automatically disappears.

In the scriptures taught by Buddha, Nāgārjuna, and others, there are many logical proofs refuting the inherent existence of everything. Nāgārjuna's *Fundamental Treatise* has twenty-seven chapters, each containing analyses proving that different types of phenomena—causes and effects, conditions, samsara, nirvana, agents and actions, coming and going, and so forth—do not inherently exist. However, when yogis begin such an analysis, they summarize all the countless phenomena into two categories: subject and object. Since everything is included within the twofold division of subject and object, the logical analysis of these two encompasses all objects of knowledge. Buddhapālita says that this is the meaning of the eighteenth chapter of the *Fundamental Treatise*. This chapter is a condensed explanation that includes all the evidence establishing the emptiness of the inherent existence of the self and of belonging to the self. In dependence on Buddhapālita's explanation of this chapter, Candrakīrti wrote a detailed exegesis of the selflessness of persons in *Introduction to the "Middle Way."*

Someone asks, "Is this not an explanation of the Mahayana way to enter into reality? If so, then the exhaustion of the grasping at the self and belonging to the self cannot be the emptiness that is the final goal. Both the emptiness of inherent existence of the self and belonging to the self are considered to be the selflessness of persons, not the selflessness of phenomena. If you wish to enter into the Dharma body, you must realize both the emptiness of persons and the emptiness of phenomena. But what is emphasized here is only the selflessness of the person; it does not include an explanation of the selflessness of phenomena. Therefore it is not correct to posit this as the path entering into reality. In short, by realizing merely what is explained here, you cannot attain the final goal of buddhahood."

The issue here concerns whether the grasping at anything other than the self of persons is the grasping at the self of phenomena. In general there is the self and there are the aggregates, which are other than the self. Candrakīrti says that first we grasp at ourselves and then we generate attachment for what we think of as our own:

> First, thinking "I," grasping at a self arises;
> Thinking "This is mine," attachment to things arises.[39]

Holding any of the aggregates to be inherently existent is grasping at the self of phenomena, whereas holding the self itself to be inherently existent is grasping at the self of persons. That much is clear. But there are various opinions expressed in different monasteries' textbooks concerning whether the mere belonging to the self—"mine" itself—is included in the self of phenomena or the self of persons. Grasping the self as inherently existent is, of course, grasping at the self of persons. But if we say that grasping at anything other than the self is grasping at the self of phenomena, we may be committed to maintaining that grasping at "mine" is grasping at the self of phenomena. Grasping at specific objects that belong to the self, things that we refer to as mine, such as "my nose," or "my house," is definitely grasping at the self of phenomena. However, Jetsun Chokyi Gyaltsen's textbook[40] says that grasping at "mine" in general, rather than the particular things that are mine, is a part of the egotistic view—which is a certain type of grasping at the self of persons. Some other textbooks disagree and say that "mine" is not "I," and therefore it is the grasping at the self of phenomena.

The question above asks, "How can the complete exhaustion of the grasping at 'I' and 'mine' be the final goal, the Dharma body?" Tsongkhapa says there is no problem here because the phrase "the complete exhaustion of the grasping at I and mine" has two meanings. One is that the mental afflictions have been completely abandoned so that they can never arise again. This permanent cessation of all the mental afflictions is the attainment of liberation, accomplished by śrāvaka and pratyekabuddha arhats. The other meaning is that all signs of elaborations of external and internal phenomena have been abandoned. Here *signs* should be understood to be the stains left by the mental afflictions previously removed. When these stains have been completely removed, there is nothing left that could give rise to the elaborations of dualistic appearance. This permanent cessation of all the mental afflictions and their stains is the attainment of the Dharma body, accomplished only by a buddha.

You may wonder, "How can there be anything left to purify once one has eliminated all desire, hatred, and ignorance from the root? Surely one must be enlightened?" According to the Prāsaṅgika system, Hinayana arhats have completely removed the mental afflictions (which are minds) and their seeds (which are not minds). Both of these constitute the obstructions to liberation. Arhats have removed grasping at inherent existence and have attained liberation from samsara. Yet they have not attained the highest goal—the Dharma body—because they still have the subtle stains, or imprints, that generate the mistaken appearance of things as inherently existent. These imprints are different from the mental afflictions and their seeds, which can be understood using the following analogy. Suppose you keep a smelly, rotten object wrapped in a piece of cloth for a long time. If you decide to clean that cloth, first you have to remove the dirty object it contains. But even after you have discarded that object and washed the cloth, a slight odor still remains in the cloth. No blemish is visible, but a subtle stain remains. This is similar to what happens within the mindstream once all the mental afflictions and their seeds have been removed; a subtle residue is left. This stain is an obstruction to omniscience—the Dharma body. Due to this kind of obscuration an arhat cannot fulfill all the aims accomplished by a buddha.

Unlike Hinayana arhats, a buddha has completely abandoned the signs of the elaborations: the imprints of the mental afflictions and their seeds (in addition, of course, to having removed their root—grasping at a self of persons and phenomena). The utter abandonment of these imprints so that they become totally nonexistent is the attainment of the Dharma body. We will reach this attainment only after purifying the wrong views that are grasping at the self and phenomena as inherently existent, including all the other mental afflictions and their seeds, as well as all the subtle imprints left over after those afflictions and seeds have been removed. In short, the removal of the mental afflictions alone does not give rise to the Dharma body. To achieve buddhahood we must remove the subtle obstructions, the imprints left by the mental afflictions and their seeds. This is done through generating within our mindstream the vast collections of profound wisdom and extensive merit, based on a sincere motivation to practice for the sake of others. We cannot attain the Dharma body without taking heartfelt responsibility for the welfare of all mother sentient beings. With that motivation alone, a future buddha engages in extensive practices for a very long period of time.

When a yogi realizes the emptiness of inherent existence of the self, he or she can reverse the grasping at the inherent existence of the aggregates, which are the limbs or parts of the self. For example, if a chariot has been totally burned up and destroyed, then its wheels and other parts will have been burned and destroyed also. It is similar here; by understanding that there is no inherently existent self, we will understand that there cannot be anything belonging to it. For if there is no inherently existent "I," then there is no inherently existent "mine." Candrakīrti's *Clear Words* says:

> Those who seek liberation analyze, "What is it that appears to own the five aggregates on which is based the manifest self-grasping of those who are totally ignorant of dependent imputation? Does that [apparent self] have the characteristics of the aggregates or does it not have the characteristics of the aggregates?" Those wishing for liberation do not perceive [such a self] when they thoroughly analyze in this way. Therefore to them [Nāgārjuna says]:
>
> > If the self does not exist,
> > How can belonging to the self exist?
>
> Because they do not perceive the self, they obviously do not perceive anything belonging to the self—the basis on which the self is imputed. When a chariot is totally burned, its parts are totally burned also; there-

fore they are not perceived at that time. Similarly, when yogis understand the absence of the self, then they understand that the aggregates, which are things belonging to the self, are also selfless.

When we realize that the self lacks an inherent nature, we realize that the aggregates belonging to that self also lack a self, an inherent nature. Usually we grasp ourselves to be inherently existent based on the five aggregates of the body and mind. The aggregates themselves are not the self; they are the bases on which we impute the self. The self is merely a conventional reality imputed on the bases of the five aggregates; but ignorance grasps this self to be inherently real. That inherently real self does not exist at all. However, the five aggregates appear to be owned or appropriated by something. An owner appears to exist. We all talk about "*my* body," "*my* hand," "*my* mind," and so on. So what is it? Why is there this appearance of an owner, ownership, and things that are owned?

There are two sides to consider here: the subject or owner and the object or the things owned. Look at what occurs when someone says to you, "You are stupid!" Suddenly a strong sense of "I" arises, and you think, "No, I am not stupid!" The "I" appears to be an owner, a dominant subject. What is the basis of this appearance? It is the aggregates. Are there any real, inherently existent aggregates or not? Is there any real, inherently existent self or not? When yogis thoroughly examine this matter, they see that there is no such thing as an inherently existent self. Therefore there is no real owning of the five aggregates. This topic is discussed extensively in Nāgārjuna's *Fundamental Treatise on the Middle Way*. As Nāgārjuna points out, if the inherently existent self does not exist, how can it own anything? If there is no owner, how can there be ownership or anything owned? When yogis realize that a self or owner does not exist as it appears, then they realize that there is no ownership by that self and therefore nothing owned in that way. Because an inherently existent self does not exist, the bases on which such a self is imputed—what belongs to the self—also do not inherently exist. The point here is that when you understand the emptiness of inherent existence of the self—the selflessness of persons—then you also understand the emptiness of inherent existence of the aggregates owned by that self—the selflessness of phenomena. Candrakīrti's *Commentary on the "Introduction to the Middle Way"* (*Madhyamakāvatāra-bhāṣya*) says:

Since you wrongly see an inherent nature of forms and so on, you do not understand the selflessness of persons, because you [wrongly] see the basis of imputation of the self, the aggregates. [Nāgārjuna] says:

> As long as there is grasping at the aggregates,
> Then there is grasping at me.[41]

As long as you hold phenomena to be inherently existent, you cannot realize the selflessness of the person. In other words, if you do not understand the emptiness of inherent existence of the aggregates, you will not understand the emptiness of inherent existence of persons.

Someone suggests there may be a problem with saying that anyone who understands the selflessness of persons must thereby understand the selflessness of phenomena, and anyone who grasps at a self of phenomena cannot understand the selflessness of persons. For does the same mind that realizes the selflessness of persons also realize the noninherent existence of the aggregates? If that is the case, then the mind realizing the selflessness of persons and the mind realizing the selflessness of phenomena must be one and the same. This is a problem. They cannot be the same because persons and phenomena are two different things. Therefore the minds that realize each one's emptiness must also be different. For example, the impermanence of a pot and the impermanence of a pillar are realized by different minds. The mind that understands a pot to be impermanent does not necessarily understand a pillar to be impermanent. Those realizations arise separately. In that case, if the mind that understands the noninherent existence of the person does not understand the noninherent existence of the aggregates, how can it be that when someone realizes the selflessness of persons they also realize the noninherent existence of the aggregates?

There are actually two questions here. The first is: "Does the mind that understands the selflessness of persons also understand the selflessness of phenomena?" The second question is: "If that is not the case, then how can you say that when a yogi realizes the selflessness of persons, he or she realizes the selflessness of phenomena?" Tsongkhapa says he does not assert the position expressed in the first question, so he will not address it. In answer to the second question, Tsongkhapa says that when a yogi realizes the selflessness of persons, the wisdom observing the selflessness of the person is not looking at the five aggregates. That particular mind understands only the self, or person, to be not inherently existent. It does not realize anything else, such as understanding the selflessness of the aggregates. However, this realization of the selflessness of persons can be used at any later moment to cut the deluded grasping at the self of phenomena. We turn the understanding of the selflessness of the person to the aggregates and investigate them in the same way. By the power of the earlier understanding of the emptiness of the self of persons, any misconceptions concerning the way in which the aggregates exist are swept away. We will naturally understand the aggregates to be empty of inherent existence.

Certain monastic textbooks add that as long as someone holds the philosophical view that the aggregates exist inherently, he or she cannot understand the selflessness of persons. Here we must distinguish between being *held by a person* and being *held by a mind*. Even if someone knows intellectually that the self does not exist inherently, he or she may still have innate minds that grasp the self to be inherently existent. The wrong view that grasps at an inherently existent self has two aspects: contrived grasping and innate grasping. Contrived or intellectually acquired grasping arises in dependence on philosophical views or faulty reasoning. Most people do not have any contrived self-grasping views at all because they simply do not think about philosophical matters. Only a person who holds a wrong philosophical view will consciously think that things are inherently existent. Yet even when such a person has rejected that wrong view and explicitly understood that things are not inherently existent, she will still have innate self-grasping minds arising naturally within her mental continuum. The innate self-grasping view is not intellectually contrived; it is a mind that naturally grasps at the self and the aggregates as inherently existent. This is not easy to eliminate, even after having developed the correct philosophical view which is an understanding that the self does not exist inherently.

To completely eliminate intellectually acquired self-grasping views, a person must gain a direct realization of selflessness by repeated meditation on a correct understanding of emptiness. Only through this direct realization does such a person see that there is no inherently existent self. At this point she attains the path of seeing and thereby eliminates the contrived self-grasping from her mental continuum; that person no longer consciously thinks that the self is inherently existent. When that person understands the self to be empty of inherent existence, then she ceases to hold a similar wrong philosophical view regarding the aggregates as well. However, even on the path of seeing, the innate grasping at a self or at the aggregates remains within the mental continuum. Although this person does not hold an inherently existent self to exist, she may have some minds arising that hold an inherently existent self to exist. But the fact that this person has innate self-grasping views arising within her mental continuum does not necessarily mean that this person is holding the self to be inherently existent.

We can interpret Nāgārjuna's above statement as follows. As long as we grasp the aggregates as inherently existent, due to holding a particular wrong tenet or philosophical view, then we have no direct understanding of the selflessness of persons. Once we have understood the selflessness of persons directly, then we cease to hold this contrived wrong view regarding the aggregates or the self. Buddhapālita clarifies this as follows:

> Given that "belonging to self" is expressed in accordance with some notion of "self" and that self does not even exist, then if it does not exist, how can it be correct to say, "This belongs to it"?

For example, the mind that understands that the son of a barren woman does not exist does not explicitly think that this child's eyes and ears do not exist. Yet through the particular mind that understands that the son of a barren woman does not exist, the person will also be able to dispel any misapprehension that his eyes, ears, and so on, exist. Similarly, when a person understands that the self does not inherently exist, the grasping at the self's eyes and so on will be dispelled. Remember, this refers to the contrived grasping that is based on false reasoning. The subtle innate grasping is still not dispelled.

Some Buddhist philosophical schools assert that functional things are truly existent. Traditionally these tenet holders—whether Vaibhāṣika, Sautrāntika, or Yogācāra—are called *Proponents of True Existence*; for simplicity, we call them *Realists*. As Buddhists they assert the selflessness of persons. However, from their perspective *selflessness* does not mean a lack of inherent existence. For Realist tenet holders, *selflessness* means that there is no self-supporting, substantially existent self.

An opponent now posits the following problem. Buddhist Realists say that the self exists as an imputation projected by the mind in dependence on something else, in this case the aggregates. So they say that the person is imputedly or nominally existent and not substantially existent.[42] However, if these Realists say that the person is not substantially existent, then they must surely say that the person is not ultimately existent. In which case they must also understand that the eyes and so on are not inherently existent.

Let us investigate some underlying assumptions of this objection. In general, *ultimately existent* and *substantially existent* are treated as coextensive categories. The Vaibhāṣikas, for example, consider a pot to be imputedly existent, nonsubstantially existent, and a conventional truth. They accept atoms, partless particles, and the smallest moments in time to be substantially existent. These substantially existent elements are considered to be instances of ultimate truth, which in this system means they are ultimately existent. Gross objects exist as imputations based on these substantially existent smallest parts or moments. Now, given that these Realists accept the person to be imputedly existent and thus not ultimately existent, does it follow that they do not accept the person to be inherently existent—and thus realize that the eyes, and so on, are not inherently existent? No, because if they understood that things do not inherently exist, this would contradict their own assertions that they truly exist. Realists accept things to be truly existent, so they cannot also accept them to be noninherently existent, because the negation of inherent existence automatically includes the negation of true existence. Furthermore, if they already understood that things do not inherently exist, then why would it be necessary to prove to them that sprouts and so on do not truly exist?

Even though the Realists do not understand the subtle view of the emptiness of inherent existence posited by the Mādhyamikas, they do differentiate between substantial existence and imputed existence. They have their own classifications and explanations of substantial existence, imputed existence, the two truths, and so on. Buddhist Realists accept that a person is imputedly existent, being designated on a basis. But they think that a person is designated on the smallest moments of consciousness and the smallest atoms of matter. These substantially existent elements function as the bases of imputation for the grosser person. Moreover, the Realists label the fully completed virtuous and nonvirtuous paths of action, which are minds, as a continuum. Therefore they also accept this continuum to be nominally or imputedly existent. All Buddhist systems agree that a continuum is imputedly existent. For example, a month is imputed in dependence on the basis of a certain number of days, and a rosary is imputed on a string of beads. Even though the Realists accept such things as imputedly existent, they do not accept that they are not inherently existent. In fact, they argue against that Madhyamaka position, saying that if one considers things to be noninherently or nontruly existent, then everything must be like a dream. This, they say, is a problem. Haribhadra's *Short Commentary on the "Ornament for Clear Knowledge"* (*Abhisamayālaṃkāra-vivṛtti*) says:

> If everything were just like a dream, then the ten nonvirtues, generosity, and so on, would also be not [truly] existent. Therefore even when you are not asleep, it would be like when you are asleep.

When we are asleep we have all kinds of fantastic dreams during which many beautiful or frightening things appear. These things only exist in dreams; they are not real. They are false. But the Realists argue that according to the Mādhyamikas there is no true existence, so even when we are awake everything is like a dream and not really existent. Therefore there would be no difference between being awake and being asleep. Why would the Realists bother to put forward this argument if they realized the emptiness of inherent existence or the emptiness of true existence?

So we can see that the criterion of whether or not something is ultimately or conventionally established for the Mādhyamikas is very different from such criteria in the systems of Realists. The terms are similar, but there is a huge difference between how the schools define them. For example, let us look at the term *conventionally existent*. Vasubandhu's *Treasury of Knowledge* (*Abhidharmakośa*) says:

> If the mind no longer apprehends something
> When it is broken or mentally split up,
> Like a pot, then it is conventionally existent;
> What is other than that is ultimately existent. (6.4)

According to the Vaibhāṣikas, anything that can be destroyed physically (as when smashed with a hammer) or mentally (as when analyzed into parts) is conventionally existent. Such things are also conventional truths according to this system, because the things—and the perception of them—no longer exist when they are dismantled. All gross things are like that, so this applies to persons too. The Vaibhāṣika interpretation is that a thing is *conventionally existent* if the identification of the perceived object as a person or anything else is lost when it is analyzed into its parts. In contrast, *ultimately existent* things cannot be divided either physically or mentally. There is no way for them to lose their identity. As such, they are the final nature of things. According to the Vaibhāṣikas, as far as physical objects are concerned the subtlest partless atoms are ultimately or truly existent. For the same reason, they assert that the shortest moments of time are ultimately existent because they cannot be divided further; thus there is no way for them to lose their identity. As such, they are the final nature of nonmaterial things. Longer periods of time, such as months, years, and so on, are imputed on these shortest moments.

The meaning of *conventionally existent* and *ultimately existent* is very different in the Madhyamaka system. According to Mādhyamikas, nothing is ultimately existent; everything is conventionally existent. Even śūnyatā itself, the ultimate truth, is conventionally existent. When we apply the Madhyamaka criterion of conventional existence to what the Realists assert to be conventionally existent, it turns out that they hold them to be ultimately existent. The Realists hold conventionally existent things to be inherently existent, so they are affirming what the Madhyamaka system considers the object of negation. Therefore, from the Madhyamaka point of view, whatever the Realists hold as conventionally existent, they in fact hold as ultimately existent. Conversely, when we apply the Madhyamaka criterion of conventional existence to what the Realists assert to be ultimately existent, it turns out that they are conventionally existent from the Madhyamaka point of view. However, it is not that the Realists are contradicting themselves; they are just operating with different criteria from the Mādhyamikas.

Furthermore, even though both the Realists and the great Mādhyamika, Candrakīrti, assert that a person is nominally existent, what they mean by *nominally existent* is very different. From Candrakīrti's point of view, the Realists do not have a realization of the selflessness of persons; in other words, they do not realize persons to be empty of inherent existence—and this is because they do not realize the selflessness of phenomena. Here we must remember the distinction made earlier between persons and minds. If a person does not realize the selflessness of phenomena, then they cannot realize the selflessness of persons. This does not mean that any mind realizing the selflessness of persons must realize the selflessness of phenomena. Candrakīrti says that as long as a tenet holder of the lower schools does not abandon the view that the aggregates are substantially existent, which they strongly hold based on logical reasoning, then they cannot understand the selflessness of persons—because they have not abandoned the view grasping the person to be substantially existent. Here the term *substantially existent* is used according to the Madhyamaka interpretation. The Vaibhāṣikas do not say that persons are substantially existent according to their own interpretation of the term. But the Mādhyamikas say that *substantially existent* means the same as truly existent—and, indeed, the same as inherently existent according to the Prāsaṅgika-Mādhyamikas. So from the Madhyamaka perspective, the Vaibhāṣikas hold persons to be substantially existent. Therefore the Mādhyamikas say that the tenet holders of the lower schools do not understand the selflessness of persons; they do not realize persons to be not ultimately existent.

Misidentifying the Object to Be Negated

(b")Actually determining reality
 (1") Identifying the object to be negated by reasoning
  (a)) Why the object of negation must be carefully identified
  (b)) Refuting other systems that negate without identifying properly
   the object to be negated
   (1)) Refuting an overly broad identification of the object to be
    negated
    (a')) Stating others' assertions
    (b')) Showing that those assertions are wrong
     (1')) Showing that those systems contradict the unique dis-
      tinguishing feature of Madhyamaka
      (a")) Identifying the distinguishing feature of
       Madhyamaka

(b") ACTUALLY DETERMINING REALITY

THE SECTION ON actually determining the correct view of reality has
three parts:

(1") Identifying the object to be negated by reasoning (chapters 4–12)
(2") Whether to use consequences or autonomous syllogisms in negating
  the object of negation (chapters 13–16)
(3") How to generate the correct view of reality within one's mental continuum by relying on that method (chapters 17–21)

In the first topic, the word *reasoning* does not refer to just any logical thought
process; it is a logical investigation that aims to determine whether or not
something is truly or ultimately existent. It is ultimate analysis: a means to

arrive at the ultimate truth. The second topic examines what type of logical process we should use to cut away the wrong view that things are truly, ultimately, or inherently existent. Should we use consequences (*prasaṅga*) or syllogisms (*svatantra*) to refute the object of negation? A consequence takes the form: if this were the case then that would be the case, for example, "If things were truly existent, then they would arise without a cause." This type of reasoning can refute an opponent's position by showing that what the opponent holds leads to a logically absurd consequence. A syllogism takes the form: this must be the case because that is the case, for example, "Things are not truly existent because they arise dependently on causes." The difference between these two logical structures is not simply their form; the important distinction concerns the ontological assumptions on which they are based. A syllogism may be based on the presupposition that things have a certain kind of independent existence—in which case it is called an autonomous syllogism. A consequence is never based on such a presupposition. Therefore in this section Tsongkhapa engages in a lengthy discussion about why we should use prasaṅga rather than svatantra reasoning to prove the nonexistence of the object of negation. The third topic shows how to generate the correct view based on this form of argument.

(1″) IDENTIFYING THE OBJECT TO BE NEGATED BY REASONING

This has three parts:

- (a)) Why the object of negation must be carefully identified
- (b)) Refuting other systems that negate without identifying properly the object to be negated (chapters 4–10)
- (c)) How our own system identifies the object of negation (chapters 11–12)

(a)) WHY THE OBJECT OF NEGATION MUST BE CAREFULLY IDENTIFIED

It is most important to correctly identify the object that we are trying to negate. In order to be sure that a certain person is not here, we must know who that person is. If we do not know who it is, we cannot properly understand the statement "He is not here." Likewise, when we say "selfless" or "without inherent nature," we must be able to identify the self or the inherent nature that is being negated. Here we are negating an object as it is held to exist by a mind of ignorance. Things and persons do not exist by virtue of their own inherent nature in the way that ignorance holds them to exist. In other words, they are "not inherently existent." Inherent nature is totally nonexistent, so we can negate it by means of valid knowledge. But in order to negate it, we first need to identify it. How can we identify as the object of negation something that does not exist? To do this we need to develop a clear general idea of what it would be like if something did exist inherently or if it were an autonomous self. Once we have clearly identified this general idea of inherent existence, we can understand its absence. If the general idea does not appear clearly to the mind, then we cannot truly understand its negation. Śāntideva says in *Engaging in the Bodhisattva's Deeds*:

> Without having identified the imputed thing,
> You cannot apprehend its absence.

In this context the "imputed thing" refers to the mental image of the object of negation itself—inherent existence—which is superimposed on the thing perceived. We cannot negate inherent existence unless we recognize this mental image, and we recognize it by developing an understanding of how something would exist if it were to exist inherently. A mental image of inherent existence occurs naturally to most people. Our ordinary sense consciousnesses perceive everything as inherently existent; it is the way that we, as ordinary beings, experience the world and ourselves. Based on this mistaken perception our conceptual consciousnesses tend to hold things as inherently existent. Such thinking arises naturally, though it may arise, in addition, owing to philosophical beliefs. In any case, as soon as an object appears to the mind, it appears to exist inherently, and a conceptual consciousness will often grasp it to exist as it appears. The object that appears to our minds is merely conventionally imputed, but we do not see it *as* imputed in this way. We see it as existing from its own side, objectively. This means that we always see it and frequently conceive of it as inherently existent—which is an additional imputation on top of the conventional thing itself. The mind that naturally grasps things as inherently existent actually grasps the object of negation—inherent existence—but cannot ascertain it as such. Only a mind of wisdom, generated through ultimate analysis, can recognize the object of negation; such a mind can clearly identify the mental image of inherent existence and then negate it.

We need to investigate whether things really exist as they appear or whether they are just conventionally imputed. There are two aspects to being conventionally imputed—internal and external, which correspond to thought and language, respectively. When we analyze this situation deeply, we can discover what it would be for things to exist inherently, just as they appear. Once we have discovered this, then we can identify the object of negation. We already see the object of negation constantly; we perceive everything as inherently existent all the time without any effort. Yet even though inherent existence always appears to us, we do not discern it. So we need to understand the measure of that object of negation. Correct analytical examination will provide us with a specific criterion: if it exists at all, then it must exist in such and such a way. Once we have understood this criterion, we have identified the object of negation.

Then we can take the next step and apply this criterion. We can ascertain that because the object of negation does not exist in such and such a way, it does not exist at all. Consider this example. You know what a horn looks like; so you can ascertain that if a rabbit had one, it would be like *this*. However, you know that a rabbit does not have anything like *this*; therefore you can negate the existence of a rabbit horn. If you did not clearly understand the criterion of a horn, then you might incorrectly reject the existence of rabbit ears. We need to have an exact criterion of the object of negation clearly in mind; only then can our negation be accurate and negate the desired object—in this case inherent existence. If we do not precisely determine the general concept of "inherent existence," the scope of our negation will be either too wide or too narrow. As a result we will not properly understand śūnyatā—the lack of inherent existence. Does this seem like a "chicken or egg" situation to you: To understand śūnyatā, we must identify the object of negation and negate it, yet at the time of identifying the object of negation and negating it, must we already understand śūnyatā? You can debate whether these two occur at the same time. Check this carefully.

There are countless objects of negation, though we do not need to negate each one individually. If we negate their shared root, we negate them all. Consider again the example of a rabbit horn. We have a fairly clear, general idea of a rabbit horn. We know what a rabbit horn would be if it existed. When we prove that a rabbit horn in general does not exist, then we will have negated all possible varieties of rabbit horns: beautiful rabbit horns, long rabbit horns, sharp rabbit horns, and so on. This is important. Gyaltsab Je's commentary on valid knowledge says:

> You should tell those people untrained in the skills of reasoning, who assert that valid knowledge cuts superimpositions like the fangs of the musk deer, that . . . when you understand the generality to be absent, then you necessarily understand its instances to be absent.[43]

In other words, when we cut away false notions we do not need to eliminate them one by one, like a musk deer that grazes by nipping one blade of grass at a time. Logical reasoning does not work that way. Rational argument negates all the instances of a generality at once by eliminating their common root—the generality itself. Consider the example of the son of a barren woman. There are innumerable objects of negation here, such as her tall son, her handsome son, her clever son, and so on. All these attributes are connected in being predicated on the barren woman's son. We eliminate them all by establishing that there is no son of a barren woman. We do not need to negate each attribute individually.

The parameters of the criterion we use to negate things as ultimately or inherently existent are very precise. We must recognize how something would exist at the subtlest level, if it were to exist inherently. If we do not understand the subtlest general idea of inherent existence, then some aspects of inherent existence will not be eliminated. If we do not go far enough to correctly identify the subtle object of negation, we will still hold things as truly existent to some degree. For example, even when we understand the level of negation reached by the Vaibhāṣikas, we are still holding things to be inherently existent. Grasping at this false way of existing is to fall to the extreme of eternalism. If we do not negate the subtlest notion of "inherent existence," we will not be able to free ourselves from samsara.

We must also be careful not to fall to the extreme of nihilism and deny the existence of something that is, in fact, there. Nihilism cuts out too much and holds existent things to be nonexistent. If our definition of *truly existent* is too broad, not only do we negate inherent existence, but we may also even negate existence itself. It is too much to assert that inherent existence means mere existence. If it did, then to say that all things are empty of inherent existence would be to deny the existence of causality and the twelve links of dependent arising. We would end up negating everything. The extreme view of nihilism is worse than the extreme view of eternalism. The extreme view of eternalism does not contradict the existence of causality; it holds causes and effects to exist in addition to their superimposed appearance as inherently existent. This is a case of grasping at existence too much. This is a little less dangerous than the nihilistic view, holding existent things to be totally nonexistent, because if we negate everything then we cannot posit any virtue and nonvirtue or karma and its results. Thus we deny that it would be possible to create the causes for a good future life or any other positive goal in the future. Such negative views and negative actions would lead us to lower rebirths.

In conclusion, it is most important to identify the object of negation because if we do not define it properly, we will definitely fall to the extreme views of eternalism or nihilism. We need to know how far we can go in negating things and the point beyond which we cannot go. We have to identify the middle way that is free of the extremes. Therefore we need to know what the extremes are and what makes something an extreme view. This kind of approach is very useful.

(b)) REFUTING OTHER SYSTEMS THAT NEGATE WITHOUT IDENTIFYING PROPERLY THE OBJECT TO BE NEGATED

Many sutras and Madhyamaka texts, such as Nāgārjuna's *Fundamental Treatise*, contain numerous examples of logical analysis of the final nature of reality. Most of these reasons involve negations: phenomena are shown not to exist as they appear. The *Heart Sutra*, for example, appears to say that nothing is accepted or held to exist. These scriptures are commonly misinterpreted and become the basis of wrong views. Because there are so many negations, some scholars and yogis developed philosophical systems that present an overly broad object of negation. This mistaken approach rejects too much and negates the existence of everything. At the other extreme some scholars present too narrow an object of negation. They negate something but not everything that needs to be negated. To correctly understand the object of negation, we must look at how others have mistakenly identified the object to be negated. This has two parts:

(1))   Refuting an overly broad identification of the object to be negated (chapters 4–9)
(2))   Refuting an overly restricted identification of the object to be negated (chapter 10)

(1)) REFUTING AN OVERLY BROAD IDENTIFICATION OF THE OBJECT TO BE NEGATED

This has two parts:

(a'))   Stating others' assertions (chapter 4)
(b'))   Showing that those assertions are wrong (chapters 4–9)

(a')) STATING OTHERS' ASSERTIONS

Here Tsongkhapa summarizes the views of some of his contemporaries as well as some earlier Tibetan Buddhist scholars who claim to be Mādhyamikas but who, in their rejection of inherent existence, go too far and negate all phenomena, from form to omniscience. The phrase "from form to omniscience" needs some explanation. To enable us to understand the characteristics and nature of all phenomena, Buddha divided all existent things into 108 categories. These are then separated into two groups: the impure side of samsara and the pure side of nirvana. The upper and lower Abhidharma literature says that there are 53 sets of afflicted phenomena on the impure side, starting with the 5 aggregates, the 12 sources, and the 18 elements. On the pure side there are 55 sets of virtuous phenomena, beginning with the 37 factors that pertain to enlightenment and concluding with the 4 buddha bodies.[44] So "from form to omniscience" encompasses all existent things: form is the first of the 5 aggregates in the first set of the impure side, and the last item of the final pure set is omniscience. There is nothing that is not included within that phrase. The *Perfection of Wisdom Sutras* teach that all these things are just empty of inherent existence.

The Madhyamaka interpretation of ultimate existence is connected with the ability to withstand ultimate analysis. Ultimate analysis is a logical search for the essential identity of an object. If something is ultimately existent then it can withstand ultimate analysis; if it is not ultimately existent then it cannot withstand ultimate analysis. The Madhyamaka approach to negating inherent existence is to analyze any proposed subject from every point of view. For example, we analyze the self in terms of the aggregates, in terms of the whole and its parts, and so on, asking, "What is that thing that I have labeled as the self?" If we analytically search for a particular person, such as Devadatta, we look for him among his five aggregates, because if he is to be found, he will be found within his aggregates of body and mind. But Devadatta is not his face, nor his body, nor any thought, feeling, or anything else among his aggregates. When we look for the real inherent nature of Devadatta, we cannot find anything. Wherever we look, outside or inside, up or down, we do not find Devadatta. Because there is nothing to be found after investigating in this way, we determine that Devadatta cannot withstand ultimate analysis.

A thing that is unable to withstand ultimate logical analysis simply disappears upon examination. We keep searching, but we cannot catch hold of anything that is the thing's essential nature. Everything that we examine loses its apparent identity, vanishing into its parts and the parts of its parts. At the end of this process, if we did indeed find something existing from its own side, as if to say, "Here I am, I am Devadatta," then this thing would be able to withstand ultimate logical analysis. However, whatever we choose to examine, whether it is the object perceived or the subject perceiving it, when we investigate its nature using ultimate analysis, in the end we find there is nothing existing from its own side. Devadatta is just nominally existent, imputed on his various aggregates. He exists, but he does not exist inherently. The Madhyamaka view is that things are imputed by conceptual or linguistic convention; terms, such as "table," "house," or "person," are labeled on a basis. What is the thing as it is labeled? When we look under the term to find the essence of that thing, we find nothing that exists from its own side as a real thing, independent of being so labeled. When we search for that thing, we eventually see just emptiness, the absence of anything existing in that way. Investigating the nature of the reality of things is like physically trying to find the core of an onion. We peel off each layer, one after another, and see that each individual layer is not the onion. We look further and further, trying to find the actual onion, but in the end we cannot find it among its parts. Another example is a distant rainbow; if we approach it to see its lovely colors in more detail, it disappears. It is unable to withstand investigation. Using this type of analysis and familiarizing themselves with it, practitioners develop a correct understanding of the absence of inherent existence, śūnyatā.

The Madhyamaka view is that nothing can bear ultimate analysis. For example, the *Heart Sutra* specifically says: "The five aggregates do not inherently exist," and lists them one by one. Then it enumerates other sets, such as the four noble truths, the twelve sources of sense consciousness, the twelve links of dependent arising, and so on, and in each case negates their inherent existence. The *Perfection of Wisdom Sutras* also explain that all things are merely empty of inherent existence in this way, expressing this idea with negations such as "They do not arise," "They do not cease," "They do not arise from self," or "They do not arise from others." Some early Tibetan scholars concluded that, for the Mādhyamikas, these scriptures and analyses negate all existent phenomena, from form up to omniscience, and they give various reasons for identifying the object of negation so broadly. Tsongkhapa shows that each of these reasons is invalid. Here he merely lists these reasons, though in later sections he negates them one by one.

The first contention of these early Tibetan scholars concerns the fact that things cannot withstand ultimate analysis. No matter what is examined, whether pure or impure, not even an atom of it can bear ultimate analysis. These scholars have a general understanding of the Madhyamaka view that "unable to withstand ultimate analysis" and "empty of inherent existence" mean the same thing. However, they expand on this view and say, "If nothing can withstand ultimate analysis, then nothing can exist at all." They consider everything to be the object of negation. They claim that nothing can be established because nothing can withstand ultimate analysis; since everything disappears when submitted to ultimate analysis, everything previously thought to exist is found to be nonexistent.

Their second point is that the teachings given in the sutras, such as the *Pile of Precious Things Collection* (*Ratna-kūṭa*), on the four alternatives— propounding that things are not existent, not nonexistent, not both, and not neither—show that nothing exists. There is nothing that is not included in one of these four alternatives; therefore everything is rejected.

Their third point is based on the knowledge of ārya beings—those who have a direct realization of emptiness. In contrast to ordinary people, whose knowledge and perceptions are not correct, āryas' direct understanding of śūnyatā is correct. Whatever is known by āryas' supreme wisdom must be real; so what their ultimate knowledge understands is the criterion of what exists. The āryas' wisdom understanding śūnyatā does not see production and cessation, bondage and liberation, and so on, to exist; it sees that these are just empty. Therefore it must be true that production and so on do not exist.

Their fourth point is that if we accept that there are such things as production, cessation, and so on, we should ask, "Can these things withstand ultimate analysis?" If they can withstand ultimate analysis, then they must be truly or ultimately existent. If they cannot withstand ultimate analysis, then they are negated by ultimate analysis—so how can they exist? These earlier scholars do not understand that there is a huge difference between "being unable to withstand ultimate analysis" and "being negated by ultimate analysis." Tsongkhapa says it is essential to be aware of this difference, so he discusses it later.

Their fifth point is that if we assert the existence of production, cessation, and so on, we should ask, "Are these things established by valid knowledge?" Usually *established by valid knowledge* is the necessary criterion for something to exist. If something is established by valid knowledge, it exists; if it is not established by valid knowledge, it does not exist. For example, a rabbit horn does not exist because there is no valid knowledge that observes it. In general there are two types of valid knowledge: ultimate valid knowledge that ascertains reality and conventional valid knowledge that perceives forms, sounds, and so on, and discerns right from wrong. But according to these scholars, it is incorrect to say that production and other conventional things are established by valid knowledge, because the āryas' wisdom perceiving reality sees that production, and so forth, do not exist. These scholars argue that since an ārya's valid knowledge does not establish conventional things, these things are not established by valid knowledge at all. If in response we say that *established by valid knowledge* means established by conventional valid knowledge, such as the sense consciousnesses, rather than by the valid knowledge of superior wisdom, then they point us to scriptures that reject conventional valid knowledge as being valid knowledge; they quote, for example, the *King of Concentrations Sutra*:

> The eye, ear, and nose consciousnesses are not valid knowledge;
> The tongue, body, and mental consciousnesses are also not valid knowledge.
> If these sense consciousnesses were valid knowledge,
> Of what use to anyone would the āryas' path be?

They also cite Candrakīrti's *Introduction to the "Middle Way,"* which says, "Ordinary knowing is always invalid." On the basis of such quotations, these earlier Tibetan scholars argue that it is incorrect to use establishment by conventional valid knowledge as the measure or criterion of existence. Hence, production and so forth are not established by valid knowledge: the valid knowledge of āryas does not perceive it, and the so-called conventional valid knowledge of ordinary beings is not really valid knowledge at all. They assert that we too, as Mādhyamikas, cannot accept the existence of something not established by valid knowledge because to claim that something exists that is not established by valid knowledge is illogical and incorrect.

Their sixth point is that, if we accept production, we must accept it conventionally because Mādhyamikas do not accept anything to be ultimately existent. However, accepting it as conventionally existent is also incorrect because Candrakīrti's *Introduction to the "Middle Way"* says:

> Whatever argument is used in the context of ultimate analysis
> To negate production from self and others,
> That argument negates it even conventionally;
> According to you, then, due to what is there production?

Ultimate analysis rejects production from self, from others, from both, and from neither, not only ultimately but also conventionally. If there is no production—neither ultimately nor conventionally—then what kind of production is there? How can we say there is production?

Their seventh point is that if we agree that there is no production from any of the four alternatives—self, others, both, and without cause—yet still assert there is production, then our negation of production using the four alternatives fails. Nāgārjuna uses the logical reasoning of the four alternatives to negate ultimate production. If something arises then it must arise in one of those four ways: there is no other way for things to be produced. If these four alternatives are eliminated, there is no production. They say that we, as is the case with all Mādhyamikas, agree that there is no production without a cause and do not accept production from self. If we do not accept production from self, then we cannot accept production from both self and others. That eliminates three of the four alternatives. Therefore, since production must be from one of the four alternatives, we must accept production from others. However, they say that to accept production from others is incorrect because Candrakīrti says in *Introduction to the "Middle Way,"* "Even in worldly terms there is no production from others." So if we maintain that something arises, yet not in one of those four ways, it becomes invalid to use the four alternatives as a proof to negate production. If using the four alternatives does not succeed in negating production, it cannot succeed in negating ultimate production.

The eighth point made by earlier Tibetan scholars is that when negating production, Mādhyamikas should not apply the qualification "ultimately," because the application of this qualification is rejected by Candrakīrti in his *Clear Words.* This is in contrast to the Svātantrika-Mādhyamikas, who say that the qualification "ultimately" must be applied in such contexts. Consider the varying interpretations of the first verse of Nāgārjuna's *Fundamental Treatise on the Middle Way:*[45]

> Not from self, not from others,
> Not from both, not without a cause;
> Any things, anywhere,
> Do not arise at any time. (1.1)

The Svātantrika-Mādhyamikas do not accept this literally. They say that the qualifier "ultimately" must be applied to certain words in this stanza so as to read:

> Not from self ultimately, not from others ultimately,
> Not from both ultimately, not without a cause ultimately.

The Svātantrika-Mādhyamikas even consider that the *Heart Sutra* is not definitive because it says "form does not exist" and "form does not exist inherently," without the word "ultimately" appearing in the text. Conversely, the Prāsaṅgika-Mādhyamikas say that the qualifier "ultimately" should not be applied here. The earlier Tibetan scholars were confused by these conflicting interpretations. Some of them would say that arising and so on cannot be accepted even conventionally, whereas others would say that they are to be accepted conventionally but not ultimately. However, all of these earlier Tibetan scholars would loudly proclaim: "There is no denying that according to the system of this master, Candrakīrti, ultimate analysis negates an essentially existent inherent nature in the case of all phenomena, because he negates inherent existence in terms of both the ultimate and the conventional. If there is no inherent nature of that kind, then what is there? Thus it is only the Svātantrika system that applies the qualifier 'ultimately' to the object of negation." These scholars argue that since the Prāsaṅgika-Mādhyamikas do not apply the qualifier "ultimately" to the object of negation, they end up negating everything by means of their ultimate analysis. Nothing exists at all.

All of the above are arguments of those who accept too broad an identification of the object of negation. Their object of negation is "the existence of all phenomena" rather than "the inherent existence of all phenomena." As a result, they reject everything, both ultimately and conventionally; they declare that all things, even conventionally existent things such as karma, are not real and do not exist. These scholars mistakenly attribute to all Mādhyamikas this overly broad identification of the object of negation.

Tsongkhapa, as a Madhyamaka scholar, defends his system from this nihilistic interpretation of Madhyamaka. He lays out all these points so that he can eliminate them and provide a response showing the genuine Madhyamaka system.

(b')) Showing that those assertions are wrong

This has two parts:

- (1')) Showing that those systems contradict the unique distinguishing feature of Madhyamaka (chapters 4–5)
- (2')) Showing that the criticisms they express are not able to disprove the distinguishing feature of Madhyamaka (chapters 6–9)

(1')) Showing that those systems contradict the unique distinguishing feature of Madhyamaka

This has three parts:

- (a")) Identifying the distinguishing feature of Madhyamaka (chapter 4)
- (b")) How those systems contradict the distinguishing feature of Madhyamaka (chapter 5)
- (c")) How a Mādhyamika responds to those who contradict the distinguishing feature of Madhyamaka (chapter 5)

(a")) IDENTIFYING THE DISTINGUISHING FEATURE OF MADHYAMAKA

To attain enlightenment we must complete the collection of merit and the collection of wisdom. Nāgārjuna's *Sixty Stanzas of Reasoning* (*Yukti-ṣaṣṭikā*) says:

> Through this virtue may all sentient beings
> Accumulate the collections of merit and wisdom
> And attain the two holy bodies
> That arise from merit and wisdom.

This stanza is a prayer that all living beings attain buddhahood. Buddhahood is a combination of perfect omniscience with a completely pure physical form that possesses thirty-two major marks and eighty minor signs and dwells in a pure land. Just as ordinary beings have a body and mind, a buddha has a perfect body called the *form body* (*rūpakāya*) and a perfect mind called the *Dharma body* (*dharmakāya*).[46] The holy Dharma body is a buddha's perfect mind free of all traces of faults; its ultimate nature is its lack of inherent existence. The Dharma body and the form body arise simultaneously—there cannot be one without the other. However, ordinary beings cannot perceive a buddha's Dharma body, so it is the holy form body that directly benefits others. The form body can manifest in various ways, give teachings, and so forth. These two bodies cannot be separated, though they have separate causes and different characteristics.

The Dharma body of a buddha is the result of the accumulation of wisdom. The collection of wisdom involves specific meditation practices, through which one gradually develops the understanding and direct realization of the ultimate truth—śūnyatā—to its fullest extent. By continually developing this wisdom directly perceiving emptiness, the mindstream is eventually purified of all mental afflictions, their seeds, and their imprints—thus becoming completely unobscured and omniscient. This is the holy mind of a buddha. However, a buddha does not only have a completely purified mind; he or she also has a pure form body to help others. The form body of a buddha is the result of the accumulation of merit. The collection of merit involves engaging in the virtuous practices of the bodhisattvas—generosity, ethical conduct, patience, compassion, love, and so on—to their fullest extent. In order to develop it we need to do millions and millions of meritorious physical, verbal, and mental deeds. This is the method side of practice.

We will achieve buddhahood only when these two collections are perfectly complete. Completing these collections depends on practicing the path that unites method with wisdom. So a practitioner must attain two kinds of knowledge: knowledge of conventional phenomena and knowledge of ultimate reality. The former is a special understanding from the depths of one's heart concerning the operation of cause and effect on the conventional level. We must know that causal relationships are specific and not arbitrary; we must clearly understand that a particular kind of cause gives rise to a particular kind of result. We must realize that beneficial results, such as peace and happiness, follow from virtuous causes, and that painful results, such as lower rebirths, follow from nonvirtuous causes. As spiritual practitioners we need to understand the truth of suffering and the truth of the cause of suffering, as well as the truth of cessation and the truth of the path to cessation. Understanding the nature of causality from the point of view of what leads to samsara and what leads to nirvana is called "attainment of the knowledge of conventional phenomena." It is especially important for a Mahayana practitioner to gain this understanding in order to practice the method side of the path that results in the holy form body.

In addition to this, Mahayana practitioners need to gain the understanding that there is not even the smallest particle of any phenomenon that exists inherently by its own nature. All existent things are dependent on other things. Everything is relative in this way; there is nothing that exists by its own inherent nature. This understanding is called "attainment of the knowledge of reality." It results in the Dharma body.

It takes many eons of practice to accumulate the two limitless collections of method and wisdom. The fortitude to engage in these accumulations for such a long time definitely depends on gaining an understanding of ultimate and conventional truth. These two are not contradictory. In fact, the understanding of śūnyatā is needed to gain a full understanding of conventional reality. If things were inherently existent, we would not be able to change them. If the mental afflictions and other imperfections existed independently by their own nature, they would always remain unchangeable. It would be impossible to attain the holy bodies of a buddha. The very function of the spiritual path is to change things: it makes impure things pure and imperfect things perfect. So the understanding of ultimate reality enhances our understanding of conventional reality and enables us to see that change, purification, and enlightenment are possible. These changes are only possible because things do not exist by way of their own nature but exist dependently on other things.

Thus the basis of the path to enlightenment is the two truths: ultimate truth and conventional truth. All phenomena fit into these two categories. We need to understand both of these two truths in order to fully develop the paths of method and wisdom. Practicing these in union eventually gives rise to the two buddha bodies. The mutual dependence of the two truths is the special quality of the Madhyamaka view. If we do not have a proper understanding of the two truths, we will not have an understanding of the paths to develop method and wisdom. If we do not have these, then we cannot develop the two buddha bodies. The correct, perfect, and complete path that is the cause to attain the two buddha bodies—the final result—is the unmistaken view of the basis: the mutual dependence of the two truths.[47] Without it, the desire to practice the complete paths of method and wisdom will not arise from the depths of our heart.

The key point of the Madhyamaka system is that the development of the two buddha bodies—Dharma body and form body—requires the attainment of both types of knowledge in union. Without an understanding of ultimate reality, we cannot understand the relativity of phenomena as dependent natures. In turn, a lack of understanding of relativity undermines our ascertainment that pleasant results are dependent on virtuous causes and painful results are dependent on nonvirtuous causes. So we need to develop an understanding of śūnyatā and of conventional phenomena together. This special training will push us to do the eons of work necessary to complete the accumulations of merit and wisdom. Only when we see the relationship between dependent arising and ultimate reality can we have the courage to seek buddhahood. In short, attainment of the two buddha bodies depends on the development of method and wisdom. In order to give rise to the proper practices to develop method and wisdom, we need the correct view of conventional things and their ultimate nature.

Other people, who do not understand the Madhyamaka approach, see the two truths as contradictory. When they posit conventional phenomena—such as causality, suffering, and liberation—they lose the understanding that such things are empty of inherent existence, because they appear to be real from their own side. When thinking about things as empty of inherent existence, they cannot accept cause and effect as being conventionally real. When the two truths appear to be contradictory in this way, they fall into the two extremes in turn. The extreme of eternalism holds things to exist too strongly; the extreme of nihilism holds nothing to exist at all. When either of these wrong views arises in their minds, they muddle Buddha's pure teachings. So they cannot explain the teachings as noncontradictory. Even during Buddha's lifetime it was difficult for his disciples to understand the relationship between the two truths. People had difficulty reconciling the presentation of conventional reality in the first turning of the wheel with the presentation of ultimate reality in the second turning of the wheel. These teachings appear to be contradictory.

Until you understand these teachings properly, free of the two extremes, you will not be able to achieve the highest goal.

There are masters possessing subtle skill and extensive wisdom who are called Mādhyamikas because they so expertly understand the two truths free of the two extremes. Having found the final meaning of the teachings, they have marvelous respect for Buddha and what he taught. These great masters praise Buddha most highly because no other religious teacher presents the profound doctrine combining emptiness and dependent arising. He alone teaches, "Wise Ones, the meaning of emptiness—being empty of inherent existence—is the meaning of dependent arising; it does not mean being unreal in the sense of being empty of the ability to function." Many special praises are offered to Buddha and his teaching of dependent arising. For example, the first stanzas of Tsongkhapa's *In Praise of Dependent Arising* are:

> I bow down to the unsurpassable teacher and sage,
> The one who sees and knows
> Dependent arising, the king of reasons,
> And explains it just as he sees it.
>
> Ignorance is the root of all
> The manifold misery in the world;
> So he teaches dependent arising—
> The seeing of which reverses it.[48]

Nāgārjuna's *Fundamental Treatise* also opens with an illuminating homage to Buddha as the teacher of dependent arising:

> I bow down to the most holy of teachers,
> The completely accomplished Buddha,
> Who teaches the peace that pacifies all elaboration,
> That whatever dependently arises has
> No cessation, no arising,
> No annihilation, no permanence,
> No coming, no going,
> No unity, no plurality.

This teaching is incomparable. Only Buddha teaches dependent arising by means of these profound eight negations, which show us the way things are: being dependent, things do not arise by their own inherent nature; having no inherent nature, they are dependently existent. This teaching gives rise to a profound understanding, an inexpressible peace that pacifies all the elaborations projected on things by ignorance.

Some great Buddhist masters are highly trained and have great knowledge of various sciences, but they adhere to the views of lower-tenet systems. They do not accept the Madhyamaka view and indeed argue that the Madhyamaka view is nihilistic. They think that if everything is empty of inherent existence, then there is no way to establish all the teachings about samsara and nirvana—the causes of bondage and how to attain liberation. In their view none of the teachings on these can be true if things do not exist by their own inherent nature. Nāgārjuna presents their argument in a stanza of his *Fundamental Treatise*:

> If all these things are empty,
> There can be no arising and no destruction.
> According to you it must follow
> That the four noble truths do not exist.

These scholars say that only if arising and destruction exist inherently can suffering arise from karma and afflictions or be destroyed by the true paths. They think that if, as Mādhyamikas state, all these things are empty, then the four noble truths must be nonexistent. Nāgārjuna elaborates their position in *Refutation of Objections* (*Vigraha-vyāvartanī*):

> If all things in every case
> Do not inherently exist,
> Then even your words do not inherently exist
> And so cannot refute inherent nature.

These scholars criticize the profound Madhyamaka position by saying that if words do not inherently exist, then words can neither negate inherent nature nor prove the absence of inherent nature. The Realists think that if there is no inherent nature and things do not exist inherently, then there cannot be anything that is produced or anything that is a producer; there cannot be anything that is rejected or proved or anything that functions to refute or prove it. In short, they claim that the Madhyamaka arguments negating inherent existence reject all functionality. Thus when the Madhyamaka and the lower schools argue about the differences between their views, the main issue is whether samsara, nirvana, and their respective causes can be established on the basis of being merely empty of inherent existence. The lower schools think that the teachings on causality and so on are incompatible with things being empty of inherent existence. The Mādhyamikas say that if they are *not* empty, then none of these things can be posited or accepted. The two sides understand the situation in opposite ways. Nāgārjuna replies in *Fundamental Treatise* to the opponents' view as follows:

> If all these things are not empty,
> There can be no arising and no destruction.
> According to you it must follow
> That the four noble truths do not exist. (24.20)

It is the special feature of the Madhyamaka system that it accepts things— such as product and producer, negation and proof, and all the explanations of samsara and nirvana—without even the smallest particle having an inherently existent nature. This is completely unsuitable for the other schools. The twenty-fourth chapter of the *Fundamental Treatise* says:

> Your consequences revealing a fault
> Do not correctly apply to emptiness;
> Thus your refutation of emptiness
> Does not correctly apply to us.
>
> Wherever emptiness is suitable,
> Everything is suitable;
> Wherever emptiness is unsuitable,
> Nothing is suitable.

Any system positing that things are not empty must accept that things are permanently fixed and unchangeable. In order to change, a thing must be relative and dependent—in other words, empty of inherent existence. Things that exist by their own nature are not dependent. So according to the Mādhyamikas, not only does the negative consequence of a lack of production not apply to those who accept emptiness, but it is only those who accept the emptiness of inherent existence who can accept the four noble truths. Nāgārjuna's view is that those who assert inherent existence cannot accept the presentations of arising and ceasing, abandonment and attainment, and so on. Candrakīrti's *Clear Words* says:

> Not only does the unacceptable consequence you state not apply to
> our position, but also all the presentations of the four noble truths and

so on are completely correct [for our position]. In order to show this [Nāgārjuna] taught, "Wherever emptiness is suitable . . ."

Everything is feasible for those who accept that everything is empty of inherent existence, because "empty of inherent existence" means "dependently existent." Everything is relative and depends on something else: causes are known in relation to effects, good in relation to bad. Things are possible because they do not exist independently or by their own inherent nature. If they did exist independently or by their own inherent nature, then we could not establish any conventional thing at all.

Nāgārjuna's explanation of dependent arising is presented in the twenty-sixth chapter of *Fundamental Treatise on the Middle Way*. Here he teaches the stages of production in the forward progression of the twelve links of dependent arising and the stages of cessation in the reverse progression of the twelve links.[49] The twenty-fifth chapter of that text mainly teaches the negation of inherent existence. The twenty-fourth chapter is an examination of the four noble truths. Here Nāgārjuna shows that if things are not empty of inherent existence, then all the explanations concerning samsara and nirvana, arising and ceasing, and so on, are untenable. Further, he demonstrates that if things are empty of inherent existence, then the explanations of causality and so on are feasible. In other words, this chapter shows that everything is possible if things are empty of inherent existence, but if things are not empty then everything becomes impossible. The detailed presentation of the analysis in this chapter should be carried over to all the other chapters.

Tsongkhapa says that some of his contemporaries miss this point. They claim to propound the Madhyamaka view, but they are actually in accord with the Realists because they say that if there is no inherent existence then causality is not possible. It is not the Madhyamaka view that causality and the absence of inherent existence are incompatible or contradictory. In fact, the genuine view of Nāgārjuna is that we understand emptiness in reliance on understanding dependent arising. If we accept that specific causes and conditions give rise to specific effects, then we can accept that they are empty of inherent existence. For example, when we say "fire burns fuel," we are looking at a number of interconnected things: the agent (fire), the action (burns), and the object of the action (fuel). Only based on the mutual dependence of these three things can we say that fire burns fuel. If these were inherently or independently existent, then they could not rely on one another and so could not function or exist in dependence on each other. We must search for the Madhyamaka view—that everything is empty of inherent existence—in reliance on the establishment of production and cessation. If the view of emptiness were unfeasible, then things would be independent; however, things are dependent on causes and conditions, and therefore the view of emptiness is feasible. The twenty-fourth chapter of the *Fundamental Treatise* says:

> Anything's dependent arising
> Is explained as emptiness;
> That dependent imputation
> Is itself the middle way.
>
> Because there is nothing
> That does not dependently arise,
> There is nothing
> That is not empty.

Nāgārjuna, the principal Mādhyamika, says that to dependently arise entails being empty of inherent existence. Things are empty of inherent existence in that they are imputed in dependence on their bases by conceptual and terminological convention. Thus the Madhyamaka view is that everything is nominally or imputedly existent. However, this does not mean things are non-existent. It means that being empty of inherent existence corresponds to being dependently or imputedly existent. This is the middle way, the view that is free of the two extremes. Those other Tibetan scholars should not mistakenly say the complete opposite: that to arise from causes and conditions entails being inherently existent. Also, Nāgārjuna's *Refutation of Objections* says:

> Wherever emptiness can exist,
> Everything can exist;
> Wherever emptiness cannot exist,
> Nothing at all can exist.
>
> I bow down to the Buddha,
> Whose incomparable supreme teaching shows
> That dependent arising and emptiness
> Have the same meaning as the middle way.

Apart from Buddha, all other religious teachers and philosophers posit truly existent causes from which results arise. They teach that all causes exist by way of their own nature. Some even posit an ultimate first cause—an external source that is permanent, partless, and absolute, such as God or a universal principle—that controls everything below it. These teachers think that things are inherently real because they arise from such causes. Buddha teaches the complete opposite: he teaches that things are empty of inherent existence because they arise dependently on causes and conditions. In other words, dependent arising and emptiness have the same meaning as the middle way.

What does the expression "same meaning" indicate here? Is Nāgārjuna saying that dependent arising is identical to emptiness? First we should understand how Buddhist logicians use the terms *same* or *one* and differentiate this from the terms *same meaning* or *one meaning*. The term *same* or *one* indicates exact identity. It means being the same in name and referent. For example, "vase" is the same as "vase." They are the same word and the same thing. In contrast, the term *same meaning* or *one meaning* is used where different names have the same referent or where different expressions are coextensive. For example, "vase" and "flower vessel" are different words, but they denote the same object. If something is a vase, then it is a flower vessel, and vice versa.[50] However, because the words are different they are not considered to be the same. If someone does not know the word "vase," he may wonder what a vase is until another person says, "It's a flower vessel." Then the first person thinks, "Oh yes, a flower vessel." Similarly, the same thing can be named in different languages. The words "table" and *chog tse* are different terms indicating the same thing; however, they are not considered to be the same, because a person may understand one term but not the other. Also, a definiendum, such as "thing," and its definition, "that which can function," are not the same expressions but have the same referent. Another classical example is the moon, which as we saw above has several names in India and Tibet, such as White Circle, One with Cooling Rays, Rabbit Bearer, and so on. Each name indicates a different function or quality of the moon; though they all refer to the moon, they do not suggest the same picture. The different names have the same referent— the moon—but are not the same. They have one referent, but they are not one. The words "moon" and "moon" are the same; but if we replace one of these terms with another here, then the two are different.

Now before going any further with this, we need to distinguish between the terms *empty* and *emptiness*. These two should not be mixed up. Things are empty. As soon as we have *empty things*, then we have *emptiness*, but they are not exactly the same. We can say "Form is empty," but we cannot say "Form is emptiness" or "Form is the emptiness of form." However, some people mix these terms up, so we need to address this confusion. All vegetables dependently arise, thus they are empty. But are they all emptiness? When you perceive a tomato with your eyes, are you seeing emptiness directly? No, of course not! You may want to say, "This lamplight is emptiness because it dependently arises," but that is not correct. Think about form and its emptiness. What is their relationship? Are they the same? Are they synonymous? Are they mutually contradictory? Form's emptiness cannot be form itself. Form itself cannot be form's emptiness. Form's emptiness is ultimate truth. Form is conventional truth. Conventional truth and ultimate truth cannot be the same; they are different. Now from a strictly logical point of view, are form and form's emptiness contradictory? There is nothing that can be an instance of both a conventional truth and an ultimate truth; in that sense there is no common basis. However, each and every thing has both a conventional nature and an ultimate nature. A conventional truth, such as form, and its ultimate nature, its emptiness, cannot exist separately. Form's emptiness is an attribute of form. So we can say that form and form's emptiness are the same nature but different isolates.[51]

Everything is empty of inherent existence; but if something is *empty* it is not necessarily *emptiness*. Form is empty of inherent existence, so any individual form has the attribute: its emptiness of inherent existence. But form is not identical with its emptiness of inherent existence. Furthermore, we can say that form is empty of inherent existence universally—anytime and anywhere. There is no moment or place in which form is not empty. Form is empty of inherent existence everywhere and forever. But we cannot say that form's emptiness of inherent existence exists all the time and everywhere. It only exists on the basis of form, wherever and whenever form happens to exist. Now, does form's emptiness of inherent existence have a cause? No, it does not depend on a cause. Is it a dependent nature? Yes, it is dependent on its parts and on being conventionally imputed. There is a lot of discussion about that!

Nāgārjuna does not say that dependent arising and emptiness are identical; he says they are, or have, the "same meaning." However, does he mean what the logicians mean by that phrase? Not quite. What Nāgārjuna is saying here is that they are, or have, the same nature. So in this context, "same meaning" denotes "same nature." The term *same nature* mainly applies to a basis and its attributes or to a generality and its instances; but it can also apply to one and the same thing, such as "pot" and "pot." Generally we say that a pot's shape is the same nature as the pot. A thing is the same nature as all of its attributes. This also applies to any given basis of emptiness, such as a form, and its attribute, emptiness. In the *Heart Sutra*, where it says "Form is empty," "form" is the basis and "emptiness" is its attribute, and where it says "Emptiness is form," this means that form's emptiness is the nature of form. So Nāgārjuna is saying here that *dependent arising* and *emptiness* are the same nature. This means that any dependently arising thing and its being empty of inherent existence are the same nature. In some places the text has the word "empty," and in other places it has the word "emptiness."[52] Here, the term *emptiness* should be understood to refer to the attribute "empty" in general, not to an abstract idea. In making these points about the terms *empty* and *emptiness*, my main concern is that you should not think that emptiness is some rarefied phenomenon that is totally separate from other things. It is simply the absence of inherent existence of anything you may care to consider, including yourself!

You should also keep in mind the different possible uses of the word "self." In the phrase "The self is empty of self," the first "self" is a causally dependent thing, a person, which is a conventional truth, whereas "empty of self" here means selfless or empty of inherent existence, which is an ultimate truth. Being selfless is not a causally dependent thing; that attribute, selflessness, is an ultimate truth, a permanent phenomenon. Moreover, "the self that is selfless" is not the same as "the selflessness of the self." Both the self and selflessness are dependent. Everything, including emptiness, is dependent. But not everything is causally dependent. "The self that is selfless" is causally dependent. "The selflessness of the self" is not causally dependent. It is a permanent phenomenon, which is dependent on its parts and on being imputed on its basis. The self that is negated, of which the causal self is empty, is totally nonexistent. This inherently existent self has never existed at all.

The term *dependent* can have different meanings. According to varying degrees of subtlety it may mean: dependent on causes and conditions, dependent on parts, or dependent on imputation. Emptiness is not nothingness. In order to exist, it is dependent on its basis of imputation. It is also dependent on its parts. However, it is not produced. The emptiness of form is dependent on form; but this does not mean that form is the cause of the emptiness of form. Being dependent is not always causal. The emptiness of form is dependent on form in the same way that form is dependent on the emptiness of form. We are not talking about causal dependence here. We are talking about being dependent on imputation. The Madhyamaka view is that everything is dependent on its own emptiness. Every form, sound, smell, and so on, is dependent on its respective emptiness. If a thing is not empty of an inherent nature, then it cannot function, it cannot arise. If a thing is empty of an inherent nature, then it is dependent; it is dependent on emptiness itself. This is not a causal dependence, but it enables causal dependence to be possible at a grosser level. Emptiness is the base or foundation of all phenomena. Everything is based on its own emptiness. If things are empty then they can come and go, arise and cease, change from one state to another. In this way all kinds of things can happen. If phenomena were not empty, then these changes could not occur.

The implication of dependent arising and emptiness having the same meaning is discussed extensively in many texts. For example, does it mean that when one understands dependent arising, one immediately understands śūnyatā? Or as some scholars claim, does it mean that when one understands śūnyatā, one immediately understands dependent arising? To understand the relationship between emptiness and dependent arising, we must be clear about the distinction between the subtle and gross levels of dependent arising. On the common or gross level, one can realize dependent arising before realizing śūnyatā. The lower schools assert karmic causality, and even ordinary people, such as farmers, understand mundane causation. Farmers know that if they plant corn seeds and provide the other necessary conditions, corn sprouts will grow and when fully ripened will result in a great crop of corn. If farmers did not understand causality, they would not till a field and throw so many good corn kernels on the ground. Understanding causality in this way is not an understanding of emptiness.

When Nāgārjuna says, "Dependent arising and emptiness have the same meaning as the middle way," he is talking about subtle dependent arising. As soon as form exists, it dependently exists. It cannot exist otherwise. There are just two possibilities: either things are dependently existent or they are not dependently existent but are inherently existent. When we analyze the situation deeply, we see that things exist merely in dependence on imputation; they do not have any independent existence themselves. This understanding of the dependent nature of form is connected to the understanding of śūnyatā. Understanding that form is empty of its own inherent nature and that it depends on something else for its identity is a very subtle understanding of dependent arising. Ordinary people do not have this level of understanding. Only as a result of engaging in ultimate analysis can someone develop this profound understanding of dependent arising.

At the subtlest level, as soon as we understand dependent arising, we see that it means that nothing exists inherently; conversely, as soon we understand emptiness—that things are not inherently existent—we realize that it means that things are dependent on something else. An understanding of subtle dependent arising is an understanding of the subtle meaning of emptiness. Instead of contradicting each other, these two kinds of understanding assist each other. By understanding one, we develop a more powerful understanding of the other, and vice versa. If we see them as contradictory, as did some of the earlier Tibetan masters, we have not understood the meaning of emptiness. Tsongkhapa says in *Three Principal Aspects of the Path*:

> As long as these two understandings appear separately—
> Nondeceptive understanding of dependently arising appearances

And assertion-free understanding of their emptiness—
You have still not understood the Subduer's thought.

When they occur together without alternating,
Whereby unmistakably seeing dependent arising
Destroys how the object is grasped by wrong thinking,
Then the analysis of the view is complete. (11–12)

Thus in the context of dependent arising and emptiness, "same meaning" indicates that by understanding one, we develop an understanding of the other, and vice versa. An understanding of subtle dependent arising brings about the understanding of emptiness. By the power of the realization that form is empty of inherent existence, we come to understand that form is dependently related in the subtlest sense. Initially when we analyze emptiness we lose sight of dependent arising, and when we analyze dependent arising we lose sight of emptiness. Eventually the two occur together: an understanding of dependent arising immediately brings forth an understanding of the absence of inherent existence, and an understanding of ultimate śūnyatā naturally brings forth an understanding of conventional dependent arising. When we understand the emptiness of form, we understand form as dependently existent.[53] Form exists only dependently; it does not exist by its own nature. Owing to this understanding of dependent arising, all wrong views holding things to exist by their own nature are destroyed. Nāgārjuna's *Seventy Stanzas on Emptiness* (*Śūnyatā-saptati*) says:

The incomparable Tathāgata taught
That because all things
Are empty of inherent existence,
Things dependently arise.

Also Nāgārjuna's *Sixty Stanzas of Reasoning* says:

Those who, not accepting them as dependent,
Cling to the self or to the world
Are, alas, captivated by views
Of permanence, impermanence, and so on.

How could false views of permanence
And so on not arise

> For those who accept
> Dependent things to inherently exist?
>
> Those who accept dependent things
> As neither real nor false
> But like a reflection of the moon on water
> Are not captivated by views.

The Madhyamaka position is that if we believe that things exist inherently, even if we accept that they arise from causes and conditions, we will fall to the extreme of eternalism. This is because we believe produced things and their causes exist from their own side. When we try to avoid that extreme, if we continue to accept things as inherently existent, we will fall to the extreme of nihilism. Mādhyamikas accept all things to be dependently existent, not from their own side but in an illusion-like way, just as a reflection of the moon appears on a body of water. The reflection appears to be the moon floating on the water, but it is not. It does not exist as that from its own side; it merely appears like that in dependence on certain conditions. Similar to a reflection, things do not exist from their own side as they appear to. Therefore Mādhyamikas accept that things are neither ultimately existent nor completely nonexistent; they are not captivated by wrong views. Nāgārjuna's *Praise of the Transcendent One* (*Lokātīta-stava*) says:

> Logicians assert that suffering
> Is produced from itself, produced from others,
> Produced from both, or produced without a cause.
> But you taught that it dependently arises.
>
> You taught that whatever
> Dependently arises is itself empty.
> "Things have no independent existence"—
> This is your incomparable lion's roar.

Logicians of various schools propound a number of wrong views about causation and reality: some assert that the factors of suffering arise from themselves; others claim that they arise from inherently existent other causes; some say they arise from both self and others; and some proclaim they arise without a cause. Buddha teaches that all suffering dependently arises, and whatever dependently arises is empty of inherent or ultimate existence. Thus all things have no independent existence or self-existence. In this sense, the meaning of dependent arising is explained as the meaning of the emptiness of inherent existence. This is the unique view of Nāgārjuna, the explicator of the Madhyamaka. This teaching is unequaled, like the most thunderous lion's roar.

This explanation of dependent arising is not just for proponents of other systems who hold certain wrong views. It is also for those who claim to be Mādhyamikas, in that they accept the emptiness of inherent existence yet are uncomfortable accepting dependently related causality as part of their system. When Nāgārjuna says, "Wherever emptiness is suitable," he shows that the dependent arising of samsara and nirvana is acceptable for a philosophical system that teaches the emptiness of inherent existence. Emptiness of inherent existence and dependent arising are not contradictory; they are logically admissible in the same philosophical system. Even emptiness itself dependently arises, and anything that dependently arises is itself empty of inherent existence.

DEPENDENT ARISING AND EMPTINESS

Someone may wonder, "How is the existence of samsara and nirvana explained in a system that accepts śūnyatā according to the Madhyamaka view?"[54] Tsongkhapa says that things such as causes, effects, abandonment, and practice are possible only when there is no inherent existence. Suffering can only be established based on causation. It could not possibly exist without causes and conditions. Therefore if suffering exists, then there must be a cause from which it arises. If suffering and its cause exist, there must be a cessation that is the end of suffering and a method leading to that cessation. In other words, the four noble truths exist. If the four noble truths exist, then the activities connected with them exist: practitioners can know suffering, abandon its cause, actualize its cessation, and cultivate the path leading to cessation. If these activities relating to the four noble truths exist, then the Three Jewels of refuge exist. How are these two connected? Practitioners in the process of accomplishing these activities are called Sangha; their realizations and attainments, the true paths and true cessations within their mindstreams, are called Dharma; and those who have completely perfected the true paths and true cessations are called Buddha. A buddha, having attained perfection, presents the teachings to others. All these are acceptable in the purview of the emptiness of inherent existence. Candrakīrti's *Clear Words* says:

> Wherever emptiness of inherent existence of all things is suitable, all the above-mentioned things are suitable. If you ask "How can this be?" it is because we explain dependent arising as emptiness. Therefore

wherever emptiness is suitable, dependent arising is suitable. Wherever dependent arising is suitable, the four noble truths are suitable. If you ask "How can this be?" it is because suffering occurs only as dependently arising, not without dependently arising. Since it does not exist by its own nature, it is empty.

If there is suffering, then the cause of suffering, the cessation of suffering, and the path leading to cessation are suitable also. So fully understanding suffering, abandoning its cause, actualizing its cessation, and cultivating the paths leading to it are all suitable too. If the truth of suffering and so on—and fully understanding it and so on—exist, then their spiritual results must also be suitable. If those results exist, then those who abide in those results must be suitable. If there are abiders in those results, then those who are entering that state must be suitable. If both enterers and the abiders in the fruits exist, then the Sangha is suitable.

If the four noble truths exist, then the Dharma is suitable. If the holy Dharma and the Sangha exist, then Buddhas are suitable too. Therefore the Three Jewels are also suitable.

Given that all the higher realizations of mundane and supramundane things are suitable, virtue and nonvirtue, as well as their results, and all worldly conventions are suitable. Therefore, as [Nāgārjuna] says:

Wherever emptiness is suitable,
Everything is suitable;
Wherever emptiness is unsuitable,
Nothing is suitable.

The latter follows because there would be no dependent arising [if emptiness were unsuitable].

Here you should understand the term *suitable* to mean "can exist" and the term *unsuitable* to mean "cannot exist."

Tsongkhapa refers back to an earlier quote from Nāgārjuna's *Refutation of Objections* representing the opponent's critique of this Madhyamaka position:

If all things in every case
Do not inherently exist,
Then even your words do not inherently exist
And so cannot refute inherent nature.

Then he quotes another stanza from that text, which is Nāgārjuna's response showing that functionality is correct within the context of emptiness:[55]

> Whatever is the dependent arising of things,
> That is called "emptiness";
> Whatever is that dependent arising
> I say is the lack of inherent existence.

To elaborate on this point, Nāgārjuna wrote in his *Commentary on the "Refutation of Objections"* (*Vigraha-vyāvartanī-vṛtti*):

> Without fully understanding the meaning of the emptiness of things, you criticize me, saying, "Your words do not inherently exist and so cannot refute the inherent nature of things."
>
> Now, whatever is the dependent arising of things, that is emptiness. Why? Because it is the lack of inherent existence. Any things that dependently arise do not have inherent nature because they do not inherently exist. Why? Because they depend on causes and conditions. If things existed inherently, then they would exist even without causes and conditions. Since that too is not the case, they do not have inherent nature. Thus, so as to explain, I say, "They are empty."
>
> Likewise, my words dependently arise because they do not inherently exist; because they do not inherently exist, it is correct to say, "They are empty." For example, because pots, woolen shawls, and so on merely dependently arise, they are empty of inherent existence. Yet the former can hold and carry honey, water, and milk, and the latter can protect one from cold, wind, and sun. Likewise, because my words too dependently arise, they do not inherently exist, yet they have the ability to prove that things do not have inherent nature. Therefore it is not correct to say to me, "Your words do not inherently exist and so cannot refute the inherent nature of all things."

Tsongkhapa comments that this passage clearly states that if things depend on causes and conditions, it follows that they are not inherently existent, and if things are inherently existent, it follows that they do not depend on causes and conditions. The first statement expresses a logical relation called the forward pervasion: whatever is dependent on causes and conditions is not inherently existent; the second statement expresses its counterpervasion: whatever is inherently existent is not dependent on causes and conditions. Moreover, this passage says that although words are not inherently existent, they are able to perform the functions of affirming and negating or proving and refuting.

The lower tenet systems say that the dependent arising and ceasing of afflicted and pure phenomena is contradictory to a lack of inherent existence. In the Madhyamaka system these are shown to be harmonious. Not only does the acceptance of one enable the other to be accepted, but the existence of one also enables the other to exist. In short, the attributes "empty of inherent existence" and "causally produced" are united within a common locus. If two attributes have a common base or instantiation, then they are not contradictory. The reverse is true of contradictory attributes: they cannot share a common base because if one exists within a certain locus, then the contradictory attribute cannot exist there. Later in the text we will encounter different types of contradictions, but this is the basic meaning of *noncontradictory*. Here, one thing can both dependently arise and be empty of inherent existence. In other words, causality and not existing by way of its own nature are not contradictory. Since these two are not contradictory, they can be instantiated within a common base. In the present context, the term *common base* is used in the most restrictive way; it indicates that two attributes have the same meaning in the technical sense explained above. So there is no occasion when something is one but not the other. In other words, they are coextensive: whatever dependently arises is empty of inherent existence; whatever is empty of inherent existence dependently arises.

Therefore even though dependent arising (a conventional truth) is not itself emptiness (an ultimate truth), and vice versa, dependent arising and emptiness should not be seen as contradictory. Each is an attribute of the other. Anything that dependently arises is empty, and anything that is empty dependently arises. We should understand that one acts as a reason for the other: because this is dependent, it is empty; because this is empty of inherent existence, it is dependent. In fact dependent arising is the most effective reason for generating an understanding of the emptiness of inherent existence. Various logical reasons can be used to prove śūnyatā, such as the argument that none of the four alternatives of inherent causation is plausible, the argument that none of the four extremes of inherent existence and nonexistence is plausible, and the argument that things are neither inherently one nor many. But Madhyamaka scholars say that dependent arising is the "king of reasons" establishing emptiness.

Only Madhyamaka masters have this special knowledge. Others hold that whatever arises and ceases in dependence on causes and conditions must exist by way of its own nature. They believe that if a thing does not inherently exist, it cannot arise or cease: therefore, if things do not exist by way of their own nature, they do not exist at all. They consider *existence* to be the same as *inherent existence*. In short, they use the very reason that proves emptiness to negate dependent arising; in this way, they transform logic into a huge obstacle to understanding the meaning of the middle way. It is said to be like a god having fallen into a demonic state. It is generally accepted that gods are helpful; if such a supportive being were to become harmful, we would say that he or she has become a devil. The same applies here. If you use logic incorrectly, like these non-Mādhyamikas do, then when you convince yourself that all phenomena lack even the smallest particle of inherent existence, you will have no ground for ascertaining within your own system the relationship between cause and effect. So you will have to posit conventional reality—cause and effect—only for the benefit of others. When you ascertain emptiness, you lose the understanding of dependent arising; conversely, when you ascertain dependent arising, you lose the understanding of emptiness. Thus you are viewing both sides wrongly. This contradiction occurs if you accept literally the *Perfection of Wisdom Sutra*'s words "There is no form, no sound . . ." and so on to mean that these things do not exist at all. If the ultimate and the conventional seem contradictory, then you lack a genuine understanding of the Madhyamaka view. It is crucial to recognize this as a misunderstanding and not proclaim it enthusiastically to be the correct Madhyamaka view.

In order to develop a correct understanding we must continue to study and practice all aspects of the teachings. We will not get anywhere if we just sit in a room thinking, "I want to gain insight into śūnyatā right now; I am not going to bother with morality and other irrelevant things." Guarding our vows and ethical conduct is the cause of finding the correct Madhyamaka view. Pure ethical conduct is the foundation of all good qualities, just as the earth is the ground for all animate and inanimate things. Based on pure morality, we need to accumulate a great mass of virtuous karma and purify our nonvirtuous karma through confession and so forth, so that we can free ourselves of obstacles to the correct understanding of emptiness. Also we need to rely on a spiritual teacher; we must make an effort to listen to his or her instructions, contemplate them, and integrate them using meditation. We need to focus on the conventional aspects of the teachings too, not only on śūnyatā. Otherwise we will not find the correct śūnyatā at all.

The practices of ethical conduct, hearing, and thinking are all dependently arising conventional appearances: this cause produces this result and that cause produces that result. If we practice ethical conduct and so on in accordance with this understanding of cause and effect, then we can practice correctly.

However, by holding these practices to be independently existent, we fall to the extremes of nihilism or eternalism. Therefore we need to free ourselves of this wrong view.

It is very rare for an understanding of dependent arising, or conventional appearances, to be combined properly with an understanding of the emptiness of inherent existence. However, when we succeed in combining them, we find that they support each other. Only then do we understand mere existence, which is the limit of existence. This view of the middle way is most difficult to find. Nāgārjuna says in the *Fundamental Treatise on the Middle Way*:

> Having understood that those with weak intelligence
> Would have difficulty realizing the depths of his teaching,
> Buddha's mind turned away
> From teaching the Dharma.

After Buddha attained enlightenment, he did not teach for a period of seven weeks. He went to a place near Vārāṇasī and remained silently by himself. The fact that even Buddha did not teach demonstrates how rare and how difficult to understand these teachings are. The first words Buddha spoke about śūnyatā indicate his opinion that no one could understand it. A stanza from the *Extensive Sport Sutra* that we looked at previously says:[56]

> Profound, peaceful, free of elaborations, radiant, unproduced:
> I found a truth like nectar.
> No one I teach this to will understand it.
> So I will not speak about it; I will hide in the forest.

Although a realization of the ultimate truth—that everything is empty of inherent existence—removes all suffering and the causes of suffering and brings about spiritual development culminating in the everlasting, deathless state of buddhahood, Buddha did not teach it. He feared that everyone—other religious teachers and scholars as well as ordinary people—would misunderstand it. In fact, he feared that if they listened to what he said they might develop the wrong view that nothing exists. This stanza does not mean that nobody will ever be able to understand, but at that time there was no one suitable to receive this teaching. Nāgārjuna's *Precious Garland* says:

> If this impure body,
> A gross object directly seen,
> Even while continually appearing

Does not stay with the mind,
Then how could the holy Dharma,
Nonabiding and very subtle,
Profound and not directly seen,
Easily come to mind?

Thinking that this Dharma, so profound,
Is too hard for ordinary folk to fathom,
The Sage, after becoming a buddha,
Turned away from teaching it.

We do not need to rely on logical proof or the testament of others to identify a coarse thing such as the body. Our ordinary senses continuously perceive it. Nevertheless if we try to focus on it, taking our posture or breathing as an object of meditation, our mind soon wanders off. We find it hard to concentrate on any part of it, even though it is fully manifest. An awareness of its qualities is even more difficult to maintain. The body is impure and in the nature of suffering; however, we see it as attractive and as a source of pleasure. The body changes moment by moment, but it appears to be enduring. The body is selfless and is not owned by a soul, yet it seems as though there is an owner, an ultimate subject to which this body belongs. This is opposite to the way in which things exist. Even though we meditate on them, these actual qualities of the body do not stay in mind. Furthermore, the ultimate nature of the body—its lack of inherent existence—has no real place of abiding. This nonabiding is very subtle. It is not the object of any ordinary direct perception.

If something as obvious as the body is hard for us to understand and focus on, then how could something as profound and subtle as emptiness easily come to mind? So do not get disheartened if you find it difficult. The scriptures of Buddha and his commentators all say that the profound teaching on ultimate reality is most difficult to understand. But do not become discouraged. Do not think, "No matter how much I have listened to teachings, studied, and analyzed, I still don't know what emptiness is! I am tired and fed up. I don't want to do this anymore." The process of realizing is like chewing a hard bone to get the juicy marrow deep inside. Think about how fortunate you are to have this chance to learn about emptiness. Your efforts will not be wasted; they will bear great fruit in the fullness of time. Even if you do not understand the teachings right now, the results of engaging in virtuous practices and searching for ultimate truth will arise.

Remember to create the causes for a direct realization of the ultimate truth—do not forget to generate merit by engaging in virtuous activities.

Otherwise if we are only interested in investigating emptiness and do not engage in accumulating merit, when we read valid Madhyamaka texts, we will not understand them correctly. For example, one of the Madhyamaka arguments to show that there is no inherent existence establishes the lack of things being one or many. This is an investigation into the relationship between a thing and its parts. Do the whole and the parts exist by their own nature independently of each other? Or does the whole depend on the parts and the parts depend on the whole? If we want to determine how a vase exists, we begin by looking at it. The definition of a Tibetan vase is a thing that has a spout, a neck, a round belly, a flat bottom, and can perform the function of holding water. Now does the vase exist inherently as a single entity? No, it has many parts. Next we examine each of these parts to see if it is the vase. But we find that the vase is not the spout, or the neck, and so on. When we analyze it, we cannot find the vase; it is not any of the parts nor is it something other than these parts. This nonfinding of the vase is in fact emptiness.

However, some people misunderstand this point. Because they are looking for something inherently existent, when they do not find it, they conclude that there is no vase at all. They become convinced, "The vase does not exist." Then they analyze the person who is examining the existence of the vase: they look at themselves and think, "My head is not me; my hands are not me; my legs, stomach, and so on, are not me." No matter where they look they cannot find the analyzer. Because an analyzer cannot be found, they conclude, "The person knowing that there is no vase does not exist either." In this way the early Tibetan Madhyamaka scholars interpret the Madhyamaka view to be: "Things are not existent nor are they totally nonexistent." Holding this view of neither existence nor nonexistence, they interpret the sutras and the śāstras such as those of Nāgārjuna to mean that things are not existent, not nonexistent, not both, and not neither. They think that if you say that things exist, you develop a view of eternalism, and if you say that things do not exist at all, you fall into nihilism. So they conclude that the only comfortable place in between these two extremes is to believe that things neither exist nor do not exist. Even Je Tsongkhapa, at an early stage in his investigation of Madhyamaka, tentatively accepted this view. Although this view is easier to grasp, it is drawn from incorrect logic and yields a misunderstanding. If the real Madhyamaka view were indeed found by this kind of reasoning, it would be the easiest thing in the world to understand.

Therefore intelligent people rely on the definitive scriptures and the commentaries on them. These teach that the meaning of emptiness is the meaning of dependent arising. To be the "same meaning" here means to be the "same nature" as explained above. So the lack of existence from a thing's own side means that it exists in dependence on or in relation to something else. If a thing exists in relation to something else, then it is empty of existing by its own power alone. Therefore anything that dependently arises is empty, and anything that is empty dependently arises. There are various ways to debate the interpretation of emptiness and dependent arising, but this is the basic meaning. The special quality of the Madhyamaka masters is to show how the correct understanding of emptiness arises from an understanding of subtle dependent arising, and vice versa. This is how an understanding of emptiness and of dependent arising mutually influence and rely on each other. This is the intent of the works composed by the peerless founders of the Madhyamaka system, Nāgārjuna and Āryadeva, and explained in full by the great commentators Buddhapālita and Candrakīrti. The subtle point is that in reliance on understanding dependent arising you understand the emptiness of inherent existence, and through understanding emptiness you come to understand dependent arising.

We should develop a firm and stable understanding of the depth and subtlety of this profound view. Without certitude about the way in which things that are empty of inherent existence arise as causes and effects and the way in which things that dependently arise are empty of inherent nature, we can easily be led astray. If someone says, "That is wrong," we drop our position and follow them. If someone else comes along and says, "Oh, you have got that wrong, it is this way," we are led off in another direction. But when we understand this profound view correctly, there is no danger of this sort.

⁎ 5 ⁂
Dependent Arising and Emptiness

(b")) How those systems contradict the distinguishing feature of
    Madhyamaka
(c")) How a Mādhyamika responds to those who contradict the
    distinguishing feature of Madhyamaka

THE SPECIAL QUALITY of the Madhyamaka system is that it not only
propounds emptiness, it also upholds conventional reality. In teaching
emptiness the Madhyamaka specifies what is negated and then shows what is
left over—conventional reality. In fact the Madhyamaka clearly explains conventional reality, ultimate reality, and the necessary connection between them
better than any other philosophical system. What is this necessary connection? We can express it as: "Everything is empty of inherent existence because
of being dependent, and everything is dependent because of being empty of
inherent existence." Both permanent and impermanent things are dependent:
the former depend on their parts and on being imputed by the mind on a suitable basis; the latter depend on those two as well as on causes and conditions.
It is because everything is empty of inherent existence that causation, change,
and existence itself are possible. Therefore those who genuinely understand the
emptiness of inherent existence also accept dependent arising.

(b")) HOW THOSE SYSTEMS CONTRADICT THE
DISTINGUISHING FEATURE OF MADHYAMAKA

According to the great master Nāgārjuna, no phenomena have even a particle of essentially existent inherent nature. Nothing exists from its own side at
all. If things were inherently existent, none of the teachings about causality,
samsara, nirvana, and so on could be established. It would be foolish not to

accept causality and so on, because they do in fact exist. In order to allow for these phenomena, we must accept that things do not exist by way of their own nature.

Tsongkhapa now addresses some earlier scholars who claim to be Mādhyamikas yet misunderstand the correct view. They say, "If things have no essentially existent inherent nature, then what else is there? It is not necessary to apply a qualifying term like 'ultimately' to the reasoning negating production, cessation, bondage, and liberation, for they are negated by the reasoning negating inherent existence." In brief, these earlier so-called Mādhyamikas say that if things do not inherently exist, they do not exist at all. Tsongkhapa points out that according to the genuine Madhyamaka view, bondage and liberation, cause and effect, arising and disintegration, and so on are established only in the total absence of inherent existence. These scholars do not acknowledge this relationship, so they contradict the actual Madhyamaka position. Therefore he urges them to consider how not to negate this special quality of the Madhyamaka.

These scholars reply that, just like Nāgārjuna and Candrakīrti, they assert that samsara and nirvana, bondage and liberation, and their causes are established only conventionally. Therefore their position is not incorrect; they do not have the fault that Tsongkhapa levels at them. But it turns out they are incorrect. Candrakīrti's view is that inherent existence is not only nonexistent ultimately, it does not exist conventionally either. Inherent existence is like a rabbit horn; it is totally nonexistent. It has to be negated on every level. Candrakīrti's point is that the same logic negates inherent existence both ultimately and conventionally. If these scholars admit to accepting Candrakīrti's rational analysis negating inherent existence, then they should reject inherent existence ultimately and conventionally. They should reject inherent bondage, inherent liberation, an inherent path, inherent causes, and so on even conventionally. This is very clear in Candrakīrti's view.

In brief, either these scholars consider that the absence of inherent existence contradicts the establishment of causality, samsara, nirvana, and so on, or they do not. If they do, then having accepted the emptiness that is the lack of inherent existence, it becomes impossible for them to establish causality and so on in terms of either of the two truths. Thus they repudiate the unique special quality of the Madhyamaka system: the noncontradiction of the two truths. If they do not consider that the absence of inherent existence contradicts causality, then they have no good reason to say that causality and so on are negated by the reasoning disproving inherent existence, where there has been no need to apply any special qualification, such as "ultimately," to the object of negation. Since these scholars, having accepted the lack of inherent existence, consider that the reasoning disproving inherent existence negates causality, they negate arising and ceasing. This makes their position no different from the Realists' argument against the Mādhyamikas summarized in the twenty-fourth chapter of Nāgārjuna's *Fundamental Treatise*:

> If all these things are empty,
> There can be no arising and no destruction.
> According to you it must follow
> That the four noble truths do not exist.

These earlier scholars object to being characterized as Realists similar to the Vaibhāṣikas and Sautrāntikas, but their view does not differ from another Realist argument as presented in Nāgārjuna's *Refutation of Objections*:

> If all things in every case
> Do not inherently exist,
> Then even your words do not inherently exist
> And so cannot refute inherent nature.

An opponent objects: "In both cases—whether things are empty of inherent existence or not—causality cannot be accepted; however, since we do not accept either inherent existence or its emptiness, this problem does not arise for us." These people too are misguided, for this is another misunderstanding of the Madhyamaka view. Simply to not accept anything is not the meaning of the Madhyamaka texts. These scholars incorrectly assert that both positions—inherent existence and the emptiness of inherent existence—are at odds with causality, so they are not going to accept either one. This approach is completely wrong. Candrakīrti's *Clear Words* demonstrates that not only do we Mādhyamikas not succumb to the fault that arising, ceasing, and so on are unacceptable, but we are also able to accept the four noble truths and so on as correct (see chapter 4). Also, Nāgārjuna's *Fundamental Treatise* shows that everything—arising, ceasing, and so on—is acceptable within the context of the emptiness of inherent existence, and that none of these are acceptable from the point of view of inherent existence. Candrakīrti's *Introduction to the "Middle Way"* says:

> It is not unknown that empty things,
> Like reflections, depend upon a collection.
> Likewise, here, from an empty reflection
> A consciousness with that aspect arises.

> Similarly, even though all things are empty,
> From their being empty production occurs.

Even ordinary people know that their reflection in a mirror does not exist as it appears. When we see our reflection in a mirror, it looks as though a face existing from its own side appears there. But we know that this reflection is illusion-like; its appearance depends on a gathering of many conditions: space, light, our eyes, the position of our head, and so forth. Similarly, there are many conditions necessary for the reflection of the moon to appear in a body of water: the sky, the moon, somebody looking at the water, and so forth. In this sense, the illusion-like nature of things such as reflections, echoes, and mirages is not unknown even to worldly people who have not realized subtle śūnyatā. Although ordinary people accept that a reflection lacks objective existence as it appears, they recognize that from a reflection a visual consciousness arises. When we see our face in a mirror, a visual consciousness ascertains all the particular aspects of our face. In dependence on various causes and conditions we see something unreal: a face that looks exactly like our face appearing to exist from its own side in the mirror. Visual consciousness arises in the aspect of that face, but that face does not exist as it appears. Similarly, even though things are empty of inherent existence, they function as causes and conditions in dependence on which many things arise.

Moreover, according to these mistaken scholars, Madhyamaka analysis rejects not just inherent existence but also negates mere existence. Thus it would not be suitable to negate such things as bondage and liberation ultimately, since they would have to be negated conventionally. If that were the case, then the establishment of everything in samsara and nirvana would be rejected even conventionally. Such a strange kind of Madhyamaka never existed before!

(c")) How a Mādhyamika responds to those who contradict the distinguishing feature of Madhyamaka

In this section Tsongkhapa responds to many objections to the genuine Madhyamaka view, which shows that emptiness and dependent arising are not in the least contradictory. Each of the opponents' points is countered using logical reasoning and reference to scriptures and commentaries. The presentation of these arguments in the great Madhyamaka texts can be difficult to follow. We must treat them in the context of specific situations. The main point is that total nonexistence and emptiness of inherent existence are not the same.

When we negate inherent existence, we should leave space for the existence of things such as causality, the four noble truths, and so on. If you think you understand śūnyatā but cannot accept those things, then you have not properly understood the middle way.

The Realists criticize the Mādhyamikas, saying, "If things are empty of inherent existence, then the causes and effects of samsara and nirvana cannot be established." Nāgārjuna responds that since the opponents have taken the fallacy he was going to aim at them and turned it around to throw it back at him, so he will turn it around again and throw it back at them. This is part of a long argument in the twenty-fourth chapter of the *Fundamental Treatise on the Middle Way*. Nāgārjuna begins by presenting the opponents' position where they reverse the fallacy that he was going to aim at them (see above):

> If all these things are empty,
> There can be no arising and no destruction.
> According to you it must follow
> That the four noble truths do not exist.

Obviously, Nāgārjuna does not accept this contention. In the same text he says:

> You take your own fallacies
> And say these are my faults.
> That is like, while riding a horse,
> Forgetting the horse you are riding.
>
> If you view things
> As inherently existent,
> Then according to your view
> Things have no causes and conditions.

The horse example illustrates the fact that we recognize everyone's faults except our own. A Tibetan anecdote may make this clearer. People from Lhasa often make jokes about people from Tsang, like me. One day a Tsangpa was going to Lhasa to trade and had a lot of donkeys to carry his goods. When he got near the city he counted the donkeys to make sure they were all there. He got quite worried because he was one short. The problem was that he counted all the donkeys but completely forgot to include the one he was riding!

Nāgārjuna says that the consequence of asserting that things exist by their own nature is that one must accept that things exist without causes and conditions. The Realists themselves never say that there are no causes and conditions; not only do they accept karma, the four noble truths, and so on, but they also believe them to be truly existent. Nevertheless, the implication of things being truly existent is that there are no causes and conditions. Nāgārjuna pushes the Realists to see the consequence of their belief. His argument takes the form, "You accept *P*, and *P* implies *Q*, so you must accept *Q*. You may not want to accept *Q*, but you must, because you accept *P*." The consequence *Q* is contrary to what the opponent wants to believe. If the Realists continue to hold that all things exist by their own nature, then they must accept the unwanted consequence of that belief—all things are without causes and conditions.

Thus it is clear that those who say, "If there is no essentially existent inherent nature, then what else is there?" are unable to distinguish between a noninherently existent sprout and a nonexistent sprout. For them a lack of inherent existence is the same as nonexistence, and inherent existence is the same as existence. Because they do not properly understand the meaning of inherent existence and noninherent existence, they say that the reasoning disproving inherent existence negates mere existence and mere causality. They claim that if sprouts and so on exist, then they exist inherently by way of their own essential nature; if sprouts and so on do not inherently exist, then they do not exist at all. Someone who makes such assertions undoubtedly falls to the two extremes of eternalism and nihilism. A person who sees things in this way may claim to accept śūnyatā and try to explain the Madhyamaka view, but he or she is no different from a Realist follower of the lower schools who propounds things to be truly existent. Candrakīrti's *Commentary on the "Four Hundred Stanzas"* (*Bodhisattva-yoga-caryā-catuḥ-śataka-ṭīkā*) says:

> According to the Realists, as long as things exist, it will be in terms of their essential nature; when lacking that essential nature, these things will be totally nonexistent, like the horn of a donkey. Thus they have not moved beyond propounding the two extremes, so all their actual beliefs are difficult to reconcile.

A Realist believes that if things do not exist in terms of their own essential nature, or inherently, they must be completely nonexistent, like a donkey horn.[57] According to this way of thinking, a lack of inherent existence means nonexistence. So if things are empty of inherent existence, they do not exist, and there is no ground for establishing causality and so on. In short, by negating inherent existence one falls to the extreme of nihilism. To avoid this extreme the Realists say that things exist by their own essential nature.

This means that whatever exists must exist by its own characteristics, by its own nature, inherently, and absolutely, and thus one falls to the extreme view of eternalism. When one grasps the extreme of eternalism, one believes that everything—causes, effects, and every other functional thing—exists in the way it appears. However, given that everything appears inherently existent, there would be no ground for establishing that things have an illusion-like nature. The Realists cannot hold that causality and so on appear as one thing yet are empty of existing in the way they appear. They are caught in a dilemma. According to a Realist interpretation, if something exists, it exists inherently; if inherent existence is negated, then nothing exists at all. So on the one hand the Realists fall to the extreme view of eternalism, and on the other hand they fall to the extreme view of nihilism. As a result, they cannot reconcile conventional and ultimate truth.

Candrakīrti clearly distinguishes between inherent existence and existence, and between a lack of inherent existence and nonexistence. To stop falling to the extreme of permanent or eternal existence, we must understand that from the very beginning all phenomena are empty of inherent existence; that is, everything that exists, that ever has existed, or that ever will exist has no inherent nature. Things do not exist as they appear, so in this sense they have an illusion-like nature. By understanding this we avoid the extreme of eternalism. In addition, to stop falling to the extreme of nihilism we must understand that having an illusion-like nature does not imply that things lack an ability to function. For example, a sprout arises from various causes; it produces a seedling, the seedling grows and produces fruit, and the fruit functions to nourish living beings. Sprouts and so on have the power to perform their functions even though they are empty of inherent existence. Understanding this will destroy the extreme of the nihilistic view.

Similarly, in *Clear Words* Candrakīrti clearly distinguishes between noninherent existence and nonexistence. He does this in the form of a debate between himself and a Realist opponent who is confused about the matter:

> *Opponent*: By positing things to be not inherently existent, you destroy whatever Buddha taught, such as, "You, yourself, will experience the maturation of the karma you create." In repudiating karma and its fruit you are the supreme nihilists.
>
> *Reply*: We are not nihilists. Having negated those who accept the two extremes of existence and nonexistence, we illuminate the path that is free of those two extremes and leads to the city of liberation. We do not say that actions, agents, and their results are totally nonexistent.
>
> *Opponent*: Well then, what do you say?

Reply: We say that they lack any inherent nature.

Opponent: If that is the case, your fault remains the same, because for things that lack inherent nature there cannot be any agent, action, and so on.

Reply: There is no such fault because only things with an inherent nature are not seen to function, and only things lacking an inherent nature are seen to function.

Tsongkhapa employs this passage to point out that there is no difference between the Realist position—that if things are not inherently existent, then karma cannot give rise to effects—and the earlier Tibetan Mādhyamikas who say that the reasoning that disproves inherent existence also completely negates cause and effect. Neither the Mādhyamikas nor the Realists of the Vaibhāṣika, Sautrāntika, and Yogācāra schools wish to annihilate causality. They all agree that if you reject causality, you are a nihilist. The difference is that genuine Mādhyamikas do not hold that the reasoning that negates inherent existence also negates cause and effect, whereas the Realists believe that it does. The Realists assert that if inherent existence is negated, it definitely follows that causality is negated. Therefore, because the Mādhyamikas state that nothing inherently exists, the Realists call them nihilists or annihilationists. Most of the early Tibetans who claim to be Mādhyamikas agree with the Realist view that if reasoning negates inherent existence then it must also negate cause and effect. These early Tibetan scholars believe that this is the Madhyamaka position. They even seem to admire its consequence—the negation of causality and dependent existence—and claim to be spreading the Madhyamaka view by teaching that things are not existent, not nonexistent, not both, and not neither.

In the above quotation, Candrakīrti counters those who hold this position by saying, "We are not nihilists; we clear away the two extremes of existence and nonexistence; we illuminate the path to liberation." The rest of the quotation shows the way to avoid the two extremes. He says that the Mādhyamikas do not deny the existence of cause and effect, so they steer clear of the extreme of nihilism; since the Mādhyamikas hold that karma and so on do not inherently exist, they do not fall to the extreme of eternalism. The opponent is not satisfied, and says to Candrakīrti that this Madhyamaka argument still has the same fault: "Although you do not say that things are totally nonexistent, you do say that things are not inherently existent. Because things that are not inherently existent cannot function, cause and effect are impossible. Thus you cannot avoid this flaw in your position." In reply, Candrakīrti says: "It is impossible for inherently existent agents and actions to produce results; only if things are not inherently existent can they function."

A similar exchange is found in Candrakīrti's *Commentary on the "Four Hundred Stanzas"*:

> *Candrakīrti*: We do not propound nonexistence; we propound dependent arising.
> *Opponent*: Are you proponents of real things?
> *Reply*: No, because we are proponents of dependent arising.
> *Opponent*: So what do you propound?
> *Reply*: We propound dependent arising.
> *Opponent*: What is the meaning of dependent arising?
> *Reply*: It means having no inherent nature; it means not arising by its own nature; it means giving rise to effects that have the nature of such things as a magical illusion, a mirage, a reflection, a celestial city, an emanation, and a dream; it means emptiness and absence of self.

In this passage the opponent asks Candrakīrti: "What kind of a Mādhyamika are you? You overemphasize existence: you say that causality, dependent arising, and so on must be properly established. Surely Mādhyamikas should not accept these things but instead should negate everything; yet you say the opposite. So do you assert that things truly, really, inherently exist?" Candrakīrti replies, "No, we do not; this is because we say that everything dependently arises." The word "dependently" indicates that things do not arise by themselves: they are reliant on something else. The word "arise" shows that things are not totally nonexistent: they do, in fact, arise as existents. To show how things exist and function but are not real in the way that they appear, Candrakīrti lists some examples of dependent phenomena that are often presented in the scriptures. Let us look at one example: the illusion of an elephant conjured by a magician. The illusory appearance of an elephant does not arise by itself, from its own power. It arises in dependence on many causes and conditions coming together: the magician, the substances to be transformed, the magic spells, the space, a source of light, an area of darkness, an audience, and so forth. Illusions, mirages, reflections, and so on are not objectively or inherently existent; they dependently arise from a combination of causes and conditions, and each of them can function. All functioning things have a nature similar to these examples; they arise in dependence on causes and conditions and function to produce their own effects. Thus emptiness does not mean nothingness; it does not mean that things are empty of functionality. The meaning of *dependent arising* and *emptiness* is the same: both terms indicate a lack of inherent existence. The meaning of *selflessness* also indicates the lack of inherent existence. In summary, through properly understanding dependent arising, both the extremes of eternalism and nihilism are cleared away at the same time.

In the context of these two extremes—to hold that things exist and to hold that things do not exist—it is important to understand that the word *thing* is being used in two different ways. When an eternalist claims "Things exist," the word *thing* refers to anything having an inherently existent nature. Of course, such a thing does not exist. When a nihilist claims "Things do not exist," the word "thing" refers to anything having functionality. This relates to the Buddhist philosophical definition of *thing*—the ability to perform a function. All Buddhists agree on this definition of a functional thing, and they agree that functional things exist. Thus when the Realists claim "Things exist," using the word *thing* to refer to something inherently existent and thereby falling to the extreme of eternalism, Mādhyamikas deny that such things exist. But when others take up the claim "Things do not exist," using the word *thing* to refer to something able to perform a function and thereby falling to the extreme of nihilism, Mādhyamikas counter that such things do exist. Candrakīrti clears away those two extremes by negating inherent nature and establishing the illusion-like nature of cause and effect. The *Commentary on the "Four Hundred Stanzas"* says:

> *Opponent*: Is there no memory of the past?
> *Reply*: Who would say there is no such thing? We do not deny dependent arising. The master Āryadeva thoroughly establishes how memory exists:
>
> > The arising of that called "memory"
> > Is only false, in that its object is false.
>
> The object of memory is something in the past. If it existed by its own nature, then since the memory of it would observe an inherently existent object, it too would exist inherently. The past object does not exist inherently, and so the memory observing it also does not exist inherently. Thus it is established as false. "False" means not existing inherently yet dependently arising. It does not mean anything else. It does not mean that functional things do not exist. Past things are not totally nonexistent because they are objects that are remembered and their results are seen. Moreover, they are not inherently existent because if they were, they would be permanent and directly ascertained.

There are two related questions addressed here: "What is memory?" and "In what way is memory false?" When memory occurs, past things appear in the present mind. The mind that remembers something is present right now; the object ascertained by this mind is in the past. The object appears to be present, but it does not actually exist in the present as it appears to. In this sense, any memory is false. Here the term *false* does not mean that memory is wrong. *False* refers to something that does not exist exactly as it appears. Memory is false because both the object and the mind perceiving the object do not exist exactly as they appear. So memory is mistaken with regard to its appearing object, but it is not mistaken with regard to its held object. That held object exists. The past thing that is recalled appears to be present but is not present, so in this sense it is false. The mind to which the past thing appears is also false, in that it perceives its object to be present when it is not. When we remember something, it seems as if we are directly perceiving the object itself, but we are not. Memory is thought; it is not direct perception. It remembers the past thing. But its appearing object is a conceptual image of that past thing. It mixes up the appearance of the conceptual image and the actual thing that is past. However, via that appearance it can hold the object. Nonetheless the object of memory does not exist as it appears; so the memory itself and the appearance of its remembered object are both false in that they do not inherently exist.

So *false* does not mean that memory and its object are nothing. It does not mean that something appears that does not exist at all. *False* simply negates the idea "The object arises because it exists inherently." There are no inherently existent past things. If past things existed inherently, they would be permanent—existing now in the same way, without any change, as they did in the past. Not only would they exist continuously, but also the mind apprehending them would perceive them directly. But memory does not grasp its object directly; the object does not directly appear to it. If memory were a directly perceiving awareness, its objects would be in the present and those past things would still exist. If this were so, then we are back to those things being permanent.

This brings up an interesting point to debate. All types of supernormal knowledge, such as seeing past lives, perceive their objects directly, unmixed with a conceptual image. So when you have supernormal knowledge of your past lives, you perceive them directly. But how is this possible? The past life is not here in the present, so how can supernormal knowledge directly perceive it? Are those lives still there? Are they permanent? Is supernormal knowledge seeing an image of the past in the present? You can debate this!

In an ordinary sense, memory is thought. It perceives a conceptual image of a past thing through the power of certain potentialities that this thing has left on the mindstream. This means that past things are not totally nonexistent, in that their effects continue to function. When we say something is nonexistent, it means it has never existed in the past, does not exist now, and will never exist in the future. A common example of a nonexistent is a rabbit horn: a rabbit horn has never existed in the past, does not exist now, and will not exist in the future. However, past things do exist; they are not present at the moment, but they are not totally nonexistent. They are functional things because we remember them. Past things exist; they exist conventionally, though they do not exist inherently. The object of memory is not here, right now, as it appears. The object is gone; it does not exist permanently. However, there is a causal relationship functioning—a chain of related causes and effects, experienced through the ripening of a potentiality, that enables us to remember the object now. Therefore the object remembered and the memory of it do exist, but they do not exist in the way that they appear. To say that they are *false* or *mistaken* things means that they dependently arise. Past things are neither totally nonexistent nor inherently existent. Past and present things are dependently related.

AVOIDING THE TWO EXTREME VIEWS WHILE MAINTAINING THE LAW OF NONCONTRADICTION

Those who accept that things are inherently existent have fallen to the extreme view of eternalism; those who accept that all external and internal things are nonthings, without the ability to function, have fallen to the extreme view of nihilism. In contrast, those who say that these things are merely existent do not propound absolute reality or inherent existence; those who say that all these things have no inherent nature have not fallen into nihilism. Therefore on the side of nonexistence we have to distinguish between *nonexistent* and *noninherently existent*, and on the side of existence we have to distinguish between *merely existent* and *inherently existent*. These are not simply terminological differences; they are important distinctions that we need to ascertain in order to avoid falling to the two extremes. Unless we draw these distinctions, we can avoid the extremes only by claiming, "We do not say that things exist or do not exist." This is the error made by the earlier Tibetan scholars. According to their view, to say that things exist means accepting things to be inherently existent, so they avoid the extreme of eternalism by saying "Things are not existent," and to say that things do not exist means accepting things to be totally nonexistent, so they avoid the extreme of nihilism by saying "Things are not nonexistent." Thus they try to avoid falling into the two extremes simply by saying the words, "Things are neither existent nor nonexistent." But positing this view only creates contradictions. It does not explain the meaning of Madhyamaka, the middle way between the extremes, in the slightest.

These earlier Tibetan scholars, who considered themselves Mādhyamikas, allowed their opponents only two alternatives when refuting them in debate. Yet when proving their own assertions, they allowed themselves a third alternative: being neither existent nor nonexistent. But when we examine whether things inherently exist, we are faced with only two possibilities: a thing is either inherently existent or not inherently existent. There is no third possibility. If there were a third alternative—something that is not included within those two possibilities—then it would be wrong to limit our examination to just two alternatives. For example, when determining a color, it is illogical to restrict ourselves to two alternatives. We should not ask "Is it blue or is it yellow?" The question is inappropriate because there is a third alternative: a color that is neither blue nor yellow, such as red. Not every color is either blue or yellow.

However, it is appropriate to analyze whether or not things are inherently existent because this is a genuine dichotomy. It is based on the general dichotomy of whether or not objects of knowledge exist. Elementary logic textbooks in the Tibetan tradition list as synonyms: object of knowledge, object of comprehension, existent, established base, and phenomenon. The term *object of knowledge* indicates something that is known. To *exist* means to be established by valid knowledge. If something is known, then it exists; if it is not known, it does not exist. We cannot say that something is neither existent nor nonexistent. When we examine whether a thing is inherently existent or not inherently existent, or whether a thing is permanent or impermanent, or whether it is one or many, and so on, it makes sense to limit the alternatives to two. They are opposites, and our object of investigation must be one or the other. For example, when Mādhyamikas examine true existence, they consider, "If something truly exists, then it must exist as one or as many." Why? This is related to a more general dichotomy: if something exists, it is either a single entity or multiple. There is no third ground. Therefore if something truly exists, it must be truly one or truly many. When considering a dichotomy, there are only two possibilities; a third ground or possibility is excluded. To posit something that is neither of the two is utterly meaningless. Nāgārjuna says in *Refutation of Objections*:

> If it negates "Not inherently existent,"
> Then it proves "Inherently existent."

This is a powerful rejection of the view that things are not existent, not nonexistent, not both, and not neither. According to people who hold this view, there is no basis for making a definite enumeration of just two possibilities. They say that refuting one of the pair—existent or nonexistent—does not prove the other, because there are other possibilities that leave the ground wide open. In this way they are continually consumed by doubt.

It would be helpful to understand the Buddhist notion of *contradictory* here. In general if two things are contradictory, then there is nothing that instantiates both: there is no common ground or shared basis. Among various ways of being contradictory there are two basic ones: direct and indirect. Direct is the strictest; we will come to that below. There are two ways of being *indirectly* contradictory. The first is where being both things is impossible, but being neither is possible. An example of this is *red* and *yellow*. Whatever is red cannot be yellow, and whatever is yellow cannot be red. There is no positive common ground: something that is both. But there is a common ground of their negations: something that is neither red nor yellow, such as *blue*. So if something is not red, then it does not have to be yellow. It can be a color other than those two. Therefore red and yellow are not directly contradictory. In Western philosophy, they are called *contrary*.

The second way of being *indirectly* contradictory is where being both things is impossible and being neither is also impossible. There is no third ground or possibility at all, whether positive or negative. If something is not F then it must be G, and if it is not G then it must be F. These are contradictory in terms of reality, but they are not contradictory in terms of understanding—so according to Buddhist logic, they are not directly contradictory. An example of this is *permanent* and *produced*. Whatever is produced cannot be permanent, and whatever is permanent cannot be produced. There is no positive common ground: something that is both. Moreover, there is no common ground of their negations: something that is neither produced nor permanent. Whatever exists must be one or the other. It is impossible for anything to be neither. So if an existent thing is not permanent, then it must be produced, and vice versa. Permanent and produced are "contradictory in the sense of being mutually eliminating." But they are not "*directly* contradictory in the sense of being mutually eliminating." If you mentally or verbally cut out "permanent," this does not mean that you will naturally understand "produced." Or if you cut out "produced," then you do not necessarily understand "permanent." Whatever is produced cannot be permanent, and whatever is permanent cannot be produced. In terms of reality, that is the case. But in terms of its verbal expression, saying "It is not permanent" does not express that it is produced. The word "permanent" does not eliminate "produced" nor prove "not produced." Also, in terms of understanding, as soon as you know that something is not permanent, this does not mean you understand it to be produced. Or if you know that something has arisen from causes and conditions, this does not immediately eliminate the thought of it being permanent. So *permanent* and *produced* are contradictory without any third ground, whether expressed in an affirmative or negative manner. They are contradictory in the sense of being mutually eliminating, but they are not *directly* contradictory in the sense of being mutually eliminating.

Two things are *directly* contradictory if the terminology itself shows that being both things is impossible and being neither is impossible. If something is not *F* then it must be *non-F*, and if something is not *non-F* then it must be *F*. An example of this is *existent* and *nonexistent*. These are "directly contradictory in the sense of being mutually eliminating." Existent and nonexistent are directly contradictory because the word *existent* cuts out *nonexistent*, and the word *nonexistent* cuts out *existent*. In terms of terminology and understanding, one member of the pair of terms directly eliminates the other, and vice versa. If you understand the first member of the pair as being affirmed, then you automatically understand the second as being eliminated; if you understand the second as being affirmed, then you automatically understand the first as being eliminated. This concerns limitation by means of word and knowledge. Once you say "exist" you eliminate "not exist"; once you say "not exist" you eliminate "exist." There is no third ground in your mind, and the word itself does not allow for that.

The same applies in the case of selflessness and other similar terms: "the self exists truly" cuts out "the self does not exist truly," and "things exist inherently" cuts out "things do not exist inherently." These are contradictory in terms of both terminology and understanding. *Directly* contradictory means that by eliminating one side, you prove the other. This kind of proof gives rise to an immediate understanding. So if two things are contradictory in terms of reality but not in terms of understanding, then they are not directly contradictory.

In Western philosophy, being directly contradictory only concerns reality, not understanding. This is a major difference between the two logical systems. The later Mādhyamikas discuss these issues when explaining *implicative negation* and *nonimplicative* (or *mere*) *negation*, which concerns whether or not the negation implies something positive: whether by cutting out one thing, another thing is positively understood.

The early Tibetans, who consider themselves Mādhyamikas, accept that there are cases where there is no third ground between *is* and *is not*—though they do not agree that the same applies to *exist* and *not exist*. However, if they consider that there is no third ground between *is* and *is not*, treating these as directly contradictory, then they should consider *exist* and *not exist* in precisely the same way. But they do not accept that implication. Their mistake is an overly literal reading of specific passages in certain Madhyamaka texts, such as "Everything is not existent, not nonexistent, not both, and not neither." They become confused by the words and take them literally. But if, as they claim, they cannot accept that anything is "existent or nonexistent," then they should not accept that anything is "not existent and not nonexistent." For the same principle applies to all four positions. They superficially read Nāgārjuna's *Fundamental Treatise on the Middle Way*:

> Believing "It exists" is grasping at permanence;
> Believing "It does not exist" is the view of nihilism;
> Therefore those who are wise do not abide
> In either existence or nonexistence.

This passage uses the phrases "It exists" and "It does not exist" to refer to ultimate existence or inherent existence, not to mere existence. The early scholars' confusion arises because the details are left out of the stanza; the words "truly existent," "ultimately existent," or "existing from their own side" do not appear.

In general there are four alternatives: existent, nonexistent, both existent and nonexistent, and neither existent nor nonexistent. Those are taken as the basis. In terms of inherent existence the four alternatives are: inherently existent, inherently nonexistent, both inherently existent and inherently nonexistent, and neither inherently existent nor inherently nonexistent. These alternatives all concern an inherent nature, and none of them is correct. So the negation of these four alternatives is formulated as: not inherently existent, not inherently nonexistent, not both inherently existent and inherently nonexistent, and not neither inherently existent nor inherently nonexistent.

Candrakīrti explains in *Clear Words* that in the last line of the above stanza, the words "existence or nonexistence" refer to the extreme views of eternalism and nihilism. Nāgārjuna is saying that if someone holds things to be inherently existent, then he or she is holding the extreme view of eternalism, and if someone holds that things inherently do not exist at all, they become nihilists. Following this, *Clear Words* says:

> *Question*: When you have the view that things exist and the view that things do not exist, why does it follow that you have the views of eternalism and nihilism?
> *Reply*: As it says [in Nāgārjuna's *Fundamental Treatise*]:
>
> > Anything that exists by its own inherent nature
> > Is permanent, because it is never nonexistent;

Believing "It existed before but does not exist now"
Would therefore entail annihilation.

"Anything that exists by its own inherent nature" indicates that it
can never be nonexistent, because there is no reversing of its inherent nature. In that case, accepting anything as inherently existent is
the view of eternalism, and having accepted a thing's earlier inherent
nature, believing "It was later destroyed and now no longer exists" is
the view of nihilism.

As mentioned above, *exist* and *not exist* are a dichotomy. According to Buddhist logic, they are directly contradictory in the sense of being mutually eliminating. Here we are not talking about mere existence but inherent existence.[58]
Because there is no third ground at all, we must accept one side of this dichotomy. We cannot say that there is something else that is neither inherently existent nor not inherently existent. We have to come to a decision about whether
things are inherently existent or not. As Nāgārjuna says above, if we negate
noninherent existence, then we prove inherent existence.

The stanza from Nāgārjuna's *Fundamental Treatise on the Middle Way*
quoted by Candrakīrti in the above passage means that if something exists
by its own nature without depending on anything else, then it is permanently
existent. It would never be nonexistent because there would be no reason for
it to appear sometimes and not at other times. Any thing that exists by its
own inherent nature does not depend on causes or conditions, so there is no
reason for it ever to cease. Such a thing would never have been nonexistent in
the past, nor would it ever be nonexistent in the future. This is the extreme
of eternalism: if an inherently existent thing exists at any time, it is never
nonexistent—it must permanently exist. Conversely, if an inherently existent
thing does not exist, then it has never existed. If it does not exist now, then it
does not exist at all.

Also, if an inherently existent thing is ceased, then it must be ceased permanently; it is never not ceased, and thus it would be nothing at all. This is the
extreme of nihilism: if an inherently existent thing does not exist at any time,
it is never existent—it must be permanently nonexistent. Therefore to believe
that an inherently existent thing existed earlier but not later would entail a
completely nihilistic view: the total nonexistence of that thing. If it does not
exist now, then it must be permanently nonexistent. In brief, if an inherently
existent thing exists, then it must exist permanently; if it does not exist now,
then it is permanently nonexistent. This is because there would be no reason

for such a thing to change its status and to appear at certain times but not at other times. j

If a thing appears on some occasions but not on other occasions, it is a sign that it is dependent on something else. It exists when certain necessary causes and conditions are present; it does not exist when these causes and conditions are absent. If something arises only occasionally, it is proof that it is not permanent.[59] In the same way, only if something has a dependent nature can it possibly have arisen previously and no longer exist now. A dependently arisen thing can exist in the first moment and not exist in the second moment. As indicated by Candrakīrti's words above, if anything that exists by its own inherent nature can be reversed—in other words, if it can cease—then in fact it is not inherent.

If something existed earlier and it does not exist now, then it must dependently arise. This does not entail the view of nihilism. But here, when positing something that is inherently existent and independent of other things, which is the view of eternalism, to claim that such a thing ceases at any time entails the view of nihilism. Candrakīrti does not say this of *merely existing* and *merely ceasing*; holding things to merely exist and merely cease does not entail falling into the two extremes. The view of nihilism is entailed when we posit something that is inherently existent and independent of other things and believe that, having first existed, it ceases to exist. Also, according to Buddhapālita, the explanation of existent and nonexistent as the two extreme views of eternalism and nihilism clearly refers to holding things to be inherently existent, just as Nāgārjuna specifies "Anything that exists by its own inherent nature." It is holding things to be inherently existent that gives rise to these two extreme views.

In brief, the people holding a Realist viewpoint say that the emptiness of inherent existence is not the emptiness taught in the *Perfection of Wisdom Sutras*. For example, the Yogācāras say that the emptiness explained in the *Perfection of Wisdom Sutras* is the emptiness of duality, which is emptiness presented according to their own system. They think that the emptiness of inherent existence is not correct or valid. They are unable to distinguish between existence and inherent existence, so they inadvertently negate karma and causality. Moreover, in negating the emptiness of inherent existence, they abandon the perfect wisdom that realizes śūnyatā. This is the abandonment of the holy Dharma. Then they generate nihilistic attitudes toward this most profound and holy Dharma, which causes them to fall into a miserable rebirth, perhaps even the lowest hell. Although some of them may admire the teaching of noninherent existence, they think, "If there is no inherent nature, then what is there?" Thus they assert that all phenomena are totally nonexistent and fall into the abyss of the nihilistic view. Therefore Nāgārjuna says:

If they view emptiness in the wrong way,
Those with little wisdom will be ruined.

Candrakīrti comments on this in *Clear Words*:

If someone thinks "Everything is empty—nothing exists," that would be a wrong view. As it says [in Nāgārjuna's *Precious Garland*]:

If they misunderstand this Dharma,
Those lacking wisdom are ruined;
For they sink into the mire
Of nihilistic views.

Even if they do not wish to repudiate everything, at that time they wonder, "How can these things be empty when they are perceived? Therefore the meaning of *emptiness* is not that of *absence of inherent existence*." In this way they definitely abandon emptiness; having abandoned that, they definitely go to the lower realms, owing to the karma of abandoning the Dharma. As the *Precious Garland* continues:

Moreover, if they misunderstand it,
Those fools proud of their learning
Abandon this [Dharma]—so, being stubborn,
They fall headlong into the Unrelenting Hell.

AN ANCIENT DEBATE ABOUT ANNIHILATION AND NIHILISM

The earlier Tibetan Mādhyamikas—who propound the view that things are not existent, not nonexistent, not both, and not neither—say that the above critique is not applicable to them. They argue, "If we had first accepted things as existent and later as not existent, then we would hold a nihilistic view. But we do not accept these things to exist from the beginning. So what is annihilated? As there is nothing to annihilate in the first place, we do not fall into the view of nihilism." To prove their assertion they quote a stanza from Nāgārjuna's *Fundamental Treatise on the Middle Way*:

Believing "It existed before but does not exist now"
Would therefore entail annihilation.

To further their claim that this is the view of the nihilist, they quote Candrakīrti's *Clear Words*:

> A yogi, having understood that conventional things, which have arisen merely owing to ignorance, are not inherently existent, and having realized that such emptiness bears the characteristics of ultimate nature, does not fall to the two extremes; for he considers, "If something becomes nonexistent in the present, then what was it that existed before?" In this way, having seen that there were no inherently existent things before, he does not think that they become totally nonexistent later.

Tsongkhapa says that the earlier Tibetans' argument is not correct. It is based on assuming that Nāgārjuna's statement means that the criterion for nihilism is to accept that something that existed previously is later annihilated. If the meaning were that simple, then it would follow that the Cārvākas are not nihilists. The Cārvākas, or Lokāyatas, are followers of a materialist school of ancient Indian philosophy; they accept only what is perceived by the sense consciousnesses in the present moment. Sensory perception is the only source of valid knowledge, and nothing beyond this exists. They do not accept inference to be a source of valid knowledge. Therefore they do not believe in previous lives or karmic causality. According to them, the present mind arises in dependence on the present body, which is composed of the four elements. These four elements are the same as the external elements—earth, water, fire, and air. When the cohesion of the four elements of the body disintegrates, the mind expires. They say that the mind is like a butter lamp: when the butter is finished, the flame goes out. Nothing more occurs. The materialists believe that we have only this life, so we should enjoy it as fully as possible. Buddhists consider this to be the worst of all the ancient philosophies because it destroys not only our potential to prepare for a good life in the future but also our potential for attaining more distant goals, such as liberation and enlightenment. In fact, the Tibetan translation of the name Cārvāka literally means "throwing the potential for liberation far away."

Accepting only what can be proved by direct sense perception is fairly common in modern times. People often say, "Oh, there is no such thing! You cannot see it, so why do you believe it?" They deny that there is any way other than sense perception to acquire valid knowledge. However, even ordinary people use logical inference to correctly understand things that are not directly perceived by the senses. For example, farmers predict from past experience that if they plough and sow their fields, crops will grow. Likewise, if we see billowing smoke, we have no doubt that there is a fire. We do not see the fire itself, yet because we see the result of the fire—the billowing smoke—we know there is a fire. This is using logical inference based on the result. Having clearly seen the result, we can infer the cause. We can understand karma, past and future lives, and so on using similar reasoning.

So when Buddhists call the Cārvākas nihilists, they are not saying that nihilism means not believing in anything at all or believing that something that once existed is now nonexistent. The materialists clearly believe in this life and in what can be directly perceived with the senses. But they do not accept the existence of previous lives; they do not believe that something that previously existed (in a past life) ceased at a later time (in a subsequent life). They are nihilists because they do not believe in karma, past and future lives, and so on.

So when Nāgārjuna says, "Believing 'It existed before but does not exist now' would therefore entail annihilation," he is referring to Realists who accept that things have inherent existence. A belief in inherent existence definitely gives rise to the two extreme views of eternalism and nihilism. If you accept inherent nature, then that nature must be permanent or unchanging. To believe that something stays the same all the time is to hold the extreme of eternalism. If you say that the thing existed earlier but not later, then you cannot say it exists inherently or independently of anything else. If a thing existed inherently at an earlier time and at a later time is destroyed, then since its nature is unchanging, it must be permanently nonexistent. Therefore you cannot accept its earlier existence. This commits you to believing in nihilism.

The Mādhyamikas' nonacceptance of anything to have even the slightest particle of inherent nature dispels the nihilistic view that believes an inherently existent thing to have previously existed and later ceased. Because the Mādhyamikas do not believe that anything has an inherent nature, they do not fall into the extreme of nihilism or the extreme of eternalism. However, the reason "things do not have inherent existence" does not eliminate all nihilistic views. The nihilistic views of the Cārvākas, who say that there are no future lives, no past lives, and no karma, cannot be negated only by the reason that all things are not inherently existent. Someone who does not believe in previous lives needs proof of previous lives. Someone who does not believe in karma needs proof of karma. Trying to prove the existence of previous lives or karma by means of the reason of noninherent existence will not be effective. The kind of nihilism that is being rejected here is not the same as the nihilism of those who do not believe in karma or past lives.

Some people accuse the Mādhyamikas of being nihilists just like the Cārvākas. The difference between these two philosophical systems is explained in detail in Candrakīrti's *Clear Words*. In brief, the Cārvākas say that karma, the four noble truths, and so on do not exist. Then, because these things do not exist at all, the Cārvākas also claim that these things do not inherently exist. The Mādhyamikas say that karma and so on exist yet do not inherently exist. Superficially the Cārvākas and the Mādhyamikas agree about a lack of inherent existence. However, their assertions about the lack of inherent existence, their ways of understanding it, and the reasons given for it are completely different.

The Mādhyamikas assert that karma, its result, and so on are not inherently existent because they arise dependently. Nihilists, like the Cārvākas, do not use dependent arising as a reason for their assertion about the lack of inherent existence of karma and so on. They say things like "Past and future lives do not exist because we do not see them." They think the best reason for rejecting the existence of something is "Because I do not see it." If this reason were valid, then we would have to directly perceive everything that exists in this present moment. That would be a very strange situation! Thus it is quite different when the Cārvākas say that karma, the four noble truths, and so on do not exist and when the Mādhyamikas say that these things do not inherently exist. Candrakīrti's *Clear Words* says:

> Some claim that the Mādhyamikas are no different from the Nihilists. This is because the Mādhyamikas say that virtuous and nonvirtuous actions, agents, resultant experiences, and all mundane things are empty of inherent existence. The Nihilists also say that these things do not exist. Therefore, they argue, there is no difference between the views of the Mādhyamikas and of the Nihilists.
>
> This is not correct. The Mādhyamikas say that things dependently arise; it is because they dependently arise that they say this life, the next life, and so on are all without inherent existence. The Nihilists do not understand that future lives and so on are not real things, in the sense of being empty of inherent existence because they dependently arise. So what do they say? They regard the components of this life to be inherently existent; nobody sees them as having come here from a past life or as going from here to a future life. So other things, which are similar to the things seen in this life, they deny.

The "components of this life" are one's body, mind, four elements, and so on. They are not seen to come from another life to this one or to go from this life to another life. The body, mind, elements, and so on that existed in a past life are similar to those that exist in this life, but the Cārvākas deny these past things because they believe that whatever they do not see in the present life does not exist.

Someone may think that even though the Mādhyamikas and the Cārvākas do not give the same reason for it, since both schools say that karma, its results, and past and future lives lack an inherently existent nature, their views concerning the emptiness of inherent existence are the same. However, they are not the same even in this regard. The Cārvākas say that to be *not inherently existent* is to be entirely *nonexistent*. For them, a lack of inherent existence means that things do not exist either ultimately or conventionally; they are totally nonexistent. Thus they do not accept either of the two truths. In contrast, although the Mādhyamikas do not accept karma and all these other things to be ultimately existent, they do say that they exist conventionally. Candrakīrti's *Clear Words* says:

> *Opponent*: Even so, regarding this view they are similar, because Nihilists consider the lack of inherent existence of things to be nonexistence.
> *Reply*: No, they are not similar, because the Mādhyamikas accept things to be conventionally existent, but Nihilists do not accept that.

This passage from *Clear Words* indicates that someone who does not accept karma and so on even conventionally, yet believes herself to be a Mādhyamika, actually has the same view as the Cārvākas. Candrakīrti and the earlier Tibetan scholars do not give the same reason for why genuine Mādhyamikas are not similar to the Cārvākas. The earlier Tibetan scholars say, "The Cārvākas believe things to be totally nonexistent, whereas we Mādhyamikas do not have such beliefs. The Cārvākas accept things to be nonexistent, but we do not accept things to be nonexistent—we say that they are not existent. We accept things to be not existent, not nonexistent, not both, and not neither." In contrast, Candrakīrti says, "We say that things are not inherently existent, positing dependent arising as the reason for that; we say that all these things, karma and so on, are conventionally existent."

Someone may wonder, "The Mādhyamikas say that karma and so forth are not inherently existent. The Cārvākas too say that things are not inherently existent. So with respect to the assertion of a lack of inherent existence, the Cārvākas and the Mādhyamikas are similar." Actually they are very dissimilar. Although the Cārvākas and the Mādhyamikas use the same words, the meaning of those words is totally different. Consider the following example. Once there was a person who stole some money. An individual who did not know who the thief was pointed to a man out of spite and said, "He stole it." Another person, one who saw the robbery, pointed to the same man and also said, "He stole it." Both people said the same thing. However, one person was telling a lie and the other was speaking the truth. Although they spoke the same words, the meaning of what they said was different because their reasons were different. Candrakīrti's *Clear Words* says:

Objection: Their view of things is the same.

Reply: Although they are similar with regard to things not being inherently existent, they are not the same because their way of understanding this is completely different. Suppose, for example, a man stole something. Someone who does not know the truth, out of ill will toward that man, dishonestly declares, "He stole it." Someone else actually saw what happened and accuses that man. Even though there is no difference between the facts, the thought processes of the accusers is very different. One is lying and the other is telling the truth. When the first one is examined thoroughly, he will be disgraced and shown up as a fraud. But this will not happen to the other one. Likewise here, when we compare those who realize and understand the nature of things as they are and speak accordingly with those nihilists who do not understand the nature of things as they are, their knowledge and speech are not the same at all.

Some people think that when you claim that things have no inherent existence, you logically negate karma and its effects and, therefore, you cannot establish causality within your philosophical system. To say that such people are wrong about conventional appearances but right about emptiness is clearly negated by Candrakīrti's passage above. According to the Mādhyamikas both conventional appearances and emptiness are nonerroneous: on the conventional side, causes and effects are properly asserted; on the ultimate side, nothing—including causes and effects—is inherently existent.

In short, we should understand that emptiness is not the emptiness of functionality. It is not the emptiness of activity, causality, good, bad, and so on. Even though things are empty of inherent existence, we must find the grounds to properly establish dependent arising, causality, and so on. In other words, when we understand emptiness, we understand that it is emptiness that makes room for causation and dependent arising to be properly established. Candrakīrti's *Commentary on the "Four Hundred Stanzas"* says:

> If this is so, then regarding any object:
>
>> In arising there is no coming.
>> Likewise, in ceasing there is no going.
>
> This definitely has no inherent nature. Some say, "If there is no inherent nature, then what is there?" We explain this as follows. Any dependently arising nature caused by the thoroughly afflictive or the completely pure exists.

This passage clearly answers the question, "If there is no essentially existent inherent nature, then what else is there?" Although nothing inherently exists, the causal or functional nature of all phenomena exists. This includes the phenomena of the afflictive samsaric side (the truth of suffering and the truth of the cause of suffering) and the phenomena of the pure side (the truth of cessation and the truth of the path). Buddhapālita also answers this question by clearly distinguishing between merely existing and existing by its own nature. In his commentary on the twentieth chapter of Nāgārjuna's *Fundamental Treatise* he says:

> *Objection*: If time does not exist, and causes, results, and collections of aggregates also do not exist, then what else is there? If that is your view, then you are just nihilistic.
>
> *Reply*: We do not say that. We only say that your conception of time and so on as inherently existent is wrong. They are established as dependently imputed.

The Mādhyamikas do not say that the Realists are wrong about the existence of cause and effect. The Mādhyamikas do not deny causality, but they do reject the inherent existence of causes and effects. Things such as time and so on are dependently imputed; they exist in dependence on being labeled or named. They dependently arise; they do not inherently exist. It is in this regard that they say the Realists are incorrect.

The Realists, including the Vaibhāṣikas, Sautrāntikas, Yogācāras, and various non-Buddhists, argue that the Mādhyamikas are nihilists and contradict reasoning as well as scripture. According to Tsongkhapa, the Realists' contentions stem from not properly distinguishing *inherent existence* and *absence of inherent existence* from *existence* and *nonexistence*. Much confusion and many wrong views will be eliminated if we clearly distinguish between inherently existent and existent, as well as between nonexistent and noninherently existent. We will no longer think that the Mādhyamikas' logical refutation of inherent existence negates mere existence. Because understanding these differences is so important, Tsongkhapa explains it in great detail, supporting his reasons with quotations from the texts of Nāgārjuna, Āryadeva, Buddhapālita, and Candrakīrti. Tsongkhapa does not merely cite one passage; he goes through many commentaries page by page explaining different aspects of the same point.

Nowadays this may seem easy to understand. You may feel bored going over these points again and again. But it was not easy to understand in the past. Until Tsongkhapa wrote his treatises, the Prāsaṅgika view was not understood in Tibet. The Svātantrika-Madhyamaka view of Śāntarakṣita and Kamalaśīla was well established, but the unique Prāsaṅgika view of Nāgārjuna and Āryadeva was never properly explained. The quotation of so many passages from the Indian sources demonstrates that Tsongkhapa is not presenting his own personal view; he is expounding the Prāsaṅgika view. He shows that this special Prāsaṅgika explanation is found in the root texts of Nāgārjuna as well as in the commentaries by Buddhapālita and Candrakīrti.

Rational Analysis

(2')) Showing that the criticisms they express are not able to disprove the
distinguishing feature of Madhyamaka
    (a")) The distinguishing feature of Madhyamaka cannot be disproved
      by negating things from the perspective of examining whether
      or not they are able to bear ultimate analysis.

(2')) SHOWING THAT THE CRITICISMS THEY EXPRESS ARE NOT ABLE TO DISPROVE THE DISTINGUISHING FEATURE OF MADHYAMAKA

Those who criticize the unique Madhyamaka view use the sutras and śāstras as
sources to support their critiques. However, Tsongkhapa shows that none of
these opponents is able to disprove the distinguishing feature of Madhyamaka:
the mutual dependence of the conventional and the ultimate. Tsongkhapa
divides this topic into four groups:

    (a")) The distinguishing feature of Madhyamaka cannot be disproved by
        negating things from the perspective of examining whether or not
        they are able to bear ultimate analysis.
    (b")) The distinguishing feature of Madhyamaka cannot be disproved by
        negating things from the perspective of examining whether or not
        they are established by valid knowledge (chapters 7–8).
    (c")) The distinguishing feature of Madhyamaka cannot be disproved by
        negating things from the perspective of examining whether or not
        they are produced in dependence on one of the four alternative means
        of production: from self, others, both, or neither (chapter 9).
    (d")) The distinguishing feature of Madhyamaka cannot be disproved by
        negating things from the perspective of the four alternatives: as exis-
        tent, nonexistent, both, or neither (chapter 9).

(a″)) THE DISTINGUISHING FEATURE OF MADHYAMAKA CANNOT BE DISPROVED BY NEGATING THINGS FROM THE PERSPECTIVE OF EXAMINING WHETHER OR NOT THEY ARE ABLE TO BEAR ULTIMATE ANALYSIS

There are two types of rational analysis: conventional analysis and ultimate analysis. Conventional analysis is used in making everyday distinctions. We identify a horse, for example, in terms of its conventional nature and can distinguish between a horse and a cow. We can ascertain whether a particular horse is male or female, big or small, fast or slow, and so on by examining its conventional characteristics. Conventional analysis deals only with the conventional nature of things. Each thing has its own conventional identity, described in terms of its characteristics and given a name. When we search for a thing conventionally, we try to find something that fits that identity; when we look for a bearer of the name *horse*, we can find it.

In contrast, ultimate analysis is used to investigate a thing's final mode of being. We do not use it to make conventional distinctions between things nor to identify them in terms of their various characteristics. Ultimate analysis investigates only the true nature of a thing or a person. We use ultimate analysis to search for inherent identity—something that exists from the side of the object as the referent of its name. In searching for that essential nature, we are not satisfied by the usual use of a term, such as *horse*, arrived at through conventional analysis. When using ultimate analysis we are looking for the inherent nature of the horse—an entity that exists from its own side as the real referent of the word *horse*. When we start to look, we see that the term *horse* is a label imputed on the body, the head, the collection of parts, and other factors combined. It expresses a conceptual convention that combines certain factors together and thinks of them as a whole thing; this whole thing is what we call a *horse*. In ultimate analysis we search for a referent of the term *horse* existing from its own side, independently of being merely labeled. Usually we do not examine this at all; we just accept the existence of a horse. However, when doing ultimate analysis we ask, "What does the word *horse* really refer to?" First we find a group of five aggregates that functions as the basis of the name *horse*. But is this combination of the five aggregates actually a horse? No, it is not. Next we look among the aggregates to find the essential identity of the horse. We look outside and inside, part by part, from hoof to head, for a real horse that exists from its own side. Try as we might, however, we do not find anything that answers to what we originally thought of as a horse. We find only various parts and collections of parts. None of them is the real horse. So one by one, we set them aside and keep trying to find the real horse. What at first appears to be the referent of the word *horse* gradually dissolves. In the end we find nothing. We cannot find an inherently real horse—either within the aggregates or outside the aggregates. We cannot find it by analyzing the basis on which the horse is conventionally imputed. Since we cannot find any inherent identity of a horse when we search within the basis of its name, we ascertain that a horse is not able to withstand ultimate analysis.

If we did find something as a result of this type of investigation, it would virtually say to us, "Here I am, I am the horse." We would be able to say that a horse is able to withstand ultimate analysis. Some Tibetan monastic textbooks define the ability to withstand ultimate analysis as "When the referent of a conventional label is sought, it is found." Thus the meaning of not being able to withstand ultimate analysis is, "When the referent of a conventional label is sought, it is not found." If something were able to withstand ultimate analysis, then it would do so in terms of ultimate rational analysis and in terms of ultimate valid understanding. Both of these types of analysis concern understanding whether things exist in an ultimate sense, by their own nature, from their own side. Thus ultimate analysis concerns śūnyatā. Tsongkhapa emphasizes that ultimate analysis is not concerned with conventional reality; conventional things are neither sought nor found by ultimate analysis because this is a matter for conventional analysis only. Since the Mādhyamikas do not accept that conventional things are found by ultimate analysis, they do not incur the fault of implying that things are truly or inherently existent.

This can be confusing. The basis of investigation of ultimate analysis is usually a conventional thing. However, ultimate analysis does not look to find that conventional thing itself because this is a matter for conventional analysis. Ultimate analysis looks to find the referent of a conventional label. Such an entity can only be found by ultimate analysis if it inherently exists, or exists from its own side. Thus, to be found by conventional analysis and to be found by ultimate analysis are completely different. It is easy to misunderstand this point.

Suppose someone asks, "If something is not able to withstand analysis, then how can that thing, negated by reasoning, exist?" The questioner thinks that because a horse is not found by ultimate analysis, it is totally nonexistent. His mistake is to think that *being unable to withstand* ultimate analysis is the same as *being negated by* ultimate analysis. But they are not the same. Many people, including some earlier Tibetan Madhyamaka scholars, confuse being unable to withstand ultimate analysis with being refuted by ultimate analysis. Those earlier scholars claim that it is nonsense to say that production and so on exist, when they are refuted by ultimate analysis; therefore they do not accept them to exist, not exist, and so forth. According to Tsongkhapa, the meaning of a thing being able to withstand ultimate analysis concerns whether it is found by ultimate analysis. Candrakīrti's *Commentary on the "Four Hundred Stanzas"* says:

> Because our analysis focuses only on the search for an inherent nature.

The term that appears here is "nature." However, when discussing the ultimate analysis that searches for a thing's nature, it is best to clarify this by using the term *inherent nature*, or *intrinsic nature*. Ultimate analysis is used to investigate whether a conventional thing has its own inherent nature. Investigating a thing's nature is different from investigating a thing's inherent nature. What does this mean? First let us consider the notion of a thing's "nature." Do form and each of the other five aggregates have a nature? Yes, they do. They have the nature of arising, abiding, aging, ceasing, and changing every moment. We are born, change, and in the end we die. That is our nature. We exist in dependence on causes and conditions. It is correct to say that this is our nature. No one can say that a thing's mere nature does not exist. In this case, *nature* refers to conventional nature, which encompasses impermanence, suffering, and so on. However, in the context of ultimate analysis, *nature* usually refers to inherent nature. It is inherent nature that is sought by ultimate analysis. Ultimate analysis does not search for the general conventional nature of something, such as arising and ceasing. It investigates whether the arising of forms and so on exists from its own side. The result of this analysis is that we do not find even a single instance of inherently existent arising or ceasing. This nonfinding means that the object analyzed is unable to withstand such analysis; it does not mean that it is refuted by that analysis.

Thus although we do not find a basis of identity existing within the object when we search for it using ultimate analysis, this does not mean that the object itself is totally negated by such analysis. You might think that if something exists, then it must be proved by analysis, and if it is not proved, then it is negated. But we must discern what type of analysis we are talking about: conventional or ultimate. We can establish the existence of the production and cessation of forms and so on by conventional valid knowledge. Conventional things exist because they are established by conventional valid knowledge. The very term *exist* means "established by valid knowledge." If there is valid knowledge of a thing, then it exists. If it is not established by valid knowledge, then it does not exist. There is mutual entailment here. Since the production of forms, feelings, and so on are conventionally established, they exist. Yet even though they exist, they are not established by ultimate valid knowledge. So how could it be reasonable to say that things not found by ultimate analysis are negated altogether?

What is known by ultimate knowledge and what is known by conventional knowledge are completely different. For example, visual consciousness cannot identify sounds, but that does not mean it negates the existence of sounds. Each sense consciousness has a different object. If there were a sound, it would be found by auditory consciousness. Similarly, the objects of conventional knowledge and ultimate knowledge are different. Ultimate analysis cannot establish or negate conventional things. Conventional analysis cannot establish or negate ultimate things.

Any conventional thing, such as forms, sounds, smells, water, earth, the four noble truths, or anything else, has its own nature and its own identity. We can find such things by means of conventional analysis, and we can differentiate them from one another. In contrast, if anything were to have its own inherent nature or its own inherent identity, then we would find it by means of ultimate analysis. That is the appropriate method of analysis to search for a thing's truly existent nature, the final referent of its name. If anything did have an inherent nature, which objectively exists from its own side, then ultimate analysis would definitely find it. But when we do this kind of analysis, we discover that we cannot find any of those things that we are searching for. Nothing, not even śūnyatā, can withstand such an examination. Because this analysis does not find production and so on, we negate inherently existent or ultimately existent production and so on.

It is important to remember that ultimate analysis is different from conventional analysis. The conventional analysis that looks for a horse in the field, for example, is not the same as ultimate analysis, which seeks the referent of the word *horse*. Here when we use conventional analysis, we know what a horse is and what it looks like. If it actually is in the field and we search in every possible place, then we will definitely find it. If we do not find a horse in the field using conventional analysis, based on valid sense consciousness, we establish that there is no horse there. We have found the absence or emptiness of a horse in the field. Is this śūnyatā? No! In the *Lamrim Chenmo* Tsongkhapa uses the example of a pot. If there is a pot in a certain location, we can find it if we search for it properly. If we search thoroughly but do not find a pot, we negate the existence of a pot in that place. Using conventional reasoning, we know that if it existed in that place, it would be found; it was not found, and therefore we have proved that there is no pot in that place. Although this valid knowledge negates the existence of a pot in that particular place, it does not negate the existence of a pot in general. The existence of a pot in general cannot be negated by that knowledge because in general pots exist.

Similarly, if there were production that exists inherently, it would definitely be found when sought by Madhyamaka ultimate analysis. Since production cannot be found by ultimate analysis, inherently existent production, or production that exists by its own nature, is negated; we understand it to be nonexistent. Is mere production negated by this knowledge? No. When we do not find production by means of ultimate analysis, we negate inherently existent production. We do not negate production in general.

Now I have a question for you. Is śūnyatā findable by ultimate analysis? When we look using ultimate analysis, do we eventually find something? Don't we find emptiness in the end? We should find emptiness when we investigate using ultimate analysis. If we do not, then what are we doing? Ultimate analysis finds śūnyatā. When a yogi examines the aggregates using ultimate analysis and eventually achieves a direct realization of śūnyatā, he or she finds emptiness in the end. The yogi does not find anything existing by its own nature but instead finds the absence of that. What is found is the emptiness of inherent existence.

To make this clearer, let us go through an illustration of ultimate analysis. When we look for the ultimate nature of a horse, we start with the term *horse* and see what it applies to. Then we search for the actual referent of the term *horse* within its basis of designation. We analyze the parts and the whole of whatever is called a *horse* and try to find something that exists *as* the horse from its own side. Finally we see that it is not there. That very absence of anything that exists *as* a horse, independently of being imputed, is the true nature of the horse. That is the emptiness of inherent existence of the horse. You start with a horse and investigate what is its ultimate nature, and that is how you find its emptiness.

Now we may ask, "What is emptiness? What does the term *emptiness* designate? Is it something absolutely true or real? Can emptiness be found by ultimate analysis?" Just as before, we search for something called *emptiness*. We start with emptiness itself, and within its basis of designation we look for emptiness that can be identified from its own side. We find that even emptiness lacks inherent existence. We cannot find emptiness's inherent nature. So when we search for the inherent identity of a horse, we find its emptiness. This is the emptiness of the horse. When we search for the inherent identity of emptiness, we find its emptiness. This is the emptiness of emptiness. Neither the horse nor the emptiness of the horse can be found to exist from its own side. Likewise, the emptiness of emptiness is also empty of existing from its own side. However far we may take this analysis, we do not find an inherently existent nature of emptiness itself. You should debate this and meditate on it!

If something is found by ultimate analysis, then it is established by ultimate analysis. It is able to withstand ultimate analysis. If it is not found by such analysis, then it is unable to withstand ultimate analysis. Tsongkhapa quotes a passage from Candrakīrti's *Commentary on the "Four Hundred Stanzas"* to support this point:

> Therefore, when analyzed in this way, the sense organs, objects, and consciousnesses, since they have no inherently existent nature, are not established by their own nature. If they were inherently established, then they would clearly be seen to exist by their own nature when correctly analyzed, but they are not seen as such. Therefore they are empty of inherent existence.

Again and again Candrakīrti says that conventional things—such as forms and sounds—exist. However, they cannot be established by ultimate analysis. In other words, analysis of whether things are inherently existent cannot determine the existence of ordinary conventional things. If we want to establish conventional things, then we investigate with our sense consciousnesses. If we want to understand the true nature of things, then we use ultimate analysis. Nevertheless, some scholars say that conventional things cannot be established or accepted at all, simply because they are not found by ultimate analysis. Candrakīrti says that such people are unskilled in establishing conventionality: they are trying to use ultimate analysis to see whether a conventional thing is established. When their examination does not find the object of their search, they say those things are negated.

If conventional things could be negated by ultimate analysis, then we should apply that analysis rigorously. We should use ultimate analysis to investigate all conventional things, such as the five aggregates and so on. But this cannot work; it is inappropriate. In his writing, Candrakīrti negates from every angle two related assertions: first that conventional things can be established by ultimate analysis, and second that when ultimate analysis does not find conventional things, those things are negated. He clearly indicates that those who take the meaning of "not found by ultimate analysis" to be the same as "negated by ultimate analysis" are confused and have wandered far away from the Madhyamaka view.

When we use ultimate analysis to look for the inherent nature of any conventional thing, we will not find it. When an ārya is in meditative equipoise directly realizing śūnyatā, he or she sees only emptiness. Form, and every other conventional object, just disappears; there is nothing conventional to be found. At that time an ārya sees only the emptiness of inherent existence—the mere negation of a truly existent nature. The ārya sees emptiness in dependence on the conventional thing he or she began to analyze but does not see the conventional thing itself.

This meditation practice develops in the following way. First a yogi employing ultimate analysis may choose to examine a pot as his or her subject. Then he or she utilizes a reason—such as, the pot dependently arises—to prove that it is empty of inherent existence. The yogi starts off with the pot as the basis of investigation, and what he or she eventually finds is its mere emptiness of inherent existence. Initially the yogi's mind comprehends a combination of the conventional and the ultimate: that the pot is not inherently existent. But, even here, the emptiness of the pot itself, not the pot, is the principal object of awareness. Gradually the appearance of the conventional disappears altogether. At that point, when emptiness alone is utilized as the object of meditation, the yogi finds mere emptiness itself. When the yogi perceives this mere emptiness directly, he or she becomes an ārya being, and the yogi's wisdom mind becomes superior gnosis. Such a wisdom of meditative equipoise that sees only emptiness directly does not perceive the basis at all. Its object is a mere negation; it is mere emptiness. Seeing some combination of emptiness and its basis together—such as seeing emptiness directly and its basis indirectly—is an implicative negation.

Ultimate analysis finds only emptiness in the end. It does not find any conventional object. It also does not find the object's nonexistence; therefore its existence is not negated. In other words, an ārya's meditative equipoise directly realizing emptiness does not see a pot, so how can it see the nonexistence of a pot? Any phenomenon can be used as a basis, but usually we work with just one or two examples. Tsongkhapa uses the production and cessation of form. He says that ultimate analysis does not find the production and cessation of form, and it also does not find its nonexistence. Although we do not find the inherent existence of production anywhere, we cannot thereby say that production itself is nonexistent. When we meditate on our chosen example, eventually we will see that no products arise inherently. No phenomena exist inherently. But the fact that no phenomena exist inherently does not mean that they do not exist at all. When we see emptiness directly we understand that all phenomena do not exist inherently. When we understand that all five aggregates are empty, we do not actually see the five aggregates that are the basis of that realization of emptiness. They no longer appear to the mind. When meditating on their emptiness of inherent existence we pass beyond seeing them. They seem to completely disappear.

Now I want to ask you some difficult questions. Does the wisdom directly realizing emptiness see anything conventional? When Buddha sees the emptiness of a pot, does he see the pot clearly? This question concerns how we draw a distinction between Buddha's perception of śūnyatā and his perception of other things. Does he have different ways of seeing the pot and its emptiness? As soon as Buddha sees the pot, does he see emptiness? Do you think that the wisdom seeing ultimate truth does not see conventional things and that the wisdom seeing conventional things does not see ultimate truth? Or do these two kinds of wisdom see the same thing? The case of Buddha is a special exception. Some monastic textbooks say that if Buddha's ultimate knowledge—the wisdom of meditative equipoise directly realizing śūnyatā—sees the subject, or basis, then it would be seeing something false. Actually Buddha's wisdom seeing ultimate truth directly sees conventional things, but it does not see conventional things in the same manner that it sees ultimate truth. If it did, then conventional truth and ultimate truth would be the same. They would be like mush, all mixed together. Buddha clearly sees the difference between conventional and ultimate truth. Even though his mind sees them both, each of them is seen in a different way. His mind does not see conventional things in the manner of seeing ultimate truth, and his mind does not see ultimate truth in the manner of seeing conventional things.[60]

Here Tsongkhapa addresses the confusion of some of his contemporaries and a number of earlier Tibetan scholars. Their misunderstanding comes from not distinguishing between certain key points. First, as we have been discussing, some scholars think that being unable to withstand ultimate analysis is the same as being negated by ultimate analysis. Second, those scholars do not distinguish between an ārya's wisdom of meditative equipoise on śūnyatā not seeing production and cessation and that same wisdom seeing the nonexistence of production and cessation. Third, they do not distinguish between production and cessation not being found by ultimate analysis and production and cessation being found not to exist. These scholars base their views on logical reasoning, on the sutras, and on some Madhyamaka texts. However, they utilize these pristine sources and tools in a befuddled way. We should examine these issues and clearly understand these distinctions.

One such scholar of the past is the great translator from Ngog, Loden Sherab. He believes that ultimate truth is not an object of knowledge. His argument is that ultimate truth is not known by conventional knowledge and it is also not known by ultimate knowledge. For, if it were known by ultimate knowledge, then it would be found by ultimate knowledge. In that case, it would be able to withstand ultimate analysis. Mādhyamikas say that neither conventional things nor ultimate things can withstand ultimate analysis. Therefore he says that ultimate truth is not findable by ultimate knowledge. So because it is not found or seen by ultimate knowledge, and certainly not by conventional knowledge, it cannot be an object of knowledge at all.

Certain other earlier scholars, such as Chapa Chokyi Senge, say that an ārya's meditative equipoise directly realizing śūnyatā finds ultimate truth in the end. Therefore they say that ultimate truth is truly existent. These scholars believe that śūnyatā is truly existent but conventional things are not truly existent. Another famous earlier Tibetan scholar, Kunkhyen Jonangpa, says that since all phenomena can be divided into the categories of "conventional" and "ultimate," only ultimate truth is truly existent; all conventional things are false. However, he does not use the term *ultimate truth* to refer to śūnyatā understood as a mere negation.

Although Tsongkhapa defends the validity of conventional knowledge, he is not suggesting that conventional knowledge is more powerful than ultimate knowledge or that it contradicts ultimate knowledge. Genuine Mādhyamikas do not believe that ultimate and conventional knowledge conflict with each other. Some scholars say that ultimate knowledge contradicts conventional knowledge, but Tsongkhapa disagrees. It is fine to accept that when we analyze a conventional thing, such as form, by means of ultimate analysis, then we do not find form—for this is not contradicted by valid conventional knowledge. But if you believe that not finding form by means of ultimate analysis thereby negates form itself, then you are wrong—for this is contradicted by valid mundane knowledge. Proving that things are not inherently existent by means of ultimate analysis does not imply that they do not exist. Only conventional valid analysis can disprove the mere existence of a conventional thing. When conventional things are not found by ultimate analysis, this proves that they are not inherently existent; it does not negate the things themselves.

Prāsaṅgika-Mādhyamika notions of conventionalities and obscuring appearances

The Prāsaṅgika system does not reject ordinary things, such as forms, sounds, smells, external objects, arising, ceasing, and karma. This is supported by a quotation from Candrakīrti's *Introduction to the "Middle Way"*:

> If you are not contradicted by mundane knowledge,
> Then you can negate this by means of mundane knowledge.
> You should debate about it with ordinary people;
> Then I will rely on the winner.

Here Candrakīrti is addressing the Yogācāras who believe that things such as the self and consciousness are substantially or truly existent. They criticize the Mādhyamikas for saying that these things are not inherently existent yet are merely conventionally existent. They say that the Mādhyamikas' establishment of conventional things is wrong. The Yogācāras argue that the Mādhyamikas' negation of substantial existence (as posited by the Yogācāras) denies any real conventionally existent nature. The Mādhyamikas' response is that the Madhyamaka view is harmonious with ordinary, conventional, or mundane knowledge. Mundane knowledge simply understands ordinary things such as "Here is a form" or "This is good and that is bad." The Prāsaṅgika-Mādhyamikas accept things in this ordinary conventional sense. The Yogācāras' attempt to contradict the Madhyamaka view of conventional existence will fail because it is contradicted by valid mundane knowledge. If their view were not contradicted by mundane knowledge, they could refute the Madhyamaka position on that basis. So Candrakīrti urges the Yogācāras to debate with ordinary people about substantial existence. He promises to follow whoever wins the argument. Given that valid mundane knowledge is not concerned with the true nature, essence, or substantial existence of a thing, the Yogācāras will lose that argument. Candrakīrti comments on this stanza in his *Commentary on the "Introduction to the 'Middle Way'"*:

> We endure great difficulties in order to reverse mundane obscuring
> appearances, whereas you simply negate mundane conventionalities.
> If you are not disproved by ordinary understanding, we will join you.
> However, you are disproved by ordinary understanding.

Worldly people do not examine whether what appears to them is correct in an ultimate sense. They simply perceive forms, sounds, arising, passing away, and so on and accept them as they appear. Everything appears to be inherently existent to ordinary perception. According to ordinary worldly understanding, there is a duality of subject and object. Forms, sounds, and so on exist externally, and in dependence on them various consciousnesses arise internally. The Prāsaṅgika-Mādhyamikas accept that these things exist in a conventional sense. They posit external objects and causality based on external objects.

When the Mādhyamikas say that they accept things in a conventional sense, *conventional* means established by the power of subtle mental obstructions. According to the Mādhyamikas, imprints left by the arising of ignorance in the mindstream create a mistaken appearance of true existence that is mixed together with the appearance of conventional things. That appearance is not actually true, because the appearance of true existence obscures the perception of how things really exist. It is very difficult to remove this mistaken obscuring appearance. To do so we must engage in some very hard work. In order to purify mistaken perceivers (such as visual consciousness) on the subjective side and mistaken appearances (such as forms) on the objective side, we must make great effort practicing the path. These obstructions are not removed by logical analysis alone but by directly perceiving emptiness. First we need to use the logic of ultimate analysis to establish a correct understanding of the emptiness of inherent existence. Then, for a very long time, we must engage in meditative concentration directly perceiving emptiness. This is what Candrakīrti means when he says, "We endure great difficulties in order to reverse mundane obscuring appearances."

In contrast to the Mādhyamikas, the Yogācāras reject what ordinary people accept. Using their own version of ultimate analysis, they try to refute the existence of the external world entirely and prove that everything exists in the nature of the mind only. They say that there are no external objects. They reject the duality of subject and object, the perceiver and the perceived. In short, Yogācāras reject ordinary conventional things.

In general, Yogācāras divide everything into three natures: dependent nature, ultimate nature, and imputed nature. They claim that dependent nature and ultimate nature are truly existent, while imputed nature is not truly existent. Thus they are Realists. When they use their ultimate analysis to search for conventional things, such as external objects, they cannot find them. They say that this nonfinding negates these things altogether. Using the same reasoning, they try to refute the Mādhyamikas' view regarding ordinary conventionalities. They say, "If you Mādhyamikas negate dependent nature being substantially existent, then we will negate your conventionally existent things." This is what Candrakīrti means when he says, "Whereas you simply negate mundane conventionalities."

The Yogācāra method is easy to employ. It is not at all difficult to reject conventional things just by arguing that they are not real. Mādhyamikas say that if conventional things could be negated by ultimate analysis, then we would not need to practice the path to eliminate mistaken appearances. However, conventional things cannot be negated by ultimate analysis. The nature of conventional things is that as soon as they appear, they appear to exist inherently. The appearance of inherent existence occurs together with the appearance of the external objects themselves, as well as the internal subjects perceiving them. If logically negating them were effective, then they would not exist at all. Not only are they not negated in this way, but the attempt to negate them also contradicts ordinary mundane understanding. .

The Mādhyamikas do not try to negate ordinary things by means of ultimate analysis; they just leave them as conventional things. Conventional knowledge concerns conventional things that arise and cease. It does not concern śūnyatā. Conventional knowledge disproves any rational arguments that try to invalidate the existence of conventional things. Mādhyamikas consider that conventional knowledge is more powerful with respect to conventional things than the Yogācāras' fallacious logical arguments analyzing the ultimate. Consequently, they say that when the Yogācāras cannot find conventional things, such as external objects, using their ultimate analysis, this reasoning does not negate those things. Candrakīrti and Tsongkhapa say to the Yogācāras, "If you can negate things accepted by the world, then go ahead. We will even join you if your position is not disproved by mundane knowledge." In other words, if the Yogācāras were actually able to negate conventional things, such as external objects, the Mādhyamikas would assist them. However, the implication is that they could never do that. Their view is disproved by common knowledge. Furthermore, the Mādhyamikas logically refute the inherent existence of all three natures. They prove that none of them are truly existent. In summary, Yogācāras try to show that their ultimate analysis negates external objects, and they try to prove the substantial existence of a substratum consciousness, which they consider to be the receptacle of all the karmic seeds and imprints. But according to the Mādhyamikas, this false logical reasoning is disproved by conventional knowledge.

Now if a Realist were to object and say, "When we say that things are not negated conventionally, we mean that these things are not negated by ordinary people, such as cowherds. However, all these things are negated by reasoning that analyzes the ultimate." Mādhyamikas would respond that it is totally incorrect to say this. Philosophers and other educated people may wonder whether things are negated by reasoning that analyzes the ultimate, but ordinary people do not have any doubts; for them, ordinary things are not negated. If conventional things were negated by ultimate analysis, then that negation must be done in conventional terms. The result would be that things are totally nonexistent. If things—such as forms, sounds, smells, arising, ceasing, and so on—were negated by ultimate analysis, then that negation too would be nonexistent in a conventional sense. Logical reasoning analyzing the ultimate negates ultimate production; it does not negate mere production in general, nor does it negate produced things.

Candrakīrti clearly states that things such as production and so on are not negated by ultimate analysis. For example, in *Commentary on the "Four Hundred Stanzas"* he says:

> If they assert that this kind of analysis totally negates production and shows that conditioned things do not arise, then in that case things would not be illusion-like. Instead they would be proved to be totally nonexistent, like the son of a barren woman. Fearing the consequence that there would be no dependent arising, I do not follow them; rather, without contradicting things, I take them to be like illusions and so on.

The "analysis" referred to in this passage is the logical reasoning analyzing the ultimate. We use this analysis to try to find something existing from its own side. When we do not find such a thing, it is negated. This means that the thing we analyzed does not exist from its own side or inherently. We must apply a qualifier here, such as inherently, ultimately, truly, from its own side, or by way of its own characteristics. In the Prāsaṅgika-Madhyamaka system, all these qualifiers refer to the same thing. When discussing conventional reality, we can use the phrase "does not exist" only when we apply one of these qualifying terms. It is wrong to flatly say "There is no arising" or "There is no ceasing," because without one of these qualifiers we would be saying that nothing is produced at all. If production were negated without any qualification, then there would be no functionality. Production and produced things would be like the son of a barren woman, a rabbit horn, or a human horn. If a produced thing lacks the ability to function, it would be nonexistent. This would imply that there is no dependent arising.

Out of fear of that kind of extreme, Candrakīrti says that produced things are not similar to the son of a barren woman, which lacks any functionality. He says that produced things are like illusions and so on. The phrase "and so on" refers to the common examples given in the sutras: an illusion, the reflection of a face in a mirror, the reflection of the moon in water, or an echo. To say something is like an illusion means that the thing exists, although not as it appears. It does not mean that the thing is totally nonexistent. If ultimate analysis totally negated production, then things would not be like illusions; they would be totally nonexistent like a rabbit horn, the son of a barren woman, or a flower in the sky. If things were nonexistent, they would not have any dependently related causes. All results depend on causes and conditions; causes and conditions produce dependently related results. But as a consequence of the opponent's reasoning alluded to above, there would be no dependently arising things. Therefore Candrakīrti does not accept that interpretation. He accepts that things dependently arise, though they do not exist inherently as they appear; so produced things are similar to illusions. What is negated is true existence or inherent existence, not mere existence.

The *Commentary on the "Four Hundred Stanzas"* says:

> *Opponent*: If the eye and so on were totally nonexistent, then how could the eye sense organ and so on be established as things that are ripened results?
>
> *Reply*: Do we deny that the eye and so on are in the nature of ripened results?
>
> *Opponent*: When you negate the eye and so on, how could you not negate that?

Reply: Because our analysis focuses only on the search for an inherent nature, we negate things existing by their own nature; we do not negate the eye and so on being ripened results produced by causes and conditions. Therefore they exist. So whatever is explained to be merely ripened results—such as the eye and so on—does exist.

Here the term *ripened result* (*las kyi rnam smin*) has a very precise meaning. The Tibetan word *las* means "karma" or "action," and specifically refers to contaminated actions, which produce contaminated results. One action may produce different types of results: ripened result, predominant result, and result corresponding to the cause.[61] The main result of an action is a rebirth. This occurs when a karmic seed becomes the substantial cause of the next life. When we are reborn, there is a ripening of karma that results in the subtle physical sense organs and the mental sense organ of our next body. Everything we experience is perceived through these subtle sense organs. The contact between the sense organs, their objects, and the consciousnesses they produce gives rise to feeling, which may be pleasant, unpleasant, or neutral. Feeling is the main component of our experience. Thus a ripened result is experienced by sentient beings because it is intimately connected with our mental and physical sense organs. In order for such an experience to arise fully, there must be an external environment, which is the predominant result; but the external environment, though it is a karmic result, is not a ripened result because it is not included within the continuum of a sentient being.

In the above passage, Candrakīrti explains very clearly what ultimate analysis negates and what it does not negate. Inherent existence is negated and conventional existence is not negated. Madhyamaka ultimate analysis is a search for something that inherently exists. Inherent existence means that something objectively and truly exists by its own nature without depending on anything else. This type of existence is not found by ultimate analysis in the end. Hence it is negated by ultimate analysis. But mere existence is not negated. We must distinguish between logical reasoning that searches for an essential or inherent nature and ordinary logical reasoning. Logical reasoning that searches for an inherent nature can only negate an inherent nature. Having made this distinction on one occasion, we should understand that it is to be applied in all other contexts, even when it is not specifically stated. It applies to whatever is negated by Madhyamaka analysis: in an ultimate sense things are negated, but in a conventional sense they are not negated.

Candrakīrti does not negate karma and its results. Instead he says that Mādhyamikas must accept the existence of ripened results. We should accept these things simply as they are, in accordance with the views of the ordinary world. We should not reject ordinary things in our search for ultimate reality.

The above passage continues, "Therefore wise beings do not subject ordinary conventional things to the kind of analysis used for seeing ultimate reality. The ripening of karma is said to be inconceivable; all the things of this world should be accepted in a manner similar to one magical emanation giving rise to another." So we must not use ultimate analysis to arrive at an understanding of conventional reality. If we want to determine whether something exists in an ultimate sense, then that is a different question. But it is totally inappropriate to use that kind of analysis to determine conventional things. For example, if there were a rabbit in this room, we would not subject it to ultimate analysis to determine that it is a rabbit and not a cat or a dog. We use conventional analysis to identify it.

There are so many kinds of experiences in the world, both pleasant and painful, that we cannot deny them. Good and bad things happen because of virtuous and nonvirtuous karma. Candrakīrti says that Mādhyamikas must accept these things. So how do we deal with this? It is not too difficult. We negate things in one sense, and we accept them in another sense. In an ultimate sense things are not real. Yet there is causality. It is like in a dream: when a terrible murderer appears, you experience fear, and when a hero arrives who defeats him, you experience joy. In a similar way ordinary things are not ultimately real, yet one thing causes another. They do not exist in the way that they appear—as real from their own side—yet they cannot be denied. They exist in a conventional sense. It is like a magician who creates two illusory elephants that fight, and eventually one defeats the other. Both of these elephants are magical illusions, though they function in a causal relationship. They arise from causes and they produce effects—on each other and on the people who are watching the magic show. Some members of the audience may enjoy it, and others, if they are on the side of the defeated elephant, may feel upset.

Each Buddhist system, and some non-Buddhist ones too, has its own way of dividing things into ultimate truth and conventional truth. Although these systems are different, each accepts one truth as true in a real sense and the other as true in an unreal sense. Within any of their presentations of the two truths, if the explanation of the ultimate harms the establishment of the conventional, then their establishment of two truths is internally contradictory. It is unskillful to negate the conventional when explaining ultimate truth or to negate the ultimate when explaining conventional truth. How could such an unskillful person be suitable as a master to explain the two truths? Conversely, if there is not the slightest internal contradiction between the explanations of the ultimate and the conventional, then it would be contradictory to say that the analysis establishing the ultimate negates the establishment of the conventional. In other words, if one's establishment of the two truths is not internally contradictory, then the reasoning that establishes the ultimate cannot negate the conventional. It would be inconsistent to claim that it would.

Candrakīrti's *Clear Words* says:

> Since you are not skillful with respect to ultimate and conventional truth, you sometimes incorrectly apply ultimate analysis to the conventional and thereby refute it. Since we are skillful in establishing conventional truth, we remain with the world's position. In order to refute a certain conventional position, we use one appropriate reason to negate another; and, like worldly elders, we negate only you, who completely damage the traditions of the world. We do not negate the conventional. We negate only those proponents of philosophical systems that repudiate conventional phenomena, but we do not negate conventional things.

In the first sentence of this passage, "you" refers to the Realists who hold that whatever exists must inherently exist, and if something does not inherently exist then it cannot exist. In this sense it may also apply to the earlier Tibetan Mādhyamikas who identify the object of negation too broadly, as we saw in the last chapter. Candrakīrti addresses people who think this way and says that they should establish what is correct conventionally by its own ordinary criteria rather than rejecting something conventional on the basis of ultimate analysis.

There are many correct conventional logical proofs and negations. Conventional things are negated by means of other conventional logical proofs: we know that a certain horned animal is not a horse because it has horns; we know that there is a fire on a certain mountain pass because we see smoke there. There is no need to deal with these things in terms of the two truths. Candrakīrti says that imposing ultimate analysis on conventional things in a manner that negates conventional things is not a skillful way to posit the two truths. Of course, one can formulate an apparent negation of conventionality by applying ultimate analysis, saying, "There is no sprout because it cannot be found by ultimate analysis." But this is not a correct means to establish the two truths. Candrakīrti does not negate conventional reality. He does not intend that we use ultimate reasoning to negate conventional things.

In brief, the various Indian Buddhist schools of philosophy try to find logical flaws in one another's presentation of the two truths. No school asserts that its own presentation of the two truths has internal contradictions. They all try to posit the two truths properly, so that the reasoning establishing the ultimate does not negate conventional things, and vice versa. No school declares that, according to its own system, establishing ultimate truth negates conventional truth. These debates between the Madhyamaka and lower schools are not just for the sake of argument. They are trying to interpret and clearly present the teachings of Buddha as found in such scriptures as the *Perfection of Wisdom Sutras.*

⁂ 7 ⁙

Valid Establishment

(b")) The distinguishing feature of Madhyamaka cannot be disproved by negating things from the perspective of examining whether or not they are established by valid knowledge

⎯⎯⎯•◉•⎯⎯⎯

(b")) THE DISTINGUISHING FEATURE OF MADHYAMAKA CANNOT BE DISPROVED BY NEGATING THINGS FROM THE PERSPECTIVE OF EXAMINING WHETHER OR NOT THEY ARE ESTABLISHED BY VALID KNOWLEDGE

IF SOMETHING IS known, established, or proved by valid knowledge, then it exists. That is what is meant by the word "exist"; it is the common definition of "existent." If something exists, it must be established by valid knowledge. This is a specific type of awareness, of which there are two types: ultimate valid knowledge and conventional valid knowledge. According to the Madhyamaka system, the former is valid knowledge of ultimate reality, śūnyatā, and the latter is valid knowledge of conventional things, such as visible forms. The Madhyamaka view is that conventional things are established by conventional valid knowledge.

However, there are certain earlier Tibetans who consider themselves Mādhyamikas, yet they do not accept the existence of conventional things because they believe that visible forms and so on are not established by any type of valid knowing—whether ultimate or conventional. Regarding the first, they say that anything established by ultimate valid knowledge is a truly existent thing that is able to withstand ultimate analysis and can be found to exist from its own side. But when we engage in ultimate analysis, we find nothing existing from its own side. In finding that absence, we find emptiness. Thus ultimate valid knowledge only establishes emptiness; it does not establish conventional things. If conventional things were established by ultimate knowledge, then they would be truly existent. Truly existent things are not accepted in the Madhyamaka system. Regarding the second, these earlier scholars say that conventional knowledge—sense consciousness or ordinary mental consciousness—is not valid knowledge at all. Only a direct realization of śūnyatā is valid knowledge. Although conventional things are the objects of sense consciousnesses and can be established relatively, they are not established by valid knowledge. Therefore, because conventional things cannot be established by valid knowledge, these scholars say that we cannot accept that they exist. They claim that this is what Buddha means when he says, "The eye, ear, and nose consciousnesses are not valid knowledge." They also question how other Mādhyamikas can take the position that valid knowledge establishes visible forms and so on, because Candrakīrti says, "Ordinary knowing is always invalid."

Tsongkhapa says that Candrakīrti is only denying the validity of conventional consciousnesses, such as visual consciousness, with respect to the ultimate nature of reality—emptiness. He does not mean that conventional consciousnesses are not valid with respect to any object whatsoever. Candrakīrti's *Commentary on the "Introduction to the "Middle Way"'* says:

> In that case, only āryas are valid with respect to contemplating reality; non-āryas are not. Why is this so? If, wanting to employ ordinary refutation, you accept that ordinary perception is valid even with regard to analyzing reality, then consider:
>
>> If ordinary knowing were valid, it would see reality.
>> Then what need would there be for another exalted knowing?
>> What would the exalted path achieve?
>> Indeed it is wrong for obscured knowing to be valid.

Candrakīrti's words "Only āryas are valid" does not mean that āryas, the people themselves, are valid knowledge. It means that their direct realization of the ultimate is a valid knowing of emptiness. Also, when the text says that non-āryas are not valid, it means that ordinary perception is not valid knowledge of emptiness. Candrakīrti's subsequent commentary on the above stanza in *Commentary on the "Introduction to the "Middle Way"'* says:

> It would be fruitless to hear, contemplate, and meditate on the Dharma or train in ethical discipline and so on in order to realize the supreme path, because mere visual consciousness and so on would understand reality. But this is not the case. Therefore:

Because ordinary knowing is always invalid,
There is no ordinary refutation with regard to reality.

With respect to śūnyatā, only āryas' knowledge is valid; others' knowledge is not. Before becoming an ārya, an ordinary individual develops an understanding of śūnyatā by means of analyzing the ultimate based on valid reasoning. This is inferential knowledge of śūnyatā, not direct perception. In this passage, the valid knowledge understanding śūnyatā that is under discussion is direct valid knowledge. Inferential valid knowledge is not direct. So even though valid knowing can be divided into direct perception and inference, inferential valid knowing is not considered here.

In general the Madhyamaka system accepts conventional knowledge. Mādhyamikas admit that ordinary sense consciousnesses validly perceive their appropriate objects: color, shape, sound, and so on. But if they were to accept that sense consciousnesses validly perceive ultimate reality, then the above criticism would apply: "What need would there be to train in the ārya path?" If ordinary conventional knowing were valid with respect to reality, then what would be the point of doing all kinds of difficult practices to reach the exalted ārya stage? If visual consciousness already sees emptiness, then why bother to practice ethics, generosity, and so on? However, ordinary conventional knowing is never valid with respect to śūnyatā. When Candrakīrti says, "There is no ordinary refutation with regard to reality," he means that ordinary valid knowing can never negate ultimate reality.

Although sense consciousnesses are not valid with respect to reality, they are valid with respect to ordinary things. In short, ordinary valid knowing applies when analyzing conventional things. Conventional knowing perceives visible forms, sounds, smells, and so on, to be real. When we understand the true nature of these objects by means of ultimate valid knowledge, we will see that they lack inherent existence and do not exist as they appear. Nevertheless, our conventional understanding knows things at a conventional level, and this does not contradict ultimate reality. Candrakīrti's *Commentary on the "Sixty Stanzas of Reasoning" (Yukti-ṣaṣṭikā-vṛtti)* says:

> Seeing the mere existence of these things is not seeing śūnyatā. For this very reason Buddha said, "The eye, ear, and nose consciousnesses are not valid knowledge."

The line quoted by Candrakīrti above is from the *King of Concentrations Sutra* (also cited in chapter 4):

The eye, ear, and nose consciousnesses are not valid knowledge;
The tongue, body, and mental consciousnesses are also not valid
    knowledge;
If these sense consciousnesses were valid knowledge,
Of what use to anyone would the āryas' path be?

It is clear that these quotations are denying the sense consciousnesses' validity with regard to ultimate reality—a special type of object—and do not deny their validity with regard to other objects. The sense consciousnesses are valid knowledge in connection with their respective conventional phenomena: visual consciousness is valid with respect to visible forms, auditory consciousness is valid with respect to sounds, and so on. If we do not interpret these quotations in this way, then the various types of perception and their respective objects would become unrelated. Mixing up the connections between perceptions and their objects only produces nonsense. It is meaningless to say, "If the sense consciousnesses are valid with respect to conventional things, there is no need to strive for the ārya's path to perceive śūnyatā." This is as ridiculous as saying, "If visual consciousness sees form, there is no need for auditory consciousness to hear sound." Each of these perceptions is unrelated to the other's object. There is no connection between the eye validly seeing form and the ear validly hearing sound. The object is different and the subject is different. Visual consciousness perceives form. Auditory consciousness perceives sound. Just so, a sense consciousness perceives a conventional thing, and the exalted wisdom of an ārya perceives emptiness. These two perceptions are totally different; the perceiving consciousnesses are different subjects, and they have different purposes and different objects. Each is connected with its own object and has no connection with the other's object. It is ridiculous to say that if one of these subjects is valid knowing, then there is no need for the other to seek its own valid object. On the other hand, these opponents could truthfully claim, "If the sense consciousnesses are valid with respect to conventional things, there is no need to strive for the ārya's path to know forms, sounds, and so on." If that is what they are saying, then of course everyone will agree; nobody thinks you need the ārya's path in order to see forms, sounds, and so on. So what would be proved by saying this? Tsongkhapa shows that these earlier scholars cannot demonstrate that any undesired consequences follow from his understanding of Candrakīrti's words.

Another questioner asks how to interpret a difficult passage from Candrakīrti's *Commentary on the "Four Hundred Stanzas"* that focuses on a general denial of the visual consciousness and so on being valid knowledge—as presented by an opponent:

You identify sense consciousness as *direct perception*, yet you consider it to be *valid knowledge*. However, these are utterly incompatible. On the one hand, a nondeceptive consciousness is ordinarily seen to be valid knowledge. On the other hand, Buddha said that sense consciousnesses have the qualities of being deceptive, false, and illusion-like, because they are conditioned things. Whatever is deceptive, false, and illusion-like cannot be nondeceptive, because the thing exists in one way yet appears to exist in another way. In that case, it cannot be considered to be valid knowledge because it would absurdly follow that all consciousnesses are valid knowledge.

Tsongkhapa says that this passage is more difficult to understand than the words of Buddha quoted earlier, "The eye, ear, and nose consciousnesses are not valid knowledge." This is because it employs more than one meaning of *nondeceptive*. Candrakīrti's opponent here utilizes the teachings of the classical Buddhist logicians Dignāga and Dharmakīrti. In two chapters of his *Commentary on Valid Cognition* (*Pramāṇa-vārttika-kārikā*), based on Dignāga's root text, Dharmakīrti explains logical inference and direct perception and uses the term *nondeceptive* to define valid knowledge:[62]

Valid knowledge is a nondeceptive cognition.

A nondeceptive cognition is an awareness that understands its main object correctly.[63] A deceptive cognition is an awareness that is ignorant, confused, or incorrectly holds its object. Although the Prāsaṅgikas agree that any non-deceptive cognition is valid knowledge, the lower schools, such as Sautrāntika, Yogācāra, and Svātantrika-Madhyamaka, specify in addition that valid knowledge must be new. This is based on Dharmakīrti's *Commentary on Valid Cognition*, which says:

Also, it knows an object not cognized before. (2.5c)

Therefore the lower schools claim that only the first moment of knowing an object is valid knowing. The second moment of knowing, called *subsequent knowing*, is not valid—even if it knows its principal object correctly. The definition of *subsequent knowing* is "a mind that realizes what has already been realized." The Tibetan word for *subsequent knowing* can be expanded in a literal translation to be "knowing that eliminates doubt." In other words, the object is already known, so there is no doubt. Subsequent knowing realizes something that was known previously. It is like remembering.

The Sanskrit term for valid knowledge is *pramāṇa*. The root *mā* means "to measure," which in the compound *pramā* means "to know, realize, or understand." The prefix *pra* means "primary." This is ambiguous; it can mean "principal" or "first." The lower schools say it means "first." However, according to the Prāsaṅgikas, it means "principal." Therefore they say that valid knowing is not necessarily the first moment; subsequent knowing can be valid knowing if that consciousness knows its principal object nondeceptively. When something is established by a nondeceptive consciousness, then it exists.

As presented in Candrakīrti's passage above, Buddha says that sense consciousnesses are deceptive, false, and illusion-like because they are conditioned things: produced by causes and conditions. This teaching, "All products are deceptive," accords with the Prāsaṅgika view. The Prāsaṅgika-Mādhyamikas assert that all sense consciousnesses—except for those of buddhas—are mistaken consciousnesses. How are they mistaken? They are mistaken with regard to the way their objects appear to them. Forms, sounds, smells, and so on appear to sense consciousnesses to exist inherently, but they are free of inherent existence. The scriptures often give the example of visual consciousness seeing the reflection of a face in a mirror. The face seen in the mirror is not a real human face. However, when the visual consciousness, based on the subtle visual sense power in the eye, looks into the mirror, it sees what appears to be a face existing from its own side. Similarly, when a visual consciousness sees a form, it sees what appears to be a form existing from its own side; that form appears to be inherently existent, but there is no such inherently existent thing there. According to the Prāsaṅgikas, because the sense consciousnesses are mistaken in this way, they are deceptive. Their appearing objects are false because what appears to exist in one way in fact exists in another way. So these appearances are illusion-like.

The argument expressed by Candrakīrti's opponent in the above passage says that any consciousness to which things appear other than how they actually exist cannot be considered valid knowledge. This is because on the one hand, such a consciousness is deceptive, and on the other hand, valid knowledge is defined as nondeceptive. One consciousness cannot be both deceptive and nondeceptive. So there seems to be a contradiction between Buddha saying that all products are deceptive and that valid knowledge is nondeceptive. What is going on here? Candrakīrti's opponent does not understand that the word *deceptive* has different meanings in the definition of valid knowledge and in the teaching that all products are deceptive. On Candrakīrti's interpretation of these two, there is no contradiction.

To allow for a better understanding of this, Tsongkhapa refers to the presentation of the logicians' views in Candrakīrti's *Commentary on the "Four Hundred Stanzas,"* which says:

> Because these logicians are completely unaccustomed to worldly conventionalities, they have to be trained in these things from the very beginning, just like little children. So in order to teach them, you debate with them and ask, "What is direct perception according to you?" They reply, "It is a directly perceiving consciousness." "What sort of consciousness is that?" "It is one that is free of thought." "What is thought?" "It is discursive discernment that superimposes an additional name and category onto a perceived object. Owing to being free of that, the five sense consciousnesses perceive only the object's own inexpressible characteristics and thus are called direct perception."

First Candrakīrti asks his opponents, "What is direct perception?" The characterization of direct perception provided by the logicians above is, "A directly perceiving consciousness that is free of thought." In other words, direct perception must apprehend the object itself rather than know the object via a conceptual image. Here we should note that the Prāsaṅgika-Madhyamaka definition of direct perception is a little different from that of the lower Buddhist schools. The Prāsaṅgika view and their refutation of the lower schools will be discussed later. In the present discussion, the definition of direct perception accords with Dharmakīrti's *Commentary on Valid Cognition.*

In general, direct perception mostly refers to sense consciousness. Mental direct perception is very rare for ordinary people. A sense consciousness, such as visual consciousness, is a directly perceiving consciousness; it always directly perceives its object, either correctly or incorrectly. According to certain lower schools, such as the Sautrāntika, direct perception must be unmistaken. If it apprehends something incorrectly, such as seeing a white object as yellow or seeing two objects where there is only one, it is not direct perception—it is wrong consciousness. For them a direct perception is never mistaken; what we perceive does exist as we perceive it—it is reality. We directly perceive things such as color, shape, and sound. We apprehend those objects as they truly, inherently are. According to Dharmakīrti, a sense consciousness sees its object directly; what it perceives is not different from the object's reality.

As soon as a sense consciousness directly perceives something, a thought usually arises in the mind instantly. Thought is not direct perception. Thought understands what is perceived and gives a name to it. You may think "I saw that," or "I heard that," or "I smelled that." For example, if we see a tree, we can close our eyes and still know the tree; we can identify it and remember it. The direct perception in this case is a visual consciousness, but the identification is a conceptual thought. Thought does not see the tree; it knows it by means of an *object universal* (*don spyi*), which in this case is a general image generated via visual consciousness. Through this conceptual image we can identify and describe that tree. This mental image is not as clear as what was perceived directly; it is a vague likeness appearing in the mind. A similar process occurs with a *term universal* (*sgra spyi*), which is a general image generated through hearing another's words. For example, when we hear a description of Buddha, a general idea of what he is like appears in our minds. We may hold onto that image and explain it to others using similar descriptive language. Thus there are two kinds of knowing: direct and indirect. Even perception itself, let alone other ways of knowing, can be direct or indirect.

Next Candrakīrti asks his opponents, "What is thought?" To understand their answer, we need to begin with a simple example. Suppose you see a vase on the table in front of you. Your visual consciousness sees the vase directly and at the same time perceives its color, shape, and other characteristics. Then a conceptual consciousness arises and assigns a type to what you see. You identify the object and give it a name. You think, "This is a vase." Thought cannot perceive an object with all of its characteristics at the same time. It considers the object and each of its characteristics individually and labels them one by one by means of elimination (*sel ba'i sgo nas 'jug pa*). Assigning a name and mentally putting together certain attributes is the activity of thought. This activity is known as *discernment*. It superimposes an image, something extra, on what the visual consciousness sees directly, thereby enabling us to differentiate between things and apply the labels "this" and "that." In short, direct perception does not discriminate between things but simply observes what is there. Thought applies labels and distinguishes between various things and their qualities. Candrakīrti's text uses the term *discursive discernment* here, which, in addition to making distinctions, refers to the movement of the mind as it ranges all over the place. Clearly, discursive discernment is conceptual.

Direct perception is free of conceptuality. According to the lower schools, the five sense consciousnesses perceive their objects and their objects' characteristics directly; thus a sense consciousness is valid with regard to its perceived object. It perceives its object to exist by way of its own characteristics, so it is valid with regard to its object's inherent existence. In short, a sense consciousness perceives the real, inherent nature of its object, which is inexpressible.

Some earlier Mādhyamikas have a special understanding of what it means to be inexpressible and inconceivable. But for the Sautrāntika and lower schools, *inexpressible* indicates that a sense consciousness perceives ultimate reality, which cannot be expressed in the way that a sense consciousness directly perceives it. Why not try it out? Consider your awareness of taste. When you eat a candy, your tongue consciousness directly experiences it. But you cannot express in words or concepts precisely what you are experiencing; you can only say, "It is very, very sweet." The object of direct perception is inexpressible in the way that we experience it. A sense consciousness always relates directly to the reality of its object, the object's characteristics, or to its inherent nature. This cannot be expressed by thought or word in the way that it is directly experienced. Therefore a sense consciousness is called direct perception.

Tsongkhapa begins his commentary on Candrakīrti's passage above by stating the logicians' definition of direct perception to be "An unmistaken consciousness that is free of conceptuality." This definition is acceptable to the lower Buddhist schools, the Vaibhāṣika and Sautrāntika, and possibly to some non-Buddhist schools—but it does not work for the Yogācāra and Madhyamaka schools. The higher Buddhist schools agree that direct perception is free of conceptuality, but for differing reasons they do not accept that it is unmistaken. According to the Yogācāra system, any sense consciousness is mistaken, because when we perceive an object it appears to exist externally as a separate substance from the perceiving subject. They claim that an object is in the nature of the mind perceiving it because both the subject and the object arise from the same inner cause. Although objects appear to be external, they are actually in the nature of the mind. Therefore the appearance of objects as external to the perceiver is mistaken; such an object is not real in the way that we see it. According to the Prāsaṅgika-Madhyamaka system, an ordinary person's direct perception is mistaken, because an ordinary consciousness, whether direct perception or thought, is always mistaken with regard to its appearing object. Things appear to be inherently existent, whereas in reality they are not. Therefore Prāsaṅgika-Mādhyamikas do not include *unmistaken* in their definition of direct perception. This is because there are only two types of direct perception that are unmistaken: the direct perception of śūnyatā and a buddha's pure perception of both ultimate and conventional truths. All other instances of direct perception are mistaken.

The logicians and lower schools believe that direct perception is both nonconceptual and unmistaken and that the objects apprehended by the sense consciousnesses exist as they are perceived. They believe that forms and so on are inherently existent, in that they exist by way of their own characteristics.[64] Also they believe the five sense consciousnesses perceive reality correctly and the objects they perceive exist truly, objectively, by way of their own intrinsic nature, and so are ultimate truths. (The Sautrāntikas do not claim that the ultimate truth is śūnyatā because they do not recognize it.) In short, according to the logicians and other Realists, the five sense consciousnesses are unmistaken consciousnesses that perceive their objects' intrinsic characteristics. Therefore direct perception apprehends the inherent nature of form, sound, and all other such objects. It is by virtue of the sense objects' inherent nature that the five sense consciousnesses are valid knowing. Real truths are ultimate truths. In contrast, conventional truths are not real truths. They are created by thought and do not exist by way of their own characteristics. Uncaused space, for example, does not exist as a real physical object. It is a conceptual construct that exists only though being labeled and thought. For the logicians and Realists of the lower schools, conventional truths do not exist from their own side. They are conceptually created.

Now because the Madhyamaka master Candrakīrti does not accept that things exist by way of their own nature or their own characteristics even conventionally, how could he possibly be saying that the sense consciousnesses are valid with regard to the inherent nature of their five objects? He is not saying any such thing! The sense consciousnesses could never be valid with regard to their objects' own intrinsic characteristics or inherent natures because the inherent natures of objects do not exist. Things are empty of inherent existence; they lack existence by way of their own intrinsic characteristics. Therefore his refutation of sense consciousnesses being valid knowing is a repudiation of the claim that the sense consciousnesses are valid with regard to the inherent nature of their five objects. He does not deny that they are mere valid knowing in general.

This refutation is made on the grounds that Buddha declares the five sense consciousnesses to be false and deceptive. *Nondeceptive* is one of the defining characteristics of valid knowledge, as posited by the logicians. So the sense consciousnesses cannot be that kind of valid knowledge. In what way are the sense consciousnesses deceptive? They perceive things to exist in a manner that is contrary to reality. The way things exist is different from the way they appear to the sense consciousnesses. The way a thing appears to exist to a sentient being's sense consciousness is not real; conversely, a thing's real mode of existence does not appear to a sentient being's sense consciousness. Therefore the sense consciousnesses are false and deceptive with respect to what appears to them. In brief, although the five sense objects do not exist by way of their own characteristics, they appear to the sense consciousnesses as if they do. Thus the five sense consciousnesses are mistaken regarding the appearance of the inherent existence of their objects. Therefore they are not valid regarding the inherent nature or intrinsic characteristics of their objects. They are deceptive. This is likened to an ordinary mistaken eye consciousness seeing one moon as two, which is deceptive regarding the moon itself.

The Realists hold that if form, sound, and so on lack inherent existence or do not exist by way of their own characteristics, they would lack the ability to function. They would be nonexistent. Further, they think that if the sense consciousnesses are not valid with regard to the inherent nature of their objects, then there cannot be any valid knowledge of those objects. Also if the sense consciousnesses are valid with regard to their objects, then they must be valid with regard to the inherent nature of those objects. All the Buddhist schools below the Madhyamaka, as well as the non-Buddhist schools, hold versions of this Realist view: for example, the Yogācāras believe that produced things, as well as the ultimate truth, are truly existent; the Sautrāntikas and Vaibhāṣikas believe that things are truly existent.

According to Candrakīrti, if anything were to exist by its own characteristics or by its own nature, it would be truly existent. Thus if valid knowledge establishes that an object is truly existent, it must be valid with regard to its inherent characteristics. However, such an object is false. Therefore, in order for a consciousness to be valid with regard to its object, it does not need to be valid with regard to that object's inherent characteristics.

Now we have to be careful with certain words. The Prāsaṅgika-Mādhyamikas do not say that things do not have their own characteristics. They say that things *have* their own characteristics but do not *exist by way of* their own characteristics or *by* their own nature. We cannot say that things lack their own nature. Unlike a rabbit horn, which does not exist, actual things have their own characteristics: a vase has its own characteristics; earth has its own characteristics. Everything has its own conventional characteristics, its own nature, and its own attributes. It is *the way that things exist* that is being questioned. To say that something exists "by its own characteristics" or "by its own nature" means that it exists without depending on anything else. Nothing exists in that way. Things do not exist by their own characteristics; they do not exist from their own side; they do not exist by their own nature. Although things are not truly existent, they are true.

You might think that the Mādhyamikas are playing word games when they say "Things are true but not truly existent." Actually this is very profound; it is not just a play on words. Truth exists; but it is quite different to say that things are truly existent. The latter is what is rejected. Candrakīrti's *Commentary on the "Four Hundred Stanzas"* says:

> It is clearly incorrect that worldly perception sees ultimate reality, because a worldly sense consciousness is valid only from the point of view of worldly convention, and the object it sees is a false and deceptive object.

If we define *valid* in terms of what is finally found through analysis of a thing's true nature, then ordinary objects are not valid and they are not established by valid knowledge. However, the term *valid* does not always refer to the true nature of things or the way that things exist finally. Using the ordinary meaning of *valid*, we can say that a sense consciousness is valid if the thing perceived is known as it is perceived—without analyzing the thing's true nature. So the sense consciousnesses can be valid in general. For example, a valid visual consciousness perceives the moon in the sky; an ordinary visual consciousness perceiving two moons is mistaken. That difference is maintained here. Candrakīrti does not reject the mere validity of sense consciousnesses. They are valid conventionally. However, because a valid sense consciousness does not perceive the ultimate truth of its object, it is not valid with respect to that thing's true nature; and because its object appears to exist in one way but actually exists in another, it does not perceive its object's true nature. It is not valid with regard to an inherent nature of its object. Candrakīrti's refutation of the validity of the sense consciousnesses is only with regard to their apprehension of their objects' apparent inherent nature.

In summary, these passages from Candrakīrti's texts do not negate conventional valid knowledge in general. If they did, it would be incorrect for him to say, "A nondeceptive consciousness is ordinarily seen to be valid knowledge." Furthermore, it would follow that the validity of all conventional consciousnesses whatsoever would be rejected. That cannot be right. It would also contradict what Candrakīrti says in *Clear Words*, "Therefore we posit ordinary things to be known through four types of valid knowledge." The four types of valid knowledge are: direct, inferential, scriptural, and analogical. The various Buddhist schools understand these four types of valid knowing in slightly different ways. However, in general, *direct valid knowing* or *perception* understands things without relying on inference—for example, a visual consciousness seeing a color. *Inferential knowing* is gained through logical analysis, which is also known as inference based on the power of the fact or actual reasons.

The third type of valid knowing, *scriptural valid knowing*, is also inferential knowledge. It is valid knowing arising from trust. There are many things that we rely on, even though we do not directly perceive them and cannot prove them ourselves. For example, we trust the explanations of scientific experts; in a similar way, we may trust Buddha's words about causality. Ordinary people cannot directly perceive particular causal connections nor can they logically deduce the specific time, place, persons, and actions that result in a particular situation. Buddha clearly expresses everything as it is, what lies behind a situation, what we should do, and how we should do it. Even though we do not see these factors directly and do not have any logical proof, if we trust what Buddha says, we can gain knowledge.

The fourth type of valid knowing is based on *analogy*. This way of knowing is like a logical proof based on a similar instance: "This should be so because it is similar to that." Sometimes this last type of valid knowing is not listed separately. The point here is that if sense consciousnesses were not valid knowing, it would contradict Candrakīrti's enumeration of these types of valid knowledge.

Candrakīrti negates inherently existent valid knowledge and inherently existent objects that are known, but does not negate dependently established valid knowledge and dependently established objects that are known. Valid knowledge depends on the object known, and the object known depends on valid knowledge. They are established dependently on each other, just as the eastern mountain and the western mountain are established dependently on each other. There cannot be valid knowledge that exists independently of anything else. Candrakīrti accepts that valid knowledge and its object exist as mutually dependently related, for he says in *Clear Words*:

> Moreover, those are mutually dependent. If there is valid knowledge, then there are things known; and if there are things known, then there is valid knowledge. Therefore valid knowledge and the object known are not established by their own nature.

TEMPORARY CAUSES OF ERROR AND DEEP CAUSES OF ERROR

In general a sense consciousness is valid if no external or internal *temporary* causes of error impede it. What this consciousness establishes is correct. It is valid even though, owing to the power of ignorance, it is affected by a *deep* cause of error, the imprints of ignorance. *Ignorance* here refers to the innate mind holding things to be inherently existent; it is the innate self-grasping mind. That kind of ignorance leaves deep imprints on the mental continuum, and these affect all unenlightened conventional consciousnesses. These imprints cause the objects of sense consciousness and so on to appear inherently existent. However, this mistaken appearance of inherent existence does not invalidate a sense consciousness that is undistorted by any temporary cause of error.

Here we must make a distinction between a *distorted* consciousness and a *mistaken* consciousness. A distorted sense consciousness grasps its primary object incorrectly because it is affected by a temporary cause of error—for example, an eye disease that causes double vision. It sees its object in a way that is completely different from the way in which it exists; therefore it cannot be valid. An undistorted sense consciousness is mistaken in a more subtle way; it is mistaken with regard to the appearance of its object as inherently existent, whereas in reality it is empty of inherent existence. However, from a conventional perspective, there is nothing wrong with that. A mistaken sense consciousness is incorrect because it is affected by the imprints of ignorance, but it need not be distorted; it is valid if it knows its main object. In terms of being the object of that conventional valid knowledge, that object exists as it is known.

According to the Prāsaṅgika-Madhyamaka system, any unenlightened being's ordinary consciousness—including sensory direct perception—is always mistaken. Apart from a buddha's awareness, only the meditative equipoise of an ārya being directly perceiving śūnyatā is nonmistaken. This is not an ordinary awareness; it is supreme wisdom or gnosis. This uncontaminated meditative wisdom of an ārya being is manifest only during a meditation session.[65] At that time nothing but emptiness appears. However, as soon as the ārya being arises from his or her meditation, mistaken consciousnesses occur again. Until reaching buddhahood, all living beings have the imprints of ignorance within their mindstreams, which give rise to the appearance of inherent existence. Even tenth-level bodhisattvas have these imprints, which are obstructions to omniscience. High-level bodhisattvas have developed compassion and bodhicitta and have directly understood truths such as impermanence; however, all these realizations are conventional knowledge. All conventional knowing is mistaken in that its object appears to exist inherently.

Nevertheless, conventional knowledge is valid with respect to its main object. A visual consciousness seeing blue is valid with regard to its object, blue. But it is mistaken in that its object, blue, appears to exist from its own side. Here we need to distinguish between the *held object* and the *appearing object* of a sense consciousness.[66] Even though a valid sense consciousness's main object—the held object—is correct, it appears incorrectly. However, the way that a sense consciousness holds its object does not include holding it as inherently existent.[67] It simply appears to exist inherently. This mistaken appearance does not harm the validity of an undistorted sense consciousness. An ordinary visual consciousness is valid, even though it sees things as inherently existent when they are not. This is because that appearance alone does not negate the conventional validity of that consciousness. On the other hand, if there are temporary causes of error that interfere with the consciousness perceiving things correctly, then even according to ordinary worldly understanding, that sense consciousness is invalid. What that consciousness sees does not in fact exist as it appears, even at a more superficial level. Realizing this does not require an understanding of śūnyatā.

Candrakīrti says in the *Introduction to the "Middle Way"*:

> It is said that there are two types of mistaken seeing:
> With clear sense organs and with faulty sense organs.
> A consciousness with faulty sense organs is said to be wrong
> In comparison to a consciousness with good sense organs.
>
> It is taught that whatever is known by worldly beings
> Through being apprehended by the six faultless sense organs
> Is true from the worldly perspective;
> The rest is wrong from the worldly perspective.

There are two types of mistaken seeing: subtle and gross. According to the Prāsaṅgika-Madhyamaka system, sentient beings see everything as inherently existent. This is the subtle way of seeing things mistakenly. Our subtle sense organs—the five physical sense powers and the mental sense power—may be either clear or faulty. Some monastic textbooks interpret the phrase "clear sense organs" to mean sense consciousnesses that do not have any temporary cause of error; so we can say that gross mistaken seeing only occurs in connection with faulty sense organs, whereas subtle mistaken seeing occurs even in connection with clear sense organs. In any case, a faulty sense organ constitutes an internal temporary cause of error.

Temporary causes of error, whether internal or external, make an object appear in a distorted manner. If a sense consciousness is affected by an internal or external temporary cause of error, what it sees is not correct. Internal causes of error include diseases, such as cataracts or jaundice, and the effects of hallucinogenic drugs. These internal causes may make us see hairs falling in front of us even though there are none, see white things as yellow, see double images, and so on. External causes of error involve exterior conditions, such as specific locations. For example, the first time I traveled on a speeding train, I looked out of the window and saw all the trees and hills running past! My visual consciousness mistakenly saw those objects moving. Another example of an external cause of error is an airplane propeller spinning so fast that we cannot see the individual blades; we see one vibrating ring. The ring is not there; it is a mistaken perception. The cause of error is not the eye sense power; it is the external motion of the propeller. Finally, even the mental consciousness may be affected by temporary causes of error. For example, people may hold wrong views because they rely on ideas propounded by some school of thought. According to ordinary worldly understanding, these peoples' minds are temporarily influenced in a completely wrong way. I am not talking about subtle wrong views concerning inherent existence here.

When influenced by temporary causes of error, the six primary consciousnesses hold their objects incorrectly. This is gross mistaken seeing; everyone, without needing to realize śūnyatā, knows that this is wrong. The subject and object are both incorrect from the point of view of ordinary conventional knowledge. A correct object is one that is apprehended by an undistorted consciousness—a consciousness not affected by any temporary cause of error. So from the perspective of worldly or conventional understanding, there are two types of objects and two types of consciousness: correct or undistorted, and wrong or distorted.

In the context of Candrakīrti's verse above, "from the worldly perspective" has a special meaning. It refers to the perspective of those who have not realized śūnyatā at all.[68] So the following formal criteria are presented. A "correct consciousness from the worldly perspective" is a consciousness that *cannot* be established as wrong by conventional valid knowledge within the continuum of a person who has not realized emptiness. A "wrong consciousness from the worldly perspective" is a consciousness that *can* be established as wrong by conventional valid knowledge within the continuum of a person who has not realized emptiness. A "correct object from the worldly perspective" is an object that *cannot* be established to not exist as it appears by that kind of valid knowledge. A "wrong object from the worldly perspective" is an object that *can* be established to not exist as it appears by that kind of valid knowledge.

In general it is accepted that when impaired by temporary causes of error, a consciousness and its object are wrong from the perspective of ordinary conventional knowledge within the continuum of someone who has not realized śūnyatā; when not impaired by temporary causes of error, the consciousness and its object are correct from that perspective. However, there are some exceptions to this general rule. Consider the innate mind holding the person to be self-sufficient and substantially existent. This is a conventional mind unaffected by temporary causes of error. So it meets the above-stated criteria for being a correct worldly consciousness. However, it is distorted from the point of view of conventional truth, because valid knowledge can understand such a mind to be distorted without having realized śūnyatā. Such a consciousness is wrong even from the conventional point of view. So this is an exceptional case. Now consider a contrived mind that holds the person to be truly existent owing to the influence of false tenets. That profound ignorance is not wrong from the worldly perspective, because no ordinary conventional consciousness can understand it to be distorted. We cannot understand this consciousness or its object to be distorted until we understand śūnyatā. Yet this mind is affected by temporary causes of error, because it arises only through the influence of false tenets that posit things to be truly existent. So it is also a special case.

Candrakīrti's *Commentary on the "Introduction to the 'Middle Way'"* offers the following account of internal and external temporary causes of error:

> Cataracts, jaundice, and so on, as well as eating datura, are internal conditions impairing the subtle sense organs. Sesame butter, water, mirrors, sounds uttered in caves, as well as sunlight in certain places at certain times, and so on, are external conditions impairing the subtle sense organs. This is because, even without the internal causes of impairment of the sense organs, they cause the apprehension of things such as reflections, echoes, and mirages. Understand the substances and spells applied by magicians in this way as well. As for the external causes of error affecting the mental consciousness, there are those mentioned above as well as incorrect tenets and false reasoning.

Candrakīrti's list of external conditions that cause errors in perception may seem a bit odd to modern readers, but they were common examples in ancient India. You might wonder, "How does sesame butter affect perception?" Well, it could be applied to a torch, which then appears as a ring of fire when whirled around very fast. Or as a magical substance, it might be spread on the eyelids of people in an audience to assist in the creation of an illusion. Water can be an external cause of error when it reflects the moon. Mirrors may create illusions by reflecting objects so that those reflections appear to be the actual things. Echoes may sound like actual voices coming from deep inside a cave. Sunlight may cause a mirage, where a sandy area in the distance appears to be a pool of water. In ancient India, and perhaps other places, magicians would put spells on certain objects so that they would appear differently. For example, sticks and stones would appear to be living elephants and horses for as long as the power of the spell lasted. These magicians would also use certain substances, perhaps drugs, to confuse their audience. Contemporary magicians in the West use physical and psychological tricks; they do not use drugs, mantras, and spells, do they? Different types of temporary causes of error can affect the mental consciousness. Wrong views, as well as what seem to be good logical reasons but in fact are not, give rise to an incorrect mental consciousness. Sleep is also a temporary cause of error because it is the cause of dreams that affect the mental consciousness.

The impairment of being influenced by ignorance is not to be taken as the cause of error in the context of ordinary conventional knowledge; in other words, an object's appearing to be inherently existent does not damage the validity of ordinary awareness. Nevertheless, the object as held by ignorance does not exist even conventionally. Here we are talking about an object as grasped by ignorance to be truly existent—we are not referring to an object independently of how it is grasped. It is the object of ignorance's way of holding: the held object of ignorance. Whenever we ordinary beings see something, it always appears to be inherently existent; that appearance does not damage conventional validity. Then, as soon as we see it, we may immediately hold it in this way. This way of holding an object is known as "grasping at a self." To understand what this means, we should consider the relationship between the basis of the attribute and the attribute itself. The object grasped by ignorance is inherent existence (the attribute) mingled with the basis of the attribute (such as a table). The table is held to be inherently existent. That held object does not exist at all—whether you consider it to be the table as inherently existent or inherent existence itself. Tsongkhapa says he will deal with this topic later.

Here Tsongkhapa's point is that the influence of innate ignorance on what appears to the mind is not considered to be a cause of error from the worldly perspective. This is because the correctness and incorrectness under consideration here is based on ordinary mundane knowledge, to which everything appears inherently existent (though not necessarily grasped in that way). The sense powers and sense consciousnesses that are not influenced by temporary internal or external causes of error are undistorted in terms of ordinary worldly knowing, and their objects are likewise correct. When the six consciousnesses are affected by internal or external temporary causes of error, both the subject—the sense powers and sense consciousnesses—as well as any objects appearing to them, such as a mirage, are distorted and false in terms of worldly knowledge. Whether or not they are affected by temporary causes of error, the six primary consciousnesses of all sentient beings are influenced by the imprints deposited in the mindstream by the arising of innate ignorance that holds things to be inherently existent. However, this is not a temporary cause of error; it is a deep cause of error that remains until enlightenment.

This brings up the question of interpretation. Suppose someone asserts: "If the five sense consciousnesses are unmistaken in a conventional sense when unimpaired by causes of error other than ignorance, then the inherent nature that appears to them must conventionally exist. But the master Candrakīrti does not assert this. Therefore we must accept that such consciousnesses are mistaken. In that case, those consciousnesses cannot validly establish forms, sounds, and so on conventionally because in a conventional sense they are mistaken with regard to forms and so on."

THE CITTAMĀTRA AND THE SVĀTANTRIKA-MADHYAMAKA INTERPRETATIONS

Tsongkhapa gives a long answer to this point of view. He begins by discussing Bhāvaviveka's rejection of the Cittamātra position. In order to understand Tsongkhapa's point, we need to know something about the Cittamātra view as well as the view of Bhāvaviveka. The different tenet systems are based on Buddha's teachings in the three turnings of the wheel of Dharma. In the first turning of the wheel, Buddha teaches from an affirmative point of view; he presents production, karma, samsara, the four noble truths, nirvana, and so forth as though they are truly existent. In the second turning of the wheel, Buddha teaches the *Perfection of Wisdom Sutras*, where he presents birth, aging, sickness, and death as having no essential nature; he explains that no phenomena exist inherently. So in the first turning of the wheel of Dharma, Buddha says that things exist by way of their own characteristics; in the second turning he says that they do not exist by way of their own characteristics. The apparent contradiction troubled some of Buddha's disciples, and they requested further explanation. So Buddha turned the wheel of Dharma for a third time and taught the *Sutra Unraveling the Intended Meaning*. A chapter called "Questions of the Bodhisattva Paramārthasamudgata" in this sutra recounts the request and presents Buddha's clarification of the first and second turnings of the wheel of the Dharma. Here Buddha explains the three natures of phenomena to show the way in which things exist and the way in which they do not exist. The Cittamātra or Yogācāra views—which are the same in most respects—are based on this teaching. They accept the third turning of the wheel of the Dharma as definitive and the first and second turnings as provisional.

The *Sutra Unraveling the Intended Meaning* teaches that all phenomena (or *dharmas*) have three natures: a dependent nature, a thoroughly established nature, and an imputed nature. The *dependent nature* is the causally conditioned nature of a thing. The *thoroughly established nature* is the ultimate nature of a thing. The *imputed nature* is the merely nominally or conceptually constructed nature of a thing. A thing's dependent nature and thoroughly established nature are really true. They are inherently existent and established by their own characteristics. A thing's imputed nature is not really true. It is not inherently existent and not established by its own characteristics. There are two types of imputed nature: an imputed nature that is existent but not inherently existent, such as the general characteristics of a thing, and an imputed nature that is totally nonexistent. An example of an existent imputed nature is "a table as held to be an object of knowledge." This is posited merely in dependence on name and thought; it does not exist inherently. An example of a nonexistent imputed nature is "a table as held to be a different entity from the mind perceiving it." According to the Cittamātra system, this duality of subject and object, where the perceiver and the perceived object are held to be different entities, does not exist at all. It is the object to be negated by the path. Other examples of nonexistent imputed natures are a rabbit horn and a sky flower. In the case of any phenomenon, the dependent nature is taken as the basis; on this basis, a specific imputed nature, the duality of subject and object, is negated; and the absence of this imputed nature is the thoroughly established nature. So we can say that the thoroughly established nature is an attribute of the basis; it is a thing's highest attribute—its śūnyatā. However, according to the Cittamātra system, this śūnyatā is still inherently existent.

The Cittamātra view is based on the *Sutra Unraveling the Intended Meaning*, and followers of this school take this sutra to be definitive. They consider that Buddha's teaching in the *Perfection of Wisdom Sutras* that "all phenomena have no essential nature" must be interpreted to apply to each of the three natures in a particular way. Vasubandhu explains how each of the three natures is natureless in a specific sense: all phenomena have an imputed nature that lacks inherent existence, all phenomena have a dependent nature that lacks self-production, and all phenomena have a thoroughly established nature that lacks ultimately established duality. He says in *Thirty Stanzas* (*Trimśikā-kārikā*):

> Having considered the three natures,
> All three of which lack a nature,
> He teaches [in the *Perfection of Wisdom Sutras*]
> That all phenomena are natureless. (23)

Bhāvaviveka rejects the Cittamātra view that imputed natures lack inherent existence. For he accepts that everything exists inherently, or by way of its own characteristics, conventionally. According to Bhāvaviveka, anything that exists must exist inherently, by its own nature, or by way of its own characteristics. If a thing does not exist by its own nature, then it does not exist at all. Furthermore, he says that although things exist by their own characteristics conventionally, they do not exist by their own characteristics ultimately. Bhāvaviveka and the Cittamātrins have different interpretations of what it means for something to exist inherently or to exist by way of its own characteristics. According to the Cittamātra system, "inherently existent," "ultimately existent," and "truly existent" mean the same thing; according to Bhāvaviveka, "ultimately existent" and "truly existent" mean the same thing, but "inherently existent" means something different.

Bhāvaviveka argues that when the Cittamātrins assert that the imputed nature is not inherently existent, they implicitly deny the existence of the dependent nature and the ultimate nature. He says that when talking about imputation, we must consider two aspects: the object that is imputed and the agent that imputes it. The agent may be a person, a thought, or a word, which are dependent natures according to the Cittamātrins. The basis on which the imputation is made is also a dependent nature. So Bhāvaviveka argues, if the Cittamātrins deny the inherent existence of imputed objects, they deny the mere existence of imputed objects. This is because, according to Bhāvaviveka, if something does not exist inherently then it does not exist at all. Since the Cittamātrins deny the (inherent) existence of imputed natures, there cannot be anything that imputes them nor any basis on which they are imputed. If there is no imputed object, then there is no imputation going on at all. The imputer and the basis of imputation are considered to be dependent natures. If these do not exist, then the Cittamātrins are denying dependent natures. If the Cittamātrins deny the existence of dependent natures, they are committed to denying the existence of any ultimate nature. This is because there cannot be an ultimate nature without a dependent nature, because the ultimate nature is an attribute of the dependent nature. Therefore if the Cittamātrins deny the inherent existence of the imputed nature, they end up denying the existence of the dependent nature and the ultimate nature. This is how Bhāvaviveka refutes their system.

Tsongkhapa says that it is clear from Bhāvaviveka's arguments against the Cittamātrins that he accepts dependent natures to be inherently existent conventionally. According to Bhāvaviveka, "to exist" means to exist inherently or by its own characteristics; however, as a Mādhyamika, he does not accept that anything exists ultimately. So when we classify his views, we can see that Bhāvaviveka is a Mādhyamika who asserts the emptiness of truly existent things and the emptiness of ultimately existent things but does not assert the emptiness of inherently existent things or the emptiness of things existing by their own characteristics. Bhāvaviveka gives reasons for his position that things conventionally inherently exist. For example, in his *Lamp for the "Fundamental Treatise"* (*Prajñā-pradīpa-mūla-madhyamaka-vṛtti*), where he comments on the twenty-fifth chapter of Nāgārjuna's text, Bhāvaviveka says:

> If you say there is no imputed nature that is the verbal or mental expression *form*, then you are denying the existence of things because you are denying the existence of mental and verbal expressions.

Let us examine an imputed nature, such as the word *form*. How does the object "form" exist as the referent of the word *form*? In other words, when we think "This is a form," how does a form exist as the object of that thought? Does it exist by its own characteristics? Or is there some kind of imputed nature in between the word and the object? This is a difficult question to answer within the context of the Cittamātra understanding of śūnyatā. In short, the Cittamātrins do not say that the imputed nature does not exist; they say that it does not exist inherently or by its own characteristics. However, according to Bhāvaviveka, if something does not exist inherently, then it does not exist at all. So he believes that the Cittamātrins deny the existence of imputation—and therefore the thoughts and words that impute, which are causally produced and dependent; thus they deny the existence of dependent natures.

To clarify Bhāvaviveka's position, Tsongkhapa quotes from Avalokitavrata's *Explanatory Commentary on the "Lamp for the 'Fundamental Treatise'"* (*Prajñā-pradīpa-ṭīkā*):

> That [passage by Bhāvaviveka] indicates that according to the Yogācāras, the imputed nature lacks a nature because it lacks an inherently existent nature. However, since this negates dependent things conventionally, it is incorrect to say that what is mentally conceived or conventionally labeled as "form"—whether the thing itself or its attributes—lacks a nature because it lacks an inherently existent nature.

There are two types of imputation. We can impute a thing itself, such as by saying or thinking "This is a form." Or we can impute a thing's attributes, such as by saying or thinking "Form is produced." When we name something or think about something, we identify it—and this is an imputed nature. According to the Cittamātrins, that imputed nature does not exist by way of its own characteristics and therefore lacks an inherent nature. Avalokitavrata's point is that in saying this imputed nature lacks inherent existence, we are denying the existence of the dependent nature of thoughts and words even conventionally—and this is incorrect.

Tsongkhapa now examines the Cittamātra view that all phenomena have no essential nature, in terms of each of the three natures, in reliance on the *Sutra Unraveling the Intended Meaning*. It is important to clarify the use of terminology when saying that imputed natures lack an inherent nature. The Tibetan term translated here as "inherent nature" (*rang gi mtshan nyid*, Skt: *svalakṣaṇa*) is translated in most other contexts as "own characteristics," usually in a phrase referring to a thing's defining characteristics; but it does not have that meaning here. In this context, the literal term *own characteristic nature* means "inherent nature." According to the Cittamātra, "established by its own characteristics" and "established by its own nature" mean the same thing. The Cittamātra interpretation of "existing by its own characteristics" is similar to *ultimately existent* or *truly existent*. They assert that imputed natures do not exist by way of their own characteristics and thus they lack an inherent nature.

A dependent nature exists by its own characteristics and thus has an inherent nature. However, according to this sutra, a dependent nature lacks a produced nature. Someone may argue that because dependent natures have an inherent nature, they have an essential nature, and because dependent natures arise from causes and conditions, they have a produced nature. So how can Buddha have said that they lack a produced nature? In this context, *produced nature* does not refer to being produced from causes and conditions; it refers to being produced from itself. Since dependent natures are produced from other factors, they lack a self-produced nature; so it can be said that they lack a produced nature. In the first stanza of the *Fundamental Treatise*, Nāgārjuna argues that things are not produced from themselves, not produced from others, not produced from both, and not produced without cause. The position that dependent natures lack a produced nature refers to the first limb of this argument: dependent natures lack a nature in that they lack a self-produced nature.

A thoroughly established nature is an ultimately established nature. So what does Buddha mean when he says that it lacks an *ultimately established nature*? In this context, it means that it lacks an ultimately established dualistic nature.

The Cittamātrins believe that Buddha was referring to these three different ways that phenomena lack an essential nature when he taught the *Perfection of Wisdom Sutras*. Since it was not explicitly stated there, the Cittamātrins say that those teachings are provisional and require further interpretation. In other words, the negations in the *Perfection of Wisdom Sutras* are not to be taken literally; there is a deeper, implicit meaning that is Buddha's actual intention. So how should we interpret the *Perfection of Wisdom Sutras*? According to the Cittamātrins, the *Sutra Unraveling the Intended Meaning* provides the correct interpretation of the teachings given in the second turning of the wheel of Dharma. They say it expresses the implicit meaning of the *Perfection of Wisdom Sutras*, which they take as provisional. So they accept the *Sutra Unraveling the Intended Meaning* as definitive. Certain Mādhyamikas, such as Bhāvaviveka and Kamalaśīla, also accept that the *Sutra Unraveling the Intended Meaning* expresses the meaning of the phrase "All phenomena have no essential nature" found in the *Perfection of Wisdom Sutras*. They consider this phrase to mean that each phenomenon has its own three natures and corresponding lack of essential natures—rather than that all phenomena lack inherent existence. So they also accept the *Sutra Unraveling the Intended Meaning* as definitive, but they say it expresses the explicit meaning of the *Perfection of Wisdom Sutras*, which they take as definitive. Kamalaśīla says in *Illumination of the Middle Way*:

> Because that sutra teaches the middle way free of the two extremes by showing the intended meaning to be the three kinds of naturelessness, it is established as a strictly definitive scripture.

Kamalaśīla's interpretation of the three natures is not exactly the same as the Cittamātra interpretation. His view of the emptiness of the imputed nature is that of the Yogācāra-Svātantrika-Madhyamaka. According to this school of thought, if something exists then it must be inherently existent; if it is not inherently existent, then it must be nonexistent. According to Kamalaśīla, the Madhyamaka system of the *Perfection of Wisdom Sutras* teaches that all things, from form to omniscience, have a dependent nature. This dependent nature is incorrectly thought to be ultimately existent. An ultimately existent dependent nature is an imputation. Such an imputation does not exist by way of its own characteristics. That is what is meant by the phrase "imputed natures do not exist inherently." It does not mean that dependent natures do not inherently exist. When the *Sutra Unraveling the Intended Meaning* says that the imputed nature does not exist inherently, it is rejecting the ultimate existence of the dependent nature. An ultimately existent dependent nature is an imputation; that kind of imputation does not exist inherently—indeed, it does not exist at all. Dependent things are not ultimately existent; however, they do exist. They are conventionally existent; therefore, conventionally they are inherently existent. Dependent natures inherently exist conventionally but do not exist truly or ultimately. This is how the two extremes of super-imposition (ultimate existence) and repudiation (nonexistence) are avoided. This is the middle way. Therefore Kamalaśīla says that the *Sutra Unraveling the Intended Meaning* teaches the Madhyamaka path. By eliminating both extremes it establishes the teaching of the *Perfection of Wisdom Sutras* as definitive. Therefore according to Kamalaśīla, the *Sutra Unraveling the Intended Meaning* cannot be a definitive sutra for the Cittamātra, since it establishes the Madhyamaka view.

THE PRĀSAṄGIKA-MADHYAMAKA INTERPRETATION

To summarize briefly, there was a two-part assertion put forward by an opponent earlier: "If the five sense consciousnesses are unmistaken in a conventional sense when unimpaired by causes of error other than ignorance, then the inherent nature that appears to them must conventionally exist. If it does not, then such consciousnesses must be mistaken. In that case, they cannot validly establish forms, sounds, and so on conventionally because in a conventional sense they are mistaken with regard to forms and so on." In answer to this, Tsongkhapa first goes over Bhāvaviveka's Sautrāntika-Svātantrika-Madhyamaka view that the dependent nature inherently exists conventionally. Then he shows that Kamalaśīla, a Yogācāra-Svātantrika-Mādhyamika, accepts this too. Now he presents the Prāsaṅgika-Madhyamaka view based on an example in Candrakīrti's *Commentary on the "Introduction to the 'Middle Way.'"* This is the classical example of mistaking a coiled rope for a snake, which may be familiar to you. Just as a snake posited on a rope is an imputed nature, but when posited on an actual snake it is a real existent, so an ultimate nature based on something that dependently arises is an imputed nature, but as an object of a buddha's knowledge it is a real existent. In this example, the imputer is the mind thinking of the concept or forming the word "snake." When this is imputed on a rope, it is a false imputation, not a real snake; in contrast, when it is imputed on an actual snake, then it is real. Similarly, if an ultimate nature is posited on a dependent nature, it is an imputed nature; but if the ultimate nature is established as an object of a buddha's knowledge, it is perfectly real. This is because a dependent nature is a conventional nature; it does not exist as the ultimate nature. However, if the ultimate nature is established as an object of a buddha's knowledge, it is perfectly real. When a buddha sees the ultimate nature of all phenomena, that ultimate nature exists: it is the final nature of things—śūnyatā.

What a buddha sees is perfectly real. However, this does not mean that it exists inherently. Here, once again we have to be very careful about terminology. In this context, *ultimate nature* does not mean inherent existence. It would be wrong to say, "Inherent existence based on a dependent nature is an imputed nature, but as an object of a buddha's knowledge it is perfectly real." Even a buddha cannot see inherent existence, because inherent existence does not exist. So here *ultimate nature* means the final nature or ultimate truth. This ultimate nature is existent as an object of a buddha's knowledge. Candrakīrti says that this is how we should understand the presentation of the three natures, and we should explain the meaning of the *Sutra Unraveling the Intended Meaning* accordingly.

Candrakīrti's *Introduction to the "Middle Way"* says:

> Any sutra that explains what is not ultimate reality
> Explains the provisional; having realized this, you must interpret it.

Remember, according to the Prāsaṅgika system sutras that primarily explain conventional reality are provisional sutras. Even though what that sutra teaches may be literally acceptable, it is still considered provisional. For example, the statement "All products are impermanent" is literally acceptable, yet it is provisional because it does not express the definitive, final nature of reality. We must interpret it in order to reach the ultimate meaning, śūnyatā. The next line in the above verse from Candrakīrti's work is:[69]

> Those that explain emptiness are to be understood as definitive.

Sutras that directly and principally explain śūnyatā are definitive. Given that Candrakīrti explains the provisional and definitive in this way, it is clear that he considers the presentation of the three natures in the *Sutra Unraveling the Intended Meaning* to be provisional. According to his Prāsaṅgika system, the imputed nature is inherent existence, which is imputed on a dependent nature; this inherently established nature, based on a dependent nature, does not exist even conventionally. In contrast, Bhāvaviveka, Kamalaśīla, and the Cittamātrins accept that an inherently existent nature, based on a dependent nature, exists conventionally. This is one of the main differences between these schools of thought.

The Cittamātrins maintain that dependent natures and thoroughly established natures have an inherently existent nature; it is only the imputed natures that lack inherent existence. There are two types of imputed natures: imputed natures that do not exist and those that do exist. A *mere imputation* does not exist at all. For example, the Cittamātrins consider everything to be only in the nature of the mind; in their view, external objects are mere imputations because external objects, independent of the nature of the mind, do not exist at all. The Cittamātrins also assert the emptiness of duality. So the notion that subject and object are different entities is also a mere imputation. These mere, nonexistent imputations should be negated on the basis of the dependent natures that they are incorrectly imputed on. A thing's thoroughly established nature is its dependent nature being empty of such an imputed nature. The second type of imputation exists. However, these are *merely existent* in that they are imputed by name and thought; they do not exist by their own characteristics. The Cittamātra, Sautrāntika, and other systems posit many merely existent imputations: generalities (such as singularity and relationship) and abstract things (such as uncaused space). Merely existent imputations include anything that is an existent object of thought, for example the form that is the object of the thought "this is a form." In this sense, the thought and the words that express it are the subject, and the object is form. The words and thought are dependent natures. Form also is a dependent nature. However, "form as the object of that thought" is an imputation. Similarly, "form as the object of the word *form*" is an imputation. It exists, but it is an imputation. So according to the Cittamātra, it does not truly exist because it does not exist by way of its own characteristics.

It seems that the Cittamātra and Yogācāra systems rely primarily on the *Sutra Unraveling the Intended Meaning.* They contend that both the dependent nature and the thoroughly established nature exist inherently or by their own characteristics. Therefore they accept that both these natures are ultimately existent. According to the masters Buddhapālita and Candrakīrti, if anything exists by way of its own characteristics, then it must be ultimately existent or truly existent. In their Prāsaṅgika system, the following terms are synonymous: existing by way of its own characteristics, truly existent, ultimately existent, and inherently existent. Bhāvaviveka and other Svātantrika-Mādhyamikas, such as Śāntarakṣita and Kamalaśīla, consider that these terms are different; they say that merely having a nature that exists by way of its own characteristics does not entail being truly existent.

THE DEBATE ABOUT WHETHER EXTERNAL OBJECTS CAUSE SENSE PERCEPTION

The Cittamātrins deny the existence of external objects altogether and argue that everything is in the nature of the mind. They say that the mind—specifically, the substratum consciousness—contains certain seeds or potentialities that ripen as two aspects: the subject and the object. The best example to illustrate this is an object in a dream. An elephant in a dream does not exist as an external thing; it exists merely in the nature of the dreamer's mind. The dream object and the dreaming consciousness arise together; the dream object does not exist somewhere first with the dreaming consciousness arising internally later to perceive it. The dream object and the perceiving subject both arise from the same substance, the same potentiality, within the mindstream. The Cittamātrins contend that ordinary perception functions in the same way. The subject and the object appear dualistically, but they are the same nature, the same substance, because they ripen from one seed or potential. That is the general idea.

The Cittamātrins try to negate the existence of external objects as posited by other Buddhist schools such as the Sautrāntika school. The Sautrāntikas say that a perceiving subject and its perceived object are substantially different. The sense and mental consciousnesses arise through coming into contact with external things that objectively exist. Those external things are already there, and an appropriate sense consciousness then perceives them. How do external things come into existence? To begin with, there are eight types of subtle physical atoms—earth, fire, water, air, form, smell, taste, and tangible substance—which combine in different proportions to become grosser objects of the senses. The objects that are formed from various collections of atoms act as causes of their respective observing consciousnesses, such as seeing, smelling, tasting, and so on. The perceiving subject arises as a result of the external thing. This is a causal relationship; therefore the object and subject are different entities or different natures. Bhāvaviveka accepts that external objects exist in a similar way on a conventional level. Even the Prāsaṅgikas accept that on a conventional level external atoms build up and act as a cause for the arising of a sense consciousness, thus being a different entity from the perceiving consciousness; however, they do not accept that any such atoms are partless.

Vasubandhu's *Treasury of Knowledge* differentiates between two kinds of atomic particles: substantial atoms (*rdzas rdul phra rab*) and aggregated atoms (*bsags rdul phra rab*). Substantial atoms are individual atoms included among the eight substances: the four great elements—earth, water, fire, and wind; and the four substances arisen from them—form, smell, taste, and tangible substance.[70] When these substantial atoms collect together to form particles that are just about visible, they are called aggregated atoms. These tiny particles accumulate further to make grosser particles, eventually becoming things, such as pots or mountains. The Vaibhāṣika and Sautrāntika schools believe that the smallest atoms cannot be divided any further. This is equivalent to saying that these atoms are partless. Dignāga and other masters offer proof that there are no partless atoms nor indeed anything that is partless. Their argument is that if a partless atom existed, it would have no directional parts— it would be indivisible. However, that is logically impossible. Suppose there are five atoms together: one above, one below, one to the right, one to the left, and one in the middle. If those atoms are partless, then what about the middle atom? If the side of the middle atom that faces right touches the atom to the right, and that side does not touch the atom to the left, then it clearly has a part on the right and a part on the left. So it is not partless—it is divisible. Similarly, if the side of the atom that faces up touches the atom above it but not the atom below it, then it must have an upper part and a lower part. An atom can only be considered partless if in touching an atom next to itself in one direction, it thereby touches all the atoms in all the directions. Only if the whole of it touches the east and simultaneously touches the west could it be considered partless. If atoms were like that, then no matter how many atoms joined together, the whole would never get any bigger. Modern scientists seem to agree that all atomic particles are divisible and cannot be partless. That is nice—scientists are following Buddhist logic!

The Cittamātrins argue that what appear to be external objects cannot be composed of atomic substances; they cannot exist as posited by these other schools. Two reasons are presented here: first, individual atoms are not the objects of sense consciousnesses because they do not appear to those consciousnesses; and second, a collection of many atoms together is not an object of sense consciousness because it does not exist substantially—like the appearance of two moons. Although two moons may appear to some people, they lack substantial existence.

Bhāvaviveka, who mainly follows the Sautrāntika system with regard to the assertion of external objects, replies to these Cittamātra arguments in *Blaze of Reasons (Tarkajvālā)*. In response to the Cittamātrins' first reason he says:

> If you are trying to prove that a single atom unconnected with any others is not perceived by the subtle sense organs, then you are proving what we have already established.

Bhāvaviveka accuses the Cittamātrins of committing the logical fallacy of proving what has already been established by the opponent. He then responds to the second Cittamātra argument in the *Blaze of Reasons*:

> Arguing that a collection of atoms of similar type, after having gathered together, is not a cause [of sense consciousness] because it does not exist substantially is not a reason accepted by the other party: [myself]. This is because atoms of similar type assist one another in collecting together, and having formed parts of a gross object, give rise to a mind that has the collection of atoms appearing to it. We accept things like pots, which are [formed] from an aggregation of atoms of similar type, to be substances, just like the atoms. This is because even [aggregated] atoms are in the nature of a collection of the eight substances, and just as they are explicitly accepted to be substances, so the things that are collections of them, such as pots, are also substances. A solitary one is not established.

Here Bhāvaviveka is discussing aggregated atoms of similar type.[71] He himself (as the opponent in the debate against the Cittamātra position) accepts that aggregated atoms, which are subtle particles in the nature of the eight substances, are themselves substances. Each individual atom within a gross object is accepted to be a cause of the sense consciousness perceiving that object because these atoms together act as a cause of the sense consciousness. When we see a mountain we see the aggregated atoms or particles that compose the mountain. When we see a pot, it is the aggregated atoms composing it that causes the visual consciousness to arise. So each of these tiny atoms is a cause of the consciousness perceiving the aggregation—the gross object. However, a solitary atom, not conjoined with anything else, cannot give rise to visual consciousness. This is what the passage means when it says "A solitary one is not established." It is not saying that there are no partless atoms; it is saying that a single atom alone is not an object of sense consciousness. However, when an atom is conjoined with other atoms to form a particle, it is an object of the senses.

Bhāvaviveka appears to accept that individual aggregated atoms are a cause of sense consciousness and therefore substantially existent; he also seems to accept that these atoms are the smallest limit, which implies that partless atoms can function as an object condition of visual consciousness. In order for perception to occur, four conditions must be present: the object condition, the empowering condition, the immediately preceding condition, and the causal condition. The *object condition* is the perceived object. The *empowering condition* is a subtle sense organ—the sense power. If the object condition—a substantially existent aggregation of atoms—is not present, then a sense consciousness perceiving it cannot arise. For example, a visual consciousness seeing blue depends on the external existence of something blue. As explained earlier, according to the Sautrāntika-Svātantrika-Madhyamaka system, a sense consciousness that is not affected by an external or internal cause of error is unmistaken. The ordinary visual consciousness seeing blue is perfectly correct, as long as it is not affected by temporary causes of error. So there is no confusion regarding the external object: it is real, and it is seen directly in the way that it exists. That is what *direct perception* means here.

To a certain extent, Bhāvaviveka posits the object condition in a similar way to the Sautrāntikas. The difference is that the Sautrāntikas say that a sense consciousness is ultimate knowledge because its object is an ultimate truth. For them, ultimate truths are real things that causally depend on other conditions in the world; conversely, conventional truths lack that kind of substantive reality, and they exist merely in dependence on thoughts and words. Ultimate truths are established by ultimate knowledge; ultimate knowledge is direct perception that is unmistaken and directly sees its object as it is. In contrast, Bhāvaviveka considers that the object condition is not truly or ultimately existent; it is conventionally existent.

Now we have a tricky question: "Does Bhāvaviveka accept that things *appear* to be truly or ultimately existent?" He accepts that the sense consciousnesses are unmistaken in that they directly see their objects as they really exist. For example, he says that the blue perceived by a visual consciousness appears to be external, and that it is an external object. He also accepts that things appear to be inherently existent, and that they are inherently existent, just as they appear to be—but only conventionally. Direct perception, according to him, is unmistaken regarding the appearance of inherent existence. But it is illogical for Bhāvaviveka to accept that an unmistaken sense consciousness perceives its object to be truly existent—because according to him such an appearance is false; things do not exist that way. So if he says that sense consciousnesses are unmistaken, then he cannot accept that things appear to the sense consciousnesses to be truly or ultimately existent.

The Prāsaṅgikas consistently maintain that all ordinary sense consciousnesses are mistaken, in that things appear to exist inherently yet do not exist in that way. The appearance of things existing inherently is a false appearance, according to them. So they say that valid sense perception is mistaken regarding the appearance of inherent existence, or true existence, or ultimate existence—all of which are synonymous in their system. Why is there this difference in approach between the Svātantrikas and Prāsaṅgikas? We should ask Bhāvaviveka! Candrakīrti's *Commentary on the "Introduction to the 'Middle Way'"* says:

> Some say that what the Sautrāntikas explain as ultimately existent is explained by the Mādhyamikas as conventionally existent. You should understand that whoever says this is speaking with utter ignorance of the nature of reality expressed in the *Fundamental Treatise*. Similarly, anyone who thinks that what the Vaibhāṣikas explain as ultimately existent is explained by the Mādhyamikas as conventionally existent also does not understand the nature of reality expressed in the *Fundamental Treatise*. This is because it is impossible for the supramundane teachings to be like the mundane teachings. Learned scholars must know that this system is unique.

The Vaibhāṣikas say that partless moments of consciousness and partless atoms are ultimately existent; they consider them to be the ultimate truth. Vasubandhu's *Treasury of Knowledge* defines the ultimate and the conventional as follows:

> If the mind no longer apprehends something
> When it is broken or mentally split up,

> Like a pot, then it is conventionally existent.
> What is other than that is ultimately existent. (6.4)

If we break a material object—such as a pot—into parts, then we lose the identification of it as a pot. The pieces are not the referent of the thought or word "pot." Even if we do not destroy the object physically but just mentally dissect it into parts, we have nothing left that can be identified as the referent of "pot." The thought "This is a pot" does not arise. An object that loses its identity when broken up in this way is conventionally existent and a conventional truth, according to the Vaibhāṣika system. Ultimately existent things cannot be physically destroyed or lose their identity when separated into parts; in other words, ultimately existent things are not divisible. Partless atoms or partless moments of time or consciousness are real ultimate truths. They are ultimate because their identity is always preserved.

There are certain tenets unique to the lower Buddhist systems that Candrakīrti does not accept even conventionally; he does not accept partless atoms or partless moments of consciousness at all. So it is wrong to say that whatever the Vaibhāṣikas explain to be ultimately existent is accepted by the Mādhyamikas to be conventionally existent. Candrakīrti makes this very clear in his *Commentary on the "Four Hundred Stanzas"*:

> It is not correct for our own schools to accept substantially existent atoms, as do the Vaiśeṣika.

The Vaiśeṣika is one of six great non-Buddhist Indian philosophical schools.[72] They assert that all objects are included within six categories and that atoms are substantially existent. Some Buddhist schools also accept partless substantial atoms, which Candrakīrti considers to be a mistake. When he criticizes people who say that what the lower schools accept as ultimately existent is accepted by Mādhyamikas as conventionally existent, Candrakīrti is specifically referring to partless atoms. He is not saying that nothing that the lower schools assert to be truly existent is accepted by the Mādhyamikas to be conventionally existent. Some of what the lower schools assert to be truly existent *is* accepted by the Mādhyamikas to be conventionally existent. For example, the lower schools assert that form, sound, and so on are truly existent, and the Mādhyamikas accept these to be conventionally existent. However, Mādhyamikas do not accept partless atoms even conventionally.

Of the four conditions discussed above, the two main causes for a sense consciousness to perceive an object are: an internal sense power or subtle sense organ, which is the dominant or empowering condition, and an external thing, which is the object condition. In *Commentary on the "Four Hundred Stanzas,"* Candrakīrti rejects the idea that each of the atoms that combine to form a subtle sense organ is inherently a cause of a sense consciousness. He says that each one is a cause only in dependence on the others. The sense organ and its component atoms are not inherently the same or inherently different. The sense organ is not independent or separate from those atoms; the atoms are not truly different from the sense organ. They are interdependent and related like a possessor and its parts; neither exists by itself, truly, independently, or inherently. The sense organ is imputed in dependence on its parts; the parts are imputed in dependence on their whole or possessor. They are not ultimately the same or different. Therefore a sense organ that is mutually imputed on its parts functions as the causal basis of a sense consciousness. Similarly, an external object that gives rise to a sense consciousness is imputedly existent in dependence on its basis. For example, when we see a mountain, there is no mountain that exists absolutely from its own side. There are just particles on which "mountain" is imputed or labeled—and those particles themselves are merely imputed on their parts. Even something like "blue" has many parts. The perceived object is just relatively existent; it has an imputed nature. So according to the Prāsaṅgikas, both the object condition and the dominant condition are causes that are dependently imputed; they are not inherently or substantially existent causes. Thus the Prāsaṅgika account of the subject and object of perception is quite different from that presented by Bhāvaviveka or the Vaibhāṣikas.

Candrakīrti and Bhāvaviveka are similar in that they both accept external objects; but the way they posit the subtle sense organs and their objects is completely different. Bhāvaviveka accepts the sense organs and their objects to be inherently existent. Candrakīrti considers that there is no such thing as an inherently existent sense organ or its object; he says that, like consciousness, they have an imputed nature.

According to the lower schools, a correct sense consciousness is direct perception or direct knowing because it perceives its object directly. But an awareness that subsequently thinks of an object, previously directly perceived, is a conceptual consciousness; it is no longer direct. A correct thought consciousness is indirect knowing because it understands its object via a conceptual image. Inferential knowledge is a conceptual consciousness that arises on the basis of correct reasoning. In the phrase "direct perception," the word *direct* refers only to the subject side, the consciousness; it does not refer to the object of that consciousness.

The Prāsaṅgikas define *direct* in a completely different way; for them, *direct* (*mngon sum*) is virtually synonymous with *manifest* (*mngon 'gyur*) in this context. The Prāsaṅgikas consider the six sense consciousnesses to be only *nominally* direct, whereas their objects are *actually* direct. Here we must refer back to an earlier discussion about direct perception. All Buddhist systems categorize phenomena as either manifest or hidden. Manifest things can be understood or known without depending on logical reasoning; for example, we do not need to depend on anything other than our own experience to know forms, sounds, smells, tastes, and so on. In contrast, we know hidden things only in dependence on logical reasoning or some other thought process. For example, when I sit at a table, anything underneath it is blocked from my view. Although I cannot see an object underneath the table directly, I might know it through some other sign or reason. If I hear a meow coming from under the table, I can logically infer that there is a cat there. Otherwise, the cat is hidden from me. According to the Prāsaṅgika system, manifest objects are known directly through valid perception, and hidden objects are known indirectly through valid reasoning. The terms *direct* and *manifest* refer to the same things; the terms *indirect* and *hidden* refer to the same things. *Indirect* means that we must use a reason or a sign to know the object; it must be known through something else.

The difference between the lower schools and the Prāsaṅgika system is difficult to understand. According to the lower schools, an object of sense consciousness is known directly by its respective sense consciousness; so the sense consciousness is direct. According to the Prāsaṅgika system, the sense consciousness is not direct; its object is direct, or manifest. Whatever is seen, such as a color or a shape, is direct. The Prāsaṅgikas do not accept the lower schools' definition because although everyone assumes there is a visual consciousness, where is it? What does it look like? Is it a round thing like an eyeball or shaped like the subtle eye organ? No. The subtle eye organ in the eyeball acts as a basis or condition of the visual consciousness. The visual consciousness is what sees the object. Yet nobody actually knows the visual consciousness directly—it has to be proved by logic or some other method. Some of the lower schools posit a type of self-cognizing consciousness, whereby each consciousness has its own experience of itself when it arises. But the Prāsaṅgikas do not accept this. According to them, the actual direct or manifest things are the objects.

We may recall an earlier discussion in which Candrakīrti disproves the sense consciousnesses of unenlightened beings to be valid regarding inherent existence, "Because the thing exists in one way yet appears to exist in another way";[73] this shows that the sense consciousnesses are mistaken. When a sentient being's sense consciousness perceives a form, a sound, and so on, the object appears to exist from its own side; but it does not exist in that way even conventionally. Therefore Candrakīrti says that the five sense consciousnesses are mistaken even conventionally.

This mistaken appearance does not affect the conventional awareness of a buddha; it just affects those of sentient beings, which are mistaken owing to the imprints left by ignorance within the mindstream. These imprints are totally purified upon attaining full enlightenment, while ignorance itself is purified somewhat earlier. An object appearing to almost any consciousness within the mental continuum of a person prior to attaining buddhahood, including on the tenth bodhisattva stage, appears to exist inherently. The only exception is a direct realization of śūnyatā that occurs on the ārya levels of the path, where just the emptiness of inherent existence appears to the wisdom of meditative equipoise directly realizing śūnyatā. Conventional things, such as forms, sounds, and smells, do not appear to that uncontaminated wisdom; this is what it means when it says in the *Heart Sutra*, "There is no form, no sound, no smell, no taste," and so on. Prior to attaining buddhahood, any awareness that is not the direct realization of śūnyatā is mistaken, in that its object appears inherently existent. This means that except for when the uncontaminated wisdom directly realizing śūnyatā manifests in the mindstream of an ārya being, even the perception of an ārya is mistaken. This kind of mistaken perception even includes āryas' understanding of the four noble truths, impermanence, compassion, love, and conventional bodhicitta. The Prāsaṅgikas say that until the attainment of full enlightenment, an ārya's experience alternates in this way.

CONVENTIONAL AND ULTIMATE KNOWLEDGE AND THEIR RESPECTIVE OBJECTS

Now if the sense consciousnesses are mistaken regarding the appearance of inherent existence of their objects, does this mean that they are not valid knowledge? No, it does not. They are valid knowledge, even though they are mistaken consciousnesses. The only reason they are mistaken is that things do not exist inherently in the way that they appear. Although the sense consciousnesses are not valid regarding the appearance of inherent existence, they are valid regarding their particular objects themselves, such as forms, sounds, and so on. Ordinary people do not know that their sense consciousnesses are mistaken regarding the appearance of an inherent nature. That mistake cannot be understood by conventional valid knowledge. Only a mind engaging in the process of ultimate analysis that investigates whether things exist inherently can understand that those appearances are mistaken. In short, the sense consciousnesses are mistaken only from the perspective of ultimate knowledge.

Conventional knowledge cannot establish that the sense consciousnesses are mistaken regarding the appearance of inherent existence. So from the perspective of conventional knowledge, ordinary sense consciousnesses are correct and thus valid. Conventional knowledge can establish when a sense consciousness is confused by temporary causes of error. It can establish that the appearance of two moons or the appearance of a reflection as a real face do not exist as they appear. Most of us understand that these are incorrect without depending on ultimate analysis. Therefore according to the Prāsaṅgikas, a distorted sense consciousness—such as perceiving the appearance of two moons—is quite different from a normal sense consciousness unaffected by temporary causes of error, which is just mistaken regarding the appearance of inherent existence. The former is categorized as a distorted conventionality and the latter as a correct conventionality. The Svātantrika-Mādhyamikas also posit correct and distorted conventionalities, but they take these categories to apply only to the object. The Prāsaṅgikas take these categories to apply both to the object and to the subject, the perceiving consciousness. The appearance of two moons is an example of an object that is a distorted conventionality, and the consciousness to which two moons appear is an example of a subject that is a distorted conventionality. Conversely, the appearance of one moon, and the consciousness to which it appears, are correct conventionalities. So both an object and a subject can be either a distorted conventionality or a correct, nondistorted conventionality.

Now someone may raise the following objection. Although there is a difference between a mistaken consciousness that only valid knowledge analyzing the ultimate can understand to be mistaken, and a mistaken consciousness that conventional valid knowledge can understand to be mistaken, those two kinds of consciousness are the same in two respects. First, just as a reflection of a face does not exist as a real face although it appears to exist that way, an object appearing to a correct sense consciousness does not inherently exist although it appears to exist that way. Second, just as forms and so on that are empty of inherent existence do in fact exist, reflections that are empty of being an actual face also exist. So it may seem that, even in terms of ordinary conventional knowledge, no distinction can be made between distorted and nondistorted consciousnesses because both are mistaken.

Tsongkhapa agrees that a thing existing inherently and a thing existing as it appears in a reflection are similar in that both are conventionally nonexistent; things such as forms and reflections are similar in that both are conventionally existent. However, he suggests examining the following passage from Candrakīrti's *Commentary on the "Introduction to the 'Middle Way'"*:

> Some dependently arising things, such as reflections and echoes, even
> appear to be false to those possessing ignorance. Some things, such
> as blue, form, feeling, mind, and so on, appear to be truly existent to

them. The ultimate nature does not completely appear to those possessing ignorance. Therefore that nature and whatever is false even conventionally are not conventional truths.

The phrase "those possessing ignorance" refers to *minds* influenced by ignorance rather than to *persons* influenced by ignorance. The word "ignorance" is also ambiguous. Ignorance is a distorted awareness, a mental factor that holds things to be truly or inherently existent. It is the primary mental affliction: self-grasping. This fundamental ignorance is known as *afflictive ignorance*. When it arises, it deposits imprints in the mindstream that cause things to appear truly existent. These imprints are known as *nonafflictive ignorance*.[74] They give rise to the appearance of true existence even when afflictive ignorance is not actively functioning. Nonafflictive ignorance functions in all ordinary perception of sentient beings. Except for when sentient beings generate the supreme wisdom of meditative equipoise directly seeing śūnyatā, they have an appearance of true existence in the mind that conceals the ultimate nature of things. A mind affected by ignorance in this way cannot see emptiness directly. It sees only a conventional nature having an appearance of being truly existent, even though it is not. Sentient beings possessing afflictive ignorance within their mindstreams, particularly those who have not seen ultimate truth directly, may hold this appearance to be true exactly as it appears. In general, ārya sentient beings do not hold this appearance to be true, but they still have minds arising that hold them in this way.[75] This mind grasping at true existence, as well as its imprints, obscures the ultimate truth of all things. So *conventional truth* means: true from the perspective of ignorance—the total obscurer.

Candrakīrti says in *Introduction to the "Middle Way"*:

> Ignorance obscures all because it conceals true nature;
> Owing to it anything fabricated appears to be true.
> The Muni declared this to be conventional truth
> And fabricated things to be conventionally existent. (6.28)

In this verse there are three occurrences of the word *kun rdzob*, translated variously as "obscures" or "conventional." Each of these occurrences presents a different use of the term. The first refers to ignorance and the imprints it leaves on the mindstream, which *obscure* the ultimate nature of all things. The second refers to things that appear to be true to a mind influenced by ignorance; these are called *conventional* truths, or truths for the total obscurer. The third refers to how these things exist; things exist *conventionally* because they are based on conventional knowledge of phenomena. Therefore *conventional truth* and *conventionally existent* are quite different notions. According to the Prāsaṅgika system, everything that exists only conventionally exists—including śūnyatā, which is an ultimate truth. However, only what is true for a mind directly realizing śūnyatā is called ultimate truth; and only what is true for a mind influenced by ignorance, which obscures the true nature of things, is called conventional truth. There is a Tibetan analogy for conventional truth and ultimate truth: a shallow river and a deep river. A shallow river is called a foot river because it can only be crossed on foot; a deep river is called a boat river because it can only be crossed by boat. In both cases, the nature of the water is the same.

Things that are true from the perspective of a mind obscured by ignorance are conventional truths. Even people who have not realized śūnyatā can understand other things, such as reflections, the appearance of two moons, and so on, to be false. Thus such things are not conventional truths; they are conventional falsities. The Prāsaṅgikas call these false things *distorted conventionalities* rather than truths. Only the things that are correct conventionalities are called truths. Neither a reflection (a distorted conventionality) nor a form (a correct conventionality) exists as it appears: a reflection does not exist as a face, and a form does not exist inherently. So why is one established as a distorted conventionality and the other as a correct conventionality? If someone says that it is incorrect to consider them to be different, what answer can we give? Reflections and forms are the same in that they both appear to conventional knowledge. However, even conventional knowledge can understand that reflections and so on are false: that they are not in fact the object they appear to be. Therefore, in terms of that appearance, they are not considered to be conventional truths. Conversely, conventional knowledge cannot understand that blue, a person, and so on are false—that they are not inherently existent as they appear to be. Therefore these things are considered to be conventional truths. Furthermore, just as it is right for objects to be true or false in terms of conventional knowledge, so it is right for subjects, or minds, to be correct or distorted in terms of conventional knowledge.

This point relates to the Svātantrika-Madhyamaka view regarding the distinction between a distorted and a correct conventionality that was presented earlier. The Svātantrikas make such a distinction with regard to the object, but they do not make a similar distinction with regard to the consciousness perceiving that object. Now here, the Svātantrikas are being pushed to consider that if the object is determined to be correct or distorted, then the consciousness perceiving that object must be either correct or distorted. The Prāsaṅgikas are saying to the Svātantrikas, "Just as you accept two kinds of object, one true and the other false, from the point of view of conventional awareness, so likewise you should accept two kinds of subject, one correct and the other distorted, from the point of view of conventional awareness." A consciousness perceiving a reflection as a real face must be a distorted consciousness; and a consciousness unaffected by any temporary cause of error must be a correct consciousness. From the Prāsaṅgika perspective, a conventional consciousness refers to a mind not directly perceiving śūnyatā. To determine whether such a consciousness is distorted or correct, we can use the following definition. A distorted conventionality is a conventional consciousness that could otherwise know that its object does not exist as it appears—for example, seeing a reflection as a real face. A correct conventionality is a conventional consciousness that could not otherwise know that its object does not exist as it appears—for example, seeing a table as inherently existent.

A valid conventional sense consciousness is what establishes forms and so on to exist. In contrast, a mind that arises in dependence on ultimate analysis is what establishes forms and so on not to exist inherently; this is not a conventional consciousness at all. It is only after engaging in ultimate analysis and understanding śūnyatā that one can understand that valid conventional sense consciousnesses, as well as their objects, are mistaken. There is nothing wrong with conventional consciousnesses or with what they establish. Their objects exist and are perceived by conventional valid knowledge. But their objects do not exist in the way that they are perceived. For example, a pot does exist, and it is perceived by conventional valid knowledge. But the pot is perceived as inherently existent by that conventional valid knowledge. Since it does not exist inherently, this valid knowing is mistaken only with regard to the way it is seen to exist. However, this mistaken aspect is understood only after having generated valid knowledge analyzing the ultimate.

Someone may argue here, "It is contradictory for a conventional consciousness to be nondistorted and yet conventionally mistaken." Tsongkhapa replies, "No. There would be a contradiction if the conventional understanding in relation to which a conventional consciousness is considered nondistorted, and the conventional that is the cause of error of a conventionally mistaken consciousness, were the same. But these two notions of *conventional* are different, so how can they be contradictory?" You may then wonder, "How are these two notions of conventional different?" When using logic to disprove that things have an inherently established nature, we do so conventionally, not ultimately. It may seem that when refuting inherent or ultimate existence, it is refuted ultimately, not conventionally. That is wrong. You have to be careful with this. When we refute true existence by means of ultimate analysis, that ultimate refutation exists. However, it does not exist ultimately; it exists merely conventionally.

Nothing is ever refuted ultimately. The Madhyamaka view is that *to exist* means to be established by conventional valid knowledge; for a thing to exist, it must be proved by that kind of valid knowing. If it is established by conventional valid knowledge, it is said to conventionally exist. Whatever exists only exists conventionally or dependently. Even when śūnyatā is established to exist, it is established by conventional knowledge. Emptiness exists; the ultimate exists. *Exists* here means conventionally exists. Prāsaṅgikas maintain that there is a difference between *ultimate truth* and *ultimately existent*. Even ultimate truth does not exist ultimately. Although śūnyatā is the ultimate truth, it is not ultimately existent, because when we analytically search for śūnyatā it cannot be found to exist from its own side. It does not inherently exist. Therefore it exists conventionally, relatively, or falsely. It is falsely existent, not truly existent. Emptiness itself is not a conventional truth, it is an ultimate truth; but it exists conventionally, not ultimately. Moreover, the *fact* that śūnyatā exists is a conventional truth and is known by conventional understanding.

Now although sensory objects appear to sentient beings as truly existent, there are two ways of understanding that appearance. One is ordinary conventional knowledge that accepts its object just as it appears. The other is subtle conventional knowledge that understands its object to exist merely conventionally. The former lacks an understanding of śūnyatā; the latter, though not a direct knowing of śūnyatā, understands how things exist dependently, nominally, and relatively. It is the understanding that arises after negating true existence by means of ultimate analysis. It knows that things are like illusions. From the perspective of this subtle conventional knowing, the sense consciousnesses are mistaken. From the perspective of ordinary conventional knowing, the sense consciousnesses are not mistaken. Therefore there is no contradiction in saying that the sense consciousnesses are correct in relation to ordinary conventional knowledge but mistaken in relation to subtle conventional knowledge. Although the two uses of the term *conventional knowledge* may seem confusing, there is no contradiction.

Tsongkhapa makes this very clear using the following example. Suppose someone in the room asks, "Is everybody here?" You might reply, "Some people are here and some people are not here." The phrase "some people" is used twice in your response. The words are the same, but they do not have the same referent: each use of the phrase refers to a different group of people. Thus it is not contradictory to say, "Some people are here and some people are not here." Similarly, it is not contradictory to say, "The sense consciousnesses are mistaken in relation to conventional knowledge, and the sense consciousnesses are correct in relation to conventional knowledge," because they are posited from the perspective of two different kinds of conventional knowledge.

The Mādhyamikas accept the five sense consciousnesses to be unmistaken in relation to ordinary worldly knowledge; however, they do not accept them to be unmistaken in general. Someone who realizes the Middle Way understands that things do not exist inherently; he or she recognizes that things exist merely as nominally imputed. For this reason, the *Introduction to the "Middle Way"* says that any such thing "is true from the worldly perspective." Given that the Mādhyamikas establish the ordinary sense consciousnesses to be mistaken in general, it is not contradictory for them to posit the objects of those consciousnesses to be false. If they posited such objects to be true, it would be contradictory for them to say that they are established by mistaken consciousnesses. In this context, the term *false* refers to conventional truth.

In sum, the objects of sense consciousnesses are true in a conventional sense, even though they are false (i.e., conventional) objects. Conventionally, all phenomena are said to be like illusions, so conventionally they are false. Yet this does not contradict their being posited as conventional truth, within the division of phenomena into the two truths. In general the term *true* refers only to ultimate truth, śūnyatā. But that truth cannot be established by the sense consciousnesses because those consciousnesses are mistaken. On the one hand, form and all conventional things are conventional truths; on the other hand, they are falsely existent.

There is a distinction to be made between conventionally existent and conventional truth. Conventional truth is true from the perspective of a mind obscured by ignorance. The *Introduction to the "Middle Way"* says, "Ignorance obscures all because it conceals true nature." Ignorance is known as the total obscurer; it conceals the ultimate nature of all things. In the context of conventional truth, the notion of *truth* is connected with the notion of *ignorance*, the total obscurer. From the perspective of that obscuring factor, conventional things are true and are called obscurer truths or conventional truths. There is no contradiction in saying that from the point of view of ignorance, conventional things are true—yet from the point of view of a refined conventional knowledge that understands things to be nontruly existent and merely nominally existent, conventional things are false.

⚜ 8 ⚜
Conventional Existence

(b")) (continued) The distinguishing feature of Madhyamaka cannot
be disproved by negating things from the perspective of examining
whether or not they are established by valid knowledge

———⚜———

THE PRĀSAṄGIKA-MĀDHYAMIKAS do not deny that ordinary things
conventionally exist. When Candrakīrti says, "Whatever is false even conventionally is not a conventional truth," he is referring to things understood by
conventional knowledge to be false. We can rephrase his statement as, "Whatever conventional knowledge knows to be false is not a conventional truth."
This does not mean that ordinary things are conventionally false. It means that
specific things accepted by the Realists are conventionally false. The Prāsaṅgikas refute those things and prove that they do not exist even conventionally.
After that, they establish ordinary things to exist conventionally in a way that
is harmonious with worldly understanding. This is how the Mādhyamikas
present samsara and nirvana in a conventional sense and negate, even conventionally, things imputed by the Realists—which includes non-Buddhist philosophical systems as well as the Vaibhāṣika, Sautrāntika, and Yogācāra. This
manner of establishment and negation is so difficult to comprehend that it is
very rare to find someone with a correct understanding of the presentation of
the two truths.

Misunderstanding can easily arise regarding the fact that valid reasoning
must be used in refuting the Realists and in proving the Madhyamaka position.
Intelligent people accept or reject things based on whether they have proof—
which involves a sequence of logical reasons. If they have a correct proof, they
accept them; without a correct proof, they do not accept them. Many so-called
Mādhyamikas think that the things established by the Mādhyamikas as conventionally existent and the things posited by the Realists are equally affected

by logical analysis. In other words, if one is negated by reason, then both are equally rejected, and if one is not negated by reason, then both are equally unharmed. They think that if we say that a divine creator, a primal essence, and so on do not exist conventionally, then we must also say that forms and so on do not exist, and if we say that forms and so on exist conventionally, then we must also say that a divine creator, a primal essence, and so on exist. They mistakenly think that in the Madhyamaka system it is unsuitable for anything to be identified or accepted as "This is so and that is not so." In short, they consider the Middle Way to mean not accepting or rejecting anything. They say we should literally accept Nāgārjuna's statement, "I do not have any thesis because I do not accept anything."[76]

Even some genuine followers of Nāgārjuna say that the highest Madhyamaka view is to accept nothing because Buddha remained silent and did not say anything one way or the other when he was questioned on certain points. They think we simply have to shut up! I am joking; but those following this interpretation of Nāgārjuna believe that to cultivate the correct view, we should meditate without holding anything in mind. To practice the path, we purify the mind of all thoughts; whatever comes to mind is like a cloud to be cleared away. Many people appreciate this approach because it is easy and temporarily keeps one free of attachment and hatred. The alternative is to struggle to understand many difficult points and deal with apparent contradictions. If meditation practice is simply to abide without thought, then we do not have to grapple with complex ideas.

This interpretation of the Middle Way is not correct. Nāgārjuna's point is that nothing can be accepted when based on the assumption that things have an inherent nature or exist by their own nature. He is not saying that nothing can be accepted at all. Tsongkhapa sees this no-thought approach as a very powerful wrong view. He makes strong statements about it in various places in the *Lamrim Chenmo*. Here he says that it is apparent that this position does not satisfy the wise: it is utterly unsatisfactory because it does not correctly identify the object to be negated by ultimate analysis, namely, inherent existence. Those who identify the object of negation too broadly destroy the establishment of all conventional things.

It is a great mistake to equate a correct view and a wrong view, such that if one is mistaken then both are equally mistaken, and if one is unmistaken then both are equally unmistaken. Even if you were to meditate without thought for a long time, you would not get the slightest bit closer to the correct understanding of the ultimate truth. Not only will it not bring you any closer to the right view, but it will take you further away. Why? The reason is that this approach grossly contradicts all Madhyamaka teachings concerning the dependent phenomena of samsara and nirvana. The twelve links of dependent arising function as causes and effects: their arising constitutes samsara (conditioned by the arising of ignorance, karma arises, and so on, all the way through to the arising of aging and death), and their cessation constitutes nirvana (conditioned by the cessation of ignorance, karma ceases, and so on, all the way through to the cessation of aging and death).[77] So if you think that cultivating the mere absence of thought leads to nirvana, then you are denying this causal relationship.

Tsongkhapa says he will explain the apparent contradiction that all phenomena, whether pure or impure, exist conventionally but do not exist ultimately. Many people think that if something exists, it must exist inherently or ultimately; in other words, it must be findable when sought by ultimate analysis. Some people try to follow the Madhyamaka view, but because they do not understand its subtlety, they see both correct and incorrect positions to be equally valid.

To remedy this dangerous mistake, Tsongkhapa begins by quoting Candrakīrti's *Introduction to the "Middle Way"*:

> The self as it is construed by the tīrthikas,
> Who are controlled by the sleep of ignorance,
> And anything else contrived, such as mirages and magical illusions,
> Do not exist even from the worldly point of view.

According to Candrakīrti's system, things asserted to exist by non-Buddhist philosophers and by the Buddhist Realists mentioned earlier do not exist even conventionally, let alone ultimately (it is obvious they do not exist ultimately). So what does it mean to say that something is *conventionally existent* or *conventionally nonexistent*? What criteria should be used to judge whether something exists? We cannot say that a thing is both existent and nonexistent; there must be some special quality that distinguishes these categories.

There are three criteria for something to exist conventionally. First, it is known by conventional knowledge. Second, the thing known in that way is not negated by another conventional valid knowledge. Third, it is not negated by ultimate knowledge analyzing ultimate reality, which investigates whether or not something has intrinsic existence. Anything that satisfies these criteria is conventionally existent. Anything that does not satisfy these criteria does not exist at all. If something exists conventionally, that is a sufficient condition for it to exist. If something does not exist conventionally, that is a sufficient condition for it not to exist. However, if something does not exist ultimately, that is not a sufficient condition for it not to exist. There is nothing that ultimately exists, according to the Madhyamaka system. To *exist* means to exist conventionally.

The first criterion

The first criterion of something to exist conventionally is that it is known by conventional knowledge. Conventional knowledge is a consciousness that knows an ordinary thing, such as a tree, just as it appears to sense consciousness. It knows without analyzing in what way the object exists. The ordinary mind does not question whether a thing's nature is something other than what appears to a sense consciousness. When we see a jar, we do not ask ourselves "Is it real?" or "What is its nature?" If somebody says, "That is a jar," we just follow along and think, "Oh yes, that is a jar." If somebody says, "This is Peter," then we think, "This is Peter, that other person is not Peter." We do not ask, "What do you mean by 'Peter'? Where is the real Peter? Does the name Peter refer to the head, the feet, inside, or outside?" Conventional valid awareness simply engages its object as it appears without further examination. This conventional consciousness is called a *nonanalytical consciousness*; in other words, it is a consciousness that does not engage in ultimate analysis to determine whether an object's reality is something deeper than its appearance. If this kind of examination is absent, it is a nonanalytical consciousness.

We should note that conventional knowing is not entirely free from any type of inquiry. A so-called nonanalytical consciousness may examine and analyze things in a conventional manner. If we see something in the distance that looks like a human being, or possibly a tree, we may investigate to determine what it is. There are also many kinds of analytical meditation, such as on the nature of impermanence, where we analyze the object of inquiry, but we are still using nonanalytical consciousness. What is meant here by *nonanalytical consciousness* is that it does not examine or look for the ultimate identity or reality of something that appears. An ordinary or conventional mind is nonanalytical in that it engages with objects just as they appear or are known, without exploring their final mode of being. It arises when we do any normal activity.

Nonanalytical consciousness is common to everyone—whether highly educated and influenced by philosophical thought or totally unaware of philosophical distinctions. It even arises in animals. So, this kind of mind is called *mundane knowing* or *common acceptance*. It is wrong to think that mundane knowing, or a nonanalytical consciousness, exists only in those who are not influenced by philosophy. We do not need to limit ourselves to asking uneducated people about what is commonly accepted. We can ask anyone. Although philosophers frequently think about ultimate reality, not all of their consciousnesses analyze the ultimate mode of existence. We can even see how the nonanalytical mind functions when two people are involved in philosophical debate. For, although they may disagree about certain issues, they hold in common many unexamined assumptions that function as a basis for their thoughts and expressions.

What is commonly accepted in the world is whatever appears or is experienced. The two types of convention—thoughts and words—arise based on such appearances and experiences. Something must appear to the mind and be experienced before we can think or say anything about it. First, our thoughts arise based on what we experience. Then we apply a name to it and label it "good" or "bad."

We may wonder whether subtle things, such as the Dharma, can be known by a nonanalytical consciousness. Ordinary people who have not studied Buddhism do not know about karma and its results, which is the side of samsara; nor do they know about the grounds and paths to enlightenment, which is the side of nirvana. However, when ordinary people hear teachings on these subjects, they can take them as an object of study and learn to differentiate them. They can understand what they have heard based on their ordinary experience, without having to examine whether these objects can be found through ultimate analysis or are merely imputed. Because these things appear to ordinary consciousness and not just to a mind analyzing the ultimate, they can be known by conventional knowledge. The fault that these things are not known by conventional knowledge does not arise.

The second criterion

The second criterion for a thing to be conventionally existent is that it is not negated by another conventional knowledge. If one valid understanding were to perceive something while another valid understanding knew it to be the opposite, then one understanding would negate the other. If something were contradicted in this manner, then it could not be conventionally existent.

For example, your conventional consciousness is not valid if it thinks "That is a snake" when you see a coiled rope in a dark corner or "There is water" when you see a mirage in the distance. Why? Because the object that it holds—a snake or water—can be negated by another conventional consciousness that is actually valid. There is no snake there at all. If we examine it more closely we see it is just a piece of rope. There is no water there at all. If we examine the mirage we find it is just a reflection of sunlight on sand. One conventional consciousness holds a piece of rope to be a snake; another conventional consciousness understands that there is no snake there. Because the second consciousness relies on truth, it harms the first. Holding a piece of rope to be a snake or a mirage to be water is an incorrect way to grasp the object. Valid knowing contradicts incorrect belief. If something is affirmed by valid knowledge, then it exists conventionally. Whatever is negated by valid knowledge does not exist at all, not even conventionally; it is totally nonexistent.

You may wonder, "Why aren't the two consciousnesses mutually harmful? If one thing harms another simply by contradicting it, then why doesn't the reverse happen too? Why doesn't an invalid consciousness harm valid consciousness? Why is the wisdom realizing selflessness always the harmer of the egotistic view of self-grasping?" In *Commentary on Valid Cognition* Dharmakīrti says that a valid consciousness harms an invalid consciousness "because it has a different nature based on truth" (2.141c). He explains that the egotistic view and the wisdom understanding selflessness grasp their respective objects in directly opposite ways. Their natures are utterly different. Although these two ways of holding the object struggle with each other temporarily, eventually the wisdom realizing selflessness completely destroys the self-grasping egotistic view. The self-grasping mind cannot destroy the wisdom realizing selflessness because that wisdom relies on the truth, whereas self-grasping relies on falsehood. Truth harms falsehood.

The third criterion
The third criterion for something to be conventionally existent is that the thing is not proved false by correct ultimate analysis that investigates whether it exists inherently. This means that any conventionally existent thing must be established by conventional valid knowledge and it must not be negated by ultimate valid knowledge. In addition, it must definitely not be proved by ultimate valid knowledge because, if it were found by correct ultimate analysis, then it would be truly or inherently existent. Ultimate analysis is an examination of whether or not something exists by its own nature. If a thing were sought and found by correct ultimate analysis, then it would be inherently existent. If a conventional thing were established by ultimate analysis, it would exist by its own nature, inherently—which would contradict its being a conventional thing. So conventional things can neither be established by ultimate analysis nor negated by ultimate analysis.

This can be confusing. Certain people erroneously think that "not being negated by ultimate analysis" and "being established by ultimate analysis" mean the same thing. Owing to getting these mixed up, they mistakenly think that the following two propositions are equally true or equally false, even in a conventional sense: happiness and suffering arise from virtue and nonvirtue, and happiness and suffering arise from the creator god Īśvara and the universal primordial nature. Because neither proposition is established by ultimate analysis, they think that if one of them is right then the other is equally correct;

and if one of them is wrong then the other is equally incorrect. This is mistaken thinking. Ultimate analysis examines whether something is inherently existent; using this analysis we find that neither statement is proved or established as such. However, the two propositions are not equal in that conventional reasoning negates one of them and does not negate the other. Someone who has a correct understanding of these matters does not become confused in this way.

Buddhist and non-Buddhist Realists posit certain objects contrived by their own unique beliefs—such as partless subjects and objects, a permanent self, a principal cause, or Īśvara. They accept these objects based on having analyzed whether or not they exist by their own nature; believing that they are found by such ultimate analysis, they establish that they exist. Their ultimate analysis must be very different from the ultimate analysis of the Mādhyamikas, because when subjected to Madhyamaka ultimate analysis, those objects are not found. Because they cannot bear examination by faultless reasoning, their existence is negated—according to the Realists' own criteria. Therefore we must conclude that the ultimate analysis of the lower Buddhist schools and the non-Buddhists contains some error.

According to our Madhyamaka system, forms, sounds, and so on are established only as known by a conventional consciousness that is free from internal and external causes of error. Unlike those non-Buddhist systems, we do not accept that ordinary things are found by analyzing whether they exist merely conventionally or in an objective manner, thereby establishing them from their own side. We do not accept that they can be found by, or bear, ultimate analysis at all. A conventional thing, something that is commonly known, is accepted just as it is known by ordinary common sense. It would be inappropriate to try to establish it by analyzing whether or not it exists inherently. That is as foolish as inquiring whether an animal is a horse or an elephant when someone says "This is a sheep."

According to the Madhyamaka system, to be conventionally existent means to be established according to common worldly knowledge. However, Mādhyamikas do not accept everything that is accepted by the world. When we say that something is "commonly known," it does not mean *known* in the sense of being proved by valid knowledge; it simply means that it is commonly accepted. What is commonly known may also be known by conventional valid knowledge, such as understanding snow to be white. But common knowledge may include a "knowing" that is not valid; indeed, some things "known" in the world for centuries can later be negated by valid reasoning and found not to exist at all.

For example, ignorance always imputes an inherent nature onto things, yet things do not exist in the way that ignorance holds them to exist. Also, the egotistic view that grasps an inherently existent self (me) and an inherent belonging to the self (mine) has operated since time without beginning, yet what is held in that way is negated by logical reasoning and does not exist at all. This does not mean that the holder—the incorrect consciousness—does not exist. It is what that incorrect consciousness holds that does not exist—the self of persons (in the case of the egotistic view) and the self of phenomena (in the case of ignorance in a broader sense). Both of these are totally nonexistent; they do not exist either ultimately or conventionally.

Another example of something commonly accepted that in fact does not exist is a thing's permanence. We think that the mountain we see today is the same as the one we saw yesterday. We do not see the momentary changes; out of longstanding habit we invariably identify today's mountain as yesterday's mountain. In reality, a thing that exists in the first moment does not exist in the second moment. It is already gone. In short, although ordinary things may be commonly known, this does not mean that they are established or proved to exist.

Some people say that forms, sounds, and so on are not similar to the things construed by non-Buddhists—in terms of their criteria of conventional existence—because (1) the former are commonly known to all worldly beings, and (2) the latter are known only to those who hold the philosophical tenets of a particular school. Those who argue this way are not making a clear distinction; thus they are in error with regard to both of their reasons. If reason 2 were correct, then the illusion-like nature of forms and so on would not exist conventionally—because the reason they give for something not to exist conventionally is that it is *known only to philosophers*. But it is only philosophers who understand śūnyatā who can know that forms and so on are illusion-like mere appearances. Worldly people have no ordinary knowledge of this. So these opponents would have to say that forms and so on, being like illusions, do not exist conventionally because they are not commonly known to worldly people.

Next, if reason 1 were correct, namely, that forms and so on exist conventionally because they are *commonly known to worldly people*, then they must accept that inherently existent things exist conventionally. Ordinary people see and hold things to be inherently existent and, even though this is wrong from the ultimate point of view, it is correct from the perspective of worldly knowledge. Many such unwanted consequences follow from the above argument. Furthermore, Candrakīrti's *Commentary on the "Sixty Stanzas of Reasoning"* says:

> It is a distorted mind that holds what is not pleasurable to be pleasurable and so on, because things do not have that nature even con-

ventionally. It is an undistorted mind that holds what is painful to be painful and so on, because things do have that nature conventionally.

The four common distorted ways of thinking are: holding impermanent things to be permanent, holding impure things to be pure, holding things having the nature of suffering to be pleasurable, and holding selfless things to be an inherently existent self or to belong to such a self. For example, every day we regard the body as a source of pleasure, even though it is in the nature of suffering. We think that we exist continuously—in other words, we hold impermanent phenomena to be permanent. We hold selfless things as a self—in other words, we inappropriately grasp at "me" and "mine" in an egotistic manner. Even though these attitudes are very common, what they hold to be the case does not exist even conventionally. Therefore these beliefs are said to be mistaken or distorted. Conversely, even though the four undistorted ways of thinking—holding impermanent things to be impermanent, and so on—are not commonly known, they do exist conventionally. Therefore these correct attitudes are said to be undistorted, even though they are known only to supreme philosophers.

THE OBJECT AS IT APPEARS AND THE OBJECT AS IT IS HELD OR UNDERSTOOD

In general, objects of sense perception or thought can be considered in two ways: the object as it appears and the object as it is held or understood. Although the basic object may be the same, the way that it appears and the way that it is held may be quite different. This can occur with direct perception or conceptual consciousness. Consider, for example, a thought that conceives the aggregates to be impermanent. This thought is mistaken with regard to its appearing object, but it is not mistaken with regard to its held object, which is the main thing understood. That understanding is not proved false by any other valid consciousness, and so it is said to be unmistaken or undistorted. Buddhist tenet systems, from the Prāsaṅgika down to the Sautrāntika, consider that *all thought* is mistaken with regard to the object as it appears. Even a correct inferential valid understanding that knows sound to be impermanent is mistaken with regard to its appearing object, but its held object is correct.

What does it mean to say that all thought is mistaken with regard to its appearing object? Here we need to consider some basic epistemology. A moment of sense consciousness perceives an object directly. Then a thought arises, where a general image of the object previously observed by the sense consciousness appears to the mind. Thought does not perceive its object directly; it ascertains its object via a general mental image.

For example, our visual consciousness perceives a tree. Then immediately a conceptual image of the tree appears to thought. Although this conceptual image is not as clear as what was apprehended by the visual sense consciousness, this general image is the means by which we ascertain "That is a tree." Thought correctly distinguishes the tree from the mountain behind it and discerns whether it is tall or green. We understand the various aspects of the tree through our general mental image of it. The actual tree itself is the main object held by thought. What appears to this thought is a mixture of the actual tree and the conceptual image of the tree. This appearing object is not the actual tree. However, we have no comprehension that the appearing object we perceive is not the actual tree. The actual tree and the conceptual image of the tree appear the same to the mind. So thought is mistaken in that the object and the mental image appear to be exactly the same thing.

This happens with all conceptual consciousness. Every thought is mistaken with regard to its appearing object. From the Prāsaṅgika-Madhyamaka point of view there is an additional level of mistaken appearance: the appearance of inherent existence. This is a subtler kind of mistaken appearance.

Let us look a little more closely at the conceptual image *tree*. If we say or think "tree," a mental image arises that encompasses all particular trees. At first we were introduced to individual trees through direct sense perception. According to the lower schools, as well as Bhāvaviveka, the individual characteristics of an object appear directly to the sense consciousness perceiving it. We see a tree, a big tree, a deciduous tree, and so on. We perceive each characteristic directly without mixing them up. Therefore, according to those systems, a sense consciousness is unmistaken; it sees things as they are, and what it sees is true. Once we have been introduced to individual trees by means of our visual consciousness, the mind creates a mental image of *treeness*, which is a generality. That conceptual image of *treeness* encompasses all trees. Any individual tree can be placed under the general conceptual image *tree*. The particular and the general are thus brought together within thought.

A sense consciousness does not perceive any conceptual image or generality. When our visual consciousness perceives a tree, it directly sees the color, shape, and various attributes of a particular tree. Our visual consciousness also sees other qualities of that individual tree, such as impermanence, production, and so on. According to the Sautrāntika and Yogācāra schools, because sense consciousness functions through the power of the object, in that it engages its object positively, it directly perceives its object without making any distinctions between the object's various characteristics. Dharmakīrti says:

Therefore, by seeing a thing
All its qualities are seen. (1.47)

The first chapter of Dharmakīrti's *Commentary on Valid Cognition* discusses at length how thoughts are indirect and mistaken. Thoughts do not perceive things directly. There is no external *treeness* that encompasses all trees. It is the mental consciousness that conceives of abstract things, such as a generality or a particularity, by means of conceptual images. It is thought, arising on the basis of a conceptual image, that understands the various attributes one by one. For example, the visual consciousness sees all the attributes of the tree at once—tall, green, impermanent, and so on. Then thought understands each quality of the tree individually. It does not understand all these attributes simultaneously. Thought engages the object by means of elimination; comprehension of a thing arises by mentally clearing away other phenomena. The affirmation of one thing negates another; the negation of one thing affirms another. If you think "tall" you are negating "nontall." Likewise, on the basis of having a conceptual image of what it is to be green and nongreen, you can think, "This is green." Conceptual awareness does this with each quality one by one. It does not recognize all the qualities together because it does not function through the power of the object. It functions through the power of our own conceptual images.

The same applies to words. Thought and language engage the object in the same way because words come from thoughts. The direct object of thought is a conceptual image through which it recognizes the qualities of the object. A word expressing that very thought also has that very conceptual image as its direct object. When we say "This is a tree" or "That is a pot," the words follow from the object engaged by thought. Although our sense consciousness perceives green, tall, leafy, impermanent, product, and so on simultaneously, when we talk about these attributes, we mention them one by one. We say, "It is green." Then we may add, "It is tall," and so on. When we say "tall," we are not indicating "green"; we are not saying anything more than "tall."

All thoughts are mistaken with regard to their appearing object, yet they are not all distorted or wrong. As has been discussed, we must make a distinction between a mistaken consciousness and a wrong or distorted consciousness. A mistaken consciousness is mistaken with regard to its appearing object. A wrong or distorted consciousness is mistaken with regard to its main or held object. Some thoughts are correct with regard to how they understand their main object, whereas other thoughts are mistaken with regard to how they understand their main object. In the latter case, both how the object appears and how it is held or understood are completely wrong.

According to the Prāsaṅgika system, the thought that holds the aggregates to be impermanent is mistaken with regard to its appearing object, because the aggregates appear to exist inherently. But its way of holding its object—namely, holding the aggregates to be impermanent—cannot be negated by valid knowledge. Therefore this thought is not mistaken with regard to its main object, so it is said to be correct. According to the Prāsaṅgika system, all sentient beings' sense consciousnesses are mistaken because their objects appear to exist inherently. An appearance of the main object is mixed with an appearance of inherent existence. However, when there is nothing else with regard to which they are mistaken, they are simply said to be mistaken—not wrong. So here, *to be mistaken* means to be incorrect regarding the appearing object. The visual consciousness that perceives blue is mistaken because blue appears to be inherently existent. However, it is not a wrong or distorted consciousness because it is not mistaken regarding its main object—blue. The primary object is correctly held to be blue; the visual consciousness that apprehends it is valid.

Not all Buddhist schools agree. According to the lower schools, valid sense consciousnesses are not mistaken. The Sautrāntikas and below say that objects exist as they are perceived. In their opinion, when we see blue there is no aspect regarding which that visual consciousness is mistaken. The object appears to exist inherently, but according to the lower schools things do exist inherently. Therefore in their view this is a completely unmistaken appearance.

The Yogācāras agree with the Prāsaṅgikas that the sense consciousnesses are mistaken, but their reasoning is different. When we see blue, we see it as an external object. According to the Yogācāra system, all sense consciousnesses are mistaken regarding this appearance of subject-object duality. Although a visual consciousness perceiving blue is mistaken with regard to the appearance of an external object, it is a valid consciousness because the primary object held by visual consciousness is blue, not the appearance of duality. Therefore it is valid knowledge because it is not mistaken with regard to the principal held object.

From the Prāsaṅgika perspective, all sense consciousnesses, except for those of a buddha, are alike in being mistaken with regard to the appearance of inherent existence. They are differentiated in terms of being correct or distorted conventionalities, based on whether a thing corresponding to the appearance exists from the point of view of ordinary beings. For example, a visual consciousness to which a reflection of a face appears as a real face is a distorted conventionality because the main object—what is held to be a real face—does not exist from the point of view of ordinary beings. Ordinary people do not accept a reflection of a face to be a real face. A distorted conventionality can be refuted by conventional valid knowledge.

For example, the held object of the thought grasping the aggregates to be permanent—permanent aggregates—does not exist conventionally, and therefore it can be negated by valid knowledge. Distorted conceptual consciousnesses holding impermanent things as permanent, impure things as pure, selfless things as having a self, and things in the nature of suffering as being pleasant are all refuted by means of negating their held objects. The held objects of these thoughts do not exist conventionally. However, the held objects of the correct ways of thinking do exist conventionally and cannot be negated by valid reasoning: impermanent things exist as impermanent, suffering natures exist as suffering, impure things exist as impure, and selfless things exist as selfless. That is the difference on the conventional side.

From the point of view of the ultimate, however, there is no differentiation between distorted and correct conventionalities because neither of them exists ultimately. There is no ultimate existence of the aggregates held wrongly (as permanent, pleasant, pure, and possessing a self), and there is no ultimate existence of the aggregates held correctly (as impermanent, suffering, impure, and selfless). Buddha taught that if we *grasp* the aggregates in any of these eight ways—as permanent or impermanent, pleasant or miserable, pure or impure, self-existent or selfless—then we are employing signs, which is completely wrong. *Employing signs* means holding things that are not truly existent to be truly existent. This is fundamentally the wrong way to hold things. If we hold things to be ultimately, inherently, or truly existent, we are employing signs. There are many passages in the scriptures that advise, "Things are not permanent, not impermanent, not pleasurable, not miserable . . . you should not *view* things in any of those ways."

CONVENTIONAL TRUTH EXISTS CONVENTIONALLY

Someone might argue that it is contradictory to disprove the way that things are held by ignorance, which superimposes an inherent nature on them, and not to disprove conventional things, because the *Introduction to the "Middle Way"* states:

> Ignorance obscures all because it conceals true nature;
> Owing to it anything fabricated appears to be true.
> The Muni declared this to be conventional truth,
> And fabricated things to be conventionally existent.

Ignorance, as we've seen, is the root mental affliction that distortedly grasps things to be truly existent. When it arises it deposits imprints in the mindstream that cause things to appear truly existent. These imprints are known as *nonafflictive ignorance*, even though they are not actually ignorance. Both types of so-called ignorance—afflictive and nonafflictive—obstruct any direct seeing of ultimate reality, which is indicated by the Tibetan term *kun rdzob*, the total obscurer. The first syllable, *kun*, means "all" and in this context refers to the ultimate nature of all phenomena; *rdzob* means "obscure" or "conceal," which refers to the obstruction that conceals the ultimate nature. Thus, owing to the power of ignorance, fabricated things appear to exist in a way that they do not exist.

The term *fabricated* has two meanings: created by causes and conditions, and false. Owing to the power of ignorance and its imprints, things appear to be truly existent. This is a false appearance. However, because things appear to be true from the perspective of a mind affected by ignorance, Buddha declared them to be true for the total obscurer. This is conventional truth. He also declared them to be conventionally existent. Remember that according to the Prāsaṅgika system, if something exists conventionally, that is sufficient for it to exist. In contrast, if something does not exist ultimately, that is not sufficient for it not to exist. For something to exist, it does not need to exist ultimately— indeed, it cannot exist ultimately. In general, *existent* means conventionally existent and *nonexistent* means not conventionally existent—it does not mean "not ultimately existent."

The opponent is trying to demonstrate that there is a contradiction in saying that conventional truth exists conventionally. He quotes Candrakīrti to show that things such as forms, sounds, and so on are conventional truths owing to the power of ignorance. He is implying that this kind of truth—conventional truth—is false because ignorance is distorted and cannot establish existent things. In contrast, what exists conventionally actually exists, in that it is not negated by valid reasoning.

Tsongkhapa says that there is no such logical fault because the meaning of *true* in the context of "forms, sounds, and so on are true for the total obscurer" is simply that they are true owing to the power of thought; such *thought* can only refer to the grasping at true existence, so conventional things are true from the perspective of ignorance that superimposes an inherent nature onto things. However, although they are "true for the total obscurer," this does not mean they are true. What is genuinely true is emptiness or śūnyatā. Any conventional truth is false; ultimate truth is true. So in this particular context, the term *true* refers only to what is true from the perspective of a mind obscured by ignorance. That is conventional truth, and it is just conventionally existent.

Kamalaśīla's *Illumination of the Middle Way* says:

> All things that are false entities due to the power of thought are just conventionally existent.[78]

It is commonly accepted that when śrāvaka and pratyekabuddha arhats achieve their respective final goals, they have totally eliminated ignorance— the afflictive mind that obstructs liberation. Likewise, according to the Prāsaṅgika system, afflictive ignorance is totally eliminated upon entering the eighth ground of the Mahayana path. Afflictive ignorance is absent from the eighth bodhisattva level up to buddhahood. In terms of this absence of ignorance, bodhisattvas on the eighth level and above are equal to śrāvaka and pratyekabuddha arhats. As Candrakīrti explains in *Commentary on the "Introduction to the 'Middle Way,'"* these three types of beings see conventional appearances:

> As fabricated natures, not as true, because they have no grasping at manifest things as true.[79]

You may wonder, "What are the bodhisattvas on the eighth, ninth, and tenth grounds doing?" They are abandoning nonafflictive ignorance—the imprints that obstruct omniscience. Although these bodhisattvas have already abandoned afflictive ignorance, they need to get rid of the subtle imprints left by ignorance. These imprints are an obstructing force called *ignorance*, even though they are not consciousnesses. They are predispositions that give rise to the subtle appearance of things as inherently existent. This kind of obscuration is a potentiality that generates a false effect and hinders correct perception. These imprints and the false appearances they give rise to are called *obstructions to omniscience*.

Candrakīrti says that both types of arhats, as well as bodhisattvas on the three pure levels, no longer experience any incorrect grasping at things as inherently existent; they have not the slightest doubt that things are not inherently existent. During their postmeditative periods they naturally and spontaneously recognize that everything has an illusion-like nature because they have completely removed the afflictive ignorance grasping at true existence. Yet when they are not meditating directly on emptiness, things still appear as inherently existent to them. Even while knowing that things do not exist that way, they are subjected to the appearance of things being inherently existent because nonafflictive ignorance is present in their mindstreams. Arhats and bodhisattvas on the eighth ground and above clearly know that all appearances of conventional phenomena are in the nature of fabrications; they recognize that phenomena are not truly existent but are like illusions. Therefore appearing things are said to be *mere conventionalities* for them.

Forms and so on are held to be true only from the point of view of ignorance. However, forms and other phenomena are not established by ignorance. Suppose, for example, someone sees a coiled rope as a real snake. Although from the point of view of that distorted consciousness the piece of rope is a snake, the rope is not established by that consciousness. Ignorance cannot establish anything as existent because it is an utterly wrong consciousness. Forms and so on are true from the perspective of a mind influenced by ignorance—the total obscurer. Apart from that, these things are false.

So how do we establish the existence of conventional things? A conventional thing is established by a conventional valid consciousness. A conventional valid consciousness is any one of the six consciousnesses unaffected by temporary causes of error. The objects established by those correct six consciousnesses are conventionally existent; they exist through the power of thought and terminology. According to the Prāsaṅgika system, everything that exists in the world is nominally existent because it is merely imputed by thought and terminology; there is nothing that exists solely by way of its own nature. However, ignorance superimposes an inherent nature on things. This inherent nature does not exist conventionally or nominally. Any object held by ignorance does not exist, even conventionally, in the way that it is held. So valid reasoning can negate this held object. If what is held by ignorance—inherent existence— were not negated by reasoning, then we could not conventionally show that things have an illusion-like nature, and we would have to conclude that things exist as they are held by ignorance and so must be truly or ultimately existent.

Valid reasoning can also negate the way that attachment and hatred hold their objects. Attachment, hatred, and all other mental afflictions arise from ignorance. Ignorance superimposes true existence onto things, and the ordinary mind applies inappropriate attention to them, seeing them as attractive or ugly from their own side. It is important to understand *inappropriate attention*. First we have a mind of ignorance arising with regard to the object, whereby we hold it to exist inherently. Then we have a mind of inappropriate attention arising toward that object, which appears to exist inherently, whereby we hold it to be beautiful or ugly and so on from its own side. So first we hold the object to exist inherently, and then we hold that object in a further inappropriate way. The texts usually mention four kinds of inappropriate attention: holding impermanent things as permanent, holding things in the nature of suffering as pleasurable, holding impure things as pure, and holding selfless things as self-existent. The objects of these minds appear inherently existent, but these minds do not hold them to exist inherently. These minds arise from another mind that holds them to exist inherently—ignorance. The appearance of things as inherently attractive or as inherently ugly arises from the imprints deposited by ignorance grasping things as inherently existent and reflects specific tendencies within the mindstream. For example, ignorance holds the body to be truly existent, and inappropriate attention superimposes an additional property onto it, such as attractiveness or ugliness. Then, on the basis of this additional superimposed quality, attachment, aversion, and so on arise. Because attachment and aversion are indirectly influenced by ignorance, they too can be negated by ultimate logical analysis.

Candrakīrti's *Commentary on the "Four Hundred Stanzas"* says:

> Attachment and so on engage only a thing's inherent nature imputed by ignorance, based on which they superimpose particular attributes, such as attractiveness or ugliness. Therefore they do not engage differently from ignorance, and they depend on ignorance because ignorance is the principal one.

There is much debate about the meaning of the phrase "not differently" in Candrakīrti's passage above. Some scholars have suggested that it refers to the technical notion of "similarity" that exists between a primary consciousness and its accompanying mental factors. Any kind of awareness consists of a primary consciousness with a retinue of accompanying consciousnesses or mental factors. Just as attendants always surround a king, a primary consciousness always functions with an entourage of secondary consciousnesses.

The Vaibhāṣika and lower Abhidharma schools assert that there are ten omnipresent mental factors, whereas all the other schools say that there are five: feeling, discernment, intention, contact, and attention. In addition to these there may be other mental factors, such as any of the five object-ascertaining mental factors. For example, when we look at something, the primary consciousness is the visual consciousness. It is accompanied by the five omnipresent mental factors, each of which has a particular function: feeling experiences something as pleasant, unpleasant, or neutral; discernment differentiates one phenomenon from another; and so on. In addition to the five omnipresent mental factors, there may be other accompanying consciousnesses, such as faith from among the eleven virtuous mental factors or hatred from among the six root delusions. Some primary consciousnesses have a great many additional mental factors in their retinue.

A primary consciousness and all its accompanying consciousnesses are similar in five ways: support, object, aspect, time, and substance. To understand these, let us look at the example of seeing a green tree. First, *support* refers to the dominating cause, which in this case is the eye sense power. The same dominating cause or sense power is shared by the primary consciousness and all its accompanying consciousnesses. Second, the main *object* of the primary consciousness, the tree, is also the main object of the accompanying consciousnesses. Third, the *aspect* of the primary consciousness, which is the quality that the mind attributes to the object, green, is the same as the aspect of the accompanying consciousnesses, which also hold the tree to be green. Fourth, the *time* at which the primary consciousness and its accompanying consciousnesses arise, abide, and cease are the same; they are simultaneous and have the same duration. Fifth, the *substance* or *entity* of the primary consciousness and of the accompanying consciousnesses is the same, in that a single primary consciousness functions with one of each type of the accompanying consciousnesses. There cannot be two types of feelings accompanying one primary consciousness. Secondary consciousnesses, such as ignorance, attachment, and so on, must bear these five similarities to the primary consciousness they accompany. So there is no difference between the aspect of the primary mind and that of its accompanying mental factors. This means that they hold the object in the same way—as possessing a certain attribute.

If all mental afflictions arise on the basis of ignorance holding things incorrectly, then do all mental afflictions hold things as inherently existent? When mental afflictions arise, are they always similar to that ignorance in these five ways? Think about this carefully. What kind of ignorance are we talking about here? Is there attachment, hatred, jealousy, and so on that do not accompany the ignorance holding things as inherently existent but do accompany the ignorance holding impermanent things as permanent, impure things as pure, and so on? As we saw above, there are many ways to grasp things incorrectly, such as holding the aggregates to be attractive and pure, and this is called *inappropriate attention*. Inappropriate attention is based on ignorance, and attachment and hatred arise from it. When those experiences arise, in what sense do they possess similarity with ignorance? Do those minds grasp their object in the same way that ignorance does? First there is a mind of ignorance that holds the object wrongly—as inherently existent. Then there is a mind of inappropriate attention that holds the object in a further wrong way—as attractive, ugly, and so on. Then other mental afflictions arise on the basis of inappropriate attention. Seeing things as ugly usually gives rise to aversion and hatred; seeing things as beautiful usually gives rise to attachment and desire.

It is important to understand that I am talking about holding things as inherently existent, not about the appearance of things as inherently existent. As was noted above, except for the direct perception of emptiness, things appear as truly existent to any mind until one attains enlightenment. Every sentient being's awareness of conventional phenomena is mistaken in that its object appears to be inherently existent. Correct sense consciousnesses and virtuous mental consciousnesses—such as love, compassion, bodhicitta, the understanding of impermanence, the understanding of the truth of suffering, and so forth—are all mistaken consciousnesses because there is the appearance of an inherently existent object. However, they are not distorted or wrong consciousnesses.

The point to consider is how attachment holds its object in contrast to how altruistic love holds its object. We really must make a distinction here, otherwise we will have a lot of problems. What is the difference between love, which is a virtuous mind, and attachment, which is not? What is the difference between renunciation, which is a virtuous mind, and aversion, which is not? When ordinary people see something nasty, they think, "This is not good, I must get rid of it." Buddhist yogis think this way about their mental afflictions, suffering, and samsaric conditioning. They think of liberation and enlightenment as beautiful and desire to attain them. What makes one desire virtuous and another desire nonvirtuous? Desire has two modes. If desire arises on the basis of inappropriate attention, which holds its object in a distorted way, then it is attachment, which is a nonvirtuous consciousness. In contrast, if desire arises on the basis of a mind that holds its object correctly, then it is a virtuous consciousness. So the difference between them is whether we hold the object correctly.

Whatever mental afflictions we may have, all are pervaded by ignorance. They are all similar to ignorance, and ignorance is the dominating principle of them all. Therefore, if we destroy ignorance, we destroy all the mental afflictions. However, we need to understand how these various afflictive minds grasp their objects. In what way are all mental afflictions similar to ignorance? Do they all hold their objects in a similar way? We cannot say that all mental afflictions grasp inherent existence, because some hold their objects in a different way. One consciousness cannot hold everything; in fact, one consciousness cannot hold two things at the same time. Therefore we cannot say that the consciousness that holds impermanent things as permanent also holds things as inherently existent. The object certainly appears inherently existent to the mind holding impermanent things as permanent, but that mind's way of holding the object is just to hold it as permanent. Thus there are many mental afflictions that involve wrong understanding other than the grasping at inherent existence, including ways of grasping at the self, such as grasping at the self as permanent or grasping at the self as pure. We cannot say that all grasping at the self is the egotistic view grasping at inherent existence based on one's own aggregates. So we have to think about the way in which a mind is grasping its object. This distinction is significant because in order to eliminate grasping at permanence, we must logically prove that the object is not permanent. We do not need to understand that the object is not inherently existent.

What then does the phrase "not differently" in Candrakīrti's passage above mean? If we interpret these words to mean "similar" in the technical sense of bearing the five similarities, then we will face some hard problems. We would have to say that ignorance, which holds its object to be inherently existent, and attachment arising on the basis of inappropriate attention that holds an impermanent thing to be permanent have the same aspect—in that they hold their object in the same way. But clearly they do not. This attachment holds its object to be permanent, whereas this ignorance holds its object to be inherently existent. So the aspects of these two minds are different.

It would be all right to say that attachment that holds things to be inherently existent bears these five similarities to ignorance that holds things to be inherently existent—because both these minds hold their object in the same way. But we cannot say that all attachment arising indirectly on the basis of this ignorance bears these five similarities to it. Furthermore, the technical notion of possessing five similarities does not really apply here, because ignorance, being a mental affliction, is not a primary mind; it is a mental factor that is sometimes identified as a distorted wisdom.

In his commentary on Candrakīrti's *Introduction to the "Middle Way,"* Tsongkhapa glosses Candrakīrti's words as follows:

> Attachment and so on are not dissimilar to ignorance, in that the ways they engage their objects are similar to that of ignorance and are connected to it.[80]

How do attachment and ignorance engage their objects? An object, such as a pot, naturally appears to be inherently existent to an ordinary mind perceiving it, owing to the imprints of ignorance within the mindstream. This appearance is not in accordance with reality. Then a mind of ignorance, which is a mental affliction, holds that object to be inherently existent. This held object is also not in accordance with reality. Next, inappropriate attention superimposes particular attributes onto that object, such as holding it to be permanent, when in fact it is impermanent. This immediately gives rise to further mental afflictions, such as attachment. The fundamental basis of a mind of inappropriate attention, and any mental afflictions arising from it, is the ignorance that grasps things as inherently existent. Ignorance is the principal affliction; it is the basis on which all other mental afflictions arise. Other mental afflictions, such as attachment, are dominated by ignorance, so they engage their appearing objects in a way similar to ignorance. This is like saying, for example, that when two people travel to San Francisco by bus, they are traveling in the same way; but if one of them flies, they are not. So the words "not differently" in Candrakīrti's passage above do not refer to bearing five similarities in the technical sense described earlier. Attachment does not necessarily have the same aspect as ignorance, because these minds may engage their held objects in different ways. Rather, the phrase "not differently" means that attachment and ignorance are similar types of mind, in that they engage their appearing objects in a similar way. Remember, there are at least two types of objects of consciousness: the appearing object, which is the object as it appears to the consciousness, and the held object, which is the object as it is held by the consciousness.[81]

All mental afflictions are types of consciousness. There are two types of mental afflictions: innate and contrived. Contrived afflictions arise as a result of taking to heart certain philosophical systems, religious training, or other deliberate constructs. In contrast, the innate afflictions arise naturally owing to tendencies that have functioned within our mindstreams from time without beginning. A mental affliction never holds its object correctly; this means that its held object is always mistaken. So even though these mental afflictions are innate, the way they hold their objects can be eliminated by valid reasoning. In that case, the held object grasped by a mental affliction is not even conventionally existent. For example, conceiving the person to be permanent is refuted by valid reasoning that confirms the opposite, namely, that the person is impermanent. Valid knowing or valid reasoning relies on the truth, and thus it completely destroys a wrong cognition. An innate consciousness that holds its object correctly is valid. All living beings—including animals, children, and philosophers—have similar sense consciousnesses that perceive colors, shapes, sounds, and so on. These sense consciousnesses arise naturally, in dependence on innate tendencies and other causes and conditions. They do not depend on any philosophical belief system. The objects held by these naturally arisen sense consciousnesses cannot be negated by valid reasoning. This is because the objects established by these sense consciousnesses, such as forms, sounds, smells, and so on, are conventionally existent. Thus some innate consciousnesses are correct, and some—such as the egotistic view—are incorrect. In this sense, we can say that there are two types of innate mind: those whose objects are negated by valid reasoning and those whose objects are not negated by it.

Now although an object held by a valid sense consciousness cannot be negated, a conceptual consciousness that arises from it might be. When a sense consciousness perceives color, shape, and so on, a thought regarding it naturally arises. There is no special kind of reason, examination, or education involved. If the thought grasps its object incorrectly, then it can be negated. Usually as soon as we see an object, attachment or aversion naturally arises, perhaps even without our awareness of it. This is why innate afflictions, such as attachment and hatred, are so difficult to remove. In order to totally remove the innate mental afflictions, we must eliminate ignorance, because these afflictions depend on and are influenced by ignorance. Ignorance cannot be removed without engaging in ultimate analysis.

Tsongkhapa gives us some advice here. He says that in the Prāsaṅgika tradition of the great masters Buddhapālita and Candrakīrti, it is very difficult to understand how to establish conventional things, because a thing existing by way of its own nature is negated even conventionally. It often happens that when people try to negate things as inherently existent, they conclude that they are totally nonexistent, and when they try to establish things as existent, they conclude that they are inherently existent. Most people think that if things do not inherently exist, then they do not exist at all. According to them, if something exists and is properly established, then it must be inherently existent. The Prāsaṅgika system makes a distinction here: things do not exist inherently, but they do exist. Things do not exist from their own side or by their own nature. But they do exist merely based on thought and language; they exist only conventionally, relatively, dependently.

Although it is extremely difficult to understand this, we will have no certainty regarding our practice if we do not know how to establish conventional things properly. Without a clear understanding of the wisdom side, the practice or method side will be unstable. It is of utmost importance not to lose the practice side. This includes ethical discipline, taking refuge, developing love and compassion, and so forth. It is difficult to develop a definite understanding of these teachings and practices if we incorrectly view things to be inherently existent. We will not be able to establish cause and effect properly. Therefore the correct view is the most essential thing, because without it we will lose the practice side.

Tsongkhapa shows this throughout the *Lamrim Chenmo*. The first half of the text is primarily about how to develop the practice side. The final chapter—almost the entire second half of the text—is about developing insight. We need to understand how to establish our practice without losing the correct view. If through establishing the view we abandon our practice, or if through establishing our practice we lose the correct view, then our practice will not be complete. Therefore, although it is most difficult to establish these two together, intelligent people should develop mastery of the way to establish conventional truth and ultimate truth, according to the subtle Prāsaṅgika system. Tsongkhapa does not elaborate any further on this topic. He fears he has already said too much. Although there have been a lot of words, we still need more, don't we?

Production Is Not Negated

(c")) The distinguishing feature of Madhyamaka cannot be disproved by
    negating things from the perspective of examining whether or not they
    are produced in dependence on one of the four alternative means of
    production
(d")) The distinguishing feature of Madhyamaka cannot be disproved by
    negating things from the perspective of the four alternatives

---

(c")) THE DISTINGUISHING FEATURE OF MADHYAMAKA CANNOT BE DISPROVED BY NEGATING THINGS FROM THE PERSPECTIVE OF EXAMINING WHETHER OR NOT THEY ARE PRODUCED IN DEPENDENCE ON ONE OF THE FOUR ALTERNATIVE MEANS OF PRODUCTION

MOST PEOPLE ACCEPT that if something arises from causes and conditions, it must arise from one of four alternatives: from self, from others, from both self and others, or without a cause. However, all four alternatives are negated by Mādhyamikas, who base their view on the first stanza of Nāgārjuna's *Fundamental Treatise on the Middle Way*:

> Not from self, not from others,
> Not from both, not without a cause;
> Any things, anywhere,
> Do not arise at any time.

An opponent raises the following objection: "If this refutation of arising from the four alternatives negates production, then according to this

Madhyamaka system these four types of production do not exist even conventionally, so there is no need to add any special qualification such as 'ultimately.' Conversely, if it does not negate production, then ultimate production is also not negated by this refutation of arising from the four alternatives."

Mādhyamikas do not accept the first position—that refutation of arising from the four alternatives negates production in general. So Tsongkhapa addresses only the second objection—that refutation of arising from the four alternatives does not negate ultimate production because it does not negate production in general. To take this position one must assume that not every kind of production is included in the four alternatives; in other words, there is some form of production that is not any of the four alternatives. Tsongkhapa argues that if you accept ultimate production, then you must accept that production is able to withstand ultimate analysis. In that case, you must logically examine whether production is from self, from others, from both, or without a cause. Only by finding some kind of production through engaging in this analysis can we say that there is ultimate production. This analysis becomes the affirmation of ultimate arising because if something arises inherently or by its own nature, it can be found to arise from one of these four alternatives. If analysis does not find production from one of the four alternatives, there is no ultimate arising.

Tsongkhapa says that the Mādhyamikas accept mere production—the arising of a result in dependence on a cause—but they do not accept ultimate production. Because the Mādhyamikas do not accept ultimate production, they are not obliged to accept that production is able to withstand ultimate analysis. There is no need to examine mere production in general by means of ultimate analysis to determine whether it is produced from any of the four alternatives.

Now you may wonder, "Why don't the Mādhyamikas accept the second of the four alternative means of production: that results arise from other causes?" It is obvious that they do not accept the first: that results arise from themselves. Therefore they do not accept the third: that results arise from both themselves and other causes. The fourth—that results arise without a cause—is impossible. So what is the matter with arising from others? Actually, this is the basis of the difference between the Svātantrika-Madhyamaka and the Prāsaṅgika-Madhyamaka systems. The Svātantrika-Madhyamaka, Yogācāra, and other Buddhist systems assert that there is production from other causes. In a general context, when we say *arising from others*, the word "others" indicates that a cause and its effect are different from each other. However, according to the Prāsaṅgika, this is not what is meant in the context of ultimate analysis. Tsongkhapa explains:

In the context of arising from others, "others" does not mean "mere others;" it means "inherently existent others."[82]

This means that *arising from others* refers to an inherently existent other result arising from inherently existent other causes. Therefore the Prāsaṅgikas say that even production from others is conventionally nonexistent.

Moreover, *mere production* means to arise in dependence on causes and conditions. This kind of dependent arising, used as a reason, refutes *production from the four alternatives* as follows: it disproves the arising from self, and it disproves the arising from inherently existent other causes, so it refutes the arising from both of these together; and, since it explicitly indicates arising in dependence on causes and conditions, it refutes the arising without a cause. Candrakīrti's *Introduction to the "Middle Way"* says:

> Because things dependently arise,
> These notions cannot bear analysis.
> Thus all nets of wrong views are severed
> By this reason: dependent arising.

Fishermen use nets to catch fish. Similarly, wrong views entrap sentient beings. The logical reason of dependent arising cuts through all the nets of wrong views. Dependent arising itself is the reason that things are not inherently existent. Using this reason, you can prove that all things are not inherently existent and thereby conquer the ignorance that is the root of all mental afflictions. Therefore dependent arising is called the "king of reasons." Śūnyatā—the emptiness of inherent existence—can be proved in various ways, but dependent arising is the most powerful proof of all. It alone cuts through the two extremes of nihilism and eternalism. The term *dependent* eliminates anything that exists inherently, by its own nature, or without a cause. The term *arising* shows that things exist and are not completely nothing.

Tsongkhapa now addresses his opponent: "Although Candrakīrti explains that dependent arising negates production from the four alternatives, you think that if something does not arise from one of the four alternative means of production, then there is no mere production at all. You seem to be saying the opposite of what Candrakīrti says." Again, he quotes from the *Introduction to the "Middle Way"* to point out the contradiction between his opponents' positions and Candrakīrti's view:

> Because things do not arise
> Without a cause, from others such as Īśvara,

Or from themselves, others, or both,
They are produced dependently.

Candrakīrti says that because things dependently arise, they do not arise from the four ultimate means of production. In contrast, the opponents say that if something arises, it must be from one of the four ultimate means of production. The Sāṃkhyas believe in a universal principal cause, which is invisible, absolute, permanent, partless, and produces all things. Thus they believe that things arise from their own nature and are thereby self-producing. The lower Buddhist schools believe that things arise from inherently existent other causes that produce inherently existent other results. The Jains assert that things arise from both themselves and other causes. But Prāsaṅgikas assert that produced things do not arise from any of those putative causes—instead they arise dependently on causes and conditions. Dependently arising things are free of the extremes, since they are free of the four extremes of production. Therefore one should not ask, "From which of those four extremes do they arise?" The problem underlying such a question is an inability to distinguish between *not arising inherently* and "not arising" in general.

"Well then," the opponent asks, "How do you explain this statement of Candrakīrti?"

Whatever argument is used in the context of ultimate analysis
To negate production from self and others,
That argument negates it even conventionally.

On the surface it looks as if Candrakīrti is saying that the same logical analysis that negates ultimate production also negates conventional arising. In other words, if things do not arise from one of the four alternate ways of arising, then things cannot arise conventionally. That is not a correct interpretation of this passage. This stanza actually means that logical analysis of ultimate reality can prove that inherently existent production—production that exists by way of its own characteristics—does not exist even conventionally. However, that logical analysis does not negate mere production or production in general. This is shown in the linking commentary. A linking commentary is a transitional passage that connects portions of a text. These transitional passages introduce the rationale for the next section; however, they do not contain the meaning of the text itself. The linking commentary that introduces the above stanza is:

Opponent: Any cause of the thoroughly afflicted or of the completely purified must produce something with a substantial nature.

Reply: Such a statement is left as mere words [without explicating any meaning]. Why?

This is because such a statement does not establish anything. It does not demonstrate that if *this* is the case, then *that* follows. This transitional passage leads into Candrakīrti's response, given in the stanza above: "Whatever argument is used in the context of ultimate analysis . . ." His commentary explains this stanza as follows:

> Production by way of its own characteristics does not exist in terms of either of the two truths. You are obliged to accept that, even if you do not want to.

Bhāvaviveka and all the Buddhist schools except the Prāsaṅgika, as well as all non-Buddhist philosophical systems, accept production that exists by way of its own characteristics. So when Bhāvaviveka says "Things exist conventionally" he actually means "Things inherently exist conventionally," even though he denies that they ultimately exist. Inherent existence is one of the most difficult philosophical issues. All the Prāsaṅgikas' opponents say that if you reject inherent production, you totally negate the existence of anything. Therefore they claim you cannot negate inherent production. Although Bhāvaviveka accepts inherently existent production, he negates ultimate production. This is a problem. According to the Prāsaṅgikas, accepting inherently existent production is the same as accepting ultimate production. If you accept inherent production, or production that exists by way of its own characteristics, you must accept ultimate production; when you negate ultimate production, you must negate inherent production in the same way—even as conventionally existent. Therefore, because there is no difference between inherent existence and ultimate existence, from the Prāsaṅgika point of view Bhāvaviveka is uttering meaningless words. Just as he negates ultimate production, he must negate inherently existent production conventionally—even though he does not want to do so.

To prove his point, Tsongkhapa quotes from the texts of Buddhapālita and Candrakīrti many times to show that they not only negate ultimate production—which is common to all Mādhyamikas—but they also negate inherent production. Over and over again Tsongkhapa points out that production that exists by its own characteristics must be treated in the same way as ultimate production. Candrakīrti makes the point very clearly in another passage from *Introduction to the "Middle Way"*:

> A barren woman's son is not self-arisen
> Either conventionally or ultimately;
> Likewise, all these things do not arise inherently
> Either ultimately or conventionally.

To assert that something exists inherently, or by its own nature, is like introducing the son of a barren woman. Such a child does not exist either ultimately or conventionally. Because this is the profound meaning explained by the master Candrakīrti, we should not accept production that exists by its own nature even conventionally.

However, some people believe that if things are not inherently produced, or if production has no inherent nature, then there is no production at all. They argue that Candrakīrti and other Prāsaṅgika-Mādhyamikas contradict themselves by saying that things arise dependently but do not arise inherently. They say that if something does not inherently arise, then it cannot dependently arise, and if it dependently arises, then it must inherently arise. Candrakīrti responds that those who argue in this way are arguing "without ears or heart": without ears, they do not hear the word "inherently" in the phrase "not inherently produced," so they think the phrase means "not produced"; without heart, they hear the word "inherently" but do not properly understand its meaning. Nāgārjuna says in the *Sixty Stanzas of Reasoning*:

> The supreme knower of reality taught that
> Whatever is dependently produced is not produced.

Candrakīrti's commentary on this passage says:

> When you see dependent arising, you do not see things as inherently existent, because whatever is dependently produced, like a reflection, is not inherently produced.
> *Objection*: Is it not the case that whatever is dependently produced is simply produced? How can the words "dependently produced" mean "not produced"? Whatever is expressed when we say "not produced" cannot be expressed by the words "dependently produced." Therefore your position is incorrect because these are mutually contradictory.
> *Reply*: Oh, poor thing! This arguing without ears or heart puts us in a difficult spot. When we say, "Whatever is dependently produced, like a reflection, is not inherently produced," how can there be an occasion to argue?

The reflection of a face in a mirror does not arise by itself. Even ordinary people understand that many causes and conditions come together to give rise to that reflection: our eyes, light, the mirror, and someone's face before it. Similarly, dependently produced things exist, but they do not exist as they appear—that is, as inherently existent. Furthermore, if something does not arise inherently, it means that it arises dependently. If it arises dependently, it means that it does not arise inherently. The Madhyamaka position is that *inherently produced* and *dependently produced* are contradictory. However, if the opponent does not hear the word *inherently* or does not understand its meaning, he will think that the Prāsaṅgikas are saying that *produced* and *dependently produced* are contradictory. Therefore it is very important to clearly distinguish the meanings of these terms: inherent existence and mere existence, inherent arising and dependent arising, and inherently produced and dependently produced.

Next Tsongkhapa quotes from the *Question of the Nāga King Anavatapta* (*Anavatapta-nāga-rāja-paripṛcchā-sūtra*). The title of this sutra is based on the ancient name of a lake and the nāga king of the same name who lived there and asked Buddha to give a special teaching to his subjects. Buddha said:

> Whatever arises from conditions does not arise;
> It does not have the inherent nature of arising.
> Whatever depends on conditions is said to be empty;
> Whoever understands emptiness in this way is diligent.

The first line of this stanza looks like a contradiction; how can whatever arises from conditions not arise? Tsongkhapa explains that the second line, "it does not have the inherent nature of arising," explicitly qualifies the manner in which such things do not arise as expressed in the first line. So the words in the first line "does not arise" are qualified by the second line to mean: *does not inherently arise*. Thus the sutra is not saying that whatever arises from conditions is not produced in general; it means that whatever arises dependently from causes and conditions is not inherently produced, or does not inherently arise, and does not have any inherently existent production. However, those who do not understand this seem to think that the words of this sutra are contradictory. They proudly make exaggerated and contradictory announcements, such as, "Just the arisen do not arise; just the dependent are not dependent."

When something is negated, a special qualification may need to be applied. This qualification may be applied in one place and not appear throughout the rest of the text; however, it should be understood to apply in every case. For example, when the *Heart Sutra* says in one place, "Perfectly see that even the five aggregates are empty of inherent existence," the qualification "inherent" is then understood to qualify every instance when the sutra says that things are empty or nonexistent. In *Clear Words*, Candrakīrti quotes the *Descent into Laṅka Sutra* to answer the question of whether the qualification "ultimate" should be applied to the negation of production from the four alternatives. In the sutra, Buddha says to Mañjuśri:

> O Great Wise One, thinking that things do not arise inherently, I said that all phenomena do not arise.

The meaning of this statement was already given briefly above. A detailed discussion of whether the qualification "ultimately" should be applied in all cases will appear later in the context of the Svātantrika-Prāsaṅgika debate on this matter.

In summary, the Prāsaṅgika-Mādhyamikas establish cause and effect while accepting everything to be empty of inherent existence. However, their opponents try to show that the Prāsaṅgika view implies a contradiction. They say that if things are not inherently existent then you cannot establish cause and effect. Tsongkhapa says that all these attempted refutations put forward by the opponents do not succeed in refuting Candrakīrti and his followers. To understand Tsongkhapa's point here, you have to know something about Buddhist logic.

A proof statement is a type of syllogism. A syllogism has the form: A is B because of being C, for example, D. If someone has explicitly realized this inference and yet also implicitly accepts a view that implies that A is $\sim B$, then you can reveal this contradiction to him and negate his wrong view by using a refuting consequence. In general a refuting consequence is used to uproot a wrong view that the opponent holds tightly, and a syllogism is used to prove a correct view about which the opponent has some doubt. A refuting consequence shows the opponent that by accepting certain premises, which he wishes to accept, he is thereby committed to accepting certain conclusions that follow from those premises and that contradict his own views. Even though the opponent does not want to accept these consequences, he is impelled to do so because they follow from what he asserts. The unwelcome consequences entailed by his view function to disprove his view.

An opponent may object to a refuting consequence, but if it is correct then he cannot disprove it. However, sometimes in debate a person may put forward a refuting consequence that is logically incorrect. Such a fallacious refuting consequence can be disproved. In general, the height of fallacious consequential reasoning is when one's own analytical argument, aimed at refuting one's opponent, can be turned back and applied in its entirety to oneself—for this demonstrates that one's argument is fallacious in the first place. That is what is happening here. The opponents' argument—that the Prāsaṅgika-Mādhyamika view is contradicted by an examination of whether or not things can withstand ultimate analysis—can be turned back against them and applied to them. As this is the case, the Prāsaṅgikas disprove the accusation that their own view entails unacceptable consequences by demonstrating that their opponents are using fallacious refuting consequences.

Now the opponents say, "Because you accept form, causality, and so on as existent, all these refuting consequences apply to you. They do not apply to us because we do not hold any position of our own." These opponents misinterpret Nāgārjuna to mean, "Because I do not have any thesis, I do not have any assertions. I do not accept that anything exists, does not exist, both, or neither. I do not accept that anything arises or does not arise." Tsongkhapa says that this answer does not enable them to abandon all their mistakes. This will be shown in detail later when discussing whether Madhyamaka analysis should use consequences or autonomous syllogisms.

(d")) THE DISTINGUISHING FEATURE OF MADHYAMAKA CANNOT BE DISPROVED BY NEGATING THINGS FROM THE PERSPECTIVE OF THE FOUR ALTERNATIVES

An opponent criticizes the Madhyamaka system, saying that the analytical reasoning presented in Madhyamaka texts negating things as inherently existent, nonexistent, both, and neither negates everything—since there is nothing not included within those four possibilities. Therefore he concludes the middle-way approach is to not accept any of them: things are neither this nor that.

As explained in chapter 5, the word *thing* has two meanings: first, a thing is anything that exists by its own nature; and second, a thing is anything that is able to function or produce a result. The Mādhyamikas negate the former both ultimately and conventionally; a thing that exists by its own nature is totally unreal and does not exist at all. Mādhyamikas do not negate a functional thing conventionally; however, they do negate it ultimately. A real or functional thing does not exist ultimately, but it does exist conventionally. Then there is another kind of existent thing, which does not arise or cease in dependence on causes and conditions, and it does not produce any kind of result. It is not momentary. It merely exists. We call it an *unreal thing*.

Unreal things are established by valid knowledge. Within the Buddhist framework, *to exist* means to be established by valid knowledge. Based on the system of logic presented by Dharmakīrti in *Commentary on Valid Cognition*, the Sautrāntika and Yogācāra systems present an array of unreal things, such as uncaused space, emptiness, conventional truth,[83] and generally characterized phenomena. In contrast to individually characterized phenomena, which are functional or real, unreal things are merely imputed by name and thought. Unreal things are not completely nonexistent; they exist, but they are not functional. They appear to conceptual consciousness. However, not everything that is thought of or spoken about is an unreal thing. There are plenty of things that we think of and speak about that do not exist at all, such as a rabbit horn or the son of a barren woman. These are "unreal" in a wider sense of that word, but they are not *unreal phenomena* in the sense of the current discussion. They are called *nothings*. We must distinguish between *unreal things*, which exist yet do not function, and *nothings*, which do not exist at all. This categorization is common to all Buddhist schools.

To understand better the concept of "unreal things," let us look at the example of space. First we should understand that space is different from the element of space. The element of space is what we can see and feel with our sense consciousnesses. It is the empty area between things, which may be a certain color, light, or dark. But this is not space. Space is an unreal thing. Why? It does not have any material properties but is just imputed by word and thought. Space is the mere absence of obstructive contact. This absence is why we can put a physical object, such as a table, in a certain place. The fact that the table is there means that space exists; it is there to accommodate it. This mere absence cannot be seen by visual consciousness, so it is not the impermanent element of space that can be measured. But it can be known by valid knowledge. It is imputed on a real thing by thought and language.

The same is true of śūnyatā. When we say "emptiness of table" or "emptiness of form," we are not saying that the table or the form itself is emptiness. "Emptiness of form" implies an analysis that finds a pure negation. Things are not ultimately existent; they are not inherently existent. This mere negation cannot be touched or seen by the senses. Also, it cannot be created. We can say that the table is empty of inherent existence. That is the mere absence of an inherent nature. This lack of inherent existence is not created by anybody. We cannot say that the table was inherently existent before, and then later owing to certain causes and conditions or owing to certain logical refutations it became noninherently existent. The table is empty of inherent existence from the very beginning. This noninherent existence is knowable and understandable. However, this kind of uncaused phenomenon is permanent and nonfunctional. It does not change. It has always been there and will always be there, forever.

According to Buddhist logic and epistemology, there are so many uncaused things—more than all the real, functional things existing in any time and place. For example, this table is a single functional thing. Based on this table, valid knowing can understand so many unreal things. When we examine it to see whether it is inherently existent, we find it is noninherently existent. If we ask whether this table is an elephant, we find it is empty of being an elephant. So this table is a nonelephant. Nobody caused this table to be a nonelephant. Even before the table was made, it was empty of being an elephant. Now you can see how there are many more uncaused phenomena or unreal things than there are functional things. It is important to understand what is an unreal thing—and in what sense it is nonfunctional. We must also understand the difference between an unreal thing and a nonthing like a rabbit horn. We cannot establish rabbit horns by any means of valid knowing because they do not exist at all. However, we can logically prove various negations: this table is nonhuman, it is a nonelephant, and it is noninherently existent. We can understand these by valid knowledge.

It is not correct to hold that uncaused, unreal things are inherently existent. Unreal things are not inherently existent in just the same way that real things are not inherently existent. Yet they exist—as nonfunctioning phenomena. We have to negate all four extremes—existence, nonexistence, both, and neither—with respect to both real and unreal things. The style of negation here is to apply the qualification "inherently" to existence, to nonexistence, to both, and to neither, and then negate all four possibilities—with respect to both real things and unreal things. If we negate these four without applying the qualification *inherently*, we contradict ourselves. It is illogical to flatly deny that things are existent, nonexistent, both, and neither. First, when we say a thing is "not existent" and then negate its opposite by saying it is "not nonexistent," there is a contradiction. Next, when we say it is "not both" and then negate that by saying it is "not not both," the second assertion is equivalent to saying "it is both," which directly contradicts the first assertion. However, we can say that things are "not existent by their own nature" and are "not nonexistent by their own nature." The difference occurs in applying the qualification "inherently" or "by its own nature." With this qualification we can negate all of the possibilities without any problems. What we are negating is the qualification "inherently." Without that qualification, existent and nonexistent are mutually exclusive; if you reject one then you must assert the other, and vice versa. Similarly, if you negate both existent and nonexistent, then you must accept neither existent nor nonexistent; if you negate neither, then you must accept both. It is completely contradictory to flatly say: not existent, not nonexistent, not both, and not neither. Despite contradicting themselves like this, the opponents declare, "Even so, there is no fault." This is a crazy way of talking. Mādhyamikas do not want to debate with crazy people! This is Tsongkhapa's summary of Candrakīrti's points.

Moreover, when you negate a self or an inherently existent nature based on the aggregates, it gives rise to the wisdom understanding that there is no inherent nature or self. If you also negate the noninherent existence that is the object of that wisdom, you are disproving the object of the wisdom realizing that phenomena are not inherently existent. In short, you reject the Madhyamaka view. There are some people who assert that you can negate both *inherent existence* and *the absence of inherent existence*. This is not possible. If you negate *inherent existence*, then you must accept *the absence of inherent existence*; if you negate *the absence of inherent existence*, then you must accept *inherent existence*. If you say that both are negated, then how do you negate the lack of inherent nature that is the object of the wisdom understanding that the aggregates have no inherent nature? You cannot negate that.

In response to Tsongkhapa's points here, an opponent cites Nāgārjuna's *Fundamental Treatise*:

> If nonemptiness exists,
> Then emptiness also exists.
> If nonemptiness does not exist,
> Then how can emptiness exist?

The opponent thinks this stanza means that because there is nothing that is not empty, everything is empty. Therefore the emptiness of inherent existence is also empty—of itself. Thus it is not empty of inherent existence; it is inherently existent. Tsongkhapa replies that in the *Fundamental Treatise*, "empty" and "not empty" mean *empty of inherent existence* and *not empty of inherent existence*, respectively. In this context, emptiness always means emptiness of inherent existence. Therefore if something is not empty of inherent existence, it is inherently existent. It is ridiculous to say that if there is no inherent existence at all, there is no emptiness of inherent existence. What Nāgārjuna is really saying here is that where a conventional basis that is not emptiness exists, then emptiness that is based on it exists; where there is no basis of emptiness, then there is no emptiness.

Furthermore, the wisdom that ascertains that a thing, such as a sprout, has no inherently existent nature holds that a sprout does not inherently exist. But, as you will easily know when you close your eyes and look within, it does not hold noninherent existence itself to exist, nor indeed not to exist. In other words, when you find that a sprout does not have inherent existence, you are using the sprout as the basis of negation. That understanding holds the sprout to be not inherently existent. However, that consciousness does not analyze whether or not the emptiness of the sprout exists. Another consciousness, going a step further, uses noninherent existence as the basis and analyzes whether or not it exists. First you understand that a specific thing is not inherently existent. Then in a subsequent investigation you examine whether that noninherent existence itself exists. For example, when you consider whether there is an elephant in your room, you see that there is no elephant. Does that very same consciousness, understanding that there is no elephant, also consider whether the absence-of-an-elephant in your room exists? No, it does not.

The mind understanding that there is no inherent existence is not suitable to apprehend that emptiness itself exists. Although it is appropriate to negate the inherent existence of emptiness by means of ultimate analysis in order to reverse the grasping at the existence of emptiness, one must accept that the object of the mind grasping emptiness to exist is negated by another mind. In any case it is totally incorrect to try to negate the object of the wisdom understanding a sprout to be empty of inherent existence. The object of that wisdom is *empty of inherent existence* based on a sprout. The Mādhyamikas say that when we use ultimate analysis to examine whether anything, such as a sprout, is inherently existent, we eventually realize that such a basis is not inherently existent. This is the understanding of emptiness: śūnyatā. The object of this realization—the emptiness of inherent existence—exists conventionally. We understand this existence by means of conventional knowledge. Different consciousnesses examine whether something is conventionally existent or whether it is inherently existent. Conventional valid knowledge understands emptiness to be conventionally existent. The object of that understanding cannot be negated by ultimate analysis; the mere existence of the emptiness of inherent existence is not to be negated. So, after having understood that there is no inherent existence based on a sprout, we can engage in another analysis to examine whether śūnyatā itself exists. The first investigation uses ultimate analysis and the second uses conventional analysis. The mere existence of śūnyatā cannot be proved or negated by ultimate analysis. After that, we can take śūnyatā as the existent basis and use ultimate analysis to investigate whether śūnyatā itself is empty of inherent existence. In this way we negate the object of a mind that holds śūnyatā to be inherently existent. This is how we prove the emptiness of emptiness.

Some earlier scholars, notably Kunkhyen Jonangpa, say that all conventional things are empty, yet they have an ultimate nature. If we ask whether this ultimate nature is conventionally or ultimately existent, they say it is ultimately existent; emptiness is what is found by ultimate analysis, therefore it ultimately exists. Only śūnyatā is ultimately existent. Everything else is conventionally existent, not ultimately existent. In contrast, Prāsaṅgikas say that all phenomena are empty of inherent existence. Having understood things to be empty of inherent existence, you examine whether that emptiness itself inherently exists and find that it does not. Emptiness is also empty of inherent existence. Does emptiness exist? Yes, of course emptiness exists—conventionally.

You may wonder, "How could someone develop the idea that śūnyatā is inherently existent?" When someone has engaged in ultimate analysis of a sprout and comes to understand that it does not inherently exist, the object observed by that consciousness is the emptiness of the sprout. Having developed an understanding of that object—the noninherent existence of the sprout—he or she may consider this emptiness to be the inherent nature of the sprout. Sometimes the mind behaves like this. For example, where there is no vase a person does not think, "It is true that there is a vase." However, the thought "It is true that there is no vase" may arise. In a similar way, when you understand that everything is not inherently existent, the thought "It is true that everything is inherently existent" will not arise, because you have already understood the opposite—that everything lacks inherent existence. However, you might start to think, "Noninherent existence itself is truly existent."

Nāgārjuna's verse above is saying that because there is nothing that does not lack inherent existence, the noninherent existence of any phenomenon also lacks inherent existence. This applies to the śūnyatā of anything. The emptiness that is the noninherent existence of a sprout has no inherent existence. The emptiness of emptiness, or the noninherent existence of noninherent existence, also has no inherent existence. Everything, including emptiness, is empty of inherent existence. The *Commentary on the "Four Hundred Stanzas"* says:

> Here it teaches that emptiness itself is negated as inherently existent. If so-called emptiness were inherently existent, then things would be inherently existent; but that does not exist. In order to show this, Āryadeva says:
>
>> As there is nothing that is not empty,
>> How can emptiness be so?
>> As there is nothing to oppose,
>> How can there be its antidote?

If there is no object to be abandoned, then how can there be its antidote? The object to be abandoned—grasping at inherent existence, is opposed by its antidote—the wisdom realizing śūnyatā. The object to be negated—inherent existence—is opposed by emptiness. Conversely, if you negate the existence of the emptiness of inherent existence, then there would be no noninherent existence. In consequence, an inherently existent nature would exist, and inherent existence could not be negated at all. This is taught again and again because, although scholars may accept that sprouts and other phenomena are empty of inherent existence, there is a strongly held view that the emptiness of inherent existence itself is truly existent. Nāgārjuna's *Refutation of Objections* says:

> How could "not inherently existent"
> Negate *not inherently existent*?
> If it negates *not inherently existent*,
> Then it proves *inherently existent*.

Nāgārjuna explains the meaning of this passage in *Commentary on the "Refutation of Objections."* Here the opponent thinks that by negating the inherent existence of things, noninherent existence itself is negated; thus inherent existence exists and things are inherently existent. The example he gives is that sound is stopped by the sound of the words "Be quiet." However, Nāgārjuna says the example does not apply to this case. It cannot prove inherent existence.

Opponent: Just as the sound of the words "do not make a sound" stop sound, similarly the words "not inherently existent" negate the noninherent existence of things. Therefore this analogy is correct.

Reply: Here the words "not inherently existent" negate the inherent existence of things. If the words "not inherently existent" negated the noninherent existence of things, then noninherent existence itself would be negated. Thus things would have inherent nature, and since they would have inherent nature, they would not be empty.

Above, we looked at the stanza from Nāgārjuna's *Fundamental Treatise*:

> If nonemptiness exists,
> Then emptiness also exists;
> If nonemptiness does not exist,
> Then how can emptiness exist?

The next stanza is:

> The Victorious Ones say that emptiness
> Definitively negates all views.

But they say there is no proving it
To those who have a view of emptiness.

The realization of emptiness completely destroys wrong views from the root. In the last line, the phrase "view of emptiness" does not mean viewing things as empty of inherent existence. It means viewing emptiness as truly or inherently existent. There is no proving what is validly established to people holding this wrong view of emptiness. The reason for this is very clearly shown by Buddhapālita:

> To those who say "Things exist by their own essential nature" and grasp at them as real, you can explain that this so-called emptiness actually means dependent arising: they are imputed as real by the power of causes and conditions but do not exist by their own essential nature. You can reverse their grasping at inherent existence when you clearly show that things are empty of inherent existence. But there is no possible means to reverse the grasping of those who grasp emptiness as inherently existent. For example, if you say "I have nothing" and another person says "Please give me that nothing," how can you make that person understand that there is nothing?

This example of confusion over "nothing" is directly analogous to those who think that everything is empty of inherent existence, and so the emptiness of inherent existence itself exists inherently. Suppose someone says to you, "Give me some money," and you reply, "I have no money." There is no problem if the requestor understands that you do not have any money. However, if he or she thinks that "no money" is a kind of currency, then they have no basis for understanding that there is no money. Likewise, suppose someone asks, "Do things have inherent existence or not?" and is told, "No, they do not have inherent existence." There is no problem if the questioner understands by this that there is no inherent existence. It is simply a case of one person letting another know that there is no inherent existence. A problem arises when the questioner understands "not having inherent existence" to be an inherently existent thing itself. This is the opponents' position. If we analyze the example according to their interpretation of emptiness, when someone says, "I have no money," they think that the person has "no money," as if that person did have money. So this idea would have to be negated yet again. The opponents' interpretation is contradictory; it would be wonderful if they relied on what the Mādhyamikas say.

Candrakīrti's commentary, *Clear Words*, also says that the phrase "the view of emptiness" in Nāgārjuna's verse above refers to emptiness held as a real thing, which must be negated—though there is no problem with merely viewing things as empty of inherent existence. Emptiness itself is not to be negated. The *Verse Summary of the Perfection of Wisdom* says:

> If, when thinking "These aggregates are empty" a bodhisattva
> Is employing signs, then he or she lacks faith in nonproduced abiding.

"Employing signs" means to hold things as truly existent. So if a bodhisattva employs signs when thinking about the emptiness of inherent existence, he or she is holding emptiness itself to be truly existent. In that case, he or she lacks faith in noninherent existence. The term "employing signs" derives from the famous phrase, "All phenomena are in the nature of emptiness, signlessness, and wishlessness." The key factor is emptiness. Nāgārjuna's *Precious Garland* says:

> Therefore, the Great Sage refuted
> Views of self and selflessness.

Buddha explains two views of self: the grasping at a self of persons, which includes the egotistic view grasping at oneself as inherently existent, and the grasping at a self of phenomena, which is the grasping at things as inherently existent. Both the person and phenomena actually exist in the opposite way: they are selfless. Thus there are two kinds of selflessness: the selflessness of persons and the selflessness of phenomena. We need to understand selflessness in order to overcome the two views of self. However, if we hold selflessness to be inherently existent, then both our view holding the self and our view holding selflessness will be wrong; in both cases we will be grasping at inherent existence. There are many sutras and treatises that say the view of emptiness and the view of selflessness are unsuitable. It is important to understand those words as they are explained here. In short, the "view of emptiness" means holding emptiness to be inherently existent; the "view of selflessness" means holding selflessness to be inherently existent. Viewing emptiness or selflessness as real or as inherently existent is incorrect. All things are empty and selfless. The statements in the sutras and treatises are not rejecting emptiness and selflessness; they must be understood to mean that viewing emptiness or selflessness as truly real is incorrect. Otherwise, they would contradict many other statements in the scriptures. For example, in the *Heart Sutra* when Śāriputra asks the great bodhisattva Avalokiteśvara how to practice and train in the profound perfection of wisdom, Avalokiteśvara replies:

Perfectly see that even the five aggregates are empty of inherent existence.

The *Verse Summary of the Perfection of Wisdom* says:

One who understands fully that all phenomena are not inherently existent is practicing the supreme perfection of wisdom.

And the *Introduction to the "Middle Way"* says:

By seeing that the self and belonging to the self are empty,
The yogi becomes completely liberated.

These three quotations say the same thing about emptiness. The first two explicitly mention the absence of inherent existence, and the third includes it implicitly.

The root of all suffering in cyclic existence is the ignorance that superimposes an inherent nature on things. Many methods are taught to temporarily control and subdue ignorance, but they are not enough to completely get rid of it. How do we do that? We must develop the wisdom that directly and completely contradicts ignorance and its way of grasping at inherent existence. Wisdom apprehends things in a way completely opposite to the way ignorance does. Ignorance holds its object to be inherently existent; wisdom holds its object to be noninherently existent. The object does not exist in the way it is held by ignorance. Wisdom correctly understands how things exist. Because the wisdom that understands selflessness or noninherent existence directly contradicts ignorance, it is the only thing that can uproot it. This is an important point because all the Buddhist schools below the Prāsaṅgika believe that *noninherent existence* means nothingness or nonexistence.

If you negate the way that wisdom apprehends its object and say that emptiness itself is not empty of true existence, then you are rejecting the correct view of reality. You have to accept this even if you do not want to. The valid knowledge directly perceiving emptiness is the only way to achieve the peace of liberation, nirvana, the total and permanent freedom from suffering and its causes. Āryadeva's *Four Hundred Stanzas* says:

The one and only door to peace,
It destroys wrong views;
It is the object of all the buddhas,
That which is called "selflessness."

Candrakīrti, commenting on this stanza, says:

> The complete extinction of attachment is the cause of attaining nir-
> vana. Except for perceiving noninherent existence, there is no other
> Dharma that causes the complete extinction of attachment. Therefore
> this selflessness, with the nature of noninherent existence, is the door
> to peace. There is no other; it alone is the only incomparable door to
> entering the city of nirvana. Although there are said to be three doors
> to liberation—emptiness, signlessness, and wishlessness—the princi-
> pal one is selflessness. For where there is the understanding that all
> phenomena are selfless and attachment toward everything is exhausted,
> how could there be the apprehension of signs or the striving to attain
> anything? Thus this [understanding of] selflessness is the one and only
> door to peace. Therefore, the *Requisites for Enlightenment* (*Byang chub
> kyi tshogs*) says:
>
> > [In seeing] the empty to be empty of inherent existence,
> > What use would there be for signs?
> > Since all signs would be reversed,
> > What would the wise be wishing for?

At the beginning of this passage, the term "attachment" encompasses all the
mental afflictions—which arise because the mind is dominated by attachment
to "I" and "mine." Candrakīrti says that the only way to remove all of them
is to understand the emptiness of inherent existence. Now if understanding
emptiness is the only door to liberation, why do we need to meditate on other
things, such as bodhicitta and the four noble truths? Are these not also the
causes of attaining nirvana? You may remember a long explanation in an earlier volume of this series that the only door to the Mahayana is bodhicitta.
Candrakīrti's *Introduction to the "Middle Way"* says:

> Buddhas are born from bodhisattvas.
> The compassionate mind, nondual wisdom,
> And bodhicitta are the causes of bodhisattvas. (1.1)

So why does Candrakīrti not include the realization of bodhicitta among
the doors to liberation? If compassion, wisdom, and bodhicitta are the causes of
bodhisattvas and indirectly of buddhas, then are they not causes of liberation
too? Furthermore, in his commentary above, Candrakīrti mentions three doors
to liberation, not just one. So why does he say that selflessness is the only door?

There are various ways to explain why the wisdom understanding selfless-ness is the only door to liberation. First, emptiness, signlessness, and wishless-ness are ways to express selflessness from three different points of view. Once a practitioner understands that all phenomena are empty of inherent existence, he or she may pray to actualize the path and accomplish its result: buddha-hood. However, the bodhisattva does so without any thought of an inherently existent cause or an inherently existent result. The cause's lack of inherent exis-tence is signlessness. The result's lack of inherent existence is wishlessness. So it is only in terms of understanding emptiness that the three doors to liberation are designated. Second, each thing can be understood to have as attributes the three doors to liberation. A thing's nature is its emptiness of inherent existence. This thing arises from a cause, which is its sign or mark, and its cause is empty of inherent existence. This thing produces its result, expressed as a wish, and its result is empty of inherent existence. In sum, each thing is empty of inherent existence from the point of view of its nature, its cause, and its result. Third, although some phenomena are permanent and have no cause—for example, uncaused space and emptiness—we can understand them in terms of the three doors to liberation expressed as the action, the agent, and the object of action. Although emptiness is not caused and does not produce a result, it is the basis of activity or function. Therefore it has an action, an agent, and an object of action associated with it. This also applies to space because within space there is coming, going, and arising. Without space we cannot have physical move-ment because physical movement is based in space. Fourth, we can say that all phenomena, including permanent phenomena, have emptiness, signlessness, and wishlessness as a conventional expression of their identity. Every phenom-enon has a definition that symbolizes its own identifying characteristics. In this sense, these characteristics may be called a cause of identification, and the defined thing may be called an effect of identification. This kind of cause and effect is not causality in the sense of a producer and its product. Every phenom-enon has this kind of cause, effect, and nature, and the three doors to liberation can be explained in terms of them.

In summary, the three doors to liberation are aspects of the direct reali-zation of śūnyatā. Everyone who gains liberation has developed a complete understanding of emptiness in terms of every aspect: nature, cause, and result. Understanding emptiness from these three points of view is the door to lib-eration. Thus the three doors to liberation are in fact only one. In this way Candrakīrti removes any apparent contradiction between the explanation that there are three doors to liberation and the explanation that there is only one door to liberation, namely, the view understanding the emptiness of inher-ent existence. This explanation is established by reasoning and scripture.

The object held by the wisdom negating inherent existence is the antidote to grasping at the two kinds of self as inherently existent. This wisdom does not have even a mere trace of grasping at inherent existence. This understanding should not be negated. If you say that even this thought must be negated because all thoughts—whether good or bad—are defective, then it is clear that you want to establish the view of the Chinese abbot Hashang Mahayana. Throughout the *Lamrim Chenmo* Tsongkhapa emphasizes that we should not take this approach. If we follow Hashang's advice and simply stop any kind of thought, there will no studying, no learning, and no understanding of the Madhyamaka view. According to Candrakīrti and the followers of the Indian Madhyamaka, this is a very great obstacle to spiritual progress.

❖ 10 ❖
Not Negating Enough

(2)) Refuting an overly restricted identification of the object to be negated

———◆———

(2)) REFUTING AN OVERLY RESTRICTED IDENTIFICATION OF THE OBJECT TO BE NEGATED

AN OPPONENT SUGGESTS that the Madhyamaka object of negation is a nature that has three attributes: it is not produced by causes and conditions, it never changes from one state to another, and its establishment does not depend on other phenomena. The third characteristic means that it does not depend on a comparative relationship with another phenomenon. What kind of dependence is this? Consider for example "east," which cannot be established independently of "west." Likewise, "short" or "middle" and so on depend on comparative relationships. Without comparison with a counterpart, they would not have any meaning and could not be established. The opponent bases his description of the object of negation on this passage from Nāgārjuna's *Fundamental Treatise*:

> It is not correct for a nature
> To arise from causes and conditions.
> If it did arise from causes and conditions
> Then a nature would be something that is made.
>
> How could it be suitable
> For such a nature to be made?
> Therefore a nature is not fabricated
> And not dependent on others.

Tsongkhapa replies that if someone were to claim that all internal and external functional things, such as sprouts, were established as this kind of nature, then the Mādhyamikas would indeed negate it, because things are not like that. However, this is not the fundamental object of negation. When you negate the primary object of negation, then the Madhyamaka view understanding that all things are empty of inherent existence will arise in your mindstream. A nature that possesses the three attributes as described by the opponents above is not the unique object of negation of the Madhyamaka school. Negating this opponent's object of negation will not result in knowing the Madhyamaka view. The lower Buddhist schools already understand that all produced things arise from causes and conditions and change from one state to another at different times. If this were the fundamental object of negation, there would be no need to show them that things lack inherent existence.

Many Madhyamaka texts present negations of inherent existence in the form of consequences, such as, "If things were inherently existent, then they would not be changeable, and they would not be dependent on causes and conditions." This argument indicates the refuting consequences that follow if the subject—functional things—were inherently existent. This form of argument forces the opponents to abandon their wrong assumptions, given that they do not want to accept the conclusion that things are not changeable and not dependent on causes and conditions. It exposes the fault in their position in terms of the pervasion.

All logic depends on relations. Therefore all philosophical systems—Buddhist and non-Buddhist alike—set forth a theory of relations. Some non-Buddhist schools specify as many as six of kinds of relation. Most Buddhist schools, such as that of Dharmakīrti and his followers, posit only two types of relation—causal and same nature—based on which there are just three types of reason that can be used in a syllogism. These three reasons, also called signs, are: a correct effect sign, a correct nature sign, and a correct nonobservation sign. A correct effect sign is a reason based on a causal relationship; it proves the presence of a cause on the basis of the presence of its result. For example, "On a smoky mountain pass there is fire because there is smoke." A correct nature sign is a reason based on a same nature relationship; it proves one attribute on the basis of another that is of the same nature. For example, "A conch sound is impermanent because it is produced." The third type of reason, a correct nonobservation sign, is simply the negative form of the other two signs; it proves the nonexistence or negation of one thing based on the nonexistence or negation of another, which are related either causally or in terms of being the same nature. In Buddhist logic, whether we use syllogisms or consequences we have three elements: the subject, the pervaded, and the pervader. To understand what is meant by the latter two, consider a generality and its instances: the generality is the pervader and its instances are the pervaded. For example, a red pot is pervaded by being a pot: if something is a red pot, then it must be a pot. This kind of relationship is known as the pervasion.

The logical consequence we are considering here says, "If things were inherently existent, then they would not be changeable, and they would not be dependent on causes and conditions." The pervader is: inherent existence. The pervaded is: not changeable and not dependent on causes and conditions. In this argument, the pervader is the object of negation. But in this kind of argument, as opposed to a syllogism, the object of negation—inherent existence— is identified in terms of what would follow from it, not in terms of what it is. This is what it means to identify the fault in terms of the pervasion. A definition or criterion of inherent existence, which is the object to be negated, is not provided. Instead the Prāsaṅgikas reveal the unwanted consequences that follow from asserting that very object, which is thereby negated.

Moreover, according to the Prāsaṅgika-Madhyamaka system, *ultimately existent, really existent,* and *truly existent* are all synonyms of *inherently existent.* The same consequences follow from any of them, such as, "If things existed ultimately, really, truly, or inherently, then they would not be produced by causes and conditions." However, this does not mean that "not produced by causes and conditions" is the definition of ultimately existent. It is simply an expression of what would be the case if things were ultimately existent. Consider, for example, a pot. Every pot is pervaded by impermanence: there is no pot that is not impermanent. Although all pots are impermanent, *impermanence* is not the meaning, definition, or defining characteristic of a pot— because there are many other things that have the quality of impermanence, such as shawls and tables. So while we acknowledge that all pots are impermanent, the definition of *pot* is "A round-bellied, flat-bottomed thing that is capable of holding water."

In the same way, a refuting consequence follows from the above opponent's description of ultimate existence, but it does not define the object of negation. The opponent accepts that things are ultimately existent; he also contends that if something is ultimately existent, it must be established by its own nature without depending on anything else. So the refuting consequence we put to him is, "If something is established by its own nature without depending on anything else, then it cannot have parts." A whole is dependent on parts; parts are dependent on a whole. We cannot have a whole without parts nor parts without a whole. Parts and whole cannot be established without mutual dependence. Although being partless follows as a consequence of being ultimately existent, *partless* is not the definition of ultimate existence. It is simply the case that if things were ultimately existent, then they would be partless. Therefore, although the Mādhyamikas do not accept anything to be partless, *partlessness* is not their primary object of negation. It is merely a property of what is negated. It is just negated on the way, not principally.

Why is this not the primary object of negation? A quality of the object of negation, such as partlessness, is merely contrived by those who accept certain philosophical tenets. Grasping at partless phenomena is not the fundamental cause that binds sentient beings to samsara. Even if one establishes that partless things are not inherently existent and meditates on that for a long time, it would not reduce the ignorance that has tied one to cyclic existence since beginningless time. Even a thorough understanding that partless things are empty would not get rid of the innate mental afflictions. Innate ignorance would remain unscathed. Therefore this identification of the object of negation is incorrect.

We need to distinguish between two types of mental afflictions: innate and contrived. Contrived mental afflictions are intellectually acquired wrong views, such as accepting the existence of partless atoms, a creator God, permanent things, and so on, based on the fallacious reasoning of some philosophers. The innate mental afflictions do not depend on any kind of reasoning or dogma. Prior to attaining the pure bodhisattva grounds, each and every sentient being—whether human or not, whether educated or not—has innate mental afflictions arising naturally in their mindstreams. The self and other things quite naturally appear to be inherently existent, and ordinary sentient beings hold them to exist as they appear. Holding things this way does not require any rationalization, such as "This is inherently existent because of X, Y, or Z." It is innate. This innate ignorance is the main thing to be abandoned by means of the path, and its held object is the primary target to be negated by means of Madhyamaka logic. The weapon to pierce this target is the perfection of wisdom. In order to use this weapon effectively we need to identify the target—the object to be negated. Innate ignorance holds something in a wrong way. What is wrong about it? How does it hold its object?

Innate ignorance holds its object to be inherently or ultimately existent. This is the fundamental object of negation. For example, innate ignorance holds the self to be inherently existent. The self exists and is not to be negated. But the self being inherently existent does not exist, and that is to be negated. So the object of negation is inherent existence superimposed on the object perceived by innate ignorance. Innate ignorance only ever sees and conceives of things as inherently existent. It has no notion of an object apart from its being inherently existent. This combination—of an ordinary object and its way of being grasped by innate ignorance—is the so-called object of innate ignorance. This is what needs to be negated. The ordinary object itself should not be negated. But what ignorance mixes together with it does need to be negated. How can we negate this?

The main procedure is to think about what follows from the way innate ignorance holds its object. We should think, "If something were to exist as it is held by innate ignorance, then it would be like such-and-such." It is very important to be able to distinguish between the object of *innate* ignorance and the objects of *contrived* ignorance. The main point is to negate the way in which things are grasped by innate ignorance. As part of this refutation, we also disprove the ways in which things are grasped by contrived ignorance. In other words, our negation of the object of innate ignorance is primary; as a subsidiary part of that negation we negate certain things that we dogmatically believe. If we do not understand this properly, we might become confused and think the opposite—that negating innate ignorance is only a part of the more important negation of dogmatic ideas. In that case, when we try to negate the self of persons, we will take only a permanent, partless, independent self, specified by certain non-Buddhist philosophers, as the object of negation. However, most people do not hold themselves to be a permanent, partless, and independent self. They think of themselves in a more simple way, without any such analysis. Negating a permanent, partless, independent person is only a secondary branch of the genuine negation of the self of persons. It is important to understand that the main target is innate ignorance, which dominates the ordinary mental activity of living beings in daily life.

Similarly, when we negate the self of phenomena, it is completely unsuitable merely to negate what is contrived only by philosophers—such as partless atoms, partless moments of consciousness, or a nature possessing three special attributes. Some non-Buddhists and followers of lower Buddhist schools contend that the subtlest physical objects are partless atoms, which combine to make gross things, and that the subtlest subjects or perceivers are partless moments of consciousness. Thus these philosophers claim that objects are spatially partless and that subjects are temporally partless. Some others believe in a true nature that possesses the three attributes described above. All these views are superficial; they are formulated and held only by those who adhere to certain philosophical tenets. Rather than disputing or negating these shallow ideas, we should try to negate the far more important primary target. It is fine to employ those more limited negations as part of developing the Madhyamaka view. However, if this is all we manage to understand from study and analysis, then it is all we will have to meditate on. We need to understand and establish the correct object so that we can meditate on it later. If we try to establish the truth only by negating these dogmatic ideas, we will only be able to establish a superficial understanding of selflessness. The *Ornament for the Mahayana Sutras* says:

> At first, in dependence upon hearing, correct thinking arises;
> Just so, correct thinking gives rise to the wisdom realizing reality. (1.16a–b)

If we have gained only a gross understanding and then proceed to meditate on the nonexistence of the two selves imputed by contrived ignorance, in the end we will merely eliminate only the contrived mental afflictions. It is completely absurd to claim that by negating the two selves imputed by contrived ignorance we will remove innate ignorance. Candrakīrti points this out to his opponents in *Introduction to the "Middle Way"*:

> You say, "When selflessness is realized, a permanent self is abandoned,"
> Yet you do not accept this to be the object of self-grasping;
> Therefore to declare that knowing the absence of such a self
> Uproots the subtle view of self is astonishing!

He follows this up in *Commentary on the "Introduction to the 'Middle Way'"*:

> These things are mutually unrelated. This is clearly explained by means of an example:
>
> > It is as if, when seeing a snake in an alcove of your room,
> > Someone says "There is no elephant here" to dispel your fear,
> > And indeed your fear of the snake dissipates;
> > Oh, the other person must be joking!

It does not help someone overcome his fear of the presence of a snake to assure him that there is no elephant. The lack of an elephant has no relation to the presence of a snake. In the same way, there is no relation between eliminating contrived ignorance and eliminating innate ignorance. By eliminating the former we cannot eliminate the latter. Simply meditating on the nonexistence of things imputed by philosophers, such as partless atoms and so on, will not eliminate the cause of the beginningless experience of suffering—the innate ignorance holding the self and phenomena to be inherently existent.

The stanza from the *Introduction to the "Middle Way"* quoted previously concerns the selflessness of persons, but Tsongkhapa says that these words could equally apply to the selflessness of phenomena. In that case, it would read:

You say, "When selflessness is realized, a contrived self is abandoned,"
Yet you do not accept this to be the object of ignorance;
Therefore, to declare that knowing the absence of such a self
Uproots the innate view of ignorance is astonishing!

Tsongkhapa suggests this reading because of the way the Prāsaṅgika system explains ignorance and the object of negation. In order to gain liberation from samsara we must eliminate its root cause: the ignorance grasping at inherent existence. This ignorance refers to both the ignorance that grasps at a self of persons and the ignorance that grasps at a self of phenomena. Both types of self-grasping are grasping at inherent existence. They are differentiated only in terms of their basis: the first grasps at an inherently existent self of persons; the second grasps at an inherently existent self of phenomena. There is no difference between them in terms of subtlety. When we realize emptiness, the only difference between the emptiness of a self of persons and the emptiness of a self of phenomena is the difference between their bases. In one case emptiness is understood on the basis of a person and in the other on the basis of other phenomena. Only from the point of view of the bases of emptiness can we say there is any difference at all. There is no difference from the point of view of the object of negation: inherent existence itself is the same in both cases. The same applies to ignorance. If we hold things to be inherently existent, then we are grasping at a self of phenomena; if we hold ourselves to be inherently existent, then we are grasping at a self of persons. Both of them are instances of the root delusion, ignorance. Therefore both of them must be eliminated in order to gain freedom from samsara.

We should note that the Prāsaṅgika understanding of the two kinds of ignorance is different from that of the other Buddhist schools. According to the Svātantrika-Madhyamaka, in order to gain liberation from samsara we must eliminate the egotistic view—the ignorance grasping at a self of persons, specifically with regard to oneself. Here, the grasping at a self of persons is a mind grasping the self to be self-sufficient and substantially existent. Svātantrikas consider that this type of grasping is the afflictive obstruction to liberation. After removing this obstruction, the innate mind grasping at true existence still arises. Phenomena still appear to be truly existent and are held to exist as they appear. According to the Svātantrikas, even an arhat has this grasping at a self of phenomena. They contend that grasping a self of phenomena is not an obstruction to liberation; instead, it is an obstruction to omniscience. It must be removed to attain perfect knowledge, or enlightenment, but it does not need to be removed in order to gain liberation from samsara. According to the Yogācāra system, the obstruction to omniscience is the ignorance viewing the object and subject as different entities. Perceiving this duality, and grasping it to exist as it is perceived, has to be removed in order to achieve full enlightenment, but we do not need to remove it in order to achieve liberation from samsara. Thus we can see that Buddhist schools of thought define the grasping at a self of persons and the grasping at a self of phenomena differently. Their main objects of negation are completely different.

Now regarding the stanzas from Nāgārjuna's *Fundamental Treatise* quoted at the beginning of this chapter, someone asks, "When Nāgārjuna says that the defining characteristics of a nature are that it is not made by causes and conditions and not comparatively dependent on other things, is he speaking hypothetically, or does that kind of nature actually exist?"

Tsongkhapa says that the term *nature* refers to the suchness or reality of phenomena. This is śūnyatā—emptiness, ultimate nature, true nature, or final nature. The final nature is not fabricated, and it does not depend on other causes and conditions. Consider the following example. Form is empty of inherent existence. The emptiness of inherent existence of form is the nature of form. That emptiness of form is not dependent on causes and conditions, and it is not dependent on being compared with something else. It is its own true nature. Nāgārjuna also mentions a third attribute: not changing from one state to another. Emptiness is permanent. It does not change moment by moment. Moreover, the fact that form is empty of inherent existence never changes. Form is always empty. This applies to any basis.

In a more general sense, the word "nature" can refer to a temporary conventional nature: fire is hot and ice is cold. If you put a pan full of ice over a fire, the ice will melt and become hot water. The heat in the water is not the nature of water; the water is made hot by certain causes and conditions. However, every fire is hot. There is no fire that is not hot. So we can say that heat is the conventional nature of fire. However, heat is not its ultimate nature. The true nature of fire is that it is empty of inherent existence. Being empty of inherent existence is its real or final reality. That reality is the final attribute of any phenomenon. So the question becomes, "Does this highest reality, described by Nāgārjuna as possessing three attributes, exist? Or, is it the object of negation?" If we were to consider this highest reality to exist as a functional thing, then it would be an object of negation. For causally produced functional things are not this highest nature nor do they possess its attributes. However, this highest reality is not an object of negation in general. It is not totally nonexistent. If we consider this highest nature to exist as śūnyatā, then it is perfectly affirmed. It is the ultimate nature of things, and it has the three attributes specified above: not produced by causes and conditions, not established in dependence on comparison with others, and not subject to change. So when Nāgārjuna talks about a nature in this passage, he is not talking about the object of negation. Candrakīrti proves this by citing a sutra in *Commentary on the "Introduction to the 'Middle Way'"*:

> Does a nature having these special attributes exist as accepted by the master Nāgārjuna? Yes, it is the "ultimate reality" extensively taught by Buddha, such as, "Whether the Tathāgata appears or does not appear, the ultimate reality of all phenomena abides." What is this ultimate reality? It is the final nature of these eyes, and so on. What is the final nature of these things? It is something of theirs that is not made and is not comparatively dependent on others. It is their own essential nature that must be realized by the wisdom that is free from the obscurations of ignorance. Who would say that it does not exist? If it does not exist, then for what purpose would bodhisattvas cultivate the paths of the perfections? It is in order to understand ultimate reality that bodhisattvas undergo hundreds of such hardships.

A questioner asks, "Earlier, did you not disprove that all phenomena exist by their own nature?" Tsongkhapa replies, "Well, did we not already say many times that phenomena, without being imputed by the mind, do not have even the tiniest atom of an inherently established nature? So why bother to mention that other phenomena have no such nature? Even śūnyatā is not truly or ultimately established in the slightest." Ultimate reality is ultimate, true, and its own nature; however, it does not exist by its own nature. In other words, śūnyatā is existent—it is the highest nature, the final truth, and the nature of all phenomena; however, even śūnyatā does not exist inherently. Candrakīrti's *Clear Words* says:

> Just as in the three times the nature of fire does not alter, the ever-abiding nature of all things is something not fabricated; it is not something that occurs later from what did not occur before, like the heat of water, or here and there, or long and short. It is not something that has any dependence on causes and conditions. That is what is meant by *final nature*. Does such a nature of fire exist? It does not exist by its own nature, but it is not nonexistent. Although it is like that, we say "it exists" conventionally, having been superimposed, so as to remove the fear of those who are listening.

The term "ever-abiding nature" is often used in tantra and in the Nyingma tradition to mean the natural, innate mind, which is continuously present. Here Candrakīrti uses it to describe the final nature of things. The ever-abiding final nature is not created. Unlike the temperature of water, it is not dependent on causes and conditions. The final nature is not dependent on comparison, such as this side and that side or here and there. That side of the room—the side opposite from where we are standing—becomes this side of the room if we walk over there. This side and that side change in dependence on its relation to where we are. Similarly, long and short are mutually comparative. In contrast, everything has an ever-abiding final nature. This nature exists, but it does not exist inherently or by its own nature.

So how does this final nature exist if not inherently? Some people listening to this explanation may think that if things do not exist inherently, then they are totally nonexistent. Since they do not understand the true nature of reality, they risk annihilating everything: cause and effect, the four noble truths, and all phenomena in samsara and nirvana. The thought that all things are not inherently existent makes them fearful. In order to remove their fear, they are taught that even though things do not exist inherently, they exist conventionally in that they are imputed by thought and language under the influence of ignorance. Even the final nature, śūnyatā, is said to exist only conventionally.

The questioner protests, "Candrakīrti does not explain that it exists; he explains that, having been superimposed, this is taught in order to remove the fear of the listeners." Tsongkhapa replies that it is incorrect to think that therefore the final nature does not exist. This is because other phenomena, having been imputed, are taught to exist for the same purpose—so that ordinary beings who do not understand śūnyatā may abandon their fear—in which case, those other phenomena would also turn out to be nonexistent. Thus to say that the ultimate nature is taught in accordance with how things are imputed by thought and terminology does not mean that it does not exist. If it did mean that the final nature was nonexistent, it would apply not only to śūnyatā but to all other phenomena as well. In that case, a bodhisattva's practice of the perfections would be purposeless. By explaining this fault, Candrakīrti demonstrates that it cannot be totally nonexistent. Also, in the *Commentary on the "Introduction to the 'Middle Way'"* Candrakīrti says:

> This nature is accepted not only by Nāgārjuna, but others can arrive at accepting it too. Thus this nature is finally established to exist by both parties.

Otherwise, if the earlier Mādhyamikas' interpretation of Candrakīrti were correct—in claiming that the ultimate nature does not exist—then we would have to accept that within the Madhyamaka system it is impossible to attain liberation. Why? When one attains nirvana, one has a direct experience of liberation. Nirvana is said to be the truth of cessation—the permanent absence of all the mental afflictions and their seeds, which have been removed gradually by the paths of seeing and meditation.

DIFFERENT INTERPRETATIONS OF TRUE CESSATION

There is some debate about what *cessation* means here, which we already touched on in chapter 3. According to one interpretation, this true cessation is the ultimate nature, or ultimate truth; it is śūnyatā. In that case, if ultimate truth did not exist, then true cessation and nirvana would not exist; thus it would be impossible to attain nirvana, because it would not exist. Clearly this outcome is unacceptable, and its premise—that the ultimate nature does not exist—is disproved below. According to another interpretation, true cessation is not ultimate truth. Ultimate truth refers to śūnyatā. Śūnyatā is the mere absence of the object of negation, which is true existence or inherent existence. Thus ultimate truth refers to the mere absence of inherent existence. In contrast, cessation refers not to the absence of true existence, but to the absence of the mental afflictions and obstructions that have been abandoned by the paths of seeing and meditation. There are two kinds of obstructions or stains: the natural obstruction and the temporary obstructions. The natural obstruction is inherent existence, which in fact is nonexistent. Everything is pure of that natural obstruction. We do not have to purify anything in order to be rid of it—we just have to understand it. Maitreya says:

> Regarding this, there is nothing at all to be removed
> Nor the slightest thing to be added.[84]

Although everything is free of the natural obstruction from the very beginning, temporary obstructions arise from causes and conditions. They are the mental afflictions—ignorance, attachment, and so on—which must be purified. A true cessation is the permanent end of any of these afflictions, with their seeds, through the power of supreme wisdom.

So how can true cessation be śūnyatā? To understand this question, let us look at an example. Because there is no elephant in this room, there is the emptiness of elephant. Is that śūnyatā? You could say that the emptiness of an inherently existent elephant is śūnyatā, but that is not the primary object of negation in this example. The object of negation is an elephant itself; we are negating the existence of an elephant. The mere lack of an elephant is not śūnyatā. Similarly, the mere lack of certain mental afflictions is not śūnyatā. So how could the permanent cessation of the afflictions be the ultimate truth? It must be a conventional truth. This is something you can debate.

Candrakīrti, in his *Commentary on the Sixty Stanzas of Reasoning*, makes great effort to prove that when one attains nirvana one directly experiences the ultimate truth of cessation. I think this refers to the mind being naturally empty of inherent nature from the very beginning. The emptiness of inherent nature is not created; it always exists. The emptiness of the inherent nature of the mind is a natural purity possessed by everyone. Even though within our mindstreams there may be many mental afflictions and obstructions to be removed, the nature of the mind is naturally pure. It is innately free from the obstruction of inherent existence. Based on that purity we can enter the bodhi-sattva path and progress through the ten stages, removing specific obstructions on each level. When we initially become an ārya, the first moment of the direct realization of śūnyatā in meditation is an uninterrupted path. An uninterrupted path is like a war; it is like a battle against an enemy. In meditating on śūnyatā we are trying to annihilate obstructions. Eventually the force of one's realization of emptiness becomes more powerful, and the mental afflictions that it opposes are destroyed and never able to arise again. At this point a special kind of confidence arises and the very next moment of meditation is a path of liberation.

An uninterrupted path and its corresponding path of liberation occur one after the other in the same meditation session. Each of them is a type of mind. The object of both is the same: śūnyatā. In one moment, the mind perceiving śūnyatā is an uninterrupted path, the antidote to a particular obstruction; in the next moment, that mind perceiving śūnyatā becomes a path of liberation, the freedom from that obstruction. Both of these minds directly perceive śūnyatā. Also, both of these minds have śūnyatā as their ultimate nature. So when a mind becomes a path of liberation through meditating directly on śūnyatā, the śūnyatā of that mind itself becomes a cessation. As each obstruction is removed, through the various bodhisattva stages, the emptiness of the mind is said to possess two purities: purity from the natural obstruction and purity from the temporary obstruction. When the mind becomes free from a temporary obstruction, that mind's emptiness is called a true cessation. Eventually, when one has completed all the paths, one attains the final cessation: nirvana. Upon attaining nirvana, the mind becomes free of all the temporary obstructions—the mental afflictions and their seeds. The śūnyatā of that liberated mind is both ultimate truth and the final true cessation. Thus the Prāsaṅgika-Madhyamaka view is that there is no separate final cessation apart from this ultimate truth.

However, can we call the mere absence of the temporary obstructions a true cessation? This is not discussed in the texts. Perhaps we could say that, according to the Prāsaṅgika view, it could be called a permanent cessation of obstructions, in that the negated obstructions have permanently ceased. But it cannot be called a true cessation. If something is a true cessation or the truth of cessation, then it must be true or the truth, which is the ultimate truth or śūnyatā.

The phrase *established as being true* means the same as *established by valid knowledge*; but it is contradictory to the phrase *truly established*. Hence all produced things, such as our eyes, do not exist as a nature that is inherently established, nor do they exist as a nature that is established as reality. The first kind of nature is the object of negation refuted by the Mādhyamikas: true existence, ultimate existence, or inherent existence. The second kind of nature is the final nature, śūnyatā. Ordinary conventional things, such as forms, do not exist as either of these two natures: they do not exist as a nature that is the object of negation, and they do not exist as the ultimate nature of all phenomena. Conventional truths are neither of those two natures. Ultimate truth, śūnyatā, exists as a nature that is established as reality—because it is not made, and it is not dependent on others (in a specific sense—see below). According to Nāgārjuna, the meaning of "made" is when something that did not exist before has newly come into being; and in this context, the meaning of "dependent on others" is when something arises in dependence on causes and conditions. So the meaning of these two attributes is similar. However, although these two attributes—"not newly arisen" and "not dependent on causes and conditions"—are attributes of śūnyatā, they are not śūnyatā itself. They are conventional things. Also, these two attributes do not exist inherently by their own nature. They exist merely conventionally.

Śūnyatā is the final ultimate nature, yet it too exists conventionally. It is conventionally imputed in dependence on other conventionally existent things. Emptiness itself is the ultimate truth; but its attributes are conventional truths, not ultimate truth. Emptiness exists, but the property "existence" is a conventional truth. Emptiness is the object of ultimate wisdom, but the property "being the object of ultimate wisdom" is a conventional truth. Likewise, properties such as "not made" or "not dependent on causes and conditions" are conventional truths. This is because the mind directly realizing śūnyatā does not understand all the various conventional attributes of emptiness. A separate conventional knowledge is needed to understand them. Ultimate knowledge cannot understand whether or not śūnyatā exists or whether or not it depends on causes and conditions and so on.

Ordinary valid knowledge knows conventional things, but it cannot know ultimate reality. The purpose of practicing pure conduct and meditating on the path is to realize this ultimate nature or reality. Candrakīrti explains to his opponent that there is no contradiction between the utter nonacceptance of an inherently existent nature with respect to all phenomena and the acceptance of a temporary nature, such as hot and burning being the nature of fire. The *Commentary on "Introduction to the 'Middle Way'"* says:

> *Objection*: Aha, that cannot be! You do not accept things at all, yet you provisionally accept a nature that is not made and not dependent on others. Thus you are saying mutually contradictory things!
>
> *Reply*: In saying this, you do not understand the meaning of the text. The meaning is as follows. If the dependently arising nature of objects held by ordinary beings, such as the eyes and so on, were their final nature, then it would be purposeless to practice pure conduct because such a nature would be realized even by those with the wrong view. But because that is not their final nature, it is purposeful to practice pure conduct in order to see it. Moreover, I explained that it is not made by causes and conditions and not dependent on something else, in relation to conventional truth. Such a nature cannot be seen by ordinary beings. That itself is rightly the ultimate nature. Merely because of that, the ultimate is not a thing and is not nothing, because it is natural peace.

In the final sentence of this passage, "not a thing" may mean not an inherently existent thing or not a functional thing; "not nothing" means it is not nonexistent, like a rabbit horn. This is similar to what was explained in the discussion about dualism in chapter 5. Śūnyatā is neither inherently existent nor utterly nonexistent. It is the lack of inherent nature. The terms *natural peace* and *natural nirvana* refer to śūnyatā. Nirvana is the cessation attained upon having removed all the temporary obstructions by means of practicing pure conduct and meditating on emptiness. The complete cessation of the mental afflictions is called *peace*. But *natural nirvana* is śūnyatā itself, so in this sense there is nothing to purify. It is completely pure in its own nature; it is not something that is initially dirty and then purified. There is nothing to be cleared away by means of an antidote. It is naturally peaceful from the very beginning. There is nothing to be added or developed.

THE FINAL ATTRIBUTE OF EACH THING IS ITS EMPTINESS OF INHERENT NATURE

The emptiness of inherent existence, which is explained as the total absence of an inherently established nature of all phenomena, exists as an attribute

on a basis. The basis is a phenomenon, such as form. When we first understand emptiness, we do so by means of inferential knowledge. This conceptual
knowledge is not a direct realization of emptiness. Tsongkhapa says here in
the *Lamrim Chenmo* that the conceptual understanding of the emptiness of
inherent existence of form involves a combination of knowing the basis and
its attribute. In other words, this inferential knowledge has both the basis
(form) and form's attribute (śūnyatā) as its object. It is not contradictory for
both the basis and the attribute to exist as the object of this single conceptual
consciousness. The basis and its attribute are the same entity. When we understand the emptiness of form, form is the conventional nature, whereas its attribute, śūnyatā, is its ultimate nature. However, this ultimate nature is only the
imputed ultimate truth. It is not real ultimate truth because inferential knowledge is dualistic. A conceptual mind may apprehend the basis of emptiness
(form) and its attribute (emptiness). Then, to any conceptual mind knowing
emptiness, śūnyatā does not appear directly; it appears via a conceptual image
of śūnyatā. The image of śūnyatā and actual śūnyatā appear to be mixed. So
when inferential knowledge understands that form is empty, it perceives form
together with emptiness mixed with its image. That combined appearance of
the image of emptiness and emptiness is not the appearance of mere emptiness. Moreover, the conceptual image of emptiness is a conventional truth; it
is a nonimplicative negation, and this image appears to be inherently existent.
Therefore śūnyatā appears to this mind to be truly existent because the conceptual image of it appears to be so, and this mind cannot distinguish between
one and the other. Thus the inferential knowledge of the emptiness of form
is a mistaken consciousness with regard to what appears to it. The inferential
knowledge understanding the emptiness of form does not reverse such dualistic appearances. So the emptiness that is the object of inferential knowledge
is only the imputed ultimate truth, not actual śūnyatā. However, even though
this inferential understanding is mistaken with regard to what appears to it,
the way that it holds or conceives of its main object—the emptiness of inherent
existence—is correct. Therefore it is a valid mind and can be used as a basis for
developing a direct understanding of śūnyatā.

When we have accustomed ourselves for a long time to the understanding
of emptiness that appears in this dualistic manner, eventually we gain a direct
realization of śūnyatā. In a direct realization of śūnyatā, ultimate truth appears
without any duality. All mistaken appearances of a noninherent nature
appearing as an inherent nature completely cease. In a direct realization of
emptiness, only the final attribute, śūnyatā, is known. The subject or basis on
which emptiness is realized does not appear at all. Nothing but emptiness is
the object of this knowledge. The wisdom directly perceiving emptiness does

not apprehend a dualistic appearance of form as the subject and śūnyatā as the attribute. Supreme wisdom has no understanding or perception of the relationship between subject and attribute. This relationship can be established only by conventional knowledge, which is an entirely different mind. Ultimate truth is free of all the elaborations that are the objects of negation, such as being truly existent, inherently existent, or existent by its own nature. Freedom from all these elaborations is absolute peace. In addition to this, ultimate truth is free of all the elaborations of appearing to exist inherently when in fact it does not exist inherently. Only śūnyatā is the mere absence of both these kinds of elaborations; it alone is posited as the ultimate truth. Conventional truths are not inherently existent, nevertheless they appear as inherently existent to sentient beings. More precisely, they appear to their respective conventional consciousnesses within the mental continuum of any sentient being. They naturally appear as inherently existent, even though they do not actually exist inherently. Ultimate truth can never appear like that to a mind directly perceiving it. The object of a mind directly perceiving śūnyatā is always free of both elaborations: being ultimately existent and appearing as ultimately existent.

The main point that Tsongkhapa is making here is that there are two levels of understanding śūnyatā. One type of wisdom understands śūnyatā directly and nondualistically. The other type of wisdom understands śūnyatā conceptually and dualistically.

Certain texts, such as Śāntarakṣita's *Ornament for the Middle Way*, speak of the *approximate ultimate*. There are two ways to understand this notion. Some say that the direct object of the inferential knowledge realizing śūnyatā is not the real ultimate truth but is close to it. In that sense it is the approximate ultimate. Others say that because śūnyatā appears to inferential knowledge in a mistaken and dualistic way, the śūnyatā in connection with inferential knowledge is only an approximation of the real ultimate truth. When śūnyatā appears to this inferential understanding it does not cut off all the mistaken elaborations of dualistic appearance but appears together with those elaborations. In that sense it is the approximate ultimate. On both interpretations it is called "approximate" because it is almost, but not completely, correct. It is correct in that inferential knowledge of śūnyatā understands the ultimate truth, the emptiness of inherent existence. It is correct in that a conceptual mind realizing śūnyatā holds the basis—form and so on—as empty of inherent existence. Thus it accords with the real ultimate truth in terms of what is *understood*. But it is incorrect in that something else mistakenly appears to the mind apprehending that śūnyatā. Thus it does not accord with the real ultimate truth in terms of what *appears*. Therefore it is not the real ultimate truth.

Tsongkhapa does not use the expression *approximate ultimate* in the *Lam-rim Chenmo*, although he does explicitly employ it in other texts such as the *Condensed Lamrim*. In this text he uses the term *imputed ultimate*. The point is that śūnyatā may be either: (1) the imputed, or approximate, ultimate, or (2) the real, or actual, ultimate. From the point of view of a conceptual thought realizing emptiness, that śūnyatā is the imputed ultimate. From the point of view of a direct perception realizing śūnyatā, that śūnyatā is the actual ultimate. Real ultimate truth is without any duality, and it appears nondualistically to the mind directly perceiving it. An analogy used for characterizing the difference between conventional truth and ultimate truth can also be used effectively here. A river that can be crossed by foot corresponds to the approximate ultimate, and a river that can only be crossed by boat corresponds to the actual ultimate. In both cases the nature of the water is the same.

Therefore, since Mādhyamikas assert a final nature that is a mere absence of all elaborations, how could they possibly accept an inherently existent final nature? Candrakīrti's *Clear Words* says:

> Things are perceived in a certain way owing to the power of the obscurations of ignorance. A nature not perceived in that manner is the object for āryans, who are free of the obscurations of ignorance [when directly seeing śūnyatā]. That very nature is posited as the final nature of those things.

This is so even for a buddha who sees the two truths simultaneously. Although a buddha sees the object, the basis of emptiness, he or she does not see it in the manner of seeing its attribute, emptiness. Conversely, although a buddha sees emptiness, he or she does not see it in the manner of seeing its basis. Here presenting an opponent's position, Candrakīrti's *Clear Words* continues:

> *Opponent*: The lack of [inherent] arising, which is the final nature of things, is not anything. Since it is just nothing, it has no essence. Therefore it is not the final nature of things.

This position is also reflected in the traditions of certain earlier Tibetan scholars, such as the great master Kunkhyen Jonangpa. Jonangpa explains his view of the definitive meaning in the *Retreat Teaching—Ocean of Definitive Meaning* (*Ri chos nges don rgya mtsho*). This text was very popular in the old days in Tibet, but after Je Tsongkhapa's time it was no longer published much. The Tibetan government was opposed to its views and hid copies of it away so that nobody could read it. Nevertheless, some masters still presented this view. The text is available now. If you read it and find it convincing, you may completely change your view!

Jonangpa and his followers divide things into conventional and ultimate truth. They accept a certain kind of ultimate truth and claim that only ultimate truth is true—all other things are conventional truth. However, they do not consider ultimate truth to be the ultimate nature of all things—such as the emptiness of inherent existence. They do not consider it to be the elimination of elaborations that are the object of negation—such as the self of persons and the self of phenomena. These masters consider ultimate truth to be an affirmative phenomenon, like blue and yellow, and not the mere absence of a false appearance. According to them, ultimate truth appears to exist independently as the object of a nonmistaken mind understanding reality, and the realization of it to exist in this way is the view realizing the profound meaning. They also say that it is wrong to interpret the correct view as a realization that internal and external phenomena—the bases that sentient beings incorrectly hold to be an inherently existent self of persons and of phenomena—are empty of inherent existence. This, they claim, is going in completely the wrong direction.

The Jonangpas' explanation of ultimate truth is similar to what is taught in the *Buddha Nature Sutra* (*Ārya-tathāgata-garbha-nāma-mahayāna-sūtra*) and the *Sublime Continuum*. Although they support their views with many proofs and statements found in these and other texts, Tsongkhapa claims they have not understood them properly. These masters explain that all sentient beings possess an ultimate nature of the mind—the inherent buddha nature— which is naturally adorned with the thirty-two major and eighty minor marks. This buddha nature is not made by causes and conditions; it is an eternally existing, liberated nature, which does not change moment by moment. This naturally pure, true nature is called *emptiness*. Although its attributes almost match the three attributes of the final nature discussed earlier,[85] the Jonangpas' interpretation of the word "emptiness" has little in common with its interpretation by the Mādhyamikas. According to the Jonangpas, "emptiness" means the absence of all conventional phenomena. The ultimate truth is completely different and separate from conventional truth. Conventional things are considered to be false; so the ultimate nature, the only truth, is empty of all conventional things.

Tsongkhapa says that these assertions stand outside all the scriptures of the Hinayana and Mahayana traditions. Jonangpa and his followers accept that grasping at a self is the root cause of sentient beings' bondage in cyclic existence, so it must be reversed. However, they say that it is not reversed by understanding that the basis held as a self is not inherently existent. Instead, they say that the view of self is reversed by knowing as truly existent some other unrelated thing. This is completely wrong. It is similar to the following scenario. Suppose you are frightened because you think there is a big snake on the eastern side of your house, even though there is no snake there at all. To assist you someone says, "You cannot remove your fear by thinking that there is no snake on the eastern side; instead, you must convince yourself that there is a tree on the western side. That will eliminate your fear and belief in the snake." The problem and the remedy suggested here are unrelated. This is like the Jonang theory described above. Sentient beings suffer owing to grasping incorrectly the two kinds of self. Instead of negating that way of grasping, the Jonangpas claim that we should hold onto the existence of an ultimate, permanent buddha nature within the mind. By holding onto that, we will reverse the fundamental wrong view and the misery generated by it.

Tsongkhapa says that if we wish good for ourselves, we must abandon such wrong views and fling them far away. We must sever the root of the ignorance that binds us to samsara. We will eliminate ignorance by negating the way it holds its object. To do this, we need to read and study the scriptures of the definitive meaning that show the ultimate truth. When we have found the meaning of these scriptures, while carefully avoiding misinterpretation we must develop a profound understanding and take it to heart. We must go beyond the ocean of cyclic existence by depending on the scriptures of Nāgārjuna and Āryadeva, spiritual father and son, who clearly and extensively taught many reasons proving the correct view.

Tsongkhapa says he has presented this extensive explanation to refute any wrong views regarding the object of negation because it is most important to avoid going in the wrong direction when seeking the Madhyamaka view.

The Actual Object to Be Negated

(c)) How our own system identifies the object of negation
    (1)) Identifying the actual object of negation

(c)) How our own system identifies the object of negation

TSONGKHAPA STRESSES the importance of a clear identification of the object of negation, which he discusses here under three headings:

(1))   Identifying the actual object of negation
(2))   Whether to add qualifications to other objects of negation (chapter 12)
(3))   Whether to add the qualification "ultimate" to the object of negation (chapter 12)

(1)) Identifying the actual object of negation

There are two kinds of objects of negation: objects negated by the path and objects negated by reasoning.

Objects negated by the path
A path is a purified mind—a realization of truth that eliminates mental obstructions. We meditate on the stages of the path in order to remove both the afflictive obstructions, which block the attainment of liberation, and the obstructions to omniscience, which block the attainment of full enlightenment. As we progress with our meditation practice through successive stages of the path, we gradually negate, cease, or eliminate the obstructions pertaining

to each stage. It is not appropriate to use the word "refute" with respect to the obstructions eliminated by the path, although we do use it when speaking about the objects negated by reason. Maitreya's *Separation of the Middle from the Extremes* (*Madhyānta-vibhāṅga-kārikā*) says:

> It is taught that there are the afflictive obstructions
> And the obstructions to omniscience;
> It is said that all obstructions are included within these,
> And once you have removed them you are free.

The two divisions of obstructions are definitive in the sense that all mental obscurations are included within them. There is nothing left out. Therefore once we have completely removed both kinds of obstruction, we will have achieved the highest enlightenment. Both kinds of obstruction exist as objects of knowledge. If they did not exist, then we would not have to do anything to be liberated. But because these obstructions exist within our mindstreams, we are not free. We must eliminate them.

Each of the Mahayana schools describes the afflictive obstructions and the obstructions to omniscience differently. The Svātantrika-Mādhyamikas say that the ignorance grasping things as truly or ultimately existent is an obstruction to omniscience. In contrast, the Prāsaṅgika-Mādhyamikas say that this type of grasping is an afflictive obstruction, and that the obstructions to omniscience are the imprints left by the afflictive obstructions. According to the Prāsaṅgikas, a perfectly omniscient mind is able to directly realize the two truths—ultimate truth and conventional truth—simultaneously, within one moment of consciousness. A single consciousness can see everything clearly because there is no mental obstruction at all. The Vaibhāṣikas avoid using the term *obstruction to omniscience* because they do not believe that omniscience, as posited by the Mahayana, exists in the first place. They say that nothing is beyond a buddha's knowledge—therefore an awakened being is able to know everything. However, a single moment of a buddha's consciousness cannot know everything simultaneously; a different wisdom perceives each object.

The two types of obstruction accepted by Prāsaṅgikas can be discussed in terms of their function or their nature. Their function is described in their definitions in the monastic textbooks. The definition of an afflictive obstruction is "an obstruction that primarily prevents the attainment of liberation." The definition of an obstruction to omniscience is "an obstruction that primarily prevents the attainment of omniscience." Of course, afflictive obstructions are also obstructions to omniscience but only in a secondary sense—hence the use of the qualification "primarily" in these definitions. In terms of their nature, afflictive obstructions include the mental afflictions such as ignorance, hatred, and attachment, as well as their seeds. Any consciousness that grasps its object incorrectly is an afflictive obstruction. The mental afflictions are consciousnesses; their seeds are neither form nor consciousness. The seeds are potentialities left by the mental afflictions that enable the mental afflictions to arise again in the future. They are the actual causes of the mental afflictions. Therefore it is most important to remove the seeds of the mental afflictions. If we just remove a mental affliction itself but do not remove its seed, then we only temporarily subdue it. For example, we can temporarily remove hatred by meditating on love; by meditating on the mental absorptions of the form and formless realms we can temporarily remove many other mental afflictions too. In both cases, the mental afflictions can arise again because their seeds are still there.

Obstructions to omniscience are the imprints left by the mental afflictions. These are similar to the seeds of the afflictions in that they are potentialities left by the mental afflictions and likewise are not consciousnesses. However, unlike the seeds, they do not cause mental afflictions to arise again in the future. They are hidden stains, subtle influences, or predispositions left on the mindstream that give rise to a certain false appearance: the appearance of things as inherently existent. These imprints remain even after the mental afflictions together with their seeds have been completely removed. Arhats, as well as bodhisattvas on the eighth level and above, still have these obstructions to omniscience. While they are meditating directly on emptiness, no appearance of true existence arises in their minds; but when they emerge from that meditation session, then everything appears to be truly existent again owing to the ripening of these propensities. These practitioners understand that things are not real in the way that they appear—yet that appearance still occurs. So during the postmeditation period, they see everything as illusion-like; an inherent aspect of things appears, but they know that inherent existence is not real. In contrast, we ordinary beings see things as inherently existent and believe that things truly exist in the way that they appear. If something appears attractive or unattractive, we firmly hold it to be so objectively. Those who have realized emptiness directly do not hold things this way. They understand that the object does not exist in the way that it appears.

Both the mistaken appearance of inherent existence and the propensities that give rise to it are obstructions to knowledge—which we call *manifest* and *nonmanifest*, respectively. A nonmanifest obstruction to omniscience gives rise to a mistaken appearance of the object as inherently existent, even if there is no grasping at inherent existence in the mind of the perceiver. The mistaken appearance of inherent existence itself is a manifest obstruction to omniscience. When we completely remove both the manifest and the non-manifest obstructions to omniscience, we attain full enlightenment.

The presence of obstructions to omniscience in the mental continuum of an arhat might also occasionally cause him or her to act in ways that appear incorrect, even though the mental afflictions, including the grasping at true existence, have been eliminated. For example, on occasion an arhat may suddenly jump or flail, even though his or her mind is at peace. Also, strange utterances, which sound like harsh words, may involuntarily escape from an arhat's mouth. When an arhat involuntarily speaks or moves like this, the slight wrong behavior arises from subtle imprints left by the afflictions. This behavior is a subtle downfall, but because an arhat is without any mental defilement, no nonvirtuous action is created. These actions are neither nonvirtuous nor virtuous: they are neutral.

Arhats and bodhisattvas on the eighth level are equal in terms of the absence of all afflictive obstructions and the presence of obstructions to omniscience within their mindstreams. However, these pure-ground bodhisattvas are superior to arhats because, from the eighth to the tenth levels, they use special Mahayana meditation techniques involving both the practices of method and wisdom, which enable them to reach full enlightenment. These special practices remove the subtle obstructions to knowledge, which are much more difficult to remove than the afflictive obstructions. Therefore to achieve the omniscience of a buddha, we must gather an enormous accumulation of merit and cultivate the wisdom directly seeing emptiness for an extremely long time.

Objects negated by reasoning

In order to cultivate the direct realization of emptiness and eliminate the objects negated by that path, we need to identify and refute the objects negated by reasoning. Refuting an object of negation through reasoning means refuting something that we hold to exist but that in fact does not exist at all. Nāgārjuna's *Refutation of Objections* says:

> It is like someone thinking that a magical
> Emanation of a woman is an actual woman,
> Then the arising of this wrong understanding
> Is stopped by another emanation.

Things have no inherent nature of their own, but they appear to exist by way of their own inherent nature. This is similar to an illusion created by a magician that seems real to the audience. Words are also like magical illusions in that they do not exist inherently as they appear. Yet the noninherently existent words of a teaching reverse the grasping that arises in the minds of those who consider things to exist inherently. Nāgārjuna's *Commentary on the "Refutation of Objections"* says:

> Someone thinks that a magical emanation of a woman, who is empty of any such nature, is truly a woman. Thus attachment arises owing to this wrong understanding. That wrong understanding is reversed by a magical emanation created by the Tathāgata or his senior disciples. Similarly, like the magical emanation of the woman, all things are empty of inherent nature, and my words, which are empty like a magical emanation, reverse any grasping at things as inherently existent.

Tsongkhapa says that here Nāgārjuna is speaking about two types of objects of negation: incorrect grasping and the object incorrectly held to be inherently existent. The first is the subject (a type of mind) and the second is the object (what that mind is holding). Although both of these are to be negated, the latter is the primary object of negation: the object held to be inherently existent. This is because we have to negate the grasped object in order to reverse the mind that grasps it. We have to know that the grasped object is not really there. To negate the inherent existence of the self and of phenomena, we use a logical reason, such as dependent arising. If something can be negated by valid reasoning, it must be nonexistent; it does not exist as an object of knowledge. Even though this object of negation is already totally nonexistent, we need to negate it because the self-grasping mind wrongly holds it to exist. This distorted mind attaches something extra, which is not there, to the basis of negation and holds it to exist in that incorrect way. To stop this wrong view from arising we have to negate its object. Negating the object held by this wrong view is not like destroying something that actually exists. It is not like breaking a clay pot with a hammer. The point of logical refutation is to recognize that what does not exist in the first place is simply not there. When we generate an understanding that such a thing is not there, then the wrong view incorrectly holding it to exist is reversed.

In general, logic is used to refute what is unreal and prove what is real. It cannot prove the existence of something that did not exist before. It is not the creation of something new, like a sprout arising from a seed. Logic simply serves to make us recognize things as they are. Giving rise to definite understanding is what it means to prove something. When we prove that something is empty of inherent existence, we understand that it never has been inherently existent. Nāgārjuna's *Refutation of Objections* says:

Objection: That would be negating something that,
　Even without those words, does not exist.
Reply: Those words "does not exist"
　Give rise to understanding; they do not eliminate anything.

Here the words "does not exist" do not eliminate something that exists; they merely indicate that nothing exists inherently or from its own side. Inherent nature simply does not exist—whether or not anyone says so. Words do not make something nonexistent; words just clear away wrong conceptions about things. Words give rise to a correct understanding. Nāgārjuna's *Commentary on the "Refutation of Objections"* says:

> *Objection*: If you establish the negation of something that, even without your words, does not exist, then what do your words "All things have no inherent nature" accomplish?
> *Reply*: I will explain. The words "All things have no inherent nature" do not make things lack inherent nature. But, in that they do lack inherent nature, to say "Things have no inherent nature" brings about that understanding. For example, in a case where Devadatta is not at home, someone says, "Devadatta is at home." Another person, who knows he is not there, says he is not. The words "Devadatta is not at home" do not make Devadatta not at home. The words only show that Devadatta is not at home. Likewise, the words "Things have no inherent nature" do not make things lack inherent nature. All things have no inherent nature, like an illusory person. However, immature beings are ignorant about the lack of a real nature. So these words are to make ordinary beings, who are confused by ignorance and superimpose an inherent nature, understand that there is no inherent nature. Therefore it is not correct to say to me, "If there is no inherent nature, the lack of inherent nature is established without words, so what do your words 'There is no inherent nature' accomplish?"

As Nāgārjuna clearly explains, we should realize that the purpose of these words is to bring about the understanding that there is no inherent nature: nothing exists inherently. However, some people contend that using words to refute or prove things does not accomplish anything. What does not exist does not need to be refuted, and what is already existent cannot be refuted. In this sense, everything is free of negation and proof. People who engage in many refutations and proofs are simply fascinated by long words and drawn-out expressions.

Tsongkhapa replies that this comment is just senseless babble. It shows that the protagonist has no idea of what is to be negated or established by means of the path or by reasoning. The objects negated by paths—the mental afflictions and their seeds, as well as the obstructions to omniscience—exist, so they cannot be refuted by logic. Logic is used to refute the objects negated by reason—which do not exist. This opponent argues that there is no need for logical proof or refutation because words do not alter reality. He fails to recognize that logic is used to refute the nonexistent objects of misconceptions. We can all agree that logic does not alter reality; it simply establishes it. Logic proves the real and disproves the unreal.

This opponent's argument is not only senseless babble, it is self-contradictory. He begins by saying that if something exists then we cannot refute it, and if it does not exist then we do not need to refute it. Then he uses this statement as a reason to refute others' use of proof and refutation. He is trying to refute others and prove his own assertions by saying it is not suitable to refute or prove anything! It is inconsistent for him to try to disprove someone else's use of logic by using his own logical reasoning.

It is important to refute and prove things because everyone has thousands of mistaken ideas. There are an unlimited number of objects of knowledge; without knowing the truth, people perceive all of them incorrectly and usually hold them to exist as they are perceived. This is fundamentally due to ignorance. All the mental afflictions arise from ignorance; under their influence we create contaminated karma, and karma gives rise to rebirth in samsara. To stop this process, we must understand reality, and to understand reality we must correctly engage in refutation and proof. *Correctly* means that we begin by listening and studying, then we engage in analysis, and finally we meditate on what we have established. Through this practice, some things are stopped and others are developed. How can we gain the knowledge necessary to achieve our goal if we do not refute or prove anything? Correct reasoning counteracts wrong views and distorted conceptions. It can also prove to us what exists. Valid reasoning helps us to eliminate misconceptions and to develop definite, unmistaken understanding. Those who want to eradicate wrong views and develop realizations—especially with regard to ultimate truth—should follow the logical treatises of a great master like Nāgārjuna.

Tsongkhapa considers an opponent's question, "You said that logical refutation destroys a distorted way of holding an object and generates a nondistorted realization by negating the incorrectly held object. So what kind of mind holds its object in such a way as to be refuted by this logic?"

Tsongkhapa replies that although generally speaking there is no limit to the wrong ways of perceiving and holding things, we must determine as quickly as possible which distorted consciousness, among the eighty-four thousand mental afflictions, is the root of our suffering. We need to identify precisely the distorted thinking that gives rise to all the other faults.

THE DISTORTED THINKING OR IGNORANCE THAT IS THE ROOT OF SAMSARA

This distorted thinking is the fundamental ignorance that holds its object to exist inherently. To eliminate it, we must negate its conceived object.[86] By negating the conceived object of such thinking, this distorted consciousness and all the other faults arising from it will cease. The antidotes to the other mental afflictions taught by Buddha are only partial remedies. For example, the antidote to hatred is patience or love, and the antidote to attachment is meditation on impurity and ugliness. These methods reverse a particular affliction; they do not eliminate all the other afflictions. But the antidote to ignorance taught by Buddha eliminates all the mental afflictions; so this ignorance is the basis of all afflictions and faults. Candrakīrti's *Clear Words* says:

> The scriptures of the buddhas explain the two truths in nine branches,
> Correctly proclaiming vast methods in accordance with the conduct of
>   ordinary beings.
> What is taught in order to clear away attachment will not exhaust hatred.
> What is taught in order to clear away hatred will not exhaust attachment.
> What is taught in order to exhaust pride will not destroy other stains.
> So these teachings are not pervasive and do not have such great purpose.
> What is taught in order to exhaust ignorance destroys all other mental
>   afflictions.
> The Conquerors have taught that all other afflictions are based on
>   ignorance.

There are different ways to catalog Buddha's teachings that have been recorded in over a hundred volumes of scripture. These can be categorized into twelve branches of scriptures. Four of these twelve branches are sometimes counted as one, so this makes nine divisions. These can then be sorted into three, which are the three baskets of the Tripiṭaka. This all-inclusive division of the teachings accords with our conduct and mental capacity so that we can progressively eliminate our faults. Each section of the Tripiṭaka contains a specific training: ethical discipline is found in the Vinaya, meditative concentration is taught in the Sutras, and wisdom is explained in the Abhidharma. Ethical conduct is the foundation, like the earth, on which the other practices are based. The main practice built on it is the wisdom that understands ultimate truth. This wisdom will cut out all the mental afflictions from their root, thereby freeing sentient beings from the misery of cyclic existence. Training in wisdom will not be effective without the special techniques of meditative concentration. So there are three stages: first, we train in ethical conduct; then, on this basis we generate a stable, single-pointed, and completely peaceful mind; finally, we develop wisdom—and by joining mental stabilization to supreme insight, we can gain a direct realization of śūnyatā.

Buddha gave extensive teachings in this world in order to provide sentient beings with the antidotes to their problems. Many instructions are the remedy for a specific fault. Only the teachings on how to eliminate ignorance will clear away all the mental afflictions simultaneously. This is because all mental afflictions depend on ignorance; they arise from ignorance.

What is ignorance? Ignorance does not just mean not knowing. It is an innate, naturally arising mind that holds the opposite of reality to be true. There are various kinds of ignorance, which may be grouped into two: ignorance of conventional reality and ignorance of ultimate reality. Alternatively, this twofold division may be represented as: ignorance of causality and ignorance of the ultimate nature. The first kind of ignorance grasps the opposite of karmic causation—thinking that engaging in virtuous actions will not lead to happiness and that engaging in nonvirtuous actions will not result in misery. Ignorance of the ultimate nature is a mind that holds things to exist in a way that is opposite to how they actually exist. It grasps things as having an inherent nature or an intrinsic identity. In this context, pervasive ignorance is the innate mind that imputes an inherent nature onto all external and internal things. Candrakīrti's *Commentary on the "Four Hundred Stanzas"* says:

> This stanza teaches that attachment to things arises owing to the power of afflictive ignorance, a consciousness that superimposes an additional inherent nature onto things; it is the seed of samsara, and through its complete cessation samsara is reversed:
>
> > The seed of samsara is this consciousness;
> > These objects are its sphere of enjoyment.
> > When you see the absence of self in the object,
> > The seed of samsara will completely cease.
>
> According to the method taught here, the consciousness that is the seed of samsara and cause of attachment is gradually completely reversed through seeing its object's lack of inherent nature; in this way, the śrāvakas and pratyekabuddhas, as well as the bodhisattvas who have

gained patience with regard to nonarising phenomena, completely reverse samsara.

Here Candrakīrti is commenting on one of Āryadeva's *Four Hundred Stanzas* describing the origin and cessation of samsara. Bodhisattvas who have attained the eighth bodhisattva stage are similar to Hinayana arhats in that they have completely removed all the mental afflictions with their seeds and attained liberation from samsara. However, they have many other qualities besides. At this stage they are called "bodhisattvas who have gained patience with regard to nonarising phenomena." This refers to the fact that afflictive ignorance will never arise again within them, and because of this they gain a special forbearance, or patience, regarding the emptiness of inherent existence. An ordinary person naturally thinks in the opposite way—that things really exist by their own nature, and if they did not then they would become nothing. It is very uncomfortable for us to think about emptiness; we are impatient with this way of seeing things. However, after realizing śūnyatā and becoming more familiar with it, we develop a certain confidence and sense of ease about that truth. A very special type of patience arises with regard to śūnyatā when the ignorance that grasps things as inherently existent has been completely removed from the root. Bodhisattvas achieve this special patience upon attaining the eighth ground when they have completely reversed samsara. Their practice is especially powerful because they have developed great compassion, bodhicitta, and extensive skillful means.

The Prāsaṅgikas consider that grasping at true existence and grasping at inherent existence are the same: they are both ignorance. There are two types of this ignorance: grasping at a self of persons and grasping at a self of phenomena. These differ only in terms of their observed basis: persons or phenomena. The way of holding these objects is the same. Both are instances of afflictive ignorance grasping at inherent existence, and both are obstructions to liberation. The Svātantrikas do not consider that grasping at true existence and grasping at inherent existence are the same. Moreover, according to them, neither is established as afflictive ignorance. The Svātantrikas consider it is correct to hold things to be inherently existent conventionally, although wrong to hold them to be truly existent. According to them, grasping at a self-sufficient substantially existent person, within the aggregates, is the root of samsara. This is their notion of grasping at a self of persons. In their view, grasping at true existence means grasping at a self of phenomena; it is an obstruction to omniscience, which prevents the attainment of full enlightenment, not an afflictive obstruction, which prevents the attainment of liberation.

In short, according to the Svātantrikas, the two sorts of grasping at a self are different in terms of their basis as well as in terms of how the object is grasped. Grasping at a self of persons is far grosser than grasping at a self of phenomena. According to their system, we cannot totally remove the grasping at true existence—the grasping at a self of phenomena—until we attain enlightenment. That is the moment when we eliminate the obstructions to omniscience. Thus they say that śrāvaka and pratyekabuddha arhats, as well as bodhisattvas on the eighth ground and above, have not abandoned grasping at true existence.

However, the Prāsaṅgikas say that grasping at true or inherent existence is an afflictive obstruction, and the reason for this is found in Āryadeva's *Four Hundred Stanzas*:

> Just as the tactile sense power pervades the whole body,
> Ignorance abides in all [the mental afflictions].
> Therefore by destroying ignorance
> All mental afflictions are destroyed.

This indicates that ignorance and all the other mental afflictions are similar in the specific sense we already discussed in chapter 8. Here I do not mean "similar" in the technical sense of the five similarities between a primary mind and its accompanying mental factors, which we touched on initially in that chapter. There are two reasons for this: first, ignorance and the other mental afflictions are all mental factors—none of them is a primary mind; second, and more important, ignorance and the other mental afflictions may engage their *held* objects in different ways, thus their aspects—one of the five similarities— may be different. Rather, I mean "similar" here in the sense that ignorance and other mental afflictions are similar types of mind, in that they engage their *appearing* objects in similar ways. Candrakīrti comments on this stanza in his *Commentary on the "Four Hundred Stanzas"*:

> Ignorance imputes an additional truly existent nature onto things owing to being confused in conceiving them to exist truly, just as they appear.

Someone asks, "If ignorance is the root of samsara, then it is incorrect for Candrakīrti to have said in *Introduction to the "Middle Way"* and *Clear Words* that the egotistic view is the root of samsara, because there are not two different roots of samsara." In the *Introduction to the "Middle Way"* Candrakīrti says:

> All afflictions and faults without exception
> Arise from the view of the perishable collection;

Seeing this with wisdom and realizing the self to be its object,
The yogi negates the self. (6.120)

Tsongkhapa notes that he already discussed Bhāvaviveka's opinion—that
ignorance is the egotistic view (the view of the perishable collection)—in
the context of the explanation of the person of intermediate spiritual capacity.[87] Now he focuses on the Prāsaṅgika view, specifically Candrakīrti's
explication—which differs from the Svātantrika-Mādhyamikas who assert
that the mind holding things to be truly existent is an obstruction to omniscience. The Prāsaṅgikas say that the mind holding things to be truly existent
is ignorance; moreover, it is afflictive ignorance. There are two kinds of ignorance: afflictive ignorance and nonafflictive ignorance. The latter refers to the
obstructions to omniscience and is just given the name ignorance—it is not
actually ignorance because it is not a mind. This was tangentially explained
above in the discussion of a quotation from the *Commentary on the "Four
Hundred Stanzas."*[88] Further, in his *Commentary on the "Introduction to the
'Middle Way'"* Candrakīrti says:

> Ignorance, or delusion, which superimposes a nonexistent essential
> nature of things and obstructs seeing the [ultimate] nature, is the total
> obscurer in that it makes sentient beings confused with respect to seeing how things exist in reality.

A few lines later this commentary continues:

> Thus it is owing to the power of afflictive ignorance included within
> the twelve links of samsara that conventional truth is posited.

To show how sentient beings circle round in samsara, Buddha taught the
twelve links of dependent arising—the first link of which is ignorance. This
is a mental affliction. In the above passage, commenting on the two truths,[89]
Candrakīrti identifies the imputation of inherent existence onto things as the
ignorance that is the first of the twelve links of dependent arising. This shows
that, according to him, the ignorance grasping at the inherent existence of
things is a mental affliction—an obstruction to liberation, not an obstruction
to omniscience.[90]

The ignorance that is the root of samsara is a general category. It is the
grasping at inherent existence in general. The egotistic view, or the view of
the perishable collection, is a particular instance of it. It is the grasping at an
inherently existent "me" or "mine" based directly on oneself and indirectly

on one's own aggregates. Thus the egotistic view is itself ignorance. There are not two separate things that are the root of samsara; there is only ignorance. Both ignorance and the egotistic view are the root of samsara because one is included within the other. There is no contradiction here. Moreover, we can consider each of them in terms of a generality and its instances. Although ignorance grasping at inherent existence in general is the root of samsara, not every instance of this ignorance is the root of samsara. For example, the ignorance grasping at the inherent existence of a pot is not the root of samsara. Likewise, although the egotistic view in general is the root of samsara, not every instance of this view is the root of samsara. For example, my own egotistic view is not the root of samsara—it is just the root of my own samsara.

If you know something about Buddhist psychology, you may wonder how the view of the perishable collection can be a kind of ignorance. In the context of Buddhist psychology, ignorance and the egotistic view are two different mental factors. If ignorance is one mental factor and the egotistic view is another, then they must be completely different. There are fifty-one mental factors: five omnipresent mental factors, five object-ascertaining mental factors, eleven virtuous mental factors, six root afflictions, twenty secondary afflictions, and four variable mental factors. Ignorance is one of the six root afflictions. The egotistic view is an afflictive view, which is included within another of the six root afflictions. But all views, whether right or wrong, are part of wisdom or intelligence. Wisdom is divided into correct and afflictive wisdom. Thus the egotistic view is an afflictive wisdom. Wisdom is one of the five object-ascertaining mental factors. Unlike the Vaibhāṣika system, the upper schools say that the five object-ascertaining mental factors are not necessarily omnipresent, so they are listed separately. Either way, how can the egotistic view be a part of ignorance?

Wisdom and ignorance are opposites. Wisdom is knowing or holding something correctly. Ignorance is not simply not knowing; it is anti-knowing or holding something incorrectly. In his *Commentary on Valid Cognition*, Dharmakīrti defines ignorance as follows and correlates it with the egotistic view:

> Because it is the direct opposite of wisdom,
> And because it is a mental factor that is apprehending,
> And just apprehending wrongly, so it is taught
> To be ignorance; anything else is not correct. (2.213c–214c)

Ignorance does not just refer to any wrong consciousness; it is the direct opposite of the realization of ultimate truth (which, in Dharmakīrti's system, is the realization of selflessness).[91] If the first part of this definition were sufficient, then any wrong consciousness—whether a feeling, discernment, another mental factor, or a wrong primary consciousness—would be ignorance. However, according to Dharmakīrti's definition, in addition to being a consciousness that is the opposite of wisdom, ignorance must be a mental factor. Every primary mind has a number of accompanying mental factors. A mind grasping at true existence may include a primary mind as well as its accompanying mental factors. Every mental factor accompanying a primary mind that grasps at true existence is the opposite of truth, but is not necessarily called ignorance. Only the mental factor that is confused about its object through its own power is called ignorance. This is a wrong consciousness. The other mental factors, as well as that main mind itself, are confused about their object through the power of the accompanying mental factor of ignorance, not through their own power.

Do the Prāsaṅgikas accept this definition of ignorance? We have to think about this because there is no text presenting the Prāsaṅgika view of abhidharma. In general, *mind* is defined in terms of knowing: a consciousness is a knower. But, in the context of our present discussion, *knowing* refers specifically to wisdom realizing the ultimate truth. Knowing is affirmative: it knows reality. Ignorance is its negation—but it does not simply mean not knowing reality. It is more dynamic than this. Ignorance holds things incorrectly—it is the direct opposite of wisdom. It hypostatizes an inherently existent self—either a self of persons or a self of phenomena. Thus there are two types of ignorance: grasping at a self of persons and grasping at a self of phenomena. Grasping at a self of phenomena is grasping at phenomena, the aggregates themselves, as inherently existent. Grasping at a self of persons is grasping at an inherently existent person based on the aggregates. The view of the perishable collection is a type of grasping at a self of persons; it is the egotistic view grasping at an inherently existent "I" or "mine" based on one's own aggregates—not on those of someone else. Saying that the view of the perishable collection, or the egotistic view, is the root of all other afflictions does not mean that ignorance is not the root. Both kinds of imputation of an inherently existent self—of persons and of phenomena—are the root of samsara.

But can we say that the grasping at a self of phenomena is the root of all afflictions *and* that the egotistic view is the root of all afflictions? Nāgārjuna's *Precious Garland* says:

> As long as there is grasping at the aggregates,
> Then there is grasping at me.

We do not think "I" or "me" without some basis of identification, such as the body or mind. Similarly, whenever the egotistic view grasping at "me" or

"mine" arises, it is preceded by grasping at the aggregates. As soon as we ordinarily perceive any of our aggregates, they appear to be inherently existent;
so we naturally grasp them as inherently existent. Grasping the aggregates
as inherently existent is the grasping at a self of phenomena, and it is from
this that the egotistic view grasping at *I* arises. We identify ourselves based on
our aggregates because there is no other way to identify the self; and, having
grasped those as inherently existent, we immediately grasp the self to be inherently existent also. Therefore the egotistic view arises after the grasping at a
self of phenomena. Grasping at a self of phenomena is the cause of the egotistic
view; the egotistic view is a result of the grasping at a self of phenomena, not
the other way around. Because they are cause and effect, they are different—
although there is no difference between them in terms of the way that they
grasp their objects: both these views grasp their objects as inherently existent.
Nevertheless, because grasping at a self of phenomena causes the egotistic view,
we cannot say that the egotistic view is the root of grasping at a self of phenomena; it is not the root of this particular form of ignorance. However, the
egotistic view is the root of all the other afflictions such as attachment, hatred,
and so on. In summary, grasping at a self of phenomena and the egotistic view
are both ignorance; both of them are the source of all the other afflictions.
Because one form of ignorance is included within the other, it is not contradictory to say that the egotistic view is the root of samsara. Thus we must say
that the egotistic view is ignorance in this context. This means that ignorance
is not one single mental factor.

If you do not understand this way of explaining Nāgārjuna's thought, it is
difficult to avoid seeing a contradiction in Candrakīrti's discussion about the
root of samsara. There are not two different causes of samsara; there is only
one root. That is explained clearly in many places. Buddha said that there is
only one target; when you get rid of that root cause, you get rid of all afflictions
and suffering. That target is what we must identify. So although other systems
may claim that the ignorance of not knowing karmic causality is the root of
samsara, we have to realize that this is not the case. That kind of ignorance
contributes to the cause of samsara, but it is not the root cause.

GRASPING AT INHERENT EXISTENCE IS THE FIRST LINK
OF DEPENDENT ARISING

Identifying ignorance in this way is not something Tsongkhapa just made up.
It is in accord with what Nāgārjuna taught. Of course, Bhāvaviveka also claims
that his view correctly represents Nāgārjuna. All the Mādhyamikas say that
their view is Nāgārjuna's view. They all rely on the two great Mādhyamika āryas,
the father and son, Nāgārjuna and Āryadeva. Subsequent scholars' attempts

to understand and explain their view resulted in different interpretations. Following Buddhapālita in particular, Candrakīrti explains the Prāsaṅgika view in detail in a number of works: *Clear Words*, which is his commentary on Nāgārjuna's *Fundamental Treatise on the Middle Way*; his *Commentary on the "Four Hundred Stanzas"*; his own composition, *Introduction to the "Middle Way"*; as well as his autocommentary on that work, *Commentary on the "Introduction to the 'Middle Way.'"* Tsongkhapa follows Candrakīrti closely, so this way of identifying ignorance accords with Nāgārjuna's view. How can we be sure? Nāgārjuna's *Seventy Stanzas on Emptiness* says:

> Although things arise from causes and conditions,
> Any thought that they do so ultimately
> Was taught by Buddha to be ignorance—
> From which the twelve links arise.

> By seeing the truth, one knows things to be empty,
> Thus ignorance does not arise;
> That is the cessation of ignorance—
> Whereby the twelve links cease.

The first stanza shows the arising of the afflictions, which is the *forward process of arising* of the twelve links from ignorance up to aging and death. The phrase "Any thought that they do so ultimately" refers to grasping at things as ultimately existent. Candrakīrti says that this grasping at things as ultimately existent is the ignorance that is the primary cause within the twelve links of samsaric causality, which includes grasping at a self of persons and at a self of phenomena. This is quite different from the view of the Sautrāntika-Madhyamaka system of Bhāvaviveka and the Yogācāra-Madhyamaka system of Śāntarakṣita and Kamalaśīla. They do not accept that grasping things as ultimately or truly existent is the ignorance that is the first of the twelve links. For, according to them, grasping at things as ultimately existent is not grasping at a self of persons, which is an afflictive obstruction, but is only grasping at a self of phenomena, which is an obstruction to omniscience. We can gain freedom from samsara without getting rid of the obstructions to omniscience, though we must eliminate them in order to attain buddhahood.

The second stanza shows the cessation of the afflictions, which is the *forward process of purifying* of the twelve links from ignorance up to aging and death. How does this process reverse the twelve links? The wisdom that correctly and directly understands that all things are empty of inherent existence will stop ignorance from arising. Gradually, as we become accustomed to this direct realization, ignorance will completely cease. When ignorance has completely ceased, then the twelve links of dependent arising automatically stop—because their cause has been removed. The complete and final cessation of the twelve links of samsaric existence is nirvana. Chapter 26 of Nāgārjuna's *Fundamental Treatise* says:

> When ignorance has ceased,
> Conditioning action will not occur.
> Ignorance is ceased by means of
> The wisdom meditating on reality.
>
> Owing to each member having ceased,
> The next will not become manifest.
> This heap of suffering will cease
> Completely only in this way. (26.11–12)

Owing to the power of ignorance we create virtuous and nonvirtuous actions. "Conditioning action" is the second of the twelve links.[92] Although the same term is used for the fourth of the five aggregates, where it is translated as *conditioning factors*, in the context of this stanza it clearly means contaminated karma. This is the projecting karma: the cause of a future rebirth. Karma leaves propensities on the stream of consciousness—the third of the twelve links. This primary consciousness has two aspects: causal consciousness and resultant consciousness. Here we are mainly concerned with the causal consciousness, because the causal consciousness together with ignorance and conditioning action are collectively called the *projecting cause*. The projecting cause is like a seed planted in the spring. A combination of three later links is the *actualizing cause*: the eighth (attachment), the ninth (grasping), and the tenth (a type of karma called existence). The actualizing cause is the condition that enables the projecting cause to ripen. It is like the water, sunlight, and fertilizer that enable a seed to sprout and grow.

The cause of samsara is always a combination of karma and the mental afflictions. In the projecting cause, the affliction, *ignorance*, precedes and accompanies the karma, *conditioning action*. At the time of the actualizing cause, the afflictions are *attachment* and *grasping*, and the karma is called *existence*. The remaining seven links are the resultant suffering: the projected results, including the resultant consciousness, and the actualized results. Once we have stopped ignorance, conditioning action and all the subsequent links will not arise. We stop ignorance through generating a mind of supreme wisdom directly seeing ultimate reality. Only in this way can suffering end completely.

This is similar to the passage from the *Seventy Stanzas on Emptiness* quoted above. It also accords with the above passage from Nāgārjuna's *Precious Garland*. We already looked at the first two lines; however, the entire stanza makes it clear that grasping at a self of persons, together with grasping at a self of phenomena, is the root of samsara:

> As long as there is grasping at the aggregates,
> Then there is grasping at myself.
> If there is grasping at myself there is action,
> And from these there is rebirth. (1.35)

As long as we grasp the aggregates to exist from their own side, we will grasp the self to exist from its own side. The aggregates appear first, and then the self is imputed based on them. When our aggregates appear to us, they appear to be inherently existent; on the basis of that appearance, the innate mind of ignorance will grasp them to be inherently existent. When the thought of "I" or "me" arises based on the aggregates, the "I" instantly appears to be inherently existent, then the innate mind of ignorance mentally holds it to be so. So first there arises the grasping at a self of phenomena as the cause, and then there arises the grasping at a self of persons as the result. Whether we grasp the aggregates as inherently existent or the self as inherently existent, we create contaminated karma. This karma together with its cause—the ignorance grasping at inherent existence—gives rise to rebirth. The next stanza further explains:

> The three paths, without beginning, middle, or end,
> Circle around like a wheel of flaming torches;
> Continuously revolving, they cause each other:
> This is cyclic existence. (1.36)

"The three paths" here do not refer to the path to enlightenment. Just as there is the path to liberation, there are paths that go to the other side. The samsaric paths are: the path of afflictions, which mainly refers to ignorance; the path of actions; and the path of suffering, also called the path of rebirth. This is another way of presenting the twelve links of dependent arising. We can divide the twelve links into the categories of afflictions, karma, and suffering. A collective name for these three categories is the "three sufferings." In this context the term "suffering" may also mean affliction. In that sense, we can say that there are afflictions arising from each of the three paths: afflictions arising from other afflictions, afflictions arising from actions, and afflictions arising from suffering or rebirth. Sentient beings cycle round and round these three sets of paths that lead continuously to misery. None of them can be posited as the beginning, middle, or end.

Surely that cannot be right? We have just read that first there is ignorance, then there are the middle links, and finally there is aging and death. Yet this stanza says that the wheel of existence, samsara, appears to be like a whirling wheel of flaming torches. When this wheel of flaming torches is spun around fast, it creates the illusion of being a continuous ring of fire. Which point is first and which is last? We cannot see any beginning or end. Likewise, for as long as we grasp the aggregates to be inherently existent, the wheel of samsara revolves; one part comes after another, continuously turning round and round.

Nāgārjuna, the founder and father of the Madhyamaka, considers ignorance—grasping at the inherent existence of phenomena or of the self—to be an obstruction to liberation rather than an obstruction to omniscience. Āryadeva, his spiritual son, shares this view, as demonstrated in the previous quotations, beginning: "Just as the tactile sense power pervades the whole body . . ." and "The seed of samsara is this consciousness." These quotations clearly show that the ignorance holding the aggregates to be truly or inherently existent is the root of samsara. This is compatible with the root of samsara being the ignorance holding the self to be truly or inherently existent, because both types of ignorance grasp the same thing: inherent existence. Moreover, all the reasoning that Nāgārjuna presents in each of the twenty-seven chapters of the *Fundamental Treatise* refutes inherent existence, which is the object of negation. By refuting that kind of nature, he not only shows that nothing has an inherent nature, but he also shows that it is ignorance—the first link of dependent arising—that imputes an inherent nature onto things. Each chapter of the *Fundamental Treatise* deals with a specific topic for the sole purpose of negating the way that ignorance holds its object. In *Buddhapālita's Commentary on the "Fundamental Treatise,"* Buddhapālita says:

Question: What is the purpose of teaching dependent arising?
Reply: The master Nāgārjuna, whose nature is great compassion, having seen sentient beings harmed by various sufferings, wanted to show them the true nature of things in order to completely liberate them. So he composed the text that teaches dependent arising:

> Those seeing incorrectly are bound.
> Those seeing correctly are totally liberated.

Question: What is the reality of things just as they are?

Reply: It is the absence of inherent nature. Unskillful beings, whose eye of wisdom is obscured by the darkness of ignorance, conceive of things as having an essential nature, which gives rise to attachment and hatred. When the wisdom understanding dependent arising appears, the darkness of ignorance is cleared away. The eye of wisdom sees things as empty of an inherent nature. Then, lacking any foundation, attachment and hatred do not arise.

Buddhapālita's transitional commentary introducing the twenty-sixth chapter says:

Question: Having explained the way to enter into the ultimate by means of the Mahayana texts, now please explain how to enter into the ultimate by means of the Hinayana texts.
Reply: "Rebirth occurs owing to the obscuration of ignorance . . ."

The remainder of this passage is not quoted in the *Lamrim Chenmo*, but it says that owing to ignorance we create karma, which causes rebirth, and so on. In the transitional commentary to the twenty-seventh chapter Buddhapālita says:

Question: Now please show how the types of views based on the extremes do not exist according to the sutras of the śrāvakas.
Reply: "Declaring, 'I existed in the past' . . ."

This passage alludes to the fourteen questions that some non-Buddhist scholars put to Buddha, which he refused to answer. Questions like "Does the world have an end or not?" and "Is the world permanent or impermanent?" and "After death will the Tathāgata arise again or not?" are all based on the assumption that everything has an ultimate identity. If Buddha had said, "Yes, there is an end to the world" or "No, there is not an end to the world," the questioner would have interpreted this in an extreme way to mean that there is a permanent self or that there is none at all. Therefore it was not useful to say either yes or no. Buddha remained silent about these topics and instead gave a teaching on dependent arising or the four noble truths. In any case, he did not answer these questions directly because the questioners were not sincerely trying to learn, they were just testing him. The point in the above passage is that whatever has been explained in the Hinayana sutras is also taught by Nāgārjuna: prior causes are dependent on ignorance and the twelve links of dependent arising.

The above passages quoted from Buddhapālita's commentary show that he identifies the ignorance that is the first of the twelve links to be what imputes inherent nature onto things, and that he considers the śrāvakas and pratyeka-buddhas to realize the emptiness of a self of phenomena. This is an important topic discussed in many texts, and Tsongkhapa presumes that his readers are familiar with this issue. Tsongkhapa is keen to show that the great masters— Nāgārjuna, Āryadeva, Buddhapālita, and Candrakīrti—assert that without the wisdom understanding the emptiness of inherent existence there is no lib-eration from samsara, let alone buddhahood. Although I am trying to follow the *Lamrim Chenmo* closely, I will have to digress here and discuss this topic in a bit more detail for Western students to understand it.

In general, the lower schools, including the Svātantrika-Madhyamaka, say that grasping at a self of phenomena is not an obstruction to liberation. Therefore those who seek liberation for themselves do not need to realize the selflessness of phenomena. In order to attain arhatship, śrāvakas and pratyeka-buddhas only need to realize the selflessness of persons: the emptiness of a self-sufficient, substantially existent person. This definition is common to the Vaibhāṣika, Sautrāntika, Yogācāra, and Svātantrika-Madhyamaka schools. When they say "selflessness of persons" they are not referring to the emptiness of an inherently existent self as taught by the Prāsaṅgika school. In their view, in order to attain nirvana one must understand emptiness and selflessness in the context of the sixteen attributes of the four noble truths. Each noble truth has four attributes. The four attributes of the truth of suffering are: imperma-nence, suffering, emptiness, and selflessness. In this context, *emptiness* refers to the lack of a permanent, partless, and independent self. This negates the view of the self held by the non-Buddhists who believe that a self, or ātman, is unitary and not dependent on causes and conditions. These non-Buddhists say that the self and the aggregates are substantially different entities: the self is permanent and the aggregates are temporary; the aggregates are like clothing that the self carries around for a while, just as we wear a jacket. Buddhists negate this view by propounding emptiness: the lack of a self that is substantially different from the aggregates in this way. In the context of the four noble truths, *selflessness* is subtler than emptiness; it refers to the lack of a self-sufficient, substantially existent self. There is a twofold division of the grasping at a self: contrived grasping at a self and innate grasping at a self. Contrived grasping at a self is based on philosophical views or religious dogma, which the believer con-sciously asserts. Innate grasping at a self is completely natural; it is not based on any reasoning and usually goes unnoticed. The innate grasping at a self is what must be negated in order to attain liberation.

The Prāsaṅgikas present the subtlest interpretation of the innate grasping at a self. According to other Buddhist schools, however, it is an innate mind of ignorance holding the person to be self-sufficient and substantially existent. In general, our ordinary awareness neither holds the self and the aggregates to be completely different entities nor yet exactly the same. We normally feel that our self is somewhere in between. This need not be a distorted awareness; indeed, it need not involve any kind of grasping at all. But based on it, a mind grasping at a self naturally arises within ordinary people's mindstreams. It grasps the self to exist as a self-sufficient substantially existent entity that is neither the same as nor different from the aggregates. To illustrate this subtle misconception, Tsongkhapa gives an example in his *Essential Explanation of the Provisional and the Definitive*:[93]

> When an ordinary person's arm is hurt
> He thinks, "I am hurt." Thus even the worldly
> Do not think these two are substantially different.

It is common sense to think "I am hurt" when we injure ourselves. This indicates that we do not hold the aggregates to be completely different from the self. Each one of us knows that our self and our aggregates are not as different as a man and his cows, for example. Our innate mind does not perceive a man and his cattle as one entity—we see them separately from each other. Now, although we do not think that our aggregates and self are completely different in this way, do we feel that they are exactly the same? No—we do not have that feeling either. Consider a classical example. A man who is a merchant captain is not different from the merchants under his command in that he is a merchant himself. However, he is different and somewhat independent of the others in that he is their commander. We think of the self and the aggregates in a similar way. For example, if we could exchange our ugly, old body for one that is young and beautiful, we may well do so! That thought could never arise if the innate mind felt that the body and the self were exactly the same. However, ordinary people do not think this way, as Dharmakīrti suggests:

> They will strive for other [sense faculties] that are superior.[94]

Everyone has a sense of an *I* that seems to dominate the aggregates; it appears to be self-sufficient, substantially existent, and able to stand by itself independently. According to the lower schools, a mind that holds the self to be substantially existent and independent, just as it appears, is the egotistic view—from which attachment, hatred, karma, and so on arise. Therefore it is the root of samsara. When we understand that there is no self-sufficient, substantially existent person, then we have understood the selflessness of persons. All the Buddhist schools, except the Prāsaṅgika, claim that this realization is sufficient to attain liberation from samsara. They say that we do not need to realize the selflessness of phenomena to attain nirvana, because grasping at a truly or ultimately existent self of phenomena is not the ignorance that is the first of the twelve links of dependent arising. Śāntideva articulates the lower schools' argument that the Prāsaṅgika-Madhyamaka view of emptiness is not necessary:

> One will be liberated through seeing the truths.
> So what is the point of seeing emptiness?[95]

In other words, a realization of the sixteen aspects of the four noble truths will lead to liberation. The emptiness and selflessness that are aspects of the first noble truth are also expressed in the four seals of Buddhism:

> All causally conditioned things are impermanent;
> All contaminated things are in the nature of suffering;
> All phenomena are empty and selfless;
> Nirvana is peace.[96]

Generally all Buddhist schools accept that causally conditioned things are impermanent. In the second seal, "suffering" does not refer to our ordinary feeling of suffering. It refers to all contaminated things, including our happy experiences, because they arise from ignorance and karma. All our contaminated experiences and their objects are in the nature of suffering. In the third seal, "All phenomena are empty" refers to the nonexistence of a self dogmatically held to be permanent, partless, and independent. "All phenomena are selfless" refers to the nonexistence of a self innately held to be self-sufficient and substantially existent. In general all Buddhist schools, including the Prāsaṅgikas, accept the four seals. However, the Prāsaṅgikas present a more subtle level of selflessness: the lack of an inherently existent self. According to this most subtle understanding, once we have individuated something—whether it is the self or the aggregates—we look for what really exists as the referent of that label. We search but cannot find anything and finally arrive at a non-finding. Focusing single-pointedly on the absence of what is sought to exist from its own side leads one to nirvana. This is how we gain true peace or cessation, which is freedom from the afflictive obstructions. The primary afflictive obstruction, according to the Prāsaṅgikas, is the ignorance holding the self or any other phenomenon as inherently existent.

SELFLESSNESS IS THE ABSENCE OF INHERENT EXISTENCE

The main point here is that even other Mādhyamikas do not believe that selflessness is this subtle. They do not accept selflessness to be the absence of inherent existence. The subtlest object of negation that they propound is the absence of true or ultimate existence, defined in their own way on the basis of phenomena, not persons. They say we can achieve liberation without removing the ignorance that grasps phenomena as truly existent, although it must be removed to attain full enlightenment. According to all schools other than the Prāsaṅgika, the ignorance that is the root of samsara and the cause of all the other afflictions is explained in the two Abhidharmas. It has nothing to do with grasping at things as truly existent. The two Abhidharmas are the lower Abhidharma, Vasubandhu's *Treasury of Knowledge*, and the upper Abhidharma, Asaṅga's *Compendium of Knowledge*. Vasubandhu's text is based on the views of the Vaibhāṣika and Sautrāntika systems. Asaṅga's work is based on the Yogācāra, which fits very well with the Svātantrika-Madhyamaka.

In *Engaging in the Bodhisattva's Deeds*, Śāntideva says that although the two Abhidharmas teach methods to get rid of afflictions, their explanations of the afflictions that must be removed are too coarse to enable us to become an arhat. Neither Abhidharma negates grasping things as truly or inherently existent. By following those texts, we may temporarily remove the afflictions, but without getting rid of grasping at inherent existence we cannot gain freedom from samsara.

> With a mind that lacks an understanding of śūnyatā,
> Any [afflictions] that are stopped will arise again,
> Just as with the meditative equipoise without discernment.
> Therefore you should meditate on śūnyatā. (9.48)

By meditating on selflessness as presented within a basic interpretation of the four noble truths we can temporarily stop the afflictions, including grasping at the self, but we cannot eradicate them permanently. Without understanding the emptiness of inherent existence as explained in the Prāsaṅgika system, grasping at the self will arise again in the future. In this case, one is not completely free and will be born in samsara again. Śāntideva says that this is similar to the temporary cessation of consciousness that results from the meditative equipoise without discernment. This meditative state is a subtle type of concentration, which arises from developing the four form-realm and the four formless-realm concentrations. The mind becomes more and more subtle, until consciousness completely stops. Some schools say that the subtle mind is still there, but apart from that, all mental functioning has stopped. The meditator appears almost dead. During this cessation of consciousness the mental afflictions stop. However, this cessation of consciousness is not a true cessation of the afflictions by means of wisdom. It is a fake or nominal cessation because the afflictions can arise again in the future. It is just a temporary cessation because this method does not get rid of the seeds of the afflictions. The mental afflictions are sure to arise again. Similarly, when practitioners have removed the afflictions through the meditation techniques taught in the two Abhidharmas, they have only temporarily removed them. They have not removed the subtle seeds; in that case, the afflictions are stopped only temporarily, not permanently.

Therefore, according to the Prāsaṅgikas, we have to get rid of the grasping at a self of phenomena in order to gain liberation from samsara. Śāntideva says that ignorance—grasping at an inherent nature—blocks us from attaining nirvana:

> Those with minds grasping at an inherent object
> Have great difficulty attaining nirvana. (9.44c–d)

There are many scriptural passages, including the *Perfection of Wisdom Sutras*, which teach this. Śāntideva says:

> It is because, as taught in the scriptures,
> Without this path there will be no enlightenment. (9.40c–d)

In general there are three kinds of enlightenment—that of śrāvakas, pratyekabuddhas, and bodhisattvas, respectively. The Mahayana sutras say that without the wisdom that understands the emptiness of inherent existence of all phenomena, we cannot achieve any of these three enlightenments. If the śrāvakas and others believe that they have achieved arhatship inherently, they are mistaken. Those who consider phenomena to be inherently real cannot achieve liberation. The Prāsaṅgika view is that even śrāvakas and pratyekabuddhas must realize the selflessness of phenomena in order to gain liberation from samsara. There is no way to attain liberation other than by eliminating ignorance. As we have seen, ignorance means grasping at inherent existence—whether of the person or phenomena.

The strongest proof that śrāvakas and pratyekabuddhas realize this kind of emptiness—the lack of inherent existence—is that the grasping at an inherent self of phenomena is the ignorance that is the first of the twelve links of dependent arising. Āryadeva's *Four Hundred Stanzas* says:

> Seeing by means of conceiving is bondage;
> That is what must be negated here.

According to Candrakīrti, Āryadeva is not talking about just any kind of conceiving, for he says:

> Conceiving, here, means superimposing an unreal inherent nature.

It is a wrong conceiving, a distorted thinking, that superimposes an inherent nature onto things. This is afflictive ignorance. Therefore we cannot infer that Āryadeva is saying that ordinary thoughts, such as "this is a book," should be negated by reasoning.

Someone like Hashang, who says that the objects of ordinary thoughts are to be negated, has not examined the matter properly. He and his followers say that the ordinary mind is impure, so conceptual thought has no valid function; whether correct or incorrect, thought obstructs the truth—just as a dog bite is the same, whether the dog is white or black. However, if we reject all thought and negate all objects of thought, ordinary individuals would have no means of knowing emptiness. Beginners cannot perceive emptiness directly. They have to start by developing an understanding of it by means of inferential knowledge. Initially we have to realize the correct view conceptually; eventually it becomes a direct realization. There is no other method we can use to ascertain the meaning of śūnyatā. Knowledge of śūnyatā arises from analysis investigating the way in which things exist and discovering that they do not exist inherently. If all thoughts were wrong, then simply by virtue of being a thought, an understanding of emptiness would be wrong and its object must be negated. If the objects of all thoughts were to be negated by logical analysis, then even this correct conceptual understanding of emptiness would be mistaken—like the wrong consciousness superimposing inherent existence. Thus there would be no correct view leading to nirvana. In that case, all hearing, studying, and meditating based on the Madhyamaka texts would become meaningless. Āryadeva's *Four Hundred Stanzas* says:

> Some say, "I will attain nirvana."
> But [seeing] nonemptiness as emptiness is not seeing.
> The Tathāgatas have taught
> That this distorted view does not lead to nirvana.

Seeing what is not emptiness, such as a mere absence of thought in the mind, as actual emptiness is not seeing emptiness. It is a distorted view and does not lead to nirvana.

Realists, whether Buddhist or non-Buddhist, having taken as a basis the conceived object grasped by ignorance, superimpose on it many particular qualities through their own reasoning and philosophical views. When the object grasped by ignorance is completely negated by means of Madhyamaka ultimate analysis, all these wrong tenet systems collapse and their extreme views are destroyed. It is like razing a big tree from the root. Therefore those who are intelligent understand that the main object to be negated is the object grasped by innate ignorance, rather than the objects imputed by philosophical thinking. This does not mean that the objects imagined by philosophers should not be negated. Indeed, in order to understand what would follow if an object did exist as it is held by the innate mind of ignorance, we first need to negate many philosophical views. Then we can eliminate the fundamental source of the problem. So in the beginning we must analyze, examine, and think about our own innate ignorance and how that innate ignorance holds its object—because that way of holding the object is the root of the problem.

The main point to realize here is that the principal object of negation is the object as it is held by the innate mind of ignorance, rather than the object as it is held by mistaken theoretical understanding. We must ascertain why this is so and why we are trying to negate that particular object. We are not trying to negate it simply because we are bored and have nothing else to do! We are doing it because we see that sentient beings are tied to samsara owing to their wrong view grasping this object of negation—and that refuting this object of negation is the only way to gain liberation. Every sentient being, apart from arhats and bodhisattvas on the pure grounds, has this innate ignorance. It does not rely on any special reasoning or education; as soon as a sentient being is born, this ignorance is there. That is why it is called *innate*. The speculative or contrived wrong views of philosophers do not bind sentient beings to samsara because these are not universal: only philosophers have them. It is extremely important to gain a firm and clear understanding of this point.

The primary wrong conceptual consciousness grasping the object of negation is innate ignorance—the first of the twelve links of dependent arising. All the contrived objects of negation of the philosophical schools are just superimposed on what is grasped earlier by this innate mind of ignorance. The way that a nonconceptual direct perception holds its object is never negated by ultimate analysis. Direct perception includes sense consciousness and mental direct perception, such as yogic direct perception. We do not negate the primary object of a sense consciousness—as long as there is no internal or external temporary cause of error. If a consciousness is not a sense consciousness, it is a mental consciousness. Mental consciousness includes thought, mental direct perception, and wrong perception. Thought is a mental consciousness but not a direct perception. Thought apprehends its object mixed with a conceptual image of that thing—so a valid thought is mistaken only with regard to what appears to it, not with regard to its main apprehended object. A nonconceptual mind, on the other hand, directly perceives whatever appears to it—such as a color or shape—unmixed with a conceptual image. We use logic to negate only the way that a conceptual mental consciousness grasps its object. But this cannot apply to every thought, for otherwise it would include an initial realization of śūnyatā. We must negate only distorted thoughts or wrong views. More specifically, we must negate the distorted thoughts grasping at a self of persons and at a self of phenomena. In addition we must negate the particular thoughts that superimpose something extra onto the objects of these two kinds of self-grasping—such as the grasping at a self of persons as held by non-Buddhist philosophers.

It is reasonable to ask, "How does innate ignorance impute an inherent nature?" First we should consider what is meant by the term *nature* (*rang bzhin*). Tsongkhapa explains that there are various ways to understand this word, according to Candrakīrti's texts. Things have a conventional nature—for example, the nature of fire is hot and the nature of water is wet. Things also have a final or ultimate nature—their own śūnyatā. But here, in the context of a nature that is imputed by ignorance, it refers to the way in which everything seems to exist by means of its own reality, rather than as merely imputed by thought or terminology. Whatever appears to our ordinary awareness—whether it is a mountain, a tree, or a person—it seems to exist from its own side; it does not appear to exist in dependence on the power of our mind perceiving or thinking of it or the terminology used to identify it. If we see a tree, it appears to be there already—as if it might introduce itself and say, "Hello, I am a tree." When we identify things ordinarily, we do not think they are established by the power of our mind in any way. Things appear to exist from their own side; the innate mind of ignorance holds them to exist from their own side, through their own reality or way of existing, just as they appear to. The grasped object, as it is held in this way by innate ignorance, is called a *self* or a *nature*. In fact, everything is established by the power of mind, and such a self as it is conceived does not exist at all. An inherent nature as held by the innate mind of ignorance is completely and totally nonexistent. Nevertheless, in order to understand how this ignorance functions so as to gradually remove it, we must hypothetically identify that self in terms of certain criteria.

Therefore when searching for the self or inherent nature, a yogi considers, "If there were an inherent nature of persons or things, then how would it exist?" Āryadeva's *Four Hundred Stanzas* says:

> All these things have no autonomous nature
> Therefore they have no self.

Here "have no autonomous nature" does not mean simply that things depend on causes and conditions. It means that things are not independently or inherently existent from their own side. In *Commentary on the "Four Hundred Stanzas,"* Candrakīrti comments on this stanza:

> This indicates anything that exists by its own nature, inherently, independently, without depending on others . . .

In the phrase "without depending on others," the word "others" does not refer merely to causes and conditions that give rise to things; it refers to the subject that conventionally knows them—the thought and terminology that identifies them. According to the Prāsaṅgika system, things are established conventionally—by the power of thought and terminology. If something were not established by the power of thought and terminology, then it would be established "without depending on others." If something were to exist by its own power, without depending on imputation by thought or terminology, then it would exist by its own entity or nature. The word "independent" indicates a thing's special, unique, intrinsic nature—through which it exists by means of its own reality or way of being. These terms, along with *inherent nature* or *essential nature*, are synonymous and refer to the object of negation that is hypothetically identified. This *nature* is what the Madhyamaka ultimate analysis negates. It is presented in terms of how it is thought to exist; we hypothesize, "If it existed, this is how it would be."

As an illustration, let us look at the classic example of a coiled rope lying in a dark corner, which the perceiver mistakenly takes to be a snake. We could examine how the concept "This is a snake" is imputed by our thought consciousness on that basis. We could ask, "How is our distorted thought consciousness functioning here?" But if we leave out the subjective side of the process, without examining that at all, and focus only on the object, we cannot find anything. No snake exists within that objective basis, so it has no qualities or attributes to examine. This is the example given here, and the same principle applies to other things.

We need to examine how things appear to our conventional awareness. But usually we leave this out and simply examine the things themselves, assuming that they exist objectively just as they appear to. Things are not established merely objectively, so when we examine them on this basis alone, we cannot find anything. The distorted mind of innate ignorance does not understand that all phenomena are established by the force of the conventional mind and the process of naming, but instead grasps everything to have its own unique way of existing from its own side. So when this mind of ignorance is functioning, we hold the object of our perception to exist exactly as it appears from its own side, as if based on its own reality; we believe that what we are seeing, whether good or bad, objectively and independently exists as such from its own side. Candrakīrti's *Commentary on the "Four Hundred Stanzas"* says:

> Things that exist only when established by conventional thought and do not exist when not established by conventional thought are definitely not inherently existent, just like a snake imputed on a coiled rope.

In this way, Candrakīrti teaches the way in which things do not exist by their own nature objectively. What is being negated here is the concept that phenomena are established not by thought, but by their own nature as objectively existent.

THE ABSENCE OF INHERENT NATURE OF PERSONS AND OF PHENOMENA

The quality of objectively existing in its own right is called *self* or *nature*. The absence of this attribute—inherent nature—on the basis of a person is the selflessness of persons. The absence of this attribute on the basis of the eyes, nose, and so on is the selflessness of phenomena. So the attribute we negate is the same, but the bases on which we negate it are different. Candrakīrti's *Introduction to the "Middle Way"* says:

> In order to liberate sentient beings, this selflessness
> Is taught in terms of two aspects: persons and phenomena. (6.179a–b)

Through this clear explanation of the distinction between the selflessness of persons and the selflessness of phenomena, we can implicitly understand that holding an inherent nature to exist on the bases of persons and phenomena is wrongly grasping at the two types of self. Candrakīrti's *Commentary on the "Four Hundred Stanzas"* says:

> Regarding that, "self" refers to an intrinsic nature of things that does not depend on something else. That does not exist, so the self does not exist. Understanding this in terms of the twofold division of persons and phenomena, there is the selflessness of persons and selflessness of phenomena.

As explained earlier, "depending on others" refers to depending on being perceived and identified by thought. Because nothing exists without depending on being perceived and identified, everything is selfless.

Someone says that it cannot be right that grasping at an inherently existent person is the grasping at a self of persons. If it were, then the grasping at some person other than oneself as inherently existent would be the grasping at a self of persons, and thus it would be the view of the perishable collection—the view that grasps in a manner of thinking "I." However, this view does not hold any thought of "I" on the basis of another person. Therefore grasping at an inherently existent person cannot be the grasping at a self of persons.

Tsongkhapa replies that, as explained earlier, Candrakīrti says that the self of persons is the inherent nature of a person, and the grasping at the self of persons is the grasping at a person as inherently existent. Although the view of the perishable collection—the egotistic view—is necessarily the grasping at a self of persons, the grasping at a self of persons is not necessarily the egotistic view. So what quality must the grasping at a self of persons have to make it the egotistic view? The egotistic view has two divisions: self-grasping that is the contrived egotistic view and self-grasping that is the innate egotistic view.

First, let us consider the *contrived* egotistic view. There are many such views, so there is no certainty regarding this matter. Different systems present different ways of holding the self. Virtually all non-Buddhist schools of thought accept a permanent self or soul, and views holding that are most obviously included among the contrived egotistic views. There is even one Buddhist school that, according to Tibetan tradition, accepts a self or person: the Vātsīputrīya, a subschool of the Saṃmitīya, which is included within the eighteen schools of the Vaibhāṣika. The Vātsīputrīyas accept a certain interpretive teaching of Buddha to be taken literally, namely, that the aggregates are like a burden and the person bearing them is not said to be either permanent or impermanent. When the person dies there is physical disintegration, so the self is not completely permanent; yet the person endures, for he or she goes from one life to the next, so the self is not completely impermanent.

There is a great deal of discussion about this in Jangkya's monastic textbook. Also, Phurbu Cog Jampa Gyatso Rinpoche discusses whether this school is even Buddhist because it accepts a self. Some scholars say that if you accept a self then you cannot be considered a Buddhist, because generally all Buddhist schools accept the four seals, and these include the insight that all phenomena are empty and selfless. Others say that, in general, a Buddhist is anyone who accepts the Three Jewels; so not accepting selflessness does not automatically make one non-Buddhist. Here it should be noted that Buddha sometimes offers teachings in order to draw people into practice. So this teaching may have been given as a temporary measure, for the benefit of those not yet ready to hear about selflessness. There are also a number of other Buddhist views that might be included in this category, though this is debatable: some Saṃmitīyas say that the aggregates are identical with the self or person, some other Vaibhāṣikas say that the continuity of the five aggregates is the basis of identity of the person, and some say the group of the aggregates is the basis of identity of the person.

Second, let us consider the *innate* egotistic view, which is the root of samsara. Tsongkhapa says that in *Introduction to the "Middle Way"* Candrakīrti demonstrates that the aggregates are not the object of the innate egotistic view, and in *Commentary on "Introduction to the 'Middle Way'"* he says that the object of this view is the dependently imputed self, or mere I. We have to be careful when talking about the object of the innate egotistic view because there are two kinds of objects of that view: the basic object and the held object. According to Tsongkhapa, the basic object of the innate egotistic view is the dependently imputed self, which conventionally exists. This is the self that creates karma, experiences its results, and tries to gain enlightenment. What Tsongkhapa is saying here is that the innate egotistic view directly observes this dependently imputed person or self; it does not directly observe the aggregates as its basic object. The innate egotistic view also has a held object, which is the basic object held to have a certain attribute: inherent existence. The held object is a combination of the basic object, the self, and the attribute that it is held to possess, inherent existence. The held object is the conventional self grasped in this incorrect way—as inherently existent. In other words, it is the inherently existent self. It is this object that the yogi recognizes to be the culprit—the object grasped by the distorted mind of ignorance, the root of samsara. So the yogi strives to negate this object—the inherently existent self—by means of analytical meditation.

It is crucially important to distinguish between these two objects of the innate view of the perishable collection—the basic object and the held object. Accordingly, we must differentiate two kinds of self: the self that is to be accepted and the self that is to be negated. The basic object of the innate egotistic view, the mere self, exists. However, this distorted view grasps its basic object as inherently existent—which is the held object. The held object of the innate egotistic view, the inherently existent self, is to be negated. This held object does not exist at all.

To clarify this, consider someone who holds sound to be permanent. Certain non-Buddhist schools claim that sound is a quality of space, space is permanent, and therefore sound is permanent. To counter them, Buddhists prove that all sound is impermanent. In this case, the opponent has a wrong view that holds "sound as permanent." That object is the held object, the object held in the wrong way—as permanent. But even though this wrong view holds or grasps "permanent sound," the basic object of this wrong view is *sound* itself. Sound itself exists. But an attribute, "permanent," is added onto sound. That is what is wrong. The held object is the combination of the basic object and the attribute—in this case "permanent sound." This held object does not exist. We should not assume, however, that any held object is nonexistent. Buddhists hold "sound as impermanent," and since this is the actual conventional nature of sound, "impermanent sound" exists.

The innate view of the perishable collection is a mind of ignorance that grasps an inherently existent self. That grasping must have an existent basis. The basis on which this wrong view arises is the conventionally existent self or person. This basic object must be oneself rather than another person. It cannot be a person who is a different continuum from oneself, because we cannot think "me" or "mine" on the basis of someone else. This is true of everybody's innate self-grasping mind. The object of your egotistic view is only you.

Now how does this self-grasping mind hold its basic object? In *Commentary on the "Introduction to the 'Middle Way'"* Candrakīrti says:

> The view of the perishable collection grasps in a certain manner of thinking "me" or "mine."

The "certain manner" in which the egotistic view grasps its object is to hold "me" or "mine" as inherently existent. It does not grasp inherent existence alone; it grasps "me" or "mine" qualified as being inherently existent. There are two divisions of this view: the view of the perishable collection grasping at me, and the view of the perishable collection grasping at mine. Candrakīrti says in *Introduction to the "Middle Way"*:

> First, thinking "I," grasping at a self arises.
> Thinking "This is mine," attachment to things arises. (1.3a–b)

When the innate egotistic view arises, first there is the thought of "I" or "me." We feel "this is me" and naturally grasp that "I" as an inherently existent self. Then we think of our sense consciousnesses, body parts, or other aggregates as "mine" and naturally grasp this "mine" itself to be inherently existent. So there is the view of the perishable collection regarding "me" and the view regarding "mine." The objects of both of these are included within the self of persons, not the self of phenomena. Even though my aggregates are considered to be instances of mine, my aggregates are not the object of the egotistic view grasping at "mine," as will be shown below.[97] They are the object of the ignorance grasping at a self of phenomena. Nevertheless, neither aspect of the egotistic view could arise without having observed the aggregates, so the aggregates function as an indirect basis for that view, but they are not the direct object of it, according to this system. Candrakīrti's *Commentary on the "Introduction to the 'Middle Way'"* says:

> Just the view of the perishable collection is to be abandoned. It will be abandoned by fully realizing the selflessness of the self.

In the phrase "selflessness of the self," "self" refers to the conventionally existent self. This self is empty of inherent existence. In other words, the conventional self or person has the attribute "selflessness." The egotistic view grasps the conventional self as inherently existent. More specifically, it grasps "me" as inherently existent. We get rid of that wrong way of holding the conventional self by means of the wisdom seeing the selflessness of the self. This correct view is the complete opposite of the egotistic view. The wisdom realizing selflessness or emptiness contradicts the way that the self is held by the egotistic view, hence the selflessness of the self.

We can understand the view of the perishable collection grasping at "mine" in this way too. However, there is some debate about how we classify this object. Is the object of the egotistic view holding "me" different from the object of the egotistic view holding "mine"? The former observes "me" and holds it to inherently exist. The second observes "mine" and grasps that to be inherently existent. So if you look at your own hand and think "mine," holding it to be inherently existent, is this grasping at phenomena as inherently existent? If not, how can "mine" be a person? If it is not a person, then since it exists must it be a phenomenon? Holding a phenomenon as inherently existent is not grasping at a self of persons because the basic object is not a person; it is grasping at a self of phenomena. So even though the egotistic view is divided into these two aspects—grasping "me" and grasping "mine" as inherently existent—you should understand that they both observe the self and they both grasp at a self of persons. You should not consider that either of them observes phenomena or grasps at a self of phenomena. The object of this egotistic view does not concern the self of phenomena.

Different scholars present different interpretations of this point. Most scholars agree that the egotistic view holding "me" observes the person. Some scholars say that the egotistic view holding "mine" also observes the person—because if it does not, then it would be grasping at a self of phenomena. Certain other scholars, while accepting that "me" refers to the person, try to avoid the problem regarding "mine" by appealing to the notions of "generality" and "particularity." They say that "mine" as a generality is the person, but particular instances of "mine" are not; they are things such as my hand and my cup. But, we may ask, if "mine" is the generality of the person, then how can a hand be a particular instance of it? That is impossible. If the subject is a person, how can a hand or a face be included among its instances?

Jetsun Chokyi Gyaltsen says that "mine" itself is not the person, but when we grasp something as "mine," then grasping the person as inherently existent must be present in the mindstream. When we think "this is my hand," first there is the thought "hand" and then the thought "mine," which is that hand in connection with "me." However, here we are not grasping "hand" as inherently existent. What we are grasping finally is "mine" itself. Without "me," "mine" cannot appear. So when we grasp "mine" as inherently existent, we are also grasping "me" as inherently existent. Therefore the main object of the grasping at "mine" is "me"; so grasping at "mine" is the grasping at a self of persons. According to Jetsun Chokyi Gyaltsen's view, we can say that "mine" is a phenomenon in general because everything that exists is a phenomenon. However, we cannot say that it is a phenomenon within the context of the division between phenomena and persons. When this division is made, it is not counted as a phenomenon; however, it is not a person either. But since you cannot hold "mine" without holding "me," it arises in connection with the egotistic view grasping at "me." Therefore both aspects of the view of the perishable collection—grasping at me and grasping at mine—observe the self and grasp at the self of persons. We should not regard either one as observing phenomena or grasping at a self of phenomena. Moreover, although grasping at a substantially existent person without the thought of "me" or "mine" is not the egotistic view, this grasping is still a mental affliction—it is ignorance grasping at the self of persons.

In conclusion, the word "self" can refer to two different things—one that exists and one that does not. The conventionally existent self actually exists; the mere "I" or "me" is an ordinary object of awareness and is not negated. The inherently existent self does not exist at all; it is the object wrongly held by the egotistic view, and it is negated by the wisdom understanding selflessness. In other words, the former is the basic object of the innate egotistic view and should not be negated. The latter is the held object of the innate egotistic view and should be negated. There is no contradiction here. It is similar to not negating the basic object of the view that grasps at sound as permanent, which is *sound*, yet negating the held object of the view that grasps at sound as permanent, which is *permanent sound*.

The noble father Nāgārjuna, his spiritual son Āryadeva, as well as the two masters Buddhapālita and Candrakīrti show what is to be negated using expressions such as "if things were inherently existent," "if things existed by their own nature," "if things existed by their own characteristics," and "if things were substantially existent." When these great masters employ words such as "inherently" and so on, you should understand them as explained earlier. When they say that things do not exist in a certain way or do not have a nature, it means that things do not exist in the way that they are held by ignorance. Generally, in a conventional sense things do have a nature, they have their own characteristics, and some things even have substance. However, we cannot say that things exist inherently, exist by their own characteristics, exist by their own nature, or substantially exist. It is the mind of ignorance that holds things to exist in these ways; a thing existing in any of these ways is to be negated. We must differentiate between what is conventionally existent and what is to be negated. The fundamental problem is the way that innate ignorance grasps its object. Negating that object correctly gives rise to a mind of wisdom that understands emptiness. When fully developed, the wisdom seeing emptiness gradually removes innate ignorance and its potentialities from the mindstream forever.

⚜ 12 ⚜
Qualifying the Object of Negation

(2)) Whether to add qualifications to other objects of negation

(3)) Whether to add the qualification "ultimate" to the object of negation

———————

(2)) WHETHER TO ADD QUALIFICATIONS TO OTHER OBJECTS OF NEGATION

WHEN INDICATING that a nonexistent thing does not exist, we do not need to add the qualification "inherently." We can simply say, "A rabbit horn does not exist" or "The son of a barren woman does not exist." Similarly, we do not need to add the modifier "inherently" when speaking of things that exist in certain times and places but not in other times and places. If there is no elephant in this room, we do not need to say, "There is no inherently existent elephant in this room." We just need to deny the existence of an elephant here—for we are discussing conventional reality. Moreover, when negating the various superimpositions uniquely asserted by Buddhist and non-Buddhist Realist systems, which Mādhyamikas do not accept even conventionally, we do not need to apply the qualification "inherently"—except in a few cases where it must be added in order to negate the Realists' underlying assumption that those things are inherently existent.

We must apply this qualification "inherently" when negating, in the context of ultimate analysis, anything conventionally established by the Mādhyamikas. If we do not, then the logic we use to refute our opponent can be turned around and applied equally to our own position. For example, the Mādhyamikas accept the conventional existence of the aggregates, the elements, and cause and effect. Therefore the Mādhaymikas specify that they are negating inherently existent aggregates, inherently existent elements, and so forth. Without the qualification "ultimately" or "inherently" our position would be subject to the same faults that result from the opponent's position. In short, we would be employing fallacious refuting consequences.[98]

Moreover, as explained before, neither ultimate analysis nor conventional valid knowledge can disprove what the Mādhyamikas conventionally establish. If they could, then no distinction could be made between things that are accepted conventionally and things that are not accepted conventionally. For example, the Mādhyamikas deny the existence of an eternal, unchanging god who is the universal cause of all things; but they accept forms, sounds, and so on to be conventionally existent. If things that are conventionally existent could be negated either by ultimate analysis or by conventional valid knowledge, then we could not make any distinctions at the mundane level or at the supramundane level—such as "This is the path and that is not the path" or "This philosophy is correct and that is not correct." Without the ability to make this kind of distinction, the special quality of the Madhyamaka—that all the presentations of samsara and nirvana are reliable and acceptable although empty of inherent existence—would not be feasible. Wise people would find it ridiculous if someone wanted to negate things that cannot be negated by valid knowledge. Therefore in teachings where conventionally established things are denied, this special qualification must definitely be applied.

In his *Commentary on the "Four Hundred Stanzas"* and *Commentary on the "Sixty Stanzas of Reasoning,"* Candrakīrti usually applies this qualifier when he refutes the object of negation. This is also the case in Nāgārjuna's *Fundamental Treatise*, Buddhapālita's *Buddhapālita's Commentary on the "Fundamental Treatise,"* as well as Candrakīrti's *Clear Words* and *Commentary on the "Introduction to the 'Middle Way.'"* However, in order to avoid being too repetitive, these authors did not apply the qualifier "inherently" in every passage. They thought it was easy to realize that it must be understood, even where it is not explicitly stated. So when "inherently" does not appear in a particular passage in these texts, it means the same as if it did. For example, the *Perfection of Wisdom Sutras* sometimes explicitly say "inherently" and sometimes they do not. Even when a sutra does not say "inherently," such as "There is no form, no sound, no smell...," we must understand that it means "There is no inherently existent form, no inherently existent sound," and so forth.

Moreover, these authors often apply the qualification of "analysis," which is to say, "When analyzed, it does not exist." As explained earlier, this means that if anything were to exist by its own nature, then we would find it when we critically examine how it exists. Since we do not find it, that thing is not able to bear ultimate analysis: it does not inherently exist. The *Commentary on the "Four Hundred Stanzas"* says:

> All these things are deceptive, like a wheel of fire, a magical emanation, and so on; therefore they are not inherently existent. If that were not the case, then when you analyze them correctly, you would definitely see their essential nature very clearly, like examining pure gold. These things have distorted causes; therefore when they are burned by the fire of ultimate analysis, they will never not be without essential nature.

Things are not real in the way that they appear; they do not exist inherently. If they did exist inherently, then they would be findable by correct ultimate analysis. We would be able to ascertain their intrinsic nature, just as we can find pure gold beneath a dirty surface by burning, cutting, rubbing, and correctly testing a specimen rock. But when things are burned by the intense fire of ultimate analysis, we can find only a lack of essential nature. Instead of finding a thing's intrinsic nature, it disappears. Therefore things do not exist inherently. Their appearance as inherently existent is a false projection and arises from a distorted cause.

(3)) WHETHER TO ADD THE QUALIFICATION "ULTIMATE" TO THE OBJECT OF NEGATION

Some philosophers contend that only the Svātantrika-Madhyamaka school applies a special qualification to the object of negation. They make this claim because Nāgārjuna's negation of production from the four extremes says:

> Not from self, not from others,
> Not from both, not without a cause;
> Any things, anywhere,
> Do not arise at any time.[99]

Bhāvaviveka and other Svātantrika-Mādhyamikas accept the production from inherently existent other causes conventionally. So in order to accept Nāgārjuna's teaching here, they must apply the modifier "ultimately" to "not from others." If they do not, then conventional production from inherently existent other causes would be ruled out. Based on this reasoning, these philosophers say that the Svātantrikas must apply the qualifier "ultimately" to each limb of the negation, because all the lines of this stanza are grammatically related; on the other hand, they say that the Prāsaṅgikas do not need to apply the qualifier "ultimately" at all.

Tsongkhapa says it is totally incorrect to think that only the Svātantrika-

Mādhyamikas add the qualifier "ultimately." In specific contexts, it is clear that the Prāsaṅgikas also add this qualification. In his *Commentary on the "Introduction to the 'Middle Way,'"* Candrakīrti quotes the *Perfection of Wisdom Sutra in Twenty-Five Thousand Lines* (*Pañca-viṃsatisāhasrikā-prajñāpāramitā-sūtra*):

> "Venerable Subhūti, is there no attainment and no clear realization?" Subhūti replies, "Venerable Śāriputra, there is attainment and clear realization but not in a dualistic manner. Venerable Śāriputra, attainment and clear realization are only worldly conventions. Moreover, stream-winners, once-returners, nonreturners, arhats, pratyeka-buddhas, and bodhisattvas are only worldly conventions. Ultimately there is no attainment and no clear realization."

Most of the practitioners listed in this passage are included within the Hinayana presentation of twenty sangha.[100] The point here is that the paths of these practitioners and the goals attained by them do not exist dualistically from their own side; in other words, the attained and the attainer do not exist ultimately. Candrakīrti, the master Prāsaṅgika, says in *Commentary on the "Introduction to the 'Middle Way'"* that we must accept this passage just as it is taught—and here we find the application of the term "ultimately." Therefore, Tsongkhapa asks, "Do you want to make the foolish claim that this *Perfection of Wisdom Sutra* is definitive only for the Svātantrika? It is clear that there are many occasions where the qualification "ultimately" is applied in definitive sutras like this." Nāgārjuna's *Seventy Stanzas on Emptiness* says:

> Buddha taught that there is abiding,
> Arising, disintegrating, existing, not existing,
> Being lower, equal, or superior—
> Based on worldly conventions, not based on reality.

Here "based on reality" means "ultimately." And, according to the Prāsaṅgika system, the qualifier "ultimately" has the same meaning as truly existent, ultimately existent, existing by its own characteristics, inherently existent, and existent in reality. Nāgārjuna's *Precious Garland* says:

> It is said that the self and belonging to the self exist.
> However, they do not ultimately exist.

And it says:

How can a falsely existent seed
    Truly produce anything?

Also:

> Likewise, the illusion-like world
> Appears to arise and disintegrate,
> Although ultimately
> There is no arising and disintegrating.

Thus Prāsaṅgika texts apply the qualifiers "ultimately," "truly," and "in reality" to the object of negation in many cases. On many other occasions they use qualifiers such as "not existing by their own nature," "not existing inherently," and "not existing by their own characteristics." In *Buddhapālita's Commentary on the "Fundamental Treatise,"* Buddhapālita adds the qualifier "ultimately" to make it clear that in a conventional sense something is true, but in an ultimate sense it is not true:

> Nāgārjuna says:
>
> > The teachings given by the buddhas
> > Are completely based on the two truths:
> > Worldly conventional truth
> > And ultimate truth.
>
> We say, for example, "There is a vase" or "There is a bamboo fence" to express a worldly conventional truth; and we say "The vase is broken" or "The bamboo fence burned down" to express the impermanence of those things. However, when we begin to think in an ultimate sense about such things as a vase and a bamboo fence, they are merely dependently imputed objects, therefore they are not real. So, how can they really get broken or burned? Also, through the power of worldly conventions, we say "The Tathāgata is elderly" or "The Tathāgata has passed beyond sorrow" to express even the impermanence of the Tathāgata. When we think about it in an ultimate sense, given that the Tathāgata himself is not real, how can he really be elderly or have passed beyond sorrow?

Also Candrakīrti considers that Nāgārjuna's words "things do not arise" negate true arising but do not negate mere arising. His *Commentary on the "Sixty Stanzas of Reasoning"* says:

When we see a reflection, we see that it dependently arises and is false, but we do not say that it does not arise in any way. However, having established that it does not arise by its own nature, we say it does not arise in that way. If someone asks, "By way of what nature is it posited as not arising?" it is by way of a nature accepted to be true as it appears. ` It is not by way of a false nature, because in terms of that nature it is accepted as arising dependently.

Here, Candrakīrti does not negate falsely existent, illusion-like arising, but he does negate truly existent arising. The example he gives is a reflection. Based on our ordinary awareness, we can know that a reflection arises in dependence on causes and conditions; we can understand that it does not exist as the thing it appears to be. There is no contradiction between saying that a reflection does not exist in the way that it appears and that a reflection arises dependently. Likewise, to our ordinary awareness everything appears truly existent; things appear to exist by way of their own inherent nature. But things do not exist as they appear in this way; therefore their appearing to exist in this way is false. We need to develop the understanding that things arise in dependence on causes and on a perceiving consciousness. Once we have established that, then we will know that nothing arises by its own true nature, in the way that it appears; such a thing does not exist at all. What Candrakīrti is showing here is that "arising dependently" and "not arising inherently" are not contradictory. Candrakīrti's *Commentary on the "Sixty Stanzas of Reasoning"* also says:

> Therefore, in this way *produced* and *not produced* concern different things. So how can they contradict each other?

The terms *produced* and *not produced* may appear to contradict each other, but they refer to different things. *Produced* means that something arises in a conventional sense in dependence on causes and conditions. *Not produced* means that something does not arise in an ultimate sense from its own inherent nature. In one sense we say that a thing is *produced*, and in another sense we say that it is *not produced*. So there is no contradiction. The same commentary says:

> When we say, "Whatever is dependently produced, like a reflection, is not inherently produced," how can there be an occasion to argue?

This passage provides an answer to an opponent's argument that it is contradictory to maintain that things "dependently arise" and "do not arise inherently." Candrakīrti's *Introduction to the "Middle Way"* says:

Therefore, in this order, you should understand that from the very
  beginning
Things do not arise in reality but arise conventionally.

Thus Candrakīrti uses the qualifier "in reality" to explain how things are not produced. Again he says:

These things, vases and so on, do not exist in reality,
But they do exist as commonly known in the world.
Since all produced things are like that,
It does not follow that they are like the son of a barren woman.

Some people claim that, as a consequence of holding that everything is not inherently existent, everything is totally nonexistent, like the son of a barren woman. But this consequence does not follow, because things are shown to be conventionally existent.

All the passages cited above—from the sutras, as well as from the texts by Nāgārjuna, Buddhapālita, and Candrakīrti—clearly say that all internal and external things do not exist ultimately but do exist conventionally. Therefore it is not the case that the Prāsaṅgika system does not apply the qualifier "ultimately" or its equivalent to the object of negation. Tsongkhapa says that if we do not accept the appropriate application of this qualifier to the object of negation, then we cannot make a distinction between the two truths. In other words, without the correct use of the qualifier "ultimately" we could not show in what way things exist and in what way they do not exist; nor could we show that something is so in an ultimate sense and that something else is so in a conventional sense. No such Madhyamaka view—which excludes the use of the qualifier "ultimately"—is expressed anywhere; therefore it is completely wrong to believe it to be a Prāsaṅgika-Madhyamaka approach.

Candrakīrti's commentary, *Clear Words*, explicitly rejects the application of the qualifier "ultimately" to the object of negation in the negation of arising from self. He says that we do not need to apply the qualifier "ultimately" here, because "arising from self" is to be negated conventionally. Self-production does not exist even conventionally, so there is no need to say it does not exist ultimately. However, Candrakīrti does not reject the application of this qualifier to production in general. In his *Commentary on the "Introduction to the 'Middle Way'"* he says:

In saying "not from self," the master Nāgārjuna did not apply a qualifier but negated arising in general. Someone else has posited, "Things

ultimately do not arise from self because they exist, like a person."
However, I think this application of the qualification "ultimately" is
completely purposeless.

This passage refers to the first stanza of the *Fundamental Treatise*, which we
cited above. Nāgārjuna's words "not from self" are aimed at those Sāṃkhyas
who do not accept a creator god.[101] Those Sāṃkhyas say that everything arises
from itself because a result is implicitly contained within its cause. A thing is
said to arise when an already existent result, initially hidden, becomes manifest.
The Buddhist response is that things cannot arise from themselves, because if
they were already there in the cause, then what is produced? If the thing exists,
why would it need to be produced? If it is already there, how could it be newly
produced? This kind of argument is expressed in the syllogism put forward
by Bhāvaviveka, whom Candrakīrti refers to as "someone else" in the above
passage. Bhāvaviveka posits, "Things ultimately do not arise from self, because
they exist, like a person." Candrakīrti argues that since it is obviously impossible for something to arise from itself, what need is there to apply the qualifier
"ultimately"? Bhāvaviveka could simply have said, "Things do not arise from
self, because they exist, like a person." Candrakīrti argues that Bhāvaviveka's
application of the qualifier "ultimately" to the four types of arising, especially
to self-production, is totally unnecessary.

Although Nāgārjuna is negating all four means of production in general, he
is considering inherent production; therefore Bhāvaviveka insists on applying
the qualifier "ultimately" to all of them. He wants to say, "Any things, anywhere, ultimately do not arise at any time, because they ultimately do not arise
from self, ultimately do not arise from others, ultimately do not arise from
both, and ultimately do not arise without a cause." He believes that if he does
not apply the qualifier "ultimately" and just flatly denies them all, then he
would not be able to accept that things arise from an inherently existent other
cause conventionally. Tsongkhapa points out:

> In the context of arising from others, "others" does not mean "mere
> others"; it means "inherently existent others."[102]

According to Bhāvaviveka's position, cause and effect are different from
each other from the point of view of their inherent nature; inherently existent
other causes give rise to inherently existent other results. This is unacceptable
to the Prāsaṅgikas. So, from the Prāsaṅgika perspective, in this context we do
not need to add the qualifier "ultimately." All four types of arising are negated,
including arising from others, because they all refer to inherently existent aris-

ing and inherently existent sameness and otherness. These do not exist conventionally or ultimately. However, when discussing mere arising, Candrakīrti says we must apply an appropriate qualifier and explicitly state, for example, that it does not arise ultimately.

INTRODUCTION TO THE SVĀTANTRIKA/PRĀSAṄGIKA DISTINCTION

Therefore the distinction between the Svātantrika-Madhyamaka and the Prāsaṅgika-Madhyamaka is not made in terms of whether they apply the qualifier "ultimately" to the object of negation. It is made in terms of whether they negate the conventional existence of an inherently existent nature. The Prāsaṅgikas negate an inherently existent nature of all internal and external phenomena, both conventionally and ultimately. According to the Prāsaṅgika system, if things exist inherently, or by their own nature, or by their own characteristics, then they exist ultimately or truly. They say that this kind of nature does not exist at all. Therefore in their negation of an inherently existent nature, they do not need to add a qualifier such as "ultimately," "in reality," or "truly." In contrast, the Svātantrikas say that, although an inherently existent nature does not exist ultimately, it does exist conventionally. So according to the Svātantrika system, in any negation of an inherently existent nature, a qualifier such as "ultimately" or "truly" must be applied.

Both the Svātantrika and Prāsaṅgika schools agree that things do not exist ultimately, in reality, or truly. Yet they both accept as crucially important the conventional existence of things such as arising, ceasing, bondage, liberation, and so forth. In general, all Mādhyamikas, whether Svātantrika or Prāsaṅgika, consider that it is utterly wrong to flatly deny these things. So in any context where a conventionally existent thing is negated, Mādhyamikas agree that we must apply a qualifier, such as "ultimately" or "inherently,"[103] to the object of negation. On the other hand, a qualifier must not be applied to a thing that is not accepted to exist conventionally. Such a thing should be flatly negated because it does not exist at all.

This can be confusing. In various sutras and Madhyamaka root texts, a certain word may appear here or there; it may appear in some contexts and not in other contexts. Also, whether or not such a qualifying word appears, the meaning may be considered to be the same or different. Therefore it is very important to understand how to make a distinction between who does and who does not apply a qualification, and we must understand the meaning of the specific qualifier that is applied.

Consider the meaning of "not ultimately existent." Various commentaries present three etymological definitions of *ultimate* (*don dam pa*). According to the first, *don* means object, which refers to an existent object of knowledge, and *dam pa* may be translated as superior, supreme, special, or even holy. So, the combination means "supreme object" and refers to śūnyatā. A second explanation is that *dam pa* refers to the supreme, nonconceptual wisdom directly realizing emptiness. The object, *don*, of this direct realization is the ultimate, śūnyatā itself. So again *don dam pa* refers to śūnyatā. According to the third explanation, *don dam pa* refers to any wisdom that is an approximation of the supreme nonconceptual wisdom directly realizing the ultimate truth. In other words, it refers to a conceptual understanding of emptiness and includes: wisdom arising from hearing, wisdom arising from thinking, and wisdom arising from meditating. The object of these three kinds of wisdom is the ultimate truth, śūnyatā.

Now let us look at some of the commentaries directly. Bhāvaviveka says in *Heart of the Middle Way* (*Madhyamaka-hṛdaya-kārikā*):

> The earth and so on
> Do not ultimately arise.

He comments on this statement in the *Blaze of Reasons*:

> Regarding the term *ultimate* (*don dam pa*), the syllable *don* refers to the object to be known; it is an object to be examined and to be understood. The term *dam pa* means supreme. Putting the two together, *don dam pa* means supreme object, which refers to the ultimate. In another way, it means *dam pa'i don*, object of the highest. This is the object of the supreme nonconceptual wisdom, so it is the ultimate. Then, in another way, it refers to the approximate ultimate. Since both a direct realization of śūnyatā and a conceptual wisdom that approximates it have the ultimate as their object, the latter is called the *approximate ultimate*.

The wisdom specified in the third definition is not a direct realization of śūnyatā. After arising from a meditation directly perceiving emptiness, one has a subsequent attainment—a conceptual awareness remembering that realization. During the postmeditation period one has wisdom that arises through hearing and through logical thinking. Both these kinds of wisdom are similar to, or approximate, a direct realization of the ultimate.

These three definitions of *ultimate* are affirmative; they explain the meaning of the term. In the context of its negation, when we say that something does not exist ultimately or is not ultimately existent, then *ultimate* is used in the sense of the third definition: the wisdom that approximates the ultimate. The *Blaze of Reasons* continues:

> *Opponent*: The ultimate is beyond all [conventional] thoughts, but the negation of things' essential nature depends on words and concepts; so, would not that negation entail their nonexistence?
>
> *Reply*: There are two kinds of ultimate. The first is the direct nonconceptual experience that is supramundane, stainless, and free from mistaken elaborations. The second is the conceptual experience that accords with the collections of merit and wisdom, known as "pure conventional wisdom," which has mistaken elaborations. Since that is used as the qualifier of the thesis here, there is no fault.

When we analyze something, whether to prove or refute it, we must employ words and thoughts. If things are not found to be the objects of words and thoughts, would this not entail that they are nonexistent? To answer this question we have to recognize that there are two kinds of subjective ultimate, or wisdom understanding śūnyatā. The first is the direct realization of emptiness by an ārya being: it is an effortless, nonconceptual, direct realization that is supramundane, uncontaminated, and "free from mistaken elaborations" of dualistic appearance. *Dualistic appearance* usually refers to the dualistic appearance of subject and object, or to the object appearing as truly existent. In the context of Madhyamaka the latter is the primary meaning. A direct realization of śūnyatā lacks these mistaken elaborations.

The second kind of subjective ultimate is the conceptual understanding of emptiness: it employs analytical reasoning, utilizes effort, and perceives conventional phenomena. This wisdom operates in connection with conventional activities, such as accumulating merit and wisdom. It is pure in terms of understanding the true nature of reality, so it is called "pure conventional wisdom." Yet it still has the mistaken appearance of true existence combined with the appearance of conventional reality. This second kind of ultimate refers not only to the subsequent attainment of an ārya but also to a correct conceptual understanding of emptiness that arises from hearing and thinking on the paths of accumulation and preparation. The wisdom arising from hearing comes from listening to the teachings that logically prove emptiness, such as "Things are not truly existent because they dependently arise." The wisdom arising from thinking is of two kinds, depending on the type of reason employed: one type of reason is used to enable oneself to understand the thesis, and the other type is used to convince someone else. The understanding that arises through ultimate analysis is the wisdom arisen from thinking. This understanding is developed before the āryan stage and after it as well. During postmeditative periods, both ordinary bodhisattvas and āryas engage in reasoning when they are giving teachings on emptiness to others or when thinking it through for themselves.

This pure conventional wisdom is what is referred to by the word "ultimate" in the context of the negation "not ultimately existent." In *Illumination of the Middle Way*, Kamalaśīla explains how this conceptual wisdom, similar to the wisdom of meditative equipoise, is connected to the phrase "not ultimately produced."

> The meaning of the phrase "not ultimately produced" is as follows. Any wisdom that arises from hearing, thinking, and meditating on reality is a nondistorted consciousness because it understands ultimate truth; it is called "ultimate" because its object is supreme. There is a difference between the activity of direct and indirect [realization], but through the power of their [ultimate] analysis they both understand that all these things are simply not produced. Therefore we explain the phrase "not ultimately produced" to mean that ultimate wisdom does not establish these things to be produced.

Kamalaśīla speaks of the direct and indirect realization of śūnyatā in this passage. In order to understand what he means here, we must distinguish between the following sets of terms: *direct* and *indirect*, and *explicit* and *implicit*.[104] The terms *explicit* and *implicit* may be applied to words, teachings, and understanding. Words may explicitly or implicitly express their object. Teachings may explicitly or implicitly convey their meaning. For example, the *Perfection of Wisdom Sutras* explicitly teach about emptiness, the ultimate nature of things, and implicitly teach about their conventional nature, especially the path system. Likewise, understanding may explicitly or implicitly know its object. To *implicitly* understand something means that the object is realized without actually appearing to the mind realizing it. To *explicitly* understand something means that the object appears to the mind realizing it. Here the object may appear in one of two ways: *directly* through direct perception or *indirectly* through the medium of a conceptual image in thought. A direct realization understands its object nakedly, without the medium of a conceptual image. Only direct perception perceives its object in this manner. Also, it is impossible for the object not to appear to a valid direct perception, so this is always an explicit realization. In contrast, a conceptual understanding is only indirect, because thought always understands its object through the medium of a mental image. Nevertheless, a thought may explicitly or implicitly realize its object. A conceptual understanding explicitly realizes its object when that object's image appears to that thought; conversely, it implicitly realizes its object when that object's image does not appear to that thought. For example, when you explicitly realize that sound is impermanent, a mental image of "sound as impermanent" appears to your conceptual awareness; at the same time, you implicitly realize that sound is empty of permanence, without any mental image of "sound as empty of permanence" appearing.

Kamalaśīla is saying here that both a direct and an indirect realization of emptiness understands the ultimate truth. Regarding that, they are both correct. So what is the difference between a direct and an indirect realization of emptiness? How are they related? Prior to attaining the path of seeing, bodhisattvas on the paths of accumulation and preparation develop the wisdom that arises from hearing, thinking, and meditating on śūnyatā. They have an inferential understanding of śūnyatā, which arises on the basis of valid reasoning, such as "Things are not truly existent because they dependently arise." This kind of conceptual realization of śūnyatā understands emptiness explicitly and indirectly. It understands śūnyatā explicitly because emptiness appears to it. However, this realization is indirect, not direct, because emptiness appears mixed with an image of emptiness. Then, using this kind of inferential knowledge, a bodhisattva meditates on śūnyatā for a very long time. Progressing through the four levels of the path of preparation, the mental image of śūnyatā gradually becomes more transparent, and eventually the meditator gains a direct perception of śūnyatā exactly as it is. At that point there is just the pure appearance of śūnyatā unmixed with any appearance of conventional reality and with no mistaken appearance of inherent existence. When this direct and explicit realization of śūnyatā occurs, the bodhisattva attains the path of seeing and becomes an ārya. When an ārya emerges from a meditation session, the conceptual awareness that subsequently arises remembers emptiness clearly, but it appears mixed with its image. Subsequent attainment, therefore, realizes śūnyatā explicitly and indirectly. It is explicit because it appears, and it is indirect because it appears by means of its conceptual image.

Now we have a hard bone to chew. The last part of Kamalaśīla's passage above says that ultimate wisdom does not establish these conventional things to be produced. This means that, although conventional things exist from the point of view of conventional knowledge, they do not exist from the point of view of the wisdom realizing ultimate truth. This is true for the conceptual wisdom that arises from hearing, thinking, and meditating, as well as for the nonconceptual wisdom of meditative equipoise perceiving emptiness directly. For example, a conventional thing, such as a cup, can be found by a conventional consciousness. However, when we analyze whether the cup exists from its own side, we do not find anything that is the essential nature of the cup. Eventually we thoroughly and directly understand that cup's emptiness of existing by its own inherent nature. Does the wisdom that sees the cup's emptiness still see the cup? No. The cup disappears and only its emptiness appears. So, from the point of view of that understanding of emptiness, the cup is not there. This wisdom sees the ultimate nature of the cup; in the face of this awareness, the cup does not become clearer, it disappears. This wisdom sees only the absence of its existing by its own nature.

Thus the phrase "not ultimately produced" means not produced from the point of view of the realization of the ultimate. In other words, as it says in some of the Tibetan textbooks, "Conventional things do not exist in the face of the exalted seeing that sees things as they are." According to the Madhyamaka system, a buddha sees everything—both ultimate reality and conventional things—at the same time.[105] Every moment of a buddha's awareness sees both natures simultaneously. A buddha's exalted wisdom that sees the ultimate also sees conventional things; a buddha's exalted wisdom that sees conventional things also sees the ultimate. Nevertheless, in the face of seeing the ultimate, a buddha does not see the conventional, and in the face of seeing the conventional, a buddha does not see the ultimate. In other words, from the perspective of a buddha's exalted wisdom seeing the ultimate, conventional things do not exist; from the perspective of a buddha's exalted wisdom seeing conventional things, the ultimate does not exist. A buddha sees both, but he or she sees them from different perspectives. Similarly, from the perspective of the inferential knowledge that arises from hearing, thinking, and meditating on the ultimate, conventional things do not arise. Therefore, as Kamalaśīla says above, a phrase such as "not ultimately produced" means that from the perspective of the wisdom understanding the ultimate, conventional things are not established as produced. When we see the ultimate nature of conventional things, we do not see the conventional things themselves as arising and ceasing. This is why Nāgārjuna's *Fundamental Treatise* begins with the homage:

> I bow down to the most holy of teachers,
> The completely accomplished Buddha,
> Who teaches the peace that pacifies all elaboration,
> That whatever dependently arises has
> No cessation, no arising,
> No annihilation, no permanence,
> No coming, no going,
> No unity, no plurality.

Buddha teaches that whatever arises dependently on causes and conditions does not truly exist—owing to being dependent. Dependently arising things, therefore, are empty of the eight special attributes of truly existent things: they are without arising or ceasing, dissolution or permanence, coming or going, sameness or difference—from their own side. This teaching is presented in terms of the way in which the subject sees its object. From the point of view of how the subject realizing śūnyatā sees its object—emptiness—there is no arising, ceasing, dissolution, permanence, coming, going, sameness, or difference. Those qualities cannot be found when submitted to ultimate analysis. The same applies to the teaching that ultimately there is no production. It means that, from the point of view of how the three kinds of wisdom see the ultimate, conventional things are not found to arise. There is only emptiness from that point of view. This is the meaning of the quotation from Kamala-śīla's *Illumination of the Middle Way*. It appears to be similar to the meaning of Bhāvaviveka's *Blaze of Reasons*, where he explains the meaning of "ultimate" in the phrase "not ultimately existent" in terms of how the subject sees its object.

There are two aspects of the ultimate: the subjective ultimate and the objective ultimate. The subjective ultimate is the perceiving consciousness. The objective ultimate is this mind's perceived object—śūnyatā. The subjective ultimate has two aspects: inferential knowledge of the ultimate and direct realization of the ultimate. The objective ultimate also has two aspects: ultimate in the face of nonexalted knowledge, which is the approximate ultimate, and the real ultimate. When a bodhisattva, prior to attaining the path of seeing, perceives emptiness, he or she perceives it explicitly and indirectly as understood by the conceptual wisdom of hearing, thinking, or meditating.[106] Although this bodhisattva perceives śūnyatā, it appears mixed with a conceptual image of it. So the object of this mind appears dualistically. Śūnyatā itself is still the real ultimate, but the conceptual image of śūnyatā is not the real ultimate because it is a conventional thing. Whenever a sentient being perceives a conventional thing, he or she always perceives it to be truly existent. So when ordinary bodhisattvas see emptiness, they see it mixed with its image and therefore see it as truly existent. The object seen by this mind understanding emptiness is the approximate ultimate, not the real ultimate, because it is seen through the medium of a conceptual image of śūnyatā and appears truly existent.

Nevertheless, this inferential knowledge is a proper understanding of śūnyatā. Although an ordinary bodhisattva perceives emptiness incorrectly, he or she does not grasp or understand it incorrectly; it just appears incorrectly. There is no other way to understand śūnyatā at first, except indirectly. Even when the object, śūnyatā, appears mixed with its image, one can understand emptiness properly. Through the paths of accumulation and preparation, this inferential knowledge gradually becomes more advanced, and the perception of śūnyatā becomes steadily clearer. Eventually the direct realization of śūnyatā on the path of seeing arises. Kamalaśīla's *Commentary on the Difficult Points of the "Ornament for the Middle Way" (Madhyamakālaṃkāra-pañjikā)* says:

> *Opponent*: In what sense are things not inherently existent?
> *Reply*: When [Śāntarakṣita] says "in reality," the word "reality" refers to the nature of reality as known by inferential reasoning based on the power of the fact; it means "empty when analyzed in terms of reality." This is how to explain the phrases "in reality" or "ultimately," and so on. Also "reality" and so on may refer to just the wisdom knowing reality, because that is its object. It is a term indicating that noninherent existence is established by the wisdom analyzing reality, not by conventional knowledge.

Kamalaśīla, who is a Svātantrika-Mādhyamika, accepts that things exist inherently. So a phrase such as "not inherently existent" must have a qualifier, such as "in reality" or "ultimately," applied to it. In this context, the word *reality* refers to what is known by the wisdom of logical analysis that accords with reality. Logical reasoning must be based on fact rather than imagination. A reason proves something because of what is actually the case. For example, "There is fire on a smoky mountain pass because there is billowing smoke." When we see the smoke, we know there is a fire the other side of the mountain, even though we cannot see it directly. Emptiness must also be understood through correct inferential reasoning initially. When we analyze the final nature of things, using the three kinds of wisdom arisen from hearing, thinking, and meditating, we cannot find any ultimately existent reality. Instead we find the emptiness of ultimate existence. Therefore *ultimate* refers to the emptiness found by the wisdom analyzing the ultimate. In terms of the object, this is how to explain the meaning of such phrases as "in reality" or "ultimately" in the context of the negations "not existent in reality" and "not existent ultimately." Also, in terms of the subject, words such as *ultimate* and *reality* may refer only to ultimate knowledge, the wisdom realizing śūnyatā, because reality is its object. This use of the words "not ultimately existent" indicates that, for Kamalaśīla, conventional things are understood to be empty of inherent existence only from the point of view of ultimate knowledge—not from the point of view of conventional knowledge. That is what is meant by the phrase "not inherently existent" here. Svātantrikas sometimes use the same phrase as the Prāsaṅgikas—"not inherently existent"—but it must have a qualifier such as "ultimately" applied to it. According to the Svātantrika system, *existent* and *inherently existent* are synonymous.

Bhāvaviveka often applies the qualifier "ultimately" to phrases such as "not inherently existent" or "without essential nature" in *Lamp for the "Fundamental Treatise"* and *Blaze of Reasons*. In particular, when commenting on the fifteenth chapter of Nāgārjuna's *Fundamental Treatise* in the *Lamp for the "Fundamental Treatise,"* he says:

> *Opponent*: If it is without essential nature, how can it be a thing? If it is a thing, then it cannot be without essential nature. So your thesis incurs the fault of undermining its very meaning.

Both the Svātantrika- and Prāsaṅgika-Mādhyamikas accept that things are without essential nature, thus they are generally referred to as Non-Essentialists (see chapter 15). Yet since they consider things to be without essential nature in the sense of being not really, truly, or ultimately existent, they may also be called Non-Realists. Here a Realist opponent argues that in maintaining the thesis "Things have no essential nature," the Mādhyamikas incur the fallacy of contradicting their own words. This Realist contends that if things have no essential nature, they lack functionality. Therefore, if words have no essential nature they cannot function, and the Mādhyamikas cannot use words to establish their thesis. To answer this objection, *Lamp for the "Fundamental Treatise"* says:

> *Reply*: We do not advance the thesis that things are without essential nature after having already accepted that things have an essential nature ultimately; therefore, since we do not undermine the meaning of our own thesis, it is not a case of the meaning of the proof being not established. So there is no fault.

Bhāvaviveka explains that, in saying that things do not have an essential nature "ultimately," he does not undermine his own thesis. This clearly implies that, in saying that things do not have an essential nature "conventionally," he would undermine his own thesis. In other words, he accepts that things have an essential nature conventionally. The same text continues:

> This is because we express that all internal things have no essential nature ultimately, and because we show that it depends precisely on such a qualifying expression. This is like an illusory man created by a magician, and so forth.

When examining the illusory appearance of a man, we do not say, "There is no illusory man." We say, "There is no man." These two statements—there is an illusory man, but there is no man—are not mutually contradictory. Similarly, according to Bhāvaviveka, when we analyze reality we do not say, "Things have no essential nature." We say, "Things have no essential nature ultimately." These two statements—things have an essential nature, but things have no essential nature ultimately—are not contradictory. Thus Bhāvaviveka definitely applies the qualifier "ultimately" to the negation of an essential nature.

All Mādhyamikas agree that "not ultimately existent" means that a thing is not established as existent when thoroughly examined by reasoning analyzing how things exist in reality. This type of examination is ultimate analysis. It is inappropriate to employ ultimate analysis to investigate the conventional nature of a thing. Conventional things are established in terms of how they appear to a valid conventional awareness. So even the texts of the Svātantrika masters explain that when establishing conventional things, we should not engage in analysis conducive to seeing ultimate reality; conversely, when refuting inherent nature, we engage in ultimate analysis and find its absence. This is like the Prāsaṅgika texts we already encountered above. Thus these great masters concur that when we engage in ultimate analysis, we do not find any conventional thing; we find only emptiness.

So what is it that they disagree about? The Svātantrikas and Prāsaṅgikas disagree about what being unable to bear ultimate analysis entails. In general, Mādhyamikas do not accept that anything is able to bear ultimate analysis. If a thing is able to bear ultimate analysis, it will be found when examined by ultimate analysis; if it is found by ultimate analysis, it ultimately exists. Candrakīrti and other Prāsaṅgikas say that if a thing is not found at the end of ultimate analysis, it is not inherently existent and does not exist by its own nature. According to the Prāsaṅgikas, because nothing is found to exist from its own side, everything is merely imputed and does not exist inherently. Bhāvaviveka agrees that if something cannot bear ultimate analysis, then it is not ultimately or truly existent. However, although he and the Svātantrikas accept that nothing is ultimately or truly existent, they will not go as far as to say that if something is unable to bear ultimate analysis, then it is not inherently existent. In other words, the Svātantrikas do not agree with the Prāsaṅgikas that if something is inherently existent, it must be able to bear ultimate analysis, and vice versa. Thus the difference between the Svātantrika and Prāsaṅgika systems concerns whether being "inherently existent" means being "able to bear ultimate analysis."

What does "inherently existent" mean? According to the Prāsaṅgikas, if something is inherently existent, then when you analytically search for its real identity or the final referent behind its name or conventional identification, you can find it. If what is searched for is not found by such ultimate analysis, then it does not inherently exist. The Prāsaṅgikas say that when we search by means of ultimate analysis for the real identity of anything conventionally labeled, we cannot find it. This is what is meant by saying that everything does not inherently exist, does not ultimately exist, does not truly exist, does not exist by its own characteristics, and does not exist by its own nature. This is the emptiness of inherent existence: there is no real referent underlying nominal reality. When we search for that, we do not find it. Instead, we find its absence: emptiness. But when we take emptiness itself as the object and search for a real referent behind its conventional label, we do not find it. We find only the absence of that: its emptiness. In contrast, the lower schools, including Yogācāra and Svātantrika-Madhyamaka, say that when we search for the referent of a name by means of ultimate analysis, we find something that exists from its own side.

There is a subtle difference between the Svātantrika notion of a truly existent nature not being found by ultimate analysis and the Prāsaṅgika notion of an inherent nature not being found by ultimate analysis. The Svātantrikas say that ultimate analysis does not find an object established from the side of its own uncommon mode of existence that is not posited also through the power of appearing to a faultless awareness.[107] This is because, according to them, nothing exists *only* from its own side. Things are partially established from their own side and partially established from the side of the mind that knows them. Therefore, according to the Svātantrikas, things do not exist truly or ultimately—but they do exist inherently. This is because a thing's identity is partly established from its own side. The Prāsaṅgikas say that ultimate analysis does not find something that exists from its own side as the referent of its name. Nothing is found by such analysis because there is no objectively existent referent of a name or conventional label. Everything is merely imputed by name and thought; nothing exists from its own side in the slightest. Things are merely labeled from the side of the mind perceiving them. But in trying to understand what it means for something to be "merely imputed," we have to understand what it means for something to be *empty*. A name identifies something with specific qualities—it is just a label. When we search for the real referent of that name among those qualities, as something existing from its own side, can we find it? No—neither the thing's qualities, nor anything else, is the referent of that name. There is nothing underlying what is merely labeled that holds its identity from its own side. A thing is merely imputed by thought and name. It is merely imputed from this side, the perceiver—it does not exist from its own side, the object, at all. This is the Prāsaṅgika view of what it means to be not truly existent, not inherently existent, or not existent by its own nature. Everything is just imputedly existent.

We can use a car as an example of this kind of analysis. When we look for the final referent of the term "car," we already know it is not something separate from its parts. So we look among the parts of the car and examine whether it is the body, the doors, the floor, the roof, the wheels, the engine, the various parts of the engine, and so on. But however hard we look, we cannot find the car itself. The car is merely imputed on its parts by thought and terminology. The body of the car is the basis of the name "car." On that basis we naturally label a certain attribute, in this case "car"—which is the imputed attribute. When we search for the final identity of the car within its basis of imputation, we cannot find it. We already have a rough understanding that the body of the car is not the car, and its parts are not the car, and so on. But we need to develop a much subtler understanding. We have to employ a special kind of wisdom in our search. Finally we find the complete absence of any real identity of that car from its own side. This is its emptiness of inherent existence. When the actual understanding of emptiness arises deeply in the mind, then it functions as the antidote to ignorance. Our notion of the car existing objectively as a car from its own side, our attachment to our car, and so on, will be loosened by that special wisdom.

Certain lower Buddhist schools consider this approach to be nihilistic. In order to avoid the pitfall of nihilism, they say that the referent of the name must be found upon analysis. The Vaibhāṣikas say that when you search for the person within its basis by ultimate analysis, the continuity of the aggregates is found as its identity. The Yogācāras say it is the substratum consciousness. The Svātantrikas say it is the mental consciousness. Bhāvaviveka says in *Blaze of Reasons*:

> We also consider that the word "I" explicitly refers to the mental consciousness conventionally.[108]

Each school contends that because things can be found, they exist by their own nature and so they are inherently existent.

This view is rejected by the Prāsaṅgikas. Alone among all these schools of Buddhist philosophy, they say it is incorrect to hold that an object searched for by ultimate analysis can be found to exist from its own side. Because those other schools consider that a thing's identity does exist from its own side, even in the face of ultimate analysis, they do not understand emptiness.

☀ 13 ☀

Misinterpretations of the
Svātantrika/Prāsaṅgika Distinction

(2") Whether to use consequences or autonomous syllogisms in negating the
object of negation
  (a)) The meaning of consequence and autonomous syllogism
    (1)) Refuting other systems
      (a')) Stating others' assertions
        (1')) The first misinterpretation
        (2')) The second misinterpretation
        (3')) The third misinterpretation
        (4')) The fourth misinterpretation

(2") WHETHER TO USE CONSEQUENCES OR AUTONOMOUS SYLLOGISMS IN NEGATING THE OBJECT OF NEGATION

THERE ARE TWO different logical procedures that the Mādhyamikas traditionally use to negate the object of negation: logical consequences (*prasaṅga*) and autonomous (*svatantra*) inferences, which Tsongkhapa glosses as autonomous syllogisms.[109] Those who favor logical consequences are called Prāsaṅgikas[110] and those who favor autonomous syllogisms are called Svātantrikas. Both methods are based on the writings of Nāgārjuna and Āryadeva. The Svātantrikas say that Nāgārjuna and Āryadeva employ autonomous syllogisms; the Prāsaṅgikas say that these masters employ consequences. Which of these should we use? Before we can answer that question, we first have to understand what consequences and autonomous syllogisms are; then we can consider which procedure gives rise to the view understanding emptiness. Therefore this topic has two parts:

(a)) The meaning of consequence and autonomous syllogism (chapters 13–15)
(b)) Which system to follow so as to develop the correct view in one's mental continuum (chapter 16)

(a)) THE MEANING OF CONSEQUENCE AND AUTONOMOUS SYLLOGISM

Until around the sixth century, there was just a general, undifferentiated Madhyamaka system. The distinction between the Svātantrika- and Prāsaṅgika-Madhyamaka systems did not arise until the time of Buddhapālita's authorship of his great commentary on Nāgārjuna's *Fundamental Treatise*, called *Buddhapālita's Commentary on the "Fundamental Treatise"* (or the *Buddhapālita* for short). In his commentary, Buddhapālita uses consequences as the logical procedure throughout. He does not explicitly discuss his choice of logical method, though it is a departure from the more common use of autonomous syllogisms in Indian logic at that time. This is evident in his commentary on Nāgārjuna's *Fundamental Treatise*, all the way through from the very first stanza:

> Not from self, not from others,
> Not from both, not without a cause;
> Any things, anywhere,
> Do not arise at any time.

In this stanza Nāgārjuna is negating various views, both Buddhist and non-Buddhist, as well as a subtler type of view that underlies them. Buddhapālita presents the argument here as a consequence that reveals the contradictions implied by these views. He shows that if someone believes any of these four types of arising to be true, it contradicts another view that his or her philosophical school believes to be true. In other words, he demonstrates that each of these four possible means of arising has unacceptable consequences for those who hold it to be true. How to parse the meaning of this stanza will be discussed later in this volume; for now, it is enough to understand that Buddhapālita uses consequences rather than autonomous syllogisms to negate the four alternative ways of arising.

Some decades later, Bhāvaviveka wrote an extensive commentary on the *Fundamental Treatise* in which he criticizes Buddhapālita's methodology. He argues that Buddhapālita can neither refute his opponents nor prove his own position because he does not use autonomous syllogisms. According to Bhāva-viveka, the final step of an argument must employ an autonomous syllogism. A consequence—an argument in the form, "If you accept this, then that would follow"—does not have power from its own side to prove or refute anything. Bhāvaviveka stresses the need to use autonomous syllogisms as a final proof. Therefore he is called the reopener of the Svātantrika system.

According to legend, Buddhapālita was from a low caste, so he could not counter the high-caste Bhāvaviveka's criticism. Candrakīrti, writing about a century later, was also from a high caste, so he could defend Buddhapālita and refute Bhāvaviveka. This may not be historically accurate, but it is what I heard. In any case, Candrakīrti argues extensively that Buddhapālita does not succumb to the faults attributed to him by Bhāvaviveka. He presents many reasons to establish that the only way to help others understand the correct view of emptiness is to employ logical consequences. This cannot be accomplished using autonomous syllogisms. In showing that it is correct to use consequences, Candrakīrti clarifies the Prāsaṅgika position. Therefore he is sometimes said to be the reopener of the Prāsaṅgika system. Other monastic textbooks say that the reopener of the Prāsaṅgika system is Buddhapālita, because even though he never discusses this issue, he only ever uses consequences.

Tibetan scholars say that after Candrakīrti, the Indian Madhyamaka was clearly divided into two: Svātantrika-Madhyamaka and Prāsaṅgika-Madhyamaka. When studying Madhyamaka it is important to understand both systems because we need to develop our reasoning skills in order to rid ourselves of ignorance. Ignorance is the cause of sentient beings' bondage in samsara, and the only antidote to ignorance is to develop a correct understanding of emptiness in accordance with the Madhyamaka view. Ignorance is an innate mind that incorrectly grasps its object. We cannot dispose of it simply like an old shirt. To eliminate ignorance, we have to generate the wisdom that is its opposite. In order to do this, we must first identify the object that ignorance grasps incorrectly—and then negate it. When we realize the absence of the object held by ignorance, we start to remove the cause of suffering. Therefore we need to know how to generate an understanding of emptiness. Which method should we use? One system says we must use autonomous syllogisms; the other system says we must use consequences. This is the basis of a lot of debate. Both systems were extensively taught in Tibet, and Tsongkhapa explains them both in detail.

When discussing any philosophical subject, we must give reasons to support our position. A simple unsupported statement is not enough to dispel an opponent's questions and doubts. This psychological fact shaped the form of Tibetan philosophical literature. A text is usually divided into three parts.

The first is a refutation of others' systems. This is because the adherents of any school of thought will continue to uphold their system unless it is proved to be incorrect, and only after this is accomplished can one show them the correct way to understand an issue. The second section is known as presenting one's own system. Then, because the opponents may argue that one's own system is wrong, the final section disproves these points and is therefore known as eliminating the objections. This is the format in which the distinction between the logical methods of autonomous syllogisms and consequences is presented. It has two parts:

(1)) Refuting other systems (chapters 13–14)
(2)) Presenting our own system (chapters 15–16)

(1)) Refuting other systems

This section has two parts:

(a')) Stating others' assertions
(b')) Refuting others' assertions (chapter 14)

(a')) Stating others' assertions

There are many ways to establish the distinction between consequences and autonomous syllogisms; but who can explain them all? Tsongkhapa says he will present just a few of them.

(1')) The first misinterpretation

The first incorrect view is that of the great Kaśmīri scholar Jayānanda, whose name means Victorious Joy. In *Explanation of the "Introduction to the 'Middle Way'"* (*Madhyamakāvatāra-ṭīkā*), he says:

> *Question*: If you accept a logical consequence to be correct reasoning, is it established by valid knowledge or not? If the former, then it must be established for both parties; so how can you say "the opponent's assertion?" If the latter, then it would not be asserted by the opponent; so how can you say "the opponent's assertion?"
> *Reply*: [In the former case] you say, "Whatever is established by valid knowledge is established for both parties." But we do not know that. When a proponent sets forth a reason, although it is established by

valid knowledge for the one who set the reason, how can he know that it is established by valid knowledge for his opponent? The attributes of another's mind are not an object of direct perception or inferential knowledge. Moreover, how can he know that it is established by valid knowledge even for himself? He might be deceived, owing to the influence of faulty reasoning over a very long period of time. Therefore through the force of being accepted as valid by both the proponent and the opponent, the nature of things is accepted. Thus an opponent's position is refuted on the basis of what that opponent accepts.

Jayānanda's point is that we cannot, and do not need to, establish anything by valid knowledge in order to refute our opponent's wrong view. We can use a logical consequence, which functions by showing an internal contradiction in what our opponent accepts. A consequence works as follows: our opponent accepts something; this belief implies certain other things, which he does not want to accept; however, he must accept them too, because he accepts the reason from which they follow. This form of reasoning is based on what the opponent accepts. It is enough that both parties accept the components of the argument—the reason and the pervasion—to be valid; they do not need to establish them by valid knowledge. Jayānanda argues that the proponent does not know whether his opponent has ascertained the reason by valid knowledge. The proponent cannot know what is in the opponent's mind, either by direct perception or by inferential knowledge. However, it is enough for the opponent simply to accept the reason without establishing it by valid knowledge. The same applies to the proponent. Supposing we are the proponent, we cannot know whether we have established the reason by valid knowledge even in our own case. We may feel sure that we know it, but we could be mistaken. Therefore, given that we can never know that the reason is established by valid knowledge for both the proponent and the opponent, Jayānanda says that the only correct way to refute an opponent is on the basis of what the opponent accepts, not on the basis of what he or she knows. If the opponent accepts something to be valid, even though he or she may not really know it by valid knowledge, it can be used to reveal the internal contradictions in the opponent's assertions. According to Jayānanda, this demonstrates that the method of logical consequences is correct. We can show our opponents the contradictions that follow from their own assumptions, as consequences, without having to establish the elements of the argument by means of valid knowledge. The proponent and the opponent simply have to accept that the reason is a property of the subject and that the pervasions are valid.

Conversely, if we want to prove something to our opponent by means of an autonomous syllogism, both our opponent and ourselves must have established the reason in relation to the subject, as well as the pervasion between the reason and the thesis, by valid knowledge. To understand what this means, let us consider a simple syllogism, "Sound is impermanent because it is produced." We put forward this argument to an opponent who does not know that sound is impermanent and to whom we want to prove that it is impermanent. In our syllogism the subject is "sound." The thesis, or *probandum*, which we are trying to prove is "sound is impermanent." The reason we give is "because it is produced." In order to bring about an understanding of the thesis in an opponent's mind, a correct syllogistic reason must instantiate the three modes. The first mode is that the reason, or mark, is known to be a property of the subject. In this case, the opponent must know that the subject "sound" is produced. If our opponent does not know that sound is produced, then our reason cannot give rise to the relevant understanding in him. In other words, for a syllogism to work, the opponent must already understand the relationship between the reason and the subject. In addition, our opponent must know that whatever is produced is impermanent. In more technical terms, he must understand the pervasion between the reason, "is produced," and the predicate of the thesis, "is impermanent." This pervasion goes in two directions: forward and reverse. In our example, the forward pervasion is: if something is produced then it must be impermanent. The reverse pervasion is: if something is not impermanent then it cannot be produced. These are the second and the third modes of a valid syllogistic reason, respectively. In order for the syllogism to be valid, both our opponent and ourselves must know all three modes. Only then can we prove our thesis, "sound is impermanent," with our reason, "because it is produced."

A syllogistic argument can take one of two forms. It can be expressed either in terms of *being*, "It is this because it is that," or in terms of *existing*, "There is this because there is that." An example of the latter is: "On a smoky mountain pass there is a fire because there is smoke." The subject is "on a smoky mountain pass." The reason is "because there is smoke." Here the first mode is established by valid visual consciousness. Our opponent can see smoke billowing from behind a mountain pass in the far distance. Our opponent knows that if there is billowing smoke, then there is a fire. On the basis of that sign or reason we can prove to him that there is fire in that place. So we present to him our syllogism to generate this knowledge within his mind. In order for an autonomous syllogistic reason to be correct, both the opponent and the proponent must have established the three modes by valid knowledge.

Then, again in *Explanation of the "Introduction to the 'Middle Way,'"* Jayānanda says:

Furthermore, according to the system of autonomous reasons, if the pervasion between the reason and the thesis were established by valid knowledge, then the reason would be a valid proof. But the pervasion is not established, because the valid knowledge that establishes a pervasion is either direct perception or inferential knowledge. In the first place, direct perception does not establish the pervasion. Based on a kitchen fire, you can understand the causal relation between fire and smoke by means of direct perception as well as nonperception—that is, if the latter exists, then the former exists, and if the former does not exist, then the latter does not exist—but not based on *all objects*. In the second place, inferential knowledge does not establish the pervasion, because this only concerns a particular case. The object of inferential knowledge is not *all cases*. An understanding of impermanence and so on arises only where there is a reason that is related to the thesis being proved; it does not do so in *all times and places*. Therefore the pervasion is established merely in terms of what is accepted in the world, not in terms of being established by valid knowledge. So how could consequential reasoning not be the correct method to refute others' positions?

In general, according to those who uphold the use of autonomous syllogisms, the presence of smoke has the power to prove the presence of fire. This only happens where both parties have established the three modes. Consider our example, "On a smoky mountain pass there is fire because there is smoke, as in a kitchen." Both the opponent and the proponent must know that on the basis of the subject there is billowing smoke. This is the first mode, the property of the subject. The second mode is the forward pervasion: where there is smoke there is fire. The third mode is the reverse pervasion: where there is no fire there is no smoke. In order for this syllogism to work, the pervasion in both directions must be known not only in this particular case but in every case universally as well. The opponent and proponent must know that in every case where there is smoke there is fire, and in every case where there is no fire there is no smoke. If this relationship is not understood to be universal, the logic does not work.

Jayānanda aims to show that an autonomous syllogism is not a correct method of proof because the three modes cannot be established by the opponent's and the proponent's valid knowledge—whether by direct perception or by inference. Regarding the first, he concedes that the existence of the reason in the subject is known by direct perception. For example, you can see with your own eyes the smoke billowing from behind the mountain pass. You are familiar with smoke because you have seen smoke billowing from your kitchen fireplace at home. You can also know by direct perception that whenever there is billowing smoke in your kitchen, there is a fire there. In other words, you see the forward pervasion in that particular place by means of visual direct perception. You can also see the reverse pervasion—if there is no fire in your kitchen, then there is no smoke there. Here the connection between the reason and the predicate is a causal relation: if there is a certain result then there must be its cause, and if there is no cause then there cannot be its result. However, you do not realize this pervasion in a general sense on the basis of direct perception. Direct perception knows only what it directly sees. It cannot establish the universal pervasion that wherever there is smoke there is fire, and wherever there is no fire there is no smoke. Therefore, Jayānanda argues, direct perception cannot know the three modes.

Second, the pervasion is also not established by valid inferential reasoning. Inferential knowledge, Jayānanda argues, is concerned only with a particular object on a particular occasion. The relation between the reason and the predicate is not understood to apply in a general sense. Consider the syllogism "Sound is impermanent because it is produced." Here what is set as the reason, "produced," and as the predicate, "impermanent," are related as the same nature: whatever is produced is impermanent, and whatever is not impermanent is not produced.[111] Inferential knowledge can only understand this relation in connection with a particular object—in this case, sound. It understands the connection between the reason and what is to be proved in a particular instance. It cannot understand in a general sense that any produced thing must be impermanent. Therefore inferential knowledge also cannot establish the three modes.

However, although valid knowledge cannot understand the pervasion in a universal sense, if we have valid knowledge of the pervasion in a particular instance, then we can accept that the pervasion applies to all other instances. Therefore Jayānanda says that the universal pervasion is established by what is accepted in the world, not by valid knowledge. Generalizations such as "Wherever there is smoke there is fire," or "Whatever is produced is impermanent," or "Whatever is a dependent arising is empty of true existence" are merely accepted conventionally. They are not established by valid knowledge.

Therefore, Jayānanda argues, autonomous syllogisms cannot be our main method of reasoning because to prove the thesis we must establish the three modes by valid knowledge. In his view it would be correct to use autonomous syllogisms only if valid knowledge could establish the three modes: the reason being a property of the subject, the forward pervasion, and the reverse pervasion. This is impossible because neither direct perception nor inference can establish the necessary pervasions in all times and all places for both parties. The two kinds of valid knowledge can only know the pervasions based on individual instances with a very small scope, such as a kitchen or a pot. In contrast, a logical consequence reveals the internal contradictions within the opponent's position merely on the basis of what is accepted by both parties, not on the basis of what is validly known by both parties. This is how Jayānanda justifies the Prāsaṅgika system.

Tsongkhapa summarizes Jayānanda's distinction between the Svātantrika and Prāsaṅgika systems as follows. Svātantrikas propound the use of autonomous syllogisms, where the thesis is proved by means of a reason whose three modes are established by the valid knowledge of both the opponent and the proponent. Prāsaṅgikas propound the use of logical consequences, where the thesis is proved by means of a reason whose three modes are just finally accepted by the opponent and the proponent.

(2')) THE SECOND MISINTERPRETATION

Certain disciples of Jayānanda, including the great translator from Ngog, Loden Sherab, as well as Khu Dodaybar and some other earlier scholars, say that Mādhyamikas are only concerned with refuting others' wrong views and make no attempt to prove any thesis of their own. They claim that since the subject, the pervasion, and so on are not established as accepted in common by both the opponent and the proponent—the latter because Mādhyamikas have no thesis of their own—autonomous syllogisms are not a correct method of proof. The final goal of rational analysis is to cause the opponent to cast away his wrong view; for this purpose, a logical consequence is most suitable. Furthermore, because Mādhyamikas have no views that they seek to establish, they should never use autonomous syllogisms; they should only use logical consequences.

These disciples also say that Mādhyamikas should use only consequences that refute; they should not use consequences that affirm a positive position. Logical consequences have the form: if this is the case, then that follows. To understand the difference between a refuting and an affirming consequence, let us consider an example. Suppose someone says "There is no fire" even though we all see billowing smoke. To make him change his mind, we can present a refuting consequence that is implied by what he claims to be the case. We start by assuming the opponent's claim—namely, that there is no fire—and say, "If there is no fire, then it follows that there is no smoke." This conclusion is unacceptable to our opponent because it contradicts his own direct perception of smoke. Therefore, he has to reconsider his premise that there is no fire. This will lead him to change his opinion. If we were to present an affirming consequence, we would say, "If there is smoke, it follows that there is a fire." This is a positive statement showing a consequence that is the opposite of what the opponent originally claimed. It looks almost the same as an autonomous syllogism. The only difference is that when we say "it follows" we are presenting the consequence implied by what the opponent accepts. In this example, a syllogism would be "In that place there is a fire because there is smoke," and the affirming consequence would be "If there is smoke in that place, then it follows there is a fire." Both the affirming consequence and the syllogism indicate that because you can directly see smoke, there must be a fire. These followers of Jayānanda are saying that because an affirming consequence ends up asserting something in a manner similar to an autonomous syllogism, Prāsaṅgikas, who have no thesis of their own, should not use it. They should use only refuting consequences that reveal a contradiction in the opponent's position and thereby force the opponent to drop his wrong view.

In a refuting consequence, both the pervasions and the reason being a property of the subject are simply accepted; they are not established by valid knowledge. In the above example, when we present the refuting consequence "If there is no fire in that place, then it follows that there is no smoke," neither we nor the opponent believe that there is no smoke. We can both see it in front of us. The statement "There is no smoke" simply follows from the opponent's assertion that there is no fire. It is not expressing something that is established by valid knowledge. The assertion "There is no fire" implies that there is no smoke. The reason and the pervasion merely demonstrate what finally follows from the opponent's assertion. Therefore these followers of Jayānanda say that we can cut through our opponent's incorrect assertions by using refuting consequences where the reason and pervasion are merely accepted by both parties; we do not have to use autonomous syllogisms where the three modes are established by valid knowledge.

Tsongkhapa presents here four types of arguments used by Jayānanda's followers, all of which are based on what the opponent accepts. The four are: a consequence revealing a contradiction, an inference based on what the opponent accepts, a consequence showing that an opponent's reason and thesis are similar, and a consequence treating similar reasons as equally applicable.

The first is a consequence that reveals a contradiction to the opponent. For example, the Sāṃkhyas assert that things arise from their own nature. They say that the universal principle contains the potentiality of all things. If something does not already exist in its cause before it appears or becomes manifest, then it cannot arise. For example, a fully grown tree already exists in a hidden state in the seed that we plant. Once the tree becomes manifest, it is produced or arisen. However, that tree is not something new that results from other causes and conditions; it already exists at the time of its seed. Yet the Sāṃkhyas also consider that production has a purpose and a limit. They do not say that manifest things arise again—only that things already exist within their cause and later become manifest. However, we may argue, if a thing is already there at the time of its cause, then why would it need to be produced? It is purposeless to produce something that already exists. Furthermore, if a thing that already exists were again produced, then its production would be endless; there would be nothing to stop it continuously reproducing itself. It would arise again and again without limit. Therefore the Buddhists present the Sāṃkhyas with a consequence showing that their belief that things arise from themselves contradicts their belief that production is purposeful and limited. The argument is, "If a thing arises from itself, it follows that production would be purposeless and endless," for an already existing thing would arise again; so it would be wrong to accept that production has a purpose and a limit. Also, "If production has a purpose and a limit, it follows that a thing does not arise from itself," for it already exists; so it would be wrong to accept that things arise from themselves. When the opponent understands this contradiction, he abandons his wrong view. We use logical consequences only for the purpose of bringing about this result.

The second type of argument is an inference based on what the opponent accepts. The opponent already accepts the subject, reason, and pervasion of the inference, and we use this argument to refute his or her thesis. However, we do not need to accept the reason or the pervasion ourselves. For example, we say to someone who accepts self-production, "A sprout does not arise from itself because it already exists within itself." The Mādhyamikas do not accept that a sprout exists within itself at the time of its cause, but the person against whom they are debating accepts that this reason is a property of the subject. The opponent has also already accepted the pervasion. So we can argue that anything that exists within itself cannot arise from itself because it already exists. Also, if an already existent sprout were to arise from itself, then that would be reproduction rather than production. If someone accepts reproduction, then they must accept that a sprout is produced again. Therefore, although the Mādhyamikas say "A sprout does not arise from itself because it already exists," they are not trying to establish as their own thesis that things are not produced from themselves. They posit it merely to refute the Sāṃkhyas' view of self-production. In short, the Mādhyamikas are not trying to refute one view and establish its opposite; thus the Mādhyamikas have no thesis of their own.

The third is a consequence showing that in an opponent's argument the reason and the thesis are similar. In other words, we show the opponent that his reason states almost exactly what he is trying to prove, so it cannot function as a reason. For example, an opponent may say, "Within the five aggregates, feeling is inherently existent because form is inherently existent." His thesis is that one of the five aggregates, feeling, is inherently existent. His reason is that another of the five aggregates, form, is inherently existent. This argument does not prove anything because both the reason and the thesis amount to the same thing: an aggregate is inherently existent.

The fourth is a consequence treating similar reasons as equally applicable. For example, someone may say, "It follows that the ear consciousness apprehending sound sees form, because the eye consciousness apprehending form ultimately sees form." In general, an eye consciousness sees a form in dependence on certain conditions: a visual object, a sense organ, and an activity. However, if the eye consciousness sees form ultimately, then seeing does not depend on any conditions. The same applies to ear consciousness. If all the sense consciousnesses ultimately perceive their objects, then they must do so independently of any conditions; because they would not depend on their own uncommon conditions, they would perceive each other's objects. So just as the eye consciousness perceives form, the ear consciousness would perceive form; just as the ear consciousness perceives sound, the eye consciousness would perceive sound. This is an example of applying similar reasons equally.

Someone asks the followers of Jayānanda, "Do you want to refute what the opponent accepts, or not? If so, then you must have a thesis, because wanting to refute their position is itself a thesis. Therefore you must prove it by means of an autonomous syllogism. If you do not want to refute what is accepted by the opponent, then it is inappropriate to refute them using such reasoning."

Jayānanda's followers reply, "In the context of ultimate analysis, if we want to prove the absence of inherent existence or the absence of ultimate arising, then we would have to accept the theses and reasons of autonomous syllogisms. However, we do not want to prove anything; therefore we have no such fault. If merely having a wish entails having a thesis, then everyone would have theses about everything." Anytime we wanted to eat something or go somewhere, we would have to have a thesis.

Jayānanda's followers contend that Prāsaṅgikas do not prove their own position; they merely refute an opponent's position. They have a wish but do not have a thesis. They have no position of their own, so at the time of ultimate analysis they do not posit any thesis, such as the absence of inherent existence. However, they do not say that they have no assertions at all. They accept ordinary assertions, such as "I am going to town" or "I want a cup of tea."

Thus the distinction between a Prāsaṅgika and a Svātantrika, according to these followers of Jayānanda, appears to be as follows. At the time of ultimate analysis, a Svātantrika accepts a thesis, such as the absence of inherent existence, and tries to prove it as his or her own system, whereas a Prāsaṅgika merely refutes the opponent's assertions without accepting anything at all.

(3')) THE THIRD MISINTERPRETATION

According to certain contemporaries of Tsongkhapa, who consider themselves to be Prāsaṅgika-Mādhyamikas, there is nothing—whether ultimate or conventional—that can be accepted by Mādhyamikas even conventionally. For if they were to accept a thesis, to prove it they would have to accept a logical argument containing an example, a reason, and a pervasion; in which case they would be Svātantrikas. Therefore Prāsaṅgikas do not have any thesis of their own to prove. These contemporaries support this interpretation with quotations taken from the authoritative texts of the great Mādhyamikas. Nāgārjuna's *Refutation of Objections* says:

> If I had any kind of thesis,
> Then that fault would apply to me.
> But I do not have a thesis;
> Thus I am totally without fault.

> If anything, owing to its nature, were known
> By direct perception and so on,
> Then that would be proved or refuted.
> But that does not exist; thus I am not faulted.

These so-called Prāsaṅgikas take Nāgārjuna's words "I do not have a thesis" literally. They even consider it wrong to hold that things are not ultimately existent. However, Nāgārjuna is not saying that he has no thesis at all; he is saying that he has no inherently existent thesis. In these stanzas, Nāgārjuna is responding to the Realists, such as the Vaibhāṣikas and Sautrāntikas, whom he presents as attacking the Mādhyamikas, saying:[112]

> Then even your words do not inherently exist,
> So cannot refute inherent nature.

According to the Realists, "not inherently existent" means "nonexistent." Therefore if words do not inherently exist, then words do not exist at all. How can something nonexistent prove or refute anything? Nāgārjuna responds by saying that there is nothing to be held as a thesis ultimately.

These contemporaries of Tsongkhapa do not understand the subtle meaning of Nāgārjuna's words; they interpret them superficially to mean that the Mādhyamikas have no fault because they have no thesis at all. Nāgārjuna's second stanza means that if something were known in an ultimate sense, then it would be proved or refuted ultimately. However, because Nāgārjuna asserts no such thing, he has no such fault.

These scholars also quote Nāgārjuna's *Sixty Stanzas of Reasoning*:

> These great ones
> Have no position and no argument;
> For those who have no position
> How can there be an opponent's position?

On the surface, this stanza says that the great Prāsaṅgika-Mādhyamikas have no position. However, it means that the Prāsaṅgikas do not accept any inherently existent position; they deny that anything exists inherently—whether it is a thesis or something known by direct perception. If ultimately there is no *my* side, how can there be *your* side?

These scholars also refer to Āryadeva's *Four Hundred Stanzas*, which says:

> Even if you try for a very long time,
> You cannot demonstrate any fault
> In those who have no position
> Regarding existence, nonexistence, or both.

This stanza, like all the above quotations, literally says that the Mādhyamikas do not accept any position or thesis. Āryadeva means that the Mādhyamikas do not accept any of the extreme positions: existence, nonexistence, both, or neither. The word "existence" refers to the extreme view of eternalism— holding things to be inherently existent, not just merely existent. The word "nonexistence" refers to the extreme view of nihilism—holding things to be totally nonexistent, not just noninherently existent.

These quotations from the great, nonpartisan Madhyamaka texts literally say that the Mādhyamikas have no faults because they do not hold any thesis. So Tsongkhapa's contemporaries use them to support their position. Candrakīrti's *Clear Words* says:

> If you are a Mādhyamika, it is not correct to use autonomous inferences, because we do not accept others' positions.

Is Candrakīrti saying that Mādhyamikas cannot accept the use of autonomous inferences? What about Śāntarakṣita, Kamalaśīla, and Bhāvaviveka? Are they not Mādhyamikas? Some of the monastic textbooks say that if you are a Mādhyamika, it is not suitable to accept the use of autonomous syllogisms. We may retort that it is not contradictory for something to be unsuitable to do and yet do it. Take the example of a fully ordained monk who possesses all the root and secondary vows. It is not suitable for such a monk to break any of these vows or disobey any vinaya rules, however minor. Yet there are fully ordained monks who break some of the vows or flout some of the rules. In short, saying that something is not suitable is quite different from saying that it cannot happen. In this context, it is not suitable for a Mādhyamika to accept autonomous syllogisms, yet there are some Mādhyamikas who use them. However, even though they consent to use autonomous syllogisms, they do not accept any position, whether their own or that of another. Again Candrakīrti's *Clear Words* says:

> Even the opposite meaning of a consequence is related to the opponent,
> but not to us, because we do not have any thesis.

A consequence is just a way of revealing a contradiction in the opponent's view. Neither the proponent nor the opponent want to accept what follows from the opponent's view. In fact, the proponent of a consequence usually accepts the opposite of what follows from it. However, when Mādhyamikas employ consequences, they accept neither the reality of what follows from it nor its opposite. For example, the Mādhyamikas say to the Sāṃkhyas, "If you accept that things arise from themselves, then it follows that things' arising again would be meaningless and endless." Candrakīrti mentions that, although he puts forward this consequence to his Sāṃkhya opponent, this does not mean that he accepts the reverse. He accepts neither what follows from the Sāṃkhya assertions nor the opposite. The consequence and its opposite are connected only to the opponent. It has nothing to do with the Mādhyamika proponent because he does not accept any thesis at all.

In Candrakīrti's *Introduction to the "Middle Way,"* the words "I do not have a position" appear again:

> Does that which refutes do its refuting
> Having contacted or not contacted the refuted object?
> The previously explained faults apply to one who has a definite position;
> Because I have no such position, this consequence cannot apply to me.

Nāgārjuna's special technique is to focus on the relationship between things, such as: the destroyer, the act of destroying, and the object destroyed; the fire, the burning, and the object burned; the producer, the producing, and the object produced. If these are inherently existent, then either they really contact each other or they do not make any contact at all. If there is contact, there is one kind of fault; if there is no contact, then there is another kind of fault. These faults, which were explained earlier, only apply to those who hold an inherently established thesis. The Mādhyamikas do not hold any such position, so these faults do not apply to them.

All these quotations demonstrate that Nāgārjuna, Āryadeva, and Candra-kīrti make their amazing arguments only to guide their opponents to the correct view. Their explanations are for the sake of their opponents, not to posit any position as their own. The *Introduction to the "Middle Way"* says:

> In the way that you accept dependent things as real
> I do not accept them even as conventional.
> Yet for the sake of the result, although nonexistent, I say "they exist";
> From the worldly point of view, I speak of a self.

The Yogācāras accept the true existence of things that are dependent on other causes and conditions. The Mādhyamikas do not accept these things to be truly existent even conventionally. However, for the sake of accomplishing others' ultimate welfare, the Mādhyamikas say that things exist conventionally from a worldly perspective. Nāgārjuna's *Refutation of Objections* says:

> Since there is nothing to be negated,
> I do not negate anything;
> Therefore, in saying that I negate things
> You are disparaging me.

The words "there is nothing" do not mean that absolutely nothing at all exists. We should understand Nāgārjuna to mean that from the perspective of the wisdom analyzing the ultimate, there is nothing inherently existent. In that sense, there is no position to negate nor is there a refutation of an opponent's position. Nāgārjuna is saying that the negation and the position it negates are not inherently existent. Here he says the Realists vilify him when they accuse him of negating everything. Nāgārjuna does not negate conventional things, such as cause and effect; he simply negates their inherent existence.

(4')) The fourth misinterpretation

Some earlier Tibetan Madhyamaka scholars who are followers of Candra-kīrti, such as Chapa Chokyi Senge, reject earlier systems that claim that the Mādhyamikas have no positions of their own and no valid knowledge establishing them. Then they posit the Madhyamaka system as follows. They deny both direct and inferential valid knowledge to be established through the force of reality—as claimed by those who accept valid knowledge and its object to be inherently existent, in the sense of being able to withstand ultimate analysis. They accept valid knowledge and its object as conventionally understood in the world without engaging in ultimate analysis. They say that the Mādhya-mikas prove that things are not truly existent by means of logical reasoning set forth as a proof statement to the opponent. Nevertheless, they claim that they are not Svātantrikas because they do not establish it by ultimate analysis but by conventional knowledge accepted in the world.

Refuting Misinterpretations of the Svātantrika/Prāsaṅgika Distinction

(b')) Refuting others' assertions
    (1')) Refuting the first misinterpretation
    (2')) Refuting the second misinterpretation
    (3')) Refuting the third misinterpretation
    (4')) Refuting the fourth misinterpretation

(b')) REFUTING OTHERS' ASSERTIONS

THE FOUR MISINTERPRETATIONS of the Svātantrika/Prāsaṅgika distinction explained in the previous chapter are now to be refuted. Therefore there are four sections in this chapter:

    (1')) Refuting the first misinterpretation
    (2')) Refuting the second misinterpretation
    (3')) Refuting the third misinterpretation
    (4')) Refuting the fourth misinterpretation

(1')) REFUTING THE FIRST MISINTERPRETATION

According to Jayānanda's *Explanation of the "Introduction to the 'Middle Way,'"* the reason and the pervasion in a Madhyamaka proof of śūnyatā are not established by valid knowledge. But his rationale for this, Tsongkhapa says, is incorrect. Jayānanda argues that neither the opponent nor the proponent needs to know that the reason is a property of the subject, nor establish the relationship between the reason and the predicate; it is sufficient for both parties to accept the validity of these points. Moreover, he argues, it is not even possible for either party to know them; the proponent cannot know whether his opponent has this knowledge, and he cannot even know whether he has this knowledge himself. So, Jayānanda argues, correct reasoning is based only on what both parties accept, not on what they know.

Tsongkhapa says that Jayānanda is wrong about this. In general, according to most systems of Buddhist logic, such as that of Dharmakīrti, both the opponent and the proponent must validly establish the three modes of the syllogism. In other words, both parties must know that the specific reason presented is a property of that subject; also that this reason implies the predicate of that thesis, and conversely the negation of that predicate implies the negation of this reason. However, the proponent and opponent do not need to know each other's mind; a lack of telepathy does not invalidate logic. Thus Jayānanda's point that the proponent cannot know what the opponent has established is not a good reason for saying that the syllogism's reason is not validly established by both parties.

Tsongkhapa points out that the same argument can be applied to the opponent's acceptance of the reason, not only to his knowledge of it. Just as we cannot know whether our opponent has validly established the reason, because we cannot read his or her mind, we also cannot know whether he or she has genuinely accepted the reason. Although our opponent may say "I accept this," his or her words are not necessarily trustworthy. We, the proponent of the argument, would have to read our opponent's mind in order to know whether he or she really does accept the reason. Thus we cannot refute our opponents in terms of what they accept, because we do not know what they accept. Therefore Jayānanda's replacement of "knowing the reason" with "accepting the reason" as a requirement for the validity of a syllogism succumbs to the same fault he was trying to avoid—it cannot be known by both parties. Quite apart from this, in order to know something, you do not need to *know* that you know it. That would lead to an epistemological infinite regress. Just knowing it is enough.

Jayānanda's claim that the pervasion is not known by valid knowledge is also incorrect. The pervasion is the relationship between the reason and the predicate. For example, in the syllogism "On the smoky mountain pass there is fire because there is smoke, as in a kitchen" the pervasion is: if there is smoke, there is fire, and if there is no fire, there is no smoke. The person to whom you are trying to prove the thesis—there is fire on the smoky mountain pass— must know this relationship between fire and smoke. Jayānanda argues that the opponent's knowledge of the pervasion is limited to his or her previous experience of smoke and fire that is expressed in the example, the kitchen. In other words, Jayānanda contends that the opponent does not understand the pervasion between smoke and fire to be universal but only understands it in the context of a specific instance: if there is smoke in the kitchen, then there is fire in the kitchen. Tsongkhapa claims that this is wrong; instead the pervasion must be known to apply in general, not just in a particular case. Although someone's knowledge of the relationship between smoke and fire is initially developed in a particular context, such as a kitchen, it is not limited to that situation. Knowledge of the pervasion cannot be so narrow that the opponent only knows that if there is smoke in the kitchen then there is fire in the kitchen. If it were, then since knowledge of any pervasion is developed on the basis of an example, on what basis could knowledge of this limited pervasion have been developed in the first place?

Consider the syllogism "Sound is impermanent because it is produced, as is a pot." The opponent understands that the reason is a property of the subject: sound is produced. He also understands the pervasion: whatever is produced must be impermanent, and if something is not impermanent it cannot be produced. But he does not understand this pervasion on the basis of sound itself. However, because we use his knowledge of the pervasion in trying to prove to him that sound is impermanent, he must have gained his knowledge of the pervasion from somewhere else. In this case, he gained it on the basis of a potter making a pot. He knows that, in the case of a pot, if it is produced then it is impermanent. He also knows that the reason "is produced" is a quality common to a pot and sound. However, he does not know that the predicate "is impermanent" also applies to both. We are trying to prove to him that the quality of being impermanent does apply to both, by means of the syllogism "Sound is impermanent because it is produced, as is a pot." Therefore the predicate of the syllogism must be a general one because it is also a quality of the example, a pot. So it cannot be a particular quality—in this case the impermanence of sound—because this does not apply to a pot. For any syllogism to work, the pervasion between the reason and the predicate must be a general one because the reason and the predicate must apply to both the example and the subject.

Tsongkhapa urges us to understand from the above discussion that the inference establishing the pervasion is valid knowledge. The person to whom we demonstrate an inference must know that the reason is a property of the subject as well as know that the predicate is a property of the example.

Thus Jayānanda is also wrong in saying that, on account of the pervasion not being established by valid knowledge, a thesis is proved by means of what is merely accepted by both the proponent and the opponent. For, Tsongkhapa argues, if our opponent uses as a reason something that he merely accepts, then we cannot refute it, because neither we nor our opponent has the valid knowledge that either proves or refutes the thing accepted.

Someone may suggest, to support Jayānanda's theory, that a distinction could be made between two kinds of acceptance, whereby one way of accepting something proves the thesis, while another way of accepting something does not prove it. But how could we make such a distinction? Would we base it on what is merely accepted? Or would we base it on what is known? If it is based on what is merely accepted, then it is like the merely accepted thesis itself and provides no knowledge with which to prove it. It would simply be begging the question. If it is based on what is known, then Jayānanda has lost his point that we can prove something without depending on valid knowledge.

(2')) REFUTING THE SECOND MISINTERPRETATION

The followers of Jayānanda say that when engaging in ultimate analysis, the Prāsaṅgikas do not assert the thesis that there is no inherent existence. They only refute their opponent's position and do not propound anything. They prove that there is no inherent existence only to someone who holds that things exist inherently. This does not mean that the Prāsaṅgikas have no position at all. It means that when they are engaged in ultimate analysis they do not assert anything. If the Prāsaṅgikas were to try to prove the absence of inherent existence, then it would become the thesis of an autonomous syllogism. This is not acceptable to them. Now the difference between this second misconception of the Svātantrika-Prāsaṅgika distinction and the third misconception is that the followers of Jayānanda say it is only at the time of ultimate analysis that the Prāsaṅgikas do not have a thesis, not in an ordinary conventional context.

In order to refute this misconception, Tsongkhapa asks those who hold it, "Are you saying that the Mādhyamikas do not accept the thesis that there is no inherent existence because an inferential consciousness analyzing whether there is inherent existence or not cannot establish it? Or are you saying that they do not accept that thesis because it is during a period of analyzing reality?" Regarding the first question, if you cannot prove the emptiness of inherent existence by means of the wisdom analyzing the ultimate, then you cannot refute the opponent's view that things are inherently existent. This is because the reasoning procedure is the same in both cases. If ultimate analysis can refute that things inherently exist, then it must be able to prove that they do not inherently exist; if ultimate analysis cannot prove that things do not inherently exist, then it cannot refute that they inherently exist.

Regarding the second question, it would be illogical for the followers of Jayānanda to think that when analyzing reality they cannot refute an opponent's thesis that things are inherently existent. Three reasons are given for this. First, it would be self-contradictory because they already said that the Prāsaṅgikas engage in ultimate analysis in order to refute the opponent's system. Second, they accept that an ordinary, nonanalytical, conventional consciousness cannot refute an opponent's position concerning the ultimate nature of reality. Third, otherwise there would be no reason for them to make a special point of saying "We do not assert any theses in our own system," because they would also have to admit that a consequence cannot refute an opponent's position. They would have to allow that the Mādhyamikas neither refute an opponent's position nor prove their own position. A proof and a refutation have the same logical status. If we present a consequence refuting our opponent's tenet that things are inherently existent, that very refutation proves that things are not inherently existent. As we saw in chapters 5 and 9, Nāgārjuna says in *Refutation of Objections*:

> If it negates "not inherently existent,"
> Then it proves "inherently existent." (26c–d)

Conversely, by negating "inherently existent," this proves "not inherently existent." There is no third ground in between. If there were, then someone might say, "I am proving that things are 'not inherently existent,' but I am not disproving that they are 'inherently existent.'" How do we reply to such a statement? We will say that "inherently existent" and "not inherently existent" are directly and mutually contradictory. The reasoning process that proves one automatically refutes the other; by refuting one you positively prove the other. Therefore when you eliminate, even in thought, inherent nature, then the lack of inherent nature is established automatically; when you eliminate the lack of inherent nature, then inherent nature is naturally established. Conversely, when you positively prove the lack of inherent nature, you immediately eliminate inherent nature, and when you prove inherent nature, you immediately eliminate the lack of inherent nature.

Now Tsongkhapa demands that the followers of Jayānanda give a reason for thinking that the Mādhyamikas do not hold any thesis, such as the absence of inherent existence, simply because it is during the time of ultimate analysis. They say that the Mādhyamikas do not accept any thesis because anything that is established at the time of ultimate analysis must be ultimately existent. But this is wrong. Why? If they do not accept anything to exist at the time of ultimate analysis, then this would also apply to that occasion itself. If they do not accept that even such an occasion exists, then they would have to accept that there is no occasion when the Mādhyamikas examine anything by means of ultimate analysis. Conversely, if they admit that there is an occasion when ultimate analysis takes place, then they must accept that there is an examiner, a method of examining, a basis being examined, and an opponent against whom they are debating.[113] Nevertheless, this does not mean that all these things are ultimately existent.

Finally, it is not satisfactory to say that a logical consequence, without involving any valid knowledge, nonetheless implies something merely based on what the opponent accepts or on what is entailed by what they accept. This must be rejected, just as the first misconception was rejected above. Moreover, it is incorrect to make a distinction between not accepting any thesis in the context of ultimate analysis yet accepting a thesis conventionally, and then use this as the criterion of someone who is a Prāsaṅgika-Mādhyamika. That kind of distinction does not make sense, because no Mādhyamika accepts anything, even the context of ultimate analysis itself, to be ultimately existent; it is merely conventionally established, like everything else. This contradicts Jayānanda's disciples' view. Also, if "not existing in the context of ultimate analysis" means "not ultimately existent," those disciples cannot use the former to distinguish between Svātantrika- and Prāsaṅgika-Mādhyamikas. For just as there is no Mādhyamika who accepts anything to be ultimately existent, so there is no Mādhyamika who accepts anything in the context of ultimate analysis. Therefore this cannot be a special quality of the Prāsaṅgika system.

(3')) Refuting the third misinterpretation

The third system that Tsongkhapa refutes represents the views of some Mādhyamikas of his time who claim that nothing is to be accepted, not even conventionally. As we saw in the last chapter, they cite many passages from the great Madhyamaka texts to support their view that the Mādhyamikas present arguments only for the purpose of refuting others and have no theses of their own—neither ultimately nor conventionally.

There are indeed various root texts, commentaries, and subcommentaries that say things such as "We have no thesis," or "We have no position," or "We have no dispute." All these statements mean that the Mādhyamikas have no inherently existent thesis, position, or dispute. In the immediate context of such phrases, these texts may not explicitly use qualifying words such as "ultimately," "truly," or "inherently," so it is easy for these scholars to say that these passages support their position. Even when they do not quote a text but merely report what Nāgārjuna says in the *Fundamental Treatise* or *Refutation of Objections*, or describe what the *Buddhapālita* says, and so on, if you go back to the original text you will find that the commentators have used the original's exact words. Nowadays, some Western scholars claim that we are forcing our own interpretation onto Nāgārjuna and other authors when we insert the term "inherently" into these passages. They think we have no reason to claim that where Nāgārjuna says he has no thesis, he means that he has no inherently existent thesis; they think if he meant that, he would say it.

There is confusion about Nāgārjuna's intended meaning because many things are not explicitly stated in his works. If you read the texts exactly as they are written, you will fall into a nihilistic view. In fact, the lower Buddhist schools accuse Nāgārjuna of holding the extreme view of nihilism because he goes through every possible category of existent things and says that they do not exist. Sometimes Nāgārjuna unambiguously says that things do not exist inherently, but this does not make any difference to the scholars of the lower schools, because for them "not inherently existent" means "not existent." So there is a great deal of discussion about this. First we have to show what is wrong if we accept these abbreviated statements literally. Then we have to understand what they mean. Finally, in order to express their meaning, we may need to use some additional words. These are not arbitrary additions; we can see that Nāgārjuna adds a special qualifier such as "inherently" or "ultimately" to his negation from time to time. He does not use it in every negation, but having used it in one place we can see how he means it to be applied in other passages.

Those who say that Mādhyamikas do not accept anything even conventionally, based on the previously cited passages, have not properly recognized the object of negation. When they see that the logical reasons they use to refute others' positions regarding inherent existence can be turned on themselves and be applied equally to any position that they set forth, they cannot answer their own accusations. They have no idea how to establish their own system while avoiding the faults that they ascribe to others. Therefore they think it best not to accept anything at all. However, if they accept nothing, then the ontological status of all dependently produced causes and effects of samsara and nirvana become like that of the creator god Īśvara. Nobody can prove or refute the existence of such a being. If we cannot prove or refute the ontological status of causal phenomena, there is no way to distinguish between what is valid and what is not valid. Therefore those who hold this misinterpretation disparage the Madhyamaka in the worst and lowest way. We have already gone over Tsongkhapa's refutation of this view in chapter 4, in the section refuting those who identify the object of negation too broadly.

Tsongkhapa says that those who claim that Mādhyamikas have no thesis and do not accept anything do not understand the word "Madhyamaka." Madhyamaka means the middle way. It is the middle because it is free of the two extreme views that things are ultimately existent and that things are completely nonexistent. The criterion of being a Mādhyamika, a person who has attained the middle way, is that you understand what is to be accepted and what is to be rejected; therefore you accept certain things. A Mādhyamika accepts that not even the tiniest atom ultimately exists, yet everything exists dependently; so conventionally everything is understood to be like an illusion. The Mādhyamikas establish this position when they negate the wrong views of those who propound that things are ultimately existent or that things are totally nonexistent. Therefore they accept that there is valid knowledge that understands what is to be negated and what is to be established. Because they show others the right view based on their own understanding, and because their opponents cannot find any realistic fault with the truths that the Mādhyamikas establish, this system is totally and utterly pure.

Tsongkhapa scolds these mistaken scholars. He says that even if they cannot establish the faultless system of the great Mādhyamikas themselves, at least they should not denigrate it by claiming it does not exist. Simply accepting the reasoning that everything dependently arises completely cuts through the net of wrong views that things ultimately exist or do not exist at all. Those who have wisdom are free from all contradiction when establishing the Madhyamaka system. It is ridiculous for anyone to think that they can avoid contradictions by claiming that they do not have any assertions at all—even denying what they see—because they think that if they do not affirm anything then their opponents will not be able to disprove them. That is just crazy talk! Candrakīrti's *Clear Words* says:

> In this way, our position is utterly pure and everything that is established is maintained without contradiction, while your gross position, easily acquired, has many faults and contradictions. But through sheer stupidity you do not see how to identify qualities and faults. Those are your own faults.

The above passage indicates that the Madhyamaka system derives from two kinds of valid knowledge: valid knowledge establishing ultimate reality and valid knowledge of conventional things. Totally pure and free of faults, the Madhyamaka system allows for the establishment of cause and effect within samsara and nirvana. We must definitely understand this point. Otherwise, if we do not understand, we will think that the statement "Mādhyamikas have no system of their own" makes the Mādhyamikas irrefutable in the same way that the statement "Whatever you say is a lie" is irrefutable. If every word you say is a lie, it becomes impossible to prove or refute you because there is no truth at all. Every turn is blocked; it is beyond the realm of logic. Similarly, if we say that Mādhyamikas have no system of their own, as the opponents suggest, this does not make the Madhyamaka system irrefutable in any sensible way. A similar argument is presented in Candrakīrti's *Introduction to the "Middle Way"*:

> If any self were established as a real thing, then, like the mind,
> It would be really established; it would not be inexpressible.

Here Candrakīrti is refuting the Vātsīputrīyas, a subdivision of the Vaibhāṣika school, whom he presents as positing a substantially existent self that cannot be expressed as either the same as or different from the aggregates. Candrakīrti argues that if the self were substantially existent, then it must be either the same as or different from the aggregates.

Tsongkhapa now addresses his mistaken contemporaries directly. If you are correct, you cannot refute the Vātsīputrīyas in this way because they would respond, "We say that the self is substantially existent and cannot be expressed as either one with or different from the aggregates; so you cannot engage in such an analysis." You could reply, "To say that the self is substantially existent contradicts the view that it is neither the same as nor different from the aggregates. Therefore it must be expressed as one of these two possibilities. So this kind of analysis can be done." But if you argue in this way, then your claim "We do not accept anything, we have no assertions" would itself be an assertion—a heartfelt belief. You might now suggest that this is like someone begging for money, who responds to the reply "I have no money" by saying, "Well, give me your *no money*." But if you think these two situations are similar, then you do not understand the Prāsaṅgika position. The Prāsaṅgikas are not saying that having no assertions is itself an assertion. They are saying that when you sincerely declare from your heart "We have no assertions," then you are making an assertion. You cannot avoid contradicting your own claim. If claims like these do not belong within the Madhyamaka system, then it is absurd to try to prove them by quoting the texts of the noble Nāgārjuna and Āryadeva. These ideas cannot be found in Candrakīrti's works, nor do they belong to any other Buddhist system. They are completely outside the Dharma.

If you followers of Jayānanda propound the Madhyamaka system, specifically the system of Candrakīrti, then you contradict yourselves by claiming to have no system of your own. Likewise, you are wrong to claim that Mādhyamikas posit things only from the point of view of others, thinking they are free of assertions themselves. If you do this, then you must accept that forms and so on are posited merely from the point of view of others. To say that Mādhyamikas posit such phenomena only for the sake of others, without accepting them themselves, is itself an assertion. So in claiming this you cannot escape making assertions. Moreover, your claim implies that you accept someone for whom things are posited, and thereby things that are posited as well as those who posit them, the Mādhyamikas themselves. Thus there is an internal contradiction in what you are saying: your claim that Mādhyamikas do not have any assertions disproves your own position.

The opponents object, "We are not saying 'We have no system of our own and make assertions only for the sake of others'—it only appears to you that we are saying that." Tsongkhapa retorts, "If you deny your own direct perception, which even the Cārvākas do not deny, and cannot experience what you are speaking about, then it is astonishing that you claim to know what we perceive and hear!" The Cārvākas are non-Buddhist materialists who do not believe in past and future lives or in liberation. They say that we do not need to worry about creating karma because this life is all there is; we should enjoy ourselves—even if it involves nonvirtuous activity—just as long as we are not caught! The Tibetan name for this school can be translated literally into English as "those who throw to a far distance"; in denying causality and liberation, a follower of this school throws the possibility of enlightenment and higher rebirth far away. Yet even the Cārvākas accept what is perceived by the senses; so why not the followers of Jayānanda? Tsongkhapa adds, "Why do you even need to say 'We have no assertions'? For, whatever you claim, you can simply deny it in the end, with no possibility of being faulted."

Now the opponents bring up another point. They say they posit logical consequences only for the sake of others without accepting that logic themselves. In reply, Tsongkhapa asks why they trust the system of Candrakīrti, who refuted the Svātantrika system and established the Prāsaṅgika system. To be consistent, just as an autonomous syllogism is not acceptable to them, a logical consequence should also not be acceptable; conversely, if a consequence is acceptable to them for the sake of others, then, for a particular purpose, an autonomous syllogism should be acceptable for the sake of others. Now just as a person cannot be called a Cittamātrin if he accepts the Cittamātra system merely for the sake of others without accepting it himself, so these opponents cannot be called Prāsaṅgikas if they present consequences showing the meaning of the middle way merely for the sake of others without accepting them themselves; since they are not Svātantrikas either, they are not Mādhyamikas at all.

At the end of chapter 13, Tsongkhapa quoted a stanza from Candrakīrti's *Introduction to the "Middle Way,"* the last two lines of which are misinterpreted by the opponents:

Yet for the sake of the result, although nonexistent, I say "they exist";
From the worldly point of view, I speak of a self.

Jayānanda's followers cannot cite this as a source to support their view that all presentations are made only for the sake of others. These lines mean that, although causes, effects, and so on do not exist inherently, for the sake of others we say that the self exists from a conventional, mundane point of view. Ultimate analysis establishes that things do not have an inherently existent nature. This is not established from the perspective of ordinary conventional knowledge. If ordinary conventional knowledge were able to establish the absence of inherent existence, then the wisdom arising from analysis of the ultimate would be pointless. Because this text says "I say 'they exist' from the worldly point of view," it shows that forms and so on are established to exist from the perspective of conventional knowledge.

We must understand that Candrakīrti makes this statement while presenting the Madhyamaka refutation of the Cittamātra system. So when he says that Mādhyamikas do not accept conventional things, he means that they do not accept them in the way that Cittamātrins accept dependent phenomena. The Cittamātrins say that dependent natures are the true basis. The true attribute of dependent natures is the emptiness of duality; this is the ultimate truth. Cittamātrins assert that both the true basis and the true attribute are ultimately existent. Between these two truly existent things, they posit imputed things that are not truly existent. The Mādhyamikas do not accept truly existent things at all, so they do not accept dependent phenomena even conventionally in the way that the Cittamātrins do. Thus this passage does not mean that Mādhyamikas do not accept conventional things in their own system; the text clearly says that Mādhyamikas do not accept them "in the way that you accept dependent things as real."

The transitional passage preceding this stanza expresses the Cittamātrins' argument, "If you Mādhyamikas use valid reasoning to negate dependent things, then we will use your reasons to negate what you hold to be conventional." The Mādhyamikas logically reject the true or ultimate existence of dependent phenomena. The Cittamātrins reply that they can use the Mādhyamika's line of reasoning to negate conventional things as posited by the Mādhyamikas. However, Tsongkhapa points out that there is a great difference between the Cittamātra and Madhyamaka notions of what it means to be negated by ultimate analysis. The Madhyamaka view is that nothing can withstand ultimate analysis; everything is conventionally existent. The Cittamātra view is that dependent things must withstand ultimate analysis. For if dependent things are not ultimately existent, they do not exist at all, and if dependent natures exist, they ultimately exist. Thus the two schools do not agree about what can be negated by analytical reasoning.

The opponents suggest that in this stanza the phrase "from the worldly point of view" refers to the standpoint of those who are not Mādhyamikas. That is an incorrect interpretation. This phrase refers to worldly or ordinary valid knowledge. Ordinary valid knowledge is a nondistorted conventional consciousness. The existence of conventional things must be established from the perspective of conventional valid knowledge. A Mādhyamika, like all other people, has conventional valid knowledge within his or her mental continuum. So how are we to understand what Candrakīrti means when he says, "Although nonexistent, I say 'they exist'"? He does not mean that things are totally nonexistent; he means that they do not exist by their own intrinsic characteristics. If anything existed by its own characteristics, it would be ultimately existent. If it were ultimately existent, it could not be known by conventional valid knowledge. So the term "nonexistent" means that phenomena do not exist inherently. Although things do not exist inherently, the text says "they exist." In other words, phenomena do not exist inherently, even conventionally; yet they do exist conventionally. This is how things are established according to the Madhyamaka system. It is unsuitable to interpret this line to mean literally "Although nonexistent, they exist," or to mean "Things are totally nonexistent." In his *Commentary on the "Introduction to the 'Middle Way,'"* Candrakīrti explains this stanza to mean, "Just as worldly people accept things to be existent or nonexistent, I accept them in the same way." Thus in the line "Although nonexistent, I say 'they exist,'" the words "nonexistent" and "exist" have different referents: "nonexistent" refers to the lack of ultimate existence, and "exist" refers to conventional existence. There is no difficulty in understanding this point when we see that these words signify different attributes.

Tsongkhapa's opponents now demand an explanation of what Nāgārjuna means in *Refutation of Objections* when he says that Mādhyamikas have no position or thesis (see chapter 13). Consider the syllogism, "A sprout has no inherently existent nature because it dependently arises, like a reflection." If we are to establish the thesis—a sprout has no inherently existent nature—we must have established the three modes of the syllogism. The first is that the reason is a property of the subject: we must understand that a sprout dependently arises. The second and third modes are the forward and reverse pervasions: we must understand that if something dependently arises, then it has no inherently existent nature, and that if something has an inherently existent nature, then it does not dependently arise. We must have established this pervasion on the basis of the example: a reflection. Even Prāsaṅgikas, such as ourselves, accept that a syllogism proves the thesis—the relationship between the subject and the predicate—in this way. The opponents claim that if we accept that valid inferential knowledge of the thesis can be produced by relying on a syllogism like this, then we Prāsaṅgikas do not reject them at all but simply despise the term "autonomous syllogism"—since Prāsaṅgikas actually use them. Therefore they ask Tsongkhapa, "Why undergo the difficulties involved in rejecting the use of autonomous syllogisms?"

Tsongkhapa responds that although the opponents correctly refer to a passage in Nāgārjuna's *Refutation of Objections* that says Mādhyamikas have no thesis or position, there are many other sections of this text that say assertions must be made. How can merely quoting this one passage prove that Mādhyamikas have no position? There may indeed be some question as to whether someone is a Svātantrika if he or she holds the thesis that things do not exist inherently and uses autonomous syllogisms to prove it. This is a more difficult question involving a very subtle point, so Tsongkhapa says he will answer it later when discussing the views of Bhāvaviveka and establishing his own position.

In reference to Nāgārjuna's statement in *Refutation of Objections* that he has no thesis, we have to recall that Mādhyamikas assert that things have no inherent existence. The Buddhist Realist[114] schools respond that Nāgārjuna cannot claim that everything lacks inherent existence. In their view, if his words can prove or refute anything, they must inherently exist. If words had no inherent existence, then they would not exist at all and could not function in any way. In that case, words could not refute inherent existence. Tsongkhapa observes that other passages in *Refutation of Objections* and its commentary, which were cited earlier, say that even if words are not inherently existent they can function to prove or refute something. In the context of this statement, Nāgārjuna is not discussing whether Mādhyamikas have a thesis in general; the debate concerns whether the words expressing the thesis that there is no inherent existence are themselves inherently existent. Nāgārjuna says that if he accepted that words exist inherently, then he would be contradicting his thesis that nothing exists inherently. However, he does not succumb to such a fault because he does not accept that words are inherently existent. There is a vast difference between "not existing" and "not existing inherently." Therefore the passage that the opponents cite above does not prove that Mādhyamikas do not have a thesis.

In *Refutation of Objections*, Nāgārjuna seems to say that there is nothing known:

> If by direct perception and so on
> An object were really known,

Then it must be proved or refuted.
But that does not occur; thus I am blameless.

However, in chapter 7 we saw that Candrakīrti's *Clear Words* says that valid knowledge and its object are not established as an inherently existent perceiver and perceived,[115] yet this does not mean that they do not exist. Valid knowledge and its object are mutually dependent and therefore existent, but not inherently existent. According to the opponents, the Madhyamaka view is untenable. They concede that, having established a thing's inherent nature by direct perception, it may be possible to negate it; but because Mādhyamikas say "All things are empty of inherent existence," this must apply also to direct perception and its object. In other words, because a perceiver and what is perceived are included in "all things," they too must be empty of inherent existence and therefore totally nonexistent. Something that does not exist cannot prove or refute something else. In support of their argument the opponents cite a passage from *Refutation of Objections* that sets forth the Realist view:

> If the things known by direct
> Perception were negated,
> There would be no direct perception
> Knowing those things.

The *Commentary* on this passage expands the Realist argument against the Madhyamaka position:

> If you think you can negate all things known by direct perception, claiming "All things are empty," then you are mistaken. Why? Valid direct perception itself is included within "all things," so it too would be empty, and any act of perceiving things would also be empty. Thus there would be no valid knowledge. Without that, negation is impossible. Therefore any claim that all things are empty is incorrect.

Candrakīrti's commentary on Āryadeva's *Four Hundred Stanzas* explains the verse containing the line "Regarding existence, nonexistence, or both" as showing that no matter how long you try to refute those who propound emptiness, you cannot do so. Here Tsongkhapa inserts a challenge to the opponents: "How can you cite these great texts to prove that Mādhyamikas do not assert anything, not even emptiness?" The works quoted above clearly demonstrate that Mādhyamikas have particular views, and that they specifically assert that everything is empty of inherent existence. This cannot be refuted. Candrakīrti explains in *Commentary on the "Introduction to the 'Middle Way'"*:

Those who propound that things are imputedly existent cannot propound dualism; therefore those who respond by refuting dualism
cannot fault the Madhyamaka position at all. As the four lines of Āryadeva say:

> Even if you try for a very long time,
> You cannot demonstrate any fault
> In those who have no position
> Regarding existence, nonexistence, or both.

Candrakīrti refers to this stanza to explain that neither Realists, who accept
things to be inherently existent, nor Nihilists, who negate the functionality of
everything, can refute those who accept dependently imputed existence while
rejecting substantial or inherent existence. This passage is clearly addressing
those who hold one of the four extreme positions and those who propound
a dualistic position. Therefore it is not correct to use this quotation to try to
prove that Mādhyamikas do not have any position of their own. This is similar
to earlier occasions where quotations from the commentaries have been used
to negate the four extremes and refute those who propound inherent existence
or total nonexistence. These passages, and the context in which they appear,
need to be examined carefully (see chapter 9).

Candrakīrti's commentary on a similar passage in Nāgārjuna's *Sixty Stanzas of Reasoning* (see chapter 13) says:

> Since there are no such things, it is impossible for there to be one's own
> or another's position; the afflictions of those who see it this way will
> definitely cease.

Here "things" refers to inherently existent things. To say that there are no such
things indicates that there are no things that exist by way of their own characteristics. In certain other contexts, the phrase "no things" might indicate that
functional things are totally nonexistent. However, that is not the meaning
here because seeing functional things as nonexistent is not an antidote to the
mental afflictions. In this passage, "no things" is the reason proving that there
is no position, whether of the Mādhyamikas or others, which accepts inherently existent things, or things that exist by way of their own characteristics.
This is also made clear in an earlier part of Candrakīrti's *Commentary on the
"Sixty Stanzas of Reasoning"*:

> Those who have not understood the depth of this reality of dependent
> arising are convinced that things exist by their own characteristics:

> If they accept things as real,
> They are holding an almost irremovable view
> That gives rise to attachment and hatred
> And will result in disputation.

Those who have not properly understood śūnyatā cannot see the depth of the truth of dependent arising, just as one cannot judge the depth of a body of water merely by looking at the surface. As a result, they totally believe that things exist by their own characteristics. This passage is addressing the Realists, who think that things are truly existent. Here "accept things as real" means imagining that things exist by way of their own characteristics.

Thus none of the texts cited here show that Mādhyamikas have no system or make no assertions. You should understand these texts in accordance with Candrakīrti's explanation in *Clear Words*, where he quotes the *Refutation of Objections* and the *Four Hundred Stanzas*, saying, "Because we do not accept that there are others' positions" (see chapter 13). Moreover, although it looks as though Nāgārjuna is saying that Mādhyamikas do not negate anything in *Refutation of Objections*, when he says, "Since there is nothing to be negated, I do not negate anything," that is not a correct interpretation of this passage. As touched on earlier, there are two objects of negation: the subjective object of negation, which is the wrong view grasping things as inherently existent, and the objective object of negation, which is what is held to be inherently existent by that wrong view. When Nāgārjuna says, "Since there is nothing to be negated," he is referring to only one of these. It would make no sense if he were referring to the objective object of negation; he is not saying that because an inherently existent thing does not exist, I do not negate anything. This passage refers to the subjective object of negation: the wrong view that grasps things to be inherently existent. This fabricating mind holds as existent that which does not exist. So this wrong view must be negated.

THE NEGATION OF INHERENT NATURE IS ONLY CONVENTIONALLY EXISTENT

The point is that we do not get rid of this wrong view by means of an inherently existent negation. Candrakīrti's commentary on this passage shows that there is no inherently existent negating agent or thing negated. Also, there is no inherent negating of the object of negation. Holding (a) the subjective object of negation, (b) its antidote, and (c) the act of negating to be inherently existent must itself be negated by the wisdom realizing emptiness. Thus we should understand this passage to mean: since there is no inherently existent object[116] to be negated, I do not inherently negate anything. The Realists deprecate Nāgārjuna's views by saying that he holds the negating agent and the negated object to be inherently existent and then negates them in an inherently existent manner.

When a yogi meditates on śūnyatā, he or she recognizes that neither the object to be destroyed (the mental afflictions along with their seeds and imprints) nor the antidote that destroys them (the wisdom realizing śūnyatā) is inherently existent. They both have an illusion-like nature. In *Refutation of Objections*, Nāgārjuna asserts that the objective and subjective objects of negation are like illusions:

> Just as a magical emanation can emanate,
> And an illusory being can stop
> An illusion by illusory means,
> So it is with this refutation.

There is a story about a man who developed attachment for a magically created woman. An emanation of Buddha showed this man how inappropriate it is to be attached to an illusion. This enabled the man to destroy his wrong perception. Likewise, just as an emanation can accomplish something within its own sphere of reality, this refutation can negate wrong views. It does not need to be truly existent in order to function. The *Refutation of Objections* continues:

> If that grasping were inherently existent,
> It could not arise dependently.
> Any grasping that arises dependently
> Is empty, is it not?
>
> If grasping were inherently existent,
> Then who could reverse that grasping?
> This is the way to understand everything else;
> Therefore there is no retort.

The naturally arising mind of ignorance grasps things to be inherently existent. The functioning of ignorance leaves imprints on the mindstream that give rise to the appearance of inherent existence. Owing to this process, everything appears inherently existent to sentient beings—except when they are directly realizing śūnyatā. Now if things were inherently existent as they appear, then they would exist by their own nature, independently, and without depending on causes and conditions. There would be no cause of their arising and no cause of their cessation. They would be permanently existent. So if things were inherently existent, how could anyone ever destroy them? For example, if the apprehension of a mirage as real water existed inherently, it would not arise in dependence on causes and conditions. In that case, no one could recognize that this apprehension of water was mistaken. We have been affected since time without beginning by mental afflictions, their seeds, and the imprints they leave on our mindstreams. Mental afflictions arise from their seeds in conjunction with certain other causes and conditions. When these causes and conditions are present, mental afflictions arise; when these causes and conditions are not present, they do not arise. Because the mental afflictions arise dependently, they can be destroyed; their seeds can be removed and eventually so can their imprints. According to Nāgārjuna, we should understand everything to dependently arise in the same way. No one can find any fault with this view; there is no overturning this understanding.

Also, the passage in Candrakīrti's *Clear Words* that says "because we do not have any thesis" cannot be used to prove that the Mādhyamikas have no system of their own. This passage occurs in a discussion of a thesis that is established by an autonomous syllogism instantiating the three modes. In that context, these words mean that Mādhyamikas have no inherently established theses. Candrakīrti is not referring simply to a thesis existing within one's mental continuum. Similarly, when Candrakīrti says in *Introduction to the "Middle Way"* that he has no position, he means that within the Madhyamaka system neither the wrong view that is being refuted nor the arguments refuting it are inherently existent. Candrakīrti challenges the Realists to examine whether, in a logical refutation, there is contact between the position being refuted and the reasoning refuting it.

This is part of the larger question about how causes give rise to their effects. For example, when heat destroys the chill in a room, is there contact between the heat and the cold? If things were inherently existent, as the Realists claim, then we would find them by means of ultimate analysis. In response to this, Candrakīrti asks a series of questions. When a cause produces a result, do the two actually come into contact? Is the cause present when the result arises? Or has the cause ceased by the time the result arises? If cause and effect were ultimately existent, then, by definition, they would exist by their own nature. If something is a cause in an inherent sense, then its result must exist at the same time. Why? Because if the result did not exist, there would be nothing of which we could say it is a cause. But how can a result already exist at the time of its cause? If a result already exists, then the cause is not really its cause. These conundrums arise if one believes that causes and their effects are ultimately existent. No such problems occur if we accept that a cause and its result are merely relatively existent; they are dependently related as cause and effect and do not exist by their own nature. Because they exist nominally and dependently, but not ultimately, we can say that at the time of the cause its result has not yet arisen, and at the time of the result its cause has already ceased.

This ultimate analysis, regarding whether two things contact each other or not, may also be applied to a refutation and the position it refutes, a proof and the position proved, or a producer and what it produces. Because Mādhyamikas do not accept that things such as the cause and the effect, the proof and the proved, or the destroyer and the destroyed exist in an ultimate sense, they do not have to assert that these things can withstand examination by ultimate analysis. The Madhyamaka system accepts that these things are dependently related. So Candrakīrti's statement "I do not have a position" means that the Mādhyamikas have no inherently established position. It does not mean that the Mādhyamikas have no system at all. Therefore the faults revealed by this kind of analysis, which apply to the Realists' positions, do not apply to the great Mādhyamikas. The reason is given in Candrakīrti's *Commentary on the "Introduction to the 'Middle Way'"*:

> The same fault is not entailed for our position because, according to our system, the refutation does not refute what is refuted by making contact, and the refutation does not refute what is refuted without making contact. This is because neither the refutation nor what is refuted inherently exists. Therefore we do not think that they make contact or do not make contact.

Here Candrakīrti states why the Mādhyamikas are not faulted, like the Realists, by this ultimate analysis: it is because things do not inherently exist, not because "we have no assertions" as some earlier Mādhyamikas claim—for that is not an effective reason. Candrakīrti explains that functional things, including the elements of reasoning, cannot be found by ultimate analysis—because they do not inherently exist. If anything inherently existed, then ultimate analysis would reveal it to be independent and static. He also explains that a proof and what is proved, and a refutation and what it refutes, are able to function—because they exist dependently or relatively.

In support of this Candrakīrti cites the *Perfection of Wisdom Sutra in Twenty-Five Thousand Lines*, where Śāriputra asks Subhūti, "Will an attainment that has not yet arisen be attained by means of a realization that has already arisen or by means of a realization that has not yet arisen?" Attainment by each of these is then refuted. So Śāriputra asks, "If neither a realization already arisen nor a realization not yet arisen gives rise to an attainment in the future, then is there no attainment and no realization?" The response, as we have seen earlier, is that these exist conventionally but not ultimately (see chapter 12). Liberation, spiritual attainments, and the meditative realizations that lead to them all exist. These exist dependently but not ultimately or inherently. If they were inherently existent, they would not be able to function. So the Mādhyamikas say "There is no attainment and no clear realization" to those who assume that things are inherently existent. In other words, attainments and realizations do not exist in the manner of the two extremes; they are neither ultimately existent nor completely nonexistent. In between those two extremes, dependently arising things—both those that have already arisen and those that are yet to arise—give rise to realizations and attainments. Candra-kīrti's *Commentary on the "Introduction to the 'Middle Way'"* says:

> This passage denies any attaining of an attainment by something already arisen or not yet arisen because that would lead to the two extremes. Since it is not correct that these two are totally nonexistent, attainment is accepted conventionally without analysis. Likewise, although the refutation and what is refuted are not posited in terms of having contact or not having contact, conventionally the refutation refutes the refuted. This is what you should understand it to be saying.

This passage clearly shows that if we analyze whether a refutation comes in contact or lacks contact with what it refutes, we find that it does not exist in either way—because this analysis is searching for inherent contact or lack of it. So a refutation does not exist ultimately. However, this analysis does not negate the existence of a refutation in general. One must accept that Mādhyamikas conventionally refute others' positions and assert their own position. It is wrong to hold that Mādhyamikas do not have any assertions. Moreover, Mādhyamikas also accept that a logical reason proves the thesis of a syllogism. The thesis, or probandum, of a syllogism is the conjunction of the subject and the predicate. For example, in the thesis "Things are not truly existent," the subject is "things," and the quality predicated to belong to the subject is "a lack of true existence." Mādhyamikas accept this thesis and the relationship between the thesis and the reason proving it. Tsongkhapa establishes this by quoting the passage that immediately follows the preceding one in Candra-kīrti's commentary:

> Although you can see the qualities of the orb of the sun,
> Such as an eclipse, in a reflection of the event,

> You cannot ask whether the sun and its reflection come into contact,
> For a reflection arises merely conventionally and dependently.
>
> And just as [a reflection] is not truly existent yet, because it can be used
>   for beautifying your face,
> It exists, so in the very same way the face of wisdom
> Can be purified by an inferential seeing of the truth,
> Which although free of being [inherently] correct, realizes the object to
>   be proved.

That is how it should be understood. Since what is called a "reflection" does not exist [as the reflected object] in the slightest, there is no possibility of conceiving of it to arise either having contact or lacking contact with the orb of the sun. Yet from its condition, a form, you see a reflection and can understand what you want to know. Likewise, a refutation that is empty of inherent existence refutes what is to be refuted; a reason that is empty of inherent existence and free of being [inherently] correct proves what is to be proved. Since this does not lead to the two extremes, it is not correct that our words succumb to faults similar to yours. That is how it should be understood.

Candrakīrti's opponents believe that things exist ultimately and thus merit ultimate analysis as to whether or not a subject and object meet. As we have seen, their view entails certain faults. The opponents contend that if these faults apply to their own position, they also apply to the Mādhyamikas' position. Candrakīrti disagrees and explains that for the Mādhyamikas, a reason that is empty of inherent existence can prove what is to be proved or refute what is to be refuted, without entailing the faults arising from the opponents' views. A Madhyamaka refutation or proof does not imply that things either truly exist or do not exist at all. So the refutation used against the opponents cannot be turned back against the Mādhyamikas themselves. To illustrate how a reason that does not exist as it appears can nevertheless prove or refute a wrong view, Candrakīrti gives two examples: an eclipse and a reflection in a mirror.

There is an ancient custom whereby some people believe that a solar eclipse is caused by a celestial being, Rāhula, eating the sun; Rāhula has a big hole in his throat, so when he swallows the sun, it soon slips out of the opening. This belief has continued until modern times. When I was young, I really thought that the poor old sun was being eaten in the sky. Many people were frightened by eclipses. Some people would blow horns, and others would cry loudly, "Please stop! Let go of the sun!" Out in the wilds of Tibet, and perhaps India, some religious practitioners believe that if they engage in Dharma practice while the sun is being consumed, the power of their Dharma practice will increase hundreds of times. Such a view can be beneficial; if you believe it, you will do serious religious practice for the duration of the eclipse. It seems that contemporary Westerners have too much education; they do not do anything special during that time.

In an eclipse it looks as though Rāhula's contact with the sun is making it smaller and smaller until it disappears. This appearance suggests that we could find, in an ultimate sense, where the contact between those two actually exists. However, this is impossible because what we are seeing is just a reflection or shadow that appears owing to certain causes and conditions, including our position, the trajectory of the sun and the moon, their shadows, and so on. A big event is taking place on a conventional level, but it does not exist in the way that it appears. Yet based on this false appearance, which is just a reflection, we can consider the event and respond to it accordingly.

Candrakīrti's second example is the functionality of a reflection in a mirror. You can use a reflection of your face in order to clean your face, apply makeup, and so on, even though your face is not actually there before you. The reflection does not exist as it appears—it does not exist as your face from its own side—yet it can show you your face in dependence on certain conditions, such as clear glass, light, and your position in front of the mirror. In the same way, a correct logical reason does not exist as it appears—it does not exist inherently—yet it can give rise to insight in dependence on certain conditions. By using reasoning we remove wrong views and come to understand the emptiness of inherent existence. That logic is free of inherent existence; it has no inherent correctness. The refutation, what is refuted, and the act of refuting are all dependently existent. A reason does not exist from its own side, yet a reason that is empty of inherent existence and lacks inherent correctness can refute wrong views or prove a position, and it can purify the mind. Candrakīrti is not saying that the Mādhyamikas have no system—for they do have theses, assertions, and views. They succeed in refuting others, establishing their own position, and supporting their arguments with relevant sources. However, because they show that everything is dependently existent, their views and arguments do not lead to the extremes of eternalism or nihilism. This kind of conventionally existent reasoning can be used to refute the opponent's acceptance of inherent existence yet not negate the Madhyamaka view that nothing inherently exists.

Furthermore, those who accept inherently existent causes and effects should engage in the ultimate analysis of causation—investigating whether a cause arises in contact or lacking contact with its result. Their views will be negated by what this analysis reveals. But this analysis does not rebound on the Mādhyamikas themselves—not because the Mādhyamikas have no system of their own, but because they accept that nothing is inherently existent. That is the main point here. Candrakīrti's *Commentary on the "Introduction to the 'Middle Way'"* says:

> So how do we explain it?
>
>> It is because both [cause and effect] are like illusions
>> That for us those faults do not occur, and worldly things exist.
>
> According to those who accept inherent producers and produced objects, this analysis will entail such faults. But according to those who accept that things are like illusions, being produced by distorted imputation and not produced inherently—and yet, although not inherently existent, are the objects of such conceiving, like falling hairs seen by a defective visual consciousness—it is impossible to think in those terms. Therefore, since there is no opportunity for the faults explained here to apply to us, and since worldly things exist when left unanalyzed, everything is established.

Candrakīrti is saying here that the faults revealed by ultimate analysis apply to others because they accept things to exist by their own characteristics; but these faults do not apply to the Mādhyamikas because they accept things to be like an illusion. When you understand this, you will know how to establish the Madhyamaka system as free of such faults leading to the extremes. Otherwise, you may claim to be a Mādhyamika and find fault with others' systems, yet you have no defense when your own arguments are turned around and directed back at you. That would be the worst kind of logical error.

There are innumerable statements in the definitive scriptures and Madhyamaka commentaries in the form "It is like this and not like that" and "This exists and that does not exist." So clearly one cannot say that the Mādhyamikas do not have views or assertions. In general these statements express the views of their author. What need is there to prove this by citing other passages by the same author? If that were necessary, we would not be able to distinguish between an author's view and his opponent's view in passages lacking such phrases as "I assert this" or "I accept that." Nevertheless, if you think that an author has to say words such as "I believe," "I accept," or "I assert" to express his view, there are many such instances. For example, Nāgārjuna says in *Refutation of Objections*:

> We do not explain anything
> Without accepting conventional things.

An in *Sixty Stanzas of Reasoning*, Nāgārjuna says:

> Just as the disintegration of an arisen thing
> Is labeled a "cessation,"
> Similarly, the wise ones consider
> Cessation to be like an illusion.

In this passage, "cessation" refers to the absence of the mental afflictions and their seeds, the continuum of which is stopped by specific antidotes produced in the mindstream through meditation. Wise beings understand that this true cessation is like an illusion. They do not accept any ultimate cessation or production. The same text says:

> Whoever believes that dependently arising things
> Are like a reflection of the moon in water—
> Neither truly existent nor totally nonexistent—
> Will not be captivated by views.

The reflection of the moon in a pool of water does not exist from its own side. It appears in dependence on many causes and conditions: the moon in the sky, clear water beneath it, no obstacle in between, and so forth. Only when such conditions are present will a vivid reflection of the moon appear. It will not appear by itself without these conditions. Although the reflection does not exist from its own side, it does exist. Those who accept that things are like this, neither inherently existent nor totally nonexistent, will not be captivated by wrong views. Nāgārjuna's *Praise of the Transcendent One* says:

> Whatever arises from causes
> Cannot exist without them;
> So why not accept it
> As clearly like a reflection?

And further:

> Without its object there is no feeling;
> So feeling is not self-existent;
> You [Buddha] accept that feeling
> Does not exist inherently.

We all experience feeling; feeling is one of the five aggregates. When we meet with an attractive object we experience a pleasant feeling; when we come across an unattractive object we experience an unpleasant feeling; when we encounter a neutral object we experience a neutral feeling. For a pleasant feeling to arise we must encounter an object, such as delicious food, that acts as its condition. Without such an object we do not experience that pleasant feeling. Thus feeling does not exist by its own nature. Nāgārjuna praises Buddha, for only he accepts that feeling exists in relation to the one that feels, the act of feeling, and the object felt, and thus all of these are empty of inherent existence. In contrast, others believe that these things are inherently real and that there is ultimate causality. The same text says:

> You teach that the agent
> And the object of action are conventional.
> You accept them to be established
> Dependently on each other.

Without an agent, there is no action and no object of action; without an object of action, there is no agent and no action; and without action, there is no agent or object of action. None of these exist independently of the others. Buddha accepts them to be mutually, dependently established. The same text says:

> Only you accept that a result cannot arise
> From a cause that is already destroyed
> Nor from one not yet destroyed,   .
> But is produced as in a dream.

Among spiritual teachers, only Buddha accepts that there is no inherent arising. Buddha teaches that production occurs in an illusion-like way, as in a dream with no real or substantial events, causes, or effects. Other teachers accept things to be inherently real and that cause and effect ultimately exist. The same text says:

> Whatever dependently arises
> You accept to be empty.

Nāgārjuna says that Śākyamuni Buddha's most striking doctrine is that whatever arises in dependence on causes and conditions thereby lacks inherent existence. Other religious teachers say that things are truly existent because they arise from causes and conditions. The very reasons that others use to prove that things are truly existent Buddha uses to prove the opposite. He uses dependent arising as a reason to demonstrate that things are empty of inherent existence.

Candrakīrti's *Commentary on the "Introduction to the 'Middle Way'"* says:

> The masters consider this position to be faultless and beneficial. So it should be accepted without hesitation.

Thus the founder of the Prāsaṅgika system clearly states that there is a position to be accepted. The same text says:

> Because we accept that things are dependently imputed, just as we accept mere dependently arising conditionality, our position does not entail the annihilation of conventional things. Others should accept this also.

This is Candrakīrti's answer to accusations that he is a nihilist because he believes that things are not inherently existent. He clearly states that certain things should be accepted and advises the proponents of lower systems to accept them too. There are many other passages like this. For example, the same text says:

> Having stated the four theses, in order to logically prove them we say:
>
> It does not arise from itself; how could it arise from others?
> It does not arise from both; how could it do so without a cause?

Here, Candrakīrti quotes two lines from his *Introduction to the "Middle Way,"* which refer to the first stanza of Nāgārjuna's *Fundamental Treatise*:

> Not from self, not from others,
> Not from both, not without a cause;
> Any things, anywhere,
> Do not arise at any time.

Candrakīrti disagrees with the way that Bhāvaviveka interprets the logical structure of Nāgārjuna's argument here. Bhāvaviveka presents the argument in the form of a syllogism, specifically as a thesis with a fourfold reason. The subject of the syllogism is "Any things." The predicate is "Anywhere, do not arise at any time." So the thesis is "Any things, anywhere, do not arise at any time." Bhāvaviveka says that this is proved by the fourfold reason "Because they do not arise from self, from others, from both, or without a cause." He further argues that the qualifier "ultimately" must be applied to the predicate

"Anywhere, do not arise 'ultimately' at any time." He uses this syllogism to refute ultimate arising. If a thing arises ultimately, then it must arise either from self, or from others, or from both, or without a cause. It must arise in one of those four alternative ways. But nothing arises in any of those ways. Therefore nothing arises ultimately.

However, in *Ocean of Reasoning*, Tsongkhapa shows that Candrakīrti does not interpret the logical structure of Nāgārjuna's argument in this way. He quotes Candrakīrti's *Commentary on the "Introduction to the 'Middle Way'"*:

> The final phrase "do not" is connected with "arise from self," which is used as a reason for true existence, and not with "exist," because the negation of the latter is established indirectly.[117]

Candrakīrti is saying here that the negating phrase is applied to arising from self and so on, because by negating the four ways of arising you indirectly negate true existence. This does not negate true existence directly. Tsongkhapa refers to this passage to show that Candrakīrti does not interpret this stanza as a syllogism in which the reason "Not from self, not from others, not from both, and not without a cause" proves the thesis "Any things, anywhere, do not arise at any time." Instead we must apply the phrase "do not arise" from the fourth line to all four positions stated in the first two lines: from self, from others, from both, or without a cause. In short, we should understand this stanza to propose four theses:

1. Any things, anywhere, do not arise at any time from self.
2. Any things, anywhere, do not arise at any time from others.
3. Any things, anywhere, do not arise at any time from both.
4. Any things, anywhere, do not arise at any time without a cause.

Nāgārjuna proves these four theses one by one later in the text. They can then be used as reasons to demonstrate that there is no ultimate arising. Although they will later function as the main proof to refute truly existent production, first each one must be treated as a thesis and proved by other reasons. We have to show why things do not arise from self, from others, from both, or without a cause, because other schools use these as reasons to prove that things are truly existent and that there is ultimate production. For example, the Svātantrika-Mādhyamikas and lower Buddhist schools say that inherently existent other causes produce inherently existent other results. Among the non-Buddhists, the Sāṃkhyas say that a thing ultimately arises from itself, the Jains say that things are produced from both self and others, and the Cārvākas say that everything arises without a cause. Each system gives reasons to prove true existence or ultimate production. The reasons that they use to prove inherent existence we then use in reverse to prove the emptiness of inherent existence, and only then can we refute ultimate production using the summary argument: "If things were to arise ultimately, then they would arise from self, from others, from both, or without a cause; because they do not arise from any of these, they do not arise ultimately."

Tsongkhapa quotes this passage to show that Candrakīrti clearly says that these positions must be expressed as four theses. Therefore the opponents cannot say that the Mādhyamikas have no theses.

(4')) Refuting the fourth misinterpretation

It seems that these scholars accept inherent existence conventionally, and yet they deny that it is able to bear ultimate analysis conventionally. This is wrong. As explained earlier, if inherent nature is accepted conventionally it must be able to bear ultimate analysis (see chapter 7).

These scholars also believe that according to the system of Candrakīrti, the Mādhyamikas prove something to their Realist opponents using an inference for another's purpose, employing a reason that instantiates the three modes established by both the proponent and the opponent. However, this is not correct because in *Clear Words* Candrakīrti pointedly rejects Bhāvaviveka's use of such syllogisms. In fact, he rejects the possibility of any debate using a mutually accepted subject and reason that instantiates the three modes, when one party accepts things to be truly existent and the other party rejects true existence. He further argues that if you accept this kind of syllogism, then you are committed to accepting all the characteristics of an autonomous logical reason, even if you do not use terminology such as "a reason proved by the power of reality." For example, the lower schools, such as the Sautrāntika and the Yogācāra followers of reasoning, accept that an inherently existent reason has the power to prove a thesis by its own nature. Such a reason proves its thesis objectively through the power of reality.[118]

The meaning, as well as the implications, of accepting autonomous syllogisms and autonomous reasons will be dealt with in the context of differentiating between the logical methods used by the Svātantrika and the Prāsaṅgika systems to refute arising from self. There we will examine Candrakīrti's powerful refutation of this kind of logic in great detail (see chapter 15). For now, Tsongkhapa says it is sufficient to note that it is completely wrong to claim that, according to Candrakīrti's system, Mādhyamikas try to prove a thesis to their opponents by using inferences for another's purpose rather than using consequences.

⊹ 15 ⊱

Our Interpretation of the Svātantrika/Prāsaṅgika Distinction

(2)) Presenting our own system
    (a')) Actually refuting autonomous argument
        (1')) Demonstrating the fault of the subject: the basic subject is not
            established
            (a")) Stating others' assertions
            (b")) Refuting others' assertions
                (1")) The meaning is incorrect
                (2")) The example cited does not match
        (2')) Demonstrating that, owing to that fault, the reason also is not
            established

---

(2)) Presenting Our Own System

TSONGKHAPA SAYS that in order to present the Prāsaṅgika system he will explain how the Prāsaṅgikas refute the Svātantrika system, because this informs us about both those systems. We may find it helpful to review some of the background to this discussion. The Madhyamaka system aims to establish a genuine understanding of śūnyatā. One way to do this is to refute the four extremes of production—that a thing arises from itself, from other causes, from both, or without a cause—and then use these four refutations together as a reason to refute ultimate production. In *Clear Words*, first Candrakīrti presents an extensive explanation of how Buddhapālita interprets each of these negations to have the form of logical consequences mainly. Next he presents Bhāvaviveka's criticisms of Buddhapālita's methodology: Bhāvaviveka finds fault with the latter's presentation of these negations as consequences and argues that the meditator here needs to use autonomous syllogisms. Finally,

Candrakīrti shows how the faults identified by Bhāvaviveka simply do not apply to Buddhapālita's use of consequences but in fact apply to Bhāvaviveka's own use of autonomous syllogisms. Based on quotations from Bhāvaviveka's works presenting the Svātantrika system and from Buddhapālita's works presenting the Prāsaṅgika system, Candrakīrti demonstrates how the latter is correct. Tsongkhapa is reluctant to include all this discussion here for fear of going on too long, so he presents the main points assembled into two topics:

(a')) Actually refuting autonomous argument
(b')) Why those faults do not apply similarly to our own system (chapter 16)

(a')) ACTUALLY REFUTING AUTONOMOUS ARGUMENT

Tsongkhapa's refutation of autonomous syllogisms has two divisions:

(1')) Demonstrating the fault of the subject: the basic subject is not established
(2')) Demonstrating that, owing to that fault, the reason also is not established

Svātantrikas accept the entire logical system presented by Dharmakīrti, which includes the use of autonomous syllogisms. We need to understand the difference between a syllogism and an autonomous syllogism. In general, a syllogism has the following form: the *subject* is the *predicate* because it is the *reason*. For example, a sprout is impermanent because it is produced. A syllogism is valid if, and only if, it fulfills specific criteria known as the three modes: both parties in the debate must know that the particular reason given is a property of that subject, and they must know that if something is that reason then it must be that predicate, and if it is not that predicate then it cannot be that reason. The latter two are, respectively, the forward and the reverse pervasions. This means that the syllogism must instantiate the three modes, which are three basic elements of understanding. These three basic elements of understanding are arranged in a specific way so as to generate a further understanding—namely, that the subject of that syllogism is the predicate. This is what the syllogism is set forth to prove; here, *to prove* means to engender further understanding. An autonomous syllogism requires that all the elements of the syllogism are held in common by both parties; in other words, they must be understood by the same kind of valid knowing.

A syllogism that fails to instantiate the three modes is faulty. Consider, for example, the first mode—that the reason is known to be a property of the subject.[119] If one of the two parties simply does not know the subject or does not know that the reason is an attribute of the subject, the syllogism cannot function to prove its thesis. One of the basic elements of understanding that is required is absent, so the further understanding cannot be generated. This is called "the fault of not establishing the property of the subject." A syllogism also succumbs to this fault when the subject is not established in common by both the proponent and the opponent. The Prāsaṅgika and the lower schools do not agree about what it means for a subject to be held in common. According to the lower schools, both the proponent and the opponent must similarly establish the subject by valid knowledge that is unmistaken with regard to its inherent nature. However, the Prāsaṅgikas do not accept that anything has an inherent nature—so they do not agree with the lower schools about what constitutes valid knowledge. These are crucial points of debate that will be explained below.

(1')) DEMONSTRATING THE FAULT OF THE SUBJECT: THE BASIC SUBJECT IS NOT ESTABLISHED

This section has two divisions:

(a")) Stating others' assertions
(b")) Refuting others' assertions

(a")) STATING OTHERS' ASSERTIONS

Candrakīrti's discussion of this topic in *Clear Words* is very full and rich. However, it is hard to understand, so Tsongkhapa undertakes to present a detailed explanation of his words. Candrakīrti begins by outlining Bhāvaviveka's position:

> This is how it should be. In the thesis "sound is impermanent," both the subject and the predicate are held in a general sense, not as qualified in a particular way. If they were held as qualified, there would be no accepted convention regarding the thing to be proved and the reason proving it. For if "sound that is arisen from the four great elements" is held to be the subject, then it is not established according to the opponent. But if "sound as a quality of space" is held to be the subject, then it is not established according to us Buddhists. Similarly, for the Vaiśeṣikas, if "produced sound" is held to be the subject of the thesis "sound is impermanent," it is not established according to their opponents;

but if "[sound] to be manifested" is held to be the subject, then it is not established according to themselves. Likewise, in each respective case, if "perishes having another cause" is used, then it is not established according to us Buddhists; but if "perishes not having another cause" is used, then it is not established according to the opponent. Therefore, just as previously the subject and attribute apprehended are merely general, so here a mere subject without a qualifier is to be apprehended.

In any valid syllogism there must be a commonly agreed-on subject—the basis on which the proponent tries to prove something to his or her opponent. Bhāvaviveka argues that in the syllogism "Sound is impermanent because it is produced," the subject must be sound in general rather than a particular notion of sound. If the subject, sound, were qualified in a particular way, then neither party would accept the subject put forward by the other party, and nothing could be proved.

The first example is a debate between Buddhists and certain non-Buddhists—though the school is not specified here. Tsongkhapa suggests it may be the Vaiśeṣikas. The Vaiśeṣikas believe that all objects are included within six categories: substance, quality, function, generality, particularity, and conjunction. Each of these is subdivided. For example, there are nine substances and twenty-four qualities. These qualities are the attributes of specific substances. The Vaiśeṣikas consider that sound is a quality of space and does not arise from the four atomic elements. Buddhists believe that sound, like objects of the other physical senses, arises from a combination of the four great elements—earth, fire, water, and wind. So Buddhists and Vaiśeṣikas have quite different notions of sound. If each party in a debate sets forth his or her own particular notion of sound as the subject of the syllogism, then the syllogism would not be acceptable to the other party. None of the three modes would be established by both parties, so neither party could prove anything to the other.

The second example is a debate between the Vaiśeṣikas and the Sāṃkhyas; both these schools are explicitly indicated here. The Sāṃkhyas believe that sound already exists in its cause in an unmanifest state; it is made manifest by other conditions. The Vaiśeṣikas consider that sound is freshly created; it does not already exist in its cause. So if one of these notions of sound, qualified in a particular way, were set forth as the subject of the syllogism, it would not be acceptable to the other party. When the first mode of the syllogism cannot be established, then nothing can function as a thesis, so nothing can act as a reason for it. Therefore the subject must be established as commonly appearing to both the opponent and the proponent. Because mere sound can be accepted in common by both parties, the subject of this syllogism should be the general notion of sound rather than one qualified in any particular way.

Using the same syllogism, Bhāvaviveka then gives an example showing that the attribute predicated to belong to the subject must also be held in general by both parties. In the thesis "sound is impermanent," we have the subject "sound" and the predicate "is impermanent" or "perishes." Buddhists believe that all produced things are impermanent; things arise, abide, and cease moment by moment. Produced things exist only for an instant—if they lasted longer they would be permanent.

Now I want to ask you a question: Is the perishing of a produced thing dependent on another cause or does a produced thing have the cause of its perishing already within the cause of its arising? Most Buddhists say that arising, abiding, and perishing are the nature of all produced things. The upper Buddhist schools say that these processes occur at the same time: a functional thing arises, abides, and perishes each moment throughout its existence. This subtle disintegration is not dependent on some other cause; it is a quality of all products. As soon as you are born, you are already disintegrating. Although every produced thing is in the process of perishing, this does not mean that it has already perished.

In contrast, some Vaibhāṣikas say that these processes occur sequentially: first a thing arises, then it abides, and finally it perishes. This is a description of gross impermanence. Here, in a gross sense, perishing depends on some other cause: first a porcelain cup is made, it exists for a while, and then later as a result of another cause—perhaps a blow by a heavy object—it ceases to exist. You are produced from your parents, you live for a while, and then you die some time later owing to some other cause, such as sickness. Gross disintegration does not occur as soon as a cup or a child is produced; it depends on a cause that occurs later. In a gross sense, a produced thing does not perish merely upon its arising.

However, the upper Buddhist schools say that if perishing depended on another cause, then there could be a produced thing that permanently exists; it may never disintegrate because that cause might never occur. So they accept subtle impermanence, where disintegrating is not dependent on another cause. As soon as something, such as sound, comes into existence, it is already disintegrating. This occurs naturally owing to the cause of its arising; it does not need another cause for it to perish. So in a subtle sense, from the moment we are born we do not abide for more than an instant.

It is difficult to develop an understanding of subtle impermanence. We have to use logic to prove that a produced thing disintegrates immediately, without staying for more than a moment. Nevertheless, the Prāsaṅgikas say that an ordinary person can generate a specific type of mind—an ordinary yogic direct perceiver—that realizes subtle impermanence. Conversely, according to the Svātantrikas and below, only an ārya being can directly realize subtle impermanence. Bhāvaviveka is a Svātantrika, so from his point of view ordinary people cannot directly realize subtle impermanence, though they may understand it through logical inference.

Just as the subject must appear in common to both parties, the predicate must also be established in general, without being qualified in any particular way. If a predicate, such as "is impermanent," were qualified in a particular way, it would not be accepted by both parties. If the predicate of the thesis "sound is impermanent" were taken to be "perishes owing to another cause,"[120] it would not be acceptable to most Buddhists; if it were taken to be "perishes without having another cause,"[121] it would not be acceptable to the opponents. Also, before the thesis can be proved to the opponent, whatever is set as the example must be established as appearing in common to both parties.

This applies equally when the Mādhyamikas prove to the Sāṃkhyas that the subject—an internal source of sense consciousness, such as the eye sense power, or an external source of sense consciousness, such as a form—does not arise from itself, and when the Mādhyamikas prove to the Buddhist Realists that it does not arise from other causes ultimately.[122] If the subject of the proof were qualified according to any of these schools of thought, it would not be accepted as existent by the others. The Madhyamaka view is that everything is falsely existent, whereas the opponents' view is that everything is truly existent. If the subject were taken to be a "truly existent eye," it would not be acceptable to the Mādhyamikas, and if the subject were taken to be a "falsely existent eye," it would not be acceptable to the Sāṃkhyas or other Realists. Therefore a subject with those particular qualifications should be discarded; it should not be qualified as either being truly existent or falsely existent. We should use a mere eye in general, representing the internal subtle sense organs, or a mere form in general, representing the external sense objects. A mere eye or a mere form, without any particular qualification, can function for both Mādhyamikas and Realists as a basis that is analyzed as to whether or not it has a particular attribute, such as arising from itself or arising from other causes. To avoid any problems, Bhāvaviveka says that if any two people who hold different views debate with each other, a general subject that is established as appearing in common to both parties is necessary for any meaningful discussion to take place.

Now Tsongkhapa considers what it means for something to be established as appearing in common. According to Bhāvaviveka, it means that the proponent and the opponent establish something by the same kind of valid knowledge. However, this is not possible, according to Candrakīrti, because there is a big difference between the Prāsaṅgika-Madhyamaka and other schools regarding valid knowledge. Owing to this difference, it is impossible for them to find any element of a syllogism that is validly established in common. Prāsaṅgikas say that every sentient being's valid knowledge of a conventional thing is mistaken because its object appears to exist inherently. The lower systems contend that valid knowledge is never mistaken. If it were mistaken with regard to the inherent nature of its object, then it would not be valid knowledge. The refutation of Bhāvaviveka's view is the topic of the next section.

(b")) REFUTING OTHERS' ASSERTIONS

Tsongkhapa refutes Bhāvaviveka's position in two sections:

(1")) The meaning is incorrect
(2")) The example cited does not match

(1")) THE MEANING IS INCORRECT

While reading the following quotation from Candrakīrti's *Clear Words*, which continues from the above, we should bear in mind that the autonomous syllogism implicitly referred to is, "A visible form does not arise from itself because it exists, like the pot there in front of you."[123] Candrakīrti states:

> That is not so. For in accepting the negation of arising as the predicate of the thesis, he accepts that the subject that is its basis—which is something found only by mistaken [consciousness]—is denied ultimately. Mistaken and nonmistaken [minds] are very different. Therefore, as in the case of one with diseased eyes [seeing] falling hairs, when the mistaken holds the nonexistent to exist, how can there be the slightest perception of an object that exists? But, as in the case of one without diseased eyes [not seeing] falling hairs, when the nonmistaken does not reify the unreal, how can there be the slightest perception of an object that does not exist—[ordinarily perceived] by a conventional [mind]? For the master Nāgārjuna says:
>
>> If anything, owing to its nature, were known
>> By direct perception and so on,
>> Then that would be proved or refuted.
>> But that does not exist; thus I am not faulted.

Because mistaken and nonmistaken [minds] are very different with regard to that [appearance], the mistaken does not exist during the occurrence of the nonmistaken—so how could any [such inference] have a conventional eye as the subject? For this reason, neither the fallacy of the nonestablishment of the subject nor the fallacy of the nonestablishment of the reason is avoided, so this is not an answer.

GENERAL EXPLANATION OF CANDRAKĪRTI'S PASSAGE

Tsongkhapa first explains the general import of this passage and then gives a detailed explanation of it phrase by phrase. To make it easier to understand, he bases his analysis on a syllogism used by the Svātantrikas to prove to the Sāṃkhyas that there is no production from self: "A visible form does not arise from itself because it exists, like the pot there in front of you." Here the thesis to be proved is, "A visible form does not arise from itself." The subject "visible form" is the basis. The proponent is trying to prove that this basis has the attribute "does not arise from itself."

Here Candrakīrti counters Bhāvaviveka and demonstrates that no subject can be established as appearing in common to the proponent and opponent. Although the example syllogism used in this discussion is obviously directed at a Sāṃkhya opponent, Tsongkhapa suggests that the point Candrakīrti is making applies more generally to all opponents of the Prāsaṅgika-Mādhyamikas. This includes the Realists, who accept that things exist by their own inherent nature ultimately, and the Svātantrika-Mādhyamikas, who accept that things exist by their own inherent nature conventionally but not ultimately. In order to avoid using too many words, Tsongkhapa coins specific terminology here to distinguish between the Prāsaṅgikas and their opponents. Whereas the Svātantrika-Mādhyamikas may be called Non-Essentialists, since this applies to all Mādhyamikas, he suggests using the term Proponents of Noninherent Existence to refer uniquely to the Prāsaṅgika-Mādhyamikas, and the term Proponents of Inherent Existence to refer to both the Realists and the Svātantrika-Mādhyamikas. The Realist view is held by non-Buddhists and lower Buddhist schools from the Yogācāra down. All Realists are Proponents of Inherent Existence, but not all Proponents of Inherent Existence are Realists. The Svātantrika-Mādhyamikas, such as Bhāvaviveka, are Proponents of Inherent Existence but not Realists.[124]

The subject of our example syllogism, visible form, must be established by the valid direct visual consciousness apprehending it. According to the Proponents of Inherent Existence this must be nonmistaken valid knowledge, because if it is mistaken then it cannot directly establish reality. Moreover, these opponents say that for a nonconceptual consciousness to be nonmistaken, it must be nonmistaken with regard to its appearing object. In other words, its object must exist in the way that it appears to exist. So they accept that the object of valid direct perception exists inherently as it appears. In which case, the kind of valid knowledge that the opponent utilizes to establish the subject of the syllogism is not acceptable to the Prāsaṅgikas, and vice versa. According to the Prāsaṅgikas, no phenomenon has an inherently existent nature even conventionally, so there is no valid knowledge establishing that kind of inherent nature. This is what Candrakīrti is pinpointing when he refutes the method of autonomous syllogisms.

This also explains how to refute the claim that an autonomous syllogism is needed to enable another person to initially generate an understanding that things are not inherently existent. This concerns ultimate analysis and the realization of śūnyatā. Bhāvaviveka argues that you must use an autonomous syllogism to generate a new understanding of śūnyatā in your opponent. Candrakīrti says this is impossible. According to the Prāsaṅgikas, an autonomous syllogism cannot be used when two parties have different notions of validity, because there will be no subject accepted in common. This brings up a further question. When two Prāsaṅgikas, who have the same understanding of valid knowledge, try to prove something to each other, can they agree on a commonly appearing subject and use an autonomous syllogism? Likewise, when two Realist schools debate, do they share a commonly appearing subject? Or does Candrakīrti completely reject the use of autonomous syllogisms? There are various opinions about the meaning of a commonly appearing subject. Some scholars say that according to the Prāsaṅgika view there is no commonly appearing subject for Prāsaṅgikas and Realists. Others say that from the Prāsaṅgika point of view employing autonomous syllogisms implies inherent existence, so there can never be a commonly appearing subject for any two people using that method of debate. Furthermore, because there is no inherent existence at all, autonomous syllogisms cannot even exist. These various opinions are not addressed by Tsongkhapa here. He simply mentions that, for the time being, he will not discuss whether autonomous syllogisms are necessary to give rise to the inferential understanding of conventional things that Prāsaṅgikas discuss among themselves.

DETAILED EXPLANATION OF THE FIRST SECTION

Having concluded these general comments on Candrakīrti's refutation of Bhāvaviveka, Tsongkhapa now explains the above quotation phrase by phrase. The example syllogism used here is, "A visible form does not arise from itself because it exists, like the pot there in front of you." Tsongkhapa begins by discussing the opening sentence of Candrakīrti's passage:

For in accepting the negation of arising as the predicate of the thesis, he accepts that the subject that is its basis—which is something found only by mistaken [consciousness]—is denied ultimately. Mistaken and nonmistaken [minds] are very different.

Candrakīrti is setting out to prove that Bhāvaviveka's view is self-contradictory. He argues that because Bhāvaviveka accepts the negation of arising as the predicate of the thesis, he implicitly accepts that the subject does not ultimately exist. Any subject such as an eye sense organ or a visible form is established only by a conventional consciousness, such as a visual consciousness; so it is something found only by a mistaken consciousness influenced by ignorance. Bhāvaviveka must admit this because he accepts "does not ultimately arise" as the predicate of the thesis based on such a subject. If those subjects were ultimately existent, it would be contradictory to use them as the basis of a proof that such things do not ultimately arise. It is impossible to prove the predicate "does not ultimately arise" as an attribute of a subject that ultimately exists.

"Well," someone may ask, "what follows from Bhāvaviveka's acceptance that the eyes and so on do not ultimately arise?" Tsongkhapa replies that the eyes, forms, and so on are not ultimate truth and do not exist in reality, so they cannot be found as objects of any nonmistaken consciousness. Therefore they are found by conventional consciousnesses, which apprehend false appearances. Those consciousnesses are mistaken owing to being influenced by ignorance. According to the Prāsaṅgika system, forms and colors that appear to a visual consciousness do not exist as they appear, so these consciousnesses are false perceivers. Although a visual consciousness that sees a color or a shape may be valid, what appears to such a consciousness is false because it appears to be inherently existent—yet it is not so in reality.

Bhāvaviveka does not agree. He considers that a valid sense consciousness is nonmistaken regarding its object and its object's inherent nature; its object does exist inherently, just as it appears.[125] But according to the Prāsaṅgika system, the only nonmistaken consciousness within the continuum of a sentient being is the direct realization of śūnyatā. So the only object found by a nonmistaken consciousness is the ultimate truth itself. The objects found by mistaken consciousnesses are the various conventional things—including everything except śūnyatā. Therefore conventional truths are the objects found by mistaken consciousness, and ultimate truth is the object found by a nonmistaken consciousness. Here the object found by a mind is the *main* object found by that mind. Ultimate truth is so called because it is found by the wisdom that directly perceives the ultimate. An object found by a nonmistaken consciousness does not appear to a mistaken consciousness, and an object that appears to a mistaken consciousness is not found by a nonmistaken consciousness. This is because a mistaken consciousness and a nonmistaken consciousness hold completely contradictory objects. That is the meaning of Candrakīrti's words, "Mistaken and nonmistaken [minds] are very different."[126]

DETAILED EXPLANATION OF THE SECOND SECTION

Tsongkhapa now explains the next section of the passage:

> Therefore, as in the case of one with diseased eyes [seeing] falling hairs, when the mistaken holds the nonexistent to exist, how can there be the slightest perception of an object that exists?

The word "mistaken" refers to conventional consciousnesses, which are affected by ignorance, and specifically to nonconceptual consciousnesses, whose objects appear inherently existent yet do not exist in that way. Such a consciousness "holds the nonexistent to exist." Here Tsongkhapa glosses the word "holds" in a special way.[127] When we say that a visual consciousness "holds" form as inherently existent, this means that form *appears* to a visual consciousness as inherently existent. In order to fully understand the meaning of this passage, we need to consider how conceptual and nonconceptual consciousnesses apprehend their objects and clarify the distinction between the held object and the appearing object of both these types of consciousness. (An earlier discussion of this topic is found in chapter 8.)

There is a big difference between the held object and the appearing object of a conceptual consciousness. For example, when we think "this is a tree," the tree is the held object. But what appears to this thought along with the tree is a conceptual image of the tree. This image is the reverse of nontree,[128] and that is what appears to this thought. Based on this image, this thought distinguishes the tree from everything else that is not the tree. That is how the tree appears to this thought. The tree appears together with an image of it, and this thought does not distinguish between those appearances; therefore the conceptual image of the tree appears to be the actual tree.[129] Along with the conceptual image of the tree, inherent existence also appears to this thought. But even though the tree mixed with its image appears to be inherently existent, the mind holds "this is a tree" rather than "this is an inherently existent tree." The main object of a thought is its held object, not its appearing object. A valid conceptual consciousness is valid in dependence on how it holds its main object, not on how it perceives its appearing object.

Now in the case of a sense consciousness, it is difficult to say whether the appearing object and the held object are the same or different. Various texts give slightly different explanations. According to the Prāsaṅgikas, an object appears to a sense consciousness as inherently existent owing to the influence of innate ignorance within the mindstream—particularly its imprints. As soon as we see a visible form, it appears to be inherently existent; but that sense consciousness does not hold it to be inherently existent. The main object of that valid visual consciousness is the visible form rather than inherent existence. So some texts say that the form is the held object and inherent existence is the appearing object. Other texts do not distinguish between the appearing object and the held object of a sense consciousness—though they do distinguish between those of a conceptual consciousness. In general, there must be some difference between the appearing object and the held object in both cases. Dharmakīrti's *Commentary on Valid Cognition* says:

> Therefore, by seeing a thing
> All its qualities are seen. (1.47a–b)

The word "quality" here has a very specific meaning; it does not mean just any quality of the thing perceived. It refers to a thing's attributes that are the same as it with respect to nature, time, and object—in being the same substance, duration, and establishment.[130] This includes a thing's color, shape, impermanence, functionality, and so on. According to Dharmakīrti, the difference between the appearing object of a nonconceptual consciousness and that of a conceptual consciousness rests on whether these specific attributes of the thing are perceived all together or individually. A sense consciousness engages its object through the power of reality. In reality, as soon as a table exists all its attributes exist, which are the same as it with respect to nature, time, and object, in terms of being the same substance, duration, and establishment. Therefore when an object appears to a visual consciousness, all these specific attributes appear too. A sense consciousness does not discriminate and pick out one or another attribute. It simply perceives the table together with these specific attributes all at the same time. It engages its object in a positive manner. When we directly see a table, we see its shape, color, impermanence, and so on. All these specific attributes of the table are included in the appearing object.

Conversely, when an object appears to thought, we think of it through the appearance of a conceptual image of it. First we have a mental picture, and through that image our thought identifies its object. Thought clears away what does not fit with the image, and what is left appears. In the process of thinking "this is a form," we distinguish between "form" and "nonform" on the basis of a conceptual picture in our mind; then we eliminate "nonform" and generate the thought "this is a form." In this way thought perceives each object and each of its attributes separately, which are the same as it with respect to nature, time, and object, in terms of being the same substance, duration, and establishment. These do not appear together but one by one. When we think of this particular vase, we think of it through the appearance of an image of this vase. When we think of the color of this vase, we think of it through the appearance of an image of the vase's color. When we think about its impermanence, that attribute appears through its image.

Now, the appearing object of a sense consciousness encompasses all the specific attributes of the object (in the special sense mentioned above) at the same time; therefore, it is much wider than the appearing object of a conceptual consciousness. However, a sense consciousness does not know everything that appears to it. A sense consciousness knows its main object, which is its held object. It is valid with regard to that held object. A visual consciousness seeing a table sees all the specific attributes (in the special sense mentioned above) of the table, including its impermanence. But it does not know all those attributes. It only knows its held object—in this case, the table itself. Therefore the appearing object and the held object of a sense consciousness must be different: the held object is necessarily an appearing object; but an appearing object is not necessarily the held object. We can say that the held object is the principal appearing object. A valid sense consciousness is not mistaken with regard to its principal appearing object. This is Dharmakīrti's system.

Returning to the passage under discussion, Candrakīrti closes his sentence with a question: "How can there be the slightest perception of an object that exists?" As discussed above, when an object is held by a nonconceptual consciousness, it merely appears to that mind. According to the Prāsaṅgika system, an object appears to a sense consciousness to be inherently existent, even though it is not. So how can this prove in the slightest that it is inherently existent? Candrakīrti gives an example of someone with a particular kind of eye disease who sees the appearance of falling hairs. If this person is eating a big bowl of food he may think, "Oh, my bowl is full of fallen hairs!" However, nobody else can see them; there are no hairs there. These hairs do not exist at all, even though they appear to exist to the sick person. In the same way, objects appear to our sense consciousnesses to be inherently existent, even though they are not. The object does not exist in the way that it appears. Therefore Candrakīrti says, "How can there be the slightest perception of an object that exists?" Because sense consciousnesses perceiving forms, sounds, and so on are mistaken, they cannot establish things to be inherently existent at all.

DETAILED EXPLANATION OF THE THIRD SECTION

Candrakīrti's passage continues:

> But, as in the case of one without diseased eyes [not seeing] falling
> hairs, when the nonmistaken does not reify the unreal, how can there
> be the slightest perception of an object that does not exist—[ordinarily
> perceived] by a conventional [mind]?

Here "the nonmistaken" refers to a nonmistaken consciousness—which is
compared to someone who, not having this eye disease, does not mistakenly
see falling hairs. When Candrakīrti says, "The nonmistaken does not reify the
unreal," he means that a direct realization of śūnyatā does not hold conventional things, such as forms, to exist. A direct realization of emptiness is the
only nonmistaken consciousness within the mental continuum of a sentient
being; śūnyatā itself is the only object of that realization. That mind does not
see or hold anything else as its direct or indirect object, including the basis on
which it has realized emptiness, such as a form. The analogy is a visual consciousness that is free of disease, which does not see the mistaken appearance
of falling hairs. A mind directly perceiving emptiness is free from the influence
of ignorance, so conventional things do not appear. "Ordinarily perceived by a
conventional mind" refers to forms and so on, which are objects that appear to
a consciousness obscured by ignorance. These objects do not appear to the nonmistaken consciousness directly realizing śūnyatā. Every one of these conventional things "does not exist" in that they do not inherently exist, even though
they appear that way to ordinary perception. A nonmistaken consciousness,
which directly sees śūnyatā, does not establish even one particle of any conventional thing. This does not mean that it negates them. A nonmistaken consciousness simply does not see or know conventional things, because they are
not the objects of that awareness.

In general, each Buddhist school of thought posits two types of valid knowledge: mistaken and nonmistaken. However, their ways of delineating them are
different. According to the Prāsaṅgikas, nonmistaken valid knowledge apprehends its object as it exists—there is no difference between the way the object
appears and the way it exists. So within the continuum of a sentient being,
only a direct realization of śūnyatā is nonmistaken, in that its object—the
absence of inherent existence—exists as it appears. In other words, the direct
object of any sentient being's nonmistaken valid knowledge is śūnyatā, the
ultimate truth. All other consciousnesses of sentient beings are mistaken, even

though they may be valid. The direct object of any sentient being's mistaken valid knowledge is a conventional thing. Apart from a buddha's exalted knowledge of the two truths, all valid knowledge of conventional things is mistaken because it is mistaken with regard to its object's inherent nature. So in the case of sentient beings, mistaken valid knowledge refers to valid conventional consciousness, and nonmistaken valid knowledge refers to the direct realization of śūnyatā. The objects of these two kinds of valid knowledge are completely different; what nonmistaken valid knowledge knows, and what mistaken valid knowledge knows, are completely different. Neither knows what the other knows. This is the point here.

In contrast, according to Svātantrikas such as Bhāvaviveka, mistaken valid knowledge specifically refers to inferential valid knowledge. Although it is valid with regard to its main object, it is mistaken with regard to its appearing object, because a conceptual image of its main object appears along with the object itself. Inherent existence also appears to a valid inferential cognizer, but that appearance is not mistaken according to the Svātantrika system; the appearance of inherent existence is not part of the criterion of a mistaken consciousness. Nonmistaken valid knowledge refers to direct perception, because direct perception sees its main object clearly, unmixed with a conceptual image of it.

DETAILED EXPLANATION OF THE FOURTH SECTION

Returning to the passage we are analyzing, Candrakīrti now quotes Nāgārjuna's *Refutation of Objections* to substantiate his view:

> If anything, owing to its nature, were known
> By direct perception and so on,
> Then that would be proved or refuted.
> But that does not exist; thus I am not faulted.

As Tsongkhapa explains, this stanza attests that no kind of valid knowledge can establish anything to be inherently existent. According to the Madhyamaka system, there are four kinds of valid knowledge: valid direct perception, valid inference, valid conviction, and valid analogy. Things may appear to be inherently existent, but valid knowledge cannot prove inherent existence because nothing is inherently existent. Even though direct perception sees its object as inherently existent, the object does not exist in the way that it appears. This is like the example of someone mistakenly seeing falling hairs.

DETAILED EXPLANATION OF THE FIFTH SECTION

Candrakīrti's passage continues:

> Because mistaken and nonmistaken [minds] are very different with
> regard to that [appearance], the mistaken does not exist during the
> occurrence of the nonmistaken—so how could any [such inference]
> have a conventional eye as the subject?

Here Candrakīrti summarizes the Prāsaṅgika position that the objects of
mistaken consciousnesses and those of nonmistaken consciousnesses are completely different. Therefore a conventional thing cannot be established by a
nonmistaken direct perception as the subject of a syllogism. So he asks the
reader, "How could any [such inference] have a conventional eye as the subject?" In other words, any conventional thing used as the subject of a syllogism
is an object of a mistaken consciousness. Candrakīrti is not saying that subjects, such as conventional eyes, do not exist. Rather, the subject of a syllogism
is a conventional object, so it cannot be established or known by a nonmistaken mind. It does not exist from the point of view of a nonmistaken mind. If
it were established as inherently existent then it would be found by a nonmistaken mind, in which case it could be the subject of an autonomous syllogism.
But there is nothing that is established as inherently existent by a nonmistaken
consciousness. Any subject of a syllogism is an object found by a mistaken consciousness, not by a nonmistaken consciousness.

DETAILED EXPLANATION OF THE SIXTH SECTION

Tsongkhapa now explains the final sentence of Candrakīrti's passage:

> For this reason, neither the fallacy of the nonestablishment of the sub-
> ject nor the fallacy of the nonestablishment of the reason is avoided, so
> this is not an answer.

When the Proponents of Noninherent Existence and the Realists debate using
a visible form as the subject of a syllogism, that subject is not established in
common for both parties. According to the former, the valid direct perception that knows a visible form is mistaken. According to the latter, the valid
direct perception that knows a visible form is nonmistaken, because if a valid
direct perception is not mistaken regarding a visible form, then it is not mistaken regarding an inherently existent visible form. In short, the Prāsaṅgika-

Mādhyamikas and their opponents cannot establish a mutually agreed-on faultless subject for debate, because the subject posited is an object of mistaken valid knowledge according to the Prāsaṅgikas, but is an object of nonmistaken valid knowledge according to their opponents. Each does not accept the other's valid knowledge to be valid, nor the object established by it. Thus no valid knowledge proves the subject to be established as appearing in common to both systems. As a result, any thesis that one tries to prove by means of an autonomous syllogism has a fatal flaw: the subject is not established in common by both parties. In other words, the basis of the debate is not agreed on. If a syllogism has the fault of nonestablishment of the subject, it unavoidably has the fault of nonestablishment of the reason.

These faults are a result of Bhāvaviveka's position. Although his followers may object: "Although this may be so according to the view that there is no inherently existent nature even conventionally, we followers of Bhāvaviveka do not assert that conventionally. In our view, the subject of an autonomous syllogism exists. A faultless subject exists." Tsongkhapa responds that this objection is inadequate. It was explained in great detail above, and will be examined further below, that it is incorrect to accept the existence of inherent nature even conventionally.

(2″)) THE EXAMPLE CITED DOES NOT MATCH

As we have seen, Bhāvaviveka argues that the subject of a syllogism, used in debate between proponents of different philosophical schools, should be a general subject rather than one qualified in a particular way. The example he provides of such a syllogism is "Sound is impermanent because it is produced." Here the subject should be sound in general, not some particular notion of sound upheld by a certain school, such as sound arisen from the elements, sound as a quality of space, produced sound, or already existent sound that becomes manifest owing to conditions. Only sound in general is acceptable as a subject to both the proponent and the opponent. The predicate of the syllogism, "impermanent," should also be understood in general, not qualified as either having another cause or not having another cause. Moreover, the subject, predicate, and reason do not need to be qualified as truly existent or as falsely existent. Bhāvaviveka believes that if we comply with these restrictions, there is no problem with using autonomous syllogisms to prove that things do not ultimately arise. How does Candrakīrti reply to this? In *Clear Words* he says:

> Moreover, your example does not match [our situation]. Here what is
> established for both parties is "sound" in general and "impermanent"

in general, without any qualification applied. But in our case neither the Proponents of Noninherent Existence nor the Proponents of Inherent Existence accept an eye in general either conventionally or ultimately. So your example does not match [our situation].

This passage does not mean that, although sound in general and impermanent in general can be taken as the subject and predicate respectively, there is no such thing as an eye that is neither truly existent nor falsely existent. This is not what Candrakīrti is arguing—for neither party accepts that there is something that is neither truly existent nor falsely existent; if they did, then it would be impossible to prove that the example does not match the situation.

So what does this passage mean? Candrakīrti agrees that non-Buddhists and Buddhist Realists can debate about a subject accepted in common, such as sound. In that case, both the proponent and the opponent accept that sound in general can be understood by valid knowledge—when it is not qualified as "sound arisen from the elements" or "sound as a property of space." However, Candrakīrti says that Bhāvaviveka's example is not relevant to a debate between the Proponents of Noninherent Existence, who follow the Prāsaṅgika system, and the Proponents of Inherent Existence, who follow other systems. Both parties agree that there is nothing—forms, eyes, and so on—validly established in general that is not established either by a nonmistaken or a mistaken consciousness. The Prāsaṅgikas consider it is established by a mistaken consciousness, which is not acceptable to their opponents; their opponents consider it is established by a nonmistaken consciousness, which is not acceptable to the Prāsaṅgikas. Neither party accepts the other's notion of validity, and neither party accepts that there is any third alternative—a general notion of validity that is neither mistaken nor nonmistaken.

A commonly agreed-on subject of a syllogism, even one not qualified as either truly existent or falsely existent, must be established by the valid knowledge of both parties in the debate. In this case there is no valid knowledge in general, which is neither mistaken nor nonmistaken, that can establish the elements of the syllogism. Neither party accepts such a general notion of valid knowledge. Since this case concerns opposing accounts of valid knowledge, this case "does not match" the examples given by Bhāvaviveka concerning other matters. Where the difference concerns other matters, then you can posit a general common basis as the subject. But where the difference concerns opposing accounts of valid knowledge, then there is no common basis that can be posited as the subject—for there is no general valid knowledge accepted in common to establish it.

The fact that one party holds the subject to exist inherently and the other party holds it to be empty of inherent existence is not the main point here. The crucial issue is valid knowledge itself. The Proponents of Inherent Existence say that valid knowledge must be valid with respect to the inherent nature of its object. Without that there is no valid knowledge. For example, if there is valid knowledge of sound, then this knowledge must be valid with regard to sound existing by way of its own characteristics. This means that sound must *be* inherently existent. It does not mean that this valid knowledge must *know* sound to be inherently existent. The Prāsaṅgika-Mādhyamikas hold the opposite position. They say that there is no valid knowledge with regard to anything's inherent nature. Although things appear to exist by way of their own characteristics to the valid knowledge perceiving them, they do not actually exist as they appear. So valid knowledge is mistaken regarding that appearance. Nevertheless, that knowledge is valid.

When two parties hold opposing accounts of valid knowledge, nothing can be posited as a common subject of debate. Anything validly established is established either by mistaken valid knowledge or by nonmistaken valid knowledge; there is nothing that can be established by valid knowledge that is neither of those two. There cannot be something that is established by valid knowledge in general but not established by either mistaken or nonmistaken valid knowledge. That is not acceptable to either party. They agree that there is no general valid knowledge—neither mistaken nor nonmistaken—that can establish a subject that is any of the six internal or six external sources of consciousness, such as an eye sense organ or a visible form.

As we have seen, according to the Prāsaṅgika-Madhyamaka system, a sentient being's nonmistaken consciousness and direct realization of śūnyatā are the same: every nonmistaken consciousness is a direct realization of emptiness, and only a direct realization of śūnyatā is a nonmistaken consciousness. So in general, "nonmistaken" refers to the meditative equipoise directly seeing ultimate truth. Conventional phenomena do not appear to this mind; only the ultimate truth appears. So this is called *ultimate truth* or *ultimate nature*. Why? When śūnyatā directly appears to the mind perceiving it, it does not appear in a mistaken way. Conversely, when a conventional truth directly appears to the primary consciousness of any sentient being, it always appears in a mistaken way. It appears to be inherently existent.

A sentient being's nonmistaken consciousness is just the meditative equipoise directly seeing śūnyatā. What does this mean? A practitioner on the paths of seeing and of meditation gives rise to two types of wisdom understanding emptiness: the wisdom of meditative equipoise, which directly sees śūnyatā in the meditation session, and the wisdom of subsequent attainment, which thinks about śūnyatā during the postmeditation period. The wisdom directly seeing emptiness only knows the ultimate and cannot perceive conventional phenomena. When this wisdom subsides as the meditation period ends, the wisdom of subsequent attainment arises and perceives conventional phenomena, such as objects of the senses. So in the case of a sentient being, the two truths are realized by different kinds of mind. The wisdom directly realizing śūnyatā is aware of nothing other than śūnyatā; it cannot simultaneously be aware of conventional phenomena. One moment of a sentient being's consciousness cannot realize the two truths simultaneously. Prior to attaining buddhahood, the direct realization of śūnyatā never manifests during the subsequent attainment—these two minds never occur together. But once you attain buddhahood, the two truths are realized simultaneously.

Unlike the case of a sentient being, a buddha's wisdom of meditative equipoise directly realizing śūnyatā exists at the same time as his or her wisdom perceiving conventional phenomena. However, we cannot call the latter "the wisdom of subsequent attainment" because every mind of a buddha is a meditative equipoise directly perceiving emptiness. A buddha directly perceives śūnyatā while engaging in many other activities. In that sense, a buddha never arises from meditation; he or she is continuously absorbed in a direct realization of emptiness, even while knowing conventional things. This is a unique quality of a buddha; no other being is able to know conventional truth and ultimate truth simultaneously. According to the Mahayana, when we progress from the tenth bodhisattva stage to buddhahood, we move from one meditative equipoise to another. Upon achieving buddhahood, the first moment of a direct realization of emptiness itself becomes omniscience. Omniscience directly realizes śūnyatā at the same time as it directly realizes all conventional phenomena.

What happens in the case of a sentient being? Does an ārya bodhisattva still have a direct realization of emptiness after he or she has arisen from meditative equipoise directly realizing emptiness? This is a point of debate between scholars. Panchen Sonam Drakpa and Jetsun Chokyi Gyaltsen give slightly different answers. According to the monastic textbooks written by Panchen Sonam Drakpa, an ārya bodhisattva does not have a direct realization of emptiness once he or she has arisen from meditative equipoise directly realizing emptiness. Only emptiness appears during that meditative equipoise, which means that there is no appearance of any conventional things. Now we may argue, "Does a bodhisattva not have a realization of bodhicitta while engaged in meditative equipoise directly perceiving emptiness? If great compassion and bodhicitta are not present within a bodhisattva's mental continuum during that meditation period, how can he or she be a bodhisattva?" Jetsun Chokyi Gyaltsen says that of course a bodhisattva has bodhicitta within his or her mental continuum. Bodhicitta and the direct realization of śūnyatā assist each other. During meditation on śūnyatā, bodhicitta becomes very subtle. Yet while meditating on emptiness, the mind directly realizing śūnyatā is held by the power of that nonmanifest bodhicitta. Upon arising from this meditation bodhicitta becomes manifest again, and the mind directly realizing śūnyatā becomes very subtle. At this time, bodhicitta is held or assisted by the nonmanifest direct realization of śūnyatā. This is similar to the fact that when we sleep we do not lose all our knowledge and wake up as ignorant as a baby. When we sleep, our knowledge of various things becomes very subtle and a sleep consciousness manifests. When we awake, our knowledge manifests and the sleep consciousness becomes very subtle. But sleep consciousness is just waiting for its opportunity—it can become manifest anytime, so you had better watch out in case you fall asleep right now!

A person has many different consciousnesses, some of which are manifest and some of which are subtle. What appears to the person is simply what appears to his or her manifest consciousness. In his commentary on Candrakīrti's *Introduction to the "Middle Way,"* Tsongkhapa says, "Therefore, they have meditative equipoise and subsequent attainment alternately."[131] The uncontaminated wisdom of a sentient being only manifests during the meditative equipoise directly realizing śūnyatā. The direct realization of śūnyatā never manifests during the subsequent attainment. At that time a sentient being's wisdom is contaminated. Other schools understand *contaminated* and *uncontaminated* differently, but according to the Prāsaṅgika system, contaminated wisdom is a mind to which an object naturally appears as inherently existent. It is a dualistic perception—the appearance of an object as inherently existent. A direct realization of emptiness is uncontaminated wisdom. Only emptiness appears to the wisdom directly realizing śūnyatā; the basis of that emptiness, a conventional thing, does not appear. When the bodhisattva emerges from that meditation, other consciousnesses arise and conventional things appear again as truly existent. Any consciousness that manifests during the postmeditation period is contaminated; impure things appear as pure, impermanent things as permanent, untrue things as true, and so on. During the postmeditation period a direct realization of śūnyatā is not manifest. However, at that time, although śūnyatā does not directly appear to the mind, the wisdom directly realizing emptiness exists subtly within the mental continuum of that bodhisattva. An ārya bodhisattva has the direct realization of ultimate truth both during meditative equipoise and the postmeditation period, but it only manifests during meditative equipoise. Although an ārya bodhisattva's compassion, bodhicitta, and realizations of other truths do not manifest during their meditative equipoise directly perceiving emptiness, it would be wrong to say that such a bodhisattva does not have those realizations at that time. If they did not possess them at all during those moments, then there would be the logical fallacy of a bodhisattva who does not possess bodhicitta. These are Jetsun Chokyi Gyaltsen's points, not those of Panchen Sonam Drakpa.

Although *nonmistaken* usually refers to the wisdom of meditative equipoise directly realizing ultimate truth, it can also refer to the person during moments when he or she is not confused—specifically when the ultimate truth manifestly appears during his or her meditative equipoise on emptiness. At that time nothing except śūnyatā appears; various other consciousnesses and the objects that normally appear to them do not manifest. When a bodhisattva meditates directly on śūnyatā, nothing appears to be ultimately existent, because only uncontaminated wisdom is manifest. At that time, the person also is said to be nonmistaken.

However, in this section of the *Lamrim Chenmo*, Tsongkhapa is primarily concerned with "nonmistaken" as it applies to valid knowledge—both direct perception and inferential knowledge. Here "nonmistaken" refers to a specific criterion of validity accepted by the opponents. According to these Proponents of Inherent Existence, any valid consciousness is nonmistaken with regard to its main object, including its inherent nature: valid direct perception is nonmistaken with regard to its appearing object, such as a form, which exists from its own side, and valid inferential knowledge is nonmistaken with regard to its held object, such as a form, which exists from its own side.[132] Bhāvaviveka seems to accept this criterion of validity too.

The Prāsaṅgika view is different. Any valid knowledge that establishes the subject and the three modes of a syllogism is mistaken. There is no nonmistaken valid knowledge of conventional things at all, except within the continuum of a buddha. So any subject of a syllogism, such as "an eye," is the object of mistaken valid knowledge. A subject of a syllogism is a conventional thing that cannot be found by nonmistaken knowledge. Any predicate, such as "does not arise from itself," is also the object of mistaken valid knowledge; so are the three modes of a syllogism, because they are conventional things. These can be found only by conventional valid knowledge, which is always mistaken with regard to its object's inherent nature. The Prāsaṅgikas consider that nonmistaken valid knowledge of the subject, the predicate, the reason, and the three modes does not exist at all. Those cannot be found by nonmistaken valid knowledge. But the Proponents of Inherent Existence believe that they must be found by nonmistaken valid knowledge. For according to them, valid knowledge must be nonmistaken with regard to its object's mode of existence. If it is not nonmistaken regarding its object's inherent nature, then it cannot be valid knowledge. Bhāvaviveka seems to accept this too.

AMBIGUITY OF THE TERM "OWN NATURE"

Now what is meant by "its own nature" or "its own characteristics"? What does it mean for something to be established by its own characteristics? In general, there are two kinds of phenomena: functional things and nonfunctional phenomena. According to the system developed by the Buddhist logicians, functional things are ultimately able to function, so they are ultimate truths, substantially existent, and established by their own specific characteristics. Examples of such specifically characterized things are the eye sense power, visible forms, visual consciousness, and all other impermanent phenomena. Nonfunctional phenomena are unable to function as causes and effects, yet they exist, so they are conventional truths, imputedly existent, and established by means of shared general characteristics. Examples of such generally characterized phenomena are space, oneness, mere negation, and all other permanent phenomena. A mere negation, such as the nonexistence of an elephant in this room, is a generally characterized phenomenon. It is not a real individual thing that activates something. It is not produced by anything nor does it produce anything itself. It is simply the lack of an elephant. A produced thing is totally the opposite. It actually functions; it arises from causes and conditions, and it produces a result itself. Thus the logicians' understanding of a nature established by its own characteristics simply refers to functional things. This is completely different to the Prāsaṅgikas' understanding of such a nature.

In the context of the Madhyamaka discussion regarding the valid establishment of the subject of a syllogism, the meaning of *own nature* or *own characteristics* is not limited to functional things. Every functional and nonfunctional thing *has* its own characteristics, its own nature, and its own manner of existing; all Buddhist schools accept this, including the Prāsaṅgika. However, it is only the Proponents of Inherent Existence who accept that things "exist by" their own nature. To say that something exists by its own nature implies that it has an *inherent nature*—a nature through whose power that thing exists from its own side. So, as discussed in chapter 6, the term *own nature* in this context means *own inherent nature*. The Proponents of Inherent Existence consider that both functional and nonfunctional phenomena have such a nature, so they say that inferential valid knowledge of a nonfunctional thing is also nonmistaken with regard to the inherent nature of its held object.

To understand this phrase, "inferential valid knowledge of a nonfunctional thing," let us first consider inferential valid knowledge of a functional thing. If we consider an example where the connection is shown between two functional things—fire and smoke—we can positively prove the presence of fire in a certain place by establishing the presence of smoke in that place. In technical terms, we prove the existence of the cause from the existence of the result using a *correct effect sign*. The same principle applies in the case of inferential valid knowledge of a nonfunctional thing. We can prove the absence of smoke in a certain place by establishing the absence of fire. We prove the negation of the effect from the negation of the cause using a *correct nonobservation sign*. For example, suppose one night you are sitting with a small child by a lake and see mist rising from it. The child feels anxious, thinking it is smoke. However, you can prove to the child that it is not smoke by saying, "There is no smoke on the lake because there is no fire." The darkness makes it difficult to see whether there is smoke arising from the lake, but it makes it easy to see whether there is a fire, because that would appear very brightly. If the mist rising from the lake were actually smoke, then there must be a fire. You know that there is no fire on the lake because quite clearly you cannot see one. Therefore you can infer that there is no smoke there. So first you must have the valid knowledge that there is no fire. Then, by means of a valid logical inference, you can ascertain that there is no smoke. The held object of that inferential knowledge is the lack of smoke on the lake. But that object is not a functional thing. It is just a mere negation, a mere lack of smoke in that place. That lack of smoke itself does not function in any way; it does not produce anything, and it is not produced by some other cause. According to the Proponents of Inherent Existence, the lack of smoke on the lake is inherently existent. So they consider that this inferential knowledge of a lack of smoke on the lake is nonmistaken with regard to its inherent existence—for if it were mistaken with regard to that, then it would not be valid.

Now if there were valid knowledge that is nonmistaken with regard to that kind of inherent nature, then it would be nonmistaken regarding the appearing object (of direct perception) or the held object (of conceptual thought). However, this would entail that it is nonmistaken with regard to its object's ultimate nature—and this is unacceptable to the Prāsaṅgikas. Therefore they assert that the type of valid knowledge accepted by the opponent does not establish the subject of a syllogism and the three modes. It is important to note that the Prāsaṅgikas are not saying that the proponent and opponent do not have any conventional valid knowledge at all; they accept that everyone has valid knowledge, such as valid visual consciousness seeing forms. The Prāsaṅgikas merely deny that valid knowledge is nonmistaken regarding its object being inherently existent. Their disagreement is over whether the criterion of validity includes being nonmistaken with regard to the inherent nature of the main object. They do not deny the mere existence of objects of conceptual thought, such as forms and so on, based on valid sense consciousness. For example, first you have a visual consciousness directly perceiving a form. This is nonmistaken if it is unaffected by temporary causes of error, such as cataracts, as explained earlier. This sense consciousness draws forth various conceptual thoughts about the object, involving judgments and enabling memory. The held object of the thought "There is a form" is not incorrect. There is nothing wrong with the main object of a thought that understands forms and so on to be merely existent.

THREE POSSIBLE WAYS OF HOLDING SOMETHING TO EXIST

This is an important point, so Tsongkhapa explains it in detail. There are three possible ways of holding something, such as a sprout, to exist. First, one can hold the sprout to be truly existent—holding it to exist by its own inherently established nature. Second, one can hold the sprout to be falsely existent—holding it to lack inherent existence yet to exist in an illusion-like way. Third, one can hold the sprout to be merely existent in general—without differentiating it as truly existent or as falsely existent. Tsongkhapa says that every other way of holding a sprout to exist, such as holding it to be impermanent or permanent, fits into one of these three, so there is no need to explain them here.

The main point is that sentient beings who have not realized the emptiness of inherent existence can hold an object to exist in only two of these ways: the first way (as truly existent) or the third way (as merely existent). They cannot hold it in the second way—as lacking inherent existence yet existing in an illusion-like way. So, holding things to exist in general and holding things to exist inherently are both present within the mindstreams of sentient beings who have not given rise to the correct view understanding that things do not exist inherently. However, it is totally wrong to assume that before we understand that things exist in an illusion-like way, everything we conceive to exist we hold to be truly existent. To think that something is existent is not the same as to think it is inherently existent; to think that something is not inherently existent is not the same as to think it is nonexistent. Even those who do not understand śūnyatā can hold things to exist without necessarily holding them to be truly existent. This was explained extensively in chapters 7 and 6, where we discussed conventional valid knowledge and the distinctions between existence, nonexistence, inherent existence, and noninherent existence, respectively.

Otherwise, if all the thoughts concerning conventionalities of non-āryas—sentient beings prior to perceiving emptiness—were thoughts grasping at true existence, then everything established by ordinary conventional minds unaffected by temporary causes of error would be negated by Prāsaṅgika-Madhyamaka analysis. However, this is contrary to the Prāsaṅgika-

Madhyamaka approach. The Prāsaṅgika-Mādhyamikas accept the existence of ordinary things commonly established by conventional knowledge, free of ultimate analysis. These are conventional truths. But if all conventional valid thoughts of ordinary beings were thoughts grasping at true existence, then they would all be wrong views; the objects held by them would be objects of negation. As a result, there would be no way to differentiate between the ontological status of conventionally existent things and things that do not exist at all, such as a permanent, uncaused, creator god called Īśvara. According to Buddhists, Īśvara is a mere fabrication; he is not real in any way. To believe in his existence is a wrong view. Similarly, according to Prāsaṅgikas, to believe in the existence of inherently existent things is a wrong view. Prāsaṅgika-Mādhyamaka analysis negates the objects held by thoughts grasping at inherent existence. So if every thought of ordinary sentient beings were a wrong view holding things to be inherently existent, then all the objects held by those thoughts would be negated. In short, the conventional truths accepted by Prāsaṅgika-Mādhyamikas would be denied.

Believing that any ordinary being's thought holds its object to exist inherently is a misconception that greatly hinders any understanding of the Madhyamaka position regarding conventional existence. It is an indication that we have not properly understood śūnyatā. A person suffering from this misconception assumes that Buddha taught the practice of virtuous activities only for those who have not yet found the definitive ultimate truth. On earlier stages of the spiritual path, prior to realizing emptiness, such a practitioner employs conceptual thought while engaging in various virtuous practices. However, after having realized śūnyatā, he or she abandons those thoughts and practices, believing them to be grasping at signs that tie us to samsara. Employing or grasping at signs, you may remember, refers to the ignorance grasping at true existence, which is the cause of samsara.[133] But someone who holds the wrong view mentioned above mistakenly identifies grasping at signs as any conceptual thought at all, without differentiating between virtuous and nonvirtuous thoughts. This is an overly broad notion of grasping at signs. From this mistaken perspective, all conceptual thoughts—not just the grasping at true existence—are seen to be faulty and the root of samsara. A person afflicted with this view ends up abandoning a vast amount of Dharma.

This view is like that of the eighth-century Chinese abbot Hashang Mahayana. According to traditional Tibetan accounts, when Hashang came as a missionary to Tibet he taught that if we do anything or think anything at all, we are grasping at signs and are bound to cyclic existence. For example, he said things such as, "It does not matter whether clouds are black or white, they both block the sun," and "It does not matter whether chains are made of iron or gold, they both bind you," and "It does not matter whether dogs are white or black, they both bite." In short, it does not matter whether one's actions and thoughts are virtuous or nonvirtuous—they both cause rebirth in samsara. The virtuous ones cause high rebirth and the nonvirtuous ones cause low rebirth, but both bind us to temporary samsaric rebirths. Therefore in order to gain enlightenment, we must do nothing and think nothing. Hashang's approach is to eliminate all actions of body, speech, and mind. Then a clear pure mind with no object will arise. This is the realization of the truth. Therefore his view is called the view of no thought.

Of course Hashang may not have taught this, but Tsongkhapa uses him as an example to warn us against this view. Hashang's teachings are attractive to many people. We do not need to study, we do not need to think, we do not need to chew these hard philosophical bones. All we need to do is sit with a blank mind. Even an illiterate person can do this with ease. We just sit down, and when a thought arises we mentally blow it away. Tsongkhapa says we are in great danger if we literally accept this view; it will stop us from studying, learning, and engaging in virtuous activities. It will even prevent us from receiving Buddha's teaching. Our spiritual progress will be blocked. Therefore Tsongkhapa refutes it many times throughout the *Lamrim Chenmo*.

Those who, like Hashang, have not yet found the correct view of the emptiness of inherent existence cannot distinguish between mere existence and inherent existence. They think that if something exists, it inherently exists—and if inherent existence is negated, existence itself is negated. This is because, as indicated by Candrakīrti's *Commentary on the "Four Hundred Stanzas"* cited earlier, they hold that whatever exists must exist by its own nature.[134] For this reason they believe that whatever does not inherently exist cannot exist at all. They cannot establish causality, because if something lacks inherent existence, it cannot be subject to cause and effect. There are many, including Bhāvaviveka, who argue in this way because they are not able to make these subtle distinctions.

Those who have generated the view of the emptiness of inherent existence within their own mindstreams can hold things to exist in any of all three ways: as truly existent, as falsely existent, and as merely existent. After having generated that view of śūnyatā, and for as long as its influence lasts, when they analyze whether or not things truly exist, the contrived grasping at true existence does not arise within their mindstreams for the time being. However, the innate grasping at true existence still arises.[135] At this point, Tsongkhapa is referring to ordinary bodhisattvas who have generated a conceptual understanding of emptiness. Nevertheless, it is important to understand that the innate grasping at true existence still arises even within the mindstreams of those who have generated a direct realization of śūnyatā—right up until attaining the eighth ground.

According to the Prāsaṅgika-Madhyamaka system, the innate grasping at inherent existence[136] is the root of samsara—the ignorance that is the first of the twelve links of dependent arising. It is the fundamental obstruction to liberation, and it is present within a Mahayana practitioner's mental continuum up to the eighth bodhisattva stage. According to the Svātantrika-Madhyamaka system, the innate grasping at true existence is an obstruction to omniscience and thus it is present throughout all ten bodhisattva stages up to buddhahood. According to the Hinayana system—as presented within Tsongkhapa's tradition—it is present within the mental continuum of a śrāvaka or a pratyekabuddha right up to the attainment of liberation from samsara. The main goal of a Mahayana practitioner is the attainment of complete buddhahood for the benefit of other sentient beings; so the main obstacle to be removed is the obstruction to omniscience rather than the obstruction to liberation.

According to the Prāsaṅgika system, the obstructions to liberation include ignorance and other mental afflictions together with their seeds. The obstructions to omniscience are the subtle imprints left by them. These subtle imprints, being so deeply embedded, are very difficult to remove. So in order to remove them, bodhisattvas first have to remove the mental afflictions and their seeds. The obstructions to liberation are completely and finally removed upon attaining the eighth level of the bodhisattva path. After that, with enormous effort bodhisattvas gradually remove their imprints on the eighth, ninth, and tenth bodhisattva levels. On these three pure grounds, the innate grasping at true existence and other mental afflictions arising from it are no longer present within their mindstreams. Only the imprints left by that innate grasping remain. However, until reaching these pure stages, the innate grasping at true existence is still present within the mental continuum of an ārya bodhisattva. Thus grasping at signs can arise, even though it may not be very strong or active.

The innate grasping at true existence has been present in all beings, including children and animals, from beginningless time. It is a specific type of mind that arises naturally. Other types of mind, such as sense consciousnesses, do not hold their objects to be truly existent. Yet because they are influenced by the innate grasping at true existence, when anything appears to a sense consciousness it appears to exist inherently. So inherent existence is an appearing object to the sense consciousness. But a sense consciousness itself does not hold its object to be inherently existent. If it did, then that sense consciousness would be a distorted consciousness. Although a visual consciousness seeing blue holds it as blue, it does not hold it as ultimately or inherently blue. A sense consciousness does not conceive of the object in any way; it does not hold things in this sense.

However, when something appears to a sense consciousness, a mind grasping it as truly existent may naturally arise within the mental continuum of the perceiver. That kind of grasping is not dependent on philosophical views, logical reasoning, or religious belief. Even when an ārya bodhisattva not yet on the pure grounds meditates directly on śūnyatā, the innate grasping at true existence is still present within his or her mental continuum, though it is not manifest at that time. Innate grasping at true existence is very different from contrived grasping at true existence. Contrived grasping is developed on the basis of incorrect reasons, mistaken philosophy, or wrong religious beliefs. Tsongkhapa says here that if someone has realized emptiness, then while engaging in ultimate analysis during meditation the contrived grasping at true existence does not arise for the time being.

Does Tsongkhapa's use of the words "for the time being" (*re zhig*) here mean that sometimes they give rise to contrived grasping at true existence? Do those who have realized that everything is empty of inherent existence sometimes have doubt about this and occasionally accept certain things to be inherently existent? To answer these questions we must understand how ultimate analysis is employed. There are two kinds of logical reasoning that can be used to refute a wrong view or prove a correct view, whether to oneself or others. Depending on what the opponent knows, we can use either consequences or syllogisms to prove that things are not inherently existent.

HOW TO USE LOGICAL CONSEQUENCES AND SYLLOGISMS

When our opponent has a wrong conception focused on one point, which he has no doubt about at all, then we use a logical consequence. This kind of grasping occurs prior to the arising of a doubt about the matter. Let us suppose that our opponent has engaged in ultimate analysis on the basis of a vase. On that basis he understands that whatever is a dependent nature is empty of inherent existence, and that whatever is not empty of inherent existence cannot be a dependent nature. But our opponent has not yet been able to relate that knowledge to a sprout; he continues to think that a sprout is truly existent. Our opponent has no doubt about this; based on incorrect reasoning, he has a wrong conception that a sprout is truly existent. Nevertheless, he understands other aspects of the situation perfectly well: he knows that a sprout is a dependent nature, and on the basis of a vase he knows the general pervasion that if something is dependent then it cannot be truly existent. But he has not been able to put these pieces of knowledge together, so he thinks that a sprout is truly existent.

In this situation we use a logical consequence because our opponent has both a correct view that understands śūnyatā on the basis of a vase and a wrong view that grasps at true existence on the basis of a sprout. In order to help him get rid of the wrong view that grasps at true existence, we can say, "If a sprout were truly existent then it would be an independent nature because of being truly existent." The opponent does not want to admit that a sprout is independent because he already knows it is dependent. He wants to say that a sprout is truly existent but at the same time does not want to say that it is independent. He already knows, on the basis of a vase, the general pervasion that whatever is a dependent nature is empty of true existence. So by using his wrong view about a sprout as a reason (that it is truly existent), we show him the consequence following from it, which he does not want to accept—that a sprout is independent. This kind of consequence reveals the logical contradiction between a correct view that he accepts and what is entailed by a wrong view that he also accepts. It demonstrates that if he accepts this wrong view, he must accept a consequence that he knows to be incorrect. Thus our presentation of a consequence generates a doubt in his mind. He begins to think that perhaps a sprout is not truly existent after all, because it is dependent.

When our opponent develops such a doubt wavering between two points, one of which is correct and the other incorrect, then we present to him a logical reason in the form of a syllogism to help him validate the correct view. As will be discussed in chapter 16, accepting the use of syllogisms does not entail accepting the use of autonomous syllogisms. A syllogistic proof, such as "A sprout is not truly existent because it is a dependent nature, like a vase," requires that both parties know the pervasion between the reason (dependent nature) and the predicate (not truly existent). They must know the forward pervasion: if something is a dependent nature then it must be empty of true existence. Also they must know the reverse pervasion: if something is truly existent then it cannot be a dependent nature. On what basis must they know it? Not on a sprout but on another more familiar example, like a vase. The opponent knows that whatever is a dependent nature must be empty of inherent existence, but he does not know it in relation to that particular object. He has a doubt about a particular instance and wonders, "Is a sprout empty of inherent existence?" He knows that a sprout is a dependent nature. He knows that whatever is a dependent nature must be empty of inherent existence. But he has not brought both these realizations to mind and put them together. In order to develop a definite understanding, the opponent must bring together in his mind the three modes of the syllogism. Then he understands that a sprout is empty of inherent existence because it is a dependent nature, like a vase. It totally depends on what the person to whom you are presenting the syllogism knows and believes. That is how syllogistic reasoning works.

How correct understanding eliminates distorted viewing

Do you think it is possible to understand emptiness on the basis of one thing, such as a vase, and at the same time hold another thing, such as a sprout, to be truly existent? Is it possible for someone to understand emptiness and still grasp at true existence? Tsongkhapa says here that when someone understands the view of emptiness, then the contrived grasping at true existence does not arise for the time being. Does a person who knows through the process of investigating emptiness that all dependent natures are empty of inherent existence ever accept that a thing is truly existent during that period of analysis? Dharmakīrti's *Commentary on Valid Cognition* says:

> Because this understanding and that falsely elaborating mind
> Have the nature of being the harmer and the harmed,
> This [understanding] is known as:
> Entering into the absence of false elaboration. (1.51)

Imagine someone who already knows that sound is produced, but who thinks that sound is permanent. We can prove to him that sound is impermanent by saying, "Sound is impermanent because it is produced." Once he realizes the forward and reverse pervasions between impermanent and produced, he can no longer strongly hold sound to be permanent. One of these thoughts harms the other. The wisdom understanding the pervasion eliminates the falsely elaborating mind conceiving sound as permanent. So that person cannot hold these thoughts at the same time. When one is manifest the other subsides, and vice versa.

When you gain an inferential realization of śūnyatā, the contrived grasping at inherent existence subsides within your mindstream at that time. It is no longer present, but its seed exists within your mindstream—though it cannot arise while the realization of śūnyatā is exercising its influence. However, the innate grasping at things as inherently existent still arises at that time. Therefore when you initially generate a conceptual realization of śūnyatā on the basis of a sprout, you give rise to an understanding that holds the basic object, the sprout, to exist in an illusion-like way. But after the influence of that meditative realization fades, you do not necessarily hold every sprout you encounter to exist in an illusion-like way. If that were not the case, then it would follow that once you realize emptiness, the innate grasping[137] at true existence would never again manifest in your mind. However, it is clear that innate grasping at things as truly existent does continue to arise after a realization of emptiness. Moreover, even though you may understand śūnyatā on the basis of some objects, you can still strongly hold other things to be truly existent.

Various interpretations of "mistaken" according to different Buddhist systems

Bhāvaviveka, Śāntarakṣita, Kamalaśīla, and so on are Mādhyamikas who negate true existence but accept that all phenomena are inherently existent conventionally—though not ultimately. Since they accept inherent existence conventionally, they accept autonomous syllogisms within their own system of reasoning. Therefore they are called Svātantrika-Mādhyamikas. The Prāsaṅgikas do not accept autonomous syllogisms mainly because they do not accept inherent existence at all. So, whether a school accepts the use of autonomous syllogisms depends on whether they accept the subtlest object of negation— inherent existence. This is the crux of the argument between Bhāvaviveka and the Prāsaṅgikas. If one accepts autonomous syllogisms, one must accept that the three modes of the syllogism exist by their own nature.

Therefore, according to Bhāvaviveka's Svātantrika tradition, any sense consciousness unaffected by a temporary cause of error is conventionally nonmistaken with regard to its appearing object—including its appearance as inherently existent. Moreover, a conceptual thought holding a conventional thing, such as a sprout, to exist inherently as it appears is nonmistaken with regard to its held object. So in their system both sense and conceptual valid consciousnesses are nonmistaken with regard to their main objects—the appearing object and the held object, respectively. Otherwise, if these Svātantrikas conceded that those consciousnesses are mistaken with regard to their main objects appearing to be inherently existent, then any valid knowledge accepted in common by themselves and their Realist opponents would establish that things do not exist inherently as they appear to the sense consciousnesses— just as Candrakīrti explained. So when the subject of a syllogism is established, it would already be understood by both parties to be noninherently existent, contrary to how it appears. Therefore what use would there be for an autonomous syllogism?

Some people may suggest that there is no need for the subject of a debate to be established in common by both parties—it is enough to let the Realists establish the subject in their own way. However, Bhāvaviveka does not accept this suggestion. If it were sufficient, then any syllogistic proof would be appropriate only for the opponent—which is the Prāsaṅgika approach. When Prāsaṅgikas debate, they do not need to posit a mutually accepted subject, because they prove or refute something by constructing a consequence based on what follows from their opponent's beliefs.

Valid sense consciousness is treated differently by the two kinds of Svātantrika-Mādhyamikas—the Sautrāntika-Svātantrika and the Yogācāra-Svātantrika. The former is closer to certain aspects of the Sautrāntika system and the latter is closer to certain aspects of the Yogācāra system. The main differences concern whether they accept external objects and whether they posit a self-cognizing consciousness.

Bhāvaviveka follows the Sautrāntika-Svātantrika-Madhyamaka system. Like the Sautrāntikas, he accepts that an external object is a different entity from the mind perceiving it, in that they do not arise from the same substantial cause. Moreover, he accepts that external objects exist inherently, by their own nature. Therefore a sense consciousness is completely nonmistaken, both with regard to the way the object appears and the way that it is held. There is nothing wrong with the appearance of an external, inherently existent form. According to the monastic textbooks, Sautrāntikas say that valid direct perception must be nonmistaken and free of conceptual thought. Being nonmistaken means that the object is known as it is perceived. However, not every direct perception is valid knowledge. A visual consciousness is a direct perception, but it does not necessarily know its object. This may occur when you are in a concert hall listening to music. Your mind is completely absorbed in the melodious sounds. At the same time, your visual consciousness may apprehend many colors and shapes—perhaps of people moving around—but you do not pay attention to them. Your visual consciousness sees what appears to it, but your mind is completely captivated by the sound. So during the concert, although your visual consciousness holds an object, later you have no memory of that sight. You have no idea of what you saw, even though you saw it directly. This is direct perception, but it is not valid knowledge. In this example your mind paid attention to the sound, so your auditory consciousness constitutes valid knowledge. According to Bhāvaviveka and the Sautrāntikas—but not the Prāsaṅgikas—in addition to being nonmistaken and free of conceptual thought, valid knowledge must newly understand its object. Memory is not valid knowledge because it involves previously acquired knowledge rather than new knowledge.

In general, a distinction must be made between "mistaken" consciousness on the one hand and "distorted" or "wrong" consciousness on the other. Mistaken consciousness is mistaken with regard to what appears to it, but it does not hold or understand its object in that way. If something wrongly appears, then the consciousness perceiving it is a mistaken consciousness. Distorted consciousness is mistaken with regard to what it holds or understands. If something wrongly appears and is held to be as it appears, then the consciousness perceiving it is a distorted consciousness. It is mistaken regarding how it holds its main object.

According to the Svātantrika-Mādhyamikas—specifically the Sautrāntika-Svātantrikas—a valid direct perception is nonmistaken with regard to its appearing object. Valid sense consciousnesses are not mistaken, because their objects exist just as they appear; they exist inherently and are substantially different from their perceiving consciousness, just as they appear. According to Bhāvaviveka, if a sense consciousness is mistaken in any way at all, it cannot be valid knowledge. Conversely, in his opinion any valid conceptual consciousness is mistaken with regard to its appearing object, though not its held object. A conceptual consciousness holding a sprout to be inherently existent is not mistaken with regard to its held object because in reality a sprout exists inherently. But because the appearing object of a thought is a combination of the actual object and its conceptual image, which appear indistinguishable, any thought is mistaken.

Now what does "mistaken" mean according to the Yogācāra-Svātantrika-Mādhyamikas such as Śāntarakṣita and Kamalaśīla? Their interpretation is similar to the Yogācāra in certain ways—yet because they are Mādhyamikas, there are some differences.

According to the Yogācāras, a sense consciousness unaffected by any temporary cause of error is nevertheless mistaken because it is affected by a deep cause of error—the imprints left by the innate grasping at the subject, a mind, and its perceived object as different substances. The Yogācāras consider that this grasping at duality is the innate grasping at a self of phenomena. The imprints of this grasping at a self of phenomena affect the senses so that when something appears to a sense consciousness it appears in a dualistic way—as a separate substance to the mind perceiving it. However, although such a consciousness is mistaken with regard to its appearing object, it is still considered to be valid knowledge. In the Yogācāra system dependent phenomena, which are under the power of other causes, are accepted to be truly existent, so a sense consciousness is not mistaken with regard to that. However, it is mistaken with regard to its object appearing dualistically as a separate substance. Thus a sense consciousness is mistaken with regard to its appearing object.

According to the Yogācāra-Svātantrika-Mādhyamikas such as Śāntarakṣita, any sense consciousness is mistaken with regard to the dualistic appearance of its object, but it is not mistaken with regard to its appearance as inherently existent. However, although the Yogācāras believe that causal things are truly existent, the Yogācāra-Svātantrika-Mādhyamikas do not accept anything to be truly or ultimately existent. Moreover, like the Yogācāras, Śāntarakṣita does not accept the existence of any external object that is not in the nature of the mind. Both consider that everything is in the nature of mind only—not that everything is the mind. Although everything is of a mental nature, when things appear to the sense consciousnesses they appear to exist externally, as if separate from the consciousness. The mind and its object appear to be different entities. Therefore according to Śāntarakṣita and the Yogācāra-Svātantrika-Mādhyamikas, even the nondefective five sense consciousnesses are mistaken with regard to the dualistic appearance of their objects. They say that valid sense consciousnesses are mistaken with regard to the appearing object but nonmistaken with regard to the held object. A visual consciousness seeing blue is mistaken with regard to the dualistic appearance of its appearing object. However, it is nonmistaken with regard to its main object, blue. It is also nonmistaken with regard to the appearance of blue as inherently existent. Such a consciousness is valid because it is nonmistaken with regard to its held object.

Conversely, if a sense consciousness is mistaken with regard to its held object—such as a visual consciousness perceiving white snow as blue or one moon as two—then it is a distorted consciousness. A distorted or wrong consciousness is not valid. A visual consciousness that sees its object, snow, as blue in color is mistaken; however, the person in whose mindstream that consciousness arises may simply see the object, snow, as snow—and therefore be nonmistaken. But if the person is similarly confused about this and perceives the snow to be blue, then that person is also mistaken. In short, according to the Yogācāra-Svātantrika-Madhyamaka system, valid knowledge does not require a consciousness to be nonmistaken with regard to its appearing object. It only requires that it must be nonmistaken with regard to its held object.

So, like the Prāsaṅgikas, the Yogācāra-Svātantrika-Mādhyamikas say that both conceptual and nonconceptual valid knowledge are mistaken consciousnesses in general. However, the way in which they are considered to be mistaken is not the same. The Prāsaṅgikas say that they are mistaken with regard to their objects appearing to be inherently existent. Ordinary consciousnesses are influenced by the innate grasping at true existence and its imprints, so when something appears to them, it appears to exist inherently, even though there is no inherent existence. The Yogācāra-Svātantrika-Mādhyamikas disagree; they say that the mistake does not concern the appearance of inherent existence, because things do exist this way conventionally. They say that a valid consciousness within the continuum of an ordinary person is mistaken, in that the subject and object appear dualistically as different entities.

From among various types of Yogācāras, such as the True Aspectarians and the False Aspectarians, the Yogācāra-Svātantrika-Mādhyamikas follow the True Aspectarians. They say that an object of sense consciousness, such as blue, exists as a mental substance conventionally. An object of visual consciousness appears to be external, at some distance from the perceiver, but conventionally it is in the nature of mind. It arises from the same substantial cause as the consciousness perceiving it. The Yogācāras believe that objects of the senses are like dream objects. In a dream we see mountains, rivers, people, and cities, but none of them exist outside of the mind. A dream mind and its object arise together from the same seed, so they are substantially the same. The primary cause of the arising of the consciousness creates both subject and object simultaneously. The object only seems to exist independently and externally. Although the mind and its object are the same substance, when one sees a mountain in the distance, it seems to be over there—while oneself, the perceiver, seems to be over here. The object appears to exist from its own side without depending on the consciousness perceiving it. Thus the subject and object appear to be different entities. They are perceived dualistically.

The visual consciousness perceiving blue has two appearing objects: the appearance of blue and the appearance of blue as external. The True Aspectarian Yogācāras say that the appearance of blue is correct. Blue actually exists as blue inherently, by its own characteristics. Therefore a sense consciousness perceiving blue is neither mistaken in perceiving blue nor in perceiving blue to be inherently existent. However, it is mistaken in perceiving blue to be an external object separate from the mind perceiving it. Since it is mistaken with regard to this dualistic appearance, a sense consciousness is mistaken with regard to its appearing object. However, although such a consciousness is mistaken with regard to its appearing object, it is still considered to be valid knowledge—because the object that it holds is correct. The visual consciousness perceiving blue depends on blue. This is according to the True Aspectarians. The False Aspectarians have a slightly different philosophical view; they say that seeing blue as blue is also mistaken.

ALL VALID KNOWLEDGE IS FINALLY BASED ON PERCEPTION

In general the Buddhist philosophical schools consider that direct perception is the principal form of valid knowledge. Inferential knowledge is valid in dependence on logical reasoning, but at the root of any inferential understanding there is a direct perception. If there were no direct perception involved at all, the process of proof would be endless: first the subject must be proved, then the predicate must be proved, then the reason must be proved, then that which proves the reason must be proved, then that which proves the thing that proves the reason must be proved, and so on *ad infinitum*. If nothing relates back to direct perception, it would be like the blind leading the blind. If a blind person follows another blind person, who follows another blind person, who follows another blind person, and so on, then none of them can see the path. They cannot get where they want to go. They have to rely on a sighted person who can see the path and lead all of them in the right direction. Similarly, understanding the subject, predicate, and reason of a valid argument finally relies on direct perception.

When we have valid knowledge, the object of our knowledge is either a manifest object or a hidden object.[138] Everything is one or the other to the consciousness apprehending it. Manifest objects, such as colors and sounds, can be directly perceived via our senses. Hidden objects cannot be apprehended by ordinary direct perception. Clearly, however, it is wrong to say that something does not exist simply because it cannot be directly perceived. Many things are hidden, but they do exist. There is no way to know things such as śūnyatā, subtle impermanence, past and future lives, or the visual sense power by means of ordinary direct perception; these objects must be known through inference initially. Yet at the root of the inference there must be something that is known by direct perception. When we posit a hidden object as the subject of an inference, we establish it through valid reasoning. Once we have established the subject, such as the subtle eye organ, we can prove our thesis—that it is empty or impermanent and so forth. Even though the subtle eye organ is known through logical reasoning, that inference finally depends on a direct perception.

In Buddhist thought the eye sense power and the other subtle sense organs are not identical to what Westerners call the sense organs. We can see an eyeball, but ordinary people cannot see the subtle eye organ or sense power—a very tiny, subtle physical thing that is the immediate dominating condition producing visual consciousness. The Yogācāras believe that the eye sense power is a kind of consciousness based on the substratum consciousness. The Sautrāntikas and others say it is an almost invisible, very subtle form within the eyeball that can be proved only by logical inference and scriptural testimony; according to the *Treasury of Knowledge*, it is shaped like a tiny sesame flower. There is a subtle sense organ specific to each sensory consciousness; these are located in the respective gross organs, such as the eye or the ear. A subtle sense organ empowers its respective sense consciousness. For example, the eye sense power produces and controls visual consciousness; visual consciousness can only experience color and shape—it cannot experience sound, smell, taste, or touch. The ear sense power directs consciousness so that it can hear sounds, but it cannot produce awareness of objects of other senses. The same applies to the other sense powers and their consciousnesses. A subtle sense organ dominates its respective consciousness, like a king controls his subjects, in that a subject must obey whatever the king commands; or a specific drum controls the type of sound that arises from it, in that it is the dominating cause of that drumming sound but not of other sounds. Similarly, the eye sense power controls visual consciousness. The existence of the subtle eye organ is proved by inference, but the line of reasoning finally reaches back to some kind of direct perception.

How does inferential knowledge arise? How did we first get the knowledge that, for example, sound is impermanent? We came to know it through a valid reason. In the syllogism "Sound is impermanent because it is produced," the subject, "sound," is perceived by ordinary direct perception. The predicate, "impermanent," is a hidden object. It is the subtle momentariness that has to be proved by a reason. The reason, "it is produced," may be directly perceived. Usually we do not need a reason to establish that fact. But if we did, we could give another reason to prove it. In general we directly perceive that the reason is a property of the subject. The pervasion, "whatever is produced must be impermanent," is known through valid reasoning. Thus some of the modes and parts of the syllogism are known through reasoning and some are known by direct perception. In this example we know that sound is impermanent through reasoning; however, our understanding of impermanence arises based on direct perception of the subject, "sound," and the reason, "produced."

When an object that is usually manifest is not visible to the perceiver, there is no way to know it other than through reasoning. For example, fire is typically a manifest object but not always. Sometimes we need to provide proof, such as "There is a fire because there is smoke." The point of our argument is to show that a hidden object, in this case fire, exists in a particular place beyond our field of vision. The reason is "there is smoke." We can directly see the smoke, but we cannot directly see the fire beneath it. We construct an inference and come to know that a fire is there based on our direct perception of the smoke. If we do not see the smoke, then we cannot know that there is a fire. If we see neither smoke nor fire yet need to prove that a fire is there, then we would have to find some other reason to prove the existence of smoke or fire in that place. In the end the reason must be directly perceived. The same principle applies when we are proving anything else, even śūnyatā. Inferential knowledge must be based on a direct perception in the end.

The sense consciousnesses are called *other-cognizers* or *other-knowers* because they understand objects other than the perceiving subject. Some schools posit *self-cognizers* that observe these other-cognizing consciousnesses.

A self-cognizer is a special type of subtle, nonmistaken, direct perception. For example, when a visual consciousness sees blue, that consciousness is an other-cognizer that perceives the object blue. At the very same time, a corresponding consciousness arises and apprehends that visual consciousness. The sense consciousness, the other-cognizer, looks outward, and simultaneously the self-cognizer looks inward. The visual consciousness sees blue, and the self-cognizer perceives the visual consciousness looking at blue. The same applies to the other senses; every other-cognizer has a self-cognizer. In contrast to a primary consciousness, which is always accompanied by the five omnipresent secondary consciousnesses, a self-cognizing consciousness is called a *solitary apprehender*. A self-cognizer does not have any accompanying secondary consciousnesses when it is looking inward at the consciousness itself. It is solitary. Because a self-cognizer does not have any accompanying mental factors, it is not a main mind. However, a self-cognizer is not a mental factor either. A self-cognizer is always nonmistaken. It is always direct perception, never conceptual thought.

Bhāvaviveka does not believe in a self-cognizing consciousness, and nor do the Vaibhāṣikas or the Prāsaṅgikas. All the other schools say that a self-cognizer is the only way we can account for the subjective side of memory. Memory is always drawn from experience. First we experience something, and from that we have a memory. There are two kinds of memory. One is objective, where you remember an object and recall, "I saw *this*." The other is subjective, where you remember the sense consciousness itself or its way of apprehending the object and recall, "*I saw* this." Memory of the subject, or perceiver, signals the existence and functioning of a self-cognizer. Without a self-cognizer we could not remember the subjective experience. For example, sometimes we remember feeling happy or sad in the past. This memory exists because a self-cognizer apprehended the consciousness that experienced happiness or sorrow. Otherwise, how could we prove that we experienced happiness? This is how the other schools account for memory. At some point we may need to consider how the Prāsaṅgikas account for memory, but we will leave it for now. It is enough to note that those who accept a self-cognizer say it is a nonmistaken direct perception.

As explained earlier, the Svātantrika schools believe that what appears to a direct perception is an inherently existent thing, which must exist objectively just as it appears; therefore there is no nonmistaken direct perception that is accepted in common by both the Madhyamaka schools—the Prāsaṅgikas, who propound the absence of an inherently existent nature, and the Svātantrikas, who do not. Even in cases that are not traced back to direct perception, we can also say that the Prāsaṅgikas do not accept the same valid knowledge that is accepted by the Svātantrikas. According to those who believe that things are inherently existent, if a thing—whether produced or unproduced—is established by valid knowledge, it must be established based on its objective nature according to its own way of existing. This valid knowledge does not need to know that; it just needs to know its object. But the object that it knows must be inherently existent. Valid knowledge exists based on the object itself. The thing exists from its own side. This means that when we search for an object referred to by conventional terminology, we can find it. The Prāsaṅgikas say that this can be refuted logically, without needing to refer back to direct perception. Such valid knowledge does not exist at all and therefore is not suitable to prove anything.

(2')) Demonstrating that, owing to that fault, the reason also is not established

Bhāvaviveka is a Mādhyamika, but in one respect he is like the Realists: he accepts that things are inherently existent (though only conventionally). Candrakīrti argues in *Clear Words* that, as a Mādhyamika, Bhāvaviveka should not accept inherent existence at all; so, as a logical method he should not accept autonomous syllogisms. *Clear Words* states:

> The same reasoning that was used to point out the fault that the thesis is not established because the subject is not established should also be used to point out the fault that the reason "because it exists" is not established.

Candrakīrti has already explained earlier that there is no valid knowledge that establishes a subject acceptable in common to both the proponents and the opponents of the emptiness of inherent existence. Since there is no mutually accepted subject of an autonomous syllogism, the thesis—which is a combination of the subject and an attribute predicated to belong to it, for example "visible form is not produced from itself"—also does not exist. This argument applies similarly to the reason "because it exists." Just as there is no valid knowledge that establishes a subject or a thesis appearing in common, so there is no valid knowledge that establishes a reason appearing in common to both the proponents and the opponents of inherent existence. When a reason is established in a syllogism, it has to apply to the subject. In this case an inherently existent reason is not established as acceptable in common to both parties. So just as Candrakīrti earlier in *Clear Words* refutes Bhāvaviveka's use of an autonomous syllogism by showing that a subject does not appear in common to those who accept and to those who reject inherent existence, so this same fault is explained here regarding the reason. When we examine the criteria used by the two debating parties to establish the subject, the predicate, and the reason, we find that the former relies on nonmistaken valid knowledge and the latter relies on mistaken valid knowledge. In short, the two systems are quite different.

Bhāvaviveka refutes the Realist method of argument in a similar way. He analyzes their assertions and explicitly says that if what they are speaking about is something conventional, then it is not acceptable to them, and if what they are speaking about is something ultimate, then it is not acceptable to himself. His argument is based on the two truths. Candrakīrti describes Bhāvaviveka's position and its consequence in *Clear Words*:

> That kind of method is applied here because this logician himself admits what was explained earlier. How so? His opponent says, "The causes producing the internal sources [of sense consciousness] and so on are merely existent because the Tathāgata taught it to be so. What-ever the Tathāgata taught is exactly so, for example, 'nirvana is peace.'" [Bhāvaviveka] presents a refutation of his opponent's proof by saying, "What do you consider to be the meaning of the reason 'because the Tathāgata taught it to be so'? Is it because the Tathāgata taught it to be so in terms of the ultimate or taught it to be so in terms of the conven-tional? If in terms of the conventional, then the meaning of the reason is not established for yourself.[139] If in terms of the ultimate, then since neither what is proved nor what proves it is established, the reason is not established and/or is contradictory."
>
> So using a criterion he himself accepts, which shows that the reason is not established, it follows that the reason and so on are not estab-lished for him[140] because all autonomous inferences have an inherently existent thing set as the reason. Thus all such proof collapses.

Certain followers of Candrakīrti explain the meaning of this passage by relat-ing it to a syllogism put forward by Bhāvaviveka in *Blaze of Reasons* to prove to the Realists that the four great elements are not ultimately existent. There Bhāvaviveka says, "Earth is not ultimately the nature of hardness because it is a great element, like wind."[141] These scholars believe that Candrakīrti crit-icizes Bhāvaviveka for positing the reason "because it is an element." Why? Bhāvaviveka already argued that if a logical reason is not acceptable to both parties, it cannot function to prove anything. In this case, if the reason is pos-ited as "because it is ultimately an element," then it is not acceptable to the

Mādhyamikas; if the reason is posited as "because it is conventionally an element," then it is not acceptable to the Realist opponent. Therefore the reason is not established as a property of the subject. If Bhāvaviveka does not accept that the reason is not established, he is contradicting his own earlier argument.

Then some other people raise another objection: "If 'because it is merely an element,' is set forth as the reason, then that is not established by the wisdom of ultimate analysis. Thus Bhāvaviveka's position is refuted." But this is not the way that Candrakīrti explains the refutation of Bhāvaviveka in *Clear Words*. Bhāvaviveka's position is not as they have presented it, and Candrakīrti does not refute Bhāvaviveka's position in the way that they have argued. The refutation made by these followers of Candrakīrti is mistaken with regard to both Bhāvaviveka's system and Candrakīrti's system.

So in the above passage from *Clear Words*, what does Candrakīrti mean when he says, "This logician himself admits what was explained earlier"? What was explained earlier is not, as the mistaken followers of Candrakīrti claim, the refutation of Bhāvaviveka's syllogism in *Blaze of Reasons*, "Earth is not ultimately the nature of hardness because it is an element." Candrakīrti's mention of an earlier explanation refers to the previously accepted way of showing that the subject is not established, and likewise that the reason is not established. In short, the subject and the reason must be accepted in common by the opponent and the proponent in the debate, otherwise syllogistic reasoning cannot function. This explanation revolves around the valid direct perception that establishes the elements of the syllogism. It must be either mistaken or nonmistaken. There is no other alternative. If objects found by mistaken consciousness are posited as the subject, the predicate, and the reason, they are not acceptable to the Realists. If objects found by nonmistaken valid knowledge are posited as the subject and so on, they are not established by valid knowledge according to the Mādhyamikas—from Candrakīrti's point of view. Thus the subject and the reason of an inherently existent autonomous syllogism are not established in common for both parties in the debate.

Candrakīrti claims that Bhāvaviveka implicitly admits this in *Blaze of Reasons*. Although Bhāvaviveka does not explicitly accept that the subject and reason are not established in this way, Candrakīrti analyzes his position and shows that in the end Bhāvaviveka is forced to accept this also. To demonstrate, Candrakīrti cites Bhāvaviveka's critique of the syllogism put forward by the Realists, "The causes producing the internal sources [of sense consciousness] and so on are merely existent, because the Tathāgata taught it to be so. Whatever the Tathāgata taught is exactly so, for example, 'nirvana is peace.'" In this syllogism, the reason is "because the Tathāgata taught it to be so." Now in order to refute the opponents' position, Bhāvaviveka engages in an examination of the reason from the point of view of the two truths. He asks, "What do you mean by 'because the Tathāgata taught it to be so'"? Some scholars suggest that this question can be rephrased as, "Is the reason 'because the Tathāgata taught it to be so conventionally' or 'because the Tathāgata taught it to be so ultimately'"? However, this interpretation is completely wrong. Bhāvaviveka would not analyze the reason in this way. This manner of critique would lead Bhāvaviveka to contradict his own view. As shown earlier, in Bhāvaviveka's analysis of the syllogism "Sound is impermanent because it is produced," he does not approve of applying any qualification to the subject of the syllogism. He clearly says that the subject of a syllogism must be expressed in general terms, without applying any specific qualifications such as "real" or "unreal," "permanent" or "impermanent." Bhāvaviveka holds that otherwise, if the subject were qualified in either way, it would not be acceptable to one of the two parties. Just as he accepts this with regard to the subject, he would consider that this applies in the same way to the reason and the example. Thus the reason "because the Tathāgata taught it to be so" cannot be qualified as "conventionally" or as "ultimately." If it were qualified in one or the other of these ways, then neither interpretation would be acceptable to both parties in the debate. The Mādhyamikas would not accept as a reason "because he taught it to be so ultimately," and the Realists would not accept as a reason "because he taught it to be so conventionally." Bhāvaviveka is a supremely great scholar. He would not refute his opponent in a way that entails a gross internal contradiction in his own view.

Moreover, Bhāvaviveka is not asking whether the Tathāgata taught something conventionally or ultimately, because this is not an all-inclusive division of phenomena. The Tathāgata taught many things in a general unspecified way; an examination of this reason in terms of whether the Tathāgata taught it ultimately or conventionally would not be exhaustive.

So what is Bhāvaviveka's analysis of his opponents' syllogism? His inquiry is based on the two truths. He says that the meaning of the reason "because the Tathāgata taught it to be so" should be examined in terms of whether the referent of the Tathāgata's speech is a conventional truth or an ultimate truth. This is a suitable question because everything fits into those two categories. Although the different Buddhist philosophical schools define the two truths differently, they all agree that there is nothing that is not included within them; whatever exists must be either a conventional truth or an ultimate truth. There is no third possibility. The appropriate question to ask would be, "Is the referent of what the Tathāgata taught an ultimate truth or a conventional truth?" If the referent of what is set as the reason is a conventional thing, then it is not acceptable to the Realists because they do not accept real things to be conventional truth. If the referent of what is set as the reason is an ultimate thing, then it is not acceptable to the Mādhyamikas, because they reject phenomena that are ultimately produced from causes that exist, do not exist, both exist and do not exist, or without a cause. Something qualified as ultimate is not acceptable to the Mādhyamikas. Moreover, because both parties do not accept anything that is neither of the two truths, there is no need to clear away any third ground.

In the *Blaze of Reasons*, Bhāvaviveka's implicit question to his opponent is, "Which of the two truths is the element that is posited as the reason?" This is similar to the question discussed above. It is suitable to ask whether the element set as the reason is a conventional truth or an ultimate truth, because both parties accept that there cannot be anything that is neither. However, it is not suitable to interpret this question as, "Is a conventional element or an ultimate element set as the reason?" As noted earlier, Bhāvaviveka argues against having a qualification, such as "ultimate" or "conventional," in any part of a syllogism. He insists that we must use a general term that is not qualified in any particular way—so that both parties in a debate can have mutually accepted terms of discussion. Therefore to interpret his question as an inquiry into whether what is set as the reason is a conventional element or an ultimate element is to entirely misunderstand his intention. Now, having asked whether what is set as the reason is ultimate or conventional, it is suitable to claim that if it is ultimate then it is not valid for ourselves, the Mādhyamikas. But how could it be suitable to claim that if it is conventional then it is not valid for the other party? That cannot be accepted literally, since the internal sources of sense consciousness, the subtle sense organs posited as the subject of the syllogism, are conventionally existent and are established or known by these opponents as well as by the Mādhyamikas. If someone interprets Bhāvaviveka's argument as saying that the opponents do not accept the mark because it is conventional, then how could the opponents accept the subject of the syllogism, the internal sources of sense consciousness—the sense organs—since those are conventional also? Therefore it is not acceptable to claim that this way of analyzing is exactly Bhāvaviveka's way.

Tsongkhapa explains Candrakīrti's contention that Bhāvaviveka admits what was explained earlier, in that he analyzes the reason "because the Tathāgata taught it to be so" in terms of the two truths. The master Candrakīrti identifies the ultimate to be something found by nonmistaken valid knowledge and the conventional to be something found by mistaken valid knowledge. Thus in his view analyzing whether something is found by mistaken or nonmistaken valid knowledge and analyzing whether something is a conventional truth or an ultimate truth comes to the same thing. Something that is neither a conventional truth nor an ultimate truth cannot exist; an existent thing must be one or the other. Similarly, something that is neither found by mistaken valid knowledge nor by nonmistaken valid knowledge cannot exist; everything fits into these two categories. According to Candrakīrti, the dichotomy between ultimate truth and conventional truth and the dichotomy between being found by mistaken valid knowledge and being found by nonmistaken valid knowledge are the same. So Candrakīrti considers that Bhāvaviveka's question, "Which of the two truths is it?" and his own question, "By which of the two kinds of knowledge is it found?" come to the same thing. In other words, Candrakīrti considers that if what is set as the reason is neither a conventional truth nor an ultimate truth, then it is not established; if what is set as the reason is neither found by a mistaken consciousness nor by a nonmistaken consciousness, then it is not established. In short, Candrakīrti considers Bhāvaviveka's question, phrased in terms of being ultimate or conventional truth, to mean the same as asking the question phrased in terms of being found by mistaken or nonmistaken valid knowledge. Candrakīrti believes these categories are coextensive and pushes Bhāvaviveka into the position of implicitly accepting this too, by showing that Bhāvaviveka employed the same logical method to refute his opponents.

Candrakīrti does not claim that Bhāvaviveka explicitly admits this. Bhāvaviveka does not talk about whether something is found by a mistaken or a nonmistaken consciousness. For Bhāvaviveka, *ultimate truth* and "an object found by nonmistaken valid knowledge" are not the same; likewise, for him *conventional truth* and "an object found by mistaken valid knowledge" are not the same. Nevertheless, he agrees that what is set forth as a subject or as a reason must be found either by nonmistaken valid knowledge or by mistaken valid knowledge—just as it must be either an ultimate truth or a conventional truth. There is no third ground. If an object cannot be found by either mistaken or nonmistaken valid knowledge, then it cannot exist. Although Bhāvaviveka would accept this much to be true, he says that the two sets of categories are not coextensive. In his system, for something to be valid knowledge it must be valid with regard to the object's inherent nature. So in the above passage from *Clear Words*, Candrakīrti purposely states "an inherently existent thing" when he represents his opponents' position, saying, "because all autonomous syllogisms have an inherently existent thing set as the reason." Both Bhāvaviveka and the Realists maintain that every valid reason must finally relate back to direct perception. Bhāvaviveka considers that some reasons and elements of a syllogism are directly established by nonmistaken direct perception, whereas others are indirectly established by nonmistaken direct perception. Inferential knowledge is not a direct perception. However, as we have seen, even in a logical proof of something that is not directly perceived, the final source of knowledge must be a direct perception. This is why a similar example plays an essential role in a syllogism; when the predicate of the thesis is not directly known, it can be understood in dependence on the similar example that is directly known. Thus Bhāvaviveka believes that a valid inference must finally rely on a direct perception that is nonmistaken with regard to the inherent nature of its object.

Candrakīrti refutes this view. He says that Bhāvaviveka cannot accept such things if he is a Mādhyamika who follows Nāgārjuna. Candrakīrti draws out the contradictions implied by Bhāvaviveka's position that the subject, the reason, and so on are established in the end by a nonmistaken direct valid perception. To support his contention that it is incorrect to accept inherently existent things, Candrakīrti says in *Clear Words*, "A Mādhyamika does not accept the opponent's position," and cites Nāgārjuna's *Refutation of Objections*:

> If anything, owing to its nature, were known
> By direct perception and so on,
> Then that would be proved or refuted.
> But that does not exist; thus I am not faulted.

In other words, if an object's inherent nature were known by direct perception or by inferential knowledge that relies on direct perception in the end, then something could be proved or refuted ultimately. But because Nāgārjuna does not accept ultimately existent things, he does not succumb to such a fault. Candrakīrti cites quotations such as this one to prove to those holding Bhāvaviveka's position that there is no valid knowledge that knows inherently existing things.

16

Our Critique of Svātantrika Does Not Hurt
Our Own Arguments

(b')) Why those faults do not apply similarly to our own system
(b)) Which system to follow so as to develop the correct view within one's
mental continuum

———◦◉◦———

(b')) WHY THOSE FAULTS DO NOT APPLY SIMILARLY TO
OUR OWN SYSTEM

SUPPOSE SOMEONE CRITICIZES the Mādhyamikas by arguing, "Surely the faults that apply to others' inferences, such as the nonestablishment of the subject and the reason, also apply to your inferences? If they do, you are in no position to condemn others." The Prāsaṅgikas reply, "Those previously explained faults apply to others because they accept *autonomous* inferences." Candrakīrti's *Clear Words* states that since Prāsaṅgikas do not accept autonomous inferences, they do not have those faults. Tsongkhapa points out that in this context, *inference* means "syllogism." In other contexts it can refer to inferential knowledge, but here it specifically refers to the arrangement of logical elements into a syllogistic argument. In *Ocean of Reasoning*, which is his commentary on Nāgārjuna's *Fundamental Treatise*, Tsongkhapa discusses Bhāvaviveka's definition of *autonomous*:[142]

> Suppose someone asks, "Now what is the meaning of *autonomous*?" According to Cog ro's translation of *Lamp for the "Fundamental Treatise on the Middle Way,"* where the faults of the opponent's position are presented, [Bhāvaviveka] says, "Is it stated in terms of an independent [proof] or in terms of a refutation?" Thus *autonomous* means "independent" here.

To accept autonomous inferential reasoning is to admit that a thesis is proved by way of both parties establishing the three modes by means of valid knowledge that is unmistaken regarding inherent nature. However, according to the Prāsaṅgikas this kind of valid knowledge does not exist; therefore the subject and so on cannot be established by means of it. Although the Prāsaṅgikas do not accept autonomous reasoning, they consider it sufficient to allow their Realist opponents to accept it; syllogistic reasoning can still work on that basis. The main requirement is that the subject, the predicate, and other elements of the syllogism are accepted in common; they do not need to be established by a shared notion of valid knowledge. This is because the purpose of every syllogism in the Madhyamaka texts is simply to refute others' wrong theses. Therefore the reason and other elements are taken as valid according to how they are accepted in the opponent's system. Based on what the opponent accepts as validly established, the inference shows them the contradictions entailed by their views. So when the Prāsaṅgikas use a syllogism to prove something to their opponents, they do not call it an autonomous inference; they call it "an inference based on others' assumptions." An example of this type of inference is found in the third chapter of Nāgārjuna's *Fundamental Treatise*:

> Seeing does not see
> Its own self.
> How can what does not see itself
> See other things?

Tsongkhapa says that if we rephrase Nāgārjuna's question "How can what does not see itself see other things?" in the form of a syllogism, it would read, "The eye does not see other things because it does not see itself." This is a stock example: here "eye" usually refers to the visual sense power or to the visual consciousness, not to the fleshly eye. Why is this syllogism based on others' assumptions? The syllogism is constructed based on the opponents' belief in inherent existence. Its purpose is to show the opponents that the eye does not inherently see things such as colors. If it saw things in an ultimate sense, it would have to see itself too. But because it does not see itself, it does not ultimately or inherently see anything. As we will discover, Nāgārjuna uses this form of reasoning on many occasions to prove the lack of inherent existence.

In the syllogism under analysis, both the Mādhyamikas and the Realists accept the reason "because it does not see itself" in a straightforward sense. The predicate of the thesis, "does not see other things," is more difficult to interpret. Tsongkhapa explains in *Ocean of Reasoning* that Nāgārjuna's argument here concerns "inherent" seeing, not mere seeing, because this is the kind of seeing accepted by the Realists. The Realists believe that the eye "sees other things 'inherently.'" So the Mādhyamikas argue that the eye "does not see other things 'inherently.'" They are not arguing that the eye "does not see other things" in a straightforward sense. Although the Mādhyamikas accept the thesis, the eye "does not see other things 'inherently,'" they do not accept it to be inherently established. In other words, the Mādhyamikas do not accept the elements of the syllogism in the same way that the Realists accept them. Nevertheless, the Mādhyamikas do accept the use of such a syllogism to prove a point to their opponents. Based on what the opponents accept, this syllogism shows the internal contradiction implicit in their view. This is quite different from using an autonomous syllogism. Candrakīrti's *Clear Words* says:

> We do not use autonomous inferences because our inferences have the effect of merely refuting others' theses.

A syllogistic inference, when used by the Prāsaṅgikas, is a cause that produces a refutation of someone else's thesis as its result. Some people think that the Prāsaṅgikas only use logical consequences and never use syllogisms at all. That is not correct. The Prāsaṅgikas use both forms of argument. However, their syllogisms are not autonomous syllogisms—they are syllogisms based on their opponents' assumptions and are posited merely to refute their opponents' theses.

Now, having posited the use of a syllogism, in the passage immediately following the previous quotation from *Clear Words*, Candrakīrti shows how to use one:

> Those who think that the eye "sees other things" also accept that the eye has the attribute of not seeing itself. They accept that if it does not have the attribute of seeing other things, then seeing does not occur at all. So we argue as follows: "Anything that does not see itself does not see other things, for instance, a vase. In the case of the eye, it does not see itself, so it does not see other things either. Therefore to say it sees other things, such as blue, is contradicted by the fact it does not see itself. So [your position] is contradicted by this inference based on your own assumptions." Thus he is refuted by an inference established for him.

Both parties accept that the eye consciousness has the attribute of not seeing itself. The opponent also accepts that the eye sees other things inherently. But if, as the opponent believes, "not seeing itself" is established inherently, then "not seeing" must be established inherently; if "seeing other things" is established inherently, then "seeing" must be established inherently. So within the opponent's position, there is a contradiction: the eye inherently does not see and the eye inherently sees. Only if seeing is dependent on conditions can we say that the eye sees other things but does not see itself. The point here is that if there is inherent seeing of anything, then seeing has no causes or conditions. It is not dependent on anything else. If the action of seeing is independent of any causes and conditions, then it must see everything all the time. We could not say that it sees other things in an ultimate sense and yet does not see itself. Therefore eye consciousness must see itself. If it does not see itself, then it cannot see any other things in an ultimate sense. If it did, that would be contradictory.

To say to one's opponent "based on your own assumptions" means the same as saying "based on others' assumptions," from the point of view of a Mādhyamika proponent. The Mādhyamikas' method of presenting syllogisms based on their opponents' assumptions is extremely important. Therefore Tsongkhapa explains it in detail. Superficially it may look as if the phrase "established for him" at the end of the above quotation means that the Mādhyamikas do not accept the subject, "the eye," the example, "a vase," the reason, "does not see itself," and the predicate of the thesis, "does not see blue and so on"; however, that is not a correct interpretation. This phrase does not mean that the reason, the pervasion, and so forth are only established for the opponent.

So what does it mean? The Mādhyamikas accept the subject, the predicate, the reason, and the example of the syllogism, but they do not accept that there is any valid knowledge that proves or establishes them to be inherently existent. The Prāsaṅgika system does not accept, even conventionally, that there is any valid knowledge that establishes inherently existent things. According to the Proponents of Inherent Existence,[143] establishment of the elements of the syllogism definitely depends on valid knowledge that is not mistaken with regard to its object's inherently existent nature. Valid knowledge of inherently existent things is acceptable only to the opponents. Therefore there is no valid knowledge establishing its object to be inherently existent that is acceptable to both parties in common—even though the opponents think there must be. So because the elements of the syllogism are established by valid knowledge acceptable only to the opponent, they are said to be "based on others' assumptions" or "established for others." Nevertheless, these objects are accepted by both parties—though the way of establishing them is not. This important point will be explained further below.

An opponent may ask, "If that kind of valid knowledge does not exist even conventionally, then anything accepted to be established by it can be logically refuted—just as reason proves false the imputation of inherent existence. So how could the correct Madhyamaka view be found in dependence on reasons established by that kind of valid knowledge? If an unmistaken understanding of śūnyatā is found in dependence on such reasons, then all the distorted tenets would be found also."

In reply, Tsongkhapa explains that the objects held by this opponent to exist—the subject, "the eye," the example, "a vase," the reason, "does not see itself," and the predicate, "does not see blue and so on"—are undeniable. Even the Prāsaṅgika-Madhyamaka system accepts these things to exist conventionally. How could Mādhyamikas negate things that are established by conventional valid knowledge? These things cannot be logically refuted. The problem is that the opponent does not differentiate between these things as existing and these things as inherently existing. The opponent claims that these things are established by valid knowledge that realizes the inherent nature of its object. In other words, he believes these things to exist inherently. So according to the Prāsaṅgikas, the way in which he holds them to exist can be logically refuted.

Although the opponent's way of holding these things to exist is wrong, he or she nevertheless does have correct conventional knowledge that establishes these things to exist. The opponent's correct conventional knowledge cannot be disproved by logical reason—for example, his unimpaired eye consciousness perceiving blue. The Prāsaṅgikas do not reject the vast amount of ordinary conventional knowledge within their opponent's mindstream. The opponent knows the subject, the reason, the pervasion, and so on. That much is correct. But the way in which he or she establishes these things and believes them to exist is incorrect. So we need to differentiate between correctly establishing the object as existent and incorrectly establishing the object as inherently existent. Because there is no valid knowledge that establishes inherently existent objects that is acceptable to both a Proponent of Inherent Existence and the Prāsaṅgikas, nothing can be proved using an autonomous syllogism. Only a syllogism based on the opponent's assumptions can be used; this is used simply to show the contradictions implied by what the opponent accepts.

The main point here is that the Prāsaṅgikas do not need to accept the way that their opponent believes things to exist. They do not need to share the opponent's way of establishing the elements of a syllogism in order to use it as a means to refute the opponent's wrong view. Even if there is no mutually accepted valid knowledge, a syllogism based on what is accepted by the opponent can demonstrate to them that their views entail contradictions. For example, let us look further at the syllogism based on others' assumptions adapted from Nāgārjuna's root text, "The eye does not see other things because it does not see itself." The reason, "does not see itself," conventionally exists as a property of the subject, "the eye." However, the attribute predicated by the opponent to belong to the subject, "sees other things, such as blue, 'inherently,'" does not exist even conventionally. Therefore the former, which exists, can refute the latter, which does not exist; in other words, the reason, "does not see itself," can refute the predicate to be negated, "sees other things, such as blue, 'inherently.'" Both the reason and the predicate to be negated are based on the eye—something that conventionally exists. If both the reason and the predicate to be negated were equally existent or equally nonexistent, then how could one be the refuter and the other the refuted? To be equally existent or equally nonexistent means that if one exists then both exist, and if one does not exist then both do not exist. If they were both existent, based on the subject, then the reason could not contradict the existence of the predicate to be negated. If they were both nonexistent, then the reason could not function to prove anything. Therefore even in a syllogism based on others' assumptions, the elements must conventionally exist according to the Mādhyamikas too. In other words, a syllogism based on others' assumptions must have a subject, a predicate, and a reason that are conventionally existent. It is not enough for them to be accepted only by the other party.

The opponents accept that the subject, the reason, and so on exist—so why should the Mādhyamikas have to prove the existence of the elements of the syllogism? It is the thesis that must be proved to the opponents, not these other elements. Yet even though the opponents know these elements conventionally, they may deny it and paradoxically say, "These are not established for us, so prove them." In which case, there is nothing that these people would not deny, so who would debate with such partners? It is fruitless to argue with them.

Someone may ask, "When you Mādhyamikas say that you demonstrate a contradiction in your opponent's acceptance of 'the eye does not see itself' and his acceptance of 'the eye sees other things, such as blue' having an inherently established nature, how do you know these to be contradictory? If valid knowledge establishes them as contradictory, then it must be established for both parties; so it would not be 'based on others' assumptions.' In any case, the contradiction cannot be posited based on what the opponent assumes because he does not see any contradiction between 'the eye does not see itself' and 'the eye sees other things.' Also it would be absurd to posit the contradiction based only on what you Mādhyamikas accept. You cannot say to your opponent, 'It is wrong for you to accept them as noncontradictory because we say they are contradictory.' Nobody would accept this as a reason."

Tsongkhapa replies that his position has no such problem. Valid knowledge establishes that if the eye does not see itself, it cannot have an inherently existent nature. This simple fact, that the former contradicts the latter, is established by valid knowledge; it is not posited as a mere assertion. Underlying Tsongkhapa's point is that if seeing and not seeing are dependent or relative, then we can say that in relation to one set of circumstances there is seeing, and in relation to another set of circumstances there is no seeing. We can say that the eye sees one thing and does not see another because of particular causes and conditions. However, if seeing and not seeing are established by their own inherent nature, then once the eye sees anything, we cannot say that it does not see something else; once the eye does not see anything, we cannot say that it sees something else. If it inherently sees, then by its very nature it can never not see; if it inherently does not see, then by its very nature it can never see.

"Well," the questioner may wonder, "if this valid proof being shown to our opponent is sufficient to make him understand the contradiction, why must it depend on his assumptions?" Tsongkhapa replies that, according to the Realists, the valid knowledge that proves this contradiction depends on knowledge that is valid with regard to its object's inherent nature. However, that does not exist according to our system. So how can we demonstrate this contradiction to our opponent based on what we accept? Therefore proving this contradiction to our opponent is based on what he or she accepts. Now, having proved to our opponent that an object's lack of inherent nature does not contradict its valid establishment, he or she will have already found the view that realizes the absence of inherent existence. Based on this proof, he or she will already know that the fact that the eye does not see itself contradicts inherently established seeing. So why do we need to prove it?

Is it possible that someone can understand emptiness in general but not know it based on a particular subject? When you try to prove to someone "A sprout does not inherently exist because it dependently arises," this person knows that anything that dependently arises cannot truly exist. She knows the pervasion in general, so she has a general understanding of śūnyatā. Yet although she knows in general that if something dependently arises it cannot truly exist, and if something truly exists then it cannot dependently arise, she may not be able to put this together with a particular thing. She may strongly believe that a sprout truly exists—even though she knows that it dependently arises. So we present her with a logical consequence that reveals the contradiction implied by her beliefs: "It follows that the subject, a sprout, does not dependently arise because it truly exists." Realizing that this contradicts her conviction about the dependent nature of a sprout, she may develop a doubt about her other assumption and think, "Oh, that is right! Anything that dependently arises cannot truly exist. So maybe a sprout does not truly exist." If she is left with this doubt, we can help her to gain a clear understanding by reformulating our argument as the following syllogism: "A sprout does not truly exist because it dependently arises, like a vase." Other opponents may develop a complete understanding on the basis of a consequence alone; the consequence takes care of the problem and they immediately understand, "It follows that a sprout does not truly exist, because if it did truly exist then it would not dependently arise." They do not need to have the consequence reformulated as a syllogism in order to understand the contradiction implied by their previous assertions.

So there are these two types of people. Surely both of them have understood śūnyatā, have they not? In the case under discussion here, we are trying to prove to our opponent, "The eye does not inherently see other things because it does not see itself." But if our opponent has already understood that the eye not seeing itself contradicts the eye inherently seeing other things, then why should we have to prove this? She already understands the pervasion. Her only doubt concerns a specific subject: the eye. She holds a wrong belief on the basis of the eye. So we present her with a consequence showing a contradiction arising from her view, "The eye sees itself because it inherently sees other things." This consequence enables her to develop an understanding that extends to all subjects. We must carefully examine these things and fathom their meaning if we want to understand Candrakīrti's system.

Someone asks, "But how can we establish the pervasion 'if it does not see itself it cannot inherently see other things' in dependence on our opponent's assumptions?" Tsongkhapa says that this is explained in *Buddhapālita's Commentary on the "Fundamental Treatise"*:

> For example, perceiving earth with water to be moist, water with fire to be hot, and clothing with jasmine flowers to be sweetly scented, depends on perceiving the three, water and so on, to have the three qualities, moistness and so on. You also accept that. Similarly, if things had some inherently existent nature, you must first perceive this inherent nature itself and then perceive that other things have it. If initially you do not perceive it in itself, how could you see it in other things that have it? For example, if you do not perceive a bad smell in jasmine flowers, then you will not perceive a bad smell in clothing with jasmine flowers.

If water did not have the quality of being wet, then no matter how much we water our garden, the earth would never be moistened; if fire did not have the quality of heat, then a kettle of water placed over a fire could never become hot; if jasmine flowers did not have a sweet scent, clothing stored with those flowers could not acquire that pleasant scent. Buddhapālita uses these examples and reasoning, which are familiar to his opponent, in order to help him understand the forward and reverse pervasions in the refutation of inherent nature. This understanding is applied to the syllogism under consideration, "If the eye's inherent nature were to see, then first we would perceive it to see itself, and next we would perceive it to see other things based on an aggregation of forms and so on; however, because the eye does not have the quality of seeing itself, it cannot have the quality of inherently seeing other things." This is how the pervasion is shown based on the opponent's assumptions.

Āryadeva uses the same argument. He says that if seeing were the eye's inherent nature, then nothing—including itself—would be excluded as an object of its seeing. In other words, if the eye inherently sees, then it would see itself. The *Four Hundred Stanzas* says:

> If the inherent nature of all things
> First appears within themselves,
> Then why would not the eye
> Also see itself?

Someone may object, saying, "Just as fire does not burn itself yet burns other things, it is not contradictory for the eye to see other things even though it does not see itself." Tsongkhapa replies that the Mādhyamikas do not deny, in a general or conventional sense, that fire burns other things or that the eye sees forms and other things. They deny that fire inherently burns things and that the eye has the inherent nature of seeing other things. The opponent accepts everything to be inherently existent, so we can rephrase his example more explicitly as "Fire burns fuel inherently." This example is totally incorrect, and what the example is supposed to demonstrate is also incorrect. If fire burns fuel in an ultimate sense, then fire and fuel must each have their own inherent nature. If that is so, then they must be inherently the same nature or inherently different natures. Which of these two alternatives is it? If the opponent says that they are ultimately the same nature, he implies that they are exactly the same and there is no difference at all between them. If that were the case, then how could one be the burner and the other be the object burned? Just as fuel is burned by fire, fire would burn itself. If the opponent wants to say they have the same inherent nature yet insists on maintaining a distinction between the burner and the burned, then we could say, "Because they have the same inherent nature, fire is the object burned and fuel is the burner."

How could he or she respond to that? If the opponent picks the other alternative—that fire and fuel are inherently different—then these must be completely unrelated. To be inherently different is not the same as being merely different. The Madhyamaka view, as expressed in the *Introduction to the "Middle Way"* and many other places, shows that if things are ultimately different then they are completely unrelated, like a horse and a cow. Since there is no relation between them, a cow can exist without a horse, and vice versa. In the same way, if fire and fuel were inherently different, then they would be totally unrelated and fire could be perceived to exist even in the absence of fuel. The Mādhyamikas do not deny that in a general sense fire and fuel are different, relative, and dependent. Fire depends on fuel; without fuel there cannot be any fire. This is a causal relationship between conventionally different entities. But although fire and fuel are different from each other, they are not inherently different. The *Four Hundred Stanzas* says:

> Fire, having the nature of heat, burns.
> If it were not hot, how could it burn?
> In that case there is nothing called "fuel,"
> And without that there is no fire.

Āryadeva's point is that fuel and fire exist relatively and dependently; they are not independently or inherently existent. Fuel is burned when heated by fire. Heat is a defining characteristic of fire. Without heat, fire cannot burn fuel. Therefore it is in connection with heat that fuel is burned. There is no ultimately existent fuel. "Fuel" means something burned by fire. Without fire there is no fuel. Also, without fuel a burning fire does not exist. The object burned and the burner are dependently related. Similarly, we label a mountain in terms of its location depending on our own position. Someone who lives to the east of a mountain calls it the mountain in the west. Someone who lives to the west of that same mountain calls it the mountain in the east. Nobody can say that the mountain is inherently the eastern mountain or inherently the western mountain; it depends on where we are situated. Likewise, the burner and the object burned, the perceiver and the object perceived, the producer and the object produced are relative.

LOGICAL REASONING ITSELF IS NOT INHERENTLY EXISTENT

Even in a logical proof there is no independent reason and no independent thesis to be proved. Nothing is fixed in a certain way by its own nature; nothing is inherently existent. If something had an inherent nature independent of other conditions, it would have that nature all the time, in every situation, and in relation to everything. If we were to accept that burning occurs owing to its own inherent nature, then fire, in having the nature of burning, would burn inherently; so fire must even burn itself. It cannot behave differently toward different objects at different times or in different situations. If we accept that burning occurs owing to its own inherent nature, yet also say that fire, with the inherent nature of burning, does not burn itself, then we find ourselves concluding that burning fire cannot inherently burn other things. Thus because fire does not burn itself, it does not inherently burn fuel; fire burns fuel only in dependence on certain relationships and conditions. Likewise, if we accept that the eye consciousness has the inherent nature to see, we must accept that if it sees other things it must also see itself, because seeing is its inherent nature independent of any other causes and conditions. Thus if it does not see itself, it cannot inherently see other things. Nāgārjuna uses this kind of logic throughout the twenty-seven chapters of his *Fundamental Treatise* to show that if we accept things to be inherently existent we cannot be free of these faults.

When you see that any acceptance of inherent existence is subject to these refutations, you will drop the intellectually acquired Realist tenets grasping at the existence of an inherently established nature. Once you let go of the contrived view that grasps at an inherent nature, you can examine how things function as an agent and the object acted on, a producer and the produced, and so on. You will understand that all such activity is plausible and logically consistent only in the absence of an inherently established nature. Through this you will understand the vast difference between a lack of inherent existence and complete nonexistence, and on the affirmative side you will differentiate between existence and inherent existence. Thus you will understand that noninherently existent valid knowledge realizes noninherently existent objects of knowledge.

Someone asks, "The valid knowledge that initially realizes that fire and fuel are not inherently existent cannot be a direct perception, so it must be an inference. Hence what reasoning is this inferential knowledge based on?"

Tsongkhapa responds by showing how logical reasoning functions, using as an example the syllogism "Fire and fuel are not inherently existent because they are neither inherently the same nor inherently different." He explains that the Prāsaṅgikas accept this reason to instantiate the three modes. The first mode is established when the opponent understands that the reason, "neither inherently the same nor inherently different," is a property of the subject, "fire and fuel." The forward pervasion is established when he understands that if something is neither inherently the same nor inherently different, then it cannot be inherently existent. The reverse pervasion is established when he understands that if something is inherently existent, then it must be either inherently the same or inherently different. When the opponent ascertains, through depending on such reasoning, that fire and fuel are not inherently existent, this is inferential knowledge.

The Prāsaṅgikas accept the existence of a logical reason that is the three modes, but they do not accept any logical reason to be the three modes inherently. There is no valid knowledge that is valid with regard to these modes' inherent existence. Nevertheless, there is valid inferential knowledge that is generated according to the method explained above. This is the way to generate the three modes and the inferential knowledge based on them within the opponent's mindstream, using a syllogism based on others' assumptions such as the one posited earlier, "The eye does not see other things because it does not see itself." This is not an autonomous syllogism, because the Prāsaṅgikas do not consider the three modes to be inherently existent, nor do they try to prove that anything exists from its own side. They are simply trying to disprove their opponent's view of inherent existence. However, a syllogism of the same form posited by Bhāvaviveka is called an autonomous syllogism, because he considers the three modes to be inherently existent and his aim is to prove something that exists from its own side based on these three inherently existent modes.

The Prāsaṅgikas do not always consider it necessary to use a reason that instantiates the three modes to prove something to the opponent. A consequence can be used to show the opponent his contradictory beliefs. The above argument put into the form of a consequence reads, "If fire and fuel were inherently existent, then they would be either inherently the same or inherently different." Suppose the opponent believes that fire is inherently the same as fuel. We use that belief as the reason to show him something that he does not wish to accept—fire burns itself. Therefore the next stage of our argument would be, "If fire and fuel were inherently the same, then just as fire burns fuel, fire would burn itself." This could also be expressed as, "It follows that fire would burn itself because it is inherently the same as fuel." This shows the opponent that what he does not want to accept follows from his current assumptions. It exposes a contradiction in his beliefs. By means of this example you should understand how to construct other consequences.

As long as an opponent has not let go of his Realist tenets propounding inherent existence, he will believe that valid knowledge establishes its referent in dependence on knowing inherently existent objects. When the opponent has developed valid inferential knowledge that some functioning things are empty of inherent existence, he will drop his Realist tenets. What does Tsongkhapa mean by saying that this opponent will "drop the Realist tenets"? First of all, Tsongkhapa is referring to a correct opponent. A correct opponent has some wrong views, but he comprehends other things correctly. A correct opponent is not too far from understanding; we can present an effective argument to him in the form of a syllogism or a consequence. As before, the choice of which logical form we use will depend on whether our opponent is in doubt about a view or if he strongly, but incorrectly, believes something that is contradicted by a correct view that he simultaneously accepts.

In either case we can take some things that our opponent accepts and arrange them in a way to help him target the incorrect view and adopt the correct view. An incorrect opponent is someone who denies everything. No matter how much we debate, no matter what we say, he contradicts everything. It is very difficult to prove anything to an incorrect opponent because he never accepts anything; since such a person argues against every point, he is very far from any understanding. In describing correct and incorrect opponents, Tsongkhapa's disciple, the great scholar and debater Kedrup Je, said, "I do not fear a hundred masters, but I fear a single idiot." In other words, he found it easy to debate with great masters because they accept certain things to be right and others to be wrong. However, an individual who persists in denying everything is petrifying; you cannot get anywhere, no matter how much you reason with such an idiot.

So who is the correct opponent here? It is someone who believes that a certain thing, such as a sprout, is inherently existent, yet who understands that something else, such as a reflection, dependently arises, and that if something dependently arises then it must be empty of inherent existence. This opponent accepts Realist tenets in that he believes that a sprout is inherently existent. However, he understands that a reflection dependently arises. He also understands the relationship between inherent existence and dependent arising in general: he knows that if something dependently arises then it cannot be inherently existent. He knows this to be the case based on a reflection; nevertheless, he still believes that a sprout is inherently existent. This is a correct opponent to whom we can present such a consequence.

Do you think he would be a follower of a lower Buddhist school? Could he be a Svātantrika-Mādhyamika? Could he be someone who does not understand anything to lack inherent existence? The correct opponent must already know that being empty of inherent existence follows from the logical reason "because it dependently arises." Tsongkhapa says that when the opponent understands certain things to be empty of inherent existence, from that point on he drops his Realist tenets. Once he knows the emptiness of inherent existence, even just based on a single object, then the opponent must be a Mādhyamika. He must have already dropped his previously held Realist tenets. What do you think? Are those tenets dropped or not? Candrakīrti's *Clear Words* says:

> *Question*: Moreover, is there a logical refutation by means of an inference established for just one party and not the other?

Reply: Yes, there is reasoning established for the opponent himself but not established for others, as can be seen even in the world. In a worldly situation, sometimes victory or defeat is brought about through the words of a witness considered to be reliable by both the prosecutor and the defendant. Sometimes it is brought about through their own words, while others' words do not bring about a win or a loss. Just as it is in the world, so it is with logical reasoning, because it is only worldly conventionalities that are dealt with in the logical treatises.

When you try to prove something to your opponent using a syllogism instantiating the three modes, that syllogism must be valid for the person to whom the argument is presented. The syllogism does not need to be validly established for the other party. In this passage, the word "others" refers to the Mādhyamika proponents. The Mādhyamikas can prove the absence of inherent existence to their opponents using reasons that the opponents accept but that the Mādhyamikas do not. This happens even in ordinary situations. When two people have a serious disagreement, they may go to court to present their claims to an arbitrator or a judge. Sometimes victory or defeat is established based on the words of a witness; in other cases it is determined based on the words of the parties in the argument themselves. When trying to prove or refute something, it is much more powerful to utilize logical arguments rather than to merely state your own opinion. Just as personal opinion is known to be unreliable in the ordinary world, so it is true of a logical system. Indeed, it is eminently suitable to use logic to establish conventional knowledge.

In this passage Candrakīrti indicates that in a proof it is enough to use an inference that is merely based on the opponent's knowledge. The opponent can accept whatever he or she wishes—and the Prāsaṅgikas can prove or refute something using reasoning based on what is familiar to the opponent. The logic is founded on what the opponent accepts rather than on what the Prāsaṅgikas accept. The Prāsaṅgikas do not have to hold the tenets of the opponent's system in order to use them in a debate. When the Prāsaṅgikas use logic, all the components of an inference are presented specifically for the opponent. The three modes of the syllogism and the example are dependent on being established by the opponent alone. The reason does not function through its own independent power; it is a conventional device that is dependent on many factors rather than being established from its own side.

This is the fundamental difference between inferences based on others' assumptions employed by the Prāsaṅgikas and autonomous syllogisms utilized by the logicians of the lower schools. Dignāga, Dharmakīrti, and their followers, who base their approach on the Sautrāntika and Yogācāra systems, firmly believe that any valid knowledge that establishes the three modes for the opponent must do so for the proponent in the same way. There must be a commonly established subject, reason, and example. If the opponent accepts these to be inherently existent, the proponent must do so likewise. In short, the logicians believe that a syllogism must be autonomous. In an autonomous syllogism the three modes are accepted to be established from their own side and function through the power of their own reality. The Prāsaṅgikas hold the opposite view; the three modes are accepted in dependence on being established by others alone. This is the fundamental difference between an autonomous inference and an inference based on others' assumptions.

In the above passage Candrakīrti indicates that reasoning based on the opponents' assumptions is appropriate for proving or disproving something to them. In the next passage from *Clear Words* he refutes those who accept the use of autonomous syllogisms.

> Those who think, "Only a statement in which any [component] is ascertained by both parties can function as a proof or refutation, but not a statement that is doubted by either or ascertained by just one party," should accept the logical method we explained: inference based on what is conventionally accepted. Similarly, a scriptural refutation is made not just in terms of scriptures established by both parties. So what else? It is also made based on those that just the opponent himself accepts. An inference based on the opponent's understanding is stable, in that it is always established for him; but one based on what is established for both parties is not. For this very reason it is pointless to state the defining characteristics [of an inference] in accordance with the logicians; the buddhas help disciples who do not understand reality by using what those individuals accept themselves.

Here Candrakīrti first paraphrases and then comments on Dignāga's position. According to Dignāga, a correct inferential proof or refutation must be known to both parties in the debate. A valid inference cannot be established by just one party nor can it be doubted by one of them. In the above passage "a statement" refers to a syllogism or formal inference and "where any [component] is ascertained" refers to any of the three modes, but particularly to the relationship between the subject and the reason. In short, both parties must definitely know or establish the components of the inference. Candrakīrti says that because the logical system of Dignāga and his followers was refuted extensively earlier, they should accept the Prāsaṅgikas' system of inference that is based on what the opponent conventionally accepts.

Valid inference is used to develop knowledge of hidden phenomena, and valid direct perception is used to develop knowledge of manifest phenomena. But there are some things we cannot know either by direct perception or by inference. Very hidden phenomena can be known based only on Buddha's teachings. For example, we must rely on the scriptures to know that great wealth is the result of the practice of generosity in a previous life. Although this is not posited as a general cause, there are certain sutra passages where a disciple questions the omniscient Buddha about why a particular person enjoys particular conditions. Buddha explains in great detail about that person's former life—their place of birth, their father and mother, and so on; finally, he relates how that person engaged in certain charitable deeds, as a result of which he or she enjoys great wealth in this life and future lives. Buddha similarly explains the practice of morality to be the cause of beauty and a blissful life, the practice of patience to be the cause of attractiveness, and the practice of joyous effort to be the cause of long-lasting great happiness. There is no logical proof that particular results of this sort arise from particular causes. However, we can trust Buddha's teachings about these very hidden phenomena because there is good reason to trust the most important things that he taught elsewhere. This is the valid knowledge of trusting the scripture.

In general, it is not sensible to accept something just because a text or a person says so. Someone's words are not a valid reason for believing something or claiming to know something. A proof based on the scriptures is not appropriate to establish things that can be known by inferential reasoning or direct perception. Only when you have no way to prove something by direct perception or by logical reasoning—in other words, when the object is very hidden—can words from a reliable source be taken as valid proof. Nevertheless, this is an important way of knowing things. In the West people often believe only what they see or know directly themselves. Such individuals think, "If something exists, then we should be able to ascertain it ourselves. If we cannot ascertain it, then it does not exist." However, Buddhists understand that there are manifest things, slightly hidden things, and very hidden things. We can know a manifest thing by our own direct perception. We can know a slightly hidden thing, such as impermanence, by means of valid logical reasoning. But there is no direct perception or logical proof of the most hidden objects. In order to know them, we must rely on valid scripture. To determine whether a scripture is valid it must be examined using three levels of analysis, like a goldsmith examines a piece of gold. According to certain ancient practices, to verify the purity of gold a goldsmith burns it to examine its color, cuts it to see whether it is as good on the inside as it is on the outside, and rubs it with a particular material to reveal any hidden impurities. If these tests show that there are no impurities, then the gold is considered to be pure. Buddha himself uses this analogy:[144]

O monks and masters,
Accept my words not out of devotion
But by thoroughly examining them,
Just as gold is tested by burning, cutting, and rubbing.

Buddha urges us not to accept his words simply out of devotion to him. We should thoroughly analyze his teachings, like a goldsmith examines gold, to see whether what he says can be contradicted by direct perception, or by valid reasoning, or by what he says elsewhere. We must check whether what Buddha says explicitly in one place is contradicted by what he says implicitly elsewhere. We should see if what he says about very hidden phenomena can be contradicted by other teachings that are verifiable by direct perception or by inference. If we examine his teachings in this way and find that there are no contradictions, then we should accept his word as valid. The teachings on the various spiritual paths and goals are accepted in this way. Even people who are not spiritual practitioners accept certain things that are beyond their own direct perception and inferential knowledge. For example, we believe certain scientific hypotheses because contemporary scientists declare them to be true. But this does not mean that people accept these things just because the scientists say so; the scientists can support their claims in certain ways. Ordinary people accept these things based on what the experts say because they have no other way of knowing them.

In conclusion, Candrakīrti made the distinction between the Svātantrika and Prāsaṅgika methods very clear. An autonomous reason, *svatantra*, refers to proof of a thesis using a reason established for both parties by means of valid knowledge that is valid with regard to the inherent nature of its object. A consequence, *prasaṅga*, does not refer to that method but instead refers to proof of a thesis using a reason where the three modes are merely accepted by the opponent. In such a proof, the reason need not be established by both parties. This kind of proof is effective enough. Candrakīrti is the master who established the use of inferences based on what the opponent accepts and refuted the use of autonomous inferences.

(b)) WHICH SYSTEM TO FOLLOW SO AS TO DEVELOP THE CORRECT VIEW WITHIN ONE'S MENTAL CONTINUUM

The various great Madhyamaka disciples of Nāgārjuna and Āryadeva each followed one of two different traditions: the Svātantrika-Madhyamaka and the Prāsaṅgika-Madhyamaka systems. Which one should we follow? Tsongkhapa explains that he follows the Prāsaṅgika system and urges us to do so as well. He gives two important reasons. First, as explained earlier, the Prāsaṅgika system negates, even conventionally, an inherently existent nature. Second, despite negating a nature that exists intrinsically from its own side, Prāsaṅgikas successfully maintain everything presented by Buddha concerning samsara and nirvana. Specifically, the Prāsaṅgikas' rejection of inherent existence is perfectly compatible with the explanation of the twelve links of dependent arising. This teaches the generation of samsara from the arising of ignorance up to the arising of aging and death, and the liberation from samsara from the ceasing of ignorance up to the ceasing of aging and death. It is absolutely essential to maintain the presentation of this process. It would be a disaster if our negation of inherent existence entailed negating these phenomena. That is the extreme of nihilism. However, it would also be disastrous if our acceptance of all the phenomena of samsara and nirvana forced us to accept them to be inherently existent. That is the extreme of eternalism. As a follower of the Prāsaṅgika system you should develop a firm understanding of how to establish emptiness without negating dependent arising, and vice versa. You must establish them as noncontradictory.

Candrakīrti and Buddhapālita often say in their texts that if we accept things to have an inherently established nature, we should employ ultimate analysis to examine their way of being—because if things did exist inherently, we would find them by such analysis. Seeing that Buddhapālita's and Candrakīrti's explanations closely adhere to the texts of Nāgārjuna and Āryadeva, Tsongkhapa accepts their system. He says that we too should definitely accept the Prāsaṅgika position as explained above.

17

Analyzing a Chariot

(3") How to generate the correct view of reality within one's mental continuum by relying on that method
    (a)) Determining the selflessness of persons
        (1)) Actually determining that the self lacks inherent nature
            (a')) Setting up the example
                (1')) Showing that a chariot exists imputedly in that it lacks inherent nature
                (2')) Eliminating the objections to that
                (3')) How a chariot is established in terms of being labeled
                (4')) The advantage that you find the view quickly by using this example

---

(3") HOW TO GENERATE THE CORRECT VIEW OF REALITY WITHIN ONE'S MENTAL CONTINUUM BY RELYING ON THAT METHOD

IN THIS SECTION of the *Lamrim Chenmo*, Tsongkhapa shows how to use the Prāsaṅgika method to produce an understanding of the ultimate truth within one's mindstream. This topic has three parts:

    (a))   Determining the selflessness of persons (chapters 17–19)
    (b))   Determining the selflessness of phenomena (chapter 20)
    (c))   How to eliminate obstructions by cultivating these views in meditation (chapter 20)

(a)) Determining the selflessness of persons

The way to determine that there is no inherent self of persons is explained in three sections:

- (1)) Actually determining that the self lacks inherent nature (chapters 17–18)
- (2)) Thereby showing that belonging to the self also lacks inherent nature (chapter 19)
- (3)) How to apply these lines of reasoning to other phenomena (chapter 20)

(1)) Actually determining that the self lacks inherent nature

This has two parts:

- (a')) Setting up the example
- (b')) Showing what the example illustrates (chapter 18)

(a')) Setting up the example

In his *Commentary on the "Introduction to the 'Middle Way'"* Candrakīrti quotes an early Buddhist sutra:[145]

> Conceiving "self" is an evil mind:
> You have a [distorted] view.
> The group of aggregates are empty of it,
> There is no sentient being within it.
>
> Just as a chariot is spoken of
> In dependence on the group of parts,
> So the convention "sentient being" is used
> In dependence on the aggregates.

What does "conceiving 'self'" mean? The Prāsaṅgikas interpret this to be the innate self-grasping mind that holds the self to be inherently existent. The lower schools say it is the innate self-grasping mind that holds the self to be self-sufficient and substantially existent. In any case it is the innate self-grasping mind or egotistic view, which wrongly holds the self to exist in a way that it does not. This mind is the internal devil or *māra*.[146] It is the source of attachment, hatred, and all mental afflictions. From the very beginning of samsara this distorted mind has clung to the self, convinced that it is truly existent and all-important. According to the Prāsaṅgika view, our subtlest self-grasping mind is innate; it arises naturally without depending on religious or philosophical views. It *directly* observes the self and it *indirectly* observes the basis of imputation of the self—any of our five aggregates that have arisen from contaminated causes and conditions. This self-grasping mind influences us to believe that there is an inherently existent "I" or "me," though in reality there is no such inherently existent thing. The self is merely imputed or labeled on the group of aggregates—it does not exist from its own side, and the aggregates themselves also do not inherently exist.

In this sutra, the example of a chariot is given to help us understand emptiness and selflessness. When people see a chariot, they generally think it exists from its own side. That perception and conception of an inherently existent thing is very powerful and persistent. But the chariot does not exist as an object in its own right; it exists merely in dependence on the assembly of its parts, such as wheels, spokes, hubs, and nails. Most people understand this at a gross level but fail to comprehend it at a subtler level. Candrakīrti's analysis of a chariot helps us to see clearly how a chariot is labeled based on its parts. This analogy is then applied to the self, a sentient being. When we investigate using Candrakīrti's analysis, we will understand that the self is conventionally labeled based on the five aggregates. The details of the analogy are explained in four divisions:

(1')) Showing that a chariot exists imputedly, without any inherent nature
(2')) Eliminating the objections to that
(3')) How to establish the chariot under various names
(4')) The advantage that you find the view quickly by using this example

(1')) SHOWING THAT A CHARIOT EXISTS IMPUTEDLY IN THAT IT LACKS INHERENT NATURE

There are just a limited number of ways in which a thing might conceivably exist from its own side. But when we analyze the thing itself, to see if it exists in any of those ways, we cannot find it. In this way, we realize it does not exist inherently. Focusing on the example of a chariot, Candrakīrti's *Introduction to the "Middle Way"* says:

> Like a chariot, it is not thought to be different from its parts,
> Not nondifferent, not possessing them,
> Not within its parts, not containing its parts,
> Not the mere collection and not the shape [of them].

This stanza presents seven different ways of analyzing a chariot in terms of how a chariot must exist if it were inherently existent. There is no way, other than these seven, in which a chariot could possibly exist in relation to its parts, if it were truly or inherently existent. The same applies to the self in relation to the aggregates. The analysis works as follows. If a chariot were truly existent, then without doubt we would find it by means of at least one of these seven ways of analyzing it. But we cannot find it to exist in any of these seven ways. Thus we realize that it does not exist by its own nature but exists as a mere imputation. The general question underlying this ultimate analysis is, "If a chariot were ultimately existent, what relationship would it have with its parts?" Based on this, we have seven specific questions: (1) Would the chariot and its parts be the same entity? (2) Would they be different entities? (3) Would the chariot possess its various parts inherently? If so, would the chariot and its parts be different entities—like Devadatta possessing cattle? Or would they be the same entity—like Devadatta possessing his ear? (4) Would the chariot be found within its parts—like a person sitting inside a tent or wrapped in a blanket? (5) Would the chariot be the support for its parts—like a container supports the yogurt inside it? (6) Would the chariot be the mere collection of its parts? (7) Would the chariot be more than a random heap of its parts—existing as a special arrangement of those parts?

These seven ways of existing are the only possible ways in which a chariot could exist, if it were ultimately existent. But when we investigate whether it exists in each of these ways, we do not find anything identified as a chariot from its own side. Having exhausted all possibilities, we realize that the chariot does not exist by its own nature. It exists as a mere imputation in dependence on its parts. Once we understand this analysis on the basis of a chariot, we can apply it to our own self. This is the general idea.

We begin the analysis by individually negating each of the seven ways that a whole and its parts could possibly be related. The chariot is the whole, or the possessor of parts, and its parts are the axle, wheels, nails, and so on. Likewise, the person is the whole, and the aggregates are the parts. If a chariot were inherently existent, then it must be findable, in relation to its parts, as an entity in its own right. So it must exist from its own side either as identical with its parts or as entirely separate from them. We must bear in mind the difference between a relationship of sameness or difference, and an inherent relationship of sameness or difference. What is being negated in the sevenfold analysis is inherent existence, so we are concerned here with inherent relationships. The first two parts of the analysis pose the question, "If a chariot were inherently existent, it would be found to be either inherently one with its parts or inherently different from them. So which is it?" Either way there is a problem. First, if the chariot and its parts were inherently the same, then because the chariot is a single thing, its parts also would be a single thing—or because its parts are multiple, the chariot itself would also be multiple. Why? If the chariot were inherently the same as its parts, then there would be no difference at all between them. The axle, wheels, nails, and so on could not be separately identified. The chariot would exist from its own side as identical with its parts; or, the parts would exist from their own side as identical with the chariot. Therefore the chariot would have to be multiple things, just as the parts are multiple things; or, those parts would all have to be one thing, just as the chariot is one thing. If the possessor of its parts were inherently the same as its various parts, then the agent and object of action would be the same. Here the chariot is the agent—the possessor, and the parts are the object of action—the possessed. If the agent and object of action were the same, then each would lose its meaning and function. Such a fault is clearly unacceptable.

Second, if the chariot and its parts were inherently different, then they would be different from their own side. They would be independent of each other and without any connection. They would be as unrelated as a pot and a woolen shawl. If a chariot and its parts were completely different in this way, then they would be unconnected things that could be seen separately. However, we do not see them independently of each other, we always see them together. We cannot see a chariot in one place and its parts in another. Moreover, if the chariot and its parts were inherently different, there would be no basis on which to impute the chariot. Language and thought identify a thing on a basis. A chariot is an entity imputed on the basis of its various parts. If these two were absolutely different in nature, then there would be no way to identify the chariot on the basis of those parts. Such a fault is unacceptable.

The third and fourth analyses investigate whether a chariot is inherently the basis of its parts and whether it is inherently dependent on its parts. In general, we can say that a chariot is dependent on its parts because it is identified on the basis of its parts. However, if a chariot were inherently existent, then ordinary dependence of this kind would not occur. If a chariot existed from its own side, its existence would not depend on being imputed on anything. It would not have that kind of dependence on its parts; nor would its parts have that kind of dependence on it. So those who believe that things exist inherently must accept that a basis and what is dependent on it exist as different entities—

just as yogurt is supported by a pot or Devadatta sits inside a tent. When we have some yogurt in a pot, the pot holds the yogurt. In that sense, the yogurt depends on the pot; the pot does not depend on the yogurt. So the pot is the basis and the yogurt is dependent. If a chariot were inherently the basis of its parts, then it would support its parts in the way that a pot holds yogurt. They would be different entities. The parts would be found to exist from their own side within the chariot. But the chariot and its parts are not different entities in this way. Similarly, from the opposite angle, when Devadatta is sitting in a tent, the tent is the basis within which sits the dependent Devadatta. If the chariot were inherently dependent on its parts, then it would be found to exist from its own side within its parts—just as Devadatta can be found sitting inside the tent. But the parts of a chariot are not an external basis like a tent, with the chariot abiding dependently within them. The tent and Devadatta are different entities, as are the pot and the yogurt. If the chariot and its parts were inherently existent and one was the basis and the other dependent on it, they would both exist as such from their own side. They would exist without any conceptual or linguistic dependence on each other. Thus they would have to be completely different entities, utterly unrelated to each other, like the examples given here. But a chariot is nothing outside its parts. We cannot find it without them, and we cannot find them without it. A thing and its parts cannot exist as different entities, so they cannot inherently depend on one another. In which case they cannot inherently exist in this way. The argument here is not a negation of mere mutually dependent existence; it is a negation of the inherent existence of a basis and what depends on it. The two examples of a basis and what depends on it are presented in terms of what is accepted by those opponents who believe things to be inherently existent. The Mādhyamikas never refute mere dependence.

The fifth analysis is an examination of possession. In general the notion of "possession" can be applied in two ways: to different entities, such as Devadatta possessing many cows, or to the same entity, such as Devadatta having ears. In a conventional sense it is fine to say that Devadatta possesses his cows or his ears. But if we say that he possesses them in an ultimate sense, then Devadatta and his cows would have to be inherently different entities, and Devadatta and his ears would have to be inherently the same entity. Being inherently different means being different from the side of the object, in which case such things would be totally unrelated. Being inherently the same means being the same from the side of the object, in which case such things would be utterly indistinguishable (they would be one and the same thing). In a conventional sense, we can say that a chariot has many parts. However, it is incorrect to say that a chariot ultimately has parts. Conventionally, when a possessor has something, there are only two possible relationships between them: either they are different entities, like Devadatta and his cows, or they are the same entity, like Devadatta and his ears. Likewise, if a possessor inherently has something, then it must be limited to these two options. We can refute both of them in turn.

First, a chariot cannot inherently possess its parts in the way that Devadatta possesses his cows, which are different entities, because then the chariot would be seen separately from its parts—and it is never seen that way. Furthermore, if a chariot did inherently possess parts that are different entities from itself, then they would be inherently different entities and therefore totally unrelated. We already refuted a chariot and its parts being inherently different entities: if the chariot were utterly independent of its parts, it would be unrelated to them as a basis of imputation. So the notion of possession that is applied to different entities cannot occur here. Second, a chariot cannot inherently possess its parts in the way that Devadatta possesses his ears, which are the same entity, because then they would be inherently the same entity and therefore utterly indistinguishable. We already refuted a chariot and its parts being inherently the same entity: if the agent and object of action were conflated, then language and thought would be meaningless. So the notion of possession that is applied to the same entity cannot occur here. Thus both notions of possession are refuted.

Of course, we cannot deny that Devadatta possesses his ears in a conventional sense, and we cannot deny that a chariot conventionally possesses its parts. Things can be the same nature in a conventional sense, though they may have different names. What is being negated here is inherent possession. Like conventional possession, inherent possession can only apply to things that are either different entities or the same entity. In the case of inherent possession, if things are different entities, then they must be inherently different entities; if they are the same entity, then they must be inherently the same entity. Both of these were already refuted earlier. It is when we say that things are the same or different, while accepting them to be ultimately existent, that big problems arise.

The sixth analysis examines whether the chariot is the mere collection of its parts. The seventh analysis examines whether the chariot is the shape of those parts assembled in a particular way. Neither of these two are the chariot. Candrakīrti's *Introduction to the "Middle Way"* says:

> If the mere collection [of parts] were the chariot,
> Then even when dismantled somewhere, the chariot would be there.
> Since there are no parts without a whole,
> It is also incorrect for the mere shape to be the chariot.

This stanza brings up two points. First, if the mere collection of parts were the chariot, then we would have to say that the chariot is present even in a chaotic pile of spokes, hubs, bolts, and so on. If all the parts are there, then the chariot must be there. Second, if there is no chariot as a whole, then we cannot say that there are parts of a chariot; if there are no parts, then the shape of those parts cannot be the chariot. These two points represent the sixth and seventh analyses, respectively.

The first point is that the chariot cannot be the mere collection of its parts. To assert that it is a mere collection of its parts leads to two contradictions— it contradicts reason, and it contradicts the assertions of the lower Buddhist schools. It contradicts reason to say "Here is the chariot" when there are only the parts of a chariot randomly thrown into a heap. But we would have to admit this if the mere collection of parts were the chariot. The Prāsaṅgika's main target of refutation is the belief that the objective referent of a name can be found when it is sought.[147] When we think "This is a table" we differentiate between something being a table and something not being a table. It looks as though the thing identified as a table exists from its own side and can be found. Actually the table is just conventionally labeled based on its parts. In terms of certain worldly conventions, we think that this table and that table are different and that oneself and others are different. These conventions are either the names given to identify things or the internal thoughts that accompany these names. Using such conventions we make distinctions between this and that, between what is beautiful and what is ugly, and so on. If a chariot or any other thing were found by ultimate analysis, then what is found? Is it the parts of the chariot? If so, then is it each of the individual parts? Or is it the collection of them? You should try this kind of analysis. But as we have seen, if the chariot were the collection of all the parts together, it would exist even in a pile of disconnected pieces. This contradicts reason.

This position also contradicts the assertions of the Buddhist Realists, who hold things to be truly existent and who say that the aggregation of parts exists but the part possessor or whole does not exist. If they accept this, however, then they must accept that the parts also do not exist—because the whole does not exist. These Realists are thinking that if you put all the pieces of a chariot together in a pile, the collection of parts is there—but the chariot itself is not there. The Prāsaṅgikas argue that if the whole itself is not there, then how can its parts be there? The parts depend on the whole. If the whole is not there, then a collection of pieces cannot be its parts. Therefore because the aggregation of parts does not exist, the collection of parts cannot be the chariot. The master Candrakīrti does not need to apply a special qualifier, such as ultimately, when refuting the mere collection of parts to be the chariot. This can be refuted even conventionally because the mere collection of parts is the basis of imputation of the chariot. The basis of imputation and the thing imputed on it cannot be the same. Thus the collection of parts, in being the basis of imputation of a chariot, cannot be the chariot. Similarly, the collection of aggregates, in being the basis of imputation of the self, cannot be the self.

The Buddhist Realist schools generally say that a collection exists as an imputation based on its components that are substantially existent. A collection—such as a rosary, a forest, and an army—is imputedly existent. However, the individual elements—such as beads and string—are substantially existent. The collection is not substantially existent. Also the whole, or part possessor, is not substantially existent—it is just an imputation based on its substantially existent parts. According to these systems, if the parts were not substantial, then a chariot could not be imputed on them because any imputed thing must be based on a substantial thing. Without a substantial thing, we cannot have a quality or attribute that is an imputed thing. This applies to persons also. The aggregates, such as body and feelings, are themselves substantially real things, and a person is imputed on that. A person is imputedly existent but has a substantially existent basis. Yet this does not mean that such things are totally nonexistent or that they are nonfunctional. Imputed things, like a person or a chariot, are functional. However, the Prāsaṅgika-Madhyamaka system does not accept anything to be substantially existent, so they say that everything is merely imputed.

Now we come to the second point outlined above. A Realist opponent suggests, "We do not accept that the mere collection of the parts is the chariot; rather, we accept that the chariot is all the parts put together in a particular arrangement." Tsongkhapa replies that, as just explained, we can talk about parts only if there is a whole. If there is no whole—in this case a chariot—then there are no parts of a chariot. If a possessor of parts does not exist, its parts cannot exist. When we dismantle a chariot, we cannot call those disassembled pieces the parts of a chariot—because there is no chariot there at all. We can call each piece by an individual name, but we cannot say it is a part of a chariot. If the parts do not exist at that time, then we cannot put them together and call the resultant shape of their arrangement a chariot. The opponent accepts that when the chariot is disassembled into a group of parts, the chariot does not exist; so it is illogical for him to claim that a chariot is the special arrangement of all its parts.

In the stanza from the *Introduction to the "Middle Way"* quoted above, we find the word "also." It clearly means that not only is the mere collection of parts not the chariot, but also the shape of the parts is not the chariot. Moreover, if we accept the shape to be the chariot, does this refer to the shape of each individual part or to the shape of the collection of parts? Here the word "shape" may indicate a special arrangement of pieces. If it is the shape of the individual parts, are these shapes the same before we put them together as they are after we assemble them? Or when we put them together, do they become new shapes different from what they were before? These are the two possibilities. In discussing the first option, Candrakīrti's *Introduction to the "Middle Way"* says:

> If you say the shapes that the individual parts had before
> Are the same as what we know [when assembled] into a chariot,
> Then just as in the case where they are separate
> So too in this case there is no chariot.

Each piece of a chariot—the hub, axle, seat, and so on—has its own shape. Their individual shapes remain the same after they are assembled as they were before we put them together. They do not suddenly change their shapes depending on whether we randomly pile them up or arrange them in a special way. The shape of a spoke is the same when lying on a workbench as it is when assembled into a wheel. If the individual shapes remain the same, how can the assemblage be a chariot? Just as there is no chariot when the pieces are separated, there is still no chariot when we put them together. Moreover, if the individual shapes were the chariot, the chariot would exist before it is built.

Does the second alternative sound any better? Suppose when the individual pieces are put together they have a shape different from what they had before. The new arrangement of pieces causes them to change their shapes, and so the final formation becomes a chariot. In response to this, Candrakīrti's *Introduction to the "Middle Way"* says:

> Now at the time of the chariot itself,
> If there were a different shape to the wheels and so on
> It would be apprehended, but it is not;
> Therefore the mere shape is not the chariot.

When we assemble the pieces in a special way we think the chariot exists. However, if the shape of each part were different after assembling them, we would be able to see that. But when we examine them, we cannot discern any difference in their shapes from before they were assembled. The shape of each spoke remains the same. It has not changed. Each round part remains round. Each square piece is still square. If they were different we would be able to see it. No matter how much we look, the shapes of the parts remain the same after being put together as they were prior to assembly. Therefore it is not correct to say that a chariot is the special shapes of the parts after they have been put together. These are no different from the shapes they had before.

Now the opponent may say, "We do not claim that the individual shape of each part is the chariot. It is the general shape of all the assembled parts together that is the chariot." What follows from this? What is the difference here? Candrakīrti's *Introduction to the "Middle Way"* says:

> According to you, the mere collection does not exist [substantially],
> Therefore it is not the shape of the collection of parts.
> Since it would depend on what is not anything,
> How can you view it as that shape?

The Realists believe that a collection of parts is not substantially existent—it is imputed on substantially existent individual parts. Since a collection does not substantially exist, it is not a suitable basis of imputation. We cannot take a collection as a basis and impute anything—not even a shape—on it. Thus the shape of the collection is not even an imputedly existent thing because its basis—the collection—is not substantially existent. So the general shape of the collection of parts does not exist at all, because it is neither substantially existent nor imputedly existent. How can such a nonexistent shape be a chariot? According to the Prāsaṅgikas, if the collection did substantially exist, it would inherently exist: the lack of substantial existence is the same as the lack of inherent nature. If a collection of parts were inherently existent, then it would have to be inherently the same as or inherently different from the parts. There is mutual possession between the parts and the whole. The parts possess the collection, so they are the collection possessor. The collection possesses the parts, so it is the part possessor or whole. If the collection were inherently existent, it would have to be either inherently the same as or inherently different from the collection possessor or parts themselves. There is no other possibility. Both positions can be refuted using the same logic employed at the beginning of this chapter.

According to the Prāsaṅgikas, everything is imputedly existent. Nothing is substantially existent. We do not accept that something substantially existent must be the basis of an imputedly existent thing. Therefore it is fine to say that the shape of all the parts assembled together is the basis of imputation of the chariot—though we do not say that it is the chariot. The chariot is an imputedly existent phenomenon. It is imputed on the basis of the shape of the collection. It is important to understand that the basis of imputation and the imputed phenomenon are not identical. The basis and the thing imputed on the basis are not the same. In this case, the shape of the assembled parts is the basis of imputation of the chariot. In addition, the chariot is imputed based on the shape of the individual parts. However, this does not mean that the parts themselves, their individual shapes, or their collective shape is the chariot. So once again, because we can conventionally refute that the special shape of the collection is the chariot, we do not need to apply a qualifier, such as ultimately, to the object of negation.

At this point an opponent suggests, "There is nothing wrong with accepting that a shape that lacks true existence is imputed in dependence on a collection that lacks true existence." Tsongkhapa replies, "In that case, you must accept that causes lacking true existence—such as ignorance and seeds—give rise to effects lacking true existence—such as conditioning action and sprouts." Thus the opponent is compelled to acknowledge that all causality is falsely existent. Candrakīrti's *Introduction to the "Middle Way"* says:

> Just as you assert here,
> Likewise, you should understand
> That all results, which have nontruly existent natures,
> Arise in dependence on nontruly existent causes.

The earlier explanation about the relationship between a chariot and its parts also serves to show that other composite phenomena—such as pots and so on—are not the assembled collection of eight elementary atomic substances. The eight elementary atomic substances are the four great elements (earth, air, fire, and water) and the four substances arisen from those elements (the objects of sight, smell, taste, and touch). When we engage in the analyses explained above, we can see that a pot is not the elementary substances that compose it, nor the collection of those substances, nor the arrangement of the collection of those substances. These simply function as the basis on which a pot is labeled. The Prāsaṅgikas do not accept anything to be substantially existent, including the bases on which a thing is imputed, because these are not inherently produced and so have no inherent nature. However, as we have seen, the Realists say that the basis of imputation must be substantially existent. Buddhist schools agree that a pot is imputed on its basis, and all except the Prāsaṅgikas believe it is findable within its basis of imputation. They are convinced there must be something among the bases of imputation that can found to be the thing itself. Because of this, they consider it to be inherently existent. So what is a pot? What is the entity referred to by that name? Where is the real, actual pot? Is it the eight substantially existent atomic particles? Or is it a special arrangement of substantially existent forms and so on? Or is it imputed on the eight substantially existent atomic particles? The Prāsaṅgika-Mādhyamikas reject all these possibilities with the arguments presented earlier. Candrakīrti says in *Introduction to the "Middle Way"*:

> Because of this, it is incorrect to think of a pot
> As a certain combination of forms and so on.
> Also, because forms and so on are not produced, they do not exist;
> Therefore it is incorrect for it to be their shape.

The opponent objects and says, "Each thing has its own defining characteristics. If, as in the example of the chariot, the pot is not the shape of the collection of parts, then the pot cannot be defined as bulbous-bellied, flat-bottomed, and able to contain water. Something having these special characteristics, with this specific function, is called a pot. We cannot say that just anything is a pot. You are implying that the elementary substances combined into a shape that is bulbous-bellied and flat-bottomed is not the defining characteristic of a pot."

Tsongkhapa replies that he accepts that whatever fits that definition is a pot. However, the shape of each individual part, such as the bulbous belly, cannot be the pot. If it were, the shape of the belly would be the pot and the shape of the neck would also be a pot. The shape of the belly and the shape of the neck each have to be the basis for the belly and the neck, respectively. The belly has its own basis. The neck has its own basis. The definition of a pot differentiates what is a pot from what is not a pot in terms of its basis. It is a way of pointing out something as a pot. The attributes function to point to the referent that we call a pot. The definition is the referent itself.

(2')) Eliminating the objections to that

The Buddhist Realists object to the upshot of Candrakīrti's analysis investigating whether something inherently exists. They say that if we search for a chariot by means of the sevenfold analysis and do not find it, then we must conclude that the chariot does not exist. In that case, we cannot use the conventional term "chariot." But this is obviously not the case. There are many statements about chariots, such as "Bring the chariot," or "Buy a chariot," or "Build a chariot." If there were no such thing as a chariot, how could these things meaningfully be said? Because these expressions exist, we must conclude that chariots exist.

Tsongkhapa says that in *Commentary on the "Introduction to the 'Middle Way'"* Candrakīrti gives two reasons to show that this fault does not apply to the Mādhyamikas. First, only the Realists, who believe that things are inherently existent, have this problem. Common conventional expressions, such as "Bring the chariot," cannot exist in their worldview. Why? This is because they accept that everything is inherently existent, and the way to establish a thing's inherent existence is to examine it by ultimate analysis. So on their view, a thing must be found when searched for by ultimate analysis. However, they offer no other way to establish the existence of things. So when they search for the referent of the term "chariot" by means of the sevenfold ultimate analysis, they cannot find a real chariot. Therefore, according to their system, the chariot is nonexistent. Thus this fault applies only to the Realists.

Tsongkhapa says that although some of his contemporaries claim to be Mādhyamikas, they also hold the view that if we do not find something existing from its own side when we search for it using ultimate analysis, then this nonfinding means that the thing is nonexistent. These so-called Mādhyamikas deny the existence of everything in this way, yet they worry about falling into nihilism. To avoid that, they declare the Madhyamaka position to be, "Things are not existent, not nonexistent, not both, and not neither." Superficially this may look like the Madhyamaka position, but this is wrong. Those who accept such an interpretation will never be able to establish conventional phenomena; there is no way that someone with this view can establish causality and functionality. The correct Madhyamaka view is that if you search for a chariot in any of the seven ways, you will not find its inherent or essential nature. But this does not mean that the chariot is completely nonexistent. It does exist conventionally, even though it does not exist ultimately or inherently. Although you do not find the thing when you search for it using ultimate analysis, this does not entail that this thing does not exist at all. Do not be confused about this.

The second reason that this fault does not apply to the Mādhyamikas is introduced by a quotation from Candrakīrti's *Introduction to the "Middle Way"*:

> Although not established through the seven ways
> In terms of ultimate reality or worldly convention,
> Yet from the unanalyzed worldly point of view
> It is imputed in dependence on its parts.

When we use the sevenfold ultimate analysis to investigate whether a chariot exists inherently, we do not find the chariot ultimately or conventionally. Nevertheless, how could not finding the chariot through this reasoning totally negate the chariot? We do not use ultimate logical analysis to prove any assertion about a chariot. Instead we drop ultimate analysis and use correct conventional knowledge, free of temporary causes of error, to establish that the chariot exists. The chariot is established as imputedly existent. It is imputed in dependence on its parts. According to the Prāsaṅgika-Mādhyamikas, this applies to everything because everything has parts, including permanent phenomena such as uncaused space. A thing with parts is dependent on its parts; it cannot exist without its parts. Thus all things are imputed on their parts. Everything exists imputedly.

The opponent now says, "When a yogi engages in ultimate analysis, he does not find the chariot. So the chariot does not exist by its own nature. However, its parts do inherently exist." The opponent accepts that the chariot itself is not findable and therefore not inherently existent. But once again he states his belief that the chariot is imputed based on parts that are substantially and inherently existent.

Tsongkhapa retorts, "This is ridiculous. It is like searching for the threads of a woolen shawl that has been completely burned to ashes." Candrakīrti's *Introduction to the "Middle Way"* says:

> At a time when the chariot does not exist,
> The whole does not exist, so its parts also do not exist.

If there is no whole or part possessor, how can there be its parts? The opponent contends, "That is not correct, because when the chariot is dismantled or falls apart, we can still identify the collection of its parts, such as the wheels and so forth."

Tsongkhapa says that the opponent is mistaken. Only if we saw a whole chariot at some earlier point could we later think that a pile of separate items were the parts of a dismantled chariot. Otherwise that thought would not arise. When the chariot is dismantled there is no whole chariot, so we cannot say that we see the parts of the chariot. At that time the pieces have no connection with a chariot because there is no chariot there. They cannot belong to something that does not exist. If something is a part of a chariot, there must be a whole chariot. If there is a whole chariot, we can say there are parts of that chariot. The parts and the whole cannot be separated. If there is no whole, then there cannot be parts of that whole. In other words, when the chariot is destroyed there are no parts of a chariot nor is there a whole chariot that possesses its parts. Neither of them exists. If we have one piece, such as a wheel, we cannot say it is part of a chariot. However, that wheel is a part possessor itself; it is dependent on its own parts, such as the spokes and hub. A spoke too has many parts, such as small particles. We cannot establish parts independently of a whole. Thus it is incorrect for the opponent to think that the chariot does not exist but the parts of the chariot do exist. Candrakīrti's *Introduction to the "Middle Way"* says:

> Just as when a chariot is burnt up, its parts no longer exist,
> When the fire of wisdom has burnt up the whole, its parts have vanished.

We should understand how to meditate on selflessness through this example. When the self that is held to be inherently existent is consumed by the fire of analytical wisdom, we see that the inherently existent self does not exist. In other words, we cannot find any self that exists by its own nature. At that point we recognize that both the self and its parts are empty.

(3')) HOW A CHARIOT IS ESTABLISHED IN TERMS OF BEING LABELED

Candrakīrti's *Commentary on the "Introduction to the 'Middle Way'"* says:

> This system not only very clearly establishes that a chariot is conventionally designated from the point of view of what is commonly known in the world, but also that any particular name of it must be accepted from the point of view of what is known in the world without analysis. It is like this:
>
> > This part possessor or whole,
> > This chariot itself is commonly called an "agent";
> > It is established for living beings as an "appropriator."

A chariot is called a composite, literally a limb possessor, because it has many components, and it is called a whole, literally a part possessor, because it has many parts. It is also called an agent in relation to the objects acted on, such as the wheels, and it is called an appropriator in relation to the appropriated parts. In the same way, living beings are called appropriators of the aggregates. These different terms show the way that things are established: they are linguistic conventions. Things are nominally established; they do not inherently exist by their own nature. A chariot is established as the conventional referent of the terms *whole* and *part possessor* in dependence on parts and components such as wheels. Therefore in relation to its parts, which are the appropriated objects, the chariot is called an appropriating agent. In relation to the function of owning these parts, it is called an appropriator. It is imputed as the referent of these different names from the point of view of its different functions. These terms do not refer to inherently different substances. The referents are established by worldly conventions. This is the way language is used. We are familiar with one object having many names. For example, in Asian countries the moon is poetically called One Having Cooling Rays, Light Possessor, and Rabbit Bearer. The last name refers to the image of a rabbit that we can see on the full moon.

Some lower Buddhist schools say that the mere collection of parts or components exists, but a whole does not exist because it is not seen separately from that collection. So a collection of parts exists, but a part possessor does not; a group of components exists, but a component possessor does not. These schools accept the existence of parts and components and of groups of parts and components. But they do not accept the existence of a part possessor or a component possessor, because that is not seen separately from the parts themselves or a group of them. In short, there are no wholes. These schools may be addressing the non-Buddhist Vaiśeṣika system, which asserts that a thing has a part possessor pervading all its parts, which is not connected to the parts themselves; it is separate from them and partless itself, though it always pervades all the parts. Perhaps in response to this, these lower Buddhist schools adopt an extreme position denying the existence of wholes or part possessors, though they accept collections of parts and components. Similarly, they say that there is action but no agent. Action exists, but an agent of action does not exist because it is not seen apart from the action itself. Also, although there is appropriation, there is no appropriator apart from the act of appropriating. There is function and activity in terms of the object acted on but not in terms of the subject acting. Likewise, parts exist but a whole does not, because it is not seen separately from the parts themselves. This way of speaking about things is completely contrary to linguistic conventions and ordinary understanding.

An obvious objection arises: "If there is no whole, how can there be parts? If there is no component possessor, how can there be components?" As we have seen, once the whole does not exist, the parts cannot exist—because the parts and the whole exist dependently on each other. Without a whole we cannot speak of parts. Without an agent we cannot speak of action. Candrakīrti's *Introduction to the "Middle Way"* says, "Do not destroy the conventions accepted in the world." Therefore just as wholes do not exist ultimately, parts do not exist ultimately; just as parts exist conventionally, wholes or the possessors of parts exist conventionally. This way of thinking will not contravene the two truths.

(4')) The advantage that you find the view quickly by using this example

We can quickly come to understand emptiness by depending on the example of a chariot. If a thing—such as a chariot—were inherently existent, the chariot and its parts would exist in one of the ways specified in the sevenfold ultimate analysis. A chariot and its parts do exist in such relationships conventionally but not inherently. Inherent existence means that something is identified in terms of its own inherent nature, not simply in dependence on a name. Ultimate analysis is the search for that nature comprehensively through those seven ways. When we do not find anything of that nature, we understand that the thing being analyzed is without inherent existence. Candrakīrti's *Commentary on the "Introduction to the 'Middle Way'"* says:

> Worldly conventional things do not exist in terms of this analysis; yet they exist in terms of being commonly accepted without analysis. Therefore when a yogi analyzes things by means of this very process, he very quickly fathoms the depths of reality. How is this so?
>
>> How could what does not exist in the seven ways be said to exist?
>> A yogi does not find it to exist,
>> Thus he also easily enters into reality.
>> Here you should accept it to be established in this way too.

The word "yogi" here does not refer to just any ordinary meditator; it refers to someone who, through engaging in ultimate analysis, realizes śūnyatā. Candrakīrti makes the extremely important point that if we analyze a chariot in these seven ways, we will quickly understand the meaning of ultimate truth—that things do not inherently exist. If there were an inherently existent chariot, we would undoubtedly find it when we examine its mode of existence using this process. Why? This is because if something is inherently existent, it must exist in one of those seven ways; if it exists in any of those seven ways, then it would be findable. However, when we use this analysis, we do not find a chariot existing by its own nature. Nevertheless, we cannot deny that a nominal chariot appears. This so-called chariot, which appears to exist inherently, is only imputed by ignorance, which is like a cataract distorting the eye of wisdom. Through engaging in ultimate analysis, a yogi will develop a firm understanding that a chariot imputedly exists but does not exist by its own nature. Thus he or she will easily realize the ultimate nature of reality.

In the stanza above, the word "also" in the line "Thus he also easily enters into reality" indicates that a yogi will understand how things exist conventionally in addition to understanding ultimate reality. Thus it is clear that such a realization will not damage conventionalities.

This sevenfold analysis offers a clear way to determine the lack of inherent existence of a chariot. By depending on this analytical method one can easily understand that a chariot is not inherently existent yet is conventionally existent. In brief, the presentation of the sevenfold analysis based on a chariot has three special qualities. First, it is easy to refute the eternalist view that superimposes inherent existence on all phenomena. Second, it is easy to refute the nihilistic view that denies the dependent arising of things that do not inherently exist. Third, by following this method of analysis, which possesses the first two qualities, a yogi can easily attain the stages of realization and accomplish the Madhyamaka view.

Let us look at these advantages in more detail. First, it is difficult to understand a refutation of inherent existence using reasoning that is very much abbreviated, such as an argument that only presents the negation of sameness and difference. Conversely, it is difficult to understand such a refutation when too great a variety of different reasons are used. So the sevenfold analysis is just right. Second, in the beginning of the sevenfold analysis, the qualifier "ultimately" is applied to the object of negation. Thus we negate inherent existence but do not harm how things conventionally exist. Third, a yogi benefits supremely from pursuing this analysis. How does this happen? A yogi must first have a definite understanding of the relationship between (a) the pervaded—inherent existence—and (b) the pervader—the seven possible modes of existence, such as the thing being the same as its parts and so on. In other words, if something is inherently existent then it must exist in at least one of those seven ways; if it does not exist in any of those seven ways, then it is not inherently existent. A yogi then analyzes the object's existence in each of those seven ways and sees that all seven ways of existing are logically invalid. When the yogi realizes this, he will understand that since the pervader is negated, the pervaded object is negated too. In other words, there is no inherent existence—because if something were inherently existent, then it must exist in one of the seven ways and every one of those has been negated. Thus the yogi arrives at a firm and definite understanding. He or she goes through this logical process again and again to generate unambiguous certainty that there is no inherent existence: everything is empty of inherent existence.

What are we left with after having developed a firm understanding of emptiness? Nothing? No! Even though there is no inherent existence, there are still conventional functioning things. A chariot fulfills its function; it carries people from place to place. There is cause and effect. Everything named or labeled conventionally exists; we cannot deny that. After developing an understanding of emptiness we see that everything exists nominally. When we comprehend this, we cannot deny conventional things—we realize their illusion-like nature.

What kind of reaction is there within a yogi who sees that things are empty of inherent existence and yet they do exist conventionally? How does this influence a practitioner? He or she feels a special joy and amazement: "Wow! Conventional things in samsara are created by karma and mental afflictions, just like illusions conjured up by a magician. Even though things are not inherently existent—without the slightest trace of their own nature—each thing arises from its own causes and conditions without the slightest mistake. It is amazing!" In this way, practitioners become certain that the meaning of dependent arising is the absence of inherent arising. They definitely recognize that dependent arising and the emptiness of inherent existence imply each other; they see that they are not incompatible. Candrakīrti's *Commentary on the "Four Hundred Stanzas"* says:

> When you analyze such things as pots in the five ways, in terms of being the same or different from their causes and so on, they do not exist. Although this is so, they are imputed and can perform functions, such as scooping up and holding honey, water, and milk. Is this not amazing?

Also:

> What lacks inherent nature and yet is seen, is empty of inherent existence, like the circle of a whirling firebrand.

❖ 18 ❖

The Person Lacks Inherent Nature

(b')) Showing what the example illustrates
    (1')) The example illustrates how the self lacks inherent nature
        (a")) Refuting the position that the self is the same as the aggregates
        (b")) Refuting the position that the self is different from the
            aggregates
        (c")) How those arguments also refute each of the remaining positions

———❖———

(b')) Showing what the example illustrates

IN THE LAST chapter we examined how a chariot would have to exist if it were to exist inherently. We learned that there are only seven possible ways in which it could exist from its own side in relation to its parts. A search for the chariot existing in each of these seven ways constitutes ultimate analysis. When the chariot cannot be found to exist from its own side in any of those seven ways, its inherent existence is negated. Having understood how this method works on the basis of a chariot, we apply it to the main object of analysis—the self. This has two parts:

    (1')) The example illustrates how the self lacks inherent nature
    (2')) The example illustrates how the self is established in terms of being labeled (chapter 19)

(1')) The example illustrates how the self lacks inherent nature

The aggregates are the basis of imputation of the self. The self is imputed on the basis of the aggregates. If the self existed inherently it would have to be either inherently the same as or inherently different from the aggregates. This twofold analysis of the relationship between the self and the aggregates encompasses all possible alternatives. This is explained in four parts:

(a")) Refuting the position that the self is the same as the aggregates
(b")) Refuting the position that the self is different from the aggregates
(c")) How those arguments also refute each of the remaining positions
(d")) How the person appears like an illusion in dependence on that refutation (chapter 19)

(a")) REFUTING THE POSITION THAT THE SELF IS THE SAME AS THE AGGREGATES

In order to succeed with this refutation we must have ascertained certain points already. We must know that being single and being multiple are mutually exclusive. When we understand that something is single, it eliminates our understanding of it as multiple; when we understand that something is multiple, it prevents us from thinking of it as single. The terms "single" and "multiple" are strictly contradictory. Something is either single or multiple; there is no other possibility. Likewise, sameness and difference are dichotomies. If things are the same, that excludes them from being different; if they are different, that excludes them from being the same. There is no third ground—no other alternative in between those two. When we understand that there is no third ground between singularity and plurality or between sameness and difference in general, then we must accept that this applies to every particular instance of them—including those that inherently exist. So if anything inherently exists, it must be either inherently one or inherently many. Also if things inherently exist, then they must be either inherently the same or inherently different. There is no third possibility.

If the self or person had an inherently existent nature, it would either be inherently one with the aggregates or inherently different from the aggregates. There is no other option. You can explore this point further. Ask yourself, "Is the self inherently the same as the aggregates or inherently different from them? Would there be a logical problem if the self and the five aggregates were inherently the same?" Buddhapālita presents three undesirable consequences that would occur if the aggregates and the self were inherently the same: first, it would be meaningless to propound a self; second, there would be many selves; and third, the self would be changing every moment. Let us look at these three faults in more detail.

If we accept that the self and the aggregates are inherently the same, there would be no point in propounding a self because there could be no self separate from the aggregates. The self would merely be the aggregates; there would be no self other than the aggregates. It would be meaningless to speak of a self as something more than the aggregates because such a thing would not exist. The word "self" would merely be another term for the aggregates, just as the names Moon and Rabbit Bearer both refer to the moon. In the Indo-Tibetan literary tradition there is a list of at least ten names for the moon, such as White Circle, One with Cooling Rays, and Rabbit Bearer. All these names refer to exactly the same thing: the moon. In the same way, if the self and the aggregates were inherently the same, the word "self" would be just another name for the five aggregates. This was taught by Nāgārjuna in the twenty-seventh chapter of the *Fundamental Treatise*:

> When you say there is no self
> Except for the appropriated,
> The appropriated themselves are the self;
> Your proposed self does not exist.

Buddhapālita comments that if there is no self other than the appropriated aggregates, the notion of a "self" would not exist. It would be meaningless to speak about a self at all; we would simply talk about the aggregates.

The second unwanted logical consequence that would occur if the self and aggregates were inherently the same is that the self would become multiple. A single person would have many selves because a person has many aggregates. Or the opposite would occur: the aggregates would become single. A person could have only one aggregate because a person has only one self. Thus the one would become many, or the many would become one. Candrakīrti's *Introduction to the "Middle Way"* says:

> If the aggregates were the self,
> Then, since they are many, the self would be many also.

The third fault is that the self would arise and cease by its own nature. Of course the self and the aggregates are impermanent; they arise and disintegrate. There is nothing wrong with them arising and ceasing conventionally. But if the aggregates were inherently the same as the self, they would be exactly the same. So the self would come into being and go out of being every moment, along with the aggregates. The problem with this consequence will be explained below. Stating the issue, Nāgārjuna says in the eighteenth chapter of the *Fundamental Treatise*:

> If the self were the aggregates,
> It would arise and disintegrate.

Also, the twenty-seventh chapter says:

> The appropriated are not the self;
> They arise and disintegrate.

Tsongkhapa mentions that we should understand the word "appropriated" in this context as referring to the five aggregates.

What is the problem with accepting that the self has the nature of arising and ceasing moment by moment? In a conventional sense there is no problem. Things arise owing to previous causes and conditions. One moment causes the next moment; the second moment arises in dependence on the first moment. Causes and conditions bring about certain results. On a gross level persons change throughout their lives. When they are born they arise, and at death they cease. Logical faults occur here only if we assert that the self and the aggregates inherently exist. Although Nāgārjuna does not explicitly use the terms "inherently" or "ultimately" in the above stanzas, they are implied. "Inherently" means ultimately, by its own nature, without depending on causes and conditions. If a thing inherently arises, it arises by its own nature, without any cause; if it inherently ceases, it permanently ceases, every moment, without depending on causes and conditions. Each moment would exist independently, unconnected to anything else. The first moment would have no relation to the second moment, nor the second to the third, and so on. Once a moment ceases it is gone, permanently, completely, and absolutely; the next moment arises without depending on any cause. If the self and the aggregates had the inherent nature of arising and ceasing, these would not depend on causes and conditions. A person's former life and future life would be unrelated, as different as a cow and a horse. When a cow dies, it does not harm the horse. Moreover, each moment within a person's life would arise and cease in an absolute sense, independently and without causes and conditions. Consecutive moments would be unrelated. This is the kind of arising and ceasing that is under consideration here.

In *Introduction to the "Middle Way"* and *Commentary on the "Introduction to the 'Middle Way,'"* Candrakīrti says there are three reasons why inherent arising and ceasing cannot exist. First, no one could remember their past lives, and even the memory of things that took place previously in this life would be untenable. Second, karma would be wasted; it would not have any result because your next life would be unrelated to your previous one. Third, you would meet with the results of karma that you had never created.

THE FIRST REASON WHY INHERENT ARISING AND CEASING IS FALLACIOUS

The first problem with inherent arising and ceasing is that it blocks any possibility of memory. If moment by moment the self inherently arises and ceases by its own nature, then every earlier instance of the self would be inherently different from every later instance of the self. These selves would be absolutely different unrelated entities. How could memory then be possible? If this were the case, Buddha would not have been able to remember his past lives. He could not have recounted, "At that time, in that life, I was a king called Māndhātṛ."[148] If past and future lives were inherently existent, there would be no relationship between them; the self of the king Māndhātṛ and the self of Buddha would be completely and inherently different. This difference would be absolute, not just relative and conventional. The king Māndhātṛ would not have been the cause, and Buddha would not have been the result. Even with his clairvoyant power, Śākyamuni Buddha would not remember having been this king because there would be no relationship between those two lives.

If you think that an inherently existent person can recollect an inherently existent past life, why could not two completely unrelated contemporaries, such as Devadatta and Yajñadatta, remember each other's prior experience? We know that Yajñadatta cannot remember something experienced earlier by Devadatta. Devadatta cannot recall or claim, "At that time I was Yajñadatta." They are completely different people, each with a separate mental continuum. Is this situation any different from an inherently existent person trying to remember an inherently existent past life? No. The past and future of an inherently existent person are just as unconnected as the mindstreams of Devadatta and Yajñadatta. The point here concerns difference in an absolute and inherent sense. If there is inherent difference, then there is no relationship and no possibility of recollection. If the previous self and the present self were completely independent and unrelated, then just as Devadatta and Yajñadatta cannot remember each other's experiences, the same would apply to Buddha and his former lives.

This is similar to the argument that refutes production from others as explained in *Introduction to the "Middle Way."* Production from others means that an inherently existent result arises from its inherently existent other causes. But if cause and effect were inherently existent, then they would be totally different and unrelated. The Buddhist Realists believe that a seed of corn and the sprout of that corn seed have inherently existent natures, yet they are cause and effect. This is not possible. When refuting production from inherently existent others, Candrakīrti says:

> If another thing were produced by a different thing,
> Then pitch darkness would be produced by blazing fire.
> Everything would give rise to everything because
> Both causes and noncauses likewise would be different. (6.14)

If you assert that a seed and a sprout are inherently existent as well as being, respectively, cause and effect, then the seed and the sprout must be inherently different entities. This is problematic because if things are inherently different entities, then they cannot be dependently or causally related to each other. You would have an independent seed and an independent sprout. If you maintain that such unrelated things are cause and effect, then why not say that fire is the cause of complete darkness? It is common knowledge that fire creates light and so destroys, rather than produces, darkness. Yet if a cause and its effect have no relationship, then why could not fire produce its opposite? An absurd conclusion—that anything could cause anything—follows from accepting production from an inherently different cause. This shows that it is untenable to accept that an inherently existent seed produces an inherently existent sprout. The same argument can be applied to refute the view that a later moment of an inherently existent self can remember an earlier moment of that inherently existent self.

This fallacy does not occur if one accepts that a cause and its effect are merely different from each other in a conventional sense or that a later moment of a conventionally existent self can remember an earlier moment of it. Cause and effect are different conventionally. What about someone's past self and future self—are they the same or different conventionally? In certain sutra passages, when Śākyamuni Buddha said, "At that time I was an animal," or "At that time I was a hell being," or "At that time I was the king Māndhātṛ," to whom was he referring? When he spoke about this to his disciples, Buddha was not the king Māndhātṛ nor any of those other beings at that time. So what did he mean when he said, "I was the king Māndhātṛ"? Can we ever correctly speak of what we were at a previous time? Even in one life we are changing continually. There is a lot of discussion about this. Many of you were not brought up to believe in karma or past and future lives. But assuming there are other lives, a previous life is not the same as the life occurring right now. That past life is completely gone. This life is completely new, even conventionally. Do you think that something from that past life comes through and remains up until now? Most non-Buddhists say that there is a permanent soul or self that exists continuously and experiences the results of its previous actions. According to them, the soul is permanent yet it has many temporary aspects, rather like a person wearing different clothes. Is Śākyamuni Buddha indicating that an unchanging soul of this kind goes from life to life?

Buddha taught that persons are impermanent, arising and disintegrating moment by moment. So how can we explain karmic causality? Is there a self that experiences the misery of lower rebirths and the happiness of a god's life? Gods are gods, humans are humans, and hell beings are hell beings; no sort of being undergoes the experiences of other kinds of rebirth in that very life. But is there a self connecting these different rebirths? If not, then why do Buddhists consider karma and past and future lives so important? Why do Buddhists say that each person's samsaric life arises through the power of previous contaminated actions? Why do we try to purify negativities and strive to create virtue so that we can attain buddhahood? Are we fools or what?

The question of whether anything continues from life to life depends on what we mean by continuity and impermanence. Even if you do not accept that you had other lives prior to this one, you would agree that you have a past in this life. You have yesterday's life, last year's life, and so on. Each of us can remember, "Several years ago I did this and that." That younger person and this older person are different. But is there something that abides throughout all these stages of one's life? Are the younger person and the older person parts of a larger whole?

Some monastic textbooks speak about "I" as a part possessor.[149] For example, today's person has many temporal parts: the person of this morning, of this afternoon, and of this evening. We can say "I was that" when talking about the past, or "I will be that" when talking about the future. At each time there is I in a general sense, as well as a particular instance of I. We can say that I was here yesterday, I am here today, and I will be here tomorrow. However, the particular I who created some karma yesterday, and the particular I who experiences its result today, are not the same particular instance of I—though they are both instances of the same I in general. The I is specific to a certain person—it is not just anybody's I. The person who previously created a certain cause and the person who later experiences its result must be based on the same mental continuum. If not, then yesterday's person and tomorrow's person would not be you: they would be somebody else. Your I in general and any particular instance of it are both imputed on the continuum of your own aggregates—not someone else's aggregates of body and mind.

According to the Prāsaṅgika system, the I is the conventional basis of actions created in former lives; when those karmic seeds ripen, the I experiences their results in a later life. The karma created by the I produces results that are experienced by the mere I in general. This I—the I that is the support of karma and its result—is what we refer to when we say, "I am creating this karma so I will experience that result." Here "I" refers to the entire I that has countless parts, not just to the particular I of right now. The individual instance of I that creates an action is not the same as the individual instance of I that experiences the result of that action. Those are not mixed together. However, the earlier and later instances of I are based on the same continuum of mind. When we speak of ourselves in an ordinary sense, as in "I really enjoyed that movie yesterday," the word "I" does not refer to the particular I present now; it refers to I in general, of which the present I is just a part.

Even the entire part possessor I is not an absolute thing; it exists nominally or conventionally. The mere I in a general sense and every instance of it are all imputed on the same mental continuum. All these are dependent on causes and conditions. As long as the I and its instances are not inherently existent, we can say that the I of Devadatta today and the I of whatever he was in the past or will be in the future are the same continuum. They are not identical, but where Devadatta was born in a past life as an animal, that animal is also the I of Devadatta; where he is born in the future as a god, that god is also the I of Devadatta. Likewise, Buddha's I pervades all his former lives in the six realms. Therefore the I is called a part possessor or general I. Buddha's continuum of lives began like everyone else's continuum of lives; Buddha has been born in all six realms at different times, including as a hell being, an animal, and so on. The mental continuum of each of those beings is not different from that of Śākyamuni Buddha. They are all one individual continuum.

In the *Descent into Laṅka Sutra*, after explaining his former rebirth as the king Māndhātṛ, Buddha says, "Do you think that the person in that lifetime was someone else? Do not view it like that." Buddha's denial of it being "someone else" other than himself indicates that it is his own continuum of I in a general sense. Candrakīrti explains that Buddha's words do not indicate that the two people are exactly the same; to be the same is to be the same referent and have the same name. Buddha only denies that they have different mindstreams. This does not mean that he and this king were the same being; it means they have the same mental continuum. The previous moment of consciousness gives rise to the next in a continuous stream of cause and effect, which takes rebirth in one form or another at different times. The persons imputed on the parts of the stream of consciousness in various rebirths are different instances of the self, but they are not inherently different. If they were inherently different, then they would be totally unrelated, like Devadatta and Yajñadatta; they would not be the same mental continuum at all.

In many sutras Buddha recounts his former lifetimes as a bodhisattva who engaged in accumulating merit and making offerings. The Jātaka tales give lengthy accounts of those lives. They all begin, "At that time I was born as so-and-so, my father was this person, my mother was that person," and so on. For example, in one sutra when teaching his disciples about his past lives, Buddha tells the story of the prince and the tigress. The story goes that in a previous life Śākyamuni Buddha was born as a royal prince. One day the bodhisattva prince went into a forest and saw a starving tigress and her little cubs. The tigress was so weak and hungry that she was about to eat her babies. To save the tigress and her cubs, the young prince decided to give her his body as food. He lay down by the tigress, but she was too frail to eat him. So the prince cut himself and began to drip his blood into her open mouth. After drinking some blood, she revived and was able to eat him. The prince gave himself completely and died right there. Because of this act of powerful compassion, he was born into the heaven of the thirty-three. Soon afterward, he appeared in the sky and spoke to the grieving members of his former family. He told them what he had done and urged them not to worry about him. After recounting the story, Buddha asks his disciples, "At that time, who was that prince? Do not think that he was someone other than me." This means that the prince was the same continuum as Buddha. The main point here is that when Buddha says, "At that time I was so-and-so," the word "I" does not refer only to Śākyamuni Buddha at the time he was teaching. It refers conventionally to his I in a general sense, which includes all his former rebirths as a bodhisattva and every other sort of sentient being.

Some people are mistaken about the meaning of statements in the sutras like "In the past I was so-and-so." They think that Buddha and his previous incarnations are one and the same. Moreover, they reason that if something is a produced thing, it must be impermanent; if a thing is impermanent, it arises and ceases moment by moment. So if those previous incarnations and Buddha are impermanent, they cannot be the same; if they are the same, then they must be permanent. This is the first of the four wrong views regarding the past: the self and the world are eternal, finite, both, or neither.[150] The view that the self and the world are permanent or eternal is refuted in the twenty-seventh chapter of the *Fundamental Treatise*:

> It is incorrect to say,
> "I already existed in the past."

That which existed previously
Is not the very thing existing now.

This passage means that it is wrong to think that something that existed in the past is exactly the same as what exists in the present. If the thing that is present now were the same as what existed in the past, then one sentient being would be all six kinds of sentient beings simultaneously. Over a period of time everyone has taken rebirth as a hell being, a hungry ghost, an animal, a human, and two types of gods, in turn. So all these beings that each of us has been, serially, would be us now at the same time. All these beings, past and present, would be permanently one.

This fault is implied by accepting an inherently existent self. In a conventional sense, you can say that you were all those beings in your past lives without implying that these are all permanently one. But can you say that the self you were in a past life as an animal exists? It would be wrong to say it does not exist; yet it does not exist right now. It is impermanent and has passed away. Nevertheless the mental continuum on which it was imputed is here now. Conversely, if you become a buddha in the future, does this buddha's name, environment, and circle of disciples exist? This buddha is not present now, but we cannot say that this buddha does not exist! It is dependent on causes and conditions within your mental continuum and will arise as soon as they are complete. Once we accept rebirth in different realms, we cannot accept a permanent self. It must be impermanent and changing.

This applies even in the context of a single lifetime. One life can be divided into youth, middle age, and old age. Each of these can be divided into days. The Devadatta of one day, for example, June 1, exists only on June 1. The Devadatta of June 2 is another thing. So is the June 1 Devadatta the same all day until June 2? When does the June 1 Devadatta cease? We cannot say that he is there in the first minute of June 1 and gone the second minute of June 1. The June 1 Devadatta exists until June 2. So there is a general June 1 Devadatta, within which there are many particular June 1 Devadattas. The June 1 Devadatta is not one solid thing; he can be divided into many moments, and within each moment change occurs. Even in one day there are so many Devadattas! At the time of the second moment, the first moment of Devadatta has gone. Devadatta is momentary. However, at each moment the I of Devadatta is present. Therefore "I" is understood in a general sense.

In a conventional sense, one self has many parts included within the past, the present, and the future. These are imputed on the same mental continuum, which also has many temporal parts. There is no problem accounting for things if they are not inherently existent. If things are merely existent, they can arise momentarily as a result of causes and conditions. If the causes and conditions to maintain the thing's existence are absent, the thing ceases. But if the self were inherently existent, the earlier and later parts of its continuum would have to be either inherently the same or inherently different. If we say that they are inherently the same, we fall into the view of eternalism. These temporal parts would be absolutely the same and remain so without any change. Conversely, if we say that the earlier and later parts of the self's continuum are inherently different, we fall into the view of nihilism. There would be no relationship between these temporal parts and no causal link to bring a thing into existence. So if something has an inherent nature, it must be either permanently existent or absolutely nonexistent. Both possibilities are illogical. Therefore wise beings should not accept that the self has an inherent nature.

THE SECOND REASON WHY INHERENT ARISING AND CEASING IS FALLACIOUS

The second problem with inherent arising and ceasing is that karma would be wasted. If the self were inherently existent, it would arise and cease every moment independently of any other moments. So the earlier self and the later self would be unrelated. A person would create karma and never experience the result of that karma, because that inherently existent person would create karma and then disappear in the next moment. The self who created the karma ceases before experiencing its result. Usually we say that a person who creates specific karma unavoidably experiences its result. But in this case, an inherently existent self would already have ceased; because there is nobody else suitable to experience the result of that karma, that karma is wasted. Someone may object, "Nevertheless, the results of the karma created by a previous self would be experienced by a later self." We will deal with this point below when responding to the third problem. Here the point is that an inherently existent earlier self is not related to an inherently existent later self. So the later self does not experience the result of karma created by the earlier self, and thus that karma is wasted. This is one suggested outcome. Furthermore, because earlier and later things are not inherently different, there is no self that is inherently different from the self that created that karma. Therefore there is no later self that exists absolutely separate from the earlier self. If the earlier person does not experience the result of the karma that he or she creates, since the result ripens after the person ceases to exist, then there is no one at all who experiences that result. To respond that the earlier person does experience the result of that karma, because the later person and the earlier person are of the same mental continuum, is acceptable only in a conventional sense. Here, in a system propounding inherent existence, an earlier self and a later self are completely different, independent, and unrelated. Therefore that kind of answer is untenable and will be refuted below. In short, the fault that karma will be wasted because nobody will experience its result cannot be resolved within a system propounding inherent existence.

THE THIRD REASON WHY INHERENT ARISING AND CEASING IS FALLACIOUS

The third problem with inherent arising and ceasing is that a person would experience the result of karma they had not created. Some claim that karma is not wasted because even though the previous self who created the karma has disappeared, a later one arises and experiences its result. However, since the self inherently arises and ceases, the later self is completely unrelated to the earlier self who created the karma. In that case, a person who never created the slightest karma that caused its resultant experience would experience the result of that very karma created by someone else. This is because the ripening of an action accumulated by one inherently existent person would be experienced by an utterly different inherently existent person. Candrakīrti's *Introduction to the "Middle Way"* says:

> In the moments preceding nirvana there would be
> No agent arising and ceasing and therefore no results.
> What one accumulates, another will experience.

Prior to attaining nirvana, there would be no agent who disintegrates at the end of one life and arises at the beginning of the next life. The earlier self and the later self would be inherently different, so there would be no self connecting the arising and the ceasing. When the later one arises, the creator of that karma has gone. So the person who experiences the result is not the one who created the cause. Thus if the self were inherently existent, the outcome would be that either nobody experiences the results of actions done in previous lives, and thus karma is wasted, or a later person experiences the results of actions done by a completely different earlier person.

Tsongkhapa says that Candrakīrti discusses three additional faults of inherent arising to refute other Buddhist schools' positions. But in the *Lamrim Chenmo* he does not present them because here he is refuting the misconceptions held in common by Buddhists and non-Buddhists. Two of the faults explained here—that karma is wasted and that one person experiences the results of karma created by another—are found in the twenty-seventh chapter of Nāgārjuna's *Fundamental Treatise*:

If this self were different from that of a former life,
It would arise without that past one having existed.
Likewise, that past one would remain,
And without that one dying, the next one arises.

Strange consequences would follow:
The continuum being cut, karma being wasted,
Someone experiencing the results
Of karma created by another, and so forth.

In the stanzas above, the phrase "If this self were different" means "If the self of a previous life and that of the present life were inherently different." If the self of a former life were inherently different from the self of the next life, there would be no relationship between them. If there is no connection between earlier and later lives, the self of the next life could arise without depending at all on the previous life. In other words, if a dependent relationship between lives is denied, the second self could be born without the first one ever having existed. Or because there is no relationship between the two lives, the present self could arise even when the past self has not yet ceased. It is a situation similar to making a vase and not destroying a woolen shawl; because the shawl and the vase are unrelated, nothing happens to the shawl when we make the vase.

The opponent counters, "The selves of past and present lives are inherently different; however, faults such as karma being wasted or experiencing the results of karma that one did not create do not occur because the previous self and the self that is experiencing the karmic result are of the same mental continuum."

Tsongkhapa replies that if past and future selves are of the same mental continuum, then they are not inherently different; therefore the opponent needs to prove his assertion—that they are inherently different. For it has already been shown that if the self of the earlier life and that of the later life were inherently different, they could not be of the same mental continuum. The earlier and later selves would be two completely different and independent persons, like Maitreya and Upagupta; Upagupta does not experience the results of Maitreya's actions, nor vice versa, because they do not share the same mental continuum. Candrakīrti's *Introduction to the "Middle Way"* says:

If you say, "There is no problem if they exist as one continuum in reality,"
I already explained the faults of them being one continuum in a previous
analysis.

The analysis found earlier in that text is:

The qualities belonging to Maitreya and Upagupta
Are completely different, so are not considered one continuum;
Likewise, whatever things are inherently different
Cannot be considered as the same continuum.

If two persons are completely different, each must have his or her own mental continuum. They cannot share one continuum. The same would apply to two inherently existent selves at different times. An earlier self that is inherently different from a later self would have no causal connection with it—as explained earlier. The twenty-seventh chapter of Nāgārjuna's *Fundamental Treatise* says:

If a deity and a human are different,
They cannot be one continuum.

In a conventional sense, a person can take birth as a hell being, a hungry ghost, an animal, a human, a deity, and even become a buddha. In a dependent, relative sense, these different lives are of the same mental continuum. But if all these beings were inherently different, then they could not be of the same mental continuum. In brief, if things were different by their inherent nature, their unique essential nature would be able to bear ultimate analysis. Being able to bear ultimate analysis means that when we look deeply for a thing's inherent nature, it eventually becomes apparent—as if to say, "Here I am." We would find it existing from its own side. However, when we search for a thing's intrinsic nature, we do not find even an atom that is able to bear that kind of analysis. While we analyze in the utmost detail and search for the thing in relation to its basis of imputation—its parts, their collection, the whole, the shape of the parts, and so on—we continually discover, "This is not it, that is not it." The thing seems to disappear as we look, until finally we find emptiness. Not even the tiniest particle can be found among the parts, their collection, and so on that can qualify as the thing's inherent essence or identity. We do not find anything that is ultimately the thing itself. In short, the thing cannot bear ultimate analysis.

If you maintain that an earlier person is inherently different from a later person within the same continuum, the earlier and later persons would be totally independent beings. So the person who creates karma would be different by his or her intrinsic nature from the person who later experiences that karma's result. If this were possible, then why could not two separate individuals— each having a completely different mental continuum, like Maitreya and Upagupta—experience the results of each other's actions? These cases are similar in every respect; there is no way to differentiate between them. Tsongkhapa says that this Madhyamaka logic should be understood to apply to all cases. For example, we considered earlier whether an inherently existent cause could produce an inherently existent other result. If that were possible, then everything would be able to arise from anything: a blazing fire could actually cause darkness. Nāgārjuna logically examines so many different things; each of the twenty-seven chapters of the *Fundamental Treatise* has a different emphasis. But the final point is that there is no ultimate or inherent existence. Everything is relative and dependent. That is what emptiness means. It does not matter whether or not the words "inherently" or "ultimately" are mentioned in every instance. You should understand that this logic is applied to all contexts.

Another Mādhyamika may ask, "Since the person who earlier experienced happiness or misery is not the same person as the one who later remembers that experience, then even according to our own system it is not possible for the later one to remember what the earlier one had experienced, nor is it possible for the later one to experience the result of karma created by the earlier one. It is similar to the case of completely different individuals like Maitreya and Upagupta." Tsongkhapa replies that this fault does not occur in our system. Why not? In the Madhyamaka system there is no contradiction implied by the earlier self and the later self being the same continuum, since they are not independently and inherently existent. The later self depends on the earlier self. To say that these beings are of the same continuum only becomes contradictory within other tenet systems, which assert ultimately different earlier and later lives.

If something were inherently existent then it would be stuck, fixed, and solid. Madhyamaka logic demonstrates that everything exists dependently, and thus there is no absolute, independent thing. The most amazing things can be explained based on dependent nature. One odd example given in ancient Indian tradition is that of a white pigeon who stood on a thick thatched roof and made a footprint in a pot of yogurt below inside the house. Even though the pigeon remained on the roof and never touched the yogurt, its footprint appeared in the surface of the yogurt below. Do you think that could happen? The example is not referring to a shadow. The footprint on the yogurt is an analogy for a person remembering the experiences of a prior life. Even though the present person did not actually exist in that previous life, he or she can remember, "At that time, when I was so-and-so, I experienced such-and-such." Memory of this kind can occur owing to many dependent causes and conditions coming together. There is a special relationship, a continuation, which dependently connects the earlier and later persons. So even though this present person was not there at that time, it is possible for him to remember it. It is not contradictory for the earlier and later persons to be different and yet be of one continuum. The main point is that owing to dependent nature all kinds of things are possible.

Tsongkhapa did not make this up. Candrakīrti's *Commentary on the "Four Hundred Stanzas"* says:

> Abandon thinking that cause and effect are ultimately the same or ultimately different. There is only an impermanent continuum of conditioning factors—particular causes bringing forth results—so it is correct to say that its appropriator, the imputedly existent self, remembers [its previous] births. Things are not inherently existent—for they are intimately involved with such conditions, and changing itself is not incorrect. Therefore since things are not inherently existent, they function in ways that are inconceivable and beyond imagination. Thus the footprint of a white pigeon sitting on a thickly layered thatched roof can be seen in a vessel of mud-like yogurt in the house below, even though his feet never touched it.

Candrakīrti's *Commentary on the "Introduction to the 'Middle Way'"* has a more extensive explanation of this point.

So far Tsongkhapa has been explaining this topic in accordance with the commentaries of Buddhapālita and Candrakīrti, but now he explains it in ordinary terms. In the twenty-seventh chapter of *Fundamental Treatise*, when investigating the assertion that the self and the aggregates are inherently one, Nāgārjuna asks:

> How could the appropriated
> Be the appropriator?

Here the aggregates or attributes are the appropriated, and the self is the appropriator, the one who takes the attributes. Alternatively, the person who is reborn is the appropriator, and the rebirth he or she takes is the appropriated. In this sense, when we create karma we are determining the situation that we will have in the next life. The terms can be used in either of these ways. We may say, "This person has appropriated this body." The body is what is taken up or appropriated, and the person or self is the taker. If the taken and the taker were (a) inherently existent and (b) the same entity, then they would be exactly the same. In that case, whatever happens to the aggregates must happen to the self in the same way. The aggregates are constantly changing—they arise and cease every moment. It would follow that exactly the same thing must happen to the self if it were inherently the same as the aggregates. But that does not happen. The self and its aggregates function in different ways. We can easily see the aggregates change; the person does not seem to change so much. A person maintains his or her identity throughout an entire lifespan; the aggregates do not.

If the self and the aggregates were accepted to be ultimately the same, there would be no difference between them. The agent (the appropriator) would be the object of action (the appropriated). Agent and object would be indistinguishable. To understand this powerful argument from the *Fundamental Treatise*, we need to comprehend the three interrelated spheres of activity: the action, the agent, and the object.[151] Nāgārjuna frequently uses these three spheres of activity to explain emptiness. Consider, for example, a person cutting wood with an axe. The cutting activity is the action, the person with the axe is the agent, and the wood is the object of the action. The primary agent is the person, but a secondary part of the agent is the axe. These are all interconnected: there is no independent agent, there is no independent action, and there is no independent object of action. Each is related to the others. Nothing exists independently, absolutely alone, by its own nature. Consider another activity: fire burning fuel. Fire is the agent, burning is the action, and fuel is the object of the action. Fuel is not independent; fuel is so-named in dependence on the activity of burning. The burner and the thing burned are likewise related. Without the thing that is burned, there is no burning; if there is no activity of burning, how could there be a burner? Connections like this can be made with regard to anything, including the self and the aggregates. The person is the agent, the taker, or appropriator. Taking is the activity. What is taken, the appropriated object, are the five aggregates—the next rebirth. When the scriptures explain samsara and the truth of suffering, they use the expression "the five aggregates of contaminated appropriation."

If the person and the aggregates were inherently the same, the agent and the object of action could not be differentiated, not even conventionally. They would be one and the same. What is wrong with accepting that they are the same? Well, when you cut wood, the agent (the person doing the cutting) and the object cut (the wood) would be the same. Similarly, a potter, his activity of potting, and his clay pot would be the same. Likewise, the agent (fire), the action (burning), and object of action (the fuel burned) would all be the same. This objection is presented by Nāgārjuna in the tenth chapter of the *Fundamental Treatise*:

> If that which is the fuel were the fire,
> Then the agent and object of action would be one.

Through this example of fire and wood
We explain the entire analysis to apply
To the self and what it appropriates
And to everything else, such as pots, shawls, and so on.

Also Candrakīrti's *Introduction to the "Middle Way"* says:

The appropriator and its appropriated object cannot be the same.
If they were, the agent and object of action would be the same.

In summary, Buddhapālita and Candrakīrti explain that there would be six faults if the self were inherently the same as the aggregates: first, it would be meaningless to accept a self at all; second, there would be many selves because each person has many aggregates; third, the agent and action would be one; fourth, no matter what good or bad karma is created, it will never be experienced in the future and so would be wasted; fifth, a person would meet with karmic results without ever creating their causes; and sixth, Buddha's words recounting his past lives would be incorrect. Seeing that there are at least these six faults, we should not accept the self and the aggregates to be the same.

(b")) REFUTING THE POSITION THAT THE SELF IS DIFFERENT FROM THE AGGREGATES

Someone may think, "The self and the aggregates are not inherently the same, but what is wrong with accepting them to be inherently different?" The eighteenth chapter of Nāgārjuna's *Fundamental Treatise* specifies the problem:

If the self were utterly different from the aggregates,
It would not have the characteristics of the aggregates.

If the self were inherently different from the aggregates, it would not have the characteristics of the aggregates, such as arising, abiding, and ceasing. It would be completely unrelated to the aggregates, just as a horse is unrelated to a cow. A horse is completely different from a cow, so it does not have a cow's characteristics. If someone thinks that the self and the five aggregates are unrelated, like a horse and a cow, we can change their opinion by arguing, "Such a self[152] is not the object held as a self nor the basis of the term 'I,' because it is uncaused, like nirvana or a sky flower." This is a syllogism based on the opponent's assumptions, outlined in Candrakīrti's *Clear Words*. In general the conventional self is imputed on the aggregates. We identify a person and give them a name based on their aggregates—a combination of their mental and physical qualities. But if the self were totally unrelated to the aggregates, then we could not identify a person nor name them on the basis of their aggregates. This is because the person or self would not have the characteristics of the aggregates. The aggregates are changing continuously—arising, abiding, and ceasing—in dependence on causes and conditions. If the self did not change in the way that the aggregates do, then it would not be produced by causes and conditions. Therefore it would be nonproduced, like nirvana (which is a mere negation) or a sky flower (which is nonexistent). The Mādhyamikas do not accept that the self is nonproduced; they merely posit this as a reason in the above syllogism just to refute their opponent's view.

Buddhapālita points out a further fault with the view that the self is inherently different from the aggregates. If the self did not have the characteristics of arising and ceasing, then it would be permanent; since there is no change in something permanent, it could not function at all. Therefore it would be purposeless to posit a self, because it could not engage in or reverse samsara.

Moreover, if the self were a completely different nature from the characteristics of the aggregates, then we would have to see them separately. For example, we see the defining characteristic of a form—that is, being suitable to be a form—separately from that of the mind. However, we do not perceive the self separately from the characteristics of the aggregates nor hold it to be a different entity from them. Therefore the self that is the basic object of self-grasping is not completely different from the aggregates. The twenty-seventh chapter of Nāgārjuna's *Fundamental Treatise* says:

> It is utterly incorrect that the self
> Is different from the appropriated aggregates;
> If it were different, it could be apprehended
> Without the appropriated, yet it is not.

Also, Candrakīrti's *Introduction to the "Middle Way"* says:

> Therefore there is no self that is different from the aggregates,
> Because it is not apprehended apart from the aggregates.

Our natural notion of the self is always mixed with a notion of the aggregates. We can never see, experience, imagine, or think of the self as something completely different and separate from them. Yet some non-Buddhist philosophers posit a soul or a self that is independent of the aggregates. They already know that it is wrong to view the self as exactly the same as the aggregates, but they do not understand that the self is merely imputed. Thus they believe the self to be something permanent, partless, and independent of the aggregates. This mistaken notion that the self is completely different from the aggregates is a view solely founded on a philosophical system. Even these philosophers do not naturally apprehend the situation in this way. Candrakīrti's *Introduction to the "Middle Way"* says:

> Merely because of having sown the seed,
> Worldly people say, "I produced this son."
> Likewise, they think, "I planted this tree."
> So even in worldly terms, there is no production from others. (6.32)

Do we ordinarily consider the seed that gives rise to a tree and the tree that is its result to be utterly, inherently, different? No, we do not. When we plant a seed in a certain place and later see a big tree there, we think, "This is the tree I planted years ago." The ordinary innate mind does not imagine that what was planted earlier and what arose later as its result are inherently different and independent. It does not imagine that inherently existent things arise from other inherently different causes. We could only think of them as inherently different if we had developed a wrong view based on a philosophical system. But we do not naturally understand it like that.

Tsongkhapa says that this also applies to the relationship between the self and the aggregates. An ordinary, naturally arisen, self-grasping mind does not apprehend the self as inherently different from the aggregates. Moreover, that type of mind holds the earlier and later self to be the same person. This is evident in the linguistic conventions of ordinary people. When your hand is hurt you say, "I am hurt." The logic is the same. Tsongkhapa says in *Essential Explanation of the Provisional and the Definitive*:[153]

> When an ordinary person's arm is hurt,
> He thinks, "I am hurt." Thus even the worldly
> Do not think these two are substantially different.

Such expressions show that we do not have an innate mind grasping at the self and the aggregates as inherently different and unrelated. This proves that the innate egotistic view does not hold the self and the aggregates to be completely different. Of course, we may have contrived grasping at this based on certain philosophical views, but that is a different issue.

Now conversely, does the innate self-grasping mind hold the self and the aggregates to be exactly the same entity? No, it does not. The contrived view may hold them to be the same, based on certain tenet systems, but the innate mind does not hold them to be exactly the same entity. The reason is given in Dharmakīrti's *Commentary on Valid Cognition*:[154]

> They will strive for other [sense faculties] that are superior.

If we consider our own sense powers, physical attributes, or mental capacities to be inferior, we might strive to change them for better ones. Although we may not be able to actually do this, it is possible for this thought to arise naturally, without depending on any kind of reasoning or philosophical tenets. This indicates that the innate egotistic view does not regard the aggregates and the self to be completely the same. If we thought they were exactly the same, we could not even conceive of exchanging our aggregates for more attractive ones. However, a person can imagine exchanging his old body for a younger one or his dull mind for a brighter one. The point here is that this thought is possible, even if the reality is not.

So how is the relationship between the self and the aggregates naturally regarded? We usually regard the self as something based on the aggregates—as a kind of inherently existent "I" or "me" on top of them. We think of the self and the aggregates as almost the same but not exactly the same, yet different but not absolutely different. Their relationship seems to be something in between—neither the same nor different. However, our innate self-grasping mind does not inquire whether the self is the same or different from the aggregates. It does not examine the situation or think about their relationship at all. Although our innate self-grasping mind has been present within us since time without beginning, it is very difficult for us to recognize it. Its active operation, grasping at inherent existence, is what gives rise to all the mental afflictions and contaminated karma. It is this that binds sentient beings to samsara— therefore we must urgently remove it. How do we remove it? We have to identify the object it is holding and how it holds it. Then we must gradually see that the object held by that mind does not exist in the way it is held. When we negate that held object, we can eliminate the mind that grasps it wrongly. That is the primary target of our meditation practice.

If the self existed as it is held by the innate egotistic mind, it would be inherently existent. In which case it would have to be inherently the same as the aggregates or inherently different from the aggregates. If we negate both of these alternatives using ultimate analysis, then we negate the inherent existence of the self. However, we must make a distinction between a mind that "grasps the self as inherently existent" and a mind that "grasps the self as inherently same as the aggregates" (or as inherently different from them). These are not the same mind. A mind that grasps the self to be inherently existent does not itself hold the self to be inherently the same as the aggregates (or inherently different from them). Therefore we need to examine whether an understanding of the emptiness of the self being inherently the same as the aggregates (or inherently different from them) is a genuine understanding of ultimate truth—the emptiness of the self being inherently existent.

In order to engage in ultimate analysis we start with a series of questions: If there were an inherently existent self, how would it exist? What would its relationship be with its basis—the aggregates? How would it be connected with them? Would the self be inherently the same as the aggregates or inherently different from them? Would it inherently be their support or be supported by them? Would the self inherently possess the aggregates? In this way we examine all the previously explained seven ways in which the self and the aggregates might be related—because if something were inherently existent, then it must be related to its basis in one of these ways inherently. When we have refuted all these alternatives through ultimate logical analysis, we eventually see that the self cannot possibly be ultimately existent—it can only exist relatively and dependently. But all these logical reasons themselves are not necessarily the opposite of the innate mind grasping at an inherently existent self. Taken together, they are the means that give rise to its opposite—a correct understanding of the emptiness of an inherently existent self.

Therefore, as mentioned earlier, negating the object as held by contrived wrong views is just preliminary to negating the object as held by the innate wrong view. In order to negate the way that things are held by the innate self-grasping mind, we have to negate contrived wrong views, such as grasping at the self as permanent, as different from the aggregates, as the same as the aggregates, and so on. This sevenfold analysis forms part of the negation of the self as held to be inherently existent by the innate egotistic mind. But in order to identify that subtle object of negation, we must clearly imagine how the self would be if it actually existed as it is held. We need a special meditative wisdom to recognize the object of negation. This arises as a result of sharp logical analysis that extensively searches for whether the self actually exists in the way that it is held. Eventually we see into the depths of this grasping and recognize it as a wrong view. Gaining a clear understanding of its nature takes a very long time. For this purpose we have to continuously train in developing a definite understanding of the sharp logical reasons that refute the self as being inherently different from or inherently the same as the aggregates—just as explained by the great Mādhyamikas. Yet even though we may follow the logic and conclude that the self is not inherently existent, if we have not drawn forth from this process a clear understanding[155] that validly refutes these two positions, then we will still not know what that really means. It will be a mere thesis that we have adopted. We will not have actually understood and so not have found the pure view or realization.

When we want to examine whether or not the person ultimately exists, we analyze whether the person—if it were ultimately existent—would be one with the aggregates or different from them. Then we analyze what is wrong with each of these positions. The final and sharpest refutation of the view that the self is inherently the same as the aggregates is that the agent and object of the action—such as fire and fuel—would be one and the same. Even our common sense recognizes that these cannot be the same. Fire is the burner, and fuel is the object burned. Similarly, the self is the taker, and a body or a rebirth is what is taken. People generally accept that the body belongs to the self, thus they are different in some sense. But if someone cannot understand this directly we use a logical proof, which leads back to direct perception in the end. Ordinary direct perception is the final step in refuting the wrong view that the self is the same as the aggregates. This wrong view cannot be refuted, finally, by the unique views of the opponent or proponent or by what is posited by their philosophical systems. That is not enough. The final refutation must be based on ordinary valid knowledge.

Similarly, the refutation of the opposite position, that the self and the aggregates are inherently different, is based on ordinary valid knowledge, not on some unshared philosophical position. If the self and the aggregates were inherently (and thus completely) different, then they would be seen separately, but they are not. Most people know this using their common sense.

Tsongkhapa's point is that, even in the context of examining ultimate reality, the final step of the logical refutation of a wrong view is nondistorted conventional knowledge shared by the opponent and the proponent. When we logically prove or refute something, our reasoning should reach back to conventional understanding. Without depending on commonly accepted conventional knowledge we cannot prove anything, including śūnyatā. For example, when we propose the thesis "All internal and external things are empty of inherent existence," we have to give a reason. We cannot use as a reason something that is peculiar to our own system. We must give a reason that is commonly known to us and the person to whom we are talking. We may have to present a series of reasons, one after another like links in a chain, until in the end our logic is proved by direct valid knowledge. Everything finally links back to the opponent's conventional knowledge.

Candrakīrti is making a very different point when he says, "There is no ordinary refutation with regard to reality."[156] Candrakīrti's words mean that ordinary knowledge is not valid knowledge with regard to ultimate reality itself. When we search for ultimate reality on the basis of conventional things, we are engaging in ultimate analysis. Our knowledge of emptiness is ultimate knowledge, not conventional knowledge. Conventional knowledge cannot understand the object of ultimate knowledge. This is quite different from the issue at hand, namely that when you prove something to your opponent, your reason must be established by shared conventional knowledge. This applies even when proving śūnyatā. The main point is that in the context of analyzing ultimate reality, nondistorted conventional knowledge is eventually employed to refute misconceptions. If a reason refuting a misconception were not finally based on nondistorted conventional knowledge, then that logical refutation would only be based on the proponent's or opponent's particular views. One's own idiosyncratic view is not grounds for proving to the other party that their view is faulty.

There are various opinions about whether to accept scriptural quotation as proof in a debate. Usually the term *valid* describes knowledge that knows its object correctly; this refers to direct perception and inference.[157] But we can also use the term to describe Buddha. He is a valid being because what he teaches is never deceptive; his instructions are unmistaken with regard to their object.[158] Moreover, since his teachings are expressed in the Buddhist scriptures, they too may be taken as valid. However, even if both people involved in a debate accept the use of scripture, they may disagree about whether a particular text is definitive or to be interpreted. So the literal truth of the scripture also has to be proved logically. If we have to prove it, what other kind of logic is there than that linked back to shared nondistorted conventional knowledge? There is no other kind. For example, when we prove something to an opponent by means of a consequence, the argument goes, "If you accept this, then you must accept that; if you do not accept that, then you cannot accept this." We must give a reason for this consequence. The final step in our proof must be based on nondistorted conventional knowledge shared by our opponent and ourselves. In this way, they will see that what they assert is contradicted by their own experience. Recognizing that, they will cease to accept that view.

In short, logic relies on our shared conventional knowledge. In the end, the final source of inferential knowledge must be a nondistorted direct perception, not another inference. This is like the example given earlier, where the guide of any number of blind people must be a sighted person, not another blind person. This approach is followed by the Mādhyamikas, such as Candrakīrti, as well as by the Sautrāntika and Yogācāra logicians, such as Dignāga and Dharmakīrti. No matter what form of logic these scholars employ, the final step in a proof with many stages of inferential reasoning always depends on nondistorted direct perception.

Although the final reason of a proof showing the lack of inherent existence relies on direct perception, this does not mean that the thesis—a lack of inherent existence—is known by direct perception. It simply means that the chain of reasoning finally reaches back to a direct perception. The emptiness of inherent existence is not directly perceived by ordinary conventional knowledge. Nevertheless, there is no fault in saying that conventional knowledge is used in proving śūnyatā. To get a clear idea of what this means, let us consider the sample syllogism given earlier, "Sound is impermanent because it is a product." Here the subject is "sound." The thesis to be proved is "sound is impermanent." The reason is "it is a product." This syllogism is directed to somebody who knows that sound is produced but does not understand that sound is impermanent. An underlying assumption here is that this person, on the basis of another subject, already knows the general pervasion: if something is produced then it must be impermanent, and if it is not impermanent then it cannot be produced. If this person does not already directly know that sound is produced by causes and conditions, we must construct another syllogism to prove that. We have to prove each point until he knows the reason directly. Assuming that this opponent knows that sound is produced by certain causes, he still might not directly perceive that sound is impermanent. How does he come to know that it is impermanent? The final reason is that sound is produced—which is something that he has perceived directly; for example, when we beat a drum a sound comes forth.

Thus the final reason that proves the thesis relies on direct perception. It is the same when proving "Sound is not inherently existent because it dependently arises." If the opponent does not know that sound dependently arises, then we prove it by appealing to his direct perception. He can perceive directly that sound is dependent on causes and conditions: the sound of a drum arises when it is beaten, and the sound of a voice arises from the position of the tongue and throat and the expelling of air. When what he has directly perceived is used as a reason, we can progress to proving subtler things. In sum, the final reason of a proof or refutation relies on direct perception. However, although the chain of reasons must reach back to a direct perception, it is not necessary for the original thesis to be known by direct perception.

(c")) How those arguments also refute each of the remaining positions

The remaining five ways that the self and the aggregates might relate, if they were inherently existent, are implicitly refuted by the logic disproving that the self and the aggregates are inherently the same or inherently different.

For if they were inherently different, then the self would either support the aggregates as a separate entity or the self would depend on the aggregates as a separate entity. In chapter 17 there is a discussion about the support and the supported in this sense, using the examples of yogurt in a bowl or Devadatta in a tent. If we assume that the self and the aggregates are inherently dependent and therefore separate entities, the yogurt supported by the bowl illustrates how the aggregates would depend on the person, and Devadatta sitting in a tent illustrates how the person would depend on the aggregates. It is not necessary to spell this out again; the same logic applies here as was put forward in the case of the chariot. Because the self and the aggregates are not inherently different, they cannot inherently exist as the support and the supported. However, in a conventional sense the self and the aggregates are mutually dependent. But they cannot depend on each other inherently or in an ultimate sense. Candrakīrti's *Introduction to the "Middle Way"* says:

> The self does not exist based on the aggregates,
> And the aggregates do not exist based on the self.
> If there were a real difference here, that thinking would follow.
> But there is no real difference, so it is a misconception.

Next, the view that the self is the possessor of the aggregates is also similar to what was explained in the context of the chariot. The notion of "possession" can be applied in only two ways: where the possessor and the possessed are different entities, such as Devadatta possessing his cattle, and where the possessor and the possessed are the same entity, such as Devadatta possessing his body. Neither type of possession could occur if the self and the aggregates—the possessor and the possessed—were absolutely, inherently different entities, or completely, inherently the same entity. Of course, in a conventional sense the self can possess a form and all the other aggregates. But this is not possible for inherently existent entities. The refutation of ultimate possession rests on the refutation of the self and the aggregates being inherently the same or inherently different entities. Candrakīrti's *Introduction to the "Middle Way"* says:

> We do not accept that the self possesses form,
> Because the self does not really exist so has no connection with the
>   meaning of possession,
> Whether in terms of different entities (e.g., having cattle) or not different
>   entities (e.g., having form),
> The self is neither inherently the same as nor inherently different
>   from form.

The sixth analysis considers whether the collection of the aggregates is the self. This too is incorrect. Some lower schools believe that the self is the collection of the aggregates and some that it is the continuum of the aggregates. Some upper schools believe that the self is the substratum consciousness and some that it is the primary mental consciousness that goes on to the next rebirth at the time of death. Even Bhāvaviveka accepts the latter. All these positions are similar in considering that the self is findable by ultimate analysis among the aggregates. However, according to the Prāsaṅgikas, it is incorrect to think that the mere collection of the five aggregates is the self. Why? This is primarily because the collection of five aggregates is the basis on which the self is labeled. The aggregates are the basis of imputation; the self is what is imputed on that basis. The collection of aggregates cannot be the self because that conflates the basis of imputation and the imputed thing. If the aggregates were the self, then the aggregates would be both the basis of imputation and the imputed thing. That is impossible. Candrakīrti's *Introduction to the "Middle Way"* says:

> The sutras teach that the self is dependent on the aggregates.
> Therefore the mere collection of aggregates is not the self.

According to the Prāsaṅgikas, to say that the self is dependent on the aggregates means that it is imputed based on the aggregates. This is the subtlest of the three forms of dependence: dependence on causes and conditions, dependence on parts, and dependence on imputation on a basis.

Moreover, if the mere collection of the aggregates were the self, there would be the logical fault that the agent and the object of action would be identical. The agent or self is the appropriator or possessor; the activity is that of appropriating or possessing; the object of action, or five aggregates, are the things appropriated or possessed. The agent (the self) and the object of action (the aggregates) cannot be the same. This is taught in Candrakīrti's *Introduction to the "Middle Way"* and *Commentary on the "Introduction to the 'Middle Way.'"* The problem is that we would have to accept that each of the individual aggregates is taken as an object of possession by the self. By accepting that, we must accept that all five aggregates are taken as objects of possession by the self. In which case, the whole group of aggregates is taken as an object of possession by the self. Now if we accept the collection of the five aggregates to be the basis of imputation of the self and thus not the self, then clearly we must accept this about the continuum of the aggregates. In other words, if it follows that because the aggregates are the basis of the imputation of the self, they are not the self—similarly it must follow that because the continuity of the aggregates is the basis of the imputation of the self, it cannot be accepted as the self.

The last of the seven refutations dispels the notion that the special shape of the collection of aggregates is the self. As we saw in chapter 17, when we throw the pieces that make up a chariot into a random pile, we obviously do not have a chariot. But when we put them together properly, we have something with a particular shape that we recognize as a chariot. Similarly, we may accept that each of the aggregates, or the collection of aggregates, or the continuity of aggregates, are not the self; but when the five aggregates are gathered together as a person, that special formation is the instantiation of the person. What is wrong with thinking this way? The problem is that this self could not be established in connection with a mind, because such a formation of shape and color exists only with regard to physical things. Candrakīrti's *Introduction to the "Middle Way"* says:

> If you say it is the shape, then since this exists only for physical things,
> Those would be the self according to you.
> If that were so, then the mind and so on could not be the self
> Because they do not have any shape.

Now although a chariot does not inherently exist in any of the seven ways when sought by ultimate analysis, a chariot does exist as something merely imputed based on its parts. Likewise, the self does not inherently exist in any of those seven ways—as identical with the aggregates or different from them and so on—yet the self exists conventionally because it is imputed or labeled based on the aggregates. The analyses of these two, the chariot and the self, are similar, and presenting the former as the analogy and the latter as the actual meaning is established in the sutras.

The Person Appears Like an Illusion

(d")) How the person appears like an illusion in dependence on that
refutation

    (2')) The example illustrates how the self is established in terms of being
labeled

        (2)) Thereby showing that belonging to the self also lacks inherent
nature

(d")) HOW THE PERSON APPEARS LIKE AN ILLUSION IN DEPENDENCE ON THAT REFUTATION

HAVING NEGATED an inherently existent self using the sevenfold analysis, yogis perceive the self as illusion-like. What does *illusion-like* mean here? There are two possible meanings: one refers to the ultimate nature and the other refers to the conventional nature. Ultimate truth is illusion-like in the sense that śūnyatā is established as merely existent, not truly existent. Conventional things are illusion-like in the sense that when form, feeling, and so on appear, they appear to have their own inherent nature, yet they are not inherently existent. Inherent nature appears, usually unrecognized, to the ordinary awareness of sentient beings. It does not appear to the meditative equipoise directly seeing śūnyatā nor to any awareness of a buddha. This appearance of inherent existence is mixed with the appearance of conventional things, such as forms. Ordinary people cannot differentiate these appearances, so they do not perceive conventional things as illusion-like. Things appear illusion-like to practitioners who have examined them using ultimate analysis and understood them to be empty of inherent existence. This happens as a result of a conceptual as well as a direct realization of śūnyatā. So here *illusion-like* refers to the way in which conventional things appear to these practitioners.

In order to realize that conventional things are like illusions, we must have understood that they are empty. Thus the second meaning of illusion-like, regarding conventional things, includes the first meaning of illusion-like, regarding ultimate truth. However, the reverse does not necessarily apply. The wisdom directly perceiving śūnyatā has no understanding of any conventional thing at all. For example, a practitioner may take form as the basis of his or her meditation on the emptiness of inherent existence. Gradually through that meditation a realization of śūnyatā is developed—and finally a direct realization. During a direct realization of śūnyatā, emptiness appears nakedly and clearly. At that time, only the emptiness of form appears; form itself does not appear. There is no knowledge or understanding, not even implicitly, of form. The conceptual image of form's emptiness has disappeared at this stage; there is no longer any mixed appearance of the conventional nature and the ultimate nature, which occurred during the conceptual realization of emptiness. Only emptiness appears to the wisdom directly seeing the emptiness of form.

After an ārya being arises from meditation on śūnyatā, conventional things appear again. At that time, a conceptual mind may understand a combination of both the appearance of conventional things and of emptiness. On the one hand things are empty, and on the other hand they appear. In this combined understanding of a conventional appearance and its ultimate nature, the practitioner understands the basis of emptiness together with its emptiness. This is the second meaning of the phrase *illusion-like*. This conjoined understanding of conventional things as illusion-like, which includes having realized their emptiness, can only be conceptual. In a direct realization of śūnyatā, only emptiness, a mere negation, appears. If this mixture appeared to a direct realization, then the object of the direct realization of śūnyatā would not be a pure nonimplicative negation because something in addition to emptiness would positively appear.

How do we develop a combined understanding of the appearance of conventional things and of their emptiness at the same time? As sentient beings, we all see forms, sounds, smells, and so on as inherently existent. We use these appearances as a basis and examine them by means of the sevenfold analysis— to see whether or not they really exist as they appear. To help us understand this process, Buddhist scriptures give the classic example of a magic show with magically emanated elephants and horses. First we see these animals with our visual consciousness. Then, when we analyze whether or not they are real, we develop a combination of two kinds of understanding. Our visual consciousness sees the elephants and horses as real, but our mental consciousness understands that they are not real in the way that they appear. We see them as real elephants and horses, but we understand they are not real elephants and horses. Based on this combined understanding, we ascertain that what appears to be real is in fact illusory or falsely appearing. Obviously not everyone recognizes that all magically created phenomena are false. Some people in the audience think they are real. But when someone recognizes that these elephants and horses, which appear to be real, are in fact unreal, then their appearance is understood to be illusory.

We use a similar process to understand that the self is illusion-like. To ordinary awareness, the self appears to exist by its own inherent nature. That appearance is undeniable. When we examine this self by means of ultimate analysis, we develop the wisdom understanding it to be empty of inherent existence. In dependence on a combination of these two understandings, we ascertain the person to be illusion-like or falsely appearing. It does not exist as it appears. Therefore it is like an illusion because what appears is not its true nature. When we have generated an understanding of the person as illusion-like, we realize that it is not truly existent yet it appears to be truly existent.

This combined understanding develops gradually. The wisdom analyzing the ultimate does not establish conventional appearances, and conventional valid knowledge does not establish the emptiness of inherent existence. This is why we need both minds in order to understand that such appearances are illusion-like—both the wisdom analyzing whether there is inherent nature and the conventional valid knowledge apprehending things such as forms. Prāsaṅgikas say that all conventional valid knowledge within the mindstreams of sentient beings is mistaken with regard to its appearing object, because its object appears to be inherently existent. However, they accept that it is non-mistaken with regard to its held object, because there is no temporary cause of error involved and it cannot be refuted by other valid knowledge. Conventional valid knowledge establishes its main object, a conventional thing; it also perceives it to exist inherently, though it does not necessarily hold it to exist inherently. Even though this mind is unmistaken with regard to its main object, the conventional thing, it is mistaken with regard to how it sees it as inherently existent. Because it is mistaken in this way, it cannot function to establish emptiness. So to understand that what appears is illusion-like, we need both conventional valid knowledge and ultimate valid knowledge.

We sentient beings do not need to make any special effort to develop conventional valid knowledge. Our awareness of conventional appearances arises quite naturally. Moreover we naturally see them as inherently existent— due to the influence of the imprints of ignorance within our mindstreams. Having heard some wonderful Buddhist teachings as presented by the great

Mādhyamikas—that forms and so on are illusion-like—we may have a great wish to see them as illusion-like. However, we cannot force ourselves to see them this way. We naturally see things as inherently existent. We see good things as good, beautiful things as beautiful, and ugly things as ugly—from their own side! We cannot brainwash ourselves into seeing them as noninherently existent. If we want to see them as illusion-like, we need to develop genuine understanding and insight. How can we accomplish that?

For this purpose we must repeatedly engage in the sevenfold analysis—the most effective method to negate inherent existence. If things exist inherently, they must exist in one of these seven ways. Investigating this again and again, with very precise wisdom, we gradually realize that they do not exist in any of those seven ways. Eventually we generate a profound and unshakeable understanding of the absence of inherent existence. Then when we arise from our meditation we perceive conventional things again—and they still appear to exist from their own side! But there is a difference now. Having developed an understanding of emptiness, when we look at what appears we realize that this appearance is false and illusion-like. We clearly understand that things do not actually exist in the way that they appear. This is the illusion-like appearance. There is no other way to establish things as illusion-like.

Earlier teachers used specific terminology to refer to two types of emptiness. First, space-like emptiness is the mere absence of inherent arising and ceasing of conventional things that appear. When the yogi, through analyzing such a subject, establishes for herself that there is no inherent nature, an understanding of emptiness arises within her mental continuum. The appearance of inherent existence vanishes, and in its place there is the appearance of mere emptiness. In the case of a direct realization of emptiness, this is like looking into space—there is nothing but emptiness. Second, illusion-like emptiness is what appears to the yogi when she arises from that meditative equipoise. Although things appear to exist by their own nature, the yogi knows instantly that they do not exist in that way, so they appear as illusion-like. This combined understanding occurs as soon as the meditator perceives conventional things. For the yogi, there is no contradiction between this correct understanding and that false appearance. When ordinary things appear, they immediately appear as illusion-like.

With this understanding of things as illusion-like, the yogi engages in various practices to acquire merit, such as prostration, circumambulation, and recitation. The yogi understands that these practices are not inherently existent even though they appear to be so, because she has already refuted inherent nature by means of her analytical meditation. After having realized śūnyatā in this way, she brings whatever she sees or does in the postmeditation period under the influence of that wisdom. Training in this manner, things naturally appear illusion-like without any further logical analysis.

There are two branches of Buddhist practice: method and wisdom. Method practices are for accumulating merit; but just performing certain activities is not necessarily virtuous unless influenced by pure wisdom and compassionate motivation. Walking around a holy object many times thinking "I need exercise" is not likely to create any merit. Such a walk has no special purpose if it is only done out of selfish attachment to one's body. Buddhist practices of prostration, circumambulation, and so on are to be done at least with a motivation of heartfelt refuge in Buddha, Dharma, and Sangha. Motivation is crucial for everything. There is a story about a previous incarnation of Je Tsongkhapa. As a boy he offered a white crystal rosary to the previous Buddha, "For the purpose of spreading the lineage of pure view and conduct."[159] Through the power of his offering, in a later lifetime his view and conduct were as clear as crystal. Pure view refers to an understanding of the emptiness of inherent existence, and pure conduct refers to the virtuous practices of generosity, morality, concentration, and so on. For our conduct of body, speech, and mind to be pure, we need to combine our virtuous practices with wisdom. If we engage in these practices while holding them to be truly existent, we are not engaging in them fully. Various sutras explain that when you attain the fruit of an ārya being, a stream-winner, an arhat, and so on, if you think, "I have truly entered the fruit of a stream-winner," then you have not really attained that result.

So it is good to examine whether the practices we are doing to gain merit have a real essence or intrinsic nature. We should logically analyze whether these practices are inherently existent. We should ask ourselves, "Is this prostration that I am doing now inherently generating merit?" We need to understand that the three spheres of the practice—the agent, the action, and the object of action—are empty of true existence. Candrakīrti's *Introduction to the "Middle Way"* says:

> When the gift, the giving, and the giver are seen as empty,
> This is called the supramundane perfection of generosity.
> Where attachment to those three arises,
> This is called the mundane perfection of generosity. (1.16)

Sometimes the recipient of the gift is included as one of the three spheres of generosity. In any case, however we define them, when we give a gift while understanding that all these aspects are empty of true existence and have an illusion-like nature, we are engaging in the supramundane practice of the perfection of generosity. When we practice generosity while holding the three spheres to be inherently existent, this is the ordinary practice of generosity. The same applies to all other practices such as concentration, recitation of mantra, circumambulation, and so on. Many people mistakenly think that all the prostrations and recitations they do in a Nyung Ne retreat are absolutely real and inherently have the power to purify nonvirtuous karma and bring about liberation or enlightenment. If these practices were inherently existent, then they could not function. Inherently existent things cannot change; they are stuck and have to stay the same. But because things are dependent, changeable, and relative, we have tremendous potential to remove evil traits and develop virtuous qualities. That is the sign that things are not inherently existent. Thus the correct method is to think of these Nyung Ne practices as falsely appearing, dependently arising phenomena, which can therefore destroy nonvirtuous traits and bring about virtuous qualities, just as one magical elephant can destroy another. If we engage in these practices with even a rough understanding of this, our practice will be much more effective. Tsongkhapa wrote a passage about the importance of the above method that is often recited:[160]

> Having cultivated both meditative equipoise on space-like emptiness
> And the subsequent realization of illusion-like emptiness,
> The union of method and wisdom
> Is praised as the perfection of the bodhisattva conduct.

The point is that first we have to understand emptiness, which then influences whatever else we do. Owing to the power of meditating on space-like emptiness, upon arising from that concentration everything appears as illusion-like without any additional effort. We can understand this kind of experience based on a familiar example. When we see the reflection of our face in a mirror, we know that we are seeing an image, not our actual face. The reflection appears to be a real face but we immediately know it is not. We are familiar with this double nature, so we understand that it is an illusory face as soon as it appears. Some of the audience at a magic show may not realize that the elephants and horses they see are the magical creations of the magician; they believe they are real. Even though the magician sees exactly what the audience sees, he or she knows that these animals are empty of true reality.

To gain a realization of space-like emptiness we need to develop a clear understanding of what is to be negated by ultimate analysis. The object of negation, as explained in chapter 4, is specified in terms of how things would be if they were inherently existent. It is hypothetical: if things were inherently existent then they would have to be like *this*. We need to work through all

seven logical analyses in order to thoroughly understand this criterion. Then
we can demonstrate that if things existed in *this* way there would be such-and-
such a fault. However, if we do not properly identify the object of negation in
accordance with this criterion, then when we refute the person to be either the
same as or different from the aggregates, and so on, we might think that they
are entirely nonexistent. We might think, "If things exist, then they should
be the same as their parts or different from them; neither of these is possible, therefore nothing exists." Such a view is nihilistic. Thinking in this way
would force you to believe that persons and all conventional things are like the
horns of a rabbit—empty of functionality and utterly nonexistent. Nihilism is
a totally wrong view. It is completely off track. You must recognize that it is not
the way to seek a correct understanding of the truth; it is going in a different
direction altogether. If everything were totally nonexistent, like a rabbit horn,
then things could not be like an illusion. Āryadeva's *Four Hundred Stanzas*
says:

> If that were the case, then how could
> Samsaric existence be like an illusion?

We need to analyze correctly in order to see that things are not inherently existent, yet not totally nonexistent—they exist in an illusion-like way.
Candrakīrti's *Commentary on the "Four Hundred Stanzas"* says:

> When you see dependent arising exactly as it is, then things become
> like an illusion for you, but not like the son of a barren woman. How-
> ever, if by this kind of analysis you were to negate all aspects of produc-
> tion and accept that functional things are shown to have no arising,
> then those things would not be like an illusion for you but would be
> judged to be like the son of a barren woman and so on. In that case,
> dependent arising would be totally nonexistent. So out of fear of this,
> you should not rely on those [misinterpretations] but should take it to
> be noncontradictory that things [exist and yet] are illusion-like.

It is wrong to think that the wisdom of ultimate analysis, searching for
whether things are inherently existent, finally determines that a mere illusion-
like nature exists and is the ultimate truth. You should not hold that the
illusion-like nature is the true nature of anything. Nevertheless, there is no
fault with generating the understanding that conventional things have a merely
illusion-like nature, after having refuted inherent existence through examining things by ultimate analysis. It would be wrong to have nothing whatsoever

left over; what remains is the illusion-like nature. Candrakīrti's *Commentary on the "Four Hundred Stanzas"* says:

> Therefore when things are thoroughly examined and not established as having an inherent nature, what is left over is the illusion-like nature of individual things.

Having refuted the inherent nature of a sprout by means of ultimate analysis, as long as the effectiveness of this analytical understanding remains in force we will not give rise to the thought that the sprout has an inherent nature. In other words, a logical understanding of the emptiness of the sprout cuts the wrong view holding it to be inherently existent. As long as the power of this realization has not degenerated, the thought of the sprout as inherently existent will not arise.

Now I want to return to a point we touched on earlier.[161] Does a person who understands the sprout's lack of inherent existence have the wrong grasping that holds the sprout to be inherently existent? Yes, this person has the subtle innate mind grasping the sprout to be inherently existent. Innate grasping cannot be blocked by this realization. But as long as this realization is functional, contrived grasping at the sprout as inherently existent will not arise. When a person believes that a sprout is inherently existent, it is the result of some kind of logical reasoning or philosophical system, not because of the innate mind. Consciously thinking that things are truly existent and grasping them to exist in this way is contrived grasping. Eliminating contrived grasping does not eliminate the innate mind that grasps things as inherently existent. It is the same situation here.

Moreover, it is wrong to think that the sprout's emptiness of inherent existence is truly existent and thus hold śūnyatā to be truly existent. It is also wrong to hold its illusion-like appearance to be inherently existent. Although conventional things are illusion-like, in that they are not inherently existent yet appear to be so, it is incorrect to hold this illusion-like nature to be truly existent. We should not hold śūnyatā to be a truly existent emptiness nor hold the illusion-like nature to be a truly existent illusion-like nature. That is wrong grasping. But it is not wrong to hold things to be illusion-like, conventionally. All illusion-like natures are illusion-like, in that they are empty of true existence. Emptiness is also empty.

Some scholars think that holding things to be illusion-like involves holding them to have truly existent illusion-like natures—and thus the notion of an illusion-like nature should be cast aside. That is totally incorrect. We should not reject holding things as illusion-like in nature. When we realize that things exist as illusion-like, we understand that they *merely exist* as illusion-like. In other words, holding things to exist conventionally does not mean that we hold them to be truly existent. Things dependently arise in an illusion-like way; they exist as causes and effects, empty of an inherent nature. All these things are to be accepted. If you reject them, you negate everything that should be established: dependent arising, causality, good and bad, virtue and non-virtue, samsara and nirvana. Not establishing these would be a very great fault because that would make it impossible to be certain about dependently arising things. As explained before, this is another example of the nihilistic view. Undoubtedly this kind of view arises from not being able to distinguish between the mere existence of an illusion-like nature and its true existence.

Furthermore, when we examine an object using ultimate analysis, we separate it into parts, because if a thing were inherently existent then it would exist from its own side within its basis. When we look into that basis bit by bit, we find nothing there. Everything seems nonexistent. At first we may develop an almost nihilistic view regarding the object. Next, we look at ourselves in the same way, investigating bit by bit. When we analytically examine the subject, again we find nothing there. We, the examiners, do not appear to exist. We have no ascertainment of either the subject or the object. Wherever we look, we find no basis for determining whether something is the case or is not the case. With that kind of confusion occurring, everything appears in a dispersed or fragmentary manner. There is nothing solid to hold onto. Fragments appear here and there, some looking like the subject and some like the object. These kinds of confused appearances arise when we begin to meditate on the subject and the object in an imprecise way—because we are not able to distinguish between inherently existent and merely existent or between non-inherently existent and nonexistent. We mix these notions together. When we try to negate the inherent existence of something, it seems to become nonexistent. If we understand that the object cannot be totally nonexistent and try to establish its existence, it appears to be inherently existent. When we proceed in this manner, strange appearances arise. The fragmentary appearances drawn forth by this kind of understanding are not the illusion-like emptiness. This incorrect understanding of emptiness totally destroys dependent nature. This understanding leads to nothingness. It is not the meaning of the phrase *illusion-like*.

So how do we arrive at the correct meaning of *illusion-like*? When we engage in ultimate analysis we develop the understanding that the person and so on does not exist in a way that is objectively established by its own nature, not even in the slightest. Based on this understanding, everything that usually appears to be solid, existing in its own right—such as forms, smells, tastes, and so on—cannot be found to exist in that way. These familiar things now appear strangely, and we do not quite understand how they exist and how they do not exist. Such appearances arise naturally for anyone who has heard some Dharma teachings on noninherent existence and who begins to devote him- or herself to the Madhyamaka teachings on śūnyatā. On the one hand, there are the appearances of familiar conventional things; on the other hand, when we examine them using ultimate analysis, they become indistinct. These kinds of fragmentary appearances are different from those mentioned earlier, because these kinds arise on the basis of correct analysis. They are common at an early stage of meditating on śūnyatā.

The most difficult point is this. We must negate inherent nature completely so that we understand emptiness fully; we must draw forth conviction from the depths of our hearts that, even though we are not inherently existent, we create karma and later experience its result. We need to see that there is no contradiction in establishing both emptiness and functionality. Very few people are able to establish the combination of these two—whether in terms of the subject, the object, the action, or anything at all. This understanding is very rare, because the Madhyamaka view is most difficult to find. Even when we understand emptiness, it is not easy to apprehend conventional things as illusion-like and functional. As mentioned previously, we do not need to make any special effort with regard to the appearance of conventional things. We already have direct experience of them and do not need any additional proof. However, we need to work very hard to develop a profound understanding that things do not exist inherently as they appear. We must completely understand their empty nature and not just partially refute their true existence.

In order to give rise to an understanding that fully refutes the object of negation, the *Lamrim Chenmo* and other texts in the lineage explain how to engage in ultimate logical analysis. We need to study this system thoroughly. In addition, we need to accumulate merit. We need many wholesome virtuous conditions in order to give rise to such profound understanding. Without the great accumulation of merit from aspirational prayers and so on, our analysis will not be effective. Likewise, only praying for a realization of śūnyatā, without engaging in any analytical meditation, will not be effective either. We need to utilize all the proper methods. This is really the case, so I am emphasizing it here. If we do not have a combined understanding of emptiness and causality, then the more we try to develop certainty about emptiness, the less certain we will be about practicing ethical discipline. Or the greater our understanding of the practice of virtue, the less we will understand emptiness. In short, without properly understanding the combination of emptiness and illusion-like appearance, a realization of one appears to harm the other. The two sides appear to be contradictory. When the view is strong, we lose the method side; when we build up the method side, we lose the correct view. Eventually we must understand both sides simultaneously, without alternating between them. At that point, the two realizations help and support each other; each becomes the reason for the other. They become equal in power. Thus when we understand subtle dependent arising, the ignorance that holds things to be inherently existent is gradually destroyed. At that point a practitioner has completed his or her analysis of śūnyatā. Tsongkhapa succinctly says this in *Three Principal Aspects of the Path*:

> When they do not alternate but are simultaneous,
> Merely correctly seeing dependent arising
> Destroys all ignorance wrongly grasping things.
> At that time the analysis of the view is complete. (12)

However, if these realizations are not equal in power and one understanding does not help to generate the other, then it is definite that the practitioner will fall into a wrong view. Some will fall to the extreme of permanence—which is a view that things truly exist, in that a superimposing mind grasps them to be inherently established. Others will fall into the extreme of nihilism—which is a view that things do not exist, in that a repudiating mind holds everything to be empty of functionality. The point here is that the understanding of emptiness and the understanding of dependent arising must assist each other; they must draw each other forth. If they simply alternate, there is no way to develop equal certainty about both. The *King of Concentrations Sutra* says:

> At that time the Victorious One, who has no sin
> And has the ten powers, taught this supreme meditation:
> Traveling in samsara is like a dream;
> No one is born here and no one dies.
>
> Sentient beings, humans, and life itself are not found;
> All these things are like bubbles, like water reeds,
> Like magical illusions, like flashes of lightning,
> Like reflections of the moon in water, and like mirages.
>
> There are no humans who die in this world
> And are born or transmigrate to another world.
> Yet once karma is created it is never wasted;
> Good and bad results will be experienced in samsara.

Neither permanent nor annihilated,
Karma does not accumulate or endure.
Yet once it is created, never do you not meet with its result;
You will never experience that which is created by another.

The wisdom of ultimate analysis does not find an inherently existent migrating person. All things arise and cease in an illusion-like manner. Even though they are illusion-like, the results of virtuous and nonvirtuous karma are definitely experienced. It is always the case that the person who creates any karma will experience its result. And we never meet with a karmic result that we have not created. People often complain about what happens to them. They say, "I did not do anything, but this terrible thing happened to me." They grumble, "I am completely innocent; it is someone else's fault." Or maybe they blame God for their problems. People seem to think they are experiencing the results of karma created by someone else. But the reality of the situation is that not even the smallest experience occurs without a cause. In this particular lifetime we may not have created the nonvirtuous actions that caused our present difficulties. However, all our experiences, whether good or bad, are the results of our own karma. If we create the karma, we will experience the result; if we have not created the karma, we will never experience its result. We certainly never experience the karmic results of others' actions. In cases where we have created the karma jointly with others, such as by forcing someone else to act, we experience some sharing of the effect.

The *Lamrim Chenmo* describes and explains how to meditate on karma at great length.[162] In brief, an account of karma has four parts: karma is definite; a person who has not created the karma will never experience its result; once you have created the karma, it will never disappear or be wasted—it will be experienced unless you purify it; and karma increases—a little karma may grow to unimaginable proportions over time. To use a farming analogy, we may plant a tiny seed that eventually grows into a huge tree with many branches, all covered in leaves, flowers, and fruit. A tree can be so big that even a hundred chariots can fit in its shade. If we see this much increase in material causes, we can infer that the increase of karmic causes is even greater. Internal karmic causes are far more powerful than physical causes. Thus one karmic cause can result in a rebirth of overwhelming misery and other aspects of the result may be experienced as suffering in many lifetimes. Such results would be impossible if things existed by their own nature, without depending on causes and conditions. But because things are relative and dependent on causes and conditions, a vast increase of results can and does occur on many occasions. We need to develop a firm understanding that this is how things work.

In short we need a clear understanding of the two truths: the ultimate nature—emptiness, and the conventional nature—dependent arising. The way to seek a firm and definite understanding of these has already been explained. To summarize, first we should form a clear image of the object of negation. We must clearly define how something would exist if it were truly existent. This object of negation does not exist, so it cannot actually appear. But the image of how it would appear if it did exist must be hypothetically developed. Then, without reference to somebody else's mind or anything else, we should observe how the ignorance within our mental continuum grasps things to truly or inherently exist. We must think deeply about how this ignorance imputes a self onto objects and recognize how it functions. If an inherent nature did exist in the way that it is imputed by ignorance, then it must exist as either one or many. For example, an inherently existent self must be either the same as the aggregates or different from the aggregates. We should consider with an open mind how adopting either of these positions is logically untenable, analyzing the points explained earlier. This is how to develop valid knowledge that logically refutes the object of negation. We need to contemplate precisely in this way, again and again, defining the target and then negating it. Eventually we will acquire a firm understanding that the person does not exist inherently by its own nature even to the tiniest degree. This is the wise way to train the mind to understand the depths of śūnyatā.

After that, on the affirmative side we must think about illusion-like appearances. The conventional nature of the person cannot be denied, even when we understand emptiness. When a person appears to us, they are established as someone who creates karma and later experiences its results. All the things that we perceive with our senses appear to the mind. We should think analytically about dependent nature and how cause and effect come about. Dependent arising is perfectly appropriate in the absence of inherent existence. These two—causality and emptiness—are harmonious. We should strive to realize that there is no contradiction between the negative aspect of a thing's true nature—emptiness—and the affirmative aspect of its appearance—dependent arising. If they appear contradictory, with emptiness on one side and causality on the other, we should take the example of a reflection in a mirror and think about how the two aspects of appearance and real nature are not contradictory. When we look in a mirror we see the reflection of our face. We use this reflection to show us how to clean and beautify our face, even though what we see is not actually our face. The eyes that we see in the mirror appear to be our eyes, but they are not real eyes. The reflected eyes, nose, and so on are empty of being those things. The reflection depends on conditions, such as our face in proximity to a clean and reflective mirror. In dependence on the conjunction of these causes and conditions, the reflection of our face appears and we can see it. When any of these conditions is absent, the reflection is no longer there. We know that the reflection is empty of being a real face, yet it arises in dependence on certain causes and conditions. Even someone who has not realized śūnyatā can understand this rough analogy of emptiness and appearance. In accordance with this analogy, a person does not have even an atom of inherent existence yet is an accumulator of karma and the experiencer of its results. This is not a contradiction. You should train your mind to understand that things are empty and yet arise from causes and conditions. This applies to every situation. The negative side, emptiness, does not contradict the affirmative side, causality. Emptiness and appearance exist together.

HOW A REFLECTION ILLUSTRATES THE LACK OF TRUE EXISTENCE

Someone asks, "Does a person who understands that a reflection in a mirror is empty of being what it appears to be thereby realize that things are empty of inherent existence? If so, then ordinary individuals would understand emptiness by direct perception and would therefore be āryas. If not, then how can things such as reflections be suitable examples of the lack of inherent existence? For the example's lack of inherent existence itself must be understood through inferential knowledge rather than direct perception, which would require another syllogism with a suitable example. Then that example's lack of inherent existence must be proved by another syllogism with a suitable example, so there would be an infinite regress." Every example would require another syllogism to prove it, then that further syllogism's example would require the proof of another syllogism. The reasoning would just go on endlessly. Consider the syllogism, "A sprout is empty of inherent existence because it arises from causes and conditions, like a reflection." If we have to prove that a reflection is a suitable example in being noninherently existent, we might say, "A reflection is empty of inherent existence because it arises from causes and conditions, like a pot." The lack of inherent existence of any example we may offer would also be understood by inferential knowledge, so it must be proved by a syllogism with another example. How can anyone arrive at an understanding of emptiness if the reasoning used to prove it goes on endlessly like this?

So what is the solution? An earlier scholar says, "An ordinary person who directly realizes that a reflection is not inherently existent does not thereby become an ārya, because he or she realizes the lack of inherent existence with respect to just a single thing—a reflection. That person has not understood emptiness in a more general or pervasive way. In order to become an ārya, one must directly perceive the emptiness of all phenomena."

Tsongkhapa says this answer is incorrect. Why? First of all, Āryadeva says in the *Four Hundred Stanzas* that by seeing the lack of inherent existence of one thing we see the emptiness of inherent existence of all things:

> Whoever sees one thing
> Is said to see all;
> The emptiness of one thing
> Is the emptiness of all.

There is no difference between the emptiness of one thing and the emptiness of any other thing. When you understand the emptiness of one thing, that understanding pervades everything else; you thereby understand the lack of inherent existence of all phenomena.

This earlier scholar seems to think we have to realize the emptiness of each phenomenon one by one. From that point of view, understanding the emptiness of one object does not enable us to understand the emptiness of anything else. Each object of negation must be eliminated individually. This is like an opponent's system of valid knowledge criticized earlier by Dharmakīrti, who comments that their way to eliminate wrong views would be like the way a musk deer grazes—cutting one blade of grass at a time with its two tiny fang-like teeth. He shows that this is an unfeasible account of inferential valid knowledge because it does not employ any general concepts. Likewise, we could never understand the emptiness of all phenomena if we had to realize each thing's emptiness one by one, because there are endless objects. But by understanding that if a thing existed inherently it would have to be a certain way—and that such a way of existing is impossible—we cut off the superimposition of inherent existence in a general way. When we understand the emptiness of one thing by valid knowledge, this understanding applies to all other instances simultaneously.

So then, does the mind that understands "A sprout is empty of inherent existence because it dependently arises" comprehend that everything is empty of inherent existence? If that is not the case, then what is being said here? When one mind understands the emptiness of inherent existence of a particular thing, that mind is not considering other objects in that moment. However, as soon as we apply our understanding to another thing, that too is seen as empty for the very same reason. The reason—in this case "because it dependently arises"—carries over to the new object. There is a pervasion between the reason, "because it dependently arises," and the predicate of the thesis, "is empty of inherent existence." The forward and reverse pervasions apply not only to the particular subject of the syllogism; they are also understood in a general way. If something dependently arises, then it must be empty of inherent existence.

If something is not empty of inherent existence, then it cannot dependently arise. These pervasions have a wide application; they carry over to anything, anywhere, at any time. We do not need to prove "This is not inherently existent because it dependently arises" each time we encounter something.

Our original hypothetical questioner suggested that if an ordinary person does not understand the emptiness of all phenomena when he or she understands that a reflection in a mirror is empty, then a reflection is not a good example of emptiness. Tsongkhapa says this is incorrect, but not for the reasons given by the earlier scholar above, which have been rejected. There are two different issues here. First, can ordinary people understand the emptiness of a reflection? Second, can ordinary people understand the emptiness of a sprout? The latter is far more difficult to realize than the former. It is easy to understand that what appears in a mirror is not the actual thing. Ordinary people can understand the emptiness of reflections, illusions, and other such false things. But this is not real emptiness. It is not an understanding that the reflection is empty of inherent existence. To say "The reflection of a face is not a real face" is totally different from saying "The reflection of a face is not inherently existent." Ordinary people understand that the reflection of a face appears to be a real face, but it is empty of existing as it appears. Everyone knows this, except perhaps for very young children and animals. When preverbal children see their reflection, they want to play with the other child inside the mirror. They hold the reflection to be real from its own side. Similarly, when animals see their reflections they may try to fight them. Older people with experience of worldly conventions understand that the reflection of a face is not a real face, although it appears to be a face. They understand that the real face is here on this side, not in the mirror. When looking at the reflection they try to clean their face; they do not try to clean the dirt off the face in the mirror. Although they do not hold the reflection to be a true face, they still hold the reflection to be truly existent. In other words, they understand that the reflection of a face appears to be a real face yet is empty of being a real face, but they do not understand that the reflection of a face is empty of being inherently existent. Thus ordinary people who directly understand the conventional characteristics of a reflection do not become ārya beings, because they do not understand śūnyatā at all.

So why is the reflection of a face suitable as an example of the emptiness of inherent existence? Even ordinary people directly perceive that reflections are empty of existing in the way that they appear. Likewise, everything is illusion-like in that its nature does not exist as it appears. These categories are similar. According to common worldly understanding, reflections, mirages, magical illusions, and so on are not true; most people understand that they do not exist as they appear. However, according to ordinary understanding, things such as forms, sprouts, the self, or the aggregates are true. Knowing that something like a reflection is empty of existing as it appears is an understanding of a very gross kind of emptiness. Knowing that things commonly accepted to be real are empty of existing as they appear is an understanding of a subtler kind of emptiness—the subtlest level of which is the understanding of the lack of inherent existence. Therefore understanding that a sprout or some other thing is empty of existing as it appears is different from understanding that a reflection is empty of existing as it appears.

When you understand that a reflection is empty of being a face, you understand it is empty of all instances of being a face, including an inherently real face. Logically, if we refute the generality, we thereby refute all its instances. For example, if someone says that a rabbit does not have horns, we know that a rabbit does not have big horns, small horns, yellow horns, red horns, inherently existent horns, or any other kind of horns. Similarly, when we understand that a reflection of a face in the mirror is not a face, we understand that it is not a beautiful face, an ugly face, a big face, a permanent face, or an inherently existent face. When the reflection is refuted to be a face, every particular instance that comes under the category "face" is refuted. So understanding that the reflection of a face is empty of existing as an inherently real face is just a refutation of an instance of a real face. It does not mean that you understand that the reflection is empty of inherent existence. You only understand that the reflection is empty of being an inherently real face. In other words, although we understand that an inherently existent face is not there in the mirror, it does not mean that we understand that the reflection of a face is not inherently existent. We have not refuted inherent existence.

Nevertheless, it is not inconsistent to use a reflection's lack of existing as it appears as an example of subtle emptiness. We can understand reflections, magical illusions, echoes, mirages, and so on to be illusion-like without realizing śūnyatā. We know that a combination of conditions gives rise to their appearance and that mirages and so on do not exist as they appear. These phenomena are examples of gross illusion-like nature. Even though we understand their gross illusion-like nature, such things as reflections still seem to be there by their own nature. We ordinary people do not understand that a reflection does not inherently exist. We do not understand its subtle illusion-like nature; we grasp it to be truly existent. So we have not completely negated the object of negation. We only negate a reflection's existing as it appears on a gross level; we are not able to refute its existing inherently as it appears on a subtle level.

Therefore what we have understood is a partial emptiness. "Partial emptiness" does not mean that we understand emptiness on the basis of some but not all phenomena. Partial emptiness is not actually emptiness at all, just as the partial illusion-like nature is not the subtle illusion-like nature at all. There have been many discussions about partial emptiness over the centuries. Some scholars say that when we initially realize śūnyatā things do not appear illusion-like, so to develop an understanding of their subtle illusion-like nature we use the example of a reflection in a mirror. However, this does not mean that simply by understanding a reflection in a conventional manner we fully understand the subtle illusion-like nature. The example of a reflection illustrates partial emptiness; it is not an instance of subtle emptiness. We understand that a reflected face does not exist as a real face; however, we are not able to fully negate that the reflection itself does not truly exist as it appears. Part of the object of negation is refuted and part is not. According to the Cittamātra system, a pot is not real as it appears, because it appears to be an external object yet does not exist in that way. According to the Prāsaṅgika system, that is only a partial emptiness. It is not subtle emptiness. Candrakīrti says to the Realists, particularly the Vaibhāṣikas:

> Just as pots and so on do not exist in reality,
> Nevertheless, they exist based on worldly knowledge.

Candrakīrti uses a pot and so on as an example of noninherent existence. Here this indicates partial emptiness, just as a reflection was used above, in that the object is not fully negated—because his opponents cannot accept the Madhyamaka understanding of subtle emptiness. This is a reference to a stanza in Vasubandhu's *Treasury of Knowledge*, which presents the Vaibhāṣika interpretation of the two truths:

> If the mind no longer apprehends something
> When it is broken or mentally split up,
> Like a pot, then it is conventionally existent;
> What is other than that is ultimately existent. (6.4)

The Vaibhāṣikas say that pots and so on are conventional truths. Why? A pot appears to be real, but when it is broken into pieces it loses its identity. Even if we do not physically destroy it but simply mentally separate it into parts, we no longer have the thought of a pot in mind. According to this system, a pot is made up of very subtle partless atoms that cannot be further divided physically or mentally. Because they are irreducible, these atoms are ultimate truths. So according to the Vaibhāṣikas, a pot is not ultimately existent; but this does not mean the same as what the Mādhyamikas mean when they say that a pot is not ultimately existent. From the Madhyamaka point of view, the emptiness posited by the Vaibhāṣikas is only a partial emptiness; it is not the ultimate or final emptiness. Although the Realists say that a pot or a chariot is conventionally existent and not ultimately existent, their understanding of these terms is different from the Mādhyamikas' understanding. As explained earlier, we have to use many different means to prove to the Realists that chariots and so on are not inherently existent.

There are other examples of partial emptiness commonly used in Buddhist texts. When a magician creates illusory horses and elephants, some members of the audience apprehend them to be real horses and elephants. The magician's eyes are also affected by the magic trick, so like the audience he too sees the horses and elephants. However, he never considers these to be real animals. He knows that these horses and elephants are false; he understands that the magical elephants do not really exist as elephants. Nevertheless, they undeniably appear to be elephants and to function as elephants. So the magician has some kind of understanding that they are empty and yet are functioning things. This emptiness is a partial emptiness, not a complete emptiness. Similarly, when we interact with animate and inanimate things in a dream, we hold them to be real. When we awake, we realize that the people and places in the dream do not exist as they appeared. Although we understand that they are not real, this does not mean that we realize that the things in the dream or the dream itself are empty of inherent existence. This is the same as understanding that a reflection of a face is not a real face, yet not understanding that the reflection lacks inherent existence. As cited in chapter 8, Candrakīrti's *Introduction to the "Middle Way"* says:

> And anything else construed, such as mirages and magical illusions,
> Do not exist even from the worldly point of view.

A mirage appears to be water, a magical illusion appears to be horses and elephants, and men and women appear to be genuine people in our dreams. Holding these to be real is negated by ordinary conventional valid knowledge. Mundane knowledge understands that these things do not really exist as they are held; however, this is not an understanding that things are empty of inherent existence. It is a comprehension of a partial emptiness. Nevertheless illusory things, such as mirages and so on, are used as examples in the profound sutras to show that things are not truly existent yet function in an illusion-like manner. We should recite and reflect on stanzas such as these from the *King of Concentrations Sutra*:

Like a mirage or a celestial city,
Like a magical illusion or a dream,
Signs that are meditated on are empty of essence.
You should understand all phenomena are like this.

As when the moon shines in a clear sky
And its reflection appears on a clear lake,
The moon has not fallen into the water.
You should understand the characteristics of all phenomena are like this.

As when people in a cave of the forested mountains
Hear echoes of singing, talking, laughing, and crying,
These do not exist as they appear.
You should understand all phenomena are like this.

As when echoes arise on the basis of things
Like singing, music, and even crying,
They never have the tonal quality of the original.
You should understand all phenomena are like this.

As when in a dream you enjoy sexual intercourse,
But when you awake you do not see the object of your desire,
Ordinary beings, however, still long for it and cling to it.
You should understand all phenomena are like this.

As when magicians create illusory forms,
Such as horses, elephants, chariots, and various things,
None of them exists as they appear.
You should understand all phenomena are like this.

As when a young woman sees herself in a dream
Bearing a son who suddenly dies,
Is joyful at the birth, then bereft at the death.
You should understand all phenomena are like this.

As when at night an appearance of the moon
Is reflected in a body of clear pure water,
The water contains no moon and cannot be held to have it.
You should understand all phenomena are like this.

As when traveling at noon in the summer sun,
A person suffering from dire thirst
Sees mirages as great pools of water.
You should understand all phenomena are like this.

Although in a mirage there is no water at all,
Ignorant sentient beings want to drink it;
But it is not real water, so they cannot imbibe it.
You should understand all phenomena are like this.

As when wanting the solid essence of a moist water plant
Someone splits open its thick stem,
But it has no solid essence—neither inside nor out.
You should understand all phenomena are like this.

Just as shown by these examples, everything has a dual nature: they are empty, yet they appear; they do not truly exist, yet they function. We can contemplate this by reciting and chanting stanzas like these. There is a common saying, "Riding the horse of pure words, the mind reflects on the profound meaning." Meaningful words chanted rhythmically in a suitable voice are like a horse. Thinking carefully about the deep meaning of this sound is like riding the horse. Contemplating the meaning of the words, not just focusing on the sound of the music, is a form of meditation. There is a similar saying that goes:

Depending on the cane of the words,
The mind knowing the meaning can arise, like an old man.[163]

Elderly people rely on canes to stand up and walk. Similarly, words are like a cane—the mind can rely on them to give rise to understanding. Here we depend on the words of the great Madhyamaka texts to develop an understanding of śūnyatā and that all things have an illusion-like nature.

(2')) THE EXAMPLE ILLUSTRATES HOW THE SELF IS ESTABLISHED IN TERMS OF BEING LABELED

When a chariot is imputed or labeled based on its parts, the chariot is the appropriator and the parts are the appropriated. The same subject-object relationship exists between the person and its basis. The person or self is imputed on the five aggregates, the six elements, and the six sources of sense consciousness. In this context, the elements are the four basic elements (earth, water, fire, and air) and the two additional elements included within a person (space and consciousness). Although we usually discuss twelve sources of sense consciousness, here only the six internal sources are considered (the five physical sense powers and the mental sense power); this is because a person is not imputed based on the six external sources, which are the objects of the senses such as visible forms, sounds, smells, and so on. The self is the whole (the appropriator or agent), which takes possession of these parts (the appropriated or object of action). Sometimes when discussing this relationship we find mention of three spheres of activity: the action, the agent, and the object of action. At other times, as here, only two of these three are mentioned: the agent or subject, and the object of action. Candrakīrti's *Introduction to the "Middle Way"* says:

> Likewise, according to common understanding,
> The self is considered to be the appropriator
> In dependence on the aggregates, elements, and six sources;
> The self is the agent and the appropriated are the objects.

The self is conventionally known based on the five aggregates, the six elements, and the six internal sources of sense consciousness. The self is the subject that takes the aggregates and so on as its possessions. This relationship of subject and object is important to consider. The object is what is taken, such as a rebirth or the aggregates; the subject or agent is the one that takes them. This is like the classic explanation of fire and fuel: the object, fuel, is what is burned; the subject or agent, fire, is the burner. Moreover, just as when we engage in ultimate analysis of a chariot and cannot find it in any of the seven ways, so when we employ ultimate analysis of the self we cannot find it. Therefore the self has no inherent nature at all. Yet it exists conventionally, from the point of view of worldly understanding that does not engage in ultimate analysis.

(2)) THEREBY SHOWING THAT BELONGING TO THE SELF ALSO LACKS INHERENT NATURE

When we employ ultimate analysis in search of whether the self inherently exists, we do not find any such thing by means of the sevenfold analysis. Having negated the inherent nature of the self, how could we find any instance of belonging to it? Through understanding that the self is not inherently existent, we understand that the self's eyes and so on do not inherently exist. Nothing considered to be its own or to be "mine" can be found by ultimate analysis. This applies particularly in relation to the aggregates because they are the primary instances of belonging to the self. There are many discussions about what the self is and what being its own, or "mine," involves. Although an inherently existent self and belonging to such a self are negated, there is a self and belonging to the self in general. These conventionally exist. If they were not conventionally existent, then their lack of inherent existence would not be genuine emptiness because the basis of that emptiness would be nonexistent. Therefore the self and belonging to it are conventionally existent.

This brings up a topic discussed in chapters 3 and 11: the egotistic view, or the view of the perishable collection. There we examined this view in the context of the first two lines of a stanza from Candrakīrti's *Introduction to the "Middle Way"*:

> First, thinking "I," grasping at a self arises;
> Thinking "This is mine," attachment to things arises.
> Thus sentient beings are powerless like a bucket on a water wheel;
> I bow to the bodhisattvas' compassion for them. (1.3)

There is a twofold division of the view of the perishable collection: the egotistic view observing the self or "me" and the egotistic view observing the self's, or "mine." Attachment arises initially toward the self and then toward the self's—which primarily encompasses one's aggregates of body and mind. The egotistic view grasps oneself or belonging to oneself as inherently existent.

When you look at your hand and think, "This is mine," while subtly grasping it as inherently existent, is that an instance of the egotistic view? Surely grasping at anything other than the person to be inherently existent is grasping at a self of phenomena? The held object of the egotistic view must be the self of persons, right? There is a lot of discussion in monastic textbooks about the object of the egotistic view. Jetsun Chokyi Gyaltsen says that the object of the egotistic view must be the person and cannot be phenomena such as eyes, nose, aggregates, and so on. These things are instances of what belongs to the self. In his view, the general notion of "mine" is the object of the egotistic view grasping at belonging to the self. The object is not any specific thing belonging to the self, such as one of the aggregates. It is the mere belonging to the self itself. The instances of what the self owns, such as the aggregates, are phenomena and so are not objects of the egotistic view. In other words, the way the egotistic view grasps "mine" is not focused on the body and other aggregates. "Mine" cannot be separated from "me." Thus the primary object of the egotistic view is the self—"I" or "me," and belonging to the self—"mine." Other than that, nothing is the object of that view, not even the instances of "mine." If it were otherwise, then your body, mind, house, and anything else you possess would become the object of this view. Things we consider to belong to us are everywhere: my home, my town, my world, and so on. Eventually this could extend so far that everything could be taken as objects of the egotistic view.

When yogis correctly identify the object of the egotistic view, they meditate on it using ultimate analysis. When they search for that object as something that exists from its own side, they do not find any inherently existent self or belonging to the self. Through realizing that the self and belonging to the self are not to be found, they will be liberated. This does not happen immediately upon first understanding. It means that once yogis have this realization, they can be liberated eventually, because now they can create the actual causes of liberation from samsara. Before this realization, the causes were beyond reach. This will be further explained later. In the eighteenth chapter of the *Fundamental Treatise*, Nāgārjuna says:

> If the self does not exist,
> How can belonging to the self exist?

Also, Candrakīrti's *Introduction to the "Middle Way"* says:

> Since without an agent there is no object acted on,
> Without a self, there is no belonging to the self.
> By seeing that the self and belonging to the self are empty,
> The yogi becomes completely liberated.

Through understanding that the self is not inherently existent, you will understand that belonging to the self is not inherently existent. You must eliminate any doubts about this based on what has been explained above. Develop firm ascertainment of this matter by engaging in the sevenfold analysis. This is how to realize the emptiness of the self.

✣ 20 ✣

Objects Lack Inherent Nature

(3)) How to apply these lines of reasoning to other phenomena
(b)) Determining the selflessness of phenomena
    [(1)) Refuting production from self]
    [(2)) Refuting production from others]
    [(3)) Refuting production from both self and others]
    [(4)) Refuting causeless production]
    [(5)) How to infer that inherent production does not exist]

---

(3)) HOW TO APPLY THESE LINES OF REASONING TO OTHER PHENOMENA

JUST AS WE analyze the relationship between the self and the aggregates in accordance with the example of the chariot and its parts, so we should understand other things, such as pots and woolen shawls, in this way. We identify the self in relation to its basis, the aggregates. Likewise, we label a pot based on a combination of the four substantial elements (earth, fire, wind, and water) and the four things that arise from those elements (form, smell, taste, and texture).[164] A pot is a physical object that has certain attributes, which include color and shape (objects of visual consciousness), as well as smell, taste, and texture (objects of other sense consciousnesses). These attributes are its basis of imputation. When we investigate by means of the sevenfold analysis whether a pot has an inherent nature, examining whether the subject and its basis of imputation are inherently the same or inherently different, we do not find any inherent sameness or difference between the pot and its parts—either conventionally or ultimately. Nevertheless, the self, pots, and so on are established from the point of view of nonanalytical conventional knowledge. Buddha says in the *Chapter Teaching the Three Vows* (*Tri-saṃvara-nirdeśa-parivarta-sūtra*):

Worldly beings dispute with me but I do not dispute with worldly
beings. Whatever worldly beings commonly accept to exist or not exist,
I also accept.

In this sutra, in the course of explaining the prātimokṣa, bodhisattva, and
tantric vows, Buddha says that he accepts whatever is known by conventional
knowledge—just as ordinary people and non-Buddhist philosophers do—
because this is not negated by ultimate analysis. Candrakīrti's *Introduction to
the "Middle Way"* says something similar:

Anything spoken of in various ways by ordinary beings,
Whether a vase, woolen shawl, canvas, army, forest, rosary, tree,
House, carriage, or guesthouse, should be understood to be established,
Because Buddha never disputes with worldly beings.

Parts, attributes, desire, characteristics, fuel, and so on,
As well as the attribute possessor, the part possessor, the desirous, the basis
    of characteristics, the fire, and so on,
Do not exist in any of the seven ways when analyzed in the same way as a
    chariot.
But other than that they do exist from the point of view of common
    worldly knowledge.

When any object and subject—such as parts and a whole possessing those
parts—is subjected to ultimate analysis, it is found not to exist in any of the
seven ways. We analyze the relationship between the subject and object—a
whole and its parts, a desirous person and their desire, fire and its fuel—by
examining whether they are inherently the same or inherently different from
each other, in just the same way that we analyze a chariot and its parts. By
doing this kind of examination we see that the subject and object do not exist
inherently. However, they do exist based on ordinary conventional knowledge.

Buddha does not refute what is conventionally known in the world. As the
above passage says, without engaging in ultimate analysis we too should accept
things commonly agreed on to exist. We can understand what this means by
taking the example of a vase. A clay vase is a whole; it is the possessor of attributes and the basis of characteristics. The clay itself is included among its parts,
as are its color and shape. Not every container is a vase; a vase has certain defining characteristics—a specific shape and function—known by everyone. For
example, it is round-bellied, spout-lipped, and long-necked. When all these
characteristics occur together, we understand the object to be a vase. The same
analysis can be applied to woolen shawls.

In Candrakīrti's verses above there are a number of related pairs: "desire" refers to strong grasping or attachment, and the basis of that attachment is the person who has the desire, namely, "the desirous"; likewise "fire" is the burner, and the object burned is "fuel." These pairs are not independent things. One is imputed on the other. A whole is imputed on its parts, and those parts are imputed on the whole. Each member of the pair has a mutually dependent relationship with its counterpart. A basis and its characteristics or an agent and the object acted on cannot exist without each other. The same applies to any subject-object relationship. This notion of "mutually dependent relationship" is specific to Madhyamaka philosophy.

According to the lower schools, there are only two ways of being related: causally related, where the components of the relationship are different entities; and related as the same nature, where the components of the relationship are not separate entities yet they are not the same thing, for example, a generality and its instances or an object and its attributes. In *Commentary on Valid Cognition*, Dharmakīrti expresses the meaning of a relation as follows:

> If this does not exist
> Then definitely that does not occur. (1.33c)

This definition applies to both types of relation: causal and same nature. In both cases, strictly speaking, the relationship is one-way, not mutual. In a causal relation, such as between smoke and fire, fire produces smoke but smoke does not produce fire. Buddhist logicians express this by saying that smoke is causally related to fire, but fire is not causally related to smoke. Smoke is dependent on its cause, fire; it cannot exist without being caused by fire. However, fire does not causally depend on smoke. A fire can exist without smoke— for example, a gas fire. In another example, a seed can exist without ripening into its fruit; however, a fruit cannot exist without having grown from a seed. Thus a causal relation operates only in one direction. There is a causal relation between a result and its cause; there is no causal relation between a cause and its result. That is what Buddhist philosophers say, though Western philosophers may reject this way of expressing it. In a same-nature relation, such as between an oak tree and a tree, an oak tree is dependent on a tree because an oak tree cannot exist unless a tree exists. However, a tree can exist even if there is no oak tree because there can still be another type of tree, such as beech or pine. Similarly, a particular person, such as Devadatta, is related to the generality "person," but not the other way around. Devadatta cannot exist unless some person exists; however, even if Devadatta does not exist, another person, such Peter or John, may exist. Devadatta is related to person, but person is not related to Devadatta, because the existence of a person does not depend on the existence of Devadatta in particular. However, if the components of a same-nature relation are coextensive, then there will be a two-way relationship, because each is an instance of the other: an impermanent thing is a product, and vice versa. This two-way relationship, however, is very different from the Madhyamaka notion of "mutual dependence" described above.

Candrakīrti's notion of "mutual dependence" is much wider than the two kinds of relation presented by Dharmakīrti. Candrakīrti says that cause and effect are mutually dependently related. The effect is dependent on the cause, but the cause is also dependent on the effect. This is not causal dependence as such; it is terminological dependence, which has much wider application than causal relations and same-nature relations. A whole is imputed in dependence on its parts because if there are no parts there cannot be a whole; similarly, the parts are imputed in dependence on the whole because if there is no whole there cannot be any parts. This applies to all the cases mentioned in Candrakīrti's verses above. Fuel depends on fire because it is given the name "fuel" in dependence on being burned by fire; fire depends on fuel because it requires something to burn and it is labeled in dependence on that. There are many more examples of these mutually dependent relationships in the *Fundamental Treatise* and *Introduction to the "Middle Way."* More obvious examples of terminological dependence are: the eastern mountain and the western mountain, a big man and a small man, a tall tree and a short tree. These are all mutually dependent. A thing established as big depends on establishing some other thing as small. A thing established as the eastern mountain depends on establishing another mountain as the western mountain. Without establishing a mountain in the west, we cannot say that there is a mountain to the east. However, are those two mountains related? The eastern mountain exists even if there is no western mountain, right? If there is a big man and a small man or a tall tree and a short tree, are those men or those trees related? No, they have no actual relationship. But are they completely unrelated? According to the Prāsaṅgika system, these things are mutually, terminologically established. The same applies to fire and smoke. Fire is the producer, and smoke is what is produced. A produced thing cannot be established without a producer, and a producer cannot be established without a produced thing. Terminologically they are mutually dependent; they do not need to be actually related. However, we can say loosely that the Prāsaṅgikas accept three kinds of relation: causal relation, same-nature relation, and terminological relation. In terms of a causal relation, smoke depends on fire—but not vice versa. In terms of a terminological relation, smoke and fire are mutually dependent.

The eighteenth chapter of Nāgārjuna's *Fundamental Treatise* says:

> The agent depends on the object of action;
> And the object occurs in dependence on the agent.
> Apart from this, we do not see
> Any other way of being established.

The next stanza in that text concludes:

> Through [the analysis of] agent and object
> You should understand all the remaining things.

The agent and the object of action are mutually dependent. This applies to everything: the product and the producer, the path gone over and the goer, the viewed and the viewer, and the knower and the known. There is no product without a producer, and there is no producer without a product. These things do not exist inherently—they are interdependently established. We must understand how to establish the two truths even on the basis of just one thing. For example, although from the perspective of ultimate analysis the self is empty of inherent existence, as an agent or object of action it functions in a conventional sense. Our understanding of these two natures based on the self can then be applied to all phenomena. The *Introduction to the "Middle Way"* says:

> By means of the correct and the deceptive seeing of all things,
> Any given thing is apprehended as having two natures. (6.23)

Each thing has two natures: ultimate and conventional. Correct seeing apprehends ultimate truth—the object's true nature. Deceptive or false seeing apprehends conventional truth—the object's appearance and function. We first understand these two truths on the basis of one example, and then we apply that insight to everything else. Based on the example of the chariot, we need to gain a firm understanding of how to analyze the self and then extend that understanding to all phenomena. The *King of Concentrations Sutra* says:

> In just the way that you discern the self,
> Mentally apply that same understanding to everything.
> The nature of all phenomena is completely pure, like the sky.
> By understanding one, you will understand them all.
> By seeing one, you will see them all.
> No matter how extensively you can explain this,
> Do not give rise to conceit regarding it.

The statement "By understanding one, you will understand them all" refers to a conceptual understanding of emptiness. The next line, "By seeing one, you will see them all," refers to direct perception of emptiness. No matter how well we understand these things, we must not give rise to the conceit that holds them in the wrong way—as inherently existent.

There is a great deal of debate about whether by understanding śūnyatā on the basis of one thing we can understand all things as empty. Does it mean that the moment we understand the emptiness of one thing, we understand the emptiness of everything? Not exactly. In a general way, understanding one thing to be empty of inherent existence enables us to understand all things as empty. Nevertheless, even though you understand a certain thing to be empty of inherent existence, you may not correctly understand something else to be empty. Once we come to understand śūnyatā by logically analyzing a particular object, we will understand another object to be empty as soon as we apply that reasoning to it. However, before we can understand emptiness in a general way, we must direct the mind to one particular example and gradually develop an understanding of emptiness on the basis of it. Even so, when we initially turn our attention to another object, we may still grasp some aspect of it incorrectly. But when we recall our earlier reasoning and analyze this object in the same way we analyzed the earlier one, the power of the earlier reasoning immediately brings about an understanding that this object too—and everything else—is empty. We do not need to employ different logical inferences to prove the emptiness of each and every subject. The reasoning based on one subject can be carried over to apply to each new case. This is how logical reasoning generates a general understanding. In short, having understood śūnyatā on the basis of one thing, when you direct your mind toward another thing and apply the same reasoning, you generate an understanding of everything as empty of inherent existence.

(b)) Determining the selflessness of phenomena

The selflessness of phenomena refers to the lack of inherent nature, not of the person but of the basis on which a person is labeled: the five aggregates, the six elements, and the six internal sources of sense consciousness. These phenomena are not the self; they are the basis of imputation of the self. Their lack of inherent existence is the selflessness of phenomena. Tsongkhapa says that there are many ways to demonstrate the emptiness of phenomena. Here he follows Candrakīrti's *Introduction to the "Middle Way"* and *Commentary on the "Introduction to the 'Middle Way'"* and establishes the emptiness of phenomena by refuting production from the four alternatives: arising from self, arising from others, arising from both, and arising without a cause. This refutation is based on the first stanza of Nāgārjuna's *Fundamental Treatise*:

> Not from self, not from others,
> Not from both, not without a cause;
> Any things, anywhere,
> Do not arise at any time.

The Svātantrikas say that this stanza presents one thesis with a fourfold reason. For example, Bhāvaviveka says that the first reason is: "Any things, anywhere, do not ultimately arise from self at any time, because production has a purpose and a limit, for example a vase." In contrast, the Prāsaṅgikas say that this stanza presents four different theses, with reasons presented later in the text. Tsongkhapa says that we should interpret the first thesis to be: "Any external or internal things, anywhere, do not arise from self at any time." We should expand the wording of the other three positions in the same way: any external or internal things, anywhere, do not arise from others at any time; any external or internal things, anywhere, do not arise from self and others at any time; and any external or internal things, anywhere, do not arise without a cause at any time. According to Buddhapālita's commentary on this stanza, we should not establish these theses using a positive proof with a reason and an example—which is Bhāvaviveka's way of establishing a thesis. Instead we should use a refuting consequence to negate what would follow from the opposite of these theses, with the following structure: "If any things, anywhere, arise from self at any time, then such-and-such a fault would follow." The fault in question expresses something that contradicts the opponent's tenets, so the argument proves that he cannot accept that things arise from self. This is applied to all four alternatives. By showing the consequences of the opposite of each thesis, which contradict the opponent's tenets, we negate the opponent's position. This is how we use refuting consequences.

This argument works in the following way. If something inherently arises, then there are only two logically possible ways in which it could do so: either it depends on a cause or it does not depend on a cause. There is no third ground or possibility. Next, if it inherently arises in dependence on a cause, then the cause and its result must be either the same entity or different entities. If the cause and effect are the same entity, then this is called "arising from self." If the cause and effect are different entities, then this is called "arising from others." Again, there is no third possibility. In terms of the refutation, arising from self and arising from others are refuted individually first. Then, because each is already refuted individually, their combination is automatically refuted.

Finally, arising without a cause is refuted, since this is completely beyond question. So if we want to investigate whether anything arises inherently, there are only four alternatives to explore: arising from self, arising from others, arising from both, and arising without a cause. If we refute all four alternatives, we eliminate every possible mode of inherent production.

According to the Prāsaṅgikas, we do not need to apply the qualification "ultimately" in our logical consequences because these four modes of production are all refuted even conventionally. There is no arising from self even conventionally, and there is no arising from other causes even conventionally, because in this context the term *others* means "inherently existent others." There is no arising from both conventionally because each has been refuted individually; there is no arising without a cause conventionally because that is impossible. Thus, taken together, the refutation of production from the four alternatives is a complete refutation of ultimate production. Once we have refuted production from the four alternatives using logical consequences, we can easily refute inherent production. There is no need to refute the four ways of arising one by one again in order to establish this. Therefore we investigate the refutation of production from each of these four alternatives in turn.

[(1)) Refuting production from self][165]

The main opponent here is the Sāṃkhya tradition. According to the Sāṃkhyas, every produced thing arises from a cause that is the same nature as itself. They contend that if a resultant thing did not already exist within its cause, it could not arise. Production occurs when a result that exists hidden in its cause becomes manifest. For example, Sāṃkhyas believe that a sprout exists in a nonmanifest way within a seed. When the seed gives rise to a sprout visible to the eye, the previously invisible, nonmanifest sprout has been produced. It has now become manifest. Buddhist schools do not accept that things arise from themselves in this way. So they present two refuting consequences against that position: "If a sprout arises just from itself, production would be meaningless" and "If a sprout arises just from itself, production would be endless."

The first consequence—if a sprout arises just from itself production would be meaningless—is based on the meaning of *produce* or *arise*. "To be produced" or "to arise" is defined as the coming into existence of a thing that did not previously exist. A thing arises from causes and conditions; it is produced by them. If *production* means "to bring into existence something that did not exist before," then the Sāṃkhya position is untenable. If a manifest sprout already exists as itself at the time of its seed, it is meaningless for it to be produced again—in both senses of the word "meaningless." It makes no sense to say that an already existent thing is produced, because "produced" would lose its meaning, and it is purposeless to bring into existence something that already exists, because it is already there and nothing further is accomplished. The second consequence—if a sprout arises just from itself, production would be endless—follows because an already produced seed would give rise to itself again. Any produced thing would give rise to itself repeatedly without end, because no other cause is involved. If the already produced seed continuously gives rise to itself, there would never be an opportunity for it to transform into a sprout. This consequence is demonstrated in the twentieth chapter of Nāgārjuna's *Fundamental Treatise*:

> If a cause and its result were the same,
> The produced and the producer would be the same.

Candrakīrti's *Introduction to the "Middle Way"* says:

> It is meaningless for a thing to arise from itself.
> It is illogical for something that has arisen to arise again.
> If you think that what has already arisen arises again,
> Then you will not find the arising of a sprout and so on.

The same text says:

> Therefore this notion that a thing arises from itself
> Is untenable in both conventional and ultimate terms.

In summary, production from self entails two sets of consequences. First, if things were produced just from themselves, as asserted by the Sāṃkhyas, then they would exist at the time of the cause; if they already exist at the time of the cause, then it would be meaningless for them to be produced again. Second, if things were produced just from themselves, then they would arise repeatedly; if they arise repeatedly, then their production would be endless.

[(2)) Refuting production from others]

All Buddhist schools except the Prāsaṅgika-Madhyamaka accept production from other causes. Even the Svātantrika-Madhyamaka school accepts that results arise from other causes and conditions conventionally. These schools try to prove their position by using logical reasoning and citing scriptures. In certain sutras Buddha teaches that there are six causes, four conditions, and four results. So, these followers argue, because Buddha says that a sense consciousness arises from four conditions, there is production from others. What are these conditions? The four necessary conditions for a visual consciousness that sees blue, for example, are: the empowering condition, the object condition, the immediately preceding condition, and the causal condition. The empowering condition is the sense power, in this case the subtle eye organ. Any sense consciousness functions under the power of a subtle sense organ, which enables it to perceive its respective object. A sense consciousness dominated by the eye organ cannot perceive objects of other senses. The second necessary condition required for sense perception is the object itself. Without the presence of its object, in this case blue, a visual consciousness that sees blue cannot arise. The third necessary condition is the immediately preceding condition. Every moment of consciousness arises from an earlier moment of consciousness; so here the cause and the effect are the same in being moments of consciousness. In order to see a color or a shape, there must have been another moment of consciousness prior to that moment of visual perception. It may be an earlier moment of visual consciousness or a moment of mental consciousness that directed the eye to look at the object. In any case, the immediately preceding condition of any consciousness is also a consciousness; so more precisely, it is a "similar" immediately preceding condition. In contrast, although external things may also be said to have an immediately preceding condition, that cause is not necessarily similar to the result. The fourth necessary condition, the causal condition, is a general category that includes all the other causes of a sense consciousness apart from the three conditions already mentioned. There are so many other causes of visual consciousness, such as karma, the body, the eyeball that houses the eye organ, light, and so on. In brief, many followers of Buddhist tenets claim that there is arising from other causes.

It is important to bear in mind that in this context *others* means inherently existent others. Those who propound that things arise from other causes basically assume that causes and conditions exist inherently or from their own side. Thus the lower schools' position is that an inherently existent result arises from inherently existent other causes. According to the Prāsaṅgikas, if a cause and its effect exist inherently, then they must be ultimately different from each other by nature; if a cause and effect are ultimately different from each other, they must be independent. Ultimately different entities are independent of each other because they exist inherently by their own power and do not depend on each other or anything else. Based on this understanding of inherent existence, the Prāsaṅgikas present two refuting consequences to disprove production from other causes. First, if results arise from inherently different other causes, then darkness would arise from a burning flame, because these would also be inherently different from each other. Second, if results arise from inherently different other causes, then anything, whether a result or not, would arise from anything else, whether a cause or not, because these would likewise be inherently other. There would be no way to identify an appropriate cause of something, because both an appropriate cause and an inappropriate cause would be inherently different from the result, in exactly the same way. In other words, nobody could say that a certain cause produces a particular result and not another, because all causes are similarly unrelated to their effects. A bright flame could cause complete darkness because a flame would be inherently other than that result. Generally, in our noninherently existent universe, light is the opposite of darkness, which is why lamps are lit in the evening. But if things were to arise from inherently different causes, then a burning flame and its quality of eliminating darkness would be unrelated, so there would be no reason for darkness not to be produced by a burning flame. If all causes and effects were inherently different, then anything could arise from anything else, because everything would be similarly unrelated.

Tsongkhapa explains this consequence using the example of a seed and a sprout. It is commonly accepted that a seed transforms into a sprout; they are cause and effect. But for someone who accepts that a seed and its sprout exist by their own independent nature, then the difference between a rice sprout and its seed, which is its cause, and the difference between a rice sprout and fire, which is not its cause, would appear the same. In each case, their way of differing would not be merely nominal but by their own nature. So since cause and effect—in this case a seed and its sprout—would be different by their own natures, they would appear to be just as unrelated and independent from each other as two things that cannot be causally related, such as a seed and fire. There would be no way to distinguish between appropriate and inappropriate causes, because the difference between each set of things would appear the same to our mind—an inherent difference. So how could we say that a rice sprout arises from a rice seed but does not arise from fire?

This argument reveals an internal contradiction in the view of inherent existence. If we make a distinction between a sprout being produced from one thing and not from another, then the difference between a sprout and its seed and the difference between a sprout and fire cannot be the same. It must be possible to distinguish between the way in which these two sets of things are different. However, if all these things are asserted to be inherently existent, then we cannot discern any disparity between the way an effect differs from an appropriate cause and the way it differs from an inappropriate cause. For the arising of a sprout would have no dependence on either an appropriate or an inappropriate cause. Candrakīrti's *Commentary on the "Introduction to the 'Middle Way'"* makes this point clearly:

> Just as a rice seed that is the cause of a sprout and the rice sprout that is its result are different, so fire, charcoal, a barley seed, and so on, which are not its cause, are different from it. Just as a rice sprout arises from a rice seed that is different from it, so it would arise from fire, charcoal, a barley seed, and so on. And just as from a rice seed there arises a rice sprout that is different from it, so a pot, a woolen shawl, and so on would arise. But that is never seen. Therefore this [arising from an inherently different cause] does not exist.

If a rice seed and its resultant rice sprout were completely, independently, and inherently different by their own nature, the difference between them would be absolute. They would be as different as a rice seed and a pot, or a rice seed and anything else unrelated to it. A rice seed would no more cause a sprout than it could cause a pot or a fire, because they would all be equally unrelated. Therefore a rice seed could give rise to anything, and anything could arise from it. Consequently, anything would arise from anything.

The opponents believe that we cannot establish such a general pervasion. They say that logical inference works only in a specific case; they do not accept that what follows in one context also follows in other contexts. They do not accept that we can know a general pervasion, such as "Wherever there is smoke there is fire, so if there is no fire then there is no smoke." They assert that we can know only a specific instance of this pervasion, such as "There is fire on that mountain pass because there is smoke up there," or "There is fire in the kitchen because there is smoke in the kitchen." As a result, they may not see that if a rice sprout arises from a rice seed that is inherently different from it, then a rice sprout could also arise from fire or a barley seed. They do not accept a pervasion to be carried over to other cases but accept it to be limited to a specific case. We already considered the refutation of such a limited pervasion in chapter 14 where Tsongkhapa demonstrates the problems in Jayānanda's position. In brief, although knowledge of a pervasion is initially developed on the basis of a particular example, it cannot be limited to that basis. If it were, then this limited pervasion itself would need to be established by some other example, and so on, ad infinitum.[166] It is clear that Candrakīrti does not propound such a limited notion of a pervasion.

For someone who accepts that a result arises from an inherently different cause, it follows that everything would arise from everything; or if did not arise, it would never arise. Furthermore, for someone who believes that causes and effects are utterly unrelated things, there would be no basis on which to distinguish a correct cause from an incorrect cause. By accepting that causes and effects are independent and inherently different, one loses the special relationship between an actual cause and effect. A possible cause would be just as different from its result as an impossible cause. The twentieth chapter of Nāgārjuna's *Fundamental Treatise* says:

> If cause and effect were utterly different,
> Then a cause and a noncause would be equal.

Also, Candrakīrti's *Introduction to the "Middle Way"* says:

> If a separate thing arises in dependence on another separate thing,
> Then heavy darkness would arise from tongues of flame,
> And everything would arise from everything,
> Because everything [causally related] would be utterly separate, like
> noncauses.

This kind of consequence cannot be rebutted by saying that a rice seed and its sprout belong to the same continuum, whereas a rice seed and a barley seed or fire do not. As explained earlier, if things are inherently different rather than dependently different, then they cannot belong to the same continuum (see chapter 18). Moreover, this kind of consequence cannot be countered by saying that it is only ever seen that a rice seed produces a rice sprout and not barley. Although it is true that specific things are definite causes of other particular things, this point cannot be used to refute the argument here. Why not? The subject under discussion is the notion of difference established on the basis of an object's inherent nature. We are not arguing about the notion of difference established by conceptual or linguistic convention, where it is certain that cows do not give birth to horses and so on. We are discussing how things exist or do not exist in an ultimate sense. When the question concerns what is examined by ultimate analysis, we cannot answer it by appealing to objects of conventional understanding.

[(3)) REFUTING PRODUCTION FROM BOTH SELF AND OTHERS]

Certain non-Buddhists, such as the Jains, accept the view that things arise from both self and others. For example, they say that a clay pot is produced from self and others. The resultant clay pot is made of clay; the pot and the raw material used to make it are the same entity and belong to the same substantial continuum. So a clay pot is produced from itself. In addition, a clay pot is produced by a potter using a wheel, a kiln, and so on. So a clay pot is produced from others. Taking the example of the continuum of a sentient being, for instance Devadatta, they say he arises from himself, in the sense that he takes rebirth in this life in dependence on his vital life force—something that exists throughout his former lives—and he is the same entity as this vital life force. They say that Devadatta arises from others, in the sense that his birth depends on his father, mother, and his karma, and these are different from Devadatta. The Jains conclude that because Devadatta does not arise just from self or just from others, he arises from a combination of self and others.

Arising from both self and others, in the sense in question, is production from something that exists inherently within the cause and from something that exists as an inherently different entity from the cause. So this view is refuted by the logical reasons explained above: the first part—arising from self—is disproved by the reasoning refuting inherent self-production; the second part—arising from other causes—is disproved by the reasoning refuting inherent production from others. Therefore we do not need an additional, separate, refutation of this view. Candrakīrti's *Introduction to the "Middle Way"* says:

> Production from both is untenable
> Because it succumbs to the faults explained earlier.
> It does not exist conventionally and it does not exist ultimately,
> Because arising from each individually is not established.

[(4)) REFUTING CAUSELESS PRODUCTION]

The Cārvākas posit production without a cause. They do not believe in karma or in past and future lives. They accept only this life, which they say arises by its own nature without depending on previous causes. We already saw in chapter 5 that the Cārvākas believe that this body and life spring from the elements; they do not arise from a life that existed before. The mind also is no different; it too arises by itself. In their view, only direct perception is valid knowledge. If something is not directly perceived, it does not exist. We never see anyone making the roots of the lotus flower rough or making its leaves and petals smooth and soft, therefore this must occur by itself. Likewise, we never see anyone painting the beautiful, multicolored eyes on peacocks' tail feathers, so they must arise naturally, uncaused by anything or anyone. Therefore the Cārvākas do not believe in a creator or in karma and so on.

Nowadays people sometimes make claims similar to the Cārvāka position, that fire naturally flares upward and that water naturally flows downward. This is inaccurate. We can see that certain things arise in particular places, at particular times, because they depend on specific causes and conditions. Things arise when their causes and conditions are present, and when they are not present they do not arise. There are two extreme consequences that would result if things arose without a cause. First, if things do not arise in dependence on certain times, places, or conditions, then there is no reason for them to arise in some places and not others or at some times and not others. Thus if something were to arise without a cause, it would have to arise everywhere all the time because its arising would not require any causes or conditions. Second, assuming that things arose without a cause, if something does not arise, then it cannot arise anywhere at any time. If it does not exist right now, there is no reason or cause for it to come into existence at any other time or place. Applying this to one of the above examples, if things do not depend on any causes and conditions, the colorful eyes of a peacock's tail could appear on a raven. There is no reason why this could not occur.

In brief, if everything is causeless, then if something arises in one circumstance, it must arise in all; or if it does not arise in one circumstance, it cannot arise anywhere, at any time, at all. So there would be no point in making a great effort to obtain certain results. All the energy that people, like farmers, expend on specific tasks would be purposeless because the resultant harvest would arise by itself. Candrakīrti's *Introduction to the "Middle Way"* says:

> If something arises simply without a cause one time,
> Then it would also arise everywhere all the time.
> So, ordinary beings would not have to do hundreds of things—
> Gathering seeds and so on—in order to obtain certain results.

[(5)) How to infer that inherent production does not exist]

Through seeing these arguments that refute production from the four alternatives, we can establish that there is no arising from any of the four extremes. Those four alternatives are the objects pervaded, and inherently existent production is the pervader: if a thing inherently arises, it must arise in one of those four ways; if it does not arise in any of those four ways, it cannot inherently arise. This pervasion was explained earlier in this chapter where we saw that the four alternatives encompass every possible type of production. There is no other way in which something could arise. We can argue that there is no inherent production because there is no production from any of the four alternatives. Inherent production mutually entails inherently existent things. So we can prove our main thesis, "Things do not inherently exist," using the reason "because there is no production from any of the four alternatives." We can develop inferential understanding that things do not inherently exist through seeing the unwanted consequences that would occur if things were to arise from any of the four alternatives: from self, from others, from both, and without a cause. Our inferential understanding may be expressed as follows: "Things are empty of inherent existence, because if they were inherently existent then they would be inherently produced, and if they were inherently produced then they would arise from one of the four alternatives—every one of which implies unacceptable consequences."

When we see those unacceptable consequences, which contradict our assumptions about how things exist, our assumptions are decimated and we can generate an inferential understanding of emptiness. There is no need to put forward a syllogism here directly proving the thesis, such as: "Things do not inherently arise because they do not arise from self, others, both, or neither." Although Bhāvaviveka and others say that a positive syllogism is needed to give rise to inferential knowledge of emptiness, the Prāsaṅgikas disagree; they contend that it is possible for intelligent people to gain inferential knowledge by understanding a consequence that reveals an implied contradiction. They do not need to see a thesis set forth in a separate syllogism. As soon as a person with a sharp mind sees the logical contradiction involved, then he or she will generate inferential understanding. Candrakīrti's *Introduction to the "Middle Way"* says:

> Because there is no arising from self, from others, from both,
> Or without depending on a cause, all things lack inherent existence.

Some people claim that the Prāsaṅgikas only use logical consequences and never use syllogisms at all. That is a misunderstanding. Although the Prāsaṅgikas consider that a syllogism is not needed to give rise to inferential knowledge, this does not mean that they never use them. To gain an understanding of emptiness, less intelligent people may need both consequences and syllogisms. First, to loosen their strong attachment to their wrong view, they need to see the contradictory consequences that follow from it. Then they develop some doubt about that view and begin to think that their previously held position is probably wrong. Having single-mindedly held a wrong belief initially, they consider the consequences of that view and now waver between two possibilities. At this stage, a syllogism—composed of a subject, a predicate, a reason, and an example—based on the opponents' own assumptions, can convince them. So both methods of inference—a consequence and a syllogism—can be used to assist less intelligent people. We do not start the process with syllogistic inference. We only use this if a consequence is not fully effective. And we certainly do not employ an autonomous inference—which the Prāsaṅgikas do not accept at all.

By refuting inherent arising in this way, we gain a firm understanding that things are not inherently existent. Nāgārjuna and Candrakīrti refute inherent existence mainly by analyzing produced things. Everything that exists is either a product or a nonproduct. Produced things arise from causes and conditions. Nonproduced things are nonfunctional; they do not arise from causes and conditions, and they do not produce any results. They do, however, exist. To *exist* means to be known by valid knowledge. For every functional thing, such as a pot, there are several nonfunctional things, such as the pot's isolate, the generality of pot, the emptiness of pot, and so on. These nonproducts are objects of knowledge; they can be understood and proved to exist. These too are empty of inherent existence.

Emptiness can be proved on the basis of a product or a nonproduct. However, the main emphasis is on the ultimate analysis of products, because most of the things that we hold to be truly existent—which engenders the egotistic view, the root cause of samsara—are functional things. In other words, our wrong views usually concern produced things that we hold to be truly good or truly bad. The non-Buddhist and lower Buddhist schools hold functional things to be truly existent and real. They say that virtuous causes really or inherently give rise to virtuous results; nonvirtuous causes truly or inherently give rise to nonvirtuous results. The Realists emphasize produced things rather than nonproduced things, so Nāgārjuna uses the same approach. He begins the *Fundamental Treatise* by praising Buddha for his unique teaching of dependent arising in terms of an eightfold refutation of inherent existence based on produced things:

I bow down to the most holy of teachers,
The completely accomplished Buddha,
Who teaches the peace that pacifies all elaboration,
That whatever dependently arises has
No cessation, no arising,
No annihilation, no permanence,
No coming, no going,
No unity, no plurality.

Once we have understood how produced things lack inherent arising, we can easily refute the inherent existence of nonproduced things. Nonproduced things exist only through imputation on produced things. Without produced things, we cannot find any nonproduced things. Consider space, for example. Nobody sees space. Space is merely the lack of material obstruction. Space exists only where it is possible for a material object to exist. So space is based on physical, produced things. All nonproduced things, such as negation, oneness, generality, and emptiness, exist this way. Therefore when you understand the emptiness of produced things, it is easy to understand that nonproduced things are not inherently existent also.[167] Nonproduced things do not need to be separately established as empty. So the refutation of arising from the four alternatives is emphasized. According to the Prāsaṅgika system, these must be negated both conventionally and ultimately. In summary, by first refuting the inherent existence of produced things, we can easily refute the inherent existence of nonproduced things. In this way, we can quickly find the Madhyamaka view with regard to all existents.

Up to this point, based on Nāgārjuna's *Fundamental Treatise* and Candra-kīrti's *Introduction to the "Middle Way,"* Tsongkhapa has explained how to establish emptiness by revealing the contradictory consequences implied by wrong views. Now, drawing on stanzas from these and other texts, he explains how to prove that things are empty of inherent existence by using a syllogism in which dependent arising is the reason. The seventh chapter of Nāgārjuna's *Fundamental Treatise* says:

> Anything that dependently arises
> Is peaceful by nature.

Although the structure may not be obvious, these two lines present a syllogism: "Anything" indicates the subject, "is peaceful by nature" indicates the predicate, and "dependently arises" indicates the reason. This is synonymous with saying that all external and internal phenomena are empty of inherent existence because they dependently arise. Candrakīrti's *Introduction to the "Middle Way"* says:

> Because things dependently arise,
> These misconceptions cannot withstand analysis.
> Therefore this reason of dependent arising
> Cuts through the nets of all wrong views.

We eliminate all wrong views by coming to understand that things, such as sprouts, are empty of inherent existence because they dependently arise.

The logical reason "because they dependently arise" clearly shows that things do not exist by their own intrinsic nature. This reason simultaneously cuts through the wrong views of eternalism and nihilism. The extreme view of eternalism or permanence holds that "things truly exist by their own nature." Any misconception that things exist in this way is eliminated by understanding that things are "dependent." The extreme view of nihilism or annihilation holds that "things are nonexistent." We see that this is not the case by understanding that things "arise." The Madhyamaka is the middle way, the central view, because it is free of these two extremes. When we follow the middle way we avoid getting lost on either wrong track. There are many other well-known logical reasons demonstrating that things do not truly exist—for example, because they are "neither truly the same nor truly different." However, dependent arising is known as "the king of reasons" because even the mere words undercut both of the extreme views at once.

This reason is so effective and straightforward that Tsongkhapa explains it further. He suggests we look at a syllogism based on others' assumptions: "A sprout does not inherently exist because it arises in dependence on its causes and conditions, like a reflection in a mirror." Most people are familiar with the example of a reflection. When young children see their reflection, they think that what appears in the mirror exists as a real face. They do not think that the nose, eyes, and so on that appear in the mirror exist only from the perspective of their perception. Small children think there is a face, existing by way of its own reality, there in the mirror. Similarly, ordinary sentient beings do not think that what they perceive and experience—whether beautiful or ugly, pleasant or unpleasant—is established by the power of their own minds; rather, they believe that a thing exists by its own nature, just as it appears to. Things naturally appear to sentient beings to exist from their own side, and most people hold them to exist that way—which is the grasping at inherent existence. Things never appear to ordinary beings as if merely labeled, so it never occurs to us that they could be imputed by our own minds. Instead, things appear to exist from their own side, and we hold them to exist objectively in that way. That is how we impute an inherent nature onto things.

The object of this way of imputing is called by various names: essence, nature, autonomous nature, inherent nature. The characteristics of this object—inherent nature—are that it exists objectively, from its own side, by way of its own entity, inherently, and autonomously. Now if something were to exist by way of its own inherent nature, then it could not arise in dependence on causes and conditions. These two—existing inherently and arising dependently—are contradictory. If they were not contradictory, then we could not maintain that an already existent pot does not need to be produced again in dependence on causes and conditions. In brief, using *dependent arising* as the logical reason is the most powerful way to refute inherent existence. Āryadeva's *Four Hundred Stanzas* says:

> Anything that dependently arises
> Cannot be autonomous.
> All these things have no autonomous nature,
> Therefore they have no self.

Commenting on this stanza, Candrakīrti says in his *Commentary on the "Four Hundred Stanzas"*:

> Anything that exists by its own nature, inherently, autonomously, without depending on others at all, does not dependently arise because it is established from its own side. However, all caused things do dependently arise. So anything that dependently arises cannot be autonomous because it arises in dependence on causes and conditions. Because all these things have no autonomous nature, any thing whatsoever has no inherent nature or self.

Here "self" and "inherent nature" have the same meaning. Now, what does "autonomous" mean? The Tibetan term literally means "self-powered," that is, "independent." Someone may suggest that being independent means not depending on causes and conditions; so to realize emptiness, we only need to understand that things are not independent in this way. But this is too simplistic. Do we understand śūnyatā because we know that things are causally dependent? No. We have to be careful in defining what is meant by "autonomous nature." The Prāsaṅgika notion of autonomy is linked to how things appear to ordinary beings. Anything that appears to the ordinary mind of a sentient being appears to exist through its own power, as if independent of anything else. Trees, mountains, and so on appear to exist externally from their own side. Although we understand that these things are dependent on causes and conditions, when we look at a tree it immediately appears to exist from its own side, freely, autonomously, without depending on anything else; based on this appearance, we naturally hold it to exist by way of its own nature. Existing in that sort of way is what is meant by "independent" or "autonomous" here. According to the Prāsaṅgikas, a simplistic understanding of the absence of autonomy—that a thing exists dependently on causes and conditions—is not equivalent to an understanding of emptiness. We do not need to prove to the lower Buddhist schools that things are free of an autonomous nature in this gross sense. They all accept that things depend on causes and conditions. So even though the lower Buddhist schools reject that things are independent of causes and conditions, they do not understand emptiness as explained by the Prāsaṅgika-Mādhyamikas. A far subtler interpretation is in question here. For the Prāsaṅgikas, "independent" or "autonomous" does not refer to being independent merely of causes and conditions; instead it refers to a way of existing whereby a thing is able to stand on its own, objectively, by means of its own nature. If a thing were to exist autonomously in this way, it must exist by its own power, from its own side, by its own nature, objectively. This is the subtlest notion of independence. When we negate this, then we realize śūnyatā.

According to the Prāsaṅgikas, all the following expressions have the same meaning: existing from its own side, existing by its own power, existing by its own characteristics, existing ultimately, and existing truly. All these terms indicate the object to be negated. The Svātantrikas do not agree. Although they accept that things are not ultimately existent or truly existent and identify this as the object to be negated, they assert that things do exist from their own side, exist through their own power, and exist by their own characteristics (that is, inherently). They think that an object must exist from its own side, with its own inherent identity, because if it did not exist that way then it would be totally nonexistent, like a rabbit horn. This is a very subtle point. It is not easy to express. In order to understand it you need to study, analyze, and meditate extensively. You need to look deeply at how things appear and how the egotistic view holds them to exist. A complete comprehension requires stable meditative concentration conjoined with very sharp wisdom.

Being empty of inherent existence means to lack this kind of autonomous nature. It does not mean that functional things do not exist. Therefore we can refute inherent existence using dependent arising as the reason. In the passage that follows the above quotation from *Commentary on the "Four Hundred Stanzas,"* Candrakīrti says:

> Therefore in this system, to dependently arise is to be free of an autonomous nature. Thus the meaning of "free of an autonomous nature" is what emptiness means. It does not mean that there are no functional things.

Tsongkhapa discussed this point earlier when he explained the error of interpreting the object of negation too widely. In former times, many scholars and practitioners believed that the Madhyamaka teachings refuted conventional things. This approach is completely distorted because it denies both the afflictive aspect of the twelve links of dependent arising that generates samsara as well as the pure aspect of the twelve links that leads to nirvana. This is the view of nihilism. On the other hand, believing that functional things exist by their own nature is also distorted because it involves a total fabrication. This is the view of eternalism. Candrakīrti's text continues:

> Therefore, according to this system, viewing dependent arising as non-existent is completely wrong because this repudiates both the afflictive and the pure causal processes, which are functional yet illusion-like; moreover, viewing it as real is completely wrong because it has no inherent nature. So those who claim that things have an inherent nature have no acceptance of dependent arising and succumb to the faults of views of eternalism or nihilism.

Those who want to be free of these two extreme views should accept that things do not inherently exist, and that both the afflictive and the pure aspects of dependent arising exist in an illusion-like way.

An opponent from the lower schools argues: "In what way are you refuting us when you negate an autonomous nature, using functional dependent arising as your reason—where *dependent arising* means free of an autonomous nature? We accept that things are dependent on causes and conditions and therefore are not autonomous. So there is no difference between us."

Tsongkhapa responds that although the opponent accepts dependently related causes and effects, he is like a young child who believes the reflection of his face in a mirror is truly a face. An inherent nature is superimposed on dependently arising things, and these opponents call that the essential nature of functional things. They say that things dependently arise. But they do not understand the subtle meaning of dependent arising and speak about it in a way that is not accurate. The difference between the lower schools and the Prāsaṅgikas is that the Prāsaṅgikas accept that things that dependently arise have no inherent nature and speak about it in this way. Candrakīrti's *Commentary on the "Four Hundred Stanzas"* says:

> You ask, "If to be free of an autonomous nature means to dependently arise, how can you refute us? What is the difference between you and us?" I will explain. The difference is that you do not understand the precise meaning of dependent arising nor how to express it. A young child who is not yet familiar with conventionalities firmly reifies a reflection to be true; he is ignorant of its lack of actually existing in that way, so he thinks it is a real thing. He does not know how to think of it as a reflection. Similarly, you assert dependent arising; but dependent arising is empty of inherent nature, like a reflection—and you do not

understand how it exists in terms of its nature. For although it does not exist inherently, you do not hold it to lack inherent existence; instead, having superimposed an inherent nature where there is no inherent nature, you hold it like that. Also you do not know how to express it, because you do not speak of the absence of inherent existence; instead you speak of the inherent nature of things.

Although the Proponents of Noninherent Existence, who follow the Prāsaṅgika system, and the Proponents of Inherent Existence, who follow other Buddhist systems, both accept dependently related causes and effects, the above passage says that the Prāsaṅgikas understand dependent arising exactly as it is, whereas the other schools do not, and that the Prāsaṅgikas know how to explain dependent arising correctly, whereas the other schools do not. So this passage shows that the Prāsaṅgikas are not just arguing about words. However, some people think that because both parties agree that things function causally, the difference between the Realists calling things "truly existent" and the Prāsaṅgikas calling things "nontruly existent" is merely verbal. Both accept that happiness arises from virtuous causes and that suffering arises from nonvirtuous causes, so it does not matter whether they call these things truly existent or nontruly existent. Likewise, here they may think that although the Svātantrikas claim that things exist by their own nature, and the Prāsaṅgikas strongly disagree, they are only arguing about terminology. There is no real difference between them.

This argument is similar to the absurd way that the Sāṃkhyas argue with the Buddhists. The Sāṃkhyas believe that sound, the object of auditory consciousness, is a quality of space and therefore permanent. The Buddhists reject that sound is permanent, because it is produced. However, the Sāṃkhyas reply that once you accept that sound is an object of auditory consciousness, you are talking about the same thing that they are—sound. So in their view, even though the Buddhists do not call it permanent, the Buddhists implicitly accept the nature of sound as permanent, exactly as the Sāṃkhyas understand it. They say that the Buddhist argument is just about the terminology. Actually there is a huge difference between the Sāṃkhyas and the Buddhists. Even though they both accept sound to be an object of auditory consciousness, their notions of the way in which sound exists are completely different.

When ordinary sentient beings hold things to arise in dependence on causes and conditions, they naturally believe things to have an inherently established nature. They even use dependent arising as a reason for thinking that causes and effects exist inherently. Thus they continue to be bound in samsara. Such people are like young children looking in a mirror; they hold what they see there to exist as it appears. Wise masters are like adults looking in a mirror; they know that what appears is merely a reflection, and they understand how it actually exists. According to wise masters, dependent arising is the reason that refutes inherent existence; it is the basis on which a definite understanding of the truth is founded. Since it cuts through the extreme wrong views, using dependent arising as a reason is the most skillful and marvelous method to establish the absence of inherent nature.

Tsongkhapa wrote a text in praise of dependent arising, the king of reasons, which begins:[168]

> I bow down to the unsurpassable teacher and sage,
> The one who sees and knows
> Dependent arising, the king of reasons,
> And explains it just as he sees it.

Buddha sees that all functioning things exist only through a chain of dependent arising. Only Buddha has seen this clearly and teaches others exactly how beings are bound in samsara and how they become free of it. So Tsongkhapa praises him specifically with regard to this teaching about the afflictive and purified twelve links of dependent arising. This is similar to Nāgārjuna's homage at the beginning of the *Fundamental Treatise*, which we looked at earlier. It is also similar to Nāgārjuna's homage at the end of *Commentary on the "Refutation of Objections"*:

> I bow down to the Buddha,
> Whose incomparable supreme teaching shows
> That dependent arising and emptiness
> Have the same meaning as the middle way.

There are many texts that express this point: whatever dependently arises is empty of inherent existence; whatever is empty of inherent existence dependently arises. Being empty of inherent existence means not existing by one's own nature; in other words, it means existing dependently. So are emptiness and dependent arising the same? When you understand emptiness do you understand dependent arising? When you understand dependent arising do you understand emptiness? Here we need to differentiate between subtle and gross dependent arising. If you understand emptiness then you understand subtle dependent arising. However, you do not need to understand śūnyatā in order to understand gross dependent arising. In the example of the reflection, both a child and an adult see a face in the mirror. When an adult sees a reflection of his face he understands it is not a real face, but a young child does not have this understanding. Likewise, when someone sees dependent arising, it does not mean that he sees it as empty of inherent existence. It is easy to understand dependent arising on a gross level. Even illiterate peasants understand that when you plant corn seeds, corn will grow, and when you plant rice seeds, rice will grow. They know that sprouts arise in dependence on particular causes and conditions and do not arise without them. So they understand a very gross level of dependent arising—that corn is dependent on its causes and is empty of independence. But a much higher level of understanding is required to see subtle dependent arising—that nothing exists by its own nature—which is far more difficult to achieve. Ordinary people cannot easily understand the very subtle manner in which things dependently arise and exist. This is a most important point and very difficult to understand. This is why so many complex texts are written about the Madhyamaka view of emptiness.

Having seen the power of using dependent arising as the reason to prove that things are empty of inherent existence, Buddha said:

> Whatever arises from conditions does not [inherently] arise;
> It does not have the [inherent] nature of arising.
> Whatever depends on conditions is said to be empty;
> Whoever understands emptiness in this way is diligent.[169]

The first two lines of this stanza mean that whatever arises in dependence on causes and conditions does not arise by its own nature. The third line specifies that being dependently related in reliance on conditions means the same as being empty of an inherent nature. The last line expresses the benefit of understanding emptiness in this way; it is the actual path. This sutra continues:

> Wise masters understand that phenomena dependently arise,
> And thus will never rely on the extreme wrong views.

This indicates that wise masters, through having understood dependent arising, eliminate the grasping at wrong views.

Now if things did have an inherently existent nature, Buddha and his śrāvaka and pratyekabuddha disciples would have seen it, but they did not. If things were inherently existent, they would never change because they would be unaffected by causes and conditions. In that case, liberation would be unattainable because it would be impossible to cut the net of elaborations grasping at signs. Here "grasping at signs" means to grasp at things as truly existent—which is the root of the mental afflictions. The *Elephant Ornament Sutra* (*Hasti-kakṣya-sūtra*) says:

> If phenomena existed by their own inherent nature,
> The Conqueror and his disciples would know it.
> Phenomena would be unchanging: there would be no passing beyond
>   sorrow;
> Wise masters would never become free of elaborations.

In this section of the *Lamrim Chenmo*, Tsongkhapa explains the selflessness of phenomena in general. He says that it would be good for students to study the more detailed explanation of the logical reasons that refute the inherent existence of the sources of sense consciousness, the aggregates, and the elements, as found in the third, fourth, and fifth chapters of Nāgārjuna's *Fundamental Treatise*. However, he says he will not elaborate any further here for fear of going on too long. It is already enough, isn't it? If we go into any more detail you may fall asleep!

Eliminating Obstructions

(c)) How to eliminate obstructions by cultivating these views in meditation

(c)) HOW TO ELIMINATE OBSTRUCTIONS BY CULTIVATING THESE VIEWS IN MEDITATION

THE PURPOSE OF all the preceding discussions about the self and belonging to the self is to eliminate the obstructions within one's mindstream. As discussed in earlier chapters, there are two types of obstructions: obstructions to liberation, which are the mental afflictions and their seeds, and obstructions to omniscience, which are the imprints left by the mental afflictions and their seeds. Tsongkhapa now shows us how to eliminate these obstructions according to the Prāsaṅgika system.

First, we develop the wisdom seeing that the self and belonging to the self do not have any inherent nature at all. Then, employing that wisdom, we continue to meditate on śūnyatā so as to gradually reverse the innate egotistic view and its seeds. All sentient beings, except arhats and pure-ground bodhisattvas, suffer from the afflictive view grasping at "me" and "mine." This innate egotistic view—the view of the perishable collection—is the basic ignorance that is the root cause of samsara. This view involves a certain type of attachment; it gives rise to various kinds of karma or action, and the attachment involved acts as a necessary condition for such karma to ripen. We gradually uproot the innate egotistic view from our mindstreams by meditating on the selflessness of the person. Once that wrong view is reversed, the four types of grasping are reversed. In general grasping occurs as the ninth of the twelve links of dependent arising.

SAMSARIC BIRTH BASED ON THE TWELVE LINKS OF DEPENDENT ARISING

The twelve links arise in a specific order and perpetuate samsara (for further detail, see chapter 9, volume 2 of this series). In brief, the first link is ignorance. Ignorance creates contaminated karma, or conditioning action. Action produces a specific type of consciousness, known as the *causal consciousness*, which is the immediate receptacle of the karmic seed. Taking human rebirth as an example, when this consciousness enters the mother's womb and combines with the mixture of egg and sperm, it gives rise to name and form (which refers to the five aggregates grouped as body and mind) at the moment of conception. Then the six internal sources of sense consciousness—the five physical sense powers and the mental sense power—gradually develop. These subtle sense organs are necessary to produce the sense consciousnesses. The meeting of a sense organ with its respective sensory object and sense consciousness is the sixth link: contact. Contact gives rise to feeling: we develop pleasant feeling in contact with attractive things, unpleasant feeling in contact with unattractive things, and neutral feeling in contact with things that are neither. Feeling is the main component of experience. Any feeling of pleasure or pain is caused by previous karma, including the karma that resulted in our present birth. Based on our present feeling we create yet more karma, which will ripen in a future life. Thus we are setting up a new round of causation. Feeling leads to attachment or craving, the eighth link. Pleasant feeling gives rise to attachment— wishing to remain in an enjoyable situation; unpleasant feeling gives rise to aversion—longing for the opposite of a painful situation; and neutral feeling gives rise to another kind of attachment. When attachment becomes stronger it becomes grasping, the ninth link.

There are four types of grasping: grasping at objects of desire, grasping at views, grasping at mistaken morality and asceticism, and grasping at a self. A sentient being's entire life is involved with the first type of grasping; we have strong attachment to sensory objects. The second type of grasping—grasping at views—is strong attachment to four of the five types of wrong views: holding extreme views, holding wrong views as supreme, holding distorted views, and holding mistaken morality and asceticism to be supreme. The third type of grasping is a fervent belief that certain religious practices—such as offering blood sacrifices, setting fire to one's body, or imitating dogs and cows—will purify the practitioner, bestow blessings, and lead to liberation. The fourth type of grasping—grasping at a self—is the fifth wrong view. This is the egotistic view, or view of the perishable collection; it is a strong attachment that grasps the self, imputed on the collection of perishable aggregates, to be inherently existent.

Grasping gives rise to existence, the tenth of the twelve links. Existence is the karma that causes a potential to ripen immediately into the next rebirth. The karmic potentiality itself was established earlier in the stream of consciousness by an action motivated by ignorance. Existence is its final ripening as a complete cause that brings about the next life. Although maturation or ripening itself is neutral, a cause of ripening, which occurs at the time of death and produces the first moment of the next life, must be virtuous or nonvirtuous. This kind of karma is never neutral because neutral karma has no power to propel consciousness into the next life. Vasubandhu says:

> The cause of ripening is only
> Nonvirtue or contaminated virtue.[170]

Grasping, the ninth link, is a necessary condition for this karma to come to fruition. It nourishes that karma like spring rain promotes the growth of seeds planted the preceding autumn. Spring provides the conditions that make seeds sprout and grow. Likewise, grasping compels the karmic seed to ripen. This state of karma about to ripen into the next life is called existence. The following moment is the eleventh link, birth. Aging and death begin in the very next moment after that.

Why is the cause of karmic ripening that occurs just before death and immediately brings about the next life called *existence*? Here the name of the result is given to its immediately preceding cause. In that moment, your next life does not quite exist yet. It almost exists and will definitely occur. You will be born into it immediately. Classical illustrations of the wheel of life depict this link as a pregnant woman about to give birth. There is no avoiding the next life at this point. So the cause is identified in terms of its result. There is a Tibetan analogy of this process. We identify a certain leafy green plant growing in a field by the name of that vegetable when cooked. The growing plant—*loma*—is not the cooked vegetable—*tshoma*; the raw *loma* only becomes *tshoma* when it is cooked. Yet we often call the raw plant by the name of the cooked vegetable.

If we do not have the link of existence, then there will be no next life; contaminated rebirth will be exhausted. How do we make this happen? For samsaric rebirth to occur there must be a combination of mental afflictions and karma. Three of the twelve links of dependent arising are mental afflictions: the first, ignorance, and the eighth and ninth, attachment and grasping, respectively. The second and tenth links are karma: projecting karma and completing karma, respectively. When we create virtuous or nonvirtuous actions, karmic seeds are deposited in our mindstreams. The depositing of karma in the mindstream is analogous to a farmer planting seeds in a field. The image of planting a seed connotes the possibility of it sprouting. Planting a seed does not always signify immediate growth. A seed will sprout in the future when there is the right amount of warmth, moisture, and other conditions. If you plant a seed that never gets any water or sunlight, it may never ripen owing to the lack of suitable conditions. The same happens to karmic seeds: a karmic seed can ripen quickly in the next life or two, or it could take much longer, not ripening for a hundred lifetimes or perhaps eons after being planted. Karmic seeds need suitable mental conditions to ripen and cannot ripen without them. There may be a very long time between an action and its karmic seed ripening; so we have the opportunity to purify karma before it brings about its result. Before a non-virtuous karmic seed has had a chance to ripen, you could enter the path, gain a direct realization of śūnyatā, and attain arhatship. In that case, that nonvirtuous seed would be destroyed by the antidotes and never ripen at all.

The second link of dependent arising, conditioning action, refers to the karmic seeds that we sow in the great field of our mental continuum every moment. These are called *projecting karma* because they propel us into our next rebirth and into whatever we experience in the future. They remain dormant within the mindstream until they meet the right conditions, and then they germinate. The tenth link, existence, is called *completing karma*, or *actualizing karma*, because it is a type of condition that actualizes the projecting karma; it immediately brings about the fruition of a karmic seed. For these karmic seeds to ripen, they must also be nourished by one further condition: grasping. At the time of death, the tenth link, existence, is activated by the ninth link, grasping, which is the cooperative cause of karmic ripening. The links of grasping and existence act in combination on the karmic seed, immediately giving rise to the next rebirth. The immediate cause of rebirth occurs the instant before death, so it is very important to have a wholesome mind at that time. If you die with a powerful nonvirtuous mind it will cause a nonvirtuous seed to ripen into a lower rebirth—even if you have spent most of your life engaging in virtuous activities. Conversely, if you die with a virtuous mind, it will cause a virtuous seed to ripen into a good rebirth.

If we eliminate ignorance, which is a mind grasping the self to be inherently existent, then attachment will not arise. If the links of attachment and grasping do not arise, then the link of existence will not occur; so the karma that brings about the next rebirth will not ripen. Even though past karmic seeds may still be present in the mental continuum, when grasping has been removed then the conditions that bring about the next life will not occur. Thus one attains liberation from samsara. The eighteenth chapter of Nāgārjuna's *Fundamental Treatise* says:

> Because [views of] the self and belonging to the self are pacified,
> Grasping at I and mine will not occur.

It also says:

> When thoughts of the self and belonging to the self
> Are exhausted with regard to internal and external things,
> Grasping is stopped.
> When that is extinguished, birth is finished.

In short, when we destroy ignorance, the grasping that arises from ignorance stops. When grasping is stopped, rebirth caused by the power of mental afflictions and contaminated karma ceases. In this stanza, the direct cause of impure rebirth in samsara is identified as grasping combined with existence. Usually this cause is said to have three aspects: attachment, grasping, and existence. As we have seen, attachment and grasping are very closely related; grasping is simply very strong attachment. In any case, we are looking at a combination of mental afflictions and karma. When these have been completely and permanently exhausted, we are liberated from samsara. The eighteenth chapter of Nāgārjuna's *Fundamental Treatise* says:

> You are liberated by extinguishing karma and mental afflictions.

How can we extinguish karma and mental afflictions? That text goes on to say:

> Karma and mental afflictions come from misconceptions;
> Those misconceptions come from elaboration;
> Elaboration is stopped by [realizing] emptiness.

Karma and mental afflictions arise from certain distorted conceptions. There are four fundamental distorted conceptions: holding impure things as pure, holding things in the nature of suffering as pleasurable, holding impermanent things as unchanging, and holding selfless things as the self or as belonging to the self. These four distorted conceptions are rectified by contemplating Buddha's teaching of the four noble truths, specifically the four attributes of the truth of suffering: suffering, impermanent, selfless, and empty. Everything that arises from karma and mental afflictions has these characteristics; but worldly beings hold things in the opposite way, expressed as the four distorted conceptions. These distorted conceptions arise from elaborations: grasping things as truly existent. To an ordinary unenlightened mind things naturally appear to be truly existent. Grasping things as truly existent, just as they appear to be, is the elaboration of true existence. We grasp that appearance of inherent nature to be real. That elaboration gives rise to distorted conceptions, which then give rise to further karma and mental afflictions. How do we get rid of the fundamental problem—the elaboration of true existence? That is easy to answer. The realization of śūnyatā completely and permanently stops such an elaboration. Of course, emptiness itself does not stop anything, but the realization of emptiness ends this elaboration eventually.

This samsaric cycle—being born, gradually aging and dying, then being born again, and so on—is propelled by the power of impure karma. Not every kind of action gives rise to samsara. Only physical, verbal, and mental actions contaminated by an afflictive mind produce samsara. Therefore we can define samsara as the impure cycle of lives perpetually revolving owing to the power of karma and mental afflictions.

NONSAMSARIC BIRTH BASED ON PURE CAUSES

Samsara is not caused by pure actions of the three doors. For example, an ārya bodhisattva on the pure grounds[171] engages in actions out of love, compassion, and the realization of śūnyatā. His or her actions are totally pure—untainted by any mental affliction. Therefore a pure ārya bodhisattva does not have an ordinary contaminated body; his or her body is in the nature of the mind, arising from uncontaminated karma in connection with the ground of the imprints of ignorance. What does this mean? A pure ārya bodhisattva's body does not arise from contaminated karma created by mental afflictions because all mental afflictions have been removed. Nevertheless, such beings still have subtle obstructions to omniscience—the imprints of ignorance—remaining in their mindstreams until they attain buddhahood. Within their mindstreams there is some special, virtuous, uncontaminated karma that is connected with the imprints of ignorance. Therefore the pure body of such an ārya bodhisattva is still called the māra of the aggregates. When arhats die, they too take this kind of pure body in their next life. Holy beings with this kind of body do not experience ordinary aging, sickness, and death. But this does not mean they have no birth at all. They have ended samsaric rebirth, not pure rebirth. After eliminating the causes of samsaric rebirth, they can take pure rebirth through the power of wisdom and compassion.

There is a huge difference between impure rebirth on the one hand and reincarnation in a pure body on the other. Reincarnation in a pure body occurs without depending on contaminated karma and mental afflictions. There are many such instances. Even buddhas may appear to take birth, manifesting as ordinary beings undergoing aging and death. You may remember the story about Maitreya appearing as a wounded dog. This is an example of a perfect, pure life that is merely a manifestation of a holy being.[172] However, there is also a big difference between a pure-ground bodhisattva's reincarnation and a buddha's nirmāṇakāya in terms of their nature and causes, though we need not go into this here.[173]

Samsara arises only from impure karma, which in turn arises from mental afflictions. What causes mental afflictions to arise? Mental afflictions, such as craving and hatred, are rooted in the egotistic view. They do not occur unless our minds inappropriately superimpose certain characteristics onto things, conceiving them to be inherently attractive and pure or inherently unattractive and impure. How do these distorted conceptions arise? Usually they arise in the context of the eight worldly concerns. Most of us want pleasure and well-being. We think that in order to be happy we need lots of material things, such as beautiful clothes and ornaments, an attractive physical form, various enjoyable experiences, and many wonderful friends—including a special man or woman in our life, and so on. We think that wealth and worldly goods enable us to achieve this. When we do not get satisfaction from those things, we want praise. We want our friends to tell us how wonderful, beautiful, and intelligent we are. When this no longer satisfies, we want more far-reaching admiration: we want fame. So there are four attractive worldly concerns: pleasure, wealth, praise, and fame. Ordinary people think that these are the true causes of happiness, so they spend their whole lives trying to gain these desirable things and fight off their opposites, the four repulsive worldly concerns: pain, poverty, blame, and disrepute. Acquiring and avoiding these in turn are the eight worldly goals. The crucial point is that we grasp the objects of these worldly concerns to be truly existent. Material goods, loving friends, pleasant experiences, and their opposites all appear to be real from their own side. Then a mind conceiving them to be truly real arises, whereby we grasp them to exist from their own side, just as they appear. Based on that conceiving or grasping, we generate the four distorted conceptions—holding impure things as pure and so forth. These conceptual thoughts incorrectly label their objects. The root from which these inappropriate thoughts arise is the elaboration holding things as truly existent. Candrakīrti's *Clear Words* says:

> Worldly elaboration without exception is stopped by emptiness—that is, by seeing the emptiness of all things. How? If things are seen as

real, there will be the elaboration described earlier. But [for example] not seeing the daughter of a barren woman as real, a lustful person will not give rise to elaboration with her as an object. If elaboration does not occur, then inappropriate thoughts regarding that object will not arise. If inappropriate thoughts do not occur, then the group of mental afflictions rooted in the view of the perishable collection, having grasped at "I" and "mine," will not arise. If the mental afflictions rooted in the view of the perishable collection do not arise, then karma will not be created. If karma is not created, then there will be no experience of samsara known as "birth, aging, and death."

This passage explains that by perceiving the absence of inherent existence,[174] we become free of the elaboration of true existence that gives rise to inappropriate thoughts holding the object to be blissful, pure, permanent, and a self. This passage and the next one from the same text clearly show how realizing emptiness reverses the process of samsara:

> How is this done? In dependence on emptiness, which has the characteristic of pacifying elaboration without exception, one is freed from elaboration. By being freed from elaboration, inappropriate thoughts are reversed. By having reversed inappropriate thoughts, mental afflictions are reversed. By having reversed karma and mental afflictions, rebirth is reversed. Therefore because only emptiness has the characteristic of reversing all elaboration, it is called *nirvana*.

Śūnyatā is the absence of inherent existence. That is its nature, its characteristic, and it has always been this way. It is the ultimate nature of all things. So it is called *natural nirvana*. Anyone who develops and utilizes a realization of this emptiness—natural nirvana—will permanently turn away all elaborations and be freed from samsara. So śūnyatā is called "passed beyond sorrow" or *nirvana* here. This expresses the reason for striving to realize emptiness: because this realization cuts the root of samsara. It is the very core of the path because without it you cannot attain liberation. No matter how much you meditate on other topics—such as generating renunciation, compassion, patience, or realizing impermanence—none of them can directly sever the root of samsara. They provide the power that helps you to realize emptiness, but only the realization of emptiness itself can cut the root of samsara. Emptiness is like the blade of an axe and the other practices are like the axe handle or the person wielding the axe. The other practices and realizations are necessary, but on their own they cannot break the bonds that bind us in samsara. You must gain a firm understanding that a realization of śūnyatā is necessary for that.

Nevertheless, the lower schools say it is not necessary to realize emptiness to attain liberation from samsara and enter nirvana. They contend that liberation is attained by gaining a correct understanding of the four noble truths. In their view the wisdom understanding śūnyatā is both unnecessary and nihilistic. They say that those who try to understand śūnyatā just end up arguing. Śāntideva paraphrases their contention:

> One will be liberated through seeing the truths,
> So what is the point of seeing emptiness?[175]

Śāntideva replies that without understanding emptiness there is no way for anyone—whether a śrāvaka, pratyekabuddha, or bodhisattva—to attain liberation:

> It is because, as taught in the scriptures,
> Without this path there will be no enlightenment.[176]

"This path" refers to perfect wisdom—the realization of śūnyatā. Without this wisdom we cannot attain any of the three kinds of enlightenment. The goals of the śrāvaka and pratyekabuddha practitioners are sometimes called "enlightenment," though they are not identical to the perfect enlightenment of the Mahayana path. The scripture that Śāntideva is referring to in this verse is the *Perfection of Wisdom Sutra*:

> Śāriputra, one who wants to train in the śrāvaka path must also train in the perfection of wisdom; one who wants to train in the pratyeka-buddha path must also train in the perfection of wisdom; one who wants to train in the bodhisattva path must also train in the perfection of wisdom.[177]

This passage shows that practitioners of all three vehicles must realize emptiness in order to achieve their respective goals. The realization of śūnyatā is the root of the path to liberation and enlightenment. Its opposite—the egotistic view holding both the self and belonging to the self to be inherently existent—is the root of samsara.

HOW THE PATHS DIFFER IN TERMS OF MOTIVATION, DURATION, AND REASONING

As we have seen, the treatises of Nāgārjuna, Āryadeva, and Candrakīrti clearly state that even śrāvakas and pratyekabuddhas must have the wisdom comprehending the absence of inherent existence of all phenomena because without it they would not be able to attain liberation. Therefore they realize that things are empty of inherent existence. According to the Prāsaṅgika system, only the realization of śūnyatā—the emptiness of inherent existence—can eliminate the obstructions to liberation. Also, the Prāsaṅgikas consider the grasping at a self of phenomena to be a mental affliction and therefore an obstruction to liberation, not an obstruction to omniscience. Other schools do not accept either of these points; even the Svātantrika-Mādhyamikas give a different account of the two kinds of obstructions and how to eliminate them. So how can the Prāsaṅgikas posit a difference between the Mahayana and the Hinayana paths? In their view there are several differences between the Hinayana and Mahayana paths, which include the motivation that directs them, the obstructions they remove, the lines of reasoning on which they are based, the time spent practicing them, and the assisting methods that accompany them. In order to attain omniscience for the sake of all beings, bodhisattvas meditate on śūnyatā for a very long time using extensive reasoning and are adorned with vast collections of merit and wholesome activities.

Śrāvakas and pratyekabuddhas strive to attain liberation for themselves; that is their motivation. So they meditate on selflessness—śūnyatā—just until their mental afflictions are completely exhausted. By removing the mental afflictions—the obstructions to liberation—they attain arhatship. Once they have exhausted their mental afflictions they are satisfied; for them, this is enough. They have no desire to continue meditating on śūnyatā in order to remove the subtler obstacles—the obstructions to omniscience. In contrast, Mahayana practitioners mainly strive to remove the obstructions to omniscience in order to free all sentient beings from suffering; that is their motivation. So they meditate for eons on śūnyatā, based on many different reasons and from many points of view, in order to accomplish complete buddhahood.

A realization is much more powerful when developed through using many reasons—even when it concerns the same object. The more reasons you have, the more powerful your understanding will be. We can see how this happens even in our ordinary experience. For example, if we feel angry with someone, the more reasons we find to be angry, the stronger it gets. This is how our reasoning feeds our emotional responses. Buddhist texts explain that there are nine levels of anger that arise on the basis of certain reasons. We may start off being a little angry with someone. But we can become really angry if we think, "This person has harmed me in the past, is doing so now, and will do so again in the future," and "This person harmed my friends in the past, is doing so now, and will do so again in the future," and "This person benefited my enemy in the past, is doing so now, and will do so again in the future." Even if the reasons are wrong, the more there are, the progressively stronger our anger becomes. The same principle applies to positive things such as understanding impermanence and emptiness. There is a difference between understanding something on the basis of just a couple of reasons and understanding it on the basis of a vast quantity of reasons that encompass many different features. Therefore Mahayana practitioners meditate on the emptiness of inherent existence using extensive reasons, such as those presented by Nāgārjuna in the *Fundamental Treatise*. Thus a bodhisattva's wisdom understanding emptiness is far more powerful than that of a śrāvaka or pratyekabuddha, even though the object they realize is the same: śūnyatā.[178] Bodhisattvas establish śūnyatā from many points of view, such as: the doer, doing, and the object of doing; the burner, burning, and the object burned; the past, the present, and the future; the cutter, cutting, and the object cut; the giver, giving, and the one given to. Using such extensive reasoning gives rise to a more powerful antidote.

Removing obstructions from the mindstream is similar to washing dirty clothes. Soiled laundry has both superficial dirt and subtler stains. Dust and mud on the surface of the clothing is washed away as soon as we put the clothes into hot soapy water. However, even when we have completely removed the rough layer of surface dirt from the clothes, the subtler layers of grime remain. If the clothing has not been washed for many years, then it will be very heavy with thick, greasy filth. Perhaps you have never seen this in the West, but in Tibet I saw this often: the dirt, in some cases, was thicker than the cloth itself! After soaking the clothes in hot soapy water, we need to pound them, scrub them, and so on. Gradually, layer by layer, the dirt comes off. The gross layers of dirt are easiest to remove so they come off first; much more effort is needed to clean the subtlest layers, so they take longer and come off last. Even when the clothes are almost completely clean, there may still be some very subtle stains deep down in the cloth, which are very difficult to remove. Throughout this entire process of washing, the main cleaning agent is water. We begin by soaking the clothes in water; then, in our second and third wash, we use water with added detergent, as well as a scrubbing brush and so on. Gradually, as we wash the clothes again and again, they get cleaner. Even if you have a washing machine, you set it on a longer program and put in more detergent to clean particularly dirty clothes.

The same thing applies to the mind. Meditating on śūnyatā is the remedy that eliminates both types of obscurations: the obstructions to liberation and the obstructions to omniscience. A realization of emptiness is the antidote employed in common on the paths of seeing and meditation. Emptiness is the primary object of meditation on both those paths, and the practice of meditation on emptiness is the same on both those paths. A direct realization of śūnyatā is first attained at the time of entering the path of seeing. There is no clearer realization of śūnyatā than this. Simply by attaining a direct realization of emptiness, practitioners get rid of the obstructions to be abandoned by the path of seeing; to accomplish this, they do not need to meditate on śūnyatā for a long time. However, this first moment of the path of seeing cannot get rid of the obstructions to be abandoned by the path of meditation. These obscurations are subtler and more difficult to remove, so practitioners have to repeat that meditation again and again, over a very long period of time. In this way they gradually move through the ten stages of the path of meditation. Their object of meditation remains the same: śūnyatā. The way that they see śūnyatā remains the same: they see it directly. Even though the realization of śūnyatā is the same on both the path of seeing and the path of meditation, there is a difference in the power of that realization owing to the length of time the practitioner spends meditating. Because of that difference in power, the path of seeing and the path of meditation purify different obstructions. According to the Prāsaṅgika system, the path of seeing purifies contrived self-grasping; the impure grounds of the path of meditation purify innate self-grasping and its seeds, which are the obstructions to liberation; and the pure grounds of the path of meditation purify the imprints of innate self-grasping, which are the obstructions to omniscience. All these obstructions are eliminated by the same tool: a direct realization of emptiness.

How the paths differ in terms of method for removing the obstructions

To summarize, śrāvakas, pratyekabuddhas, and bodhisattvas all realize the same object: emptiness. However, the bodhisattvas' way of understanding emptiness is much more powerful because it is based on many more reasons. Furthermore, because śrāvakas and pratyekabuddhas meditate on śūnyatā for a relatively short period of time, the power of their wisdom is very different from ārya bodhisattvas' wisdom. Śrāvakas and pratyekabuddhas meditate on emptiness just until they eliminate the obstructions to liberation. They are satisfied with merely removing their own mental afflictions and attaining liberation from samsara. They do not continue to meditate on śūnyatā after their mental afflictions have been completely removed, therefore they do not eliminate the far subtler obscurations—the obstructions to omniscience. These obstructions are removed on the pure grounds of the bodhisattva path of meditation. A practitioner must spend many more lifetimes engaging in meditation on emptiness to remove these imprints of the mental afflictions.

However, eliminating the obstructions to omniscience is not simply a matter of meditating on śūnyatā utilizing more reasons and for a longer period of time. Even this is not enough. There is a further difference between Hinayana and Mahayana practitioners. Some people say that the śrāvakas and pratyeka-buddhas do not have the same realization of emptiness as the bodhisattvas, but that is not correct. Their realization is the same. When meditating on śūnyatā, the śrāvakas and pratyekabuddhas see everything as empty of inherent existence. There is nothing missing in what they perceive. They understand śūnyatā completely. They fully comprehend the emptiness of inherent existence. Nevertheless, their meditation is not a full, complete, or perfect meditation on śūnyatā.

What does this mean? Śrāvakas and pratyekabuddhas are satisfied with meditating on śūnyatā to remove their own mental afflictions. Once that is attained, they simply abide in peace. In contrast, bodhisattvas meditate on emptiness motivated by the desire to attain enlightenment for the purpose of benefiting other sentient beings, whom they regard affectionately as their own beloved mothers. They are not satisfied with just liberating themselves from samsara. Their goal is to free all sentient beings from suffering, so bodhisattvas strive to attain perfect buddhahood for others' benefit. In order to utilize the realization of emptiness fully, which is the practice of *wisdom*, they engage in the powerful *method* practices of the Mahayana path. Bodhisattvas combine extensive meditation on śūnyatā with the practices of generosity, ethical conduct, patience, love, and compassion. The merit they generate in this way assists their wisdom to become powerful enough to remove the obstructions to omniscience completely. Removing the subtle obstructions depends on the combined practice of method and wisdom. It takes a very long time to build up the power and force of the wisdom and the method practices. According to the sutra system, even though a bodhisattva's understanding of śūnyatā may occur quite early on the path, he or she must strive for three countless great eons to gather enough merit and wisdom to attain buddhahood. Śrāvakas and pratyekabuddhas do not meditate with bodhicitta motivation. Thus the duration and depth of their practice is very different.

It is important to bear in mind that although meditation on love, compassion, patience, and conventional bodhicitta are powerful antidotes, they are not the primary tool that cuts the root of samsara. These methods do not directly contradict ignorance. The antidote that eliminates both kinds of obstructions is the wisdom realizing śūnyatā. Dharmakīrti says:

> Love and so on do not contradict ignorance,
> So cannot cut out the primary fault.[179]

Candrakīrti's *Commentary on the "Introduction to the 'Middle Way'"* says:

> Although even śrāvakas and pratyekabuddhas see the mere condition-
> ality of dependent arising, they still do not have the full and complete
> meditation on the selflessness of phenomena; however, they do have a
> method for abandoning the mental afflictions belonging to the three
> realms.

Śrāvakas and pratyekabuddhas meditate on śūnyatā just enough to eliminate
all the mental afflictions belonging to the desire, form, and formless realms.
But they cannot eliminate the obstructions to omniscience—the imprints of
the mental afflictions—because they do not engage in a complete meditation
on the selflessness of phenomena. When meditating on emptiness, śrāvakas
and pratyekabuddhas are satisfied by limited logical reasons and a restricted
method, whereas bodhisattvas use limitless logical reasons and a most extensive method. Bodhisattvas combine their detailed meditation on śūnyatā with
innumerable compassionate deeds for the benefit of others. Their vast merit
empowers their wisdom, so they develop the most powerful realization. As a
result, bodhisattvas completely eliminate the obstructions to omniscience in
addition to removing all the mental afflictions.

As we noted before, the Svātantrika-Mādhyamikas define the two kinds
of obstructions and the way to eliminate them quite differently from the
Prāsaṅgikas. The Prāsaṅgika master, Candrakīrti, says that holding phenomena to be truly existent is a mental affliction—an obstruction to liberation. In
contrast, Svātantrika masters—such as Bhāvaviveka, Kamalaśīla, and Śāntarakṣita—assert that holding phenomena to be truly or ultimately existent is
an obstruction to omniscience. In some contexts this difference is explained
using the terms *afflictive ignorance* and *nonafflictive ignorance*. Bhāvaviveka
and other Svātantrikas say that to gain freedom from samsara we must eliminate afflictive ignorance, but it is not necessary to eliminate nonafflictive
ignorance. In their view grasping things to be truly existent is not a mental
affliction; it is an obstruction to omniscience, and thus it is nonafflictive ignorance. In Candrakīrti's view, holding things to be truly or inherently existent
is included within afflictive ignorance. Therefore Prāsaṅgikas say that even
śrāvakas and pratyekabuddhas must remove it by meditating on the selflessness of phenomena in order to attain liberation from samsara. All these great
beings—śrāvakas, pratyekabuddhas, and buddhas—are victorious; they have
conquered the mental afflictions and are liberated from samsara. However, śrāvakas and pratyekabuddhas do not have a full and complete meditation on the
selflessness of phenomena, as explained here. Therefore they do not have the

power of fully enlightened buddhas—who are superior to Hinayana arhats in terms of knowledge and skill in teaching.

Now the question arises, "If the Prāsaṅgikas say that grasping phenomena to be truly existent is a mental affliction and an obstruction to liberation, what are the obstructions to omniscience in their system?" From time without beginning, our mindstreams have been contaminated by an active tendency to grasp things as real, in the sense of holding them to have an inherent nature. Whenever this grasping arises, it deposits seeds within the mindstream, which also leave imprints. Through the power of these imprints, things appear to exist inherently, even though they do not exist in that way. Even a valid conventional awareness in the mindstream of a sentient being perceives its object to exist inherently. According to the Prāsaṅgika system, this appearance of things as inherently existent is called a *dualistic appearance*, and it is completely mistaken. (We should note here that Yogācāras define *dualistic appearance* differently; they say a dualistic appearance is the appearance of the subject and object as different entities.) According to the Prāsaṅgikas, the imprints themselves, as well as any appearance of inherent existence that they produce in the mind, are obstructions to omniscience. Even once we have eliminated grasping things to be truly existent, the imprints of those seeds remain in the mindstream right up until we attain buddhahood. They obstruct our knowing phenomena fully and thus limit our ability to help others gain liberation from suffering.

Obstructions to knowing have two aspects: a manifest obstruction to knowing, which is the appearance of inherent existence, and a nonmanifest obstruction to knowing, which is the subtle imprint that causes it. Both of these exist. One is the cause: the imprint. The other is the result: the mistaken appearance. When an imprint ripens into an appearance of inherent existence, that appearance exists. However, inherent existence, which is what appears, does not exist. The appearance is an obstruction to omniscience, but inherent existence itself is not, because an inherently existent nature does not exist at all. For example, an inherently existent tree does not exist, so that cannot be an obstruction to knowing. But the appearance of a tree as inherently existent does exist, and that is an obstruction to knowing; it is a mistaken dualistic appearance that manifests through the power of one of the imprints of ignorance. The mistaken appearance is a manifest obstruction to omniscience; the imprint is a nonmanifest obstruction to omniscience. Both aspects of the obstructions to omniscience function even after the mental afflictions and their seeds have been destroyed. The obstructions to omniscience are removed only upon attaining full enlightenment.

According to Jetsun Chokyi Gyaltsen, there is no obstruction to knowledge in a bodhisattva's mindstream at the last moment of the tenth bodhisattva ground, just before the attainment of buddhahood. At that final moment, the direct antidote to all obstructions to knowledge is present in a bodhisattva's mind. He or she no longer has any obstructions to omniscience; yet a dualistic appearance of true existence still arises in the mind. Although there is a mistaken dualistic appearance, it is not an obstruction to knowledge. This dualistic appearance is not the ripening of an imprint, because there are no imprints left in the mindstream. Such highly realized bodhisattvas have dualistic appearances because they have many virtuous minds in addition to a direct realization of śūnyatā. True existence appears to these bodhisattvas when they engage in conventional bodhicitta, compassion, and so on. But at the last moment of the path, this dualistic appearance is no longer the ripening of an imprint that is an obstruction to knowledge. It is a mistaken dualistic appearance, but it is not an aspect of an obstruction to omniscience that is a mistaken dualistic appearance.

Is either aspect of an obstruction to omniscience a consciousness? No. An obstruction to knowledge is not a consciousness; and a consciousness is not an obstruction to knowledge. Obstructions to omniscience are the mistaken dualistic appearances that manifest to a consciousness, as well as the imprints within a stream of consciousness that give rise to those mistaken dualistic appearances. Prāsaṅgikas do not accept that the consciousness to which a mistaken dualistic appearance appears is an obstruction to knowledge. The only consciousnesses that are obstructions of any kind are the mental afflictions. The mental afflictions are obstructions to liberation; they are not obstructions to omniscience. After the mental afflictions have been completely removed, subtle appearances of inherent nature and the imprints that cause them remain. Neither of these are consciousnesses; they are the manifest and nonmanifest aspects of obstructions to omniscience, respectively. Candrakīrti's *Commentary on the "Introduction to the 'Middle Way'"* says:

> In the case of śrāvakas, pratyekabuddhas, and bodhisattvas who have eliminated afflictive ignorance, conditioned things—which exist only in the manner of reflections and so on—are seen as fabricated natures, not as true, because they have no grasping at manifest things as true. In the case of ordinary beings, these are deceptive. In the case of others, they are mere conventionalities, simply dependently arising, like illusions. Moreover, since they appear solely through the power of ignorance that has the characteristics of an obstruction to omniscience, they appear to ārya beings in the context of apprehending an object with such an appearance, but not in the context of apprehending an object without such an appearance.

In this passage, Candrakīrti delineates three types of sentient beings, grouped in accordance with the obstructions eliminated within their mindstreams. First, there are those who have eliminated afflictive ignorance, which includes śrāvaka arhats, pratyekabuddha arhats, and bodhisattvas on the eighth, ninth, and tenth levels—the three pure grounds. Upon attaining the eighth ground, a bodhisattva gains a special kind of confidence and ease regarding his or her direct realization of śūnyatā. Such practitioners are called "bodhisattvas who have gained patience regarding nonarising phenomena."[180] This appellation indicates that they have completely eliminated afflictive ignorance so that it will never arise again within them, owing to which they gain a special forbearance or patience regarding the emptiness of inherent existence. These bodhisattvas have eliminated all their mental afflictions and are equal to Hinayana arhats in this regard. Pure-ground bodhisattvas and arhats have no grasping at true existence, so they understand all conditioned things to be merely fabricated and not truly existent, like reflections. However, because they still have nonafflictive ignorance—which is not actual ignorance, but the imprints of ignorance—present within their mindstreams, things appear to be truly existent to them; but no part of their minds holds things to be truly existent.

Second, there are ordinary beings who always see conditioned things as truly existent and frequently hold them to be so. For ordinary beings, who have no awareness that conditioned things do not exist as they appear, such things are deceptive—with regard to both how they appear and how they are held.

Third, there are the other ārya beings apart from the three kinds mentioned above, who know that conditioned things are not truly existent because they have seen emptiness directly in meditative equipoise. During that time there is no appearance of duality; only emptiness, the total lack of inherent existence, appears. But when these ārya beings arise from this meditation and engage in postmeditation activities, then everything appears inherently existent again; also some part of their minds may hold them to be truly existent because the innate grasping at true existence is still present within their mindstreams. However, these ārya beings understand that things dependently arise and are merely conventionally existent, like illusions. When conditioned things appear, they naturally appear to be truly existent. This is due to the influence of the imprints of ignorance—the obstructions to omniscience—within the mindstream. Through the power of these imprints, everything that appears during the postmeditation period, including conventional bodhicitta, appears in a dualistic manner as inherently existent.

This mistaken appearance of inherent existence occurs right up to the attainment of buddhahood. Even in the case of arhats and bodhisattvas on the pure grounds, dualistic appearances arise during the postmeditation periods.

However, these pure beings do not hold them to be true, because they have totally eliminated innate grasping and purified all the mental afflictions. Nevertheless these holy beings still have a great many subtle imprints remaining in their mindstreams owing to having been accustomed to ignorance for such a long time; however, unlike the lower āryas, they do not create any new imprints. Bodhisattvas on the pure grounds meditate on śūnyatā for a very long time to purify these subtle imprints. When they are not in meditative equipoise, they collect great oceans of merit to strengthen their ability to remove the obstructions to omniscience. Once they completely eliminate all latent predispositions that give rise to dualistic appearances, they become buddhas.

DEVELOPING BODHICITTA TO EMPOWER WISDOM

As we have seen, Nāgārjuna and his followers, Āryadeva, Buddhapālita, and Candrakīrti, taught that there is no difference between the Mahayana and Hinayana definitive view of śūnyatā. However, although their understanding of reality is equally subtle, they utilize this realization differently and produce different results. There are two marvelous outcomes drawn from this knowledge. The first is an understanding that there is no way to attain liberation from samsara, much less attain enlightenment, without realizing that all phenomena are empty of inherent existence; so practitioners strive to engage in many different methods to find the pure view of śūnyatā. The second is an understanding that the difference between the results of the two vehicles is a function of one's motivation and actions; so practitioners strive to develop the precious mind of bodhicitta and engage in the great waves of bodhisattvas' deeds that stem from it. There is no limit to what bodhisattvas will do in order to benefit mother sentient beings. Through understanding that the difference between the two vehicles is not the view but the method, practitioners will hold the bodhisattva conduct to be the most profound and supreme instruction. Some people forget the method side; they consider the view of emptiness to be supreme and think that when they develop that supreme realization they are done. However, it is only by joining the view of śūnyatā to the bodhisattvas' motivation and deeds that we can eliminate the obstructions to omniscience and attain enlightenment. Do not remain content with understanding śūnyatā! That is not enough. We must develop the precious mind of bodhicitta based on universal compassion and love. After that we should take the bodhisattva vows to empower our practice. These vows outline how to behave for the benefit of all mother sentient beings. Once we take them, we should practice these modes of behavior.

A way to understand these two important conclusions is through the analogy of parents. In ancient India, the caste or race of a child was determined by the father's identity. A woman may have had children with many different men; but each of her children would be classified depending on the father. Without a woman, a man cannot have children at all. Similarly, wisdom is universal; like a mother, she can give birth to children of many types. The wisdom understanding śūnyatā is necessary to attain the goals of both the Hinayana and Mahayana paths, so it is like the mother. The method practice provides the differentiating characteristics of the goal, so it is like the father. Therefore "father" is the name given to the method side, and "mother" is the name for the wisdom side.

Tsongkhapa has now completed his explanation of the most important topics in the Prāsaṅgika system. In conclusion he offers eight stanzas of praise to Śākyamuni Buddha, Nāgārjuna, Buddhapālita, Candrakīrti, and the Madhyamaka tradition. He begins by recounting Buddha's teaching of the *Perfection of Wisdom Sutra* on Vulture Peak, a holy mountain in India.

> When he ascended that marvelous mountain,
> The great mountain known as Vulture Peak,
> The vast earth trembled in six ways, and magically
> Hundreds of buddha fields appeared, all filled with light.
>
> The Wise One spoke with his glorious voice
> The supremely excellent *Perfection of Wisdom*,
> The great mother from whom every ārya is born,
> The life force of the paths of sutra and tantra.

Vulture Peak is unusual in that on it there are many big rocks standing upright. I have been there and can tell you that these rocks look like vultures sitting in a cemetery waiting for a corpse to arrive. When Buddha went to the top of that famous mountain the earth trembled and shook. (Earthquakes were not always regarded as bad in ancient times; they were often taken to be good omens.) Light rays from Buddha's heart radiated out in all directions, reaching the furthest space. Upon returning they dissolved back into him and pure lands appeared all around. These miraculous signs indicated that Buddha was about to do something very special, which drew other buddhas, bodhisattvas, and deities to that place. Gathering to receive teachings, some came to rest on the ground and others remained in the sky above.

Buddha then spoke with his resonant voice the teaching of the *Perfection of Wisdom*, which is the life of the paths of both sutra and tantra. The realization of śūnyatā, the perfection of wisdom, is the essence of the śrāvaka, pratyekabuddha, and bodhisattva paths. All practices, including all tantric practices, are based on it. Because it is vital to all the goals, the perfection of wisdom is the great mother who gives birth to all āryas. In other words, without the wisdom realizing śūnyatā there is no ārya being. The original sources for this analogy only mention male children because the ancient mythical kings who could benefit all in their realms were only ever men. It is different today and we include all noble children, male and female, as objects of praise.

"Great mother" is the name given to the perfection of wisdom itself, as well as to its verbal expression, the *Perfection of Wisdom Sutra*. In this stanza "great mother" refers to the incomparable teaching, the *Perfection of Wisdom Sutra*, which was taught on this mountain. In other sutras, such as the *Descent into Laṅka Sutra*, Buddha prophesied that a man called Nāgārjuna would appear to explain this highest of teachings.

> Nāgārjuna, the hero prophesied in scripture,
> Explained precisely this unsurpassable text
> In an incomparable commentary as famous as the sun,
> Known as the glorious *Fundamental Treatise*.

> Like Buddha's offspring, Buddhapālita wrote a commentary
> Explaining that treatise extremely well; that explanation
> Candrakīrti understood exactly, and in his great commentary
> Clarified in detail both its words and its meaning.

Candrakīrti recognized Buddhapālita's work to be an excellent explanation of emptiness. In *Clear Words* Candrakīrti shows in great detail not only that Buddhapālita's explanation of emptiness is correct, but he also refutes the views of those who consider it to be wrong. Bhāvaviveka did not agree with Buddhapālita's view; because he criticized it in many ways, he is not mentioned in Tsongkhapa's stanzas of praise.

If each of these explanations is so marvelous, why do they all need further explanation? Why does Nāgārjuna have to explain Buddha's teaching, and Buddhapālita explain Nāgārjuna's treatise, and then Candrakīrti explain Buddhapālita's commentary? Each teaching is given in different circumstances for specific purposes. They are difficult to understand on their own. Even in Tsongkhapa's time, if someone were to read the texts of Nāgārjuna or Buddhapālita without a commentary they would get completely confused. Therefore Tsongkhapa brings together the main points in these great works and explains them clearly in plain language. His purpose is to make it easier to understand their pure system, which shows that things have no inherent existence and yet exist in an illusion-like way. The same difficulty occurs today. Tsongkhapa's commentary is no longer easy to understand, so students have requested my commentary.

> I give a brief explanation to help you understand
> Their stainless system that correctly presents how
> Illusion-like things lack inherent existence yet arise
> Dependently as cause and effect in samsara and nirvana.

> My friends, you who study the profound Madhyamaka texts,
> Although within your understanding it is hard to establish
> Dependently arising cause and effect with a lack of inherent nature,
> You should think, "This is the Madhyamaka system."

> It is more helpful to rely on this way of speaking.
> Otherwise, if you show the faults implied by others
> Yet cannot refute them when they are applied to you,
> You may retort, "I have no system"; so you must learn more.

Finally, Tsongkhapa offers his dedication. This dedication shows that Tsongkhapa wrote the *Lamrim Chenmo* so that Buddha's precious teachings may remain. He did not write it to achieve mere fame or for any other worldly purpose.

> Therefore, by thoroughly explaining here
> The way to search for the correct view
> According to the texts of the noble Nāgārjuna and his followers,
> May the Conqueror's teaching remain for a long time.

⁂ 22 ⁂
Insight Requires Analysis

(b') Classifications of insight
(c') How to cultivate insight in meditation
    (1') Refuting other systems
        (a") The first refutation
        (b") The second refutation
        (c") The third refutation
        (d") The fourth refutation

(b') CLASSIFICATIONS OF INSIGHT

KAMALAŚĪLA's middle *Stages of Meditation* teaches that we need to accumulate three preparatory causes for the development of insight. The first is to rely on a spiritual guide or guru. However, just relying on a great holy being will not cause us to develop insight; we need further causes. The second is to hear many teachings and study them carefully. The third cause is to deeply analyze what we have studied in a suitable way. In dependence on these three causes, we will find the correct understanding of the two kinds of selflessness. Then based on this understanding we can engage in insight meditation and gradually gain a high level of realization.

Although there are hundreds of meditation practices presented in the sutras—named on the basis of their functions, the results of their practice, and so on—they are all included within two general kinds of meditation practice: analytical and stabilizing. All analytical meditation is included within the category of vipaśyanā, or insight meditation, because any meditation that investigates its object is a type of insight. This applies whether you have accomplished vipaśyanā or are on the way to accomplishing it through practice. All stabilizing meditation is included within śamatha, or calm abiding meditation, because any meditation that eschews analysis and places attention on one object so as to develop mental stability is a type of śamatha. This applies whether you have accomplished śamatha or just are on the way to accomplishing it through practice. The practices of śamatha and vipaśyanā are common to the śrāvaka, pratyekabuddha, and bodhisattva paths. You should understand that in general all meditation practices are included within these two categories—śamatha and vipaśyanā; there is no meditation practice other than these two.

We discussed the practice of śamatha in some detail in volume 4 of this series. To review briefly, when we engage in śamatha meditation practice, we refrain from investigating the aspects and qualities of the object; rather we synthesize the various aspects into one and focus on that object single-pointedly. When our mind wanders off, we bring it back to the object and place it there again and again until it remains spontaneously. When we have completed our training in śamatha, we are able to focus on our object of meditation for as long as we wish. This is now actual śamatha meditation rather than the mere practice of it. Through having such a concentrated mind we experience the subtle pleasures of special pliancy and bliss. After having achieved śamatha, we are ready to analytically search for the nature of reality. For this purpose we practice insight meditation, vipaśyanā.

There are two aspects of reality that we need to understand: conventional and ultimate. We develop an understanding of each of these by analyzing the many different qualities and subtle aspects of the object of our scrutiny. This is how we eventually realize the characteristics of the four noble truths, the characteristics of the ultimate truth, the characteristics of the illusion-like nature, and so on. Without using sharp logical analysis we cannot understand any of these objects nor arrive at seeing them directly. So how do we embark on this method? When we practice vipaśyanā meditation, we do not try to hold everything together as one object; rather we spread the object apart and examine the various details individually. Using analytical wisdom, we identify various aspects of the object, analyzing it into parts and wholes, causes and effects, time, nature, and so on. We distinguish, separate, and identify each aspect so as to understand its nature and function. We can analyze an object in terms of many different categories, such as the five aggregates, the eighteen elements, and the twelve links of dependent arising; each of these can be subjected to further analysis.

When you investigate the aggregates, for example, you examine how they epitomize the truth of suffering. The truth of suffering has four attributes: impermanent, suffering, empty, and selfless. So when you meditate on the aggregates as exemplifying the truth of suffering, you will see that they are impermanent, changing every moment. This is one aspect of the truth of suffering. You need to analyze in this way when you meditate on the truth of suffering. Otherwise if you take any of your own aggregates as your object of meditation and simply think, without analyzing, "This is the truth of suffering, this is the truth of suffering, this is the truth of suffering," you will never gain any realization—no matter how deeply you stay focused on that thought. You need to examine reality and dig for the truth, distinguishing, separating, and analyzing. First you make rough distinctions, and then you analyze in more detail. This applies to both the conventional and ultimate objects of meditation. Even when meditating on śūnyatā, first you analyze in a rough way, and then you analyze in a subtler way, digging very deeply for the truth. This kind of meditation is called analytical meditation.

How many types of insight meditation are there? Tsongkhapa says that he will not explain any advanced insight meditations here, such as those suitable for high-level bodhisattvas, or indeed the special insight connected with tantric practice. Instead his concern here is to show those who do not have insight how to begin to develop it. To give a complete presentation of the subject, Tsongkhapa explains insight meditation in three ways: as having four aspects, three aspects, and six aspects. His presentation relies on the *Sutra Unraveling the Intended Meaning* and Asaṅga's *Levels of Yogic Deeds* (*Yoga-caryā-bhūmi*). The latter text is very extensive and contains several chapters, two of which are often referred to as separate texts: *Śrāvaka Levels* and *Bodhisattva Levels*. According to the *Sutra Unraveling the Intended Meaning*, we use the same objects in śamatha meditation as we do in vipaśyanā meditation. The difference concerns the way that we meditate on the object. In śamatha meditation we focus on one object single-pointedly. We do not allow the mind to investigate the various aspects and qualities of the object; rather, having mentally gathered all its aspects together and synthesized them as a single thing, we focus on that one thing as the main object of meditation. In vipaśyanā meditation we examine the same object, but we do not focus on it as one thing. Instead we investigate the object by analyzing it into various aspects and qualities, which we then analyze in further detail.

THE DIVISION INTO FOUR ASPECTS

The *Sutra Unraveling the Intended Meaning* teaches a fourfold division of insight meditation: differentiating, fully differentiating, thoroughly examining, and thoroughly analyzing. Differentiating is to make distinctions regarding conventional things. Fully differentiating is to make distinctions regarding the ultimate. So the first two divisions are made in terms of what object is being investigated: conventional truth or ultimate truth. The second two divisions of insight meditation are made in terms of the manner in which the object is being investigated: a rough examination or a subtle analysis. Vasubandhu says:

> Examining and analyzing are coarse and subtle.[181]

When we begin insight meditation our manner of analysis is relatively crude; later it becomes more penetrating and refined. Both items in the first division—the two truths—are roughly examined to begin with and then analyzed in more detail.

Asaṅga's *Śrāvaka Levels* further explains this fourfold division of insight:

> What are the four aspects of insight? Regarding this, monks, it is thus. In dependence on the inwardly directed mind of śamatha, you differentiate phenomena, fully differentiate, thoroughly examine, and thoroughly analyze. How do you differentiate? Regarding [meditation] objects that purify the delusions that most influence behavior, objects of mastery, and objects that purify manifest delusions, you differentiate in terms of conventional reality; then you fully differentiate in terms of ultimate reality. When a mind of analytical wisdom combined with conceptual thought examines in terms of apprehending general signs, this is thoroughly examining; when examining precisely, this is thoroughly analyzing.

This passage states that our search for the truth is founded on meditative concentration. If the mind is affected by excitement, sinking, and so on, it is impossible to develop insight. So first we engage in the mental training that makes the mind stable and calm. We start by selecting an object and bringing it to mind. As ordinary individuals our object of meditation is a mental image, not a direct perception of a thing itself. For example, if we are meditating on the emptiness of this book, we do not open our eyes, look at the book, and examine it directly. We develop an image of the book—which is like a reflection of the object—to use as the object of meditation. Now with that mental image as an object we can engage in either stabilizing or analytical meditation. But before we can actually develop insight, we must have śamatha. Śāntideva says:

> Having understood that the mental afflictions are completely overcome
> By vipaśyanā thoroughly imbued with śamatha...[182]

Only on the basis of śamatha can we develop the supreme wisdom that directly realizes the nature of reality. Therefore once we understand that only this insight can get rid of the mental afflictions, we will feel motivated to develop śamatha.

Buddha taught that objects of meditation can be divided into four types: universal or pervasive objects, objects that purify the delusions that most influence behavior, objects of mastery, and objects that purify manifest mental afflictions.[183] All four types of objects are common to śamatha and vipaśyanā meditation.

Universal objects pertain to the other three categories, in that every mental image taken as an object of meditation is an internal reflection of one of the other three types of object. Universal objects can be further subdivided into four: discursive images, nondiscursive images, the limits of existence, and the achievement of your purpose. Discursive images and nondiscursive images are posited in terms of the observing mind: vipaśyanā or śamatha. When we engage in vipaśyanā meditation we make precise distinctions to obtain a detailed mental picture. This is a discursive image. When we engage in śamatha meditation we do not make distinctions; we condense everything into a single synthesized image. This is a nondiscursive image, which is finally accomplished when we attain śamatha. The third type of universal object, the limits of existence, is posited in terms of the observed object: conventional truth or ultimate truth. The fourth type, the achievement of your purpose, is posited in terms of the mental obstructions that have been removed through your long and dedicated practice. This process is similar to physical exercise: at first the body feels heavy and stiff, but as we exercise more each day it gradually feels lighter and more agile. In the development of śamatha we progress through nine levels of meditative concentration. Initially we try to become free of the obstructions belonging to the first level. When we achieve that, we attain the second level. Then we continue to practice in order to become free of the obstructions belonging to the second level. When we have done that, we attain the third level and so on. It takes great effort, but as we eliminate the obstructions belonging to each level we spontaneously achieve our goal.

The second type of meditation object—objects that purify the delusions that most influence behavior—is divided into five because there are five mental afflictions that most influence peoples' behavior. Different people are influenced by particular delusions to various degrees: attachment is dominant in some people; hatred more dominant in others; ignorance, conceit, or distracted mental wandering may dominate others. You choose an object of meditation that is the antidote to the mental affliction most problematic for you. If attachment—say, intense sexual desire—is your primary affliction, you would meditate on the ugliness and impurity of the body. Although it will not uproot it completely, this meditation will reduce your attachment because you train yourself to view the body as unattractive. In contrast, if you are afflicted by anger or hatred, then you meditate on love as the antidote. You meditate on dependent arising—the relationship between cause and effect—as the antidote to ignorance about causality. Someone who is very conceited and thinks that they know everything should meditate on the various sets of elements of the desire, form, and formless realms. You meditate on the breath as an antidote to mental agitation. Meditation on the flow of the breath is generally very helpful if you have too many thoughts cascading through your mind like a mountain stream. We do not need to search for an object of meditation here because we are always breathing. We can just sit down and watch each breath. We may start by counting them: an out-breath and in-breath together are counted as one, the next out-breath and in-breath are two, and so on. Using this method we can easily recognize when the mind has wandered from the counting and the awareness of the breath. It is not easy to concentrate on the breath even for ten minutes. You have to let go of all distracting thoughts and focus in a gentle manner to maintain the count without mistake. But the awareness of the breath itself, not the counting, is the important thing here; it is the object of meditation.

Meditate with dedication on whichever of these objects is most appropriate for you, in connection with its conventional nature or its ultimate truth and in a manner that is rough or subtle. You can use these five objects in both śamatha and vipaśyanā meditation. For example, if you are using ugliness as your object in śamatha practice, first you should consider all the reasons why your object of desire is ugly. Then bring these together as a unitary object of focus and meditate on that single-pointedly. If ugliness is the basis of a vipaśyanā meditation, you should examine how every aspect of the object of desire is ugly in detail. While these meditations will reduce the mental afflictions, they will not remove any of them from the root.

The third type of meditation object—objects of mastery—are the objects of meditation based on which one gains philosophical and meditative mastery. There are five such objects: the aggregates, the elements, the sources of sense consciousness, dependent arising, and what is suitable and unsuitable. The five aggregates are the physical and mental constituents of the person: form, feeling, discernment, conditioning factors, and consciousness. The elements may be categorized into groups of three, six, or eighteen. The three are: the desire, form, and formless realms. The six are: earth, water, fire, wind, space, and consciousness. The eighteen are: the six internal sources of sense consciousness (the sense powers), the six external sources of sense consciousness (their objects), and the six sense consciousnesses themselves, which arise in dependence on the sense powers and their objects. This group of eighteen elements overlaps with the next object, the sources of sense consciousness: the six sense powers and the objects of the six sense consciousnesses. The fourth object is the twelve links of dependent arising. Finally, what is suitable and unsuitable involves understanding karma and its results in some detail. It is suitable to think that by engaging in virtuous actions you will experience happiness and by engaging in nonvirtuous actions you will experience misery. It is unsuitable to think that by engaging in virtuous actions you will experience misery and by engaging in nonvirtuous actions you will experience happiness. When you take any of these five objects as objects of vipaśyanā meditation practice, you investigate their characteristics, divisions, nature, and so on, in detail. When you succeed in this practice you become a master.

The fourth type of meditation object includes two objects that purify the manifest mental afflictions: one that temporarily subdues them and one that permanently eliminates them. To temporarily subdue the afflictions, we meditate on the coarseness of our current level of existence and compare it to the peacefulness of the next higher level. For example, to subdue the attachment of the desire realm, we compare the grossness of the desire realm to the first level of the form realm. In comparison to the desire realm, the first dhyāna seems like a perfect heaven. The body, mind, and environment of the first dhyāna are peaceful and pure. In that realm you do not have a body of flesh and blood; you have a special mental body endowed with long life. In contrast, the desire realm is impermanent, ugly, dirty, and full of misery. When you compare the two, you will gradually lose all interest in the desire realm. When you have temporarily subdued the nine levels of mental afflictions in connection with the desire realm, you attain the actual achievement of the first dhyāna. If you were to die at this time, you would take rebirth in the first level of the form realm because to be reborn in the desire realm you have to have strong attachment to it. So by pacifying manifest attachment to the desire realm, you temporarily block rebirth there. When you achieve the first dhyāna you do the same type of meditation: you compare the roughness of the first dhyāna with the peacefulness of the second dhyāna. When you have achieved the second dhyāna you have temporarily removed the delusions of the first dhyāna. This is how to pacify the delusions of each level from the desire realm up to the highest formless realm. The *Treasury of Knowledge* says:

> You meditate on the higher and lower levels
> As having the qualities of peacefulness and roughness. (6.49c–d)

This meditation practice is common to Buddhist and non-Buddhist traditions. Any yogi can do this after achieving śamatha. Through this method of comparison, also known as "the peaceful and the gross," we can temporarily subdue the mental afflictions, but we cannot remove them from the root. In order to completely remove them with all their seeds, we need to meditate on the four noble truths, in particular emptiness. In terms of understanding the two truths, we meditate on ultimate truth, śūnyatā, to eliminate all the mental afflictions of the three realms.

According to the above quotation from the *Śrāvaka Levels*, when we are doing vipaśyanā practice we first differentiate these four types of objects of meditation in terms of the conventional—investigating their number, divisions, nature, function, and so on. Then we fully differentiate them in terms of the ultimate, searching for their ultimate nature: emptiness. With regard to the way of investigating, first we thoroughly examine them and then we thoroughly analyze them. Thoroughly examining an object uses a mental image to dissect each characteristic of the object in a general way. Thoroughly analyzing an object dissects the object in a more detailed and subtle way. Although we can thoroughly examine and thoroughly analyze both the conventional and the ultimate, the practice of insight is primarily concerned with the ultimate, and the subtler process of thoroughly analyzing is more appropriate for the ultimate.

Asaṅga's *Compendium of Knowledge* also says that the practice of insight has the four divisions: differentiating, fully differentiating, thoroughly examining, and thoroughly analyzing. Ratnākaraśānti's *Instructions for the Perfection of Wisdom* (*Prajñāpāramitopadeśa*) identifies them in the same way that Asaṅga does in the *Śrāvaka Levels*. So all the explanations of the fourfold division of vipaśyanā are based on the *Sutra Unraveling the Intended Meaning*.

THE DIVISION INTO THREE ASPECTS

The *Sutra Unraveling the Intended Meaning* says:

> "Bhagavan, how many aspects of insight are there?" "Maitreya, there are three aspects: that which arises from signs, that which arises from thorough searching, and that which arises from precise analysis. What is that which arises from signs? It is insight that brings to mind only an image of a conceptualized object of stabilizing meditation. What is that which arises from thorough searching? It is insight that brings to mind those phenomena that have not been properly understood by wisdom, in order to properly understand them. What is that which arises from precise analysis? It is insight that brings to mind those phenomena that have been properly understood by wisdom, in order to experience perfect bliss through being completely liberated."

Tsongkhapa paraphrases Asaṅga's *Śrāvaka Levels* to explain the meaning of this sutra passage. The three types of insight meditation take as their objects the four categories explained above: pervasive objects, objects of mastery, and so on. First there is the wisdom that arises from hearing Dharma teachings and holding them in mind. When beginners consider teachings that they have received, they grab onto words, signs, and symbols because their analytical thinking is not grounded on single-pointed concentration. As a result, they do not thoroughly understand in detail the objects brought to mind through listening, studying, and so on. Practitioners who have not achieved śamatha or entered the first dhyāna need a mental picture of the various signs or characteristics of the object. They cannot examine the object of meditation in a subtle way. They engage in vipaśyanā that arises from signs, which is the wisdom that arises from hearing. This is not a ground of meditation.

A mental state of the desire realm is never a ground of meditation—even if you are meditating. In the desire realm, your mind is distracted and agitated; this is the case right up until you develop śamatha. There are nine stages of training to develop śamatha. The highest, subtlest, and most stable mental state of the desire realm is the ninth of these stages. But even the ninth stage is a mind of the desire realm. After the ninth stage you achieve śamatha; only at this point, after entering the first dhyāna of the form realm, is your mind a ground of meditation. Once you develop the śamatha of single-pointed concentration in the form and formless realms, your mind is always in a subtle meditative state. But no mental state of the desire realm is a ground or stage of meditation.[184]

Gradually as we think, assess, and examine the object of meditation more closely, in order to understand the object's characteristics, nature, and so on, we develop the wisdom that arises from thinking. This second type of insight— the vipaśyanā that arises from thoroughly searching—is also a desire-realm mental state; hence it too is not a ground of meditation.

The third type of vipaśyanā arises when you have established the object in your mind and examined it in a subtler and detailed way. This analytical wisdom is based on śamatha, so it is wisdom arisen from meditation. This vipaśyanā arises from precise analysis in conjunction with śamatha, so it is a ground of meditation. This is genuine insight meditation. It gradually frees you from all the obstructions and gives rise to the perfect bliss of liberation from samsara.

In brief, there are three doors of insight: hearing, thinking, and meditating. The first door of insight is to consider a topic you have heard teachings about, such as the meaning of selflessness. You bring to mind its basic meaning, but you have not thought about it in detail nor developed much understanding of it. The second door is to thoroughly examine its meaning so as to understand what you did not understand before. The third door is to engage in much deeper analysis, which is more subtle and precise, so as to develop familiarity with what you have already understood.

THE DIVISION INTO SIX ASPECTS

The three doors of insight can be subdivided into six. The six aspects of insight refer to thoroughly searching for reality on the basis of six objects: the meaning, the thing, the characteristics, the side, the time, and the reason. Asaṅga says in the *Bodhisattva Levels* that to search for reality means to investigate these categories in particular.

First, to search for the meaning is to investigate the connotation of the words and terms. Second, to search for the thing itself is to investigate whether it is an internal or an external thing. For example, if you consider the sources of sense consciousness, you identify the six internal sense powers and the six external objects. Third, to search for the characteristics is to investigate whether something is a specific or a general attribute—in other words, whether the trait is unique or is shared in common with other things. For example, when practicing the four foundations of mindfulness, we find that the body and feeling share general characteristics, such as impermanence, selflessness, and so on. However, the body and feeling also have characteristics that are uniquely their own. Fourth, to search for the side means to investigate whether a thing has faults and defects, thus belonging to the nonvirtuous side, or whether it has good qualities, thus belonging to the virtuous side. Some phenomena belong to the nonvirtuous side because they are among the mental afflictions that lead to samsara; every nonvirtue is caused by a fault, a mental affliction, and every nonvirtue has a detrimental result. Other phenomena belong to the virtuous side because they are among the purifying states of mind that lead to nirvana; every virtue is caused by a good quality, and every virtue has a beneficial result. So to search for the side is to investigate whether the results are detrimental or beneficial. Fifth, to search for the time is to investigate whether an event has occurred in the past, will occur in the future, or is occurring in the present. Sixth, to search for the reason involves investigating four types of reason: dependence, functionality, correctness, and nature.

The reason of dependence shows how results arise in reliance on certain causes and conditions. We investigate this from the perspective of the conventional, the ultimate, and their bases. The reason of functionality shows how things work. For example, if we examine the function of fire, we find it is the activity of burning; the function of water is the activity of moistening, and so on. The reason of correctness establishes a thing's existence without contradicting any of the three kinds of valid knowledge: direct, inferential, or based on authoritative scripture. Anything refuted by valid knowledge is incorrect; anything established by valid knowledge is correct. The reason of nature shows the reality of the object. We may investigate a thing's commonly known nature, which is the thing's actual characteristic, such as fire is hot, water is wet, and so forth. Then there are examples of an inconceivable nature, such as one we encountered earlier in the text: a pigeon's footprint appears in a bowl of yogurt inside a house, even though the pigeon never entered the house. Do not think too much about this kind of inconceivable nature—it will drive you crazy! Finally, everything that exists has an abiding nature: emptiness. Tsongkhapa mentions that a reason of nature simply shows the way something is; it does not explain why it is that way. He advises that we should not trouble our minds with wondering why!

These six ways of searching or investigating are posited with regard to the ways that yogis understand the three things to be known: the meaning of words, conventional reality, and ultimate reality. The first object to be known, the meaning of words, is connected to the first way of searching—investigating the meaning. The second object to be known, conventional reality, is connected to the second way of searching—investigating the thing itself, as well as with one aspect of the third way of searching—investigating a thing's unique characteristics. The third object to be known, the ultimate, is connected to the remaining ways of searching—investigating the side, time, and reason, as well as with the other aspect of the third way of searching—investigating a thing's general characteristics. Asaṅga's *Śrāvaka Levels* says:

> The three doors of insight practice and the six divisions of the basis are observed thus. In brief, all insight practices are included in these categories.

This indicates that the above explanations encompass all insight practices. The initial fourfold division of vipaśyanā—differentiating and so on—actually includes the three divisions of the second presentation. When these three are explained more fully, they become the six ways of investigating. So it seems that the threefold and sixfold divisions are included within the initial fourfold division.

Asaṅga's *Śrāvaka Levels* says that the four mental attentions, explained in the context of the nine stages in the process of developing śamatha,[185] also apply to insight meditation. The four mental attentions are: tight focus, intermittent focus, uninterrupted focus, and spontaneous focus. The first mental attention is employed at the start of our practice; at this point we cannot keep the mind stably fixed on an object, so we have to make the mind strong and focus on the object very tightly. Tight focus is applied during the first two of the nine stages of developing śamatha. Over the next five stages we apply intermittent focus. During this time we are able to stay on the object of meditation most of the time, although occasionally our focus is interrupted. On the eighth stage our focus is uninterrupted. Once we set our mind on the object it remains there. It still requires some effort, but our concentration is not interrupted by distractions such as someone singing. The final mental attention is the ninth stage. At this point we are just about to achieve śamatha and our focus is spontaneous and effortless. Everything is naturally calm. When we set our mind on an object it naturally remains there by itself without becoming distracted, just as a lit butter lamp continues to burn on its own.

By progressively training in the four mental attentions within the context of both śamatha and vipaśyanā practice, you gain spontaneous and effortless focus on the object. This is not yet true śamatha or vipaśyanā; however, it gives rise to a special physical and mental pliancy or suppleness, very soft and flexible. Having attained this level of practice, you develop a subtle internal wind that pervades the body. This wind makes the body light and blissful; all aches and heaviness disappear, and the senses no longer distract you. At this point you are completely under the power of śamatha and vipaśyanā. This mental pliancy combined with physical bliss is very beneficial for mental stability. Until this pliancy arises you are still engaged in the training; once it arises you have achieved actual śamatha and vipaśyanā.

To liberate yourself from both the obstructions to liberation and to omniscience you need a direct realization of the truth. To gain a direct realization of emptiness you need śamatha so that the mind remains on the object of meditation without distraction. The *Instructions for the Perfection of Wisdom* says:

> By completing the four aspects of vipaśyanā meditation, you are liberated from the bondage of taking lower rebirth. By completing the nine aspects of śamatha meditation, you are liberated from the bondage of signs.

Many other great texts say this too. In summary, the method of meditating on vipaśyanā is based on the four divisions—differentiating and so on—as explained in the *Sutra Unraveling the Intended Meaning*, and the method of meditating on śamatha is through the nine stages, without thinking or analyzing at all.

(c') How to cultivate insight in meditation

Cultivation of insight is taught in two sections:

(1') Refuting other systems
(2') The presentation of our own system (chapters 23–25)

(1') Refuting other systems

Tsongkhapa explains and then refutes four incorrect ways of cultivating insight. This discussion takes the form of a debate between Tsongkhapa and his opponent.

(a") The first refutation

The first opponent proposes, "A meditator does not have to find a correct understanding of selflessness; to meditate on the true nature of reality is simply to hold the mind still without thinking anything. This is because reality—emptiness—is free from any identification as 'this' or 'not this.' Thus the mind resting without thinking is close to reality, in that the object does not exist in any way and the mind does not hold it in any way."

Tsongkhapa asks this opponent, "Is it that the meditator has understood that things do not exist in any way and accordingly places his mind on not apprehending anything? Or is it that, without such an understanding,[186] he meditates on reality by making his mind blank without apprehending anything because an object's reality cannot be established in any way?"

"In the first case, you contradict your earlier assertion that a meditator does not have to find a view, for here the meditator realizes that things do not exist in any way and meditates on that, which you accept as the definitive view. According to the Prāsaṅgika way of thinking, however, you fail to correctly identify the object of negation. Your refutation negates too much. Because you cannot identify the boundary of what is to be negated, you think that any assertion can be contradicted by reasoning and consequently there is no ground for identifying anything. This is nihilism. Therefore placing your mind on this is not correctly meditating on emptiness." Tsongkhapa adds that he already presented the problems that arise when the object of negation is identified too broadly,[187] so he does not elaborate on them here.

In the second case, because functional and nonfunctional things cannot be established when they are examined by ultimate analysis, the meditator thinks that these things are free of elaborations of ultimate existence; so he meditates on the absence of elaborating thought, without understanding what this really means, and considers this to be meditating on emptiness. Many unacceptable consequences follow from believing that simply to stop thinking is to meditate on emptiness. For example, it would follow that all sense consciousnesses are instances of meditating on reality because they do not differentiate one thing from another. Sense consciousnesses are free of thought and judgment. They are like a mirror. They do not identify what appears to them; it is a subsequent thought that identifies such things. If this opponent were correct, then because sense consciousnesses do not identify their objects, they accord with reality: reality is free of anything existing in any specific way. Moreover, if it were sufficient for someone to recognize the concordance between reality (that nothing exists) and the mind (not thinking anything), this would imply that non-Buddhists who achieve śamatha are meditating on śūnyatā. There would be no way to refute this implication. This was explained in the later chapters of volume 4 of this series.

Objecting to Tsongkhapa's second point, the opponent says, "This is not the same. The meditator realizes that the subject and object are concordant and then sets his or her mind in a concentrated state without thinking." Tsongkhapa replies, "So you think that a person first understands reality and then sets his or her mind on it. In other words, that person has found a view. However, you said earlier that meditation on śūnyatā takes place when a person—who does not have a view—simply concentrates the mind without apprehending anything. There is a contradiction here."

The opponent contends, "Thinking anything at all binds one to samsara, so we should immediately drop all thought and make the mind blank. This is the path to liberation." Tsongkhapa replies that he has refuted this position, which is similar to the tradition of Hashang Mahayana, many times before[188] in accordance with Kamalaśīla's final *Stages of Meditation*:

> Some say that sentient beings experience the results of higher and lower rebirths and revolve in samsara owing to the power of virtuous and nonvirtuous karma produced by thoughts in the mind. Those who do not think anything and do not do anything will be liberated from samsara. Therefore you should not think anything; you should not engage in any meritorious practices, such as generosity. They believe that the practices of generosity and so on were taught only for the purpose of unintelligent beings.
>
> Those who say this are completely abandoning the Mahayana. The root of all the vehicles is the Mahayana, so if you abandon it you aban-

don all the vehicles. This is because in saying "Do not think anything," you abandon the wisdom whose characteristic is precise ultimate analysis. Because the root of supramundane wisdom of ultimate reality is precise ultimate analysis, if you abandon that you cut off its root and thus abandon supramundane wisdom. Also, in saying "Do not engage in the practices of generosity and so forth," you completely abandon the method side without leaving even a little corner. In brief, wisdom and method are the Mahayana. The *Foremost of Gayā Sutra* (*Gayā-śīrṣa-sūtra*) says:

> The bodhisattvas' path, in brief, is twofold. What are the two? They are method and wisdom.

The *Sutra of Showing the Tathāgata's Inconceivable Secret* (*Tathāgatā-cintya-guhya-nirdeśa-sūtra*) says:

> All the paths of bodhisattvas are included within the two: method and wisdom.

Therefore completely abandoning the Mahayana creates a great karmic obstruction. If this is the case, they abandon the Mahayana, they study very little, they hold their own view as supreme, they do not respect wise masters, and they do not understand the method of the Tathāgata's teaching. Having ruined themselves, they ruin others. Their poisonous words contradict scripture and reasoning, so wise beings who wish for the good should throw them far away, like poisoned food.

According to the Chinese monk Hashang Mahayana, the mind is totally pure; Buddha is already present, so enlightenment will come naturally if you do not think or do anything. Whether or not this was his view, Tibetans believe that this is what he taught in Tibet many centuries ago. Many people, including some highly educated practitioners well versed in the sutras and Madhyamaka texts, find this teaching very attractive because it does not require any study or hardship. However, anyone who adopts this view, even if it is based on a genuine interest in spiritual training, is led down a disastrous path because he or she interprets the object of negation too broadly. This is why Tsongkhapa makes so much effort to clarify the meaning of the scriptures.

The opponent now says, "We are not entirely like Hashang because we practice generosity and so on." Tsongkhapa replies that if it is just the practice of generosity and other method practices that differentiates the opponent from Hashang, then this implies that the two share a definitive view and meditation practice. If it is more than their behavior that is different, then the opponent must specify how their practices of meditative stabilization and insight differ. Since this is not mentioned, it indicates that their views are the same. Moreover, if the opponent's view is, "All thinking, whether virtuous or nonvirtuous, binds one to samsara," then why does he bother to practice generosity, ethical discipline, and so forth? All these practices involve thinking. So if the path to liberation from samsara necessitates no thinking, then is he really striving for liberation? This was discussed earlier at length.[189] If the opponent believes that all thinking binds one to samsara, then he might as well adopt Hashang's position, because his own is riddled with contradictions. For he says on the one hand that thinking binds you to samsara, and on the other hand that you must practice generosity and so on—practices that involve thinking—in order to gain liberation from samsara. This opponent claims that his position is slightly different from Hashang's, but this difference makes his view even worse!

Someone else who follows this opponent's method says, "If, by deeply analyzing the object that is held as either kind of self, you negate the subject holding it, this simply eliminates external elaborations, like a dog chasing after a stone ball." This opponent thinks that analytical meditation only cuts away elaborations externally; he does not believe that it eliminates them from within. His example is familiar to Tibetans and to anyone who has ever been chased by a dog. If you throw a stone in the direction of a dog threatening to attack you, the dog will run after the stone instead of coming for you. But do not throw the stone at the dog! Throw it near him so that he is distracted by it and runs after it. There are some fierce dogs in Tibet; we used to keep a stone handy so that if one came at us, we could chase it away like this. Now this opponent says that we must keep the mind without thinking anything. We do not let the mind go out toward the object; instead, from the very beginning, we keep the mind directed inward. In that way the mind will not be distracted, nor will it create elaborations and judgments. This cuts through elaborations from the inside rather than from the outside. It is like a dog taking the stone from the hand that would have thrown it. There is no need to throw the stone; you just keep it in your hand. Conversely, those who train in reasoning and scriptures in order to explain the view are attracted to mere words. That is the opponent's opinion.

Tsongkhapa says that this is a most distorted view. It discards Buddha's words as well as the writings of the six great Buddhist masters who are the ornaments of the world. There are six great scholars whom we Tibetans call "ornaments" because they benefit sentient beings by explaining the meaning of Buddha's words and the import of logical reasoning. Nāgārjuna and Asaṅga are the supreme ornaments, and the other four ornaments are Āryadeva, Vasubandhu, Dignāga, and Dharmakīrti. These great masters' works enable people to understand all the different approaches taught by Buddha. Some of their commentaries present the Madhyamaka view, others the Yogācāra, Vaibhāṣika, or Sautrāntika views, each with their corresponding method-side practices.

Furthermore, you use rigorous reasoning and analysis of pure scriptures to thoroughly examine how the mind incorrectly grasps the two kinds of self, and thereby you arrive at a definite understanding that nothing exists in the way that it is held. When you understand that the two kinds of self do not exist in the way that they appear, as well as how the mind holds them, then your mistaken perceptions and erroneous knowledge come crashing down. It is the collapse of a big lie, disproved by the truth. Keeping the mind still stops it from going toward the objects of the two kinds of grasping at a self. However, this does not mean that you realize selflessness at that time. If you could understand reality simply by keeping the mind within, it would absurdly follow that fainting or falling into a deep sleep would be a realization of emptiness, because at that time the mind is kept within and not attracted to any other object. For example, if you are camping overnight in an unfamiliar, deep cave, in which you fear there may be a wild beast, you will not eliminate your fear until you light a lamp, thoroughly examine the whole place, and see that there is no wild beast there. If someone urges you instead not to bother with all that but just to stop thinking about wild beasts, would it make you feel at ease? No. We need to undertake a similar analytical process to free the mind of any misconceiving. Keeping the mind within, simply without thinking anything, does not solve the problem. Kamalaśīla's third *Stages of Meditation* says:

> This is like a coward who shuts his eyes when he sees a powerful enemy in battle. In contrast, a hero opens his eyes to carefully determine where the enemy is and then directs his weapons against him. The *Play of Mañjuśrī Sutra* (*Mañjuśrī-vikrīḍita-sūtra*) says:
>
>> Daughter, how does a bodhisattva gain victory in battle?
>> O Mañjuśrī, the supreme way: all phenomena are not seen [to exist inherently] when analyzed.
>
> Likewise, a yogi opens his eye of supramundane wisdom and defeats his enemy—the mental afflictions—by means of the weapon of wisdom. He is without fear; he does not shut his eyes like a coward.

So here too it says that we must analyze phenomena. Neither Kamalaśīla nor the sutras say, "Do not think—just keep your mind within." It is upon thorough examination that we understand that all phenomena do not inherently exist. This understanding is the way to gain victory over the obstructions to liberation and enlightenment. Tsongkhapa explains this using the familiar example of someone who, upon seeing a coiled rope in a dark corner, fears that a poisonous snake is in the house. Only by investigating and determining that it is a piece of rope—and not a real snake—is his confusion and fear removed. He cannot remove his fear simply by shutting his eyes. Similarly, sentient beings make the mistake of holding an inherent nature or self of persons, and an inherent nature or self of phenomena, to exist. As a result, they create karma, and this brings about suffering rebirths in samsara. In other words, the misery of samsara is produced by the ignorance that grasps persons and phenomena to be truly existent. We come to comprehend that our ignorant view is completely mistaken only by engaging in a study of scripture and a process of reasoning, which leads to a definite understanding that nothing exists as it is held by the egotistic view. An initial realization of emptiness occurs when you realize that the object does not exist as it is held by this view. However, it is not enough to rely on this understanding alone. In order to eliminate such a mistaken view, we must develop deep and strong familiarity with it by means of meditation over a long period of time. When ignorance is removed, none of the samsaric misery that it produces can arise.

This is why the Madhyamaka texts present numerous approaches to ultimate analysis that refutes inherent existence. Āryadeva says:

> When you see the absence of self in the object,
> The seed of samsara will completely cease.

Samsara arises from mistakenly grasping yourself and other things to be truly existent. Samsara can no longer arise when you have eliminated its seed through becoming accustomed to the realization of śūnyatā. Candrakīrti's *Introduction to the "Middle Way"* says:

> If real things existed, these conceptions would be correct.
> But we already analyzed how things do not exist like that.

The conceptions grasping the extremes only arise when we hold things to be inherently existent. Therefore Buddhist texts explain many ways to analyze how the objects of extreme views do not exist. The *Introduction to the "Middle Way"* also says:

> All afflictions and faults without exception
> Arise from the view of the perishable collection;

Seeing this with wisdom and realizing the self to be its object,
The yogi negates the self.

The yogi sees, with a mind of wisdom, that all his mental afflictions and contaminated karma arise from the egotistic view; he understands that this distorted view wrongly grasps the self as its object. He knows that by negating
the object held by this view, the view itself will dissolve. So he tries to negate
the object wrongly grasped by this view. The egotistic view holds the self to
be inherently existent, even though it is not. The held object of this view is
the inherently existent self, and that does not exist at all. The basic object of
this view, the conventional self, exists. The problem is that the innate egotistic
mind holds the conventional self to exist inherently. The yogi sees that grasping the self in this way is the root of all suffering, so he strives to negate that
inherently existent self and free himself from the distorted mind that grasps
it. Since an inherently existent self is naturally nonexistent, the object held
by the egotistic mind can be negated by logical reasons. Therefore, based on
extensive study, logical analysis, and meditation, the yogi gradually develops
the wisdom understanding that such an object—an inherently existent self—
does not exist.

There is a sense in which we cannot negate an object that never existed in
the first place. Consider the classic example of someone who thinks a piece of
coiled rope in a dark corner is a snake. A piece of coiled rope is never a snake;
the snake does not exist, so there is no need to refute it. However, the mind
that mistakenly holds the coiled rope to be a snake does exist. We negate the
object of this distorted mind by investigating and coming to see that the thing
in the corner is a rope and not a snake. Similarly, we negate the object of the
distorted mind that holds the self to be inherently existent by logically investigating and coming to see that there is no inherently existent self. Dharmakīrti,
the supremely powerful logician, says:

> You cannot abandon it
> Without negating its object.
> We eliminate attachment and hatred—
> Which are responses to good qualities and faults—
> By not seeing their objects [as real].
> It is not done through external methods.

As explained in detail in chapter 8, any conventional thing, such as the self,
naturally appears to be inherently existent to an ordinary mind perceiving it.
Although the object itself is correct, the appearance of it as inherently existent

is mistaken. Based on this appearance, a mind of ignorance may arise that holds the object to exist inherently, just as it appears. Ignorance is a distorted mind, and the way that it holds its object is wrong. This incorrect way of holding the object gives rise to inappropriate attention, which superimposes certain attributes onto the object that are not true of it, such as holding the object to be a source of happiness in its own nature. Such misconceptions give rise to further mental afflictions. Attachment usually arises from holding the object to be intrinsically good, hatred usually arises from holding it to be intrinsically bad, and so on. To get rid of all these mental afflictions, we must dig out their root—the ignorance that grasps the object to be inherently existent. We gradually remove this ignorance by seeing that the object it holds to exist inherently does not exist in that way. This is how we get rid of the mental afflictions. We cannot eliminate them in any other way. There is no external method to remove them; we cannot simply extract them as we might pull a thorn out of our foot. The actual way to get rid of the mental afflictions and wrong conceptions is taught in many Madhyamaka texts as well as the logical texts of other schools. In short we must generate the wisdom that functions as the antidote to ignorance.

There are some who say that since every type of thinking binds us to samsara, when we meditate on emptiness all thinking ceases. This claim should be investigated. We may ask, "When ordinary people meditate on emptiness, is the referent of what they are meditating on—the meaning of emptiness—manifest or hidden?" If the object is manifest, then an ordinary person would have to be an ārya. A manifest object is something directly perceived by anyone—it is obvious to ordinary valid direct perception. A hidden object cannot be directly perceived by an ordinary being—it can be known only through a logical inference. Some hidden objects, however, can be directly perceived by ārya beings. If the referent of meditation on emptiness is a manifest object, then it is a directly perceived object, so the person perceiving it in meditation must be an ārya. If you say that it is not contradictory for someone to directly realize the referent object of meditation on emptiness and yet be an ordinary being, then using the same reasoning we can make the absurd statement that it is not contradictory for someone to be an ārya, and yet, when they meditate on emptiness, the referent of emptiness is a hidden object.

The opponent counters, saying, "When ordinary people meditate they directly perceive reality; however, they do not understand that the object of their meditation is ultimate reality. Someone has to prove it to them using scriptural evidence." The opponent is saying that when an ordinary person realizes emptiness, a teacher has to logically prove to her that what she has already directly realized is emptiness. This is completely ridiculous. How could there be such a situation? This kind of statement is laughable to those who understand valid cognition.

The opponent replies, "An ordinary person directly perceives reality in meditation, but others establish the conventional label for her." For example, although you can directly see a vase in front of you, you may not know the term used by the local community to refer to that thing, which has the characteristics of being round-bellied, flat-based, and able to hold water. You have already directly perceived the vase itself; you just need to learn the name "vase." The opponent's argument is that when an ordinary individual—who meditates by stopping thought and closing her mind to any object—has a direct realization of reality, someone else has to prove to the meditator that what she has realized is conventionally called *ultimate reality* or *emptiness*. The meditator has already directly understood the referent of the term; she just has to learn the term itself. So this is no big deal.

Tsongkhapa says, "You cannot get away with that." As Dharmakīrti says:

> Because it concerns simple things
> Even known to cowherds.[190]

Our monastic textbooks explain that in Dharmakīrti's system of logic there are various types of correct logical reasons, for example: that which proves the meaning or referent; and that which proves only the terminology.[191] Here the opponent is talking about a correct logical reason that proves only the terminology. The idea is that you may see something but not know what it is called. This is a very common situation. When I first came to the United States, I saw various items of food, clothing, and so on—but I did not know their names. Right now you can go into a grocery store and buy some ethnic food. When you taste it, you can directly experience whether it is sweet, salty, or sour. However, you may not be able to say what this food is. You are not stupid; the name simply has to be introduced to you. You are acquainted with the referent object. You only need to be told, "This is called such-and-such." Or when you travel abroad you might see a big black animal for the first time and not know what type of animal it is. You just need someone to tell you, "This is called a cow because it has a tail with a tip like this and horns shaped like that." This logical reason proves only the terminology, because you already know the referent object. Once this reason has been shown to you, then later, when you see a small white cow, you can say, "This is a cow because it has this kind of tail and that kind of horns." Having learned the defining characteristics of a cow, you can recognize an animal called "cow." The opponent is suggesting that the same applies to this situation, where an ordinary person directly realizing ultimate reality in meditation simply needs to learn the name of the object. Tsongkhapa counters this point, citing Dharmakīrti, to show that a reason that proves the terminology is useful only when someone is acquainted with an object of mundane knowledge—something known even to cowherds—but is ignorant of the name. "If that is the case here," Tsongkhapa asks, "what fool does not realize emptiness?"

Suppose we concede that, as the opponent insists, the meditator sees śūnyatā. We can demonstrate that this is inappropriate by means of a simple example. There is a special breed of white cow that has a dewlap on its throat and a hump on its back. Anyone can identify such an animal as a cow or a bull. But the particular characteristics of that breed, even though they enable you to identify such an animal as a cow, are not suitable to be the defining characteristics of "cow." Likewise, when an ordinary individual meditates on their own empty mind, they perceive it directly. But that kind of emptiness is not the criterion of the defining characteristics of ultimate reality; merely seeing it directly does not establish it as reality. If the opponent claims that this person perceives śūnyatā yet simply cannot label it as such, it contradicts his own assertion that a reason proving the terminology is required—for that is used only for mundane things. Tsongkhapa says that such an opponent has nothing sensible to say, so he will not discuss the matter any further.

If the referent object of an ordinary person's meditation on emptiness is a hidden object, then it is ridiculous to assert that it is apprehended by a mind free from thought. The very meaning of *hidden object* is something known to ordinary people only through inferential knowledge. In the absence of inferential knowledge, there is no way to know a hidden object. So in this case a meditator whose mind is free from thought, thereby lacking inferential knowledge, could not know what he or she is meditating on. Therefore what the opponent says is completely contradictory.

In summary, if the mind of an ordinary individual meditating on śūnyatā is not directed toward selflessness or emptiness, then it contradicts the claim that the person is meditating on śūnyatā. If this person's mind is directed toward selflessness or emptiness as an object of meditation, that object must be either a hidden or a manifest object. Now if selflessness is a manifest object, then the meditator must be an ārya being. As a corollary, you must accept that the referent of selflessness or emptiness is a hidden object for an ordinary individual. But if the referent of selflessness is a hidden object for an ordinary being, then it is understood via a conceptual image rather than by direct perception. Thus it cannot be the object of a mind free from thought.

Even someone on the highest of the four levels of the bodhisattva path of preparation is still an ordinary individual.[192] He or she is just about to attain the path of seeing but still uses a conceptual image when meditating on emptiness. According to most Buddhist systems, a conceptual mind is always mistaken because its appearing object is always a mental image mixed together with its main object; in contrast, a mind that directly realizes its object is free of any such image appearing to it, and so it is nonmistaken.[193] If even a bodhisattva who is about to attain the ārya path of seeing in the next moment knows the meaning of selflessness only via an image, how could an ordinary beginner meditate on emptiness with a mind free of all thought? If an ordinary practitioner's mind meditating on emptiness were free of thought, he or she would be realizing the object—selflessness—with yogic direct perception.[194] Yogic direct perception, the highest form of direct perception, is defined as: "An exalted cognition within the mental continuum of an ārya being that arises in dependence on its own uncommon dominant condition: the meditative stabilization that is the union of śamatha and vipaśyanā." So we would be forced to conclude that the mind of a beginner is unmistaken about selflessness because it directly realizes selflessness.

In conclusion, some people assert that we meditate on the meaning of emptiness simply by keeping the mind still and not letting it go toward the two types of self. Thus we do not have to find the right view that negates the object of the egotistic view. Their claim is that ordinary individuals meditate nonconceptually on selflessness. Many people are drawn to this idea. But those who accept these assertions have wandered far from the path of scripture and reasoning. It is important to understand the refutation of the belief that a direct realization of emptiness is achieved by keeping the mind turned inward and blocking all thoughts. In order to realize the ultimate truth we need to understand the Madhyamaka view. We have to spend a long time using scriptures and reasoning to refute the object of negation and come to a correct understanding. If this were not the case, then anyone could realize śūnyatā just by hibernating like animals that spend the winter sleeping underground. It would be so easy!

(b″) THE SECOND REFUTATION

The second opponent agrees that the position of the first opponent is incorrect: it is wrong to accept that mental stabilization without thinking anything, which lacks the view of emptiness that is selflessness, is meditation on emptiness. This second opponent's position is that once someone has understood selflessness, any of that person's subsequent mental stabilization without thinking is meditation on emptiness. Although this is a little better than the previous opponent's view, it is also incorrect.

If all meditation without thinking, by someone who has understood the definitive view, were meditation on emptiness, then why would not her meditation on bodhicitta likewise be meditation on śūnyatā? The opponent replies, "When a person who has found the definitive view of śūnyatā meditates on bodhicitta, she does not do so by remembering a previous meditation on emptiness and stabilizing her mind on that object." Tsongkhapa agrees that someone is indeed meditating on śūnyatā when she has found the definitive view and stably places her mind on a recollection of that view. But how could all of this person's subsequent mental stabilizations without thinking anything sustain the view of emptiness? Simply settling the mind in a relaxed state without thinking anything does not constitute meditation on śūnyatā. According to the Prāsaṅgikas, in this context the phrase "without thinking anything" means that the mind remains focused on one object without making analytical distinctions, such as "this is so" or "that is not so." It does not mean being free from thought. The phrase "free from thought" refers to direct perception, including sensory direct perception, which is without any conceptual image. This has been discussed on many occasions in the *Lamrim Chenmo*'s explanation of śamatha and vipaśyanā.

(c") THE THIRD REFUTATION

The third opponent says he does not accept the first position—that even without having found the view, any mental stabilization without thinking is meditation on emptiness; nor does he accept the second position—that having found the view, any mental stabilization without thinking is meditation on emptiness. His opinion is that prior to a period of mental stabilization without thinking anything, you have to analyze the object by means of precise analytical wisdom. After that is completed, all subsequent mental stabilization without thinking is meditation on śūnyatā.

The opponent seems to be saying that, after having understood the view of emptiness, you do not need to develop mental stabilization observing śūnyatā in order to meditate on it. This is incorrect. It would absurdly follow that if you fall asleep while engaged in analytical investigation of emptiness, your subsequent deep sleep without thinking anything would be meditation on śūnyatā. It is obvious that if you fall asleep or simply remain without thinking, you are not meditating on śūnyatā.

So what is meditation on emptiness? It is to analyze the view and then place your mind on the object you have understood: the absence of inherent existence. If after meditating a little while you lose that object and your mind wanders off or simply rests without thinking anything in particular, you are no longer meditating on śūnyatā. So you must not lose the object. You have to remind yourself of it continuously and refresh your understanding. While meditating on emptiness, a little corner of your mind acts as a spy; this is a kind of wisdom that checks whether the main part of your mind is staying on the object, or has wandered off, or has fallen asleep. You need to maintain sharp awareness from one moment to the next as to whether your mind is continuing to remain focused on the view. That is the correct approach according to our system.

(d″) THE FOURTH REFUTATION

The fourth opponent says he does not accept the three earlier positions. In his opinion, when meditating on śūnyatā first you draw forth a definite understanding of emptiness, then you hold your mind on that object and keep it there without examining anything else. This is a faultless meditation on śūnyatā because it does not succumb to the errors of the first three systems: unlike the first, it is not a meditation that is not directed toward śūnyatā; unlike the second, it is not a meditation where the mind remains without thinking and does not recollect the correct view; and unlike the third, it is not a meditation where, after having analyzed śūnyatā, the mind remains without thinking and does not stay on the view. This opponent says that after having understood śūnyatā, you keep your mind on it without analyzing anything else.

This sounds correct, right? Tsongkhapa says no. What is wrong with this approach? The opponent says that to meditate on śūnyatā you first analyze the view of śūnyatā and then engage in stabilizing meditation on that view. This is a description of śamatha meditation taking śūnyatā as the focal object; his approach lacks a way to maintain analytical meditation. Insight meditation cannot be mere stabilizing meditation; it must be analytical. This analytical meditation cannot be superficial; it must be subtle, sharp, and powerful because it is the method used to understand reality clearly. Genuine vipaśyanā meditation is the union of śamatha and insight. It stably abides on the object while subtly examining and analyzing it. The union of these two practices is essential. A useful analogy of this union is a little fish swimming in a calm and still pond. The fish can swim from top to bottom and from side to side without disturbing the main body of water. In just this way, a yogi's union of śamatha and vipaśyanā realizing śūnyatā can analyze every aspect of the object of meditation without disturbing the calm placement of the mind on that object. The mind of śamatha stably focuses on śūnyatā. The mind of vipaśyanā has a sharp quality that subtly checks and analyzes the object. The combination of śamatha and vipaśyanā meditation on śūnyatā is a far more powerful tool for removing the obstructions to liberation and omniscience than either method alone.

The fourth opponent's system is indeed the best of these four systems, but it is still incorrect because it does not have the union of śamatha and vipaśyanā.

✣ 23 ✣

Cultivating Insight in Meditation

(2') Presenting our own system
    (a") Why both stabilizing meditation and analytical meditation are
        necessary
    (b") Eliminating objections to that

———— ⊷◉⊶ ————

(2') PRESENTING OUR OWN SYSTEM

IF YOU DO NOT arrive at a deep understanding of selflessness, which is the
definitive meaning or ultimate truth, then none of your meditative awareness will be a mind directed toward selflessness. First you must find the view,
and then while meditating you need to recollect the view. It is not enough
to merely understand the words; you must meditate on the analysis and the
analyzed object again and again. While maintaining the view of selflessness
you continue to analyze the object with wisdom and place the mind on selflessness without distraction. Therefore you need both analytical and stabilizing
meditation—vipaśyanā and śamatha. Neither one alone is enough. There are
three topics relating to this:

    (a") Why both stabilizing meditation and analytical meditation are
          necessary
    (b") Eliminating objections to that
    (c") A summary of the key points for maintaining this meditation
          (chapter 24)

(a") WHY BOTH STABILIZING MEDITATION AND
ANALYTICAL MEDITATION ARE NECESSARY

You will not develop a realization that is genuine insight if you do not understand the meaning of selflessness to its fullest extent. Buddha teaches that a

complete ascertainment of that view is the cause of insight and that not hearing the teachings explaining śūnyatā is a hindrance to developing insight. Only by listening to these teachings can you generate the wisdom arisen from hearing, followed by the wisdom arisen from thinking, and the wisdom arisen from meditating. Tsongkhapa quotes several passages indicating this, here and elsewhere. The *Sutra Unraveling the Intended Meaning* says:

> "Bhagavan, from what causes do śamatha and vipaśyanā arise?" "Maitreya, they arise from the cause that is pure ethical conduct and they arise from the cause that is the pure view arisen from hearing and thinking."

Also:

> Not having heard the superior teaching as you would wish is a hindrance to insight.

Likewise, the *Questions of Nārāyaṇa* (*Nārāyaṇa-paripṛcchā*) says:

> From hearing arises wisdom, and wisdom eliminates the mental afflictions.

Insight arises from an understanding of emptiness as follows. You begin to develop an understanding of the correct view by analyzing many scriptures and logical investigations. Once you understand the view, you analyze it again and again with precise analytical wisdom. Stabilizing the mind on the object, without maintaining analysis, will not give rise to insight. Therefore after you have achieved śamatha—when your mind is able to stay on the object of meditation for as long as you wish and your body and mind experience a special pliancy and bliss—you must continuously analyze the object during your meditation. This is how to become very familiar with it.

An opponent comments, "We do not say that you should meditate without analysis in the beginning; but once you have understood the view through study and analysis, you should not engage in analysis while meditating." He is suggesting that we should meditate by simply placing our mind on the object already analyzed and ascertained. If we do more analysis while meditating, then we are engaging in discriminating thought. Our mind is therefore grasping at signs. In many scriptures it says that śūnyatā is signless and wishless, and three doors to liberation are specified: emptiness, signlessness, and wishlessness. So we should not employ a method that involves grasping at signs.

Tsongkhapa says that this opponent's argument has no weight. He reminds us that on many occasions he has refuted the assertion that an ordinary being's meditation on selflessness is utterly free from thought. So it is wrong not to maintain analysis of the view in meditation. Here the opponent assumes that every kind of thought is grasping at signs. However, in the scriptures *grasping at signs* is defined as holding things to be truly existent. If, as the opponent claims, all thought must be stopped during meditation because all thoughts hold their objects to be truly existent, then analyzing how things are empty of a self when establishing the view must also be stopped because it involves thought. This would bring an end to any teaching about emptiness, any debate on selflessness, any writing on this topic, and any examination of reality, because all these activities can only be done using thought; we should not distinguish between needing to stop thought during meditation and not needing to stop thought at other times, since we should always be trying to stop grasping at true existence.

The opponent replies, "We do not accept that. Until we understand selflessness, we must engage in the study of scripture and rational analysis. Once we have found the view that understands śūnyatā, we no longer need to engage in analysis during meditation." There are many people who think that when you study, you use scriptures and logical reasoning to analyze what is correct and what is not; then when you meditate, you just keep your mind on the object without analyzing anything. Their definition of meditation is single-pointed concentration. These people say that every meditation is stabilizing meditation, and therefore all thoughts are obstacles to meditation. This view is still prevalent; I have heard it stated on many occasions.

Tsongkhapa counters that if that is the case, there would be no point in āryas meditating on selflessness because they already directly realized selflessness at the first moment of the path of seeing. What does this mean? Let us look at what follows if this opponent is correct. Suppose a student studies a great deal so that upon entering the bodhisattva path of accumulation, he or she already understands śūnyatā. From the opponent's point of view, this would mean that from this moment on the practitioner would have nothing else to analyze. Also when a practitioner first attains a direct realization of śūnyatā, he or she enters the path of seeing—the first of the bodhisattva grounds; if all meditation after this first direct realization of emptiness were nonanalytical, a bodhisattva would never need to analyze śūnyatā again. It takes three great eons to complete the ten stages of the bodhisattva path, according to the sutra system. So from the second to the tenth bodhisattva stage—which are all parts of the path of meditation—what should bodhisattvas meditate on? The scriptures say that throughout the path of meditation bodhisattvas meditate on śūnyatā. But what would be the point of doing that if there were no new realizations to be gained? You would only realize yet again what you had already realized on the path of seeing. Therefore Tsongkhapa argues the opponent is totally incorrect: śamatha alone will not enable us to develop our understanding of śūnyatā. We must combine it with vipaśyanā meditation. We need both stabilizing meditation and analytical meditation; at certain times we need the former, at other times we need the latter, and eventually we need to combine them.

The opponent replies, "Bodhisattvas meditate on śūnyatā on the path of meditation because the path of seeing does not eliminate all the obstacles to enlightenment. To get rid of the obstructions to omniscience bodhisattvas must actively engage in this meditation, even though there is nothing new to understand."

Tsongkhapa says that it is the same here. Even though an ordinary person establishes an understanding of emptiness through the wisdom arisen from study and analysis, he or she needs to become more familiar with what was already established. The more you become accustomed to what you have established, the stronger that understanding will be. You need repeated analytical meditation and stabilizing meditation to develop a powerful and long-lasting realization. Elsewhere Tsongkhapa says this is analogous to the sunrise. When the sun begins to rise in the east, at first there is only a little light in the sky. Then sunbeams begin to stream forth over the top of the mountains, and gradually the sun emerges. Once the sun has fully appeared in the sky, sunrise is over; the sun in its entirety is in the sky. There is no more sun to rise that day. However, the function of the sun is not finished. It provides heat, light, and beneficial rays from its initial arising in the east to its final setting in the west. The sun remains the same as it goes across the sky; it does not change in size or strength.

Similarly, the object of meditation, śūnyatā, is the same throughout a bodhisattva's progress over the stages of the path. On the path of preparation, bodhisattvas first analyze śūnyatā rather roughly, then more subtly, though the object still appears mixed with its mental image. Gradually, as the image becomes subtler, śūnyatā becomes more vivid. Eventually the intermediary image disappears and bodhisattvas realize śūnyatā by means of yogic direct perception. This moment of direct realization is called the path of seeing because it is the first time that a yogi sees emptiness directly. After that there is nothing more to be seen. But just like the sun in its passage across the sky, the sustained perception of śūnyatā performs many functions. The remaining stages on the bodhisattva path are called the path of meditation or cultivation. The obstructions eliminated by the path of seeing are different from those eliminated by the path of meditation. On the path of seeing, the gross obstructions are eliminated. On the stages of the path of meditation, subtler obstructions are gradually eliminated. All these obstacles are removed through analytical meditation. Dharmakīrti's *Commentary on Valid Cognition* says:

> Definite understanding and false imputation
> Are in the nature of the harmer and the harmed.

"Definite understanding" refers to inferential knowledge of the truth; for example, knowing that sound is impermanent because it is a product or knowing that everything is empty because it dependently arises. Definite understanding negates its opposite—in this case the "false imputation" that sound is permanent or that everything is truly existent. So how does logical inference change a wrong view (that sound is permanent) into an understanding (that sound is impermanent)?[195] Definite understanding and its opposite, false imputation, are in the nature of the harmer and the object harmed. The harmer is true, and it is supported by correct reasoning. The harmed is false, and it is not supported by correct reasoning. Dharmakīrti says that the wisdom realizing selflessness destroys self-grasping "Because it has a different nature based on truth."[196] The truth can destroy falsehood completely; but falsehood, no matter how much you accustom yourself to it, can never destroy the truth. It may be able to challenge the truth, but it can never destroy it. The wisdom that realizes selflessness is the harmer, and the egotistic view is the object harmed. The egotistic view and the wisdom that negates it hold their object in completely contradictory ways. They are equal in the sense of holding an object, but the egotistic view is based on falsehood, whereas its opposing wisdom is based on truth. Although the afflictive mind may be more powerful at present, it is based on the false egotistic view and so can be overcome. Although wisdom may be weak at present, it can never be destroyed by mental afflictions. Wisdom knows the truth and thus it defeats the egotistic view—the view of the perishable collection—which grasps things wrongly. The more you strengthen and stabilize a definite understanding of emptiness, the more you weaken and destabilize the falsely imputing mind of self-grasping. Therefore your understanding of emptiness must be based on many lines of reasoning; you must analyze them again and again to deepen your familiarity. In this way you will eventually defeat all incorrect grasping. Virtue destroys evil in the end.

If you do not do this, you will get nowhere. Suppose you develop a basic understanding of the faults of samsara, or the relationship between virtuous and nonvirtuous causes and their respective results, or bodhicitta, love, and compassion. If you do no further analysis, your only meditation practice would be to simply fix your mind on one of these objects. For example, your meditation on impermanence might be just thinking, "I will die, I will die, I will die." You would not analyze the causes of death, or the reason to fear death, or anything else. In order to bring forth a pure understanding of impermanence, bodhicitta, and so on, it is not enough merely to fixate on a phrase such as "I will die" or "I must attain buddhahood for the sake of all sentient beings." To develop a powerful realization you need to reflect on the reasons supporting it from many different angles. For example, to get rid of obsession with this life, believing in permanence, and clinging to the thought "I will never die," the *Lamrim Chenmo* explains three rudimentary meditations on death and impermanence, each with three subsidiary reasons.[197] This may be enough for people of quick intelligence; for others, many more reasons are presented to strengthen the understanding and the feeling that arises from each rudimentary meditation. Likewise, in order to develop a firm understanding of the emptiness of inherent existence, it is not enough just to keep in mind "Everything is empty." We must think about the many reasons why things are not inherently existent, and we must consider the contradictory consequences that would follow if things were inherently existent. That is how to meditate. Tsongkhapa explains this extensively in the context of the practice of beings of smaller spiritual scope.[198]

All three volumes of Kamalaśīla's *Stages of Meditation* state that after establishing śamatha, you continue to engage in analysis when you meditate. When Candrakīrti says such things as "The yogi negates the self" in *Introduction to the "Middle Way,"* he means that yogis use logical analysis when meditating. Candrakīrti is saying that the only way to disprove the reality of an inherently existent self is to bring to mind many scriptural and logical reasons. We cannot negate such a misconception without this analysis. We cannot beat it with a stick! Even the term *yogi* indicates someone whose meditation yokes śamatha with vipaśyanā—calm concentration with analytical insight. The Tibetan translation of the term yogi is *naljorpa* (*rnal 'byor pa*). The first syllable, *nal*, refers to śamatha; the second syllable, *jor*, refers to vipaśyanā. *Naljor* indicates the union of śamatha and vipaśyanā. The final syllable, *pa*, indicates a person who meditates with this kind of mind. So we can hardly call someone who does not engage in insight meditation a yogi.

Yogis want to get rid of the mental afflictions in order to achieve liberation and enlightenment. The primary means to eliminate the mental afflictions is vipaśyanā; so why do they bother to develop śamatha? They need śamatha in order to develop vipaśyanā. But they also search for an understanding of the view prior to achieving śamatha. In terms of practice, yogis first develop an understanding of the view, then they develop śamatha, and then they analyze the view again with this more powerful mind. At that point they develop supreme wisdom. Therefore in the context of the six perfections, meditative concentration comes before wisdom. In other words, the analysis of the view is presented after the method of attaining śamatha. The order of these practices indicates the need to analyze selflessness after accomplishing śamatha. This shows that wisdom is based on śamatha. Bhāvaviveka's *Heart of the Middle Way* says:

> After the mind is placed in equipoise,
> All these things, the phenomena
> Conventionally identified,
> Are examined by wisdom in this way.

The commentary on this stanza clearly says that after developing concentration you must engage in analysis of the view. Śāntideva presents this order of practice in *Engaging in the Bodhisattva's Deeds*. He says we should first accomplish the practice of śamatha as taught in the chapter on meditative concentration and then engage in vipaśyanā meditation. In the chapter on wisdom, Śāntideva gives a detailed explanation of how yogis meditate on śūnyatā using logical analysis. At the beginning of that chapter, Śāntideva says:

> All these branches were taught
> By Buddha for the sake of wisdom.[199]

"These branches" are the method side of bodhisattva practice. They are the first five perfections: the bodhisattvas' activities after they develop bodhicitta. In the first eight chapters of the text, Śāntideva explains that each of these practices, including śamatha, either directly or indirectly assists the development of wisdom. It is wisdom that eliminates the obstructions to liberation and omniscience. So the ninth chapter is the key because it explains the most important practice of wisdom; everything else—all the method-side practices to accumulate merit—are taught for the purpose of developing wisdom. That is why Śāntideva presents the method-side practices before the practice of wisdom.

This is also the order of the last two perfections and of the last two trainings: concentration comes before wisdom. All the teachings on how to cultivate wisdom—from the point of view of analyzing ultimate and conventional reality—are organized in this way. You engage in vipaśyanā meditation after accomplishing śamatha. This progression of practices is not only found in books; it is the order of meditation practiced by yogis. Do not imagine it to be otherwise. Moreover, because many great texts emphasize this point, it is beyond doubt that when you engage in insight meditation you must analyze. It is wrong to think that these practices are only ever done separately. You should not assume that when doing vipaśyanā meditation you only engage in analysis without any stabilizing meditation, and you should also not assume that when doing śamatha meditation you only engage in stabilizing meditation without any analysis. Many texts say that if you do not establish śamatha when engaging in analytical meditation, you will destroy your previously developed śamatha. As already explained, without śamatha you cannot develop vipaśyanā. Both practices are necessary; the mind of śamatha must be maintained together with analytical meditation. When you finish a session of analytical meditation, you engage in stabilizing meditation on the meaning of that analysis for some time. By doing this you accomplish the union of śamatha and vipaśyanā focusing on selflessness. Kamalaśīla's middle *Stages of Meditation* says:

> The *Cloud of Jewels Sutra (Mahāmegha-nāma-mahāyānasūtra)* says:
>
>> One who is skillful in dealing with faults engages in the yoga of meditating on śūnyatā in order to gain freedom from all elaborations. Meditating extensively on śūnyatā, his mind reaches out anywhere: when he thoroughly searches for the nature of the object of his mind's joyful focus, he realizes emptiness; when he searches for what the mind is, he realizes emptiness; when he thoroughly searches for the nature of the mind's activity of realizing, he realizes emptiness. By realizing in this way he enters into the yoga of signlessness.
>
> This passage teaches that the practitioner must engage in thorough examination before entering into the yoga of signlessness. It very clearly demonstrates that it is impossible to engage in the yoga of signlessness merely by abandoning all thought completely and not analyzing the nature of things by means of wisdom.

This sutra passage shows that before entering into the yoga of signlessness you engage in ultimate analysis of the object, the subject, and the activity of the mind; here we are talking about the wisdom realizing emptiness. When you examine the nature of the object (emptiness) realized by the subject, and the subject (wisdom) that realizes the object, you realize that both are empty of inherent existence. When you search for the nature of the activity (realizing), you realize that it too is empty of inherent existence. Only after realizing śūnyatā by means of such analysis do you begin the practice of meditation on signlessness. Therefore Kamalaśīla shows that what Hashang asserts is impossible. You cannot engage in a signless or nonconceptual meditation on emptiness merely by abandoning thought and withdrawing the mind from any object. You must rationally investigate the object by means of ultimate analysis first and then engage in nonconceptual practice. Here *nonconceptual practice* means the direct realization of śūnyatā. In other contexts, śamatha is considered nonconceptual practice because it is nondiscursive. But the point of this passage is that merely stopping thought and maintaining nondiscursive awareness will not enable you to enter into the advanced nonconceptual practice that is the direct perception of emptiness.

Therefore as Tsongkhapa explained earlier, using the weapon of ultimate analysis, which proves that the two types of self are not established in the slightest among phenomena, we destroy grasping at them. This analysis draws forth a definite understanding of selflessness. If the reality of the two types of self does not exist, how could the nonexistence of that reality, which negates it, really exist? In other words, if we negate the ultimate existence of everything, we cannot establish that the emptiness of ultimate existence itself is ultimately existent. The negation of ultimate existence cannot be ultimately existent. This is the emptiness of emptiness. To illustrate, Tsongkhapa says that our understanding of the nonexistence of a barren woman's son first depends on whether there is a barren mother and her son. Anyone who understands that they do not exist at all would never think or say that the nonexistence of a barren woman's son is itself a really existent thing. Tsongkhapa's point is that if you see that nothing is truly existent on any basis whatsoever, you will not consider the absence of true existence itself to be truly existent.

Is that right? Certain famous Tibetan scholars of old, such as Kunkhyen Jonangpa, say that although things are empty of being truly existent—and therefore are conventional, false, and unreal—the absence of true existence itself is real. They believe that śūnyatā, the ultimate truth, is the one thing that truly exists. There have been many debates about this. Chapa Chokyi Senge says that although conventional things are not ultimately existent, ultimate truth is ultimately existent and therefore is an object of knowledge.[200] Other early scholars, such as Ngog Loden Sherab, say that the ultimate truth is not an object of knowledge because it is not ultimately existent.[201] You have to think about this.

Based on the above quotation from *Stages of Meditation*, Tsongkhapa concludes that the realization of the emptiness of the object, subject, and activity reverses the conceiving that grasps at signs because any such conceiving must grasp the true existence of the real or the true existence of the unreal. The terms *real* and *unreal* may indicate "really existent" and "not really existent," respectively; or they may indicate "functional" and "nonfunctional" phenomena, respectively, which together comprise all existents. According to Dharmakīrti's philosophy, grasping true existence is the generality; its particular instances are grasping the true existence of functional things and grasping the true existence of nonfunctional things. As we noted earlier, Gyaltsab Je said that when you understand that a generality or universal is absent, you also understand that all its instances are absent.[202] In most cases a generality is the pervader, and its instances are the pervaded. Where there is mutual pervasion between a generality and its instance, such as between impermanent and produced, this relationship is sometimes expressed as pervader-pervaded; in other words, the two have the same extension. In the present case, if something is grasped as truly existent, then it must be either a functional thing that is grasped as truly existent or a nonfunctional thing that is grasped as truly existent—and vice versa, because if there is no pervader then there is no pervaded. Kamalaśīla alludes to this in his *Stages of Meditation.*

Supreme nonconceptual wisdom directly realizing śūnyatā is achieved by alternately practicing vipaśyanā and śamatha. We engage in analysis to give rise to an understanding from the depths of our hearts that no functional or nonfunctional thing whatsoever has even the tiniest particle of true existence. We then stabilize the mind on the meaning of that analysis. By alternately engaging in these two practices, we will accomplish the supreme gnosis directly realizing śūnyatā. This cannot be achieved simply by withdrawing the mind from every object and not investigating anything at all. It may feel very pleasant to stop thinking and relax in a meditative equipoise that is the cessation of discursive activity. But the mere absence of thought cannot harm the egotistic view in any way. This no-thinking approach cannot eliminate grasping things to be truly existent. We must distinguish between not thinking of things as being truly existent and understanding that things are not truly existent. Not thinking about anything as truly existent is not the same as realizing the absence of true existence; not thinking about anything as having a self is not the same as realizing selflessness. This is a very important point. We must develop a clear and definite understanding that not thinking of anything as having either of the two kinds of self is very different from realizing the two kinds of selflessness.

(b") Eliminating objections to that

Someone says, "Analyzing the meaning of selflessness involves thought, so it cannot give rise to the supreme nonconceptual gnosis because these are contradictory and causes and their effects must be congruent." Tsongkhapa replies that Buddha himself explained that this objection is not correct. The *Kāśyapa Chapter Sutra* (*Kāśyapa-parivarta-sūtra*) says:

> Kāśyapa, it is thus. For example, the wind rubs two dry sticks of wood together, which starts a fire; once started, the fire burns those two sticks. Similarly, Kāśyapa, if you have precise ultimate analysis, the powerful wisdom of an ārya will arise; having arisen, this wisdom burns up your precise ultimate analysis.

So this sutra says that the nonconceptual wisdom of an ārya arises from analytical thinking. The middle *Stages of Meditation* says:

> Thus yogis analyze by means of wisdom in this way. When they definitely do not apprehend anything's essential nature ultimately, they enter into nonconceptual samādhi. They realize that all phenomena have no essential nature. Someone who does not meditate by means of analyzing the essential nature of things with wisdom, but meditates just by abandoning all mental activity completely, will never be rid of false conceptions and will never realize the lack of essential nature, because there is no light of wisdom. Thus, just as the Bhagavan taught, "Like the fire arising from rubbing two sticks together, the fire of wisdom seeing the ultimate exactly as it is arises from precise ultimate analysis and then burns the wood of conceptions."

If you believe that dissimilar things—such as the analysis and the direct realization of the ultimate—are totally contradictory and cannot be causally related, then you would also have to hold that it would be impossible for an uncontaminated path to arise from a contaminated path. Hence no ordinary individual could become an ārya because the cause and effect are completely different. Also if that were so, how could a green sprout come from a gray seed? How could smoke come from fire? How could a man be born from a woman? There are many more examples of a cause and its effect having completely different aspects. Nonconceptual wisdom directly realizes the meaning of the two types of selflessness; it knows that the object grasped as either of the two types of self does not exist. In order to give rise to this direct realization, you must first precisely analyze the object grasped as a self; then, having understood by means of inference that there is no truly existent self, you bring this recognition into your meditation practice. Although this is conceptual, it is a cause that is harmonious with the supreme nonconceptual wisdom directly realizing emptiness. A stanza we examined earlier from the *King of Concentrations Sutra* says:

> If you analyze the selflessness of phenomena,
> And if, having analyzed, you meditate upon it,
> This will cause the result: the attainment of nirvana.
> There is no peace from any other cause.[203]

In other words, after having thoroughly examined the self, you meditate on what you established through that analysis. This is the only cause of genuine peace. The final *Stages of Meditation* says:

> Although that [analysis] is in the nature of thought, yet because it is in the nature of appropriate attention it will give rise to nonconceptual wisdom. Anyone who desires that wisdom must rely on it.

The opponent objects, "The *Perfection of Wisdom Sutras* say that if you engage in analysis, thinking that 'forms and so on are empty and selfless,' you are employing signs. Therefore it is not right to engage in precise analysis of emptiness."

Tsongkhapa clarifies that in passages like this from the *Perfection of Wisdom Sutras*, "employing signs" means grasping śūnyatā to be truly existent. He notes that he has explained many times that merely thinking "This is empty" is not employing signs. If it were employing signs, it would contradict another passage from the *Perfection of Wisdom Sutras*:

> A bodhisattva, a great being who practices the perfection of wisdom
> and meditates on the perfection of wisdom, should closely examine
> and scrutinize like this: "What is the perfection of wisdom? Whose
> is the perfection of wisdom? Is the nonperceiving or nonexistence of
> any phenomena the perfection of wisdom?" Thus you should closely
> examine and scrutinize in this way.

This and other sutra passages state that in order to understand the perfection of wisdom we need to employ skillful thought. When we meditate on the perfection of wisdom, we investigate, examine, and analyze things in terms of their nature, function, aspect, and so on. For example, in the *Heart Sutra*, in response to Śāriputra's question, "How should any son or daughter of the lineage practice the profound perfection of wisdom?" Avalokiteśvara says, "They should perfectly see that even the five aggregates are empty of inherent existence." Also the *Verse Summary of the Perfection of Wisdom* says:

> When conditioned, unconditioned, virtuous, or nonvirtuous phenomena
> Are analyzed by wisdom, not even a tiny particle is seen.
> This is commonly called the perfection of wisdom.

In other words, when you examine the nature of phenomena, mentally separating out every aspect and part, and do not find even the tiniest atom existing from its own side, then you have realized emptiness by means of perfect wisdom.

A more literal translation of the name for this kind of realization is *wisdom that has gone to the other side*. According to the Mādhyamikas, the perfection of wisdom has two aspects: the wisdom that goes beyond and the wisdom that has gone beyond. The former is the supreme wisdom directly realizing emptiness on the paths of seeing and meditation; it is the means by which you attain enlightenment. The latter is the completely perfect wisdom of a buddha. In the context of the six perfections, the perfection of wisdom refers to both the wisdom within the mental continuum of a bodhisattva and the wisdom within the mental continuum of a buddha. According to some other schools, the perfections only belong to the continuum of a buddha. However, Mādhyamikas say the phrase "gone to the other side" is like the term "burning." "Burning" can refer to the fuel, the fire, or the action; fuel is burning, fire is burning it, and burning is occurring. Similarly, "gone to the other side" can apply to what has gone, where it has gone, and the activity of having gone. Prior to a direct realization of emptiness, an ordinary bodhisattva's practice of any of the six perfections is the practice of a perfection; however, it is a mundane perfection because it is not pervaded by a direct realization of śūnyatā. After having seen emptiness directly, an ārya bodhisattva's practice of any of the six perfections is a supramundane perfection. Candrakīrti says in *Introduction to the "Middle Way"*:

> When the gift, the giving, and the giver are seen as empty,
> This is called the supramundane perfection of generosity.
> Where attachment to those three arises,
> This is called the mundane perfection of generosity. (1.16)

In the case of wisdom, the term *perfection of wisdom* encompasses the mundane and the supramundane perfection of wisdom. Even though a bodhisattva's wisdom may not be as complete as a buddha's wisdom, it is still called the perfection of wisdom.

The opponent persists in asserting that *analysis* means to grasp at signs, and therefore all analysis is a hindrance. Tsongkhapa reminds him that the need for precise analytical investigation is taught in many sutras and other works. Therefore the opponent's position—that it is wrong to analyze because it is wrong to grasp at signs—contradicts the scriptures. Given his interpretation, the opponent cannot account for why the holy texts teach in some places that you must analyze until you find not even the tiniest atom existing from its own side, and in other places that you must not grasp at signs. The opponent has no justification for asserting that *grasping at signs* means analysis or examination. He immediately runs into contradictions similar to those that arise from holding the view of Hashang. If he asserts that *grasping at signs* refers to every kind of thought, he must accept that everything we think and do binds us to samsara. So we cannot do anything. We even have to stop thinking "I want to request teachings on emptiness and meditate on them" because that would be a thought binding us to cyclic existence. This has already been refuted many times.

In short, these scriptural passages do not support the opponent's interpretation of *analysis* to mean grasping at signs. So what is the meaning of the phrase *grasping at signs*? According to Tsongkhapa, if you examine the relevant scriptural passages, you will see that *grasping at signs* means to grasp at true existence. So the exhortation to not grasp at signs is telling us, "Do not grasp things to be truly existent." It does not mean, "Do not think." It is not contradictory to say that we must not grasp at signs and yet we must analyze. Ceasing to grasp at signs—in other words negating the thought grasping at true existence—is similar to no longer fearing the presence of a snake in your room because you now recognize that you mistook a coiled rope to be a real snake. The only way to eliminate your fear is to investigate the object. Through examination you come to understand that no real snake exists in the way that you thought it did. Similarly, in order to understand that things we hold to be truly existent do not really exist as we believe they do, we must logically analyze them. Then we must meditate and become accustomed to the meaning that we have arrived at through our examination so that it becomes spontaneous and influences our mind.

This is the meaning of meditation. It is a tool to familiarize ourselves with an object so that our understanding becomes deeper and more powerful. In order to gain a profound familiarity, we need to alternate between analytical meditation and stabilizing meditation. When we investigate using ultimate analysis, we think about how a thing is empty, why it is empty, in what way it is empty, and then focus on the meaning of that. This is how wisdom becomes spontaneous and influences our mind. Our usual experience is that the mind races here and there, holding so many things to be truly existent. We cannot solve this problem just by bringing the mind back inside, not apprehending any object, and not thinking anything. Meditation is not to merely sit still and focus on one object. Such a simplistic method cannot eliminate the mind of ignorance that grasps things to be truly existent.

We must accept that the mind grasping at true existence is mistaken. If it were not mistaken, then there would be no point in stopping it. But we cannot know that the mind grasping at true existence is mistaken unless we understand that the object held by it does not exist. Whether a mind is mistaken or not depends on whether an object exists or does not exist as it is held by that mind. So in order to understand that the grasping at true existence is mistaken, we need to prove to ourselves that the object of this grasping does not exist. We must rely on faultless logic and scripture. Simply saying, "Nothing exists as it is held by the mind grasping things to be truly existent," does not establish it to be mistaken. Therefore we engage in reasoning and scriptural study to establish the emptiness of true existence. Then we place the mind in meditative equipoise focused on that emptiness, without conceiving anything as truly existent. In brief, nonconceptual wisdom must be preceded by precise analytical wisdom that examines whether the object is real as it is held by the mind grasping it to be truly existent. It is not enough merely to stop all conceptual activity. As Kamalaśīla's final *Stages of Meditation* says:

> Thus, when [instructions] such as "without recollection" and "without mental activity" occur in the holy scriptures, you must see that precise ultimate analysis precedes them. For it is only through precise ultimate analysis that you are able to engage in meditation "without recollection" and "without mental activity." There is no other way.

Also:

> Sutras such as the *Cloud of Jewels Sutra* and the *Sutra Unraveling the Intended Meaning* say that precise ultimate analysis is the nature of vipaśyanā. The *Cloud of Jewels Sutra* says:
>
>> Having analyzed by means of vipaśyanā, you realize the absence of essential nature. This is engaging in the signless [meditation].
>
> The *Descent into Laṅka Sutra* says:

> Mahāmati, it is said that all phenomena have no essential nature because when analyzed by means of wisdom, their particular and general characteristics are not found.

> If you do not engage in precise ultimate analysis, then you are acting contrary to Buddha's instruction in many sutras that you must engage in precise ultimate analysis. So although it is acceptable to say, "I have little wisdom and little diligence, therefore I cannot study or investigate extensively," it is wrong to abandon extensive study all the time, because Buddha highly commended it.

The last sentence in this passage means that it is acceptable to say that you are incapable of studying extensively because of your personal limitations. This is very different from saying that you should not study or analyze because thoughts bind you to samsara. It is not correct to say that learning and study, which Buddha praised, should be abandoned in general. If you say that, you are abandoning what Buddha taught.

Likewise, scriptural passages that teach that the mind should not dwell on any phenomena from form up to omniscience must be understood to mean that we should not grasp anything to be truly existent. The phrase "from form up to omniscience" refers to all the impure phenomena of samsara and all the pure phenomena beyond it. None of these ultimately exist; therefore they are not suitable to be held as truly existent objects on which the mind can settle. If we do not interpret such statements in this way, then it would absurdly follow that we should not think about or practice the six perfections because they are included in the category of things on which the mind should not dwell. As already explained, all the scriptural passages that teach things like "Do not dwell on anything" or "Do not think about anything" presume that the practitioner has already engaged in precise ultimate analysis negating the object's true or inherent existence. To properly "not dwell" and "not think" about an object depends on an understanding that the object is not truly existent. So instructions such as "Do not dwell on anything" and "Do not think about anything" are not directed to those who have neither analyzed the truth nor understood emptiness.

Where the scriptures speak of śūnyatā as "inconceivable" and "beyond the intellect," it is to negate the misconception that something so profound can be fully understood through study and analysis. Some people conceitedly think that they have fully realized emptiness based only on the wisdom arisen from hearing and thinking. Although it is true that emptiness is the object of the wisdom arisen from hearing and thinking, in such cases it is understood via a mental image. Only the direct perception of an ārya actually sees śūnyatā exactly as it is. The object of that direct realization cannot be fully understood by an ordinary person's wisdom, which arises from hearing or from thinking. But this does not mean that studying and thinking about śūnyatā is unnecessary. Without thinking about śūnyatā, after having received appropriate teachings, there is no possibility of developing a direct perception that knows śūnyatā exactly as it is. Kamalaśīla's final *Stages of Meditation* says:

> Thus wherever you hear words such as "inconceivable," it is for the purpose of stopping the conceit of those who think they understand śūnyatā merely by having heard and thought about it. These words show that phenomena are to be known by an individual's direct awareness. You should understand that this rejects inappropriate thinking to be correct but does not reject precise ultimate analysis. Otherwise it would contradict a great many logical reasons and scriptures.

What scriptures is Kamalaśīla claiming that this would contradict? It would contradict this statement from the *Kāśyapa Chapter Sutra*:

> Kāśyapa, what is the middle way that precisely analyzes phenomena in terms of the ultimate? Kāśyapa, it precisely analyzes the self to be nonexistent [ultimately], it precisely analyzes a sentient being, a living being, a nourished being, a creature, a person, a vital being, an able being, to be nonexistent [ultimately]. Kāśyapa, this is called the middle way that precisely analyzes phenomena in terms of the ultimate.

The statement that śūnyatā is "inconceivable" also refutes the incorrect idea that the profound meaning of emptiness truly exists. For example, to explain the Dharma Jewel in the *Uttara Tantra*, Maitreya composed stanzas describing the true paths and the true cessations. The true paths are the direct realizations of śūnyatā within the mindstream of an ārya; the objects of these realizations are the true cessations—śūnyatā itself. The qualities of the true cessations are described as:

> Inconceivable, nondual, nonconceptual,
> Pure, clear, and remedial.[204]

Maitreya describes emptiness this way to dispel any holding of it as truly existent, not to deny the need for analytical investigation of the ultimate.

Kamalaśīla's first *Stages of Meditation* says:

The *Formula for Entering the Nonconceptual* (*Avikalpa-praveśa-dhāraṇī*) says:

> You abandon the signs of forms and so on by not thinking.

Here "not thinking" refers to a nonseeing by wisdom when analyzing. It does not mean simply not thinking; that would be like meditative equipoise without discernment. You cannot abandon the beginning-less grasping at forms and so on by merely abandoning thinking.

Kamalaśīla here explains that when the scriptures say "not thinking" we should understand it to mean that when we engage in ultimate analysis we do not find anything that exists from its own side. In other words, because there is no intrinsically existent thing to see or think about, there is no seeing and no thinking of that nature. If "not thinking" simply meant the stopping of thought, it would be no different from meditative equipoise without discernment.

To appreciate Kamalaśīla's point, we have to understand the nature of meditative equipoise without discernment. This is one of three states without thought propounded by the Vaibhāṣika system: the meditative equipoise without discernment, one without discernment,[205] and the meditative equipoise of cessation. The Vaibhāṣikas assert that there is no mind at all during these three states. The upper schools say that the subtle mind is still present because if that stops, the individual dies; so they say that mainly it is feeling and discernment that are stopped. According to the Vaibhāṣikas, although the mind has stopped during all three of these states, the person does not die because there is a special nonassociated conditioning factor within their mental continuum called *obtainment*, which enables the mind to arise again at the appropriate time. This system holds that the mind can temporarily stop for eons. It is like sleep: before falling asleep we have lots of thoughts, which cease when we fall asleep; then immediately upon waking the next morning our minds think all kinds of things again.

Of these three states, only the first is an actual meditative absorption. It arises from meditation and develops into an absorption without discernment; it is a virtuous state. The latter two states are not really meditative absorptions. The second, one without discernment, is a karmic ripening that results from extensive practice of the first, the meditative equipoise without discernment. This ripened result is a natural lack of discriminative awareness within the continuum of one who has taken rebirth in the realm of the gods without discernment—the so-called sleeping gods. In general a ripened result is not a person; it is a nonassociated conditioning factor within the continuum of a person. For example, a hell being's experience is a ripened result, but the hell being himself is not a ripened result. We humans also possess countless ripened results, though we are not ripened results ourselves. A ripened result is scripturally unspecified; it is neutral—neither virtuous nor nonvirtuous. The third, the meditative equipoise of cessation, is a cessation. It is the complete cessation of discriminative perception, arisen from meditation directed toward stopping all thought. It is a highly virtuous state, attained only by ārya beings.

Those who engage in the meditative equipoise without discernment are not āryas. They are ordinary individuals who have a rough understanding that misery is a result of karma and that karma is created through the power of the mental afflictions. These practitioners probably believe that afflictions, such as attachment and hatred, arise from thinking. Fed up with the suffering of samsara, they use a particular technique to develop mundane śamatha and vipaśyanā—which is not the special insight understanding śūnyatā. However, in combination with single-pointed concentration and the motivation to be free from the mental afflictions and rebirth in samsara, these practitioners accomplish the meditations of the first three dhyānas and attain the fourth dhyāna. The fourth dhyāna, the highest level of the form realm, is the mind most suitable for meditation. It is neither too rough, like the prior levels of the form realm and the desire realm, nor is it too subtle, like the formless-realm dhyānas. According to the Vaibhāṣika system, on the fourth dhyāna this type of practitioner first stops the sense consciousnesses from arising, then he or she stops gross thoughts from arising and eventually stops the mind altogether. At this point the mind does not arise; it is so deeply absorbed—without any thought at all—that it is like the unconsciousness of heavy sleep. The Vaibhāṣikas seem to believe that this nondiscriminating state is the attainment of a rough kind of peace or nirvana, but there appears to be some confusion here. In any case, according to their view the meditative equipoise attained by this practice is not a mind. Consciousness has been completely worn away; all that is left is the body, and based on the body there is an equipoise that stops the arising of any feeling or thought. It is a virtuous nonassociated conditioning factor; it is neither form nor consciousness.

If a human being meditates for a long time in this meditative equipoise without discernment, his or her next rebirth will be in the realm of gods without discriminating awareness. This rebirth as a sleeping god is included within the fourth dhyāna level—which contains eight of the heavenly realms. The first three realms are where ordinary individuals take rebirth as a result of great merit. The five higher realms are called the five pure lands, where only āryas can take rebirth. Beings who take rebirth as sleeping gods in an ordinary heavenly realm of the fourth dhyāna initially have one short moment of consciousness and then immediately become unconscious. They may remain in this state for eons without waking up. This is the karmic result of having accomplished the meditative equipoise without discernment in their previous life. When that karma is exhausted, after so many eons, they die. At the time of death, a moment of conceiving or grasping arises—due to the force of some other karma in their mindstreams—which propels them into their next life. But in the meantime, from the first moment of birth in this realm until the final moment of grasping at the time of death, there are no other thoughts or perceptions.

So there are three kinds of states without thought. The first and second of these are two aspects of one causal process. The first is a genuine meditative equipoise that stops the arising of consciousness in a particular lifetime. The second is the resultant rebirth as a god without discriminating awareness in the very next lifetime. The former is virtuous because it occurs through meditation motivated by some kind of wish to be free from samsara. The lack of mental activity in the following rebirth is not virtuous; it is neutral because it is a karmic ripening that naturally occurs without any intention or effort. The third state, the meditative equipoise of cessation, is also the stopping of thought. But in this case it is a virtuous state attained by āryas with a special motivation. Even arhats may sometimes utilize this practice.

Kamalaśīla warns that if we interpret the phrase "not thinking" to mean the cessation of thought, then that meditation would be like the meditative equipoise without discernment. The problem here is that a practitioner who engages in the meditative equipoise without discernment does not remove the grasping at true existence. He or she temporarily stops thought and gains a high rebirth. But most texts say that during life as a form-realm god, individuals just use up previously created virtuous karma; they do not create virtuous karma, nor do they purify any nonvirtuous karma. All their karmic seeds remain in their mindstreams. So when the virtuous karma that caused this birth as a god is used up, the individual is likely to take rebirth in a lower realm. Similarly, merely abandoning thought cannot eliminate the ignorance grasping phenomena to be truly existent.

In brief, within the Mahayana there is no view other than those explained in the commentaries of the noble Nāgārjuna and Asaṅga and their respective followers. Asaṅga explains the Yogācāra view and Nāgārjuna explains the Madhyamaka view. It is evident that the holy masters of India and Tibet rely on one of those two. Therefore we too should strive to understand one of the views as these masters explain it in their writings. How to arrive at an understanding of the Madhyamaka view based on the texts of Nāgārjuna and Āryadeva has already been explained above.

According to Asaṅga, the object apprehended and the subject apprehending it are ultimately empty of being substantially different from each other in any way. Both the subject, which is a mind, and the object that it apprehends are the same nature; they are both in the nature of the mind—hence the appellation "Mind Only." In the Yogācāra system emptiness is the lack of subject-object duality. However, to ordinary individuals the subject and its object appear to be completely different entities, and ordinary beings hold them to be substantially different, just as they appear. This false imputed nature—subject-object duality—does not exist at all. Yet ordinary beings hold it to be truly existent: this is the grasping at a self of phenomena. The false imputed nature, which does not exist, is based on an actual dependent nature, which does exist. All objects perceived and the minds perceiving them are dependent on causes and conditions, thus they are dependent natures. Dependent natures are not negated. The main target to be negated in this system is the false imputed nature—subject-object duality—held to be truly existent. Buddhist scriptures and reasoning totally negate this false imputed nature and establish its opposite: the lack of subject-object duality, which is the thoroughly established nature, śūnyatā.

Any disciple of Asaṅga, having arrived at this understanding of emptiness, engages in both precise analytical meditation as well as stabilizing meditation placed on that view. If instead you just stop thinking after having understood the correct view, you would not be meditating on emptiness. In his *Instructions for the Perfection of Wisdom*, the great Indian master Ratnākaraśānti gives a clear explanation of how to establish the view and employ the various meditation techniques according to the Yogācāra system. First you establish an understanding of śūnyatā—the emptiness of duality. Then you meditate on it using śamatha and vipaśyanā meditation, initially separately and then in union. Tsongkhapa says that if you understand this system well and meditate on it in accordance with this commentary, you will attain marvelous results. Although Tsongkhapa is not a follower of the Yogācāra, here he expresses his appreciation for that view; indeed it can act as a steppingstone to the Madhyamaka view. But the main point here is that just stopping discursive thought is neither the Madhyamaka view nor the Yogācāra view of meditation on emptiness.

There are many great Mahayana texts, from the longest sutras and śāstras to the extremely short ones, which teach the profound meaning of śūnyatā. There are also quite a few Mahayana scriptures that explain the method side of practice and do not offer a profound teaching of śūnyatā. So when you put into practice these texts' instructions regarding the bodhisattvas' extensive practices of love, compassion, and bodhicitta, you must add what they do not teach explicitly by drawing on a teaching on śūnyatā from other texts that do explain it. Conversely you need to supplement texts that only explicitly teach emptiness with instructions on the method side of practice from other texts. In this way each teaching supplements the other. An explanation that lacks either the profound view or the extensive method is an incomplete and one-sided teaching. It is not suitable to rely on such a partial explanation as a final teaching. This is why so much emphasis is placed on the characteristics of a lama who is completely qualified to show the path to enlightenment—such a teacher should be a master of all the vehicles.

⊹ 24 ⊹

Uniting Śamatha and Vipaśyanā

(c") A summary of the key points for maintaining this meditation
(d') The measure of achieving insight through meditation
   (iii) How to unite śamatha and vipaśyanā

———◈———

(c") A SUMMARY OF THE KEY POINTS FOR MAINTAINING THIS MEDITATION

AS EXPLAINED EARLIER, when you arrive at the definitive view realizing emptiness, you understand that the self and belonging to the self—the basis on which the egotistic view grasping "me" and "mine" arises—do not inherently exist. Just as you did when first establishing the emptiness of inherent existence, you must engage continuously in precise ultimate analysis again and again to produce a powerful understanding of the ultimate meaning. Then you practice stabilizing meditation—holding your mind in that view without distraction, and alternate this with analytical meditation—examining the object with precise analytical wisdom. If you do too much analytical meditation, your stabilization may become weak. In that case do more stabilizing meditation to recover it. However, it is not good to do too much stabilizing meditation, where your stability becomes so strong that you no longer wish to engage in analytical practice, because if you do not analyze you will not develop a firm and powerful understanding of śūnyatā. Without the wisdom understanding śūnyatā, its opposite—the superimposing mind grasping the two selves to exist inherently—will not be damaged at all. In order to weaken and eventually destroy all grasping at inherent existence, your wisdom must be sharp and strong. Therefore you need to meditate in a balanced way—without too much single-pointed absorption and without too much ultimate analysis. If one is strong and the other is weak, you need to increase the strength of the weaker one. You work back and forth to keep a fine balance between these two practices. Kamalaśīla's final *Stages of Meditation* says:

> When, through vipaśyanā meditation, wisdom becomes very strong and śamatha weak, the mind wavers like a butter lamp in the wind, so you are not able to see reality clearly. Therefore at that time you should do śamatha meditation. When śamatha is very strong [and vipaśyanā weak], then, like a person asleep, you cannot see reality clearly. Therefore at that time you should do wisdom meditation.

You need to know how to prepare for a meditation session, how to conclude a meditation session, and how to behave in between meditation sessions. The postmeditation period is just as important as the meditation session. If you engage in serious meditation but act wildly afterward, the qualities you developed in meditation will be destroyed. After meditating you need to study the topic of your meditation and think about it further. Tsongkhapa reminds us that he explained this earlier in the context of the person of small spiritual scope.[206] The same instructions apply when meditating on selflessness.

During the meditation session, it is crucially important to recognize mental sinking and excitement. Tsongkhapa already explained this in detail in the section on meditative concentration.[207] To review briefly, there are many kinds of mental sinking: gross sinking, subtle sinking, and so on. If the grossest kind of mental sinking or torpor occurs, you may need to get up and go for a walk to refresh yourself. Subtle mental sinking is more dangerous because it can seem like perfect samādhi. The various types of excitement are based on attachment. During a meditation session, instead of remaining on the object of meditation your mind keeps going toward other things that you previously enjoyed or hope to enjoy in the future. When sinking or excitement interferes with your meditation, taking a rest is not the right strategy on most occasions. Instead you should immediately take action to eliminate them by employing their antidotes: mindfulness and introspection. Mindfulness is a mental factor that holds the mind on its object; it does not let the mind forget or wander. Introspection is a mental factor that continuously checks to see if the mind is experiencing sinking or excitement; it is like a little spy in a corner of your mind, quietly noticing any comings and goings of other mental states. If you can identify sinking and excitement before they have fully arisen, you can stop them from interfering. If you keep the mind free from these unbalancing influences, it will naturally do what it is supposed to do without any problem. You can relax your effort and simply maintain equanimity.

There are many kinds of equanimity: the equanimity between love and hate, the equanimity between pleasant and unpleasant feelings, the balance between doing too much and doing nothing at all. Here it refers to the equanimity of mental activity: a mind free from the faults of sinking and excitement, which can stay on its object without additional effort. In the section on meditative concentration, Tsongkhapa explains that equanimity is one of the eight antidotes used to combat the five major faults affecting śamatha and vipaśyanā meditations. The first fault is laziness: you do not want to meditate or even go to your meditation seat. The second fault is forgetfulness: you want to meditate, but you cannot remember the instructions you were given. The third fault is twofold, sinking and excitement: you have the energy to meditate and remember the instructions, but these mental factors disturb your focus. The fourth fault is not applying the antidotes to sinking and excitement. The fifth fault is applying an antidote when it is not needed. To combat the last three faults you must recognize when sinking and excitement are arising and then apply their antidotes: mindfulness and introspection. When there is no sinking or excitement and your śamatha is perfect, you should not apply any additional effort; just remain in equanimity focused on the object of meditation.

In *Instructions for the Perfection of Wisdom*, Ratnākaraśānti presents a slightly different method to conjoin śamatha and vipaśyanā. He says that when you maintain śamatha on an object, a special mental and physical pliancy arises. After this, by engaging in insight meditation on that same object another kind of pliancy arises. Having accomplished each of these separately, you practice them together. According to him it is not necessary to practice śamatha and vipaśyanā in the same meditation session. You can practice them in separate sessions and combine them in a later session. This is one way of understanding how to join śamatha and vipaśyanā. Then there is another way to understand it; you practice śamatha and vipaśyanā alternately in one session, and in that same session you unite them.

Tsongkhapa emphasizes that in both methods you must completely negate the existence of the held object as it is imputed by your own ignorance and develop a powerful understanding of its opposite—the emptiness of inherent existence—and meditate on that emptiness. This is the most important point here. If you meditate on a completely different kind of emptiness—one that does not negate the self-grasping mind or the way that ignorance grasps its object—you will not remove ignorance or self-grasping in the least. For if your object of meditation is totally unconnected with your goal, then no matter how much you meditate it will not affect the situation. As Gendun Drup says, it would be like "Giving a ransom at the western door when the demon is at the eastern door." This saying refers to a tantric ritual practiced in Tibet that may have come from India. People pay a ransom to chase away a demon that is making someone ill. An image of the sick person is made out of dough, finely dressed, and offered to the demon along with butter lamps, other gifts, and a specially blessed ritual cake. In return for these, the demon is entreated to leave and no longer harm the person. The ritual also includes a threat: if the demon remains, he will be destroyed. If you offer the ransom at the western door when the demon is at the eastern door, your action is unrelated to its object and will not help. Some great lamas and scholars of old would say that if your meditation on śūnyatā is unrelated to your own problems—ignorance, the egotistic view, the mental afflictions—then it is just as useless. You should meditate on something that destroys the cause of samsara; mediating on something unrelated, but called śūnyatā, will not help. This is true indeed.

Tsongkhapa says that his explanation of these meditation techniques is quite abbreviated. So you have to rely on genuine spiritual masters. Based on their instructions you will develop your own understanding through meditative experience. When you meditate, you will discover subtle good qualities and faults. Tsongkhapa does not elaborate here.

Tsongkhapa's explanation of these meditation methods is an expansion based on earlier instructions. The *Little Digest of Instructions (Be'u bum)* by the great Kadam lama Geshe Potowa says:

> Some say that when studying and thinking, you use reasoning
> To establish the emptiness of inherent existence;
> Then when you meditate, you meditate only nonconceptually.
> If that were the case, it would not relate to emptiness.
> Since you are meditating on something else, it is not the antidote.
> Therefore when you meditate, you must analyze
> Whether things are one or many or dependently arise
> And then remain on that without the least discursive thought.
> Meditating this way is the antidote to the mental afflictions.
> For those who wish to follow the divine one,
> And who wish to practice the perfection vehicle,
> The tradition of wisdom meditation is this.
> Therefore meditate on the selflessness of persons
> And then proceed in this way.

Atiśa was often called "the divine one" by his disciples. He and his disciple Dromtonpa[208] primarily taught the perfection vehicle, though they probably taught the tantrayāna secretly. Those who want to follow the great Atiśa and his instructions should meditate in this way. In his *Introduction to the Two Truths (Satya-dvayāvatāra)* Atiśa says:

If you ask, "What is the way to realize emptiness?"
Follow the one prophesied by the Buddha,
Who sees the truth of reality, Nāgārjuna,
And his disciple, Candrakīrti.
By means of the instructions from this lineage
You will realize the truth of reality.

Tsongkhapa quotes these passages on many occasions. They are one of the reasons he follows this lineage of instruction. Some Western scholars question whether Candrakīrti was Nāgārjuna's disciple or a later follower of Nāgārjuna's teachings. The term *disciple* implies direct contact between the teacher and the student. So when did Candrakīrti live? If the two men met, did Nāgārjuna live for six hundred years? Candrakīrti is Nāgārjuna's true follower in the sense that he proved Nāgārjuna's position. But who knows if he was a direct disciple?

This explanation of the way to meditate is in accordance with Atiśa's advice in the *Madhyamaka Instructions* (*Madhyamakopadeśa*). There he explains that you alternately practice analytical meditation and stabilizing meditation on the object. There is no difference between this approach and the system of Kamalaśīla. As explained earlier, it is also the implicit meaning of Candrakīrti's *Introduction to the "Middle Way*, Bhāvaviveka's *Heart of the Middle Way*, and Śāntideva's works. Furthermore, these meditation techniques are frequently explained in the five texts of Maitreya, as well as Asaṅga's works, such as the five treatises on the grounds and the two compendiums. This is also clearly explained in Ratnākaraśānti's *Instructions for the Perfection of Wisdom*. This great paṇḍita holds Asaṅga's system without error. So it is apparent that the lineages of texts and personal instructions coming from Nāgārjuna and Asaṅga agree about the way to meditate on śamatha and vipaśyanā individually and how to unite them. This does not imply that their view of emptiness is the same, but they are in accord about the way to meditate on it.

(d') THE MEASURE OF ACHIEVING INSIGHT THROUGH MEDITATION

When you are meditating on śūnyatā ascertained by precise analytical wisdom, you are not engaging in actual insight meditation until a special blissful mental and physical pliancy arises. Up to that point your analytical meditation is a similitude of insight meditation; it is close to vipaśyanā, but it does not have all the characteristics of vipaśyanā. The nature of this mental and physical pliancy, as well as how to produce them, is explained in detail in the section on śamatha.[209] There is nothing different about it here. However, merely having the pliancy induced by śamatha is not a sign of having attained vipaśyanā. Even if you have this pliancy while engaging in analytical meditation, it is still not enough to satisfy the criterion of the attainment of vipaśyanā. What you need is the pliancy that arises from insight itself. Mental and physical pliancy first arise through the power of śamatha. Later a different kind of pliancy arises through the power of analysis. The pliancy that arises through the power of analytical meditation is the mark of fully qualified vipaśyanā. That criterion is the same whether the object observed in meditation is the ultimate or the conventional. This special pliancy can be produced by a meditation comparing the grossness of the desire realm with the peacefulness of the first dhyāna, or comparing the first dhyāna with the second, and so forth, as well as by meditation on emptiness. In all cases, as you examine the characteristics of your meditation object, your mind becomes sharper and sharper. Finally this special kind of pliancy arises and you attain genuine insight. The *Sutra Unraveling the Intended Meaning* says:

> "Bhagavan, until bodhisattvas achieve pliancy of body and mind, what do we call the meditative attention they use to carefully think about phenomena and analyze the internal images that are the object of their concentration?"
>
> "Maitreya, it is not insight, but we may say it is concordant with the mind of aspiration accompanying insight."

Here Buddha refers to the fact that every primary consciousness has many accompanying mental factors, such as wisdom, aspiration, concentration, feeling, and so on. The mental factors of concentration and aspiration that accompany this meditative attention are similar to those that accompany insight. This mind is not fully qualified insight; however, the way it analyzes is similar to insight. Ratnākaraśānti's *Instructions for the Perfection of Wisdom* says:

> That [bodhisattva] abiding in the mental and physical pliancy already attained [through śamatha] precisely analyzes with great aspiration whatever object has been contemplated. This object of concentration is an internal image. As long as [further] mental and physical pliancy have not arisen, this [analytical wisdom] is similar to insight; once they have arisen, it is insight.

This text makes the point that, no matter what is taken as the object of meditation, the criterion marking the arising of vipaśyanā is the same. Śamatha, vipaśyanā, and their union may observe conventional things or ultimate truth.

Initially it may seem that analysis and concentration interrupt each other. Having placed your mind single-pointedly on an object, you may not want to engage in analysis because it disturbs your concentration. Although analytical meditation focuses on one object, it involves searching for the depths of reality by examining many different attributes of that object; in other words, it is not single-pointed. However, when precise analytical meditation itself has the power to induce mental and physical pliancy, then it can induce single-pointed concentration. This means that śamatha and vipaśyanā need not interrupt each other. Only someone who has already accomplished śamatha can induce single-pointed concentration by means of analytical meditation. When a yogi who has developed śamatha engages in analytical meditation, that analytical meditation assists the further development of his or her śamatha. So you should not think that doing precise analytical meditation will diminish your fully focused calm awareness. Although this might be true in general, it is not the case once you have already developed śamatha. Insight meditation can give rise to a special śamatha on the basis of śamatha previously induced by single-pointed concentration.

The criterion of proper insight meditation combining analytical and stabilizing meditation on śūnyatā is to have gained a pure and faultless understanding of either of the two types of selflessness and to meditate on the object of that view. There is no other basis for identifying insight. It entirely depends on a union of analytical and stabilizing meditation focusing on emptiness. If it is focused on anything else, even on other things that are called śūnyatā, it is not true insight meditation. Here "other things" refers to experiences that follow from having achieved śamatha using emptiness as an object, such as the experience of illusion-like appearances and so on. Those of you who meditate may have experienced this; it is a bit difficult to explain to those who do not meditate. In brief, when people start to meditate there is a dualistic appearance of subject and object. Then after meditating for a long time, the gross appearance of subject-object duality eventually disappears. As a result, the mind becomes clear and vivid, like pristine space or a cloudless autumn sky. The mind is then able to stay on its object for a very long time; it is as stable as a butter lamp in the absence of wind. The appearances of external and internal things become transparent, like a rainbow or a smoky haze. These appearances cannot withstand being looked at; if you pay a little more attention to them, they just disappear. At first gross external objects, such as shapes, sounds, and so on, disappear. Then as you meditate more, the experiencing subject cannot withstand that attention either. Eventually subjective experiences and the knowledge you previously possessed also disappear. When no attention is paid to them, the subject and object seem to be there. But when you look, they fundamentally vanish. Some people say that this experience is the criterion for the accomplishment of śamatha and vipaśyanā meditation on śūnyatā. However, this is not the criterion that signifies having found the view realizing nondual reality. Also the arising of these indistinct, translucent appearances is not the measure of having realized the illusion-like nature as explained in the Madhyamaka system. Anyone can have such experiences if they engage in stabilizing meditation for long enough, even if they pay no attention to the view and have no understanding of it.

According to the Madhyamaka system, to realize illusion-like appearances means to understand that the object is empty of true existence and also that the appearance of the object cannot be denied. The experience of translucency described above does not involve understanding this combination. As explained earlier, to realize illusion-like appearances you first come to a definite understanding that things are not inherently existent; then, together with that understanding, you realize that forms, sounds, and all the other things of this world appear and cannot be denied because they are established by conventional valid awareness. There must be these two aspects: definitely understanding that things are not inherently existent, and knowing that their conventional existence cannot be denied. In other words, it is to simultaneously recognize that things do not exist as they appear and yet they conventionally exist. In dependence on knowing this, things appear like illusions to bodhisattvas who have realized emptiness. These holy beings perceive the illusion-like nature of things: things appear to them, yet they understand their emptiness. It is through a combination of conventional and ultimate knowledge that things appear illusion-like.

The perception of the illusion-like nature that arises as a result of understanding emptiness is not at all like the ordinary experience of translucency that follows the śamatha meditation described above. In that ordinary experience, gross things, such as forms, appear in the mind to be as clear and transparent as a rainbow. Meditators who have mastered this śamatha technique see things as empty of solidity and resistance, but they do not understand that what they see is empty of inherent existence. It is inappropriate to interpret the term "not inherently existent" to mean that things, which look solid and tangible, in fact do not exist that way. Understanding that things are free of solidity and yet appear is not the same as understanding that things are empty of inherent existence and yet appear. If you think these are the same, then you have conflated solidity with inherent nature and a lack of solidity with emptiness. If this equivalence were the Madhyamaka explanation of the subtle illusion-like nature, then we would never give rise to the thought that grasps a rainbow or some other insubstantial thing to be inherently existent: everyone would already know that rainbows and similar things are not inherently existent owing to the mere reason that they lack solidity. Through simply understanding the basis—the rainbow—we would know that it lacks inherent nature. Conversely when a tangible thing, such as a table, is taken as the basis, we would never understand that it lacks inherent nature, since the table is solid. Every tangible thing is held to be solid and therefore inherently existent on this interpretation, just as it appears. So if a lack of inherent nature is taken to mean having a nonsolid nature, there would be nothing to realize in either case: an insubstantial thing, such as a rainbow, is already known to be not solid, so recognizing its lack of inherent nature would not be a new realization; and a solid thing is not insubstantial, so it could never be realized to lack inherent nature.

Clearly this is not the Madhyamaka interpretation of a lack of inherent nature nor of illusion-like appearances. These ordinary meditators do not understand that the insubstantial appearances of forms and so on lack inherent reality. They do not understand the view of emptiness that negates inherent existence. Instead they think that these strange and indistinct appearances are the ultimate reality of forms and so on. According to the Madhyamaka system, a genuine illusion-like appearance arises only if you have understood and not forgotten the emptiness of inherent existence. The main point is that you must understand the emptiness of inherent existence of things and that this emptiness is their ultimate nature. Without this understanding you have not found the Madhyamaka view. Moreover, any insubstantial appearances that do not result from the realization of śūnyatā are not authentic illusion-like appearances. It is true that without having understood emptiness you may have experiences that seem similar. Yogis definitely have these kinds of experiences. Also people who have consumed alcohol, taken drugs, or suffer from certain diseases may experience strange things appearing, such as hallucinations. These insubstantial appearances might be mistaken for appearances of the illusion-like nature, but they should not be confused with the subtle illusion-like nature that appears as a result of understanding emptiness.

The lamrim lineage that comes to us from the Kadampa Geshe Gonpawa teaches that to generate a realization of emptiness, we should begin by meditating on the selflessness of persons and then meditate on the selflessness of phenomena. Mindfulness and introspection are key instruments to use in both meditations. It is best not to make the meditation sessions too long. If they are too long, then mindfulness and introspection cannot catch all the disturbances. As a result, sinking and excitement will occur and our meditation will be less effective. Normally it is said that there are four major meditation sessions each day: morning, evening, dusk, and dawn. As you can see, the sessions are early and late; there is no session at noon or in the middle of the night. Each of these sessions should be divided into four. In the morning you should do four sessions, in the evening four sessions, and so on. That comes to sixteen meditation sessions every twenty-four hours. When you experience clarity or some other experience, you should stop. Do not continue when this happens, because if you carry on you will become exhausted. Check the length of time you have been meditating. Sometimes you may feel that you have not been meditating for very long, but when you look at the time you find that an entire day has passed. When it seems that a day has gone by in an instant, it is a sign that your mind has been properly caught up in meditation. After such a session you feel that your delusions and dullness are reduced. Your mind feels fresh and clear and you wonder whether you will ever need to sleep again. In contrast, if you feel that you have been meditating a long time, but when you check the clock you find that hardly any time has passed, it means your mind has not been properly engaged in meditation.

If you meditate properly during every meditation session, a concentration possessing four special characteristics will arise. The first quality is nonconceptuality, in the sense of nondiscursiveness: your mind is concentrating so well that your breath and thought become very subtle—you do not even feel your breath going in and out. The second quality is clarity: your mind is as clear as a noon sky in autumn. In some parts of the world, including India and certain areas of Tibet, the sky is full of humidity and clouds during the summer rainy season; then in autumn, after the rains have stopped, the sky is crystal clear. The third quality is limpidity: your mind is free of impurities—as vivid and pure as a bowl of clean water in the sunshine. The fourth quality is subtlety: with a mind having the first three qualities you can see minute details—even the parts of the tip of a hair when it is split into sections. Some other texts even say that a mind having this quality of subtlety, combined with nondiscursiveness, clarity, and vividness, can see each and every piece of a hair split into a hundred sections.

A concentration with these four characteristics is very similar to, but is not, nonconceptual wisdom. Nonconceptual wisdom is a direct realization of emptiness; it is an ārya's realization of ultimate truth—the final, subtlest nature of all things. By comparison to nonconceptual wisdom, this kind of concentration is somewhat rough; it is conceptual. In that respect it is wrong or distorted because all conceptual thought is mistaken consciousness. As explained earlier, even if a conceptual consciousness correctly understands its object, it is mistaken; in the case of sentient beings, only an ārya's direct realization of emptiness is a nonmistaken consciousness. Maitreya's *Separation of the Middle from the Extremes* says, "This similar one is mistaken." According to this text an ordinary individual's meditation on śūnyatā, even the best of them, must be considered mistaken. For example, the instant before you attain the path of seeing, you are engaged in meditation on emptiness at the highest level of the path of preparation. This is very close to a direct realization; it is the last moment of realizing śūnyatā as an ordinary individual. In the next moment of that meditation session you will become an ārya. However, during that final moment of meditative equipoise on the path of preparation, your meditation on emptiness is still conceptual because a very subtle mental image of śūnyatā appears mixed together with śūnyatā. Although this meditative equipoise is similar to nonconceptual wisdom, it is a mistaken consciousness because it is a conceptual realization of emptiness.

If a yogi correctly understands emptiness and meditates on it, then this meditation is an actual meditation on śūnyatā, even if it does not possess the characteristics described above. If a yogi lacks an understanding of emptiness and is not meditating on the object of the correct view, then even if this meditation possesses all the characteristics described above, it is not a meditation on the definitive meaning, śūnyatā. In other words, the criterion to determine whether a meditation is a meditation on śūnyatā or not is as explained above: one must find a pure and faultless understanding of either of the two types of selflessness and meditate on the object of that view. After having meditated on śūnyatā, a genuine illusion-like appearance will arise in the postmeditation period. Conventional things still appear to be truly existent, but having realized in meditation that they do not exist as they appear, they naturally appear to have an illusion-like nature in the postmeditation period.

(iii) HOW TO UNITE ŚAMATHA AND VIPAŚYANĀ

You cannot unite śamatha and vipaśyanā if you have not attained each of them according to the criterion explained above. As soon as you attain vipaśyanā, you will have attained this union. However, when you first attain śamatha, you have not attained this union and will not attain it until much later. Why is this so? To achieve vipaśyanā you must first develop śamatha, and as explained in volume 4 of this series, to achieve śamatha you must engage serially in the four mental attentions: tight focus, interrupted focus, uninterrupted focus, and spontaneous focus. To review these briefly, the sutras, commentaries, and lamrim texts teach that there are nine stages in the development of śamatha. In the beginning, on the first two stages it is difficult to maintain attention on the object; if you do not apply very strong effort you will not be able to meditate for even a few minutes. Your mind just wanders off and you lose the object. Thus because you have to maintain strict control of the mind, the first two stages are called tight focus. Meditation is slightly easier on the next five stages; however, it is called interrupted focus because you are still disturbed by sinking and excitement from time to time. These two faults were so prevalent on the first two stages that you spent most of your time in sinking and excitement rather than in meditation—so there is no need to talk about those early stages as being interrupted by sinking and excitement! The eighth stage is called uninterrupted focus; by making an effort at the start of a meditation session, your meditation will be strong, continuous, and uninterrupted by sinking and excitement. You need to apply a little effort to get going, but once you have started to meditate you just go along naturally without any more exertion. The ninth stage and fourth mental focus is very close to śamatha; it is spontaneous and occurs effortlessly. This is the subtlest, highest concentration of the desire realm; from there you go to the first dhyāna of the form realm.

Having achieved śamatha, you develop insight by applying the same four mental attentions to analytic practice. You go through the same nine stages to develop the pliancy of vipaśyanā. The process is to engage in analytical meditation and then place the mind on the object analyzed and remain with that for some time. Gradually your analytical meditation will become stabilizing meditation. When you attain spontaneous focus in the context of analytical meditation, your mind is able to stay on the object analyzed naturally, without needing a separate stabilizing meditation. At this point you have achieved the union of śamatha and vipaśyanā. Asaṅga's *Śrāvaka Levels* says:

> In what way are śamatha and vipaśyanā combined and balanced? Also why is this called the path of union? It is similar to the nine steps of mental abiding, where having attained the ninth, balanced placement, you achieve meditative concentration. In dependence on that, you strive to analyze phenomena with superior wisdom. When the wisdom analyzing phenomena effortlessly engages its object without any need to apply antidotes, as when having achieved śamatha, you attain vipaśyanā that is completely pure, completely free of faults, following closely after śamatha, and completely permeated by the special bliss of pliancy. Thus śamatha and vipaśyanā are combined and balanced; this is called the path of union of śamatha and vipaśyanā.

Kamalaśīla's final *Stages of Meditation* says:

> When, through being free of sinking and excitement, these two are equally balanced and naturally focused, so that the mind directed

toward reality becomes very clear, at which point effort is relaxed and equanimity spontaneously achieved, then you should understand that you have accomplished the union of śamatha and vipaśyanā.

Why is this called union? At earlier stages of practice, analytical meditation and stabilizing meditation interrupt each other; neither one brings about the other. You have to engage in analytical meditation and stabilizing meditation separately. But once you have accomplished both practices, then precise analytical meditation itself draws forth śamatha. The analytical part of the practice is vipaśyanā. After analysis, when the mind naturally abides on the object, it is the special śamatha observing śūnyatā. This is called union. Ratnākaraśānti's *Instructions for the Perfection of Wisdom* says:

> After that you look at the internal object of analysis. When the mind investigates that object continuously and uninterruptedly, you experience both. At this point it is called the path of union (*zung 'brel*). Here śamatha and vipaśyanā are a pair (*zung*), and connection (*'brel*) means possession in the sense of being mutually bound in their engagement.

On the path of union, engaging in vipaśyanā naturally involves śamatha, and engaging in śamatha naturally involves vipaśyanā. Each assists the other; they are not separate and neither interrupts the other. Prior to achieving this level, you had to stop analytical meditation in order to engage in stabilizing meditation, and vice versa. In the quotation above, "uninterruptedly" indicates that this no longer occurs; now analytical meditation draws forth śamatha and the two types of meditation assist each other. The phrase "experience both" refers to apprehending the mental objects observed by śamatha and vipaśyanā. This does not mean that these objects are necessarily experienced at exactly the same time. It means that you engage in a continuous stream of meditation; you do not have to stop one in order to begin the other. They are a continuum within one meditation session, each one bringing about the other. Thus *union* means that śamatha and vipaśyanā induce each other continuously instead of interrupting one another.

Someone asks, "Is it not contradictory to say that, after having achieved śamatha, you engage in precise analytical meditation to accomplish śamatha?" Tsongkhapa replies that prior to having achieved śamatha, if you repeatedly alternate between analytical meditation and postanalytical stabilizing meditation, you will not be able to accomplish śamatha—because at this stage, analytical meditation interrupts stabilizing meditation. After having achieved śamatha, engaging in analytical meditation can bring forth a special śamatha.

So there is no contradiction. It is important to understand at what point śamatha and vipaśyanā interrupt each other and at what point they are united. In general, prior to having achieved śamatha, analytical meditation and stabilizing meditation interrupt each other. There is just one exception to this: the analytical meditation immediately prior to attaining vipaśyanā. This is very close to vipaśyanā and can bring forth single-pointed meditative stabilization, just as vipaśyanā itself can do. This is the one exception to the explanation that, before having achieved śamatha, you will not be able to attain postanalytical śamatha if you keep alternating the practices of analytical meditation and stabilizing meditation. After having achieved śamatha, there is no such problem. But before that, if you want to develop śamatha, you should focus only on stabilizing meditation and avoid analysis.

In summary, if you have not yet achieved śamatha, you cannot accomplish it by alternately practicing stabilizing meditation and analytical meditation. You must continuously engage in stabilizing meditation. After having achieved śamatha, but before achieving vipaśyanā, just doing a little bit of analytical meditation will not be able to draw forth single-pointed meditative stabilization. However, if you do a lot of precise analytical meditation, you will eventually achieve a firm śamatha that has a special pliancy. At this point you have achieved vipaśyanā and entered into the union of śamatha and vipaśyanā. Do not make the mistake of thinking that the union of śamatha and vipaśyanā is the mere combination of the two: it is not simply being able to analyze the meaning of selflessness while staying totally unmoved in a state of nondiscursive tranquility, the way a little fish can swim around in a calm pond without disturbing the stillness of the water. This is the combination of śamatha and vipaśyanā, not their union. Their union requires that first you have śamatha, and then you engage in analytical meditation to bring forth a special blissful pliancy, a more advanced śamatha, which is itself vipaśyanā. Prior to that you may have something similar to this union, but it is not the real thing. So be careful not to confuse these. You should understand the way that śamatha and vipaśyanā are united as explained in the texts that are authoritative sources. Do not trust other sources that are just fabricated explanations. Tsongkhapa concludes that although there are many divisions and distinctions regarding the way to maintain śamatha and vipaśyanā, he did not write about them here for fear of going on too long.

⚜ 25 ⚜
Summary and Conclusion

b' How to train specifically in the Vajrayāna

A GENERAL SUMMARY OF THE PATH

J E Tsongkhapa now summarizes the detailed explanation of the path system presented in his *Lamrim Chenmo*. You can look back over the five volumes of this commentary to find a thorough explanation of each point. Or if you want an even briefer synopsis, you can reflect on a short prayer, *Foundation of All Good Qualities* (*Yon tan gzhir gyur ma*), which outlines the same thing. You may already be familiar with this prayer by Tsongkhapa. Let us turn to his summary of the *Lamrim Chenmo* here.

First if you are interested in the spiritual path, specifically the Mahayana path, you need to search for a spiritual teacher: this is the root of the path. Your success in following the path and developing realizations depends on your reliance on your teacher. However, it is not enough just to find a teacher; once you have found him or her, you cannot relax and do nothing. You should rely on your spiritual teacher in thought, word, and deed. You need to receive teachings, study them, analyze them, and meditate on them so as to develop your faith and devotion. This is how you prepare for the final experience.

Next you need to consider what an amazing opportunity you have in this life to accomplish the highest and most meaningful goal. For this purpose you meditate on the leisure and fortune of your present life so that a wish to accomplish that goal arises spontaneously within you. You think about how difficult it is to obtain such excellent conditions and you spur yourself on not to waste this rare opportunity. To develop a sense of urgency regarding your practice, you think, "Spiritual practice is the only significant thing in life, and this is my only chance to do it." Through your own reflection, with the help of your guru and spiritual friends, you develop a heartfelt aspiration to engage in spiritual practice and accomplish the goal. Therefore this is a very, very important meditation.

After realizing how meaningful and rare a human life with leisure and fortune is, you recognize the importance of this precious opportunity. However, worldly attitudes still continue to arise within you. If you do not reverse your attitudes that seek only worldly gain, pleasure, praise, and fame in this life, you will not strive to obtain a good future rebirth. To change your focus, it is important to meditate on the fact that your body does not survive for long and you may pass away at any time. By reflecting on the impermanence of life, you come to feel that you cannot waste even a moment. You need to think not only about impermanence but also about what will happen after you die. There are two possibilities: you can go up or you can go down. You must consider that if you fall down to a lower rebirth, you will wander around in the three lower realms without any control. You may be stuck there for eons completely under the power of your past karma. In order to understand the reality of this situation, you must reflect on the general nature of the three lower realms and the specific pain that you will experience in each of these states. Once you have understood that you could be born in a lower realm at any time, you experience a great fear of the pain of the lower realms. When you first begin this meditation practice, you have to try to make this fear arise; but continued meditation will transform your way of seeing the situation, and a fear of taking a lower rebirth will spontaneously arise all the time. This fear is a good thing; fearlessness is foolish and dangerous.

When you have developed this spontaneous fear, you will yearn for something that can protect you. Searching for this, you recognize that such protection can be found only in the three objects of refuge: Buddha, Dharma, and Sangha. Buddha is the one who shows the refuge; he is like the doctor who has diagnosed our fundamental problem and prescribes the cure. Dharma is the real refuge; it is like the medicine we take to cure the cause of our pain. Sangha is the holy community that assists in taking refuge; they are like the nurses who help us to apply the medicine prescribed by the doctor. When you reflect on the perfect qualities of these Three Jewels, you develop a clear understanding of their protective power; then you take refuge in them from the depths of your heart. What does it mean to think or say "I go for refuge"? Primarily this act indicates trust: you trust that the Three Jewels have the power to protect you from what you most fear—rebirth in the three lower realms. Complete and sincere reliance on the triple gem is called "trusting faith"; this in itself is going for refuge. When you go for refuge to the Three Jewels, you must follow their guidance: they lead you to abandon evil because it is the cause of all suffering and to engage in virtue because it is the source of all happiness. That is the main Dharma practice. In order to fully engage in this practice, you may choose to take vows. The prātimokṣa vows are common to all three Buddhist vehicles; they train you to control your actions and enable you to attain individual liberation. When seriously trying to practice, it is important to abide within the precepts and not break them.

After going for refuge you develop trusting faith in karmic causality. This is confidence that all the happiness and misery we experience is produced by our own actions: virtuous actions result in happiness, and nonvirtuous actions result in misery. Even the subtlest karma gives rise to its result accordingly. Developing trusting faith in karmic causality is one of the most important aspects of the spiritual path. All Dharma practice is based on this. This trusting faith in karma is not blind faith. It is an understanding of conventional reality that is developed through extensive study and reflection. Once you have developed this understanding, you need to keep it firm. That is most important. Understanding the relationship between actions and their results is known as the conventional view; understanding emptiness is the ultimate view. Tsongkhapa praises faith in the conventional view as the basis of all meritorious causes and their effects, right up to and including enlightenment. Everything is based on this trusting faith.

Having developed trusting faith that understands conventional reality, you need to make great effort to engage in virtue and turn away from nonvirtue every day of your life. If you think, speak, or act negatively, you should immediately recognize what you have done and try to purify those actions by means of the four powers. You should do this every day because if you die before having purified your negative actions you could fall to the lower realms. Even though you may have accumulated a lot of merit by practicing generosity, completing recitations, and so on, your more powerful nonvirtuous karma will drag you down into the lower realms before your virtuous karma can ripen. As explained before, once you are in the lower realms it is very difficult to escape them; you could be stuck there for eons. Therefore continuous application of the four antidotes is most important.

The practices summarized so far are included within the instructions for a being of lesser spiritual capacity. As mentioned in the introduction to this volume, the lamrim method has three stages of teachings based on the capacities of practitioners: lesser, intermediate, and great. The primary goal of those with lesser capacity is to block the door to the lower realms. At this stage you need to develop great fear of the results of nonvirtuous karma: without it, you might fall down into the lower realms where you have no ability to attain a higher rebirth—let alone reach the distant goals of liberation and enlightenment.

When you have actualized everything that needs to be accomplished on the path of beings of lesser spiritual capacity, you become a being of intermediate capacity. Now you strive to develop a fear of samsara altogether, not just the lower realms. You reflect deeply about the general and particular faults of any samsaric rebirth, even in the upper realms. By thinking about the misery of the continuous cycle of birth, sickness, aging, and death, you come to see every aspect of it as undesirable. Now that you wish to get out of samsara completely, what should you do? There is no way to get out of samsara without getting rid of its cause. Samsara is produced by contaminated karma and mental afflictions such as ignorance, craving, hatred, and so on. So a practitioner of intermediate spiritual capacity needs to emphasize the development of a deep understanding of the causes of samsara and a spontaneous wish to eliminate them. This is the thought of definite emergence, or renunciation.

Renunciation is the first of the three principal aspects of the path; the other two are bodhicitta and the correct view. Renunciation is a genuine, spontaneous desire to definitely emerge from samsara forever. It is not an artificial or temporary wish; nor is it a matter of being troubled by the misery of samsara on one day and then forgetting about it the next—even if it brought tears to your eyes and made your hair stand up on end! Genuine renunciation arises spontaneously all the time. Once it has arisen you need to develop the actual path, which is the way to eliminate samsara's causes. There is no other way out; no airplane can fly you to freedom and no one can grant you liberation. There are some non-Buddhists who say that liberation or peace is a magnificent pure land shaped like an upside-down white umbrella; they want to be taken there and pray to an external being for help. But this has nothing to do with Buddhism. According to Buddhist teachings, peace is internal. It comes from eliminating contaminated karma and mental afflictions so that they will never arise again. That permanent cessation is pure peace and is called nirvana. The only method to attain this inner peace is to develop the three higher trainings: ethical conduct, meditative stabilization, and wisdom. It is wisdom that cuts all the mental afflictions from the root. Wisdom relies on meditative stabilization; without powerful meditative stabilization, wisdom cannot function. Meditative stabilization is dependent on ethical conduct, whereby you control your senses and prevent your body, speech, and mind from behaving in negative ways. To that end you take vows and endeavor to keep your mental, verbal, and physical actions virtuous. On this basis you can develop śamatha, and in dependence on that you can develop supreme wisdom. Trying to jump to a higher path without making an effort to keep the vows and all their attendant precepts will not work. You need to gain certainty about the three trainings and put them into practice. No one forces the vows on you; you voluntarily take the vows of individual liberation because you want to be free from the misery of samsara. Therefore you must make an effort to keep the prātimokṣa vows you have taken. The three higher trainings are the main path for beings of intermediate capacity.

When you are sufficiently trained in what is required on the path of the intermediate being and have completed those practices properly, you are ready to progress to the path of the being of great spiritual capacity. Only after you have thoroughly understood your own problem can you comprehend how all others are in the same situation; they too are sinking in the ocean of samsara, overwhelmed by all kinds of suffering. Now you begin to meditate on bodhicitta: the wish to quickly attain complete enlightenment in order to benefit all sentient beings—every one of whom has been your mother. Bodhicitta is rooted in love and compassion: love is the wish that all sentient beings have happiness, and compassion is the wish that they be free from suffering. These attitudes need to become spontaneous for bodhicitta to arise. There are two ways to train the mind in developing bodhicitta: the sevenfold cause and effect method and the exchanging self for others method. It is important to practice these methods as much as possible because without bodhicitta, the practice of the six perfections as well as the tantric path will be fruitless. To engage in the bodhisattvas' activities or to practice the two stages of tantra without this great mind is like trying to put a roof on a house without having built a foundation—it will soon fall down. Once you have developed bodhicitta and a realization of śūnyatā, you can engage in practices that make your progress to enlightenment quicker and more powerful; for example, the tantric path includes certain magical elements, various wrathful activities, and even the use of mental afflictions. But if you lack bodhicitta and engage in these activities, you will fall down—perhaps even into hell.

In order to keep your bodhicitta firm and not lose it, you reinforce this wonderful attitude by taking the bodhisattva vow. Initially you study and practice without taking the vow. When you have developed a genuine experience of bodhicitta and some understanding of the practice of the six perfections, you may feel it is time to do some serious work. At that point you take the bodhisattva vow with the ritual. The bodhisattva vow entails a great many precepts that you need to keep. It is very difficult to judge by yourself what to do and what to avoid; you must study in order to discern what thoughts and actions to engage in and what to abandon, so as to assist others in the best possible way. Bodhisattvas do not engage in these activities for their own benefit: their work is to benefit all sentient beings. They strive to save various beings from lower rebirths, as well as from samsara, and even from the Hinayana paths and goals.

When you have a strong wish to practice these activities, you are ready to take the bodhisattva vow with the ritual.

There are two rituals. First you take the bodhisattva vow in connection with aspiring bodhicitta. The prayer of aspiring bodhicitta, a promise never to give up your bodhicitta, appears in the *Six Session Guru Yoga* (*Thun drug bla ma'i rnal 'jor rgyas pa*):

> From now until I become a buddha
> May I never give up, even at the cost of my life,
> The attitude wishing to attain complete enlightenment
> To free all beings from the fears of samsara and nirvana.[210]

Then, after studying the bodhisattva deeds in depth, you take the bodhisattva vow in connection with engaging bodhicitta. The actual vow is to think, "Just as all buddhas and bodhisattvas gave rise to bodhicitta and practiced the bodhisattvas' deeds, I too will practice all these deeds." The prayer of engaging bodhicitta also appears in the *Six Session Guru Yoga*:

> O gurus, buddhas, and bodhisattvas!
> I request you please to listen to me:
> Just as all the previous buddhas
> Developed the wish to become enlightened
> And trained in the bodhisattva practices
> In accordance with their gradual stages,
> So may I too, for the sake of all beings,
> Develop the wish to become enlightened
> And train in the bodhisattva practices
> In accordance with their gradual stages.[211]

A similar wish is part of the standard refuge prayer, which is usually recited and contemplated at the beginning of any ritual, teaching, or practice:

> To Buddha, Dharma, and Sangha supreme
> I go for refuge until I am enlightened,
> Through the merit I create by giving and so on,
> May I become a buddha to benefit all beings.[212]

After having taken the vow, to mature your own mental continuum you practice the six perfections: generosity, ethical conduct, patience, joyous effort, meditative concentration, and wisdom. Then, to ripen the minds of others, you engage in the four ways of gathering disciples: generosity, pleasant speech, using the instruction's meaning, and acting accordingly. The *Ornament for the Mahayana Sutras (Mahāyāna-sūtrālaṃkāra-kārikā)* says:[213]

> A method to benefit others,
> Causing understanding, causing involvement,
> And acting in accordance oneself,
> Should be understood as the four ways to gather. (17.74)

How do you benefit others? You cannot go from door to door to help each individual sentient being; they will not listen to you even if you have something wonderful, like Buddhism, to teach. You need to employ more wide-ranging skillful methods to attract people. First you help them materially; you give them things they need, such as food, clothing, and shelter. This will draw people toward you; and as they come to trust you, they will listen to what you say. Then you give them some practical advice and gradually introduce some Dharma teachings to them. Christian missionaries do this kind of thing. First, they give people various material things; they build schools and hospitals. Gradually as people begin to trust them, the missionaries teach them about Christianity. Seen this way, the practice of generosity is almost like waving and calling to people, "Come here." You arouse their interest with generosity, so that when you instruct them they will take it more seriously. It is important to practice the teachings that you give to others. If you do not act in accordance with how you advise others to behave, they will not listen to you for very long. The *Ornament for the Mahayana Sutras* says:

> Generosity is the same. Teaching that, making them take it up,
> And following the instruction oneself,
> Are accepted as pleasant speech, utilizing the meaning,
> And acting according to the meaning respectively. (17.73)

After taking the bodhisattva vow, you need to keep the root precepts even at the cost of your life. If you had to choose between immediate death or breaking a root precept, which would you choose? Most people would make their choice based on the egotistic view "I want to live," so they would give up that vow. But a bodhisattva protects his or her vows and the enlightenment of other beings even if it means death in this life. There are eighteen root bodhisattva vows and forty-six secondary vows. Four great binding factors must be present to break a root vow: not regarding that nonvirtuous action as a fault, not reversing the wish to do that nonvirtuous action but instead wanting to do it again, having no respect for avoiding that action, and having no shame for doing that action. The worst of these is the first one: not regarding the nonvirtuous action as a fault. In comparison, the other factors alone are small downfalls. You must make a great effort not to incur any of these faults, great or small. When all four of these factors are complete, the root vow is broken; if any of them are lacking, the vow is not completely broken. Even if the first factor is present and is accompanied by one or two of the others, it is not a complete downfall, although intermediate downfalls and minor faults will have occurred. If you realize that you have incurred any of these faults you must purify them immediately. That is how bodhisattvas practice keeping their vows.

The bodhisattva vow contains a commitment to practice the six perfections. You especially need to practice the last two: meditative concentration, or śamatha, and wisdom, or vipaśyanā. You must master the method of stabilizing the mind to attain śamatha and then generate the pure view of the two kinds of selflessness free from the two extremes. When you have found the correct view and single-pointedly placed your mind on it, you must develop an understanding of how to maintain your concentration on this view. It is not correct to leave aside what you have understood through analysis and instead meditate with an empty mind. You should come to an understanding by means of analysis and then focus on the object found by that analysis. The practices of meditative concentration and wisdom are called śamatha and vipaśyanā, but they are not something different from the last two perfections; they are included within the training of a vowed bodhisattva.

Your practice is developing if your wish to progress to the higher stages increases while you are doing the lower meditations and if your wish to accomplish the lower stages becomes stronger while you are studying and meditating on the more advanced levels. Without practicing the lower stages, you cannot get to the higher ones: if you just dive into higher practices, such as meditative stabilization and wisdom, without engaging in any of the earlier practices, such as relying on the spiritual guide, it will be very difficult to get to the real point. Śamatha and vipaśyanā alone will not get you to enlightenment. You need to develop a strong and firm understanding of the entire path, not just some portion of it. You need to know how the different parts of the Mahayana path are related and how each part helps every other one from the beginning to the end. In the beginning the earlier practices are imperative and the more advanced practices are not so critical; later on the higher stages of practice become more central. Each part is equally important relative to its appropriate time. This is how to think regarding your practice; it will clear away narrow thinking like, "This is all I want to do, I do not want to do anything else because just this will get me through."

As you follow the path your main focus of practice may vary depending on what is arising in your own mind. If your respect for your spiritual teacher seems to be lessening, there is a danger that you will cut off the root of all good spiritual results; in that case you need to make an effort to refresh your practice by meditating on the earliest great teaching in the lamrim: how to rely on your spiritual guide. Using these meditation instructions, generate a sense of your teacher's profound importance and develop a feeling of deep appreciation for him or her. Similarly, if your delight in doing spiritual practice in this life weakens and you want to play around and enjoy yourself instead, the antidote is to meditate on the leisure and fortune of this life. If you continue to have strong attachment to things of this life, such as wealth and fame, the antidote is to meditate on the impermanence of this life and realize that after death you may experience the misery of a lower rebirth. If it seems that you have become careless of the vows you have taken—breaking precepts here and there and being too casual about the spiritual rules—you should recognize that this is because you do not understand karmic causality; so you should meditate primarily on karma and its results. If it seems that your sorrow regarding life in samsara—including every realm from the hells to the heavens—is declining, then your stated desire to seek liberation from all samsara will be mere words rather than a heartfelt aspiration; when that happens you should meditate on the general and particular faults of samsara. If it seems that you have no powerful wish that everything you do should be for the benefit of other sentient beings, then the bodhisattva attitude, which is the root of the Mahayana path, is cut off. If your aspiration, "Anything that I do, including seeking enlightenment, is for the benefit of sentient beings, not for me alone," is gone, you should train for a long time in one of the methods to develop aspiring bodhicitta—either the sevenfold cause and effect meditation or exchanging oneself for others. If you have aspiring bodhicitta, have taken the bodhisattva vows, and are practicing the six perfections, yet it appears to you that subject, object, and action are inherently existent, then clearly your mind is not free from the bondage of grasping at signs. In that case you need to employ various analytical meditations to negate the inherent nature of things by means of consequential reasoning. This will destroy the wrong view holding things to exist inherently. Eventually you should meditate on the emptiness that is like the sky: the emptiness of inherent existence of all phenomena. When you arise from that meditation and look at things, you will see them as unreal and yet appearing. You should practice seeing everything in this way during the postmeditation period. If it seems that your mind has become the servant of distraction and is unable to stay on a virtuous object for long, it is time primarily to engage in stabilizing meditation.

From these illustrations you should understand how to employ the other meditations that are not mentioned here. In brief, when you engage in spiritual practice you should not emphasize only one aspect of the path and ignore the rest; you should apply every virtuous practice equally. Whenever a strong delusion arises, you should meditate on the appropriate antidote and eliminate it. The Kadam lamas called this "smoothing out the bumpy afflictions." Just as you smooth out bumps in the ground to make it flat, you do the same in terms of your spiritual practice: you do not want any bumps in your mind. So, from understanding how and when to apply each antidote, you practice every aspect of the path with equal dedication.

Tsongkhapa's explanation of the practices for those of great spiritual capacity, in particular the bodhisattvas' training in the sixth perfection—the practice of the perfection of wisdom giving rise to special insight—is now complete. Up to this point Tsongkhapa has explained what is known as the common path or Sūtrayāna. The focus has been on the three principal aspects of the path: renunciation, bodhicitta, and the correct view. Renunciation, or definite emergence, is prominent on the paths of those with lesser and intermediate spiritual capacity; this is their main practice. Later the mind of enlightenment and the correct view are added to renunciation; these three comprise the path of beings with great spiritual capacity. The Mahayana also has a further method of practice known as the Tantrayāna, Mantrayāna, or Vajrayāna. Tsongkhapa concludes the *Lamrim Chenmo* with a brief summary of the tantric path. He wrote a separate, extensive text on the stages of the path of secret mantra, the *Ngarim Chenmo* (*sNgags rim chen mo*), which explains the tantric path in great detail. But it is just lightly touched on below.

b' HOW TO TRAIN SPECIFICALLY IN THE VAJRAYĀNA

There is no way to enter the tantric path without first training in all the Sūtrayāna practices; you simply cannot jump directly into tantric practice. However, you must definitely engage in secret mantra without any hesitation after you have properly trained in the practices common to both Sūtrayāna and Tantrayāna—which are the content of the *Lamrim Chenmo*. Why should you enter the tantric path? The primary reason for this is that the tantric practices enable you to complete the accumulations of merit and wisdom much more quickly. If you practice only the Sūtrayāna it can take three countless eons to attain enlightenment. But if you add the rare and precious practice of tantra to the basis of the common practices, you traverse the path as if by jet instead of by walking or riding a horse.

As Atiśa explained in *Lamp for the Path to Enlightenment*, if you enter the tantric path you must honor and respect your guru even more than the way that was explained earlier in the context of sutra practice. Your spiritual teacher gives you an initiation to enter the tantric path and then guides you through the secret practices. Therefore the way to rely on a spiritual teacher in the context of tantric practice is more advanced; your guru devotion must be highly developed, even to the point of following your guru's every word. It may be very hard to follow the instruction, but if your guru says "Jump off this cliff," you may have to jump! I am joking somewhat, but it is true that from the very beginning of your tantric practice you must pay homage, respectfully obey, and offer service to a guru who has the qualities explained in the sutras and tantras. However, there is no need to follow a spiritual teacher who lacks these qualifications.

After you find a guru, your mind must be matured by receiving the ripening initiation. This is not just any kind of initiation; it must be one that is found in an authoritative tantric textual source. During the initiation you receive the tantric pledges and vows. Some vows, such as the bodhisattva vows, are common to sutra and tantra. The path of secret mantra additionally requires special root and secondary vows. Once you have taken these, you should study the texts that explain them and make a great effort to keep them. If you break any of them, you can restore them by various methods explained in the tantric texts, such as taking them again during a proper initiation. This will purify broken vows and any faults you have incurred. However, if you have committed a root downfall, then an obstacle in your mindstream will remain even after taking the tantric vows again. It is similar to a broken leg; you can go to a hospital, get it set in plaster, and the bones will heal—but your leg will never be the same as it was before. In this case, after you break and purify a root vow it will take much longer to give rise to the special qualities of the tantric path.

The foundation of the tantric path is to receive an initiation during which you take the bodhisattva and tantric vows and then protect those vows purely. If you try to engage in tantric practice without taking and maintaining the vows, you will be like a rotten old house with a broken foundation that is ready to fall at any moment. In short, there is no way that you would achieve any attainments. Therefore from the very beginning, you should make a great effort not to be tainted by any nonvirtuous downfall.

The *Root Tantra of Mañjuśrī* (*Mañjuśrī-mūla-tantra*) says, "The Buddha did not speak of tantric attainments with regard to those who break their ethical discipline." In other words, people who do not protect the vows and pledges they make during an initiation will not gain any of the high, medium, or low attainments that come from tantric practice. According to the highest yoga tantra texts, those who do not guard their pledges and vows, or who have received an improper initiation, or who do not understand śūnyatā, will not attain any realizations, no matter how much they engage in meditation to accomplish the deity and the mandala. Those who proudly boast about being a tantric master, doing tantric meditation, and being a great tantric practitioner—and yet do not properly guard their pledges and vows—have completely strayed from the tantric path.

In order to cultivate the path of secret mantra, you must keep your tantric pledges and vows pure and begin meditating on the generation stage. This involves meditating on any completely pure mandala of a deity as explained in authentic tantric sources. The purpose of the generation stage is to eliminate certain special obstacles. While the Sūtrayāna explains two obstacles to be abandoned—obstructions to liberation and obstructions to omniscience—the Tantrayāna explains two additional ones: the appearance of ordinariness and the conception of ordinariness. The appearance of ordinariness concerns the five aggregates, the six or eighteen elements, and the twelve sources of sense consciousness. There is nothing within a person's experience that is not included in one of these categories. Normally these constituents combine and appear to be rather ordinary: our bodies, houses, food, clothes, and other objects of enjoyment. On the basis of ordinary appearance, we grasp these things to exist as they appear. We conceive ourselves to be ordinary people—not deities. We grasp our homes to be ordinary houses—not mandalas. The problem is that things appear in an ordinary way, and we hold them to exist the way that they appear—as just ordinary. However, this is an incorrect perception and a wrong conception based on that misperception. The generation stage is the antidote that gets rid of these wrong appearances and conceptions. This practice transforms the ordinary abode into the holy divine mandala, and so on.

The generation stage is cultivated primarily in the imagination. First you dissolve your body and sense of identity into emptiness, and from the sphere of emptiness you arise in the form of a deity visualized inside a mandala. You imagine that your house is the palace of the deity, your body is the body of a deity. You appear in the form of the particular deity you are practicing. Everything—your body, abode, and objects of enjoyment—are transformed into a divine appearance. Every sound is transformed into the sound of the mantra. You imagine yourself to be part of that mandala all the time: you imitate the behavior of the enlightened beings in whatever you do, whether eating, speaking, sitting, walking, or lying down. Purifying ordinary appearances and thoughts by transforming them into aspects of the deity brings special blessings from all the buddhas and bodhisattvas. These blessings flow into you constantly, quickly purifying obstructions and completing the limitless collection of merit. Thus practicing the generation stage makes you a suitable vessel for the completion stage.

When you have completed meditating on the generation stage, you meditate on the completion stage as taught in the authoritative tantric sources. During the completion stage training, instead of your imagination you use your subtle nervous system—the channels, winds, and drops—as a basis for actualizing your meditation. Some people want to practice only the completion stage practices, particularly the famous ones such as the development of inner heat, without having fully accomplished the generation stage. This is not the proper way to practice according to authoritative tantric sources and the masters who have commented on them. The essential point is that you need to practice both the generation stage and the completion stage in order to accomplish the path of highest yoga tantra. You will not achieve your desired result if either of those is missing.

This is just a verbal description showing part of the way to enter the path of secret mantra. It is impossible to explain everything in this context. To develop a more complete understanding of this subject you should read works on the stages of the path of secret mantra. Tsongkhapa's *Ngarim Chenmo* is an extensive explanation of this subject. If you practice according to what is presented in that text, as well as the one you are reading now, then your practice will become a training in the complete body of the path; it will include all the essential points of the sutras and tantras. If you can do that, you will make your life of leisure and fortune meaningful. You will be able to spread Buddha's precious teaching in your own and others' mindstreams.

CONCLUSION

To conclude this text, Tsongkhapa composed a beautiful poetic prayer. It begins by saying that the countless scriptures of Śākyamuni Buddha can be understood by viewing them through the eye of this one text, the *Lamrim Chenmo*. If you read hundreds of volumes of sutras and tantras one by one, it would be difficult to understand how all the different topics, instructions, and points of view fit together. The *Lamrim Chenmo* is like a window to the scriptures. Through an ordinary small window you can see a vast landscape that includes flowers, trees, houses, animals, lakes, and mountains. Likewise, this text expands your gaze to all the scriptures by focusing it through a single framework. Those who are wise will feel great joy when they read it because this text leads to an understanding of the vast meaning of the scriptures that encompass the entire path of sutra and tantra. Tsongkhapa says that he was able to compose this text because he relied on many great spiritual teachers, particularly his special secret guru: Mañjuśrī, the primordial buddha. Through the power of his relationship with Mañjuśrī, Tsongkhapa became a master, understanding ultimate and conventional truth. Although Tsongkhapa had many other important teachers, such as Rinchen Kyabchog Pal Zangpo and Jetsun Rendawa,[214] here he singles out Mañjuśrī as the supreme guru in whom he took refuge and through whose help he directly realized emptiness.

> The Muni's countless teachings are viewed by one eye;
> One text brings joy to the wise, who perfectly understand all the
>   scriptures through it;
> It has depended on great spiritual teachers and the primordial buddha,
>   who is Mañjuśrī,
> Who is my refuge, my nourishment, and by whose power reality is
>   discerned by a master;
> Master supreme, please always protect me!

Buddha is the source of the lineage of the lamrim teachings: the profound view explained in the lamrim comes to us from Buddha, via Mañjuśrī, and then to Nāgārjuna; the vast path system of the lamrim comes to us from Buddha, through Asaṅga. These two, Nāgārjuna and Asaṅga, are the crown ornaments of all the masters and scholars in the world; they are glorious flags of fame that fly everywhere among sentient beings. The lamrim method is magnificent because it fulfills the desires of all sentient beings. Every sentient being wants the highest happiness and peace. Following the lamrim method fulfills that goal; therefore this teaching is the most precious of all jewels. Just as the ocean is a collection of water from all rivers, this text is a glorious ocean of good explanations collected from thousands of different scriptures and commentaries.

> They are the crown ornaments of all the scholars of Jambudvīpa,
> The glorious banners of fame spreading among sentient beings:
> Nāgārjuna and Asaṅga; from these two have passed down gradually
> The lineage of the lamrim teachings.
>
> Because it fulfills the desired goals of all living beings,
> This instruction is the king of wish-granting jewels;
> Because it collects the rivers of thousands of scriptural systems,
> It is a glorious ocean of good explanations.

The lineages of Nāgārjuna and Asaṅga converge in Atiśa, the great scholar and practitioner Dīpaṃkara Śrī Jñāna. He expounded these teachings in

Tibet, the Land of Snow Mountains, where his teachings flourished. They were properly understood and practiced by the famous Kadam yogis and geshes. So in Tibet, the eyes that see the excellent path to buddhahood did not close for a long time. It is these teachings that have been passed to all the lamas of the lineage down to the present day.

> It was the great scholar Dīpaṃkara
> Who revealed them in the Land of Snow Mountains.
> Here, the eyes that see the Conqueror's excellent path
> Did not close for a very long time.

Then the great masters, scholars, and yogis who understood the essential points of the teachings passed away. Over a long period of time this excellent method deteriorated. Tsongkhapa recognized this situation, and in order to restore those teachings in Tibet he arranged all Buddha's teachings of sutra and tantra into a graduated path for a fortunate person who rides to enlightenment on the supreme vehicle of the Mahayana.

> Then, when the wise ones who properly understood
> Every essential point of the teaching passed away,
> This beneficial path declined for a long time.
> Seeing this situation, in order to spread the teachings,
>
> I brought together into a method of practice
> Everything taught by Buddha,
> Into a graduated path for a fortunate individual
> Who rides the supreme vehicle.

The lamrim is a method for someone who goes from the beginning, through all the stages of the path of the lesser being, through the path of the middle being, to the end of the path of the great being. The parts of the method are all for one person; they are not meant for different individuals who want to go in different directions. Even though there are many stages, they are all stages on the path of one person's practice. This condensed manner of practice is not too extensive, so even those with little wisdom can understand it quickly and easily. However, this method includes the essential points of all Buddha's teachings. Nothing is missing. Tsongkhapa developed the lamrim method by examining the scriptures and analyzing their meaning through a process of logical reasoning.

> I drew forth this correct path of practice
> By analyzing the scriptures and reasoning;
> It is not too long, yet it includes all the essential points;
> So even those with less intelligence can easily understand it.

Tsongkhapa notes that it is most difficult to understand the bodhisattvas' path system. He says that he is the most foolish among fools, so he confesses any mistakes that are found in this text in the presence of the great buddhas, bodhisattvas, and masters who clearly see everything exactly as it is.

> It is very difficult to understand the bodhisattva path,
> And I am the most childish among children,
> So whatever mistakes appear here
> I confess before those who see things as they are.

Dedication

> By means of the two collections vast as space that I have amassed
> Through extensive effort to compile this lamrim text,
> May I become a victorious buddha, a leader
> For all beings whose wisdom-eyes are blinded by ignorance.

> In all my lives until I attain that state,
> May I be nourished by Mañjuśrī's compassion;
> May I please the buddhas by ascertaining and accomplishing completely
> The supreme path encompassing all the stages of the teachings.

> Through skillful means drawn forth by powerful compassion,
> May my understanding of the essence of the path
> Lift the darkness from the minds of living beings,
> And may I uphold Buddha's teachings for a long time.

The Buddha's teachings are twofold: the realized teachings, which refers to the realizations you gain through practice, and the scriptural teachings, which refers to explaining what you know of the teachings to others.

> In areas where the supreme precious teachings have not reached
> And in places where they have spread but degenerated,
> With my mind moved by great compassion
> May I illumine that treasury of happiness and peace.

> May this text on the stages of the path to enlightenment,
> Well established by marvelous deeds of the buddhas and bodhisattvas,
> Bring glory to the minds of those wishing for liberation
> And long spread forth the deeds of Buddha.

Buddha's deeds are present for as long as the teachings remain; if the teachings disappear, then Buddha's deeds disappear. So by practicing the teachings, may the deeds of Buddha stretch out for a very long time.

> May all humans and nonhumans who provided the necessary conditions
> And cleared away obstacles to compiling this text on the excellent path,
> Never be separated, in all of their lives,
> From the pure path that is praised by the buddhas.

> When striving to properly practice
> The ten perfections of the supreme Mahayana,
> May the powerful Dharma protectors always be helpful,
> And may an ocean of auspiciousness pervade everywhere.

COLOPHON

The *Lamrim Chenmo* collects and summarizes the essential points of all Buddha's scriptures. It presents the great systems of the openers of the chariot-way, Nāgārjuna and Asaṅga, who were prophesied by Buddha himself. It explicates especially the systems of the great Mahayana teachers and presents them in a single comprehensive format. Unlike the Hinayana and other religious systems, it shows the complete stages of practice of the three levels of beings. Following this lamrim system leads to omniscience, the state of perfect enlightenment.

Tsongkhapa now pays his respects to those who most influenced him. Konchog Tsultrim, the regent of the great bodhisattva Ngog Loden Sherab, masterfully studied the scriptural collection of Buddha's teaching; taking it to heart he practiced its meaning and led many sentient beings, thus becoming the most important root of this precious teaching.

Konchog Pal Zangpo, the abbot of Zulpu and the regent of the great master Jadulpa Dzinpa, was unanimously praised by all earlier vow holders. Adorned with many qualities of scriptural knowledge and realizations, such as wisdom and compassion, he rose above the other masters of Tibet like the jeweled pinnacle of a victory banner.

Kyabchog Pal Zangpo previously made many requests for teachings and later became a great master of the sutras and tantras. He was a master among masters. Emphasizing continuously his practice of the three trainings, he carried the burden of the precious teachings. He was incomparable, a speaker of two languages, a great spiritual teacher, and a great bodhisattva. This holy man was very famous and was one of Tsongkhapa's gurus. He urged Tsongkhapa to write a treatise explaining the path.

Accepting this commission, Tsongkhapa studied two lineages under his guru, the holy reverend Namkha Gyaltsen: the Kadam lineage passed from Gonpawa to Neusurpa, and the lamrim lineage passed from Chenngawa. He received another two lineages from Chokyab Zangpo: the Kadam lamrim lineage passed from Potowa to Sharawa and the lineage passed from Potowa to Dolpa. All the teachings from these Kadam lamrim lineages are included in the *Lamrim Chenmo*.

Atiśa's *Lamp for the Path to Enlightenment* is the basic lamrim text. Aside from Atiśa's explanation of the general characteristics of the three kinds of spiritual practitioners, Tsongkhapa does not cite that text because he feels that it is easily understood on its own. Before Tsongkhapa composed the *Lamrim Chenmo*, Ngog Loden Sherab and Drolungpa had written short lamrim texts. Tsongkhapa based the structure of the *Lamrim Chenmo* on the framework of Drolungpa's lamrim. Thus Tsongkhapa gathered the essential points from many smaller lamrim texts and wrote a book with all parts of the path in the exact order of practice, making them easy to practice. This text is a great chariot of the Land of Snow Mountains.

Tsongkhapa now pays homage to his teachers, particularly his root guru Rendawa. He bows down and places the crown of his head at the feet of this kind, marvelous, and great bodhisattva. Rendawa had great wisdom and a heroic attitude toward all the scriptures; he practiced them properly without any fear, thus pleasing all the buddhas and bodhisattvas. Tsongkhapa identifies himself as the fully ordained monk named Lobsang Drakpa, an easterner born in Tsong kha, who studied much to become a learned master and practiced much to abandon negativities. He composed this text, the *Lamrim Chenmo*, in Reting monastery, which is situated in a solitary place below Lion Rock, just north of Lhasa. The scribe who wrote it down was Sonam Pal Zangpo.

Tsongkhapa finally makes a last great dedication. The goal of every human being is peace and happiness. The teachings are the source of peace and happiness. By writing this text, may the precious teachings spread throughout the entire world, bringing peace and happiness to the hearts of all beings.

Appendix: Outline of the Text

CHAPTER 1: *Why Insight Is Needed*

  (ii) How to practice insight [16]

CHAPTER 2: *Relying on Definitive Sources*

  (a') Fulfilling the prerequisites for insight [33]
    (1') Identifying the scriptures of provisional and definitive meaning [37]
    (2') The history of commentary on Nāgārjuna's thought [44]

CHAPTER 3: *The Stages of Entering into Reality*

  (3') How to determine the view of emptiness [51]
    (a") The stages of entering into reality [51]

CHAPTER 4: *Misidentifying the Object to Be Negated*

  (b") Actually determining reality [71]
    (1") Identifying the object to be negated by reasoning [72]
    (a)) Why the object of negation must be carefully identified [72]
    (b)) Refuting other systems that negate without identifying properly
      the object to be negated [76]
    (1)) Refuting an overly broad identification of the object to be
      negated [76]
    (a')) Stating others' assertions [76]
    (b')) Showing that those assertions are wrong [82]
      (1')) Showing that those systems contradict the unique
        distinguishing feature of Madhyamaka [82]
      (a")) Identifying the distinguishing feature of
        Madhyamaka [83]

CHAPTER 5: *Dependent Arising and Emptiness*

        (b")) How those systems contradict the distinguishing
          feature of Madhyamaka [107]
        (c")) How a Mādhyamika responds to those who contra-
          dict the distinguishing feature of Madhyamaka [110]

CHAPTER 12: *Qualifying the Object of Negation*

CHAPTER 13: *Misinterpretations of the Svātantrika/Prāsaṅgika Distinction*

CHAPTER 14: *Refuting Misinterpretations of the Svātantrika/Prāsaṅgika Distinction*

CHAPTER 15: *Our Interpretation of the Svātantrika/Prāsaṅgika Distinction*

CHAPTER 16: *Our Critique of Svātantrika Does Not Hurt Our Own Arguments*

CHAPTER 17: *Analyzing a Chariot*

CHAPTER 18: *The Person Lacks Inherent Nature*

CHAPTER 19: *The Person Appears Like an Illusion*

CHAPTER 20: *Objects Lack Inherent Nature*

CHAPTER 21: *Eliminating Obstructions*

CHAPTER 22: *Insight Requires Analysis*

CHAPTER 23: *Cultivating Insight in Meditation*

CHAPTER 24: *Uniting Śamatha and Vipaśyanā*

CHAPTER 25: *Summary and Conclusion*

Glossary

Abhidharma (*chos mngon pa*). One of three major sections of the Buddhist canon, the Tripiṭaka; this section contains texts that systemize and classify the Buddha's teachings, largely dealing with Buddhist ontology, psychology, cosmology, karmic cause and effect, the stages of the path, and resultant attainments.

accompanying consciousness (*sems byung*). Mental factor. According to Abhidharma sources, any sensory or mental awareness consists of a primary consciousness with a retinue of accompanying consciousnesses, or mental factors. The former cognizes an object, whereas the latter cognize specific qualities of the object.

action, agent, and object of action (*bya, byed, las*). The interdependence of these three forms the basis of Madhyamaka ultimate analysis, which is the search for the analyzed object existing from its own side, independently of being imputed by a mind apprehending it.

actual ultimate (*don dam mngon nas*). This refers to śūnyatā as it appears to the wisdom directly perceiving it. The object of a direct perception of śūnyatā is free of any dualistic appearance.

actualized result (*grub pa'i 'bras bu*). This refers to *birth* and *aging and death*, depicted respectively as the eleventh and twelfth links in the wheel of life.

actualizing cause (*grub byed kyi rgyu*). This refers to *attachment, grasping,* and *existence*, depicted respectively as the eighth, ninth, and tenth links of the wheel of life, which together constitute the karma that enables the projecting cause to ripen. It is also known as the completing cause.

affirming consequence (*sgrub pa'i thal 'gyur*). This is a logical consequence that states positively what follows from a given assumption.

afflictions (*nyon mongs*, Skt: *kleśa*). Nonvirtuous mental states, such as desire, hostility, and ignorance, which motivate actions (karma) that cause one to continue to be born in cyclic existence.

afflictive ignorance (*nyon mongs can gi ma rig pa*). According to the Prāsaṅgika tradition, this refers to the ignorance that is the first of the twelve links of cyclic existence. It is the root cause of suffering that gives rise to all other mental afflictions and contaminated karma; thus, along with its seeds, it is an obstruction to liberation. See also *ignorance* and *nonafflictive ignorance*.

afflictive obstructions (*nyon sgrib*, Skt: *kleśāvaraṇa*). These are the mental afflictions and their seeds, which mainly obstruct the attainment of liberation from samsara. When they are totally removed one attains arhatship, although at this point one still has the obstructions to omniscience.

aggregates of appropriation (*nyer len gyi phung po*). The five appropriated aggregates function as the basis of imputation of a conventionally existent person or self. They include the body, the primary consciousness, various mental events, and all the other causal factors within the continuum of a person, traditionally listed as: form, feeling, discernment, conditioning factors, and consciousness. They are what is grasped or appropriated in the continual round of rebirth, which occurs as a result of contaminated karma motivated by mental afflictions, especially grasping. Therefore the aggregates themselves, as well as the rebirth taken, are in the nature of suffering.

analysis (*dpyad pa*). In a general sense this refers to a mind of wisdom investigating its object of scrutiny, which may be either conventional or ultimate reality. See *analyze* and *examine*.

analytical cessation (*so sor brtags 'gog*). This is the mere absence of an obstruction that has been removed from the mindstream by means of the wisdom of meditative equipoise analyzing the ultimate, which uproots its cause and ensures that this particular obstruction can never arise again. This is a true cessation, of which there are many—each at different stages of the path—finally culminating in nirvana or omniscience.

analytical meditation (*dpyad sgom*). The practitioner investigates the aspects and qualities of the object of meditation by analyzing it into its parts or by searching for it in relation to its parts, thereby arriving at its conventional or ultimate nature. Any analytical meditation, whether conceptual or nonconceptual, is included within the category of insight meditation, vipaśyanā. See *differentiate, fully differentiate, analyze,* and *examine.*

analyze, thoroughly analyze (*dpyod pa, yongs su dpyod pa*). In a technical sense, this is a mind of analytical wisdom that mentally dissects its object of meditation in a subtle and precise way. It is more refined than examining.

appearing object (*snang yul*). This refers to what appears to a consciousness apprehending an object. In general, to a directly perceiving awareness, the object manifestly appears; to a conceptual awareness, a mental image of the object appears mixed with an appearance of the object itself. To any kind of ordinary awareness, the object appears truly existent. The appearance of true existence is a false appearance; however, according to the Prāsaṅgika system, this alone does not invalidate the consciousness to which it appears, provided the main object is apprehended correctly.

apprehended and apprehender (*bdzung dzin*). This refers to the object apprehended by a mind and the mind that apprehends it.

appropriated object, the owned (*nye bar blang bya*). This is a technical term that usually refers to the parts of an object or to the aggregates of a person; it is the object acted on, the object of action.

appropriation (*nye bar len pa*, Skt: *upādāna*). This is ambiguous between the act of appropriating and the appropriated object. As one of a pair, in conjunction with the appropriator, *appropriation* refers to the appropriated object. As one of a triad, in conjunction with the appropriator and the appropriated, *appropriation* refers to the act of appropriating. See also *action, agent,* and *object of action.*

appropriator, owner (*nye bar len pa po*). This is a technical term that usually refers to a whole object or to a person; it is the agent.

approximate ultimate (*mthun pa'i don dam*). This is synonymous with *imputed ultimate* or *nominal ultimate.* Subjectively this may refer to the subsequent attainment of an ārya, or to a non-ārya's conceptual understanding of śūnyatā. Objectively this refers to śūnyatā as it appears to a conceptual understanding of it. To such a mind, śūnyatā appears via an image of it and mixed with that image; this image, being a conventional thing, appears to be truly existent. Thus the object of a conceptual understanding of śūnyatā has a dualistic appearance.

attribute (*chos, khyad chos*). A property possessed by an object or by a subject.

autonomous inference (*rang rgyud kyi rjes dpag*, Skt: *svatantrānumāna*). Proponents of autonomous inferences assert that an inference, or syllogism, is valid if, and only if, both the proponent and the opponent establish the three modes by means of valid knowledge that is unmistaken with regard to their inherent nature. See *inference based on others' assumptions.*

autonomous syllogism (*rang rgyud kyi sbyor ba*, Skt: *svatantraprayoga*). See *autonomous inference.*

basic object (*dmigs pa'i yul*). This refers to the main object of focus of either perception or thought. When a mind apprehending it holds the basic object to possess certain attributes, then that is the held object. Thus the basic object and the held object are different.

basic object of the innate view of the perishable collection (*'jig lta lhan skyes kyi dmigs pa'i yul*). According to Tsongkhapa's interpretation of Candrakīrti, the basic object of the innate egotistic view is the dependently imputed self, which conventionally exists. This is the self that creates karma, experiences karmic results, and tries to gain enlightenment.

basis of attributes (*khyad gzhi*). An object that possesses attributes, thereby functioning as their basis.

basis of emptiness (*stong gzhi*). The object taken as a basis of analytical meditation, which searches for that object's ultimate basis of identity existing from its own side.

basis of identity (*mtshan gzhi*). A conventional basis of identity of an object includes the object itself and its characteristics, which are used to identify that object in daily life. An ultimate basis of identity of an object, according to the Prāsaṅgika system, is something found to exist from its own side, in terms of which that object is ultimately identified; however, when that object is subjected to ultimate analysis, its ultimate basis of identity cannot be found—and that absence itself is the object's emptiness of inherent existence, its ultimate nature.

basis of name or conventional label (*tha snyad btags pa'i gzhi*). See *basis of identity*.

basis of imputation (*gdags pa'i gzhi*). See *imputed phenomenon*.

belonging to the self, or mine (*bdag gi ba, nga yi ba*). The primary object of the egotistic view is the self—*I* or *me*, and belonging to the self—*mine*. Other than that, nothing is the object of that view, not even the instances of *mine*. If it were otherwise, then one's body, mind, house, and anything else one possesses, would become the object of this view.

bodhicitta (*byang chub kyi sems*). The altruistic mind of enlightenment. The aspiration motivated by great compassion to become a buddha for the sake of benefiting other sentient beings caught in the misery of samsara.

bodhisattva (*byang chub sems pa*). A person who has entered the Mahayana path. Such beings have a continuous, spontaneous wish to attain enlightenment in order to benefit other sentient beings.

body which has the nature of mind (*yid kyi rang bzhin gyi lus*). Arhats or pure-ground ārya bodhisattvas do not have gross aggregates that arise from contaminated karma and mental afflictions; instead they have subtle aggregates that arise in dependence on uncontaminated karma and the ground of the imprints of ignorance (*ma rig bag chags kyis sa dang zag med kyi las la brtan nas byung ba'i phung po*).

calm abiding (*zhi gnas*). See *śamatha*.

Cārvāka (*rgyang 'phen pa*). The Cārvākas are non-Buddhist materialists who do not believe in past and future lives or in liberation; in denying causality and liberation, a follower of this school casts the possibility of enlightenment and higher rebirth far away, as the Tibetan translation of this name suggests.

cause of error (*'khrul pa'i rgyu*). In terms of location, there are two types: external and internal causes of error. In terms of subtlety, there are two types: temporary and deep causes of error. A deep cause of error is only ever internal.

cessation (*'gog pa*). There are two interpretations of cessation. More generally, it is the absence of specific mental afflictions and their seeds within the mindstream at various stages of the path, which have been removed gradually by the wisdom seeing selflessness or emptiness. More specifically, it is the ultimate nature, or śūnyatā, of each purified stage of the mindstream. This is called *true cessation* within the Madhyamaka system. See also *nominal cessation*.

characteristics (*mtshan nyid*). See *definition*.

common basis (*gzhi mthun*). This is where two particular attributes or classes of object are instantiated in one thing, which means that they are not contradictory.

common knowledge, mundane acceptance (*'jig rten la grags pa*). Ordinary awareness that accepts what occurs in the world without engaging in ultimate analysis. Mundane knowledge has less strict criteria than valid knowledge; it may even include things that can be disproved by valid knowledge.

completing cause (*rdzogs byed kyi rgyu*). See *actualizing cause*.

conceived object (*zhen yul*). A conceived object is an object of thought only. Thought conceives something, and the object that it holds is the conceived object. A thought's conceived object is a mental image that represents its basic object held in a certain way—rightly or wrongly, depending on whether that thought is correct or incorrect.

concentration (*ting nge 'dzin*, Skt: *samādhi*). See *samādhi*.

conceptual image (*don spyi*). Mental image, generalized image, object universal. This is a technical term referring to the appearing object of a conceptual consciousness. Thought engages its basic object via a partly transparent mental image of it, which is a generality, or universal. The object appears mixed with this image.

condition (*rkyen*). There are four types of conditions listed as giving rise to a sense consciousness: object condition—what is perceived; dominant or empowering condition—a sense power; immediately preceding condition—a previous moment of consciousness; and causal condition—any other conditions required, such as a body, karma, or proximity.

conditioned thing (*'dus byas*, Skt: *saṃskṛta*). Whatever is produced by causes and conditions. Also, an object perceived by a sense consciousness.

conditioning action (*'du byed*, Skt: *saṃskāra*). The second of the twelve links of dependent arising.

conditioning factors (*'du byed*, Skt: *saṃskāra*). The fourth of the five aggregates constituting the basis of imputation of a person.

consequence, consequential reasoning (*thal 'gyur*, Skt: *prasaṅga*). A logical consequence usually has the form "If *A* then *B*," and correspondingly, "If ~*B* then ~*A*." A logical consequence can be valid without the two parties in a debate having a commonly accepted valid knowledge of its components. There are two types of consequences: affirming consequences and refuting consequences. Mādhyamikas mainly use the latter in their arguments to uproot an opponent's wrong view. See *refuting consequences*.

contradictory (*'gal ba*). Two things are contradictory if nothing instantiates both; in other words, there is no common ground or shared basis. Among various ways of being contradictory there are two basic ones. See *directly contradictory* and *indirectly contradictory*.

contrived mental afflictions (*kun btags pa'i nyon mongs pa*). Contrived afflictions arise as a result of taking to heart certain philosophical systems, religious training, or other deliberate constructs. They mainly include wrong views, such as accepting the existence of partless atoms, a creator God, permanent things, and so on, based on fallacious reasoning.

contrived view of the perishable collection, intellectually acquired egotistic view ('*jig lta kun btags*). There are many such views or apprehensions; different systems present different ways of holding the self, thus there is no certainty regarding this matter. Virtually all non-Buddhist schools of thought accept a permanent self or soul, and any view or mind grasping such a self is most obviously counted as a contrived egotistic view.

conventionality (*tha snyad pa, kun rdzob pa*). In general, conventionality concerns concepts and terminology. There are two types of conventionality to consider here: conceiving of something as that very thing, in dependence on apprehending its basis of imputation, or conceiving of something as truly existent, in dependence on apprehending that very thing. The latter is a false conception, based on a false appearance, which is caused by the *total obscurer* (*kun rdzob*). The former, depending on interpretation, may be employed even by arhats, pure-ground bodhisattvas, and possibly buddhas. However, ordinary conventional awareness cannot distinguish between these two types of conceiving. This may be why the Tibetan terms *tha snyad du* and *kun rdzob tu* are often used synonymously.

conventional analysis (*tha snyad dpyod pa'i rigs pa*). This kind of analysis is commonly used in daily life; we identify things in terms of their conventional characteristics.

conventional consciousness (*tha snyad pa'i shes pa*). In general, according to the Prāsaṅgika system, this refers to any awareness that is not a direct perception of śūnyatā. There are many ways of differentiating types of conventional consciousness. One way is to distinguish between the conventional consciousness of someone who has eliminated self-grasping and its seeds (not its imprints) from his or her mental continuum, and the conventional consciousness of someone who has not eliminated them.

conventional truth, conventional reality (*kun rdzob kyi bden pa*). This refers to things that are true from the perspective of a mind obscured by ignorance and/or its imprints. The imprints of ignorance give rise to the appearance of true existence.

conventional valid knowledge (*kun rzdob pa'i tshad ma, tha snyad pa'i tshad ma*). A conventional valid consciousness is any of the six consciousnesses unaffected by temporary causes of error. The objects established by those correct six consciousnesses are conventionally existent; they exist through the power of thought and terminology. However, we can also say that there are two types of conventional valid knowledge. One is ordinary conventional valid consciousness that accepts its object to exist just as it appears: it appears truly existent owing to the power of ignorance and/or its imprints. The other is subtle conventional valid consciousness that understands its object to exist merely conventionally, although it appears truly existent. The former lacks an understanding of śūnyatā; the latter, though not a direct perception of śūnyatā, understands how things exist dependently, nominally, and relatively.

conventionally imputed (*tha snyed btags pa*). There are two aspects to being conventionally imputed, internal and external, which correspond to thought and language respectively. See *imputed phenomenon.*

conventionally established (*kun rdzob tu grub pa*). This is synonymous with conventionally existent.

conventionally existent (*kun rdzob tu yod pa*). This is synonymous with *existent.* Everything that exists only conventionally exists. See *falsely existent.*

correct conventionality (*yang dag pa'i kun rdzob*). When not impaired by temporary causes of error, a consciousness and its object are correct conventionalities if they are correct from the perspective of ordinary conventional knowledge within the continuum of someone who has not realized śūnyatā at all. (This is only a general criterion because there are some exceptions.)

correct effect sign (*'dras rtags yang dag*). This is a reason based on a causal relationship; it proves the existence of the cause based on the existence of its result. For example, "On a smoky mountain pass there is fire because there is smoke."

correct nature sign (*rang bzhin gyi rtags yang dag*). This is a reason based on a samenature relationship; it proves one thing on the basis of another that is of the same nature as it. For example, "Sound is impermanent because it is produced."

correct nonobservation sign (*ma dmigs pa'i rtags yang dag*). This is simply the negative form of the other two types of reason—a correct effect sign and a correct nature sign; it proves the nonexistence or negation of one thing based on the nonexistence or negation of another, which are related either causally or in terms of being the same nature.

deep cause of error (*phugs kyi 'khrul rgyu*). This refers to the imprints left by ignorance within the mental continuum. These obscure the perception of ultimate reality and cause the objects of ordinary sense consciousnesses to appear truly existent. The sense consciousnesses of all sentient beings are mistaken in this way, though not necessarily distorted; they may still be valid from a conventional perspective. See *temporary cause of error.*

defined thing, definiendum (*mtshon bya*). This is a dharma, a thing, or a quality that is identified in terms of its characteristics encapsulated in its definition.

definition, characteristics (*mtshan nyid*). A definition encapsulates the particular characteristics of a dharma, a thing, or a quality in terms of which it is identified. A definition and its definiendum are coreferential or coextensive.

definitive meaning (*nges don*). For Mādhyamikas, this refers to ultimate truth, śūnyatā.

definitive scripture (*nges don kyi gsung rab*). For the Prāsaṅgika system, this refers to scriptures that principally elucidate ultimate truth, śūnyatā. There is no need for them to be literally acceptable, unlike for the Svātantrikas.

dependent arising (*rten 'brel*). According to varying degrees of subtlety, the term *dependent* may mean: dependent on causes, dependent on parts, dependent on imputation. The twelve links of dependent arising is a prime example of causal dependence; however, according to the Prāsaṅgika system, the twelve links are also dependent in the two more subtle ways. Dependent arising is utilized as the king of reasons because it simultaneously negates the two extremes: *dependent* negates eternalism—the belief that things exist from their own side, and *arising* negates nihilism—the belief that things do not exist at all.

dependent nature, under the power of another cause (*gzhan dbang*). This refers to one of the three natures taught in the *Sutra Unraveling the Intended Meaning*: the causally conditioned nature of a thing. See *imputed nature* and *thoroughly established nature*.

dependently designated (*brten nas btags pa*). See *imputed phenomenon*.

Dharma body (*chos sku*, Skt: *dharmakāya*). This is the infinitely compassionate and holy mind of a buddha; it is what a practitioner's mindstream transforms into when all gross and subtle obstructions have been removed from it.

dhyāna (*bsam gtan*, Skt: *dhyāna*). Meditative absorption. This is a type of meditative concentration that places the mind in a state beyond the desire realm. It includes four levels of the form realm and four levels of the formless realm.

dichotomy (*gnyis su kha tshon chod pa*). Limited to two possibilities. See *law of excluded middle*.

different (*tha dad*). Things that are distinct from each other in every respect.

different entity, different nature (*ngo bo tha dad, rang bzhin tha dad*). Things that exist apart from each other, though they may be causally related.

different isolate (*ldog pa tha dad*). Things that are conceptually and verbally distinct, though they do not necessarily exist apart from each other.

different unrelated things (*'brel med don gzhan*). Two things that are totally different and have no relationship at all; like a horse and a cow, they are neither related causally nor as the same nature.

differentiate (*rnam par 'byed pa*). This is a type of analytical meditation that makes distinctions with regard to conventional things.

direct perception (*mngon sum*). A mind that perceives its object directly, or free of conceptuality; free of any temporary causes of error, it is valid.

directly, manifestly (*mngon sum du*). An object appears directly, or nakedly, to the direct perception apprehending it, without the medium of a conceptual image.

directly contradictory (*dngos 'gal*). This includes *directly contradictory in the sense of being mutually eliminating* (*phan tshun spangs te gnas pa'i dngos 'gal*). Two things are directly contradictory if the terminology itself shows that it is impossible to be both things and impossible to be neither. This means that by eliminating one side you prove the other. This kind of proof gives rise to an immediate understanding. So if two things are contradictory in terms of reality but not in terms of terminology or understanding, then they are not directly contradictory. See *indirectly contradictory in the sense of being mutually eliminating.*

discernment (*'du shes*). Mentally putting together certain attributes and assigning a name to it; superimposing a conceptual image on what the sense consciousness sees directly, thereby enabling differentiation between things.

distorted conceptions (*tshul bzhin ma yin pa'i rnam rtog*). There are four fundamental distorted conceptions, also known as inappropriate attention: holding impure things as pure, holding things in the nature of suffering as pleasurable, holding impermanent things as unchanging, and holding selfless things as a self or as belonging to a self.

distorted conventionality (*log pa'i kun rdzob*). When impaired by temporary causes of error, a consciousness and its object are distorted conventionalities if they are distorted from the perspective of ordinary conventional knowledge within the continuum of someone who has not realized śūnyatā. (This is only a general criterion because there are some exceptions.)

distorted or wrong consciousness (*log shes*). A distorted consciousness is mistaken with regard to how it holds its principal object (in addition to how that object appears). A wrong perception or distorted thought is not any kind of valid knowledge. See *mistaken consciousness.*

dualistic appearance (*gnyis snang*). There are several types of dualistic appearance, each of which is considered mistaken in some way: the mind, or subject, and its object appearing as separate entities; the object appearing mixed with an image of it; the object appearing together with its attribute; and the object appearing as truly existent. Cittamātrins are more concerned with the first and Mādhyamikas with the last. A direct realization of śūnyatā lacks any of these mistaken elaborations.

egotistic view (*'jig tshogs la lta ba*). See *view of the perishable collection.*

elaborations (*spros pa*). There are several types of elaboration, including the superimposition of true existence and the appearance of true existence. In the context of Tsongkhapa's interpretation of the Prāsaṅgika system, it primarily refers to the latter. See *dualistic appearance.*

elements (*khams*, Skt: *dhātu*). The elements may be categorized into groups of three, six, or eighteen. The three are: the desire, form, and formless realms. The six are: earth, water, fire, wind, space, and consciousness. The eighteen are: the six internal sources of sense consciousness (the sense powers), the six external sources of sense consciousness (their objects), and the six sense consciousnesses themselves, which arise in dependence on the sense powers and their objects.

employing signs (*mtshan ma la dpyod pa*). See *grasping at signs.*

emptiness (*stong pa nyid*). Emptiness, or śūnyatā, is the final nature of all phenomena: the absence of true existence or the lack of ultimate existence (according to the Madhyamaka schools).

emptiness of inherent existence (*rang gi mtshan nyis kyis grub pas stong pa*). This is the subtle emptiness, or selflessness, posited by the Prāsaṅgika school.

emptiness of a permanent, partless, and independent person (*gang zag rtag gcig rang dbang can gyis stong pa*). This is the gross selflessness of persons posited by the Vaibhāṣika, Sautrāntika, Cittamātra/Yogācāra, and Svātantrika-Madhyamaka schools.

emptiness of a self-sufficient, substantially existent person (*gang zag rang rkya thub pa'i rdzas yod kyis stong pa*). This is the subtle selflessness of persons posited by the Vaibhāṣika, Sautrāntika, Cittamātra/Yogācāra, and Svātantrika-Madhyamaka schools.

emptiness of a substantial difference between the apprehender and the apprehended (*bzung 'dzin rdzas tha dad pas stong pa*). This is one type of subtle emptiness posited by followers of the Cittamātra/Yogācāra school.

emptiness of true existence (*bden stong*). This is the subtle emptiness of phenomena posited by the Madhyamaka schools. The Prāsaṅgikas interpret this in an even more subtle way and consider it to be equivalent to the emptiness of inherent existence, whether of persons or phenomena.

essential nature (*rang gi ngo bo nyid*). All phenomena lack an essential nature. The Prāsaṅgikas interpret this to mean that all phenomena lack inherent existence. The Cittamātrins interpret this in three ways, corresponding to the three natures.

established as appearing in common (*mthun snang du grub pa*). According to Bhāvaviveka, it means that the proponent and the opponent establish something by the same kind of valid knowledge. However, this is not possible according to Candrakīrti, because there is a big difference between the Prāsaṅgika-Madhyamaka and other schools regarding valid knowledge.

established as mutually dependent (*phan tshun bltos pa'i grub pa*). See *related as mutually dependent.*

established autonomously, independently, or through its own power (*rang dbang du grub pa*). See *established by its own nature.*

established by its own characteristics (*rang gi mtshan nyid kyis grub pa*). See *established by its own nature.*

established by its own essential nature (*rang gi ngo bos grub pa*). See *established by its own nature.*

established by its own nature (*rang bzhin gyis grub pa*). If something were to exist from its own side, independently of a mind that perceives or conceives it, then it would be inherently existent, or established by its own nature. Such a thing would be found by ultimate analysis; however, according to the Prāsaṅgikas, it is not found.

established by valid knowledge (*tshad mas grub pa*). This defines what it means to exist.

established from its own side (*rang gi ngo nas grub pa*). See *established by its own nature.*

examine, thoroughly examine (*rtog pa, yongs su rtog pa*). In a technical sense, this is a conceptual, analytical wisdom that mentally dissects the characteristics of its object of meditation in a general way. It is coarser than analyzing.

excitement (*rgod pa*). This mental factor is based on attachment and influences the mind to wander away from its object of focus. It is one of two main hindrances to meditative concentration.

existent, to exist (*yod pa*). To be established by valid knowledge.

explicitly (*dngos su*). To explicitly understand something means that the object appears to the mind knowing it.

falsely existent (*brdzun par yod*). Conventionally existent. This is synonymous with *existent.* Everything that exists only conventionally exists. Nothing is truly existent.

five aggregates (*phung po lnga*). See *aggregates of appropriation.*

five omnipresent mental factors (*kun 'gro lnga*). There are five mental factors that accompany every primary mind: feeling, discernment, intention, contact, and attention.

five similarities possessed in common (*mtshungs ldan lnga*). A main mind and its accompanying mental factors possess five similarities: same basis, same object, same aspect, same time, and same substance.

four extremes of production (*mtha' bzhi'i skye ba*). Production from self, from others, from both, and without a cause—all of which are based on an assumption of being truly existent. These four extremes are refuted in the process of refuting true existence.

four seals (*phyag rgya bzhi*). The four signs of someone who upholds Buddhist tenets asserting: all causally conditioned things are impermanent, all contaminated things are in the nature of suffering, all phenomena are empty and selfless, nirvana is peace.

free from thought, nonconceptual (*rtog bral, rnam par mi rtog pa*). This refers to direct perception, including sensory direct perception, which is without any conceptual image. It does not refer to a mind that is merely free of discursive thought. See *without thinking anything*.

fully differentiate (*rab tu rnam par 'byed pa*). This is a type of analytical meditation that makes distinctions with regard to the ultimate.

general characteristics (*spyi mtshan*). Characteristics shared by things belonging to the same kind or category.

grasping at a self (*bdag 'dzin*). A mind grasping at inherent nature.

grasping at a self of persons (*gang zag gi bdag 'dzin*). A mind grasping at the person as inherently existent (according to the Prāsaṅgika system).

grasping at a self of phenomena (*chos kyi bdag 'dzin*). Grasping at any phenomena, other than the person, as inherently existent (according to the Prāsaṅgika system).

grasping at signs (*mtshan mar 'dzin pa*). A mind grasping at things to exist just as they appear to exist—that is, as truly existent.

held object (*'dzin stangs kyi yul*). This may be an object of thought or direct perception. It is that mind's basic object held in a certain way—rightly or wrongly, depending on whether that mind is correct or incorrect.

held object of the innate view of the perishable collection (*'jig lta lhan skyes kyi 'dzin stangs kyi yul*). According to Tsongkhapa's interpretation of Candrakīrti, this is a combination of the basic object of the innate egotistic view (the self) and the attribute that it is held to possess (inherent existence). The held object is the conventional self grasped in this incorrect way—as inherently existent. In other words, it is the inherently existent self, which does not exist at all.

hidden (*lkog 'gyur*). A hidden object can be known only in dependence on logical reasoning or some other thought process. It is indirect. However, what is hidden on one occasion or from one perspective might not be hidden on another occasion or from another perspective.

ignorance (*ma rig pa*, Skt: *avidyā*; also *gti mug*, Skt: *moha*). This usually refers to afflictive ignorance, which is a distorted awareness. It is a mental factor rather than a primary mind. Ignorance is not simply not knowing the truth, it is the opposite of knowing the truth; it is a radical misunderstanding of reality. There are many types of ignorance, often categorized into two: ignorance of cause and effect, and ignorance of ultimate reality. See *afflictive ignorance* and *nonafflictive ignorance*.

ignorance of cause and effect (*las 'bras la rmongs pa'i ma rig pa*). This is a mind that actively misapprehends karmic causation; it holds that virtuous action does not lead to happiness and that nonvirtuous action does not bring about misery.

ignorance of ultimate reality (*de kho na nyid la rmongs pa'i ma rig pa*). This is a naturally arising mind that actively misapprehends the nature of reality; it holds things to exist inherently, from their own side, just as they appear to ordinary perception.

illusion-like emptiness (*sgyu ma lta bu'i stong nyid*). After arising from the meditative equipoise directly seeing śūnyatā, an ārya sees conventional things again. Being influenced by the previous seeing of śūnyatā, these things appear illusion-like. The combined state of being empty, yet appearing, is the illusion-like emptiness.

implicative negation (*ma yin dgag*). This is when the object of negation is directly negated and the words expressing that negation also state or infer some other positive phenomenon, whether directly or indirectly. For example, the fat Devadatta does not eat during the daytime.

implicitly (*shugs la*). The terms *explicitly* and *implicitly* may be applied to words, teachings, and understanding. To implicitly understand something means that the object is realized without actually appearing to the mind knowing it.

imprint (*bag chags*). This refers to the subtle propensities that remain in the mindstream once the mental afflictions and their seeds have been removed. These predispositions give rise to the appearance of things as truly existent and function as obstructions to omniscience. See *obstructions to omniscience*.

imputed nature (*kun brtags, kun dtags*). This usually refers to one of the three natures taught in the *Sutra Unraveling the Intended Meaning*: the merely nominally or conceptually constructed nature of a thing. See *dependent nature* and *thoroughly established nature*.

imputed phenomenon (*btags pa'i chos*). Any permanent or impermanent thing is imputed on its basis of imputation. The basis of imputation of a thing may include its attributes, its parts, or any of its other characteristics. Most Buddhists agree that a whole is imputed in dependence on its parts. However, Prāsaṅgikas posit mutually dependent imputation, so the reverse also applies: the parts are imputed in dependence on the whole.

imputed ultimate (*don dam btags pa ba*). See *approximate ultimate*.

imputedly existent (*btags yod*). Something that does not exist substantially but instead exists through being imputed in dependence on its basis of imputation. Such a thing does not bear its identity from its own side; it cannot be found by ultimate analysis. See *substantially existent*.

inappropriate attention (*tshul min yid byed*). See *distorted conceptions*.

indirectly (*rgyud nas*). An object appears indirectly to the mind apprehending it when it appears through the medium of a conceptual image. Yet since the object appears to it, that mind explicitly understands its object.

indirectly contradictory (*brgyud 'gal*). There is a less strict way and a stricter way of being indirectly contradictory. This entry deals with the first. Two things are indirectly contradictory in the less strict way if there are no instances that are both, yet there are instances that are neither. An example of this is *red* and *yellow*. Whatever is red cannot be yellow, and whatever is yellow cannot be red. There is no positive common ground: something that is both. But there is a common ground of their negations: something that is neither red nor yellow, such as *blue*. So if something is not red, then it does not have to be yellow. It can be a color other than those two. Therefore red and yellow are not strictly contradictory. In Western philosophy, they are called *contrary*. See *indirectly contradictory in the sense of being mutually eliminating*.

indirectly contradictory in the sense of being mutually eliminating (*phan tshun spangs te gnas pa'i brgyud 'gal*). A stricter way of being indirectly contradictory is where being both things is impossible and being neither is impossible. There is no third ground or possibility at all, whether positive or negative. If something is not *F* then it must be *G*, and if it is not *G* then it must be *F*. These are contradictory in terms of reality, but they are not contradictory in terms of terminology or understanding—so according to Buddhist logic, they are not directly contradictory. An example of this is *permanent* and *produced*. Permanent and produced are *contradictory in the sense of being mutually eliminating*. But they are not *directly contradictory in the sense of being mutually eliminating*. If you mentally or verbally cut out *permanent*, this does not mean you will naturally understand *produced*. Or if you cut out *produced*, then you do not necessarily understand *permanent*. See *directly contradictory in the sense of being mutually eliminating*.

individual characteristics, own characteristics (*rang mtshan, rang gi mtshan nyid*). Unique characteristics belonging to a particular individual.

inference (*rjes dpag*). The term *inference* is ambiguous between an inferential understanding and a formally structured argument designed to engender that understanding. Two types of formally structured argument commonly used by Buddhist philosophers are syllogisms and consequences.

inference based on others' assumptions (*gzhan grags pa'i rjes dpag*). This kind of inference is used merely to refute an opponent's thesis. Here the opponent already accepts the subject, the reason, and the pervasion of the inference, and may even consider that these are established by valid knowledge. However, the proponent need not accept the reason, the pervasion, or that any elements of the inference are established by a shared notion of valid knowledge.

inherent nature (*rang bzhin*, Skt: *svabhāva*). See *nature*.

inherently existent (*rang bzhin gyis grub pa*). See *established by its own nature*.

innate egotistic view, naturally arising view of the perishable collection (*'jig lta lhan skyes*). According to the Prāsaṅgika system, this is a mind of ignorance that grasps oneself to be inherently existent. Although there is no self that exists inherently, the innate distorted mind of self-grasping obscures that reality. It is a very powerful mind that gives rise to all other mental afflictions and contaminated actions; thus it is the root of samsara.

innate mental afflictions (*nyon mongs lhan skyes*). These do not depend on any kind of reasoning or dogma. Prior to attaining the pure bodhisattva grounds, each and every sentient being—whether human or not, whether educated or not—has innate mental afflictions arising naturally in their mindstream.

introspection (*shes bzhin*). This is a mental factor that continuously checks to see if the mind is experiencing sinking or excitement; it is like a little spy in a corner of one's focused mind, quietly noticing any comings and goings of other mental states.

isolate, reversal (*ldog pa*). Conceptually isolatable factors. For example, "product" and "impermanent thing" are inseparable in reality and therefore one entity, yet they are different isolates because for a conceptual consciousness the one term does not evoke the other.

law of excluded middle (*phung sum ldog pa*). Literally, third possibility excluded. In classical Western logic, the law of excluded middle affirms that a proposition either is the case or is not the case. In other words, it is true or false. A middle value between them, such as being neither true nor false, is excluded. A Buddhist equivalent is to affirm that something is either existent or nonexistent. There is no third possibility in between these two, such as being neither existent nor nonexistent. Tsongkhapa cites Nāgārjuna as saying, "By negating the nonexistence of inherent nature, you prove the existence of inherent nature; by negating the existence of inherent nature, you prove the nonexistence of inherent nature."

main object. This term is used to refer to various kinds of object. On some occasions it may refer to the *basic object* and on others to the *held object*, which is the basic object as it is held or understood. The way it is used on each occasion is made clear in its context.

manifest (*mngon 'gyur*). This can mean one of three things: activated, more gross, or clearly evident. See *nonmanifest*.

meditative absorption. See *dhyāna*.

meditative concentration. See *samādhi* and *śamatha*.

mental afflictions. See *afflictions*.

mental factor. See *accompanying consciousness*.

mere conventionality (*kun rdzob tsham*). Although conventional things appear truly existent even to arhats and bodhisattvas on the pure grounds, such things are said to be *mere conventionalities* for them because they no longer have any minds grasping at things as truly existent.

mere "I," mere self (*nga tsham, bdag tsham*). The dependently imputed, conventionally existent self, which is the basic object of the innate egotistic view.

mere negation, nonimplicative negation (*med dgag*). This is when the object of negation is directly negated, and the words expressing that negation do not state or infer some other positive phenomenon, directly or indirectly.

mindfulness (*dran pa*). Recollection. This is a mental factor that functions to keep the mind on its object; it does not let the mind forget about or move away from its object.

mistaken consciousness (*'khrul shes*). A mistaken consciousness is mistaken with regard to how its object appears, not to how it is held. A mistaken consciousness, whether a perception or a thought, need not be distorted. It is valid if it holds its principal object correctly. See *distorted consciousness*.

natural nirvana (*rang bzhin gyi yongs su mya ngan las 'das pa*). This is the ultimate nature of all things: the absence of inherent existence. It is an attribute that everything possesses naturally. Anyone who utilizes the direct realization of this natural nirvana will gradually remove the cause of samsara.

natural stain (*rang bzhin gyi dri ma*). This refers to inherent existence. However, everything is naturally free of this stain because it does not exist at all. See *temporary stains*.

nature, ultimate nature, inherent nature (*rang bzhin*, Skt: *svabhāva*). The term *nature* has at least three meanings: conventional nature, which mainly refers to a thing's conventional characteristics; ultimate nature, which refers to a thing's emptiness of inherent existence; and inherent nature, which is not an attribute of anything at all because it does not exist—nevertheless, everything appears to exist by its own inherent nature to sentient beings' conventional consciousness and is grasped to exist inherently by an innate mind of ignorance apprehending it.

nature body (*ngo bo nyid sku*, Skt: *svabhāvikakāya*). The ultimate nature of a buddha's immaculate mind: its emptiness or śūnyatā.

nirvana (*mya ngan las 'das pa*; Skt: *nirvāṇa*). The Mahayana texts present a fourfold terminological division of nirvana: natural nirvana, nirvana with remainder, nirvana without remainder, and nonabiding nirvana. Only the last three are genuinely types of nirvana. The term *nirvana* indicates a state beyond suffering and its causes. The final nirvana of the Mahayana, nonabiding nirvana, is a completely purified state that is free of both kinds of obstructions. It is a very special type of śūnyatā because not only is its basis naturally pure, but its basis is also completely purified of all temporary obstructions and faults. It is the emptiness of a buddha's holy mind, the final true cessation.

nominal or fake cessation (*rda'i dgog pa*). This is not a cessation of the mental afflictions removed by wisdom. This is merely a cessation of the stream of consciousness by means of certain methods. The mental afflictions are sure to arise again.

nominally existent (*tha snyad du yod*). See *conventionally existent*.

nonabiding nirvana (*mi gnas pa'i mya ngan las 'das pa*). This is the final true cessation. Of the two aspects of the nature body of a buddha—naturally pure and purified of all stains—it is the latter. This is a very special type of śūnyatā.

nonafflictive ignorance (*nyon mongs can ma yin pa'i ma rig pa*). This refers to the imprints of ignorance, which are obstructions to omniscience.

nonanalytical cessation (*so sor brtags min gyi 'gog pa*). This is the mere absence of an obstruction that has been removed from the mindstream temporarily by means of spiritual practice that only subdues its causes and conditions without uprooting them.

nonconceptual (*rtog bral*). See *free from thought*.

nonconceptual practice (*mi rtog par 'jug pa*). The advanced nonconceptual Buddhist practice is the direct realization of śūnyatā, which arises from ultimate analysis, vipaśyanā. In a more general context śamatha is considered nonconceptual practice because it is nondiscursive. See *without thinking anything*.

nonconceptual wisdom (*rnam par mi rtog pa'i ye shes*). A supreme mind of wisdom that directly realizes the emptiness of inherent existence.

Non-Essentialists (*ngo bo nyid med par smra ba*). Mādhyamikas only.

nonmanifest (*bag la nyal*). This can mean one of three things: dormant, very subtle, or deeply hidden. In the first sense, a karmic seed within a sentient being's mindstream may remain dormant for a long time until it meets the right conditions for it to ripen. In the second sense, a mental factor or some other type of consciousness may be nonmanifest within a sentient being's mindstream at any given moment; for example, when a realization of emptiness is manifest within the mindstream of an ārya bodhisattva, then his or her realization of bodhicitta is nonmanifest, and vice versa. In the third sense, the obstructions to omniscience are deeply hidden stains within the mental continuum.

nonthing (*dngos med*). A nonthing is a nonexistent. See also *unreal*.

not thinking (*yid la mi byed pa*). This has a technical meaning. When one engages in ultimate analysis one does not find anything that exists from its own side, so there is no seeing and no thinking of that nature. It does not mean just stopping all thought.

object to be abandoned (*spangs bya*). This refers to both the obstructions to liberation and to omniscience that exist within the mental continuum of a sentient being. These two types of obstructions are removed gradually by means of specific stages on the paths of seeing and of meditation.

object to be negated, object of negation (*dgag bya*). There are two types of objects to be negated: objects negated by paths and objects negated by reasoning. The former exist and refer to the objects to be abandoned by the paths of seeing and of meditation. The latter refer to nonexistent objects that are held to exist by a mind of ignorance grasping its object to exist truly, ultimately, or inherently. Reasoning is used to negate such an object, which gives rise to an understanding that sees its absence and gradually removes the ignorance grasping at it, along with its seeds and eventually its imprints.

object universal (*don spyi*). See *conceptual image*.

objective ultimate (*yul don dam*). This refers to śūnyatā, which is the object known by the consciousness realizing the ultimate.

obscuration (*rab rib*). This refers to an obstruction in the mindstream that blocks the perception of śūnyatā. It is likened to a cataract that blocks ordinary vision.

obscurer. See *total obscurer*.

observed object (*dmigs pa*). The main object of focus. This often refers to the main object observed by consciousness in meditation. See *basic object*.

obstructions, obstacles, obscurations (*sgrib pa*). There are two types of obstructions within the mental continuum that are removed mainly by the path of meditation: afflictive obstructions and obstructions to omniscience.

obstructions to omniscience (*shes sgrib*, Skt: *jñeyāvaraṇa*). According to the Prāsaṅgika tradition, these are the imprints of the mental afflictions and their seeds, as well as the appearance of true existence that they cause. These imprints and dualistic appearances mainly obstruct the attainment of buddhahood; respectively they are known as the nonmanifest and the manifest obstructions to omniscience. Upon their total removal one attains the path of no more learning, or buddhahood. At this point there are no obscurations left within the mental continuum; only the infinite and pure qualities of a buddha, such as omniscience, are present.

opponent in a debate (*phyi rgol*). The defender within a formally structured argument; the one to whom the proponent is trying to prove something. The term *opponent* may apply to a school of thought or to a person representing it.

ordinary being, ordinary individual (*so so'i skye bu*). A being who has not yet reached the state of an ārya, or superior being.

part possessor, composite, whole (*cha can, yan lag can*). A whole object is considered to be composed of parts and to be imputed in dependence on its parts. See *parts*.

parts, limbs (*cha, yan lag*). The parts of an object are considered to be the components of the whole thing, as well as its basis of imputation. Prāsaṅgikas posit mutually dependent imputation between the parts and the whole. See *imputed phenomenon*.

path of liberation (*rnam grol lam*). This is a direct realization of śūnyatā that occurs as an immediate result of an uninterrupted path that has removed specific obstructions from the mindstream. The path of liberation is a type of mind; its ultimate nature, or śūnyatā, is a true cessation.

perfections (*phar phyin*, Skt: *pāramitā*). Any perfection, strictly speaking, exists only within the continuum of a buddha. However, a bodhisattva practices the perfections on the Mahayana path and engages in the supreme practice of the perfections after having developed a direct insight into emptiness. The six perfections are giving, ethical conduct, patience, joyous effort, meditative concentration, and wisdom.

pervaded object (*khyab bya*). That which is encompassed by another. An instance is pervaded by any of its generalities. For example, impermanent things are encompassed by existent things; they are included within the domain of existent things. In this case, impermanent things are the pervaded.

pervader (*khyab byed*). That which encompasses another. A generality encompasses all its instances. For example, existent things encompass or include impermanent things as well as permanent things. In this case, existent things are the pervader.

pervasion, to pervade (*khyab pa*). To encompass or include; to extend over a domain. Pervasion is an expression of relationship. There are two types of relation—causal relation and same-nature relation—therefore there are two types of pervasion. As an example of the latter type, a generality pervades all its instances. For example, the generality, horse, encompasses all kinds of horse and all individual horses. Pervasion in the context of logic requires that, in a formally structured argument, the reason must pervade the predicate. See *syllogism*.

pliancy (*shin tu sbyangs pa*). This is a mental factor that enables the mind and the body to become serviceable in meditation focused on a virtuous object. It is a quality especially associated with the development of śamatha. However, after having attained śamatha, there is another more special kind of pliancy that arises from vipaśyanā meditation.

prasaṅga (*thal 'gyur*). See *consequence*.

pratyekabuddha (*rang sangs rgyas*). Solitary realizers; so called because, having studied and practiced extensively in previous lives, they attain liberation in their final lifetime without the need of a teacher.

precise ultimate analysis (*yang dag par so sor rtog pa*). A mind of wisdom that very finely analyses its object so as to ascertain its ultimate nature. Based on śamatha, this is wisdom that arises from meditation. See *ultimate analysis*.

predicate of the thesis (*bsgrub bya'i chos*). The predicate, or what is to be proved of the subject, in a formally structured argument. See *syllogism*.

predominant result, environmental result (*bdag po'i 'bras bu*). This refers to any karmic results not included within the continuum of a sentient being, such as external environment, lifespan, and success. Although predominant results are not experiences, they enable experiences to arise fully within sentient beings.

primary consciousness, main mind (*gtso sems*, Skt: *citta*). According to the Prāsaṅgika system, there are six primary minds (the six sense consciousnesses, which arise in dependence on the six sense powers), all of which are accompanied by a retinue of mental factors. See *accompanying consciousness*.

projected result (*'pang pa'i 'bras bu*). This refers to *resultant consciousness*, *name and form*, *sense organs*, *contact*, and *feeling*, depicted respectively as one aspect of the third link and the fourth through to the seventh links in the wheel of life.

projecting cause (*'phen byed kyi rgyu*). This refers to *ignorance*, *conditioning action*, and *causal consciousness*, depicted respectively as the first and second links and one aspect of the third link in the wheel of life, which together constitute the powerful karma that propels a sentient being into a particular type of rebirth.

proof (*sgrub byed*). This refers to the reason, or sign, which proves the thesis, or probandum, in a formally structured argument.

proof statement (*sgrub ngag*). See *syllogism*.

property of the subject (*phyogs chos*). See *syllogism*.

proponent in a debate (*snga rgol*). The person who is trying to prove something to an opponent within the context of a formally structured argument. The term *proponent* may apply to a school of thought or to a person who represents it.

Proponents of Inherent Existence (*rang bzhin yod par smra ba*). Any non-Prāsaṅgika.

Proponents of Noninherent Existence (*rang bzhin med par smra ba*). Prāsaṅgikas only.

provisional or interpretive meaning (*drang don*). For Mādhyamikas, this refers to conventional reality.

provisional or interpretive scripture (*drang don kyi gsung rab*). For the Prāsaṅgika system, this refers to scriptures that principally elucidate conventional reality.

quality (*yon tan*). Attribute or property; good, neutral, or bad qualities (but usually used to refer to good qualities).

Realists (*dngos por smra ba*). Proponents of true existence. Any non-Mādhyamika.

really established (*yang dag par grub pa*). See *established by its own nature*.

reason, sign, mark, evidence (*rtags*). The reason or evidence posited in a valid syllogism to show that the predicate applies to the subject. All logical reasoning depends on relations. Dharmakīrti posits only two types of relation—causal and same nature—based on which there are just three types of reason that can be used in a valid syllogism: a correct effect sign, a correct nature sign, and a correct nonobservation sign.

refuting consequence (*sun 'byin gyi thal 'gyur*). This is a logical consequence that is presented specifically to uproot a wrong view that the opponent holds tightly. It explicitly demonstrates to the opponent that by accepting certain premises, which he wishes to accept, he is thereby committed to accepting certain conclusions that contradict his own views. Even though the opponent does not want to accept these consequences, he is impelled to do so because they follow from what he asserts. The unwelcome consequences entailed by his view function to disprove his view.

related as mutually dependent (*phan tshun bltos pa'i 'brel ba*). This is a relationship of terminological dependence, which has much wider application than the stricter relations: causal relation and same-nature relation. It is presented within the Prāsaṅgika-Madhyamaka system only as the most profound meaning of dependent arising. It applies to all phenomena because everything is established as mutually dependent on its basis of imputation. This is what it means to lack inherent existence.

related as the same nature (*bdag gcig 'brel*). This is a relation whose components do not exist separately, yet they are not identical in that they can be distinguished conceptually. Consider, for example, a generality and its instances or an object and its attributes; there is no generality separate from its instances, and there is no object separate from its attributes. A same-nature relation is one-way, not mutual. An instance is related to its generality, not the other way around: an oak tree is dependent on being a tree in terms of its nature, but the reverse is not implied. Nevertheless if two components of a same-nature relation are coextensive, then a two-way relationship ensues because each is an instance of the other: an impermanent thing is a product, and vice versa. This two-way relationship is very different from the Madhyamaka relation of mutual dependence.

related causally (*de byung 'brel*). This is a relation whose components are different entities or natures. It involves impermanent things only: any cause and its effect. It is a one-way relation, not mutual. An effect is related to its cause—not the other way around: smoke is causally dependent on fire, but the reverse is not true.

relation ('*brel ba*). According to earlier Buddhist systems, there are just two ways of being related: related causally and related as the same nature. A relation holds between two different things and is characterized as follows: if this does not exist, then definitely that does not occur. This definition applies to both types of relations and in one direction only, not mutually (unless both components in a same-nature relation are coextensive). A third type of relation is presented in the Madhyamaka system: related as mutually dependent.

relationship of terminological dependence (*tha snyad rnam 'jog gi 'brel ba*). See *related as mutually dependent.*

renunciation (*nges 'byung*). This is a transformation of the mind characterized by a loss of interest in the eight worldly concerns, an identification of the root cause of suffering, and a heartfelt desire to become free from it.

repudiation (*skur 'debs*). Deprecation. This refers to the implicit or explicit denial of the existence of something that actually exists. It is the opposite of *superimposition.*

result corresponding to the cause (*rgyu mthun gyi 'bras bu*). This refers to experiences that are similar to the actions that caused them, which may occur in a lifetime subsequent to the main result of such action, the ripened result.

ripened result, fruitional result, matured result of karma (*rnam smin gyi 'bras bu, las kyi rnam smin*). This refers to the main result of the ripening of a karmic seed: the experience of being reborn into a certain type of life. A ripened result of contaminated karma is not a person; it is a nonassociated conditional factor within the continuum of a person. A ripened result is neutral—neither virtuous nor nonvirtuous.

ripening cause, fruitional cause, cause of ripening (*rnam min gyi rgyu*). This refers to the karma that causes a potential to ripen immediately into the next rebirth: existence, the tenth of the twelve links of dependent arising. A ripening cause must be powerful enough to propel rebirth, so it must be virtuous or nonvirtuous.

samādhi (*ting nge 'dzin*). Single-pointed meditative concentration. There are many levels of concentration, which may accompany different types of mind. When gradually developed in conjunction with a virtuous mind, samādhi eventually gives rise to śamatha.

śamatha (*zhi gnas*). Single-pointed meditative concentration, calm abiding, serenity. Śamatha arises as a result of having progressively developed nine specific levels of concentration. It is accompanied by physical and mental pliancy and their concurrent forms of bliss. It is united with vipaśyanā to subdue or remove the mental afflictions.

same, one (*gcig*). Absolute identity, including conceptual and terminological identity.

same entity, same nature (*ngo bo gcig, rang bzhin gcig*). This applies where the things concerned do not exist apart from one another, yet they may be differentiated conceptually and terminologically. For example, a thing and its attributes.

same meaning, same referent (*don gcig*). This applies where the referent or extension of two different terms is the same. There is a formal eightfold criterion provided: whatever is *a* is *b*, whatever is *b* is *a*, whatever is not *a* is not *b*, whatever is not *b* is not *a*, if *a* exists then *b* exists, if *b* exists then *a* exists, if *a* does not exist then *b* does not exist, if *b* does not exist then *a* does not exist.

Saṃmitīya (*mang pos bkur ba'i sde ba*). A subschool of the Vaibhāṣika (according to some classification systems); the opponent named in Candrakīrti's commentary on the selflessness of persons.

samsara (*'khor ba*). The uncontrolled taking of rebirth under the force of karma and the afflictions. The six realms of samsaric existence consist of the three lower realms (the hells, hungry ghosts, and animals) and three higher realms (humans, demigods, and gods).

secondary consciousness, mental factor (*sems 'byung*, Skt: *caitta*). See *accompanying consciousness*.

self-cognizing consciousness (*rang rig*). This is a directly perceiving, inwardly focused mind that observes an outwardly focused, other-cognizing mind. These minds are substantially identical. (Prāsaṅgikas do not posit any self-cognizing consciousness.)

self-grasping (*bdag 'dzin*). A mind grasping at inherent existence, whether of the person or of other phenomena.

self-grasping of persons (*gang zag gi bdag 'dzin*). A mind holding the person, or self, to be inherently existent.

self-grasping of phenomena (*chos kyi bdag 'dzin*). A mind holding phenomena, or dharmas, to be inherently existent.

sense basis, source of sense consciousness (*skye mched*, Skt: *āyatana*). These are the twelve sources of sense consciousness: internally, the six sense powers, and externally, the objects of the six sense consciousnesses.

sense powers, subtle sense organs (*dbang po*, Skt: *indriya*). These are the subtle sense organs, located in their grosser counterparts such as the eyeball, which function as the internal sources of their respective sense consciousnesses. However, the mental sense power is not an organ, it is a previous moment of mind.

serenity (*zhi gnas*). See *śamatha*.

similar, similarity (*mtshungs*). A formal notion of similarity may be employed in certain contexts. For example, there is a presentation of five shared features or similarities that obtain between a primary mind and its accompanying mental factors, which must have: the same substance, the same object, the same aspect, the same basis, and the same duration.

similar example (*mthun dpe*). See *syllogism*.

single-pointed concentration (*sems rtse gcig pa'i zhi gnas*). See *śamatha*.

sinking (*bying ba*). Laxity. This occurs when the mind does not hold its object strongly enough in meditation. The object still appears, but it does not appear sharply. Subtle sinking is a great obstacle to meditative concentration because it can seem like perfect samādhi.

solitary apprehender (*'dzin pa yang gar ba*). This refers to the self-cognizing mind, which has no accompanying mental factors; therefore it is neither a primary mind nor a secondary consciousness. See *self-cognizing consciousness*.

space-like emptiness (*nam mkha' lta bu'i stong nyid*). This is the mere absence of inherent existence. In a direct realization of śūnyatā only emptiness appears. This appearance of emptiness is said to be space-like.

stabilization (*ting nge 'dzin*). See *samādhi*.

stabilizing meditation (*'jog sgom*). The practitioner, instead of investigating the aspects and qualities of the object, synthesizes the various aspects into one and focuses on that object single-pointedly. When the attention wanders off, it is brought back to the object and placed there again and again until it remains spontaneously.

strictly contradictory. See *indirectly contradictory in the sense of being mutually eliminating*.

subject (*chos can*). Literally, something that has attributes. This term also refers to the subject of a formally structured argument.

subject (*yul can*). Literally, something that has an object. This term refers to persons, minds, and words.

subjective ultimate (*yul can don dam*). This refers to the consciousness that knows śūnyatā, the objective ultimate.

subsequent knowledge (*bcad shes*). A mind that realizes what has already been realized; knowledge that eliminates doubt.

substantially existent (*rdzas yod*). Lower Buddhist systems posit substantially existent things, such as indivisible atomic particles and moments of consciousness, to be the bases of imputation on which gross objects must be imputed. A substantially existent thing supposedly bears its identity from its own side and can be found by ultimate analysis. Prāsaṅgikas do not accept anything to be substantially existent.

substratum consciousness (*kun gzhi rnam shes*, Skt: *ālayavijñāna*). Foundation consciousness. Cittamātra/Yogācāra followers posit eight primary minds: the six sense consciousnesses, the afflicted mental consciousness, and the substratum consciousness. They consider the substratum consciousness to be the receptacle of the karmic seeds and imprints as well as the basis of identity of the self.

śūnyatā (*stong nyid*). Emptiness; the final nature of all phenomena. For Prāsaṅgikas this is the absence of inherent existence or lack of essential nature.

superimposition (*sgro btags*). Exaggeration. This refers to the implicit or explicit acceptance of the existence of something that does not actually exist. It is the opposite of *repudiation*.

supramundane path (*'jig rten las 'das pa'i lam*). This refers to the direct realization of emptiness, which in gradual stages removes karmic seeds from the mindstream and eventually purifies their imprints too.

svatantra (*rang rgyud*). See *autonomous inference*.

syllogism (*sbyor ba*, Skt: *prayoga*). This is not necessarily an autonomous syllogism. It is a positively stated argument that has the following form: the *subject* is the *predicate* because it is the *reason*, as in the *similar example*. For a syllogism to be correct it must instantiate the three modes, which in the case of an autonomous inference must be known by both parties using a commonly accepted notion of validity, as follows: the reason is a property of the subject, the presence of the reason entails the presence of the predicate, and the absence of the predicate entails the absence of the reason. The latter two modes are called the forward pervasion and the reverse pervasion, respectively. The similar example is provided to help the opponent recognize the relation between the reason and the predicate, based on his or her own experience. A valid syllogism, for a suitable opponent, might be: On the smoky mountain pass (the *subject*) there is a fire (the *predicate*) because there is smoke (the *reason*), as in the kitchen (the *similar example*).

syllogistic proof (*sbyor ngag*). See *syllogism*.

temporary cause of error (*'phral gyi 'khrul rgyu*). This mainly applies to sense consciousness and includes both external and internal causes of error, except the deep cause of error. Internal temporary causes of error include faulty sense organs, diseases affecting perception, hallucinogenic drugs, and so on. External causes of error include such things as the blades of an airplane propeller spinning so fast that we see it as one vibrating ring. See *deep cause of error.*

temporary stains (*glo bur gi dri ma*). This refers to the obstructions within a sentient being's mental continuum, of which there are two types: (afflictive) obstructions to liberation and (nonafflictive) obstructions to omniscience. Both types of obstructions can be removed eventually, so they are called temporary or adventitious stains. See *natural stain.*

terminologically established (*tha snyad rnam 'jog*). See *related as mutually dependent.*

thesis, probandum, that which is to be proved (*dam bca', bsgrub bya*). Combination of the subject and the predicate of a formally structured argument. See *syllogism.*

thing, impermanent thing, real thing (*dngos po*). The word *dngos po* has at least two meanings: a thing that arises and ceases in dependence on causes and functions to produce a result, and a truly existent thing.

thoroughly established nature (*yongs grub*). This refers to one of the three natures taught in the *Sutra Unraveling the Intended Meaning*: the ultimate nature of a thing. See *dependent nature* and *imputed nature.*

three doors to liberation (*rnam par thar pa'i sgo gsum*). Emptiness (*stong pa nyid*), signlessness (*mtshan ma med pa nyid*), and wishlessness (*smon pa med pa nyid*). These refer to the three aspects of understanding the selflessness of all phenomena.

three higher trainings (*bslab pa gsum*). Training in ethical conduct, meditative stabilization, and wisdom.

three modes (*tshul gsum*). See *syllogism.*

three natures (*mtshan nyid gsum*). These are taught in the *Sutra Unraveling the Intended Meaning*: the dependent nature, the imputed nature, and the thoroughly established nature. They are a fundamental feature of the Cittamātra system.

three poisons (*dug gsum*). The three root afflictions: desire, hostility, and ignorance.

total obscurer (*kun rdzob*). The mind of ignorance and/or the imprints of ignorance, both of which obscure the ultimate nature of all phenomena; the former actively grasps its object as truly existent, while the latter causes it to appear truly existent.

true cessation (*'gog bden*). The ultimate nature, or śūnyatā, of each purified stage of the mindstream, culminating in nirvana or enlightenment. See *cessation.*

truly established (*bden par grub pa*). See *established by its own nature.*

type, kind (*rigs*). A general concept under which something is classified and labeled.

ultimate (*don dam pa, dam pa'i don*). Supreme, holy object. Object of supreme wisdom. This refers to the ultimate nature of reality, śūnyatā, the mere absence of true existence, which is the object of the supreme wisdom directly perceiving it.

The yogic direct perception of ultimate reality purifies the perceiver's mindstream by gradually removing all the mental afflictions with their seeds and eventually their imprints.

ultimate analysis (*don dam dpyod pa'i rigs pa*). Ultimate analysis is used to develop an understanding of ultimate truth, śūnyatā. It is an analytical search for an object existing from its own side, that is, ultimately. The object analyzed cannot be found to exist in that way. What is found is a mere lack of its existing ultimately. This is the ultimate or final nature of the object analyzed. It is the ultimate truth, śūnyatā.

ultimate truth, ultimate reality (*don dam bden pa*, Skt: paramārthasatya). Śūnyatā, the emptiness of inherent existence.

ultimately established (*don dam par grub pa*). According to the Prāsaṅgika system, if an object were found by ultimate analysis, then it would be ultimately established, or ultimately existent. However, the object analyzed can never be found to exist from its own side, or ultimately, because it does not exist in that way. Therefore nothing is ultimately established.

ultimately existent. See *ultimately established.*

uninterrupted path (*bar chad med lam*). An uninterrupted path is a direct realization of śūnyatā that functions to remove inner obstructions: the mental afflictions, their seeds, and imprints. When the obstructions that it opposes are completely uprooted, it immediately becomes a path of liberation, which is also a direct realization of śūnyatā. These occur in the same meditation session.

union of śamatha and vipaśyanā (*zhi lhag zung 'brel*). The union of śamatha and vipaśyanā requires that first you have śamatha and then you engage in analytical meditation to bring forth a special blissful pliancy, a more advanced śamatha, which is itself vipaśyanā. Prior to that you may have achieved the combination of śamatha and vipaśyanā, which is similar to this union but not the real thing. The union of śamatha and vipaśyanā meditation on śūnyatā is needed to remove the inner obstructions.

unreal (*dngos med*). There are at least two senses of unreal: an *unreal thing*, which exists but does not arise or cease in dependence on causes and does not function to produce any result, and a *nonthing*, which does not exist at all. A nonthing is unreal, but it is not an unreal thing. An unreal thing is a permanent phenomenon. Additionally, in some contexts *unreal* can mean *not really existent* or *not truly existent.*

valid conventional knowledge (*kun rdzob pa'i tshad ma, tha snyad pa'i tshad ma*). A mind that correctly knows its principal object, a conventional thing.

valid knowledge (*tshad ma*, Skt: *pramāṇa*). A mind that correctly knows its primary or principal object. A valid sense consciousness is free of any temporary cause of error, though not necessarily of a deep cause of error; owing to the latter it is mistaken but not invalid (according to the Prāsaṅgika system).

valid mundane knowledge (*'jig rten grags pa'i tshad ma*). A mind that correctly knows what is commonly accepted in the world, conventional reality.

valid ultimate knowledge (*don dam pa'i tshad ma*). A mind that correctly knows its principal object, ultimate reality.

view, viewing (*lta ba*, Skt: *dṛṣṭi*). This mainly refers to a type of mind that holds its object in a certain way. It can also refer to a shared belief or philosophical tenet.

view of the perishable collection, egotistic view (*'jig tshogs la lta ba*, Skt: *satkāyadṛṣṭi*). This is a self-grasping mind, of which there are two types: contrived egotistic view and innate egotistic view.

view that upholds neither existence nor nonexistence (*yod min med min gyi lta ba*). Certain earlier Mādhyamikas interpret the sutras, and śāstras such as Nāgārjuna's works, to mean that things are not existent, not nonexistent, not both, and not neither. They think that to avoid the two extremes of eternalism and nihilism, one must believe that things neither exist nor do not exist. Tsongkhapa vigorously rejects this; he says it is a misinterpretation of the profound Madhyamaka view.

vipaśyanā (*lhag mthong*). Superior wisdom; highest insight. Buddhist practice includes both mundane and supramundane insight, though only the latter, combined with śamatha, is a prerequisite for attaining liberation or enlightenment. This type of vipaśyanā is unique to the Buddhist path.

visible form (*gzugs kyi skye mched*). An object perceived by a visual consciousness empowered by a visual sense organ. It includes color and shape.

wisdom (*shes rab*, Skt: *prajñā*). Wisdom is a mind that investigates the characteristics of its object.

wisdom Dharma body (*ye shes chos sku*, Skt: *jñānadharmakāya*). The conventional nature of a buddha's mind: the completely purified immaculate mind itself.

wisdom of meditative equipoise (*mnyam gzhag ye shes*). This refers to a perfectly concentrated mind of supreme wisdom that sees emptiness directly, which is generated within the mental continuum of an ārya being or a buddha. The object of this realization is known as space-like emptiness.

wisdom of subsequent attainment (*rjes thob ye shes*). This refers to a special understanding that things do not exist inherently, in the way that they appear to ordinary perception; it naturally manifests after arising from the meditative equipoise directly seeing emptiness. The object of this realization is known as illusion-like emptiness, or illusion-like nature.

without thinking anything, without discursive thought (*cir yang mi rtog pa*). According to the Prāsaṅgika system, this refers to a mind that is focused on one object without making analytical distinctions, such as "this is so" or "that is not so." It does not refer to a mind that is free from a conceptual image. See *free from thought*.

worldly convention (*'jig rten gyi tha snyad*). See *convention*.

Notes

1. *In Praise of Dependent Arising* (*rTen 'brel bstod pa*), 2, in *Dharma Practices* (*Chos spyod*), 79.

2. *Engaging in the Bodhisattva's Deeds*, 8.134.

3. *Introduction to the "Middle Way,"* 1.3.

4. The five aggregates are the basis of imputation of a person. They roughly constitute a person's body, mind, and inner forces: form, feeling, discernment, conditioning factors, and consciousness. Each of these five is an aggregation of many elements or factors, all of which are in a constant state of flux.

5. The person is even included within the aggregates—specifically the fourth aggregate, conditioning factors. This is because a person is impermanent and not uniquely any of the other aggregates.

6. The third volume of the series discusses how to develop bodhicitta and the first four perfections. The fourth volume covers the fifth perfection: meditative concentration.

7. See volume 4 of this series.

8. Sentient beings born into the formless realm have no material body though they have all the other aggregates, including those that are types of mind and those that are neither mental nor physical, such as karmic potentialities within the mental continuum.

9. "Seed" (*sa bon*) here refers to a certain type of potentiality deposited by an occurrence of a mental affliction, which leads to further occurrences of that mental affliction.

10. The Buddhist notion of "consciousness" (*shes pa / yid kyi rnam par shes pa*) is much broader than the Western notion of consciousness. It does not refer merely to a conscious state of mind but rather to the mental continuum, or moments within it, in any state at all, including in a state of sleep or unconsciousness. The distinction between "consciousness," "unconsciousness," and "subconsciousness" found in the West is not presented in Buddhist theory. Instead other distinctions are made, some of them very subtle indeed, which do not appear in Western theory.

11. This basic understanding of true cessation seems to be common to most Buddhist

systems. However, a more subtle understanding of true cessation as a special type of śūnyatā—the emptiness of inherent existence of a mind from which certain obstructions have been permanently removed—is discussed in chapters 3 and 10 of this volume.

12. *Engaging in the Bodhisattva's Deeds*, 8.4.

13. A sense consciousness arises in dependence on specific conditions including: a previous moment of consciousness, an observed object, and a corresponding sense power. The last two categories are often listed independently as the *twelve sources of sense consciousness*: six objects of the senses and six sense powers. We use the term "source" to translate the Sanskrit term *āyatana*, which is translated as *skye mched* in Tibetan. This is an abbreviation of *skye ba'i sgo mched pa* and literally means "opener of the doors of arising." In other words, the "sources" open the doors for the arising of the six sense consciousnesses. The six objects of the senses function as external sources of sense consciousness, and the six sense powers function as internal sources. A sense power may be described as a subtle sense organ (e.g., the eye sense power) that is located within its respective gross organ (e.g., the eye); however, the mental sense power, which is a source of the mental sense consciousness, is not a subtle organ but rather another type of mind. The subtle sense organs cannot be seen with the naked eye but can be seen by certain clairvoyants. For the sake of Western readers we may use terminology such as "visual sense power," as here in this passage, though in some places we may use more literal language, such as "eye sense power" and correspondingly "eye sense consciousness"—especially where the text contains concise arguments about these topics and where it uses stock examples such as the "eye" (*mig*) to refer either to the corresponding sense power or to its sense consciousness.

14. This stanza from the *King of Concentrations Sutra* (or *King of Samādhi Sutra*) was also discussed in volume 4 of this series.

15. *Basic Path to Awakening* (*Lam rim nyams mgur*), 35–37, in *Dharma Practices*, 71.

16. *Extensive Sport Sutra*, cited in Thurman, *Tsong Khapa's Speech of Gold*, 114n167.

17. In this context, which lists the objects of the sense powers and sense consciousnesses, the term *form* strictly means "visible form." This is much narrower than the notion of "form" encountered in the previous two chapters—the form aggregate and the form and formless realms—where it means "body" or "physical matter." Visible form is a subset of physical form within the threefold division of impermanent things: form, consciousness, and conditioning factors that are neither form nor consciousness.

18. According to Inada, *Nāgārjuna*, this comes from the Sagāthakam section of the *Descent into Laṅka Sutra*, verses 165–66.

19. The three worlds (*sa gsum*) should not be confused with the three realms (*khams gsum*) of cyclic existence: the desire realm, the form realm, and the formless realm.

20. *Introduction to the "Middle Way,"* 6.79.

21. An etymological examination shows the particular characteristics denoted. The Tibetan term *sems can* literally means "one who possesses consciousness" and is usually translated as "sentient being." One of the Tibetan words for "person" is *skyes bu*, which means a being born with a certain capacity or ability. The word derives from the expression *shed las skyes pa*. *Shed* means strength, vital force, or ability. Thus Bon texts often use the term *shed bu* to indicate a vital being in much the same way Buddhist texts use the term *skye bu*. Another word for "person" in Tibetan is *gang zag*, which can be explained by looking at the meaning of the term's two syllables. *Gang* means "full" and refers to the mental continuum of ordinary beings as filled with mental afflictions. When a person is filled with mental afflictions, he or she "falls down," *zag*, into the different realms of cyclic existence. This etymological explanation of the term "person" provides only the general meaning of the term; it does not imply that all persons must possess the attributes described. Śākyamuni Buddha no longer had any afflictions within his mental continuum after attaining enlightenment, yet he is considered to have been a person throughout his life. Another etymological explanation of *gang zag* may be given with regard to him: he is full of virtue and all defilements have fallen away. Similarly, he is not referred to as a sentient being, even though he possesses consciousness.

22. Searching for the inherent identity of an object analyzed in terms of this mutually related triad—action, agent, and object of action (*bya byed las gsum*)—forms the core of Nāgārjuna's Madhyamaka analysis.

23. *Illumination of the Middle Way* presents the Svātantrika-Madhyamaka view. The Prāsaṅgika-Madhyamaka view regarding the definitive meaning is different. These differences will be presented later in the text.

24. Here *valid* means "reliable."

25. There are different scholarly interpretations regarding which of Nāgārjuna's works should be included in the list of the six philosophical treatises (*rigs tshogs drug*). According to David Seyfort Ruegg (*Literature of the Madhyamaka School*, 8) the six are: *Fundamental Treatise on the Middle Way* (*Mūlamadhyamaka-kārikā*), *Sixty Verses on Reasoning* (*Yuktiṣaṣṭikā*), *Seventy Verses on Emptiness* (*Śūnyatāsaptati*), *The End of Disputes* (*Vigrahavyāvartanī*), *Pulverizing the Categories* (*Vaidalyaprakaraṇa*), and *Proof of Convention* (*Vyavahārasiddhi*). Ruegg says that the last text is not extant and the *Precious Garland* (*Ratnāvalī*) is often substituted. (Translation of the text titles in Ruegg's work may differ from the translation we provide in this volume.)

26. Ngog Loden Sherab (1059–1109), a Kadam scholar and the nephew and spiritual heir of Atiśa's disciple Ngog Legpai Sherab (1018–1115), translated many important works in the Buddhist canon. The elder Ngog founded Sangphu Monastery, and the younger greatly expanded its influence.

27. An implicative negation (*ma yin dgag*) is a negation of a particular thing that also implies something else. For example, "The fat cow is not fed at night." We know from experience that if a cow is fat, it must eat. There are only two alternatives: it is fed either during the day or during the night. Therefore we know from the negation of "fed at night" that the cow must be fed during the day. Negation is a complex logical issue that will be dealt with in greater detail later in the text.

28. A mere negation (*med dgag*) is a negation of a particular thing without implying anything else. For example, "There is no cow in the barn." This statement does not imply the existence of anything else in the barn. The barn is simply the location of the mere absence.

29. Yeshe De (Ye shes sDe, late eighth to early ninth century).

30. This is similar to a commonly accepted rule of derivation in classical Western logic, *modus tollendo tollens*: $P \to Q, \sim Q \vdash \sim P$. Some Western Buddhist commentators translate *prasaṅga* as *reductio ad absurdum*. However, the latter term has a more restricted application: if an explicit contradiction, e.g., $Q \& \sim Q$, can be derived from the premises of an argument, then the faulty premise, P, is negated using the rule of *reductio ad absurdum*, for example: $P \to Q, P \to \sim Q \vdash \sim P$.

31. According to Ruegg (*Literature of the Madhyamaka School*, 49n129), the eight great commentaries on Nāgārjuna's *Fundamental Treatise on the Middle Way* are: Nāgārjuna's *Akutobhayā*, Buddhapālita's *Vṛtti*, Candrakīrti's *Prasannapadā*, and commentaries by Devaśarman, Guṇaśrī, Guṇamati, Sthiramati, and Bhāvaviveka. Scholars dispute Nāgārjuna's authorship of the *Akutobhayā* because a stanza by Āryadeva is quoted in the text.

32. The Mahayana texts present a fourfold terminological division of nirvana: natural nirvana, nirvana with remainder, nirvana without remainder, and nonabiding nirvana. Only the last three are genuinely types of nirvana. The term *nirvana* indicates a state beyond suffering and its causes. The final nirvana of the Mahayana, nonabiding nirvana, is a completely purified state that is free of both the afflictive obstructions and the obstructions to omniscience. It is the ultimate nature of a buddha's holy mind.

33. This is an analytical cessation, which according to the Prāsaṅgika system is emptiness.

34. The term *nonabiding nirvana* indicates that a fully enlightened buddha abides neither in samsara nor in solitary peace.

35. The phrase "in this context" refers to Nāgārjuna's Madhyamaka texts.

36. *Engaging in the Bodhisattva's Deeds*, 6.93a–b.

37. The word *dmigs pa* can mean: perceive, be perceived, perception, exist, existent, know, known, or object. The Tibetan term generally shows no differentiation between noun and verb or between active and passive voice in itself; such differences are sometimes indicated by accompanying terms or the broader context.

38. This second explanation is offered to accommodate those masters who interpret the first occurrence of "self" in this verse as the *basic object*, and the second occurrence of "self" as the *held object* of the view of the perishable collection. Geshe Sopa suggests that a yogi can begin with a general notion of self, which is then analyzed into the basic object and the held object.

39. *Introduction to the "Middle Way,"* 1.3.

40. Jetsun Chokyi Gyaltsen (1469–1544), also known as Sera Jetsunpa, authored the main textbooks used at Sera Je Monastery.

41. Although in general this series follows the translation of text titles in the *Great Treatise on the Stages of the Path* published by Snow Lion, in this volume the title of Candrakīrti's *Madhyamakāvatāra-bhāṣya* is translated as *Commentary on the "Introduction to the 'Middle Way.'"* Readers of the translation will find this text called *Explanation of the "Middle Way" Commentary*.

42. Realists make a distinction between being *substantially existent* (*rdzas yod*) and *existing as a substance* (*rdzas su yod pa*). A person is not substantially existent because of being imputedly existent but does exist as a substance because of being a functioning thing.

43. *Faultlessly Revealing the Path to Liberation,* 114–15.

44. Upon attaining complete enlightenment one simultaneously attains the four buddha bodies: svābhāvikakāya, jñānadharmakāya, saṃbhogakāya, and nirmāṇakāya. The first two are respectively the ultimate and conventional Dharma body, or dharmakāya, and the second two are types of form body, or rūpakāya.

45. This verse has such far-reaching implications that Geshe Sopa quotes it several times in his commentary to illustrate Tsongkhapa's arguments.

46. See volume 3, chapter 7, for a discussion of this topic, and chapter 3 of the present volume.

47. We must know the two truths in order to attain the two buddha bodies within the Mahayana system or to attain the resultant bodies within the Hinayana system. But we do not need to attain the two buddha bodies or the resultant bodies in order to know the two truths.

48. *In Praise of Dependent Arising,* in *Dharma Practices,* 79.

49. For a complete discussion of the twelve links see volume 2, chapter 9. In brief, the twelve links begin with ignorance, ignorance gives rise to karma, karma gives rise to a specific type of consciousness, that consciousness gives rise to name and form, name and form give rise to the six subtle sense organs, the subtle sense organs give rise to contact, contact gives rise to feeling, feeling gives rise to attachment, attachment gives rise to grasping, attachment and grasping together give rise to existence that is ready to bring the next rebirth, existence gives rise to birth, birth gives rise to aging and death and all other suffering. There are four

main ways to analyze this process. We can analyze it in terms of the thoroughly afflicted elements of samsara: the forward process, which shows the causal series of their arising (beginning with the arising of ignorance); and the reverse process, which shows the resultant series of their arising (beginning with the arising of aging and death). We can also analyze it in terms of the completely pure elements of the path to nirvana: the forward process, which shows the causal series of their cessation (beginning with the cessation of ignorance); and the reverse process, which shows the resultant series of their cessation (beginning with the cessation of aging and death).

50. There is a formal eightfold criterion for X being the same meaning as Y: whatever is X is Y, whatever is Y is X, whatever is not X is not Y, whatever is not Y is not X, if X exists then Y exists, if Y exists then X exists, if X does not exist then Y does not exist, and if Y does not exist then X does not exist. This criterion is taught early in the Tibetan monastic curriculum in accordance with various Collected Topics (*bsdus gra*) textbooks while presenting the nature of definition, definiendum, and illustration.

51. Form and form's emptiness are inseparable in reality and thus are one entity, yet they are different isolates because for a conceptual consciousness the one term does not evoke the other.

52. This is true of the Tibetan text on rare occasions, whereas the Sanskrit text seems to make consistent use of the word *śūnyatā*, emptiness.

53. We should consider whether this is referring to one person or one mind. If the latter, we cannot say that the wisdom directly seeing emptiness simultaneously perceives dependent arising, or vice versa. So we may be inclined to think that the conceptual mind understanding emptiness indirectly understands dependent arising, and vice versa. But emptiness is a nonimplicative negation, according to Tsongkhapa's system—so how can there be another object appearing? Therefore it seems that this must be referring to one person.

54. For readers who are following the *The Great Treatise on the Stages of the Path to Enlightenment*, volume 3, a division is made here, and this question begins chapter 11. In Geshe Sopa's commentary we follow the presentation provided by Tsongkhapa in the Tibetan text, where no such division is made. Therefore we do not start a new chapter at this point. However, we do insert a subdivision to link this section with the English translation and to provide a breathing space.

55. This verse may be translated in various ways depending whether the focus is on things that dependently arise or on the quality of dependent arising itself. In the former case, the term *stong nyid* would be translated as "only empty," whereas in the latter case it would retain its usual translation as "emptiness." After much debate, we have adopted the second approach. Tsongkhapa explains below that to equate dependent arising and emptiness means that they are harmonious; it does not mean that they are exactly the same.

56. *Extensive Sport Sutra*, cited in Thurman, *Tsong Khapa's Speech of Gold*, 114n167.

57. Classic texts often use a rabbit horn as an example of something that does not exist. (Somebody once showed me a picture of a rabbit with big horns. It looked real but was a joke!) A donkey horn or a human horn is a similar nonexistent thing. Actually there is a myth about a Tibetan king who had horns. King Langdarma, who reigned in the ninth century, supposedly wore a special headdress made from red string tied in two elaborate knots on each side of a central parting in his hair to hide his horns. Every time his hair was washed, the person assisting him had to be killed to prevent his telling anyone else about the horns.

58. The four alternatives—exist, not exist, both, neither—concern inherent existence.

59. Dharmakīrti says in the *Commentary on Valid Cognition*: 2.179c–d, in Jackson, *Is Enlightenment Possible?*: "This suffering is proven to have a cause, because it is occasional."

60. *Ji lta ba gzigs pa'i gzigs ngor ji snyed pa ma gzigs; ji snyed pa gzigs pa'i gzigs ngor ji lta ba ma gzigs.*

61. For a complete discussion of the varieties of karmic results see volume 2 of this series, pages 96–133.

62. *Commentary on Valid Cognition*, 2.1a. This text has four chapters altogether, though different monasteries have different ways of numbering them. It is based on Dignāga's *Compendium of Valid Cognition*.

63. What Geshe Sopa calls the "main object" or the "principal object" varies slightly according to context. On some occasions he uses it to refer to the *basic object (dmigs yul)*, as he does here, and on other occasions to the *held object ('dzin stang kyi yul)*, which is the basic object as it is held or understood.

64. Each school has its own understanding of "existing by way of its own characteristics."

65. According to Jetsun Chokyi Gyaltsen, the direct realization of emptiness is present but nonmanifest within the mental continuum of an ārya being during the subsequent attainment. It is only manifest during meditative equipoise directly realizing śūnyatā. This topic is discussed further in chapter 15.

66. The held object (*'dzin stangs kyi yul*) refers to the basic object (e.g., blue) as it is held by that consciousness (i.e., as blue, in the case of a valid visual consciousness perceiving blue). This is considered to be the main object here. It is not entirely the same as the appearing object (*snang yul*).

67. *Lamrim Chenmo*, 617, last line (1985, Xining edition). Geshe Sopa recommends omitting the word *'dzin par* that appears here.

68. In other contexts, "worldly being" refers to those who have not realized śūnyatā directly. But here, "from a worldly perspective" refers to the perspective of those who have not even realized śūnyatā conceptually, let alone directly.

69. *Introduction to the "Middle Way,"* 6.97d.

70. The fifth sense object—sound, which is the object of hearing—does not incorporate atoms, so it is not counted as one of the elementary substances here.

71. An aggregation of atoms of similar type refers to the atoms that accumulate to make up a single object, such as a pot. These atoms exist within one substantial continuum. In contrast, a collection of atoms of dissimilar type refers to the atoms that constitute different individuals that together make up a collective object, such as an army or a forest. A collective object of this kind is based on atoms that compose a number of separate individuals. This collection does not exist as a substance because the components—soldiers, trees, and so forth—are unique individuals with different substantial continua. Tsongkhapa discusses this topic in *Essential Explanation of the Provisional and the Definitive*, 110.

72. The others are the Naiyāyika, Sāṃkhya, Mīmāṃsaka, Nirgrantha, and Cārvāka.

73. See the first quotation in this chapter from Candrakīrti's *Commentary on the "Four Hundred Stanzas."*

74. Although these imprints are called *nonafflictive ignorance*, they are not actually ignorance because they are not mental factors or minds; they are nonassociated conditioning factors. A *nonassociated conditioning factor* (*ldan min 'du byed*) is so called because it is a conditioning factor that is not any part of the consciousness aggregate, nor the physical form aggregate, nor any of the mental factors included within the category of "conditioning factors."

75. Arhats and pure-ground bodhisattvas do not hold anything to be truly existent, and they do not have any minds arising that hold things to be truly existent; however, except for when they see śūnyatā directly, things still appear to them to be truly existent.

76. *Refutation of Objections*, 29c–d.

77. See chapter 4, note 49, of this volume for further details about their forward and reverse processes.

78. *Illumination of the Middle Way*, quoted in Jetsun Chokyi Gyaltsen's *Complete Meaning of the Middle Way* (*dBu ma'i spyi don*), 199.

79. See chapter 21 for a more extensive presentation of this passage and commentary on it.

80. *Clarification of the Intention* (1988), 192.

81. The appearing object may also be considered in various ways. To a mind apprehending a pot as beautiful, the pot appears, being beautiful appears, and being inherently existent appears.

82. *Clarification of the Intention* (1988), 162.

83. According to the Sautrāntika system, conventional truth is synonymous with permanent phenomena. According to other traditions, conventional truth in

general is permanent because all generalities are permanent. However, if something is a conventional truth, it is not necessarily permanent—for example, a table.

84. *Sublime Continuum*, 1.154a–b. The same stanza appears in *Ornament for Clear Knowledge*, 5.21.

85. Not made by causes and conditions, not impermanent, and not comparatively dependent on others.

86. A *conceived object* (*zhen yul*) is an object of a conceptual mind only, never of a direct perception. A conceptual awareness conceives something, and the object that it holds is the conceived object—a mental image that represents its basic object as held in a certain way, correctly or incorrectly. The term *held object* (*'dzin stangs kyi yul*) has a wider meaning. The held object may be an object of a conceptual mind or of a directly perceiving awareness; likewise, it may be held correctly or incorrectly.

87. See chapter 8 of volume 2 of this series.

88. The quotation referred to begins, "This stanza teaches that attachment to things arises owing to the power of afflictive ignorance..."

89. See chapters 7 and 8 for an extensive presentation of the two truths.

90. See chapter 21 for a presentation of the obstructions to omniscience.

91. We should note that not every mind realizing selflessness is a wisdom realizing selflessness because there are also primary minds that realize selflessness (wisdom is a mental factor—a secondary mind that accompanies a primary mind).

92. The second link, *'du byed*, may also be translated as *formative activity*. For a complete explanation of the twelve links of dependent origination see chapter 9 of volume 2 of this series. We delve into it again in chapter 21 of the present volume.

93 *Essential Explanation of the Provisional and the Definitive* (1991), 159. Tsongkhapa composed these lines using the same style of reasoning employed by Candrakīrti in *Introduction to the "Middle Way,"* 6.32. See Thurman, *Tsong Khapa's Speech of Gold*, 310.

94. *Commentary on Valid Cognition*, 2.247c. Cited in Jackson, *Is Enlightenment Possible?*, 393, 449.

95. *Engaging in the Bodhisattva's Deeds*, 9.40a–b.

96. Sopa and Hopkins, *Cutting through Appearances*, 176.

97. See Hopkins, *Meditation on Emptiness*, 888–90n739.

98. The expressions *sun 'byin* (refuting consequence) and *thal 'gyur* (consequence) basically have the same meaning. These forms of argument dispel an opponent's wrong view by showing that what follows from it is unacceptable to the oppo-

nent himself. In addition, there is the logical system of *proof statements* (*grub ngag*), which includes *syllogisms* (*sbyor ba*). Mādhyamikas may use syllogisms, provided they are not regarded as valid with respect to inherent nature; in other words, they never use *autonomous syllogisms* (*rang rgyud kyi sbyor ba*, Skt *svatantraprayoga*). See chapters 13–16 for further explanation.

99. *Fundamental Treatise*, 1.1.

100. The twenty sangha is the hidden meaning of this sutra passage. This complex topic is clearly explained in Maitreya's *Ornament for Clear Knowledge*. In brief, the Hinayana system presents a list of twenty sangha. There are eight divisions in connection with the śrāvaka path: the enterers and abiders in the four fruits of the stream-winner, once-returner, nonreturner, and arhat. An abider is one who has obtained the fruit of a particular stage. There is also the pratyekabuddha, which counts as one division. These categories are subdivided to make a total of twenty. These twenty are the sangha of ordinary individuals in whom we take refuge.

The meaning of "sangha" here, understood within the context of the Hinayana vinaya system, is a community of at least four ordinary individuals who hold the prātimokṣa vows. A group of four fully ordained monks or nuns, who completely possess those vows, comprise a spiritual assembly. The spiritual assembly, or sangha, can perform many special vinaya activities, such as giving vows, making confession and purification, engaging in the summer retreat, and opening the boundaries after the retreat. Although individuals take responsibility for specific tasks, these rituals can only be fulfilled by the sangha as a whole.

There is also the ārya sangha. The ārya sangha does not need to be an assembly of four persons. When an individual achieves a direct realization of truth, that person is called sangha and has the ability to perform all the vinaya functions. He or she does not need to be a monk or nun. According to the Mahayana system, individual male or female ārya bodhisattvas, whether laypersons or monks and nuns, are the sangha.

101. The Tibetan word for Sāṃkhya, *grangs can pa*, can be translated as "enumerators." Sāṃkhyas catalog all phenomena into twenty-five objects of knowledge. Among these twenty-five, there are two permanent objects: the universal principle and the person. The *person* or *self* is a special kind of mind or consciousness that is pure, permanent, and pervasive. It is an independent, clear awareness that experiences things. It does not produce anything and it is not produced by any other cause. The *universal principle*, on the other hand, is a subtle, invisible potential. It is the permanent and absolute cause of everything except the person.

There are two divisions of the Sāṃkhya: one accepts a creator god and the other does not. Some Sāṃkhyas think that the universal principle alone cannot be the creator. They believe there must be some intelligence along with the universal principle because the world seems to have a special design. The universal principle is a bit too dull to have created such a clever design. Therefore they posit a god, Īśvara. God and the universal principle work together as a team to create everything except the person. God wishes for something, and the universal principle creates it for him. God alone cannot create the world; the universal principle alone cannot create the world. God is like an intelligent cripple with very good eyesight; he knows what to do, but has no power to produce anything. The universal principle has the potential to produce objects but lacks any clear direction, like a blind man with very good legs. When these two team up, they have the vision and ability to produce the desired results.

According to the Sāṃkhyas who do not accept god, the universal principle alone is the creator of everything else in the world for the pure, permanent, and pervasive self (the only thing not created by the universal principle). When a yogi develops knowledge of how the universal principle functions, the principle dissolves all its creations back into itself. Eventually all that remains is the person and the universal principle. The universal principle—as if ashamed, like the mistress of a man discovered by her lover's wife—withdraws from the person and disappears. All connection between them ceases. In that moment the person attains liberation. The person has always been there and does not cease to exist but is now liberated because samsara has disappeared.

102. *Clarification of the Intention* (1988), 162.

103. This second qualifier, "inherently," is applicable only within the Prāsaṅgika-Madhyamaka system—unless accompanied by the first qualifier, "ultimately," which is applicable within both systems.

104. Here Geshe Sopa is making a distinction between two sets of Tibetan terms: first, *mngon sum du* (directly) and *rgyud nas* (indirectly); and second, *dngos su* (explicitly) and *shugs la* (implicitly). These pairs do not refer to exactly the same things, though it is often the case that both sets of terms are translated into English as *directly* and *indirectly*.

105. Other systems, such as the Vaibhāṣika, say that although a buddha, being omniscient, sees everything, he does not see everything simultaneously because one moment of consciousness cannot see everything at once. The Madhyamaka system says that even one moment of a buddha's knowledge sees everything simultaneously because the omniscient mind is free of all obstructions.

106. This example is specifically mentioning bodhisattvas who did not previously gain a direct realization of śūnyatā on the Hinayana path.

107. According to the Svātantrikas, a valid mind is unmistaken with regard to its object's appearing to be inherently existent. The Prāsaṅgikas do not use this as a criterion because they consider that all conventional valid knowledge, except for that of a buddha, is mistaken regarding the appearance of inherent existence.

108. *Blaze of Reasons*, quoted by Tsongkhapa in *Clarification of the Intention* (1988), 367.

109. As presented in chapter 16 of this volume, Tsongkhapa explicitly states that in the context of this discussion the term *inference* means "syllogism." In *Ocean of Reasoning* he says that the term *rang rgyud* (*svatantra*) means "autonomous." Although Tsongkhapa frequently uses the latter term alone, we find it applied

to *inference* (*rjes dpag/anumāna*) or to *reason* (*rtags/liṅga* and *gtan tshigs/hetu*) in general, or to what Tibetan masters have identified as one specific form of inference: a *syllogism* (*sbyor ba/prayoga*). It is never applied to the other specific form of inference discussed here: a *consequence* (*thal 'gyur/prasaṅga*). Therefore to make the situation clear, in Tsongkhapa's commentary as well as his own, Geshe Sopa prefers to attach the term *autonomous* to the specific term *syllogism* rather than to the more general term *inference*.

110. Although the Prāsaṅgikas favor the use of consequences, they also accept the use of *nonautonomous* inferences, reasons, and syllogisms in their own arguments, as we shall see later.

111. See chapters 4, 10, and 20 of this volume for some discussion about what it means to be related as the same nature. The term "related as the same nature" is also presented in the glossary.

112. *Refutation of Objections*, 1c–d.

113. The term "opponent" need not always refer to another person. It can include a view that you, the "proponent," are trying to oppose—whether it is within yourself or someone else.

114. Geshe Sopa notes that although the term Realist (*dngos por smra ba*) usually refers to philosophical systems that assert that all functioning things are truly, really, or ultimately existent—that is, the lower Buddhist schools, from the Yogācāra down to the Vaibhāṣika, as well as the non-Buddhist schools of thought—sometimes it has a wider connotation. Here and in similar contexts it refers to all those who hold things to be inherently existent, and implicitly includes the Svātantrika-Mādhyamika system. Geshe Sopa declines to use the term Essentialist in translating *dngos por smra ba* in these contexts and prefers to use the term Realist. This point is touched on in chapter 12, and an account of the narrower sense of Realist is provided in chapter 15.

115. The passage from *Clear Words* referred to here appears in *Lamrim Chenmo*, 617, which we translate as follows: "Moreover, those are mutually dependent. If there is valid knowledge, then there are things known; and if there are things known, then there is valid knowledge. Therefore valid knowledge and the object known are not established by their own nature." (See chapter 7 of this volume.)

116. We are still referring to the subjective object of negation here—the wrong view grasping at inherent existence.

117. Candrakīrti, *Commentary on the "Introduction to the 'Middle Way,'"* 79. Cited in Tsongkhapa, *Clarification of the Intention*, 146, and in Tsongkhapa, *Ocean of Reasoning*, 39. See *Ocean of Reasoning* 2006, 48–49.

118. There are other kinds of inferences also, such as those based on renown and those based on belief.

119. Here Tsongkhapa uses Dharmakīrti's terminology to describe the first mode, the

combination of the subject and the reason. In most logical contexts the word for the subject is *chos can*, the word for the reason is *rtags*, and the object to be proved or the thesis is *phyogs*. However, here we find the term *phyogs chos*, where *phyogs* indicates the subject, and *chos* refers to the reason, which is a property or attribute of the subject. So the combination of subject and reason is reflected in this term. There is a lengthy discussion in Dharmakīrti's text about why the usual term for the subject is not employed in this context. There is no need to discuss it here.

120. This is gross impermanence.

121. This is subtle impermanence.

122. According to the Prāsaṅgikas, Bhāvaviveka makes a related mistake himself by the application of the qualification "ultimately" to the predicate "arise," which is an unnecessary and inappropriate addition for both the proponent and the opponent. The Madhyamaka proponents flatly negate that anything arises from itself—both conventionally and ultimately. The Sāṃkhya opponents accept without qualification that a thing does arise from itself. This is based on the opponents' assumption that everything is inherently existent. A detailed discussion of this important problem with Bhāvaviveka's logical argument will be found later in the text.

123. A *visible form* (*gzugs kyi skye mched*) is the external source of visual consciousness; it is the *observed object condition* (*dmigs rkyen*) of that consciousness—that is, the object perceived.

124. Although differentiating here between the two, Tsongkhapa sometimes oscillates between labeling an opponent a Realist and a Proponent of Inherent Existence—even in the same paragraph (see chapter 20). In such cases, the term Realist may have a wider connotation (see chapter 14, note 114).

125. However, according to Bhāvaviveka, the object is not truly existent and does not appear to be truly existent to a valid sense consciousness. Unlike the Prāsaṅgikas, he considers "truly existent" to be different from "inherently existent."

126. In the Tibetan text the term *phyin ci log* is used here. A slight distinction was made earlier between two meanings of this term: "distorted/nondistorted" or "mistaken/nonmistaken." Since this distinction is not made clearly here, it would be better to use the Tibetan word *'khrul pa / ma 'khrul pa* because *phyin ci log pa / phyin ci ma log pa* in this context means "mistaken/nonmistaken" consciousness specifically with regard to the appearing object only.

127. Tsongkhapa glosses the word *'dzin pa* here as *bzung ba*. These words are grammatically related and literally mean "hold" or "held." Tsongkhapa shows that the term *'dzin pa* has two meanings: in the context of a conceptual consciousness, *'dzin pa* has its usual meaning—"to grasp" or "to hold"—and in the context of a nonconceptual consciousness, *'dzin pa* is glossed as *bzung ba*, which here means "to appear" (*snang ba*).

128. *Shing ma yin pa'i las ldog pa snang ba.* The reverse of nontree appears to the thought apprehending a tree. But the reverse of tree's impermanence does not appear to that thought; it appears to the mind apprehending the tree's impermanence.

129. To say that the tree indirectly appears means that its appearance is mixed with an appearance of its image.

130. *Yul dus rang bzhin gang la bstod kyang grub sde rdzas gcig du yon tan tha dag.*

131. *Clarification of the Intention* (1988), 196.

132. Form is the appearing object and the held object of a direct perception apprehending form. Form is the held object of a thought apprehending form, and a conceptual image of form is its appearing object.

133. See chapters 8 and 9.

134. See chapter 11, where Candrakīrti's *Commentary on the "Four Hundred Stanzas"* says: "Here conceiving means: superimposing an unreal inherent nature."

135. See chapter 19.

136. In the Prāsaṅgika system, the innate grasping at true existence and the innate grasping at inherent existence are the same. In the Svātantrika system they are not because that system rejects things to be truly existent but accepts things to be inherently existent conventionally.

137. Geshe Sopa says that the earlier part of this paragraph refers to the contrived grasping at inherent existence, though the later part refers to the innate grasping at inherent existence.

138. It may even be a very hidden object, such as specific details about karmic cause and effect, which can only be known through relying on Buddha's word.

139. The Tibetan word *rang* (also Sanskrit *svatas*, "oneself") is highly ambiguous and leaves open the question of whether it refers to the questioner, identified as Bhāvaviveka in Geluk sources, or the person to whom the question is being addressed, Bhāvaviveka's opponent. Geshe Sopa reads it as the latter, and we have translated it as "for *yourself*."

140. This refers to the proponent, Bhāvaviveka.

141. In ancient India, things such as visible forms and so on were thought to arise from the four great elements: earth, fire, water, and wind. Each element has a special characteristic: the defining feature of earth is that it is hard and obstructing, fire is hot and burning, water is wet and moistening, and wind is light and moving.

142. *Ocean of Reasoning* (1997), 58; (2006), 66.

143. This is one of the rare occasions when Tsongkhapa uses the expression *rang bzhin yod par smra ba.*

144. *Essential Explanation of the Provisional and the Definitive*, 6.

145. These verses appear in the Pali canon, Saṃyutta Nikāya, 1.533–34, where they are attributed to Bhikkhunī Vajirā (aka Vīr[y]ā), and in the Chinese Saṃyukta Āgama, *Bhikṣuṇī Saṃyukta*, where they are attributed to Bhikṣuṇī Śailā (the transcription and order of the nuns' names differs in the two collections—see Bingenheimer 2008). They are quoted in commentaries of northern Buddhist traditions, such as Vasubandhu's *Abhidharma-kośa-bhāṣya*, where they are attributed to Arhantī Śailā (Pali: Selā).

146. According to Buddhism there are four devils, also called demons or *māras*. The first demon is the contaminated aggregates; it is a demon because all the misery of birth, aging, sickness, and death is experienced when one has a body composed of these aggregates. The gross body of an ordinary sentient being arises from mental afflictions and contaminated karma, so the second demon is the mental afflictions—the chief of which is the egotistic view that grasps "I" or "mine." Even pure-ground ārya bodhisattvas and arhats, who have abandoned the sufferings of aging, sickness, and death from the root and no longer have mental afflictions within their mindstreams, have bodies that arise from the imprints or stains of the root mental afflictions. This kind of subtle body—in the nature of the mind, not of flesh and bone—is not as perfect as a buddha's, so it is called a subtle demon of the aggregates. The third demon is the demon of death. We do not have the power to live forever; we all have to die sometime as a result of karma. The phrase "demon of death" could refer to some kind of spirit who takes your life, but here it does not refer to an external physical thing. It is a special kind of karmic cause; there is no way to prevent it from ripening. The fourth is the divine-youth demon. Usually this refers to an external spirit or subtle evil force that harms you.

147. *Tha snyad btags pa'i btags don btsal ba'i tshe na rnyed pa.*

148. In the *Descent into Laṅka Sutra*, Śākyamuni Buddha recounts that he was once Māndhātṛ, an extremely powerful and conceited king. Māndhātṛ was a *cakravartin*, an emperor of the four continents on earth, but he was not satisfied with that. He craved control over Trāyastriṃśa heaven and kingship of the desire-realm gods. With his powerful merit he rose to a position of sharing Indra's seat as the king of the gods. But when he sought sole power, owing to his egotistic attitude, he fell back down to earth.

149. *Cha can gyi nga.*

150. These four wrong views are included in a list of fourteen scripturally unspecified views. The remaining ten include: four views regarding nirvana—after death the Tathāgata continues to exist, does not continue to exist, both, or neither; four views regarding the future—the self and the world have an end, do not have an end, both, or neither; and two views regarding a permanent soul—the body and the soul are the same, and the body and the soul are different. These fourteen are part of a longer list of sixty-four wrong views that are presented in *Net of Brahma Sutra (Brahmajālasūtra)*. Tsongkhapa's commentary on these fourteen unspecified views is found in chapter 4 of *Golden Rosary of Eloquence*, a commentary on Maitreya's *Ornament for Clear Knowledge*.

151. Action (*bya*), agent (*byed*), and object (*las*). (In other contexts *las* means "action" and *bya* means "object.")

152. The subject of the syllogism is indicated by the word "that" (*de*), which refers to a self unrelated to the aggregates and lacking their characteristics of arising, abiding, and disintegrating.

153. *Essential Explanation of the Provisional and the Definitive* (1991), 159. See Thurman, *Tsong Khapa's Speech of Gold*, 310.

154. *Commentary on Valid Cognition*, 2.247c. See Jackson, *Is Enlightenment Possible?*, 393, 449.

155. This experiential understanding is still conceptual—it is not yet a direct perception of śūnyatā.

156. *Introduction to the "Middle Way,"* 6.31b (see chapter 7).

157. The term *valid* comes from Dharmakīrti's seven treatises, collectively known as the seven treatises of valid knowledge. These are a primary source of Buddhist logic. Here *valid* does not mean exactly the same as *logic*, though of course logic is used in these treatises on valid knowledge.

158. The title of the first book of Dignāga's *Compendium of Valid Cognition* (*Pramāṇasamuccaya*) uses this meaning of valid. The title is connected to the first homage of that text, which praises Buddha: "To the one who has become valid, the one who wishes to benefit beings, the teacher, the *sugata*, the protector, I bow down." There are a great many explanations of this homage, and the entire second chapter of Dharmakīrti's *Commentary on Valid Cognition* is a commentary on that homage. It discusses how Buddha became a valid teacher, from the start of developing compassion all the way up to the complete perfection of a Tathāgata. How does Dharmakīrti prove that Buddha is a perfectly valid being? He relies on the forward and reverse processes of reasoning going through the four special qualities presented in Dignāga's praise. "The one who has become valid" is what is to be proved; "the one who wishes to benefit beings" is the first step of the reasoning; "the teacher" is the second; "the sugata" is the third; and "the protector" is the fourth. The forward process of reasoning moves from the first step through to the fourth, and the reverse process of reasoning moves from the fourth step through to the first. A more detailed explanation of this can be found in Jackson, *Is Enlightenment Possible?*

159. This line appears in a prayer of the Gelug tradition, *bLo bzang rgyal bstan ma*, in *Dharma Practices*, 311.

160. *Condensed Lamrim*, verse 40.

161. See chapter 15 of this volume.

162. See volume 2 of this series.

163. Gungthang Rinpoche, *Spiritual Guide to the Jewel Island*, 14.

164. Sound is excluded here because it is not made of atoms.

165. This and the following four subsections are not part of Tsongkhapa's outline. Tsongkhapa's text has been subdivided for the ease of the reader. The square brackets indicate an editorial addition.

166. A syllogism includes a similar example because inferential knowledge is based on such an example within the knower's experience. However, if knowledge of the pervasion were limited to that example, then no general knowledge would be formed. In that case, even knowledge of the pervasion based on the example— knowing that if there is smoke in the kitchen then there is fire in the kitchen— would have to have been developed using an example other than a kitchen. Without that understanding, there would be no basis on which to understand the present case of the relationship between smoke and fire in the kitchen. Knowledge of the pervasion based on the further example would succumb to the same criticism. Hence there would be an infinite regress. For this reason, we do not accept that knowledge of the pervasion is limited to a particular case.

167. According to the Sautrāntika school, on the other hand, nonproduced things are conventional truths so are not grasped as ultimately existent. Produced things are considered to be ultimate truths because they are ultimately able to perform a function. The subtle object of negation in this system is an independent, substantially existent self.

168. *In Praise of Dependent Arising*, 1.

169. *Question of the Nāga King Anavatapta Sutra*, previously quoted and explained in chapter 9.

170. *Treasury of Knowledge*, 2.54c–d.

171. The eighth, ninth, and tenth bodhisattva grounds.

172. There are three kinds of emanation body, or nirmāṇakāya: supreme emanation, artisan emanation, and miscellaneous emanation. Śākyamuni Buddha manifested as a supreme emanation (*uttamanirmāṇakāya*) and engaged in the twelve special deeds. An artisan emanation (*śilpinnirmāṇakāya*) refers to a buddha who manifests as a person perfectly skilled in a specific field in order to subdue a particular sentient being. For example, a buddha might emanate as a superb musician to tame the pride of a talented musician who considers himself to be the best in the world. Miscellaneous emanation (*janmanirmāṇakāya*) refers to any independently manifested rebirth, especially as a deity in a pure land.

173. A pure-ground bodhisattva's mental body arises from uncontaminated karma and the ground of the imprints of ignorance (*ma rig bag chags kyi sa dang zag med kyi las*). A buddha, on the other hand, does not have any imprints of ignorance; they have all been purified. A buddha's nirmāṇakāya is simply a manifestation for the benefit of others.

174. An explanation of the word *dmigs pa* and the relationship between *existing* and

knowing or *perceiving* was given in chapter 3, note 37. Also, as Tsongkhapa eluci-
dated in chapter 5, the term *dngos po* is ambiguous; it may mean "inherent existence" or "functional thing."

175. *Engaging in the Bodhisattva's Deeds,* 9.40a–b.

176. *Engaging in the Bodhisattva's Deeds,* 9.40c–d.

177. *Perfection of Wisdom Sutra.* As discussed in Jetsun Chokyi Gyaltsen's *Complete
Meaning of the Middle Way,* 121–22.

178. According to the Prāsaṅgika tradition, selflessness and śūnyatā are the same: the
emptiness of inherent existence. Only the basis on which it is realized is different:
persons or phenomena, respectively.

179. *Commentary on Valid Cognition,* 2.212c–d.

180. This point was discussed in chapter 11, citing Candrakīrti's *Commentary on the
"Four Hundred Stanzas."*

181. *Treasury of Knowledge,* 2.33a.

182. *Engaging in the Bodhisattva's Deeds,* 8.4a–b.

183. See volume 4.

184. The nine stages of cultivating śamatha, which occur within the desire realm,
should not be confused with the nine stages of the three realms: the desire, form,
and formless realms. In the latter set, the desire realm is one stage; the form
realm consists of four stages—the four form dhyānas; and the formless realm
consists of four stages—the four formless dhyānas. Another use of the term *stage*
or *ground* (*sa*) occurs in the presentation of the ten stages, or spiritual grounds, of
the bodhisattva path.

185. See volume 4.

186. Geshe Sopa says that *de ltar na shes kyang* should be read as *de ltar ma shes kyang*.

187. See chapter 4 of this volume.

188. See chapter 5 of this volume.

189. See volume 3, chapters 7 and following, for a more detailed explanation of this
topic.

190. The syllable *mo,* as in this case, does not necessarily indicate a female; even the
title of the text we are working through contains it: *Lamrim Chenmo.*

191. This is presented in monastic textbooks on signs and reasoning within the context of the third way to delineate correct signs: delineating correct signs from the
point of view of the manner of proof.

192. There are four levels of the bodhisattva path of preparation: heat, peak, patience,

and supramundane qualities. The level of supramundane qualities is the highest ordinary state.

193. In addition, according to the Prāsaṅgika system, when a conventional thing appears—in this case, a conceptual image—it appears to exist inherently and thus is mistaken; in contrast, a direct perception of śūnyatā is free of the appearance of a conceptual image and of its appearing to exist inherently and so is nonmistaken.

194. In general there are four kinds of direct perception: sensory direct perception, mental direct perception, yogic direct perception, and self-cognizing direct perception. The Prāsaṅgikas accept only three of these; they do not accept self-cognizing direct perception.

195. This was explained more fully in chapter 8 of this volume.

196. *Commentary on Valid Cognition*, 2.141c.

197. See chapters 9 and 10 of volume 1 of this series.

198. See volume 1 of this series.

199. *Engaging in the Bodhisattva's Deeds*, 9.1a–b.

200. Chapa Chokyi Senge (1109–69), a student of Drolungpa (see chapter 1 of volume 1 of this series) and an abbot of Sangphu Monastery, is credited with introducing into Tibet the debating system using consequences rather than the formal syllogisms of the classical Indian tradition.

201. On Ngog, see note 26 in chapter 2.

202. See a more complete discussion of this point in the section "Why the object of negation must be carefully identified" in chapter 4 of this volume.

203. See chapter 1 of this volume and chapter 1 of volume 4 of this series.

204. *Sublime Continuum* (*Uttara-tantra*), 10a–b. This text presents nine "vajra points," the first three of which are the Three Jewels.

205. I have translated two different terms here: *du shes med pa'i snyoms 'jug* (*asaṃjñā-samāpatti*) and *'du shes med pa pa* (*āsaṃjñika*). The first refers to a type of mind, whereas the second refers to a conditioning factor. The second is quite ambiguous in its expression—it could even refer to a person (e.g., a sleeping god), as persons are included within the fourth of the five aggregates. However, Geshe Sopa explains that it refers to a karmic ripening within the continuum of such a person. I cannot find any other way of translating the term *'du shes med pa pa* that is acceptable and preserves its ambiguity. Some commentators might explain it to be a person. So I have translated it as "one without discernment," which leaves it open: a state, a person, a karmic ripening, and so on.

206. See chapter 5, volume 1 of this series.

207. See volume 4 of this series.

208. Dromtonpa ('Brom ston pa, 1005–64) was the foremost Tibetan disciple of Atiśa and founder of the Kadam tradition.

209. See volume 4 of this series.

210. *Collected Prayers* (*Zhal 'don gces btus*), 24.

211. *Collected Prayers*, 25.

212. *Collected Prayers*, 23.

213. Previously cited in volume 3, chapter 15.

214. Rendawa (1349–1412) was a lama of the Sakya tradition who wrote a commentary on Nāgārjuna's *Friendly Letter*. He became Tsongkhapa's root guru.

Bibliography

Sūtras and Śāstras

Blaze of Reasons
Tarkajvālā: Madhyamaka-hṛdaya-vṛtti-tarka-jvālā
dBu ma'i snying po'i grel pa rtog ge 'bar ba
author: Bhāvaviveka
P5256, vol. 96

Bodhisattva Levels
Bodhisattva-bhūmi: Yogā-cāra-bhūmau-bodhisattva-bhūmi
rNal 'byor spyod pa'i sa las byang chub sems dpa'i sa
author: Asaṅga
P5538, vol. 110

Buddha Nature Sutra
Ārya-tathāgata-garbha-nāma-mahāyāna-sūtra
'Phags pa de bzhin gshegs pa'i snying po zhes bya ba theg pa chen po'i mdo
P924, vol. 36

Buddhapālita's Commentary on the "Fundamental Treatise"
Buddhapālita-mūla-madhyamaka-vṛtti
dBu ma rtsa ba'i 'grel pa buddha pā li ta
author: Buddhapālita
P5242, vol. 95

Chapter Teaching the Three Vows
Tri-saṃvara-nirdeśa-parivarta-nāma-mahāyāna-sūtra
sDom pa gsum bstan pa'i le'u zhes bya ba theg pa chen po'i mdo
Section 1 of the *Pile of Precious Things Collection*, Ratna-kūṭa
P760.1, vol. 22

Clear Words
Prasanna-padā: Mūla-madhyamaka-vṛtti-prasanna-padā
dBu ma rtsa ba'i 'grel pa tshig gsal ba zhes bya ba
author: Candrakīrti
P5260, vol. 98

Cloud of Jewels Sutra
Mahāmegha-nāma-mahāyānasūtra

'Phags pa dkon mchog sprin zhes bya ba theg pa chen po'i mdo
P0897, vol. 35

Commentary on the Difficult Points of the "Ornament for the Middle Way"
Madhyamakālaṃkāra-pañjikā
dBus ma'i rgyan gyi dka' 'grel
author: Kamalaśīla
P5286, vol. 101

Commentary on the "Four Hundred Stanzas"
Bodhisattva-yogā-cāra-catuḥ-śataka-ṭīkā
Byang chub sems pa'i rnal 'byor spyod pa bzhi brgya pa'i rgya cher 'grel pa
author: Candrakīrti
P5266, vol. 98

Commentary on the "Introduction to the 'Middle Way'"
Madhyamakāvatāra-bhāṣya
dBu ma la 'jug pa'i bshad pa zhes bya ba
author: Candrakīrti
P5263, vol. 98

Commentary on the "Refutation of Objections"
Vigraha-vyāvartanī-vṛtti
rTsod pa bzlog pa'i 'grel pa
author: Nāgārjuna
P5232, vol. 95

Commentary on the "Sixty Stanzas of Reasoning"
Yukti-ṣaṣṭikā-vṛtti
Rigs pa drug cu pa'i 'grel pa
author: Candrakīrti
P5265, vol. 98

Commentary on Valid Cognition
Pramāṇa-vārttika-kārikā
Tshad ma rnam 'grel gyi tshig le'ur byas pa
author: Dharmakīrti
P5709, vol. 130

Compendium of Knowledge
Abhidharma-samuccaya
Chos mngon pa kun las btus pa
author: Asaṅga
P5550, vol. 112

Compendium of Valid Cognition
Pramāṇa-samuccaya
Tshad ma kun las btus pa
author: Dignāga
P5700, vol. 130

Descent into Laṅka Sutra
Ārya-laṅkāvatāra-mahāyāna-sūtra
'Phags pa lang kar gshegs pa'i mdo
P775, vol. 29

Difference Between the Views
lTa ba'i khyad par
author: Ye shes sDe
P5847

Elephant Ornament Sutra
Hasti-kakṣya-nāma-mahāyāna-sūtra
Glang po'i rtsal zhes bya ba theg pa chen po'i mdo
P873, vol. 34

Engaging in the Bodhisattva's Deeds
Bodhisattva-caryāvatāra
Byang chub sems dpa'i spyod la 'jug pa
author: Śāntideva
P5272, vol. 99

Explanation of the "Introduction to the 'Middle Way'"
Madhyamakāvatāra-ṭīkā
dBu ma la 'jug pa'i 'grel bshad ces bya ba
author: Jayānanda
P5271, vol. 99

Explanatory Commentary on the "Lamp for the 'Fundamental Treatise'"
Prajñā-pradīpa-ṭīkā
Shes rab sgron ma rgya cher 'grel pa
author: Avalokitavrata
P5259, vols. 96–97

Extensive Sport Sutra
Lalita-vistara-sūtra: Ārya-lalita-vistara-nāma-mahāyāna-sūtra
'Phags pa rgya cher rol pa shes bya ba theg pa chen po'i mdo
P763, vol. 27

Foremost of Gayā Sutra
Ārya-gayā-śīrṣa-nāma-mahāyāna-sūtra
'Phags pa gayā mgo'i ri zhes bya ba theg pa chen po'i mdo
P777, vol. 29

Formula for Entering the Nonconceptual
Ārya-avikalpa-praveśa-dhāraṇī
'Phags pa rnam par mi rtog par 'jug pa gzungs
P810, vol. 32

Four Hundred Stanzas
Catuḥ-śataka: Catuḥ-śataka-śāstra-kārikā-nāma
bsTan bcos bzhi brgya pa zhes bya ba'i tshig le'ur byas pa
author: Āryadeva
P5246, vol. 95

Friendly Letter
Suhṛl-lekha
bShes pa'i spring yig
author: Nāgārjuna
P5682, vol. 129

Fundamental Treatise on the Middle Way
Mūla-madhyamaka-kārikā: Prajñā-nāma-mūla-madhyamaka-kārikā
dBu ma rtsa ba'i tshig le'ur byas pa shes rab ces bya ba
author: Nāgārjuna
P5224, vol. 95

Heart of the Middle Way
Madhyamaka-hṛdaya-kārikā
dBu ma'i snying po'i tshig le'ur byas pa
author: Bhāvaviveka
P5255, vol. 96

Heart Sutra
Prajñāpāramitā-hṛdaya: Bhagavatī-prajñāpāramitā-hṛdaya
Shes rab snying po: bCom ldan 'das ma shes rab kyi pha rol tu phyin pa'i snying po
P160, vol. 6

Illumination of the Middle Way
Madhyamakāloka-nāma
dBu ma snang ba zhes bya ba
Kamalaśīla
P5287, vol. 101

Instructions for the Perfection of Wisdom
Prajñāpāramitopadeśa
Shes rab kyi pha rol tu phyin pa'i man ngag
author: Ratnākaraśānti
P5579, vol. 114

Introduction to the "Middle Way"
Madhyamakāvatāra
dBu ma la 'jug pa
author: Candrakīrti
P5261, vol. 98

Introduction to the Two Truths
Satya-dvayāvatāra
Bden pa gnyis la 'jug pa
author: Atiśa
P5298

Kāśyapa Chapter Sutra
Ārya-kāśyapa-parivarta-nāma-mahāyāna-sūtra
'Phags pa 'od srung gi le'u zhes bya ba theg pa chen po'i mdo
Section 43 of the *Pile of Precious Things Collection,* Ratna-kūṭa
P760.43, vol. 24

King of Concentrations Sutra
Samādhi-rāja-sūtra: Sarva-dharma-svabhāva-samatā-vipañcita-samādhi-rāja-
sūtra
Chos tham cad kyi rang bzhin mnyam pa nyid rnam par spros pa ting nge 'dzin
gyi rgyal po'i mdo
P795, vol. 31

Lamp for the "Fundamental Treatise on the Middle Way"
Prajñā-pradīpa-mūla-madhyamaka-vṛtti
dBu ma'i rtsa ba'i 'grel pa shes rab sgron ma
author: Bhāvaviveka
P5253, vol. 95

Lamp for the Path to Enlightenment
Bodhi-patha-pradīpa
Byang chub lam gyi sgron ma
author: Atīśa
P5343, vol. 103

Levels of Yogic Deeds
Yogā-cāra-bhūmi
rNal 'byor spyod pa'i sa
author: Asaṅga
P5536, vols. 109–10

Madhyamaka Instructions
Madhyamakopadeśa-nāma
dBu ma'i man ngag zhes bya ba
author: Atiśa
P5324, vol. 102

Net of Brahma Sutra
Brahmajālasūtra
Tshangs pa'i dra ba'i mdo
P1021, vol. 40

Ornament for Clear Knowledge
Abhisamayālaṃkāra: Abhisamayālaṃkāra-nāma-prajñāpāramitopadeśa-śāstra-kārikā
shes rab phyi pha rol tu phyin pa'i man ngag gi bstan bcos mngon par rtogs pa'i rgyan zhes bya ba'i tshig le'ur byas pa
author: Maitreya
P5184, vol. 88

Ornament for the Light of Wisdom That Introduces the Object of All Buddhas
Ārya-sarva-buddha-viṣayāvatāra-jñānālokālaṃkāra-nāma-mahāyāna-sūtra
'Phags pa sangs rgyas thams cad kyi yul la 'jug pa'i ye shes snang ba'i rgyan zhes bya ba theg pa chen po'i mdo
P768, vol. 28

Ornament for the Mahayana Sutras
Mahāyāna-sūtrālaṃkāra-kārikā
Theg pa chen po'i mdo sde'i rgyan gyi tshig le'ur byas pa
author: Maitreya
P5521, vol. 108

Ornament for the Middle Way
Madhyamakālaṃkāra-kārikā
dBus ma'i rgyan gyi tshig le'ur byas pa
author: Śāntarakṣita
P5284, vol. 101

Perfection of Wisdom Sutra in Eight Thousand Lines
Aṣṭa-sāhasrikā-prajñāpāramitā-sūtra
Shes rab kyi pha rol tu phyin pa brgyad stong pa'i mdo
P734, vol. 21

Perfection of Wisdom Sutra in One Hundred Thousand Lines
Śata-sāhasrikā-prajñāpāramitā-sūtra
Shes rab kyi pha rol tu phyin pa stong phrag brgya pa'i mdo
P730, vols. 12–18

Perfection of Wisdom Sutra in Twenty-Five Thousand Lines
Pañca-viṃśati-sāhasrikā-prajñāpāramitā-sūtra
Shes rab kyi pha rol tun phyin pa stong phrag nyi shu lnga pa
P731, vols. 18–19

Pile of Precious Things Collection
Ratna-kūṭa: Ārya-mahā-ratna-kūṭa-dharma-paryāya-śata-sāhasrika-granthe
'Phags pa dkon mchog brtsegs pa chen po'i chos kyi rnam grangs le'u stong phrag brgya pa
P760, vols. 22–24

Play of Mañjuśrī Sutra
Ārya-Mañjuśrī-vikrīḍita-nāma-mahāyāna-sūtra
'Phags pa 'jam dpal rnam par rol pa zhes bya ba theg pa chen po'i mdo
P764, vol. 27

Praise of the Transcendent One
Lokātīta-stava
'Jig rten las 'das par bstod pa
author: Nāgārjuna
P2012, vol. 46

Precious Garland
Ratnāvalī: Rāja-parikathā-ratnāvalī
rGyal po la gtam bya ba rin po che'i phreng ba
author: Nāgārjuna
P5658, vol. 129

Question of the Nāga King Anavatapta
Ārya-Anavatapta-nāga-rāja-paripṛcchā-nāma-mahāyāna-sūtra
'Phags pa klu'i rgyal po ma dros pas zhus pa zhes bya ba theg pa chen po'i mdo
P823, vol. 33

Questions of Nārāyaṇa
Nārāyaṇa-paripṛcchā-ārya-mahāmayā-vijaya-vāhinī-dhāraṇī
Sred med kyi bus zhus pa 'phags pa sgyu ma chen mo rnam par rgyal ba thob par
byed pa zhes bya ba'i gzungs
Not found in P, D684, vol. 91

Refutation of Objections
Vigraha-vyāvartanī-kārikā-nāma
rTsod pa bzlog pa'i tshig le'ur byas pa zhes bya ba
author: Nāgārjuna
P5228, vol. 95

Root Tantra of Mañjuśrī
Mañjuśrī-mūla-tantra
'Phags pa 'jam dpal gyi rtsa ba'i rgyud
P162, vol. 6

Scriptural Collection of the Bodhisattvas
Bodhisattva-piṭaka: Ārya-bodhisattva-piṭaka-nāma-mahāyāna-sūtra
'Phags pa byang chub sems dpa'i sde snod ces bya ba theg pa chen po'i mdo
Section 12 of the *Pile of Precious Things Collection*, Ratna-kūṭa
P760.12, vol. 22

Separation of the Middle from the Extremes
Madhyānta-vibhāga
dBus dang mtha' rnam par 'byed pa'i tshig le'ur byas pa
author: Maitreya
P5522, vol. 108

Seventy Stanzas on Emptiness
Śūnyatā-saptati
sTong pa nyid bdun bcu pa'i tshig le'ur byas pa zhes bya ba
author: Nāgārjuna
P5227, vol. 95

Short Commentary on the "Ornament for Clear Knowledge"
Abhisamayālaṃkāra-nāma-prajñāpāramitopadeśa-śāstra-vṛtti
Shes rab kyi pha rol tu phyin pa'i man ngag gi bstan bcos mngon par rtogs pa'i
rgyan ces bya ba'i 'grel pa
author: Haribhadra
P5191, vol. 90

Sixty Stanzas of Reasoning
Yukti-ṣaṣṭikā-kārikā-nāma
Rigs pa drug cu pa'i tshig le'ur byas pa zhes bya ba
author: Nāgārjuna
P5225, vol. 95

Śrāvaka Levels
Yogā-cāra-bhūmau-śrāvaka-bhūmi
rNal 'byor spyod pa'i sa las nyan thos kyi sa
author: Asaṅga
P5537, vol. 110

Stages of Meditation
Bhāvanā-krama
sGom pa'i rim pa
author: Kamalaśīla
P5310–12, vol. 102

Sublime Continuum
Uttara-tantra: Mahāyānottara-tantra-śāstra
Theg pa chen po rgyud bla ma'i bstan bcos
author: Maitreya
P5525, vol. 108

Sutra of Cultivating Faith in the Mahayana
Ārya-mahāyāna-prasāda-prabhāvanā-nāma-mahāyāna-sūtra
'Phags pa theg pa chen po la dad pa rab tu sgom pa shes bya ba theg pa chen po'i
mdo
P812, vol. 32

Sutra of Showing the Tathāgata's Inconceivable Secret
Ārya-tathāgatācintya-guhya-nirdeśa-nāma-mahāyāna-sūtra
'Phags pa de bzhin gshegs pa'i gsang ba bsam gyis mi khyab pa bstan pa shes bya
ba theg pa chen po'i mdo
Section 3 of the *Pile of Precious Things Collection*, Ratna-kūṭa
P760.3, vol. 22

Sutra Unraveling the Intended Meaning
Ārya-saṃdhi-nirmocana-nāma-mahāyāna-sūtra
'Phags pa dgongs pa nges par 'grel pa zhes bya ba theg pa chen po'i mdo
P774, vol. 29

Teachings of Akṣayamati Sutra
Ārya-Akṣayamati-nirdeśa-nāma-mahāyāna-sūtra
'Phags pa blo gros mi zad pas bstan pa zhes bya ba theg pa chen po'i mdo
P842, vol. 34

Thirty Stanzas
Triṃśikā-kārikā
Sum cu pa'i tshig le'ur byas pa
author: Vasubandhu
P5556, vol. 113

Treasury of Knowledge
Abhidharma-kośa-kārikā
Chos mngon pa'i mdzod kyi tshig le'ur byas pa
author: Vasubandhu
P5590, vol. 115

Treasury of Knowledge Auto-Commentary
Abhidharma-kośa-bhāṣya
Chos mngon pa'i mdzod kyi bshad pa
author: Vasubandhu
P5591, vol. 115

Verse Summary of the Perfection of Wisdom
Ārya-prajñāpāramitā-ratna-guṇa-saṃcaya-gāthā
'Phags pa shes rab kyi pha rol tu phyin pa sdud pa tshigs su bcad pa
P735, vol. 21

OTHER WORKS CITED

Bingenheimer, Marcus. "The *Bhikṣuṇī Saṃyukta* in the Shorter Chinese *Saṃyukta Āgama*." *Buddhist Studies Review* 25.1 (2008): 5–26.

Bodhi, Bhikku, trans. *The Connected Discourses of the Buddha: A New Translation of the Saṃyutta Nikāya*. Boston: Wisdom Publications, 2000.

Collected Prayers (*Zhal 'don gces btus*). 4th ed. Bylakuppe, India: Sera Mey Library, 2006.

Dharma Practices (*Chos spyod*). Sarnath, India: Central Institute of Higher Tibetan Studies, 1987.

Gungthang Rinpoche (Gangthang dKon mChog bsTan pa'i sGron me Rinpoche). *Spiritual Guide to the Jewel Island*. Translated by Blanche C. Olschak and Thupten Wangyal. Zurich: Buddhist Publications Institute for Buddhist Psychology and Central Asian Studies, 1973.

Gyaltsab Je (rGyal tshab Dar ma rin chen). *Faultlessly Revealing the Path to Liberation: A Detailed Commentary on the "Commentary on Valid Cognition" (Tshad ma rnam 'grel gyi tshig le'ur byas pa'i rnam bshad thar lam phin ci ma log par gsal bar byed pa)*. Karnataka, India: Drepung Loseling Library Society, 1992.

Hopkins, Jeffrey. *Meditation on Emptiness*. London: Wisdom Publications, 1983.

Inada, Kenneth K. *Nāgārjuna: A Translation of His Mūlamadhyamakakārikā with an Introductory Essay*. Tokyo: The Hokuseido Press, 1970.

Jackson, Roger R. *Is Enlightenment Possible? Dharmakīrti and rGyal tshab rje on Knowledge, Rebirth, No-Self and Liberation*. Ithaca, NY: Snow Lion Publications, 1993.

Jetsun Chokyi Gyaltsen (rJe btsun pa Chos kyi rgyal mtshan). *Complete Meaning of the Middle Way (dBu ma'i spyi don)*. Bylakuppe, India: Sera Je Library & Computer Project, 2004.

Kun mkhyen Jo nang ba. *The Retreat Teaching: Ocean of Definitive Meaning (Ri chos nges don rgya mtsho)*. Beijing: Jonang Publication Series, Mi rigs dpe sgrun khang, 2007.

Po to ba Rin chen gsal. *Little Digest of Instructions (Be'u bum)*. Arranged by Dol pa Shes rab rgya mtsho.

Ruegg, David Seyfort. *The Literature of the Madhyamaka School of Philosophy in India*. Volume 7 of *A History of Indian Literature*. Edited by Jan Gonda. Wiesbaden: Otto Harrassowitz, 1981.

Śāntideva. *The Bodhicaryāvatāra*. Translated by Kate Crosby and Andrew Skilton. Oxford: Oxford University Press, 1995.

———. *A Guide to the Bodhisattva's Way of Life*. Translated by Stephen Batchelor. Dharamsala, India: Library of Tibetan Works and Archives, 1987.

———. *A Guide to the Bodhisattva Way of Life*. Translated by Vesna A. Wallace and B. Allan Wallace. Ithaca, NY: Snow Lion Publications, 1997.

Sopa, Geshe Lhundub, and Jeffrey Hopkins. *Cutting through Appearances*. Ithaca, NY: Snow Lion Publications, 1990.

Sopa, Geshe Lhundub, with David Patt. *Steps on the Path to Enlightenment: A Commentary on Tsongkhapa's* Lamrim Chenmo, *volume 1: The Foundation Practices*. Boston: Wisdom Publications, 2004.

———. *Steps on the Path to Enlightenment: A Commentary on Tsongkhapa's* Lamrim Chenmo, *volume 2: Karma*. Boston: Wisdom Publications, 2005.

Sopa, Geshe Lhundub, with Beth Newman. *Steps on the Path to Enlightenment: A Commentary on Tsongkhapa's* Lamrim Chenmo, *volume 3: The Way of the Bodhisattva*. Boston: Wisdom Publications, 2008.

Sopa, Geshe Lhundub, with James Blumenthal. *Steps on the Path to Enlightenment: A Commentary on Tsongkhapa's* Lamrim Chenmo, *volume 4: Śamatha.* Boston: Wisdom Publications, 2016.

Thurman, Robert A. F. *Tsong Khapa's Speech of Gold in the Essence of True Eloquence: Reason and Enlightenment in the Central Philosophy of Tibet.* Princeton, NJ: Princeton University Press, 1984.

Tsongkhapa (Tsong kha pa Blo bzang grags pa). *Basic Path to Awakening* (*Lam rim nyams mgur*). In *Dharma Practices*, 64–74.

———. *Clarification of the Intention: Extensive Explanation of "Introduction to the 'Middle Way'"* (*dBu ma dgongs pa rab gsal*). Sarnath, India: Pleasure of Elegant Sayings Press, 1988. P6143, vol. 154.

———. *Condensed Lamrim* (*Byang chub lam gyi rim pa'i nyams len gyi rnam gshag mdor bsdus te brjed byang du byas pa*). P6061, vol. 153.

———. *Essential Explanation of the Provisional and the Definitive* (*Drang nges legs bshad snying po*). Mundgod, India: Drepung Loseling Library Society, 1991. Sarnath, India: Central Institute of Higher Tibetan Studies, 1997. P6061, vol. 153.

———. *Foundation of All Good Qualities* (*Yon tan gzhir gyur ma*). In *Byang chub lam gyi rim pa'i bryud pa rnams la gsol ba 'debs pa'i rim pa lam mchog sgo 'byed shes bya ba.* P6003, vol. 153.

———. *Golden Rosary of Eloquence: Extensive Explanation of "Ornament for Clear Knowledge" and Its Commentaries* (*Legs bshad gser gyi phreng ba*). P6150, vols. 154–55.

———. *Great Exposition of Secret Mantra* (*sNgags rim chen mo*): *The Stages of the Path to Becoming a Great Conquering Overlord Vajradhara That Reveals the Essential Points of All Secrets* (*rGyal ba khyab bdag rdo rje 'chang chen po'i lam gyi rim pa gsang ba kun gyi gnad rnam par phye pa*). P6210, vol. 161.

———. *The Great Treatise on the Stages of the Path to Enlightenment* (*sKyes bu gsum gyi rnyams su blang ba'i rim pa thams cad tshang bar ston pa'i byang chub lam gyi rim pa*). Zi-ling (Xining): Qinghai Ethnic Publishing House (mTsho sngon People's Press), 1985. Also, Dharamsala, India, 1991.

———. *The Great Treatise on the Stages of the Path to Enlightenment*, vol. 1. Translated by the Lamrim Chenmo Translation Committee, Joshua W. C. Cutler, editor in chief. Ithaca, NY: Snow Lion Publications, 2000.

———. *The Great Treatise on the Stages of the Path to Enlightenment*, vol. 2. Translated by the Lamrim Chenmo Translation Committee, Joshua W. C. Cutler, editor in chief. Ithaca, NY: Snow Lion Publications, 2004.

———. *The Great Treatise on the Stages of the Path to Enlightenment*, vol. 3. Translated by the Lamrim Chenmo Translation Committee, Joshua W. C. Cutler, editor in chief. Ithaca, NY: Snow Lion Publications, 2002.

————. *In Praise of Dependent Arising (Sangs rgyas bcom ldan 'das la zab mo rten cing 'grel bar 'byung ba'i sgo nas bstod pa legs par bshad pa'i snying po)*. In *Dharma Practices*, 1987.

————. *Ocean of Reasoning: A Great Commentary on Nāgārjuna's Mūlamadhyamaka-kārikā (rTsa she tik chen rigs pa'i rgya mtsho)*. Mundgod, India: Drepung Loseling Library Society, 1997.

————. *Ocean of Reasoning: A Great Commentary on Nāgārjuna's Mūlamadhyamaka-kārikā (rTsa she tik chen rigs pa'i rgya mtsho)*. Translated by Geshe Ngawang Samten and Jay L. Garfield. New York: Oxford University Press, 2006.

————. *Three Principal Aspects of the Path (Lam gyi gtso bo rnam gsum)*. In *Dharma Practices*, 304–7.

Index

according to Prāsaṅgika-Madhyamaka, 61–62, 257–60, 266, 268, 275,
386, 521, 530–38
according to Svātantrika-Madhyamaka, 243, 258, 266–68, 272, 386,
534
according to Yogācāra, 243–44
obstructions according to Tantrayāna,
616
obtainment, 586
Ocean of Reasoning (Tsongkhapa), 357,
405, 406
omniscience. *See* bodies of a buddha;
buddha's perception; buddhahood;
Dharma body of a buddha
once-returner, 296, 666n100
Ornament for Clear Knowledge (Maitreya), 665n84, 666n100
*Ornament for the Light of Wisdom That
Introduces the Object of All Buddhas,*
39
Ornament for the Mahayana Sutras
(Maitreya), 13, 242, 611
Ornament for the Middle Way (Śāntarakṣita), 46, 252

P

Padmasambhava, 24
Panchen Sonam Drakpa, 378–80
path
of accumulation, 57, 305, 307, 571
of meditation, 52, 57, 247, 377, 531–32,
572
of no more learning. *See* buddhahood; liberation
of preparation, 57, 305, 307, 564, 572,
601, 675n192
of seeing, 36, 57, 247, 305, 307–8, 377,
531–32, 571–72, 601
patience, 3, 6, 264, 266, 420, 533, 537
perception. *See* valid knowledge,
direct/perceptual
perfection of wisdom, 2, 6–7, 9, 16,
29–31, 51, 231–32, 240, 529, 539–40,
580–82, 614

*Perfection of Wisdom Sutra in Twen-
ty-Five Thousand Lines,* 296, 349
Perfection of Wisdom Sutras, 529, 580
pervasion
forward, 99, 318–20, 388–89, 415, 485
limited or particular, 321, 332–33, 506,
673n166
reverse or counter, 99, 318–20, 388–
89, 415, 485
universal or general, 320, 333, 387–88,
411, 467, 485–86, 506
Phurbu Cog Jampa Gyatso, 287
Pile of Precious Things Collection, 79
Play of Mañjuśrī Sutra, 559
pliancy, 17, 554, 570, 593, 595–97, 602,
604
postmeditation period, 207, 259, 302,
377, 379, 537, 592
potentiality, 52, 118, 177, 207, 259, 273,
523, 538. *See also* karma, imprints/
seeds of
Potowa, 594, 622. See also *Little Digest
of Instructions*
Praise of the Transcendent One (Nāgārjuna), 96, 354
pramāṇa, 155. *See also* valid knowledge
prasaṅga. *See* consequence
Prāsaṅgika-Madhyamaka
on attaining buddhahood, 258–60,
532, 535–36
on being dependent and empty,
41–43, 142–43, 214, 228, 498,
514–17
on conventional and ultimate reality,
178, 188, 190, 193, 205–14, 384
on grasping at truly existent nature,
207–8, 266–68, 270–71, 277–78,
281, 285–92, 424–25
on the history of Madhyamaka,
48–49
on ultimate analysis, 79–82, 134–40,
146–50, 310–12, 422, 440, 456,
510–12
on uprooting samsara, 51, 69, 248–49,
258–60, 530, 534

*Also Available from Wisdom Publications
by Geshe Lhundub Sopa*

Steps on the Path to Enlightenment
A Commentary on Tsongkhapa's Lamrim Chenmo

Vol. 1: The Foundation Practices
Geshe Lhundub Sopa with David Patt and Beth Newman
Foreword by His Holiness the Dalai Lama

"An indispensable companion to Tsongkhapa's elegant and elaborate
Great Exposition on the Stages of the Path."—*Buddhadharma*

Vol. 2: Karma
Geshe Lhundub Sopa with David Patt
Foreword by His Holiness the Dalai Lama

"Those of us fortunate to have studied directly with Geshe Sopa well
know what an inexhaustible fount of Buddhist learning and wisdom he is.
With the publication of volume 2 of his comprehensive commentary on
Tsongkhapa's classic *Lamrim Chenmo,* a much wider audience will
further benefit from these unending riches."—William S. Waldron,
Middlebury College

Vol. 3: The Way of the Bodhisattva
Geshe Lhundub Sopa with Beth Newman
Foreword by His Holiness the Dalai Lama

"From my first encounter with Professor Geshe Lhundub Sopa in 1962, I have
been impressed with his kindness, patience, and thorough-going scholarship,
qualities so strong that they obviously are based on profound realization.
His compassionate forbearance shines throughout the heartfelt, practical
explanations in these books."—Jeffrey Hopkins, author of *Meditation on
Emptiness*

Vol. 4: Śamatha
Geshe Lhundub Sopa with James Blumenthal
Foreword by His Holiness the Dalai Lama

"In this fourth volume of the commentary *Steps on the Path to Enlightenment*, Geshe Sopa draws from his extraordinary erudition and meditative experience to further elucidate this indispensable aspect of Buddhist meditation, which is all too often overlooked or marginalized in contemporary Buddhist practice. This should be carefully studied and practiced by all those who wish to proceed along the Buddhist path to enlightenment."—B. Alan Wallace, author of *Stilling the Mind*

LIKE A WAKING DREAM
The Autobiography of Geshe Lhundub Sopa
Geshe Lhundub Sopa with Paul Donnelly
Foreword by His Holiness the Dalai Lama

"Geshe Sopa is one of the greatest living Buddhist masters of his generation. This marvelous life story, rich in detail and told in his own words, will captivate the hearts and minds of anyone who reads it."—José Ignacio Cabezón, UC Santa Barbara, author of *Sexuality in Classical South Asian Buddhism*

THE CRYSTAL MIRROR OF PHILOSOPHICAL SYSTEMS
A Tibetan Study of Asian Religious Thought
Thuken Losang Chökyi Nyima
Translated by Geshe Lhundub Sopa
Edited by Roger Jackson

"An impressive translation of a fascinating and vitally important book. Its broad scope and keen observation makes it an invaluable resource." —Guy Newland, Central Michigan University, author of *Introduction to Emptiness*

PEACOCK IN THE POISON GROVE
Two Buddhist Texts on Training the Mind
Geshe Lhundub Sopa with Leonard Zwilling and Michael J. Sweet

"It belongs on the shelf—and a readily accessible one at that!—of every scholar and every practitioner of Tibetan Buddhism."—Roger Jackson, Carleton College

About Wisdom Publications

Wisdom Publications is the leading publisher of classic and contemporary Buddhist books and practical works on mindfulness. To learn more about us or to explore our other books, please visit our website at wisdompubs.org or contact us at the address below.

Wisdom Publications
199 Elm Street
Somerville, MA 02144 USA

We are a 501(c)(3) organization, and donations in support of our mission are tax deductible.

Wisdom Publications is affiliated with the Foundation for the Preservation of the Mahayana Tradition (FPMT).